CRIMINAL LAWS
KNOW YOUR RIGHTS

CRIMINAL LAWS
KNOW YOUR RIGHTS

R K Jatain

MD PUBLICATIONS PVT LTD
NEW DELHI
www.mdppl.com

Published by :

MD Publications Pvt Ltd
"MD House", 11, Darya Ganj,
New Delhi - 110002
Phone : +91-11-45355555
E-mail : contact@mdppl.com
Website: www.mdppl.com

ISBN: 978-81-7533-451-9

Published and Printed by Mr. Pranav Gupta on behalf of **MD Publications Pvt Ltd** at Mohit Enterprises, Delhi.

Preface

A body of rules and statutes that defines conduct prohibited by the government because it threatens and harms public safety and welfare and that establishes punishment to be imposed for the commission of such acts. The term criminal law generally refers to substantive criminal laws. Substantive criminal laws define crimes and may establish punishments. In contrast, Criminal Procedure describes the process through which the criminal laws are enforced. For example, the law prohibiting murder is a substantive criminal law. The manner in which government enforces this substantive law through the gathering of evidence and prosecution is generally considered a procedural matter. Crimes are usually categorized as felonies or misdemeanors based on their nature and the maximum punishment that can be imposed. A felony involves serious misconduct that is punishable by death or by imprisonment for more than one year. Most state criminal laws subdivide felonies into different classes with varying degrees of punishment. Crimes that do not amount to felonies are misdemeanors or violations. A misdemeanor is misconduct for which the law prescribes punishment of no more than one year in prison. Lesser offenses, such as traffic and parking infractions, are often called violations and are considered a part of criminal law.

Criminal law is distinctive for the uniquely serious potential consequences or sanctions for failure to abide by its rules. Every crime is composed of criminal elements. Capital punishment may be imposed in some jurisdictions for the most serious crimes. Physical or corporal punishment may be imposed such as whipping or caning, although these punishments are prohibited in much of the world. Individuals may be incarcerated in prison or jail in a variety of conditions depending on the jurisdiction. Confinement may be solitary. Length of incarceration may vary from a day to life. Government supervision may be imposed, including house arrest, and convicts may be required to conform to particularized guidelines as part of a parole or probation regimen. Fines also may be imposed, seizing money or property from a person convicted of a crime.

The criminal law generally prohibits undesirable acts. Thus, proof of a crime requires proof of some act. Scholars label this as the requirement of an actus reus or guilty act. Some crimes particularly modern regulatory offenses require no more, and they are known as strict liability offenses. Nevertheless, because of the potentially severe consequences of criminal conviction, judges at common law also sought proof of an intent to do some bad thing, the mens rea or guilty mind. As to crimes of which both actus reus and mens rea are requirements, judges have concluded that the elements must be present at precisely the same moment and it is not enough that they occurred sequentially at different times.

In preparation of this book, I am thankful to my family, friends and colleagues for their constant support and guidance. I am also grateful to Mr Pranav Gupta, Director of MD Publications Pvt Ltd, for his encouragement in preparation of this book.

R K Jatain

Contents

1

The Anti-Corruption Laws (Amendment) Act, 1967

ACT NO. 16 OF 1967 [25TH JUNE, 1967]

AN ACT further to amend the anti-corruption laws.

Be it enacted by Parliament in the Eighteenth Year of the Republic of India as follows:-

1. Short title and commencement.

(1) This Act may be called the Anti-Corruption Laws (Amendment) Act, 1967.

(2) It shall be deemed to have come into force on the 5th day of May, 1967.

2. Amendment of anti-corruption law in relation to certain pending trials.

(1) Notwithstanding-

(a) the substitution of new provisions for sub-section (3) of Section 5 of the Prevention of Corruption Act, 1947 (2 of 1947), (hereinafter referred to as the 1947-Act) by Section 6 (2) (c) of the Anti-Corruption Laws (Amendment) Act, 1964 (40 of 1964) (hereinafter referred to as the 1964-Act); and

(b) any judgment or order of any court, the said sub-section (3) as it stood immediately before the commencement of the 1964-Act, shall apply and shall be deemed always to have applied to and in relation to trials of offences punishable under sub-section (2) of Section 5 of the 1947-Act pending before any court immediately before such commencement as if no such new provisions had been substituted for the said sub-section (3).

(2) The accused person in any trial to and in relation to which sub-section (1) applies may, at the earliest opportunity available to him after the commencement of this Act, demand that the trial of the offence should proceed from the stage

at which it was immediately before the commencement of the 1964-Act and on any such demand being made the court shall proceed with the trial from that stage.

(3) For the removal of doubt it is hereby provided that any court-

(i) before which an appeal or application for revision against any judgment, order or sentence passed or made in any trial to which sub-section (1) applies is pending immediately before the commencement of this Act, or

(ii) before which an appeal or application for revision against any judgment, order or sentence passed or made before the commencement of this Act in any such trial, is filed after such commencement, shall remand the case for trial in conformity with the provisions of this section.

3. Repeal and saving.

(1) The Anti-Corruption Laws (Amendment) Ordinance, 1967 (3 of 1967) is hereby repealed.

(2) Notwithstanding such repeal, anything done or any action taken under the said Ordinance shall be deemed to have been done or taken under this Act.

❑❑❑

2

The Assam Criminal Law Amendment (Supplementary) Act, 1934

ACT NO. 27 OF 1934 [25TH AUGUST, 1934]

AN ACT to supplement the Assam Criminal Law Amendment Act, 1934.

WHEREAS it is expedient to supplement the Assam Criminal Law Amendment Act, 1934 (Assam 3 of 1934). It is hereby enacted as follows:-

1. Short title. This Act may be called the Assam Criminal Law Amendment (Supplementary) Act, 1934.

2. Appeals and confirmations.

(1) Any person convicted on a trial held by Commissioner under the Assam Criminal Law Amendment Act, 1934 (Assam 3 of 1934), may appeal to the High Court of Judicature at Fort William in Bengal, and such appeal shall be disposed of by the said High Court in the manner provided in Chapter XXXI of the Code of Criminal Procedure, 1898 (5 of 1898).

(2) When the said Commissioners pass a sentence of death, the record of the proceedings before them shall be submitted to the said High Court, and the sentence shall not be executed unless it is confirmed by the High Court which shall exercise in respect of such proceedings all the powers conferred on the High Court by Chapter XXVII of the Code of Criminal Procedure, 1898 (5 of 1898).

3. Bar of certain legal proceedings. The powers conferred by Section 491 of the Code of Criminal Procedure, 1898 (5 of 1898), shall not be exercised in respect of any person arrested, committed to or detained in custody under the Assam Criminal Law Amendment Act, 1934 (Assam 3 of 1934).

4. Retrospective effect of Sections 2 and 3. Section 2 and Section 3 shall have effect from the commencement of the Assam Criminal Law Amendment Act, 1934 (Assam 3 of 1934).

❏❏❏

3

The Criminal and Election Laws Amendment Act, 1969

ACT NO. 35 OF 1969 [4TH SEPTEMBER, 1969]

AN ACT further to amend the Indian Penal Code, the Code of Criminal Procedure, 1898 and the Representation of the People Act, 1951 and to provide against printing and publication of certain objectionable matters.

❑❑❑

4

The Criminal Law (Amendment) Act, 2005

Act No. 2 of 2006 [11th January, 2006]

AN ACT further to amend the Indian Penal Code, the Code of Criminal Procedure, 1973 and the Indian Evidence Act, 1872.

Be it enacted by Parliament in the Fifty-sixth Year of the Republic of India as follows:-

CHAPTER - I : PRELIMINARY

1. Short title and commencement.

(1) This Act may be called the Criminal Law (Amendment) Act, 2005.

(2) It shall come into force on such date as the Central Government may, by notification in the Official Gazette, appoint; and different dates may be appointed for different provisions of this Act.

CHAPTER - II : AMENDMENT TO THE INDIAN PENAL CODE

2. Insertion of new Section 195A. After Section 195 of the Indian Penal Code (45 of 1860), the following section shall be inserted, namely:-

"195A. Threatening or inducing any person to give false evidence. Whoever threatens another with any injury to his person, reputation or property or to the person or reputation of any one in whom that person is interested, with intent to cause that person to give false evidence shall be punished with imprisonment of either description for a term which may extend to seven years, or with fine, or with both; and if innocent person is convicted and sentenced in consequence of such false evidence, with death or imprisonment for more than seven years, the person who threatens shall be punished with the same punishment and sentence in the same manner and to the same extent such innocent person is punished and sentenced.".

CHAPTER - III : AMENDMENTS TO THE CODE OF CRIMINAL PROCEDURE, 1973

3. Amendment of Section 195. In Section 195 of the Code of Criminal Procedure, 1973 (2 of 1974) (hereafter in this Chapter referred to as the Code of Criminal Procedure), in sub-section 1, for the words "except on the complaint in writing of that Court, or of some other Court to which that Court is subordinate", the words "except on the complaint in writing of that Court or by such officer of the Court as that Court may authorise in writing in this behalf, or of some other Court to which that Court is subordinate" shall be substituted.

4. Insertion of new Chapter XXIA. After Chapter XXI of the Code of Criminal Procedure, the following Chapter shall be inserted, namely:- CHAPTER XXIA PLEA BARGAINING

265A. Application of the Chapter.

(1) This Chapter shall apply in respect of an accused against whom-

(a) the report has been forwarded by the officer in charge of the police station under Section 173 alleging therein that an offence appears to have been committed by him other than an offence for which the punishment of death or of imprisonment for life or of imprisonment for a term exceeding seven years has been provided under the law for the time being in force; or

(b) a Magistrate has taken cognizance of an offence on complaint, other than an offence for which the punishment of death or of imprisonment for life or of imprisonment for a term exceeding seven years, has been provided under the law for the time being in force, and after examining complainant and witnesses under Section 200, issued the process under Section 204, but does not apply where such offence affects the socio-economic condition of the country or has been committed against a woman, or a child below the age of fourteen years.

(2) For the purposes of sub-section (1), the Central Government shall, by notification, determine the offences under the law for the time being in force which shall be the offences affecting the socio-economic condition of the country.

265B. Application for plea bargaining.

(1) A person accused of an offence may file an application for plea bargaining in the Court in which such offence is pending for trial.

(2) The application under sub-section (1) shall contain a brief description of the case relating to which the application is filed including the offence to which the case relates and shall be accompanied by an affidavit sworn by the accused stating therein that he has voluntarily preferred, after understanding the nature and extent of punishment provided under the law for the offence, the plea bargaining in his case and that he has not previously been convicted by a Court in a case in which he had been charged with the same offence.

(3) After receiving the application under sub-section (1), the Court shall issue notice to the Public Prosecutor or the complainant of the case, as the case may be, and to the accused to appear on the date fixed for the case.

(4) When the Public Prosecutor or the complainant of the case, as the case may be, and the accused appear on the date fixed under sub-section (3), the Court shall examine the accused in camera, where the other party in the case shall not be present, to satisfy itself that the accused has filed the application voluntarily and where-

(a) the Court is satisfied that the application has been filed by the accused voluntarily, it shall provide time to the Public Prosecutor or the complainant of the case, as the case may be, and the accused to work out a mutually satisfactory disposition of the case which may include giving to the victim by the accused the compensation and other expenses during the case and thereafter fix the date for further hearing of the case;

(b) the Court finds that the application has been filed involuntarily by the accused or he has previously been convicted by a Court in a case in which he had been charged with the same offence, it shall proceed further in accordance with the provisions of this Code from the stage such application has been filed under sub-section (1).

265C. Guidelines for mutually satisfactory disposition. In working out a mutually satisfactory disposition under clause (a) of sub-section (4) of Section 265B, the Court shall follow the following procedure, namely:-

(a) in a case instituted on a police report, the Court shall issue notice to the Public Prosecutor, the police officer who has investigated the case, the accused and the victim of the case to participate in the meeting to work out a satisfactory disposition of the case:

PROVIDED that throughout such process of working out a satisfactory disposition of the case, it shall be the duty of the Court to ensure that the entire process is completed voluntarily by the parties participating in the meeting:

PROVIDED further that the accused may, if he so desires, participate in such meeting with his pleader, if any, engaged in the case;

(b) in a case instituted otherwise than on police report, the Court shall issue notice to the accused and the victim of the case to participate in a meeting to work out a satisfactory disposition of the case:

PROVIDED that it shall be the duty of the Court to ensure, throughout such process of working out a satisfactory disposition of the case, that it is completed voluntarily by the parties participating in the meeting:

PROVIDED further that if the victim of the case or the accused, as the case may be, so desires, he may participate in such meeting with his pleader engaged in the case.

265D. Report of the mutually satisfactory disposition to be submitted before the Court. Where in a meeting under Section 265C, a satisfactory disposition of the case has been worked out, the Court shall prepare a report of such disposition which shall be signed by the presiding officer of the Court and all other persons who participated in the meeting and if no such disposition has been worked out, the Court shall record such observation and proceed further in accordance with the provisions of this Code from the stage the application under sub-section (1) of Section 265B has been filed in such case.

265E. Disposal of the case. Where a satisfactory disposition of the case has been worked out under Section 265D, the Court shall dispose of the case in the following manner, namely:-

(a) the Court shall award the compensation to the victim in accordance with the disposition under Section 265D and hear the parties on the quantum of the punishment, releasing of the accused on probation of good conduct or after admonition under Section 360 or for dealing with the accused under the provisions of the Probation of Offenders Act, 1958 (20 of 1958) or any other law for the time being in force and follow the procedure specified in the succeeding clauses for imposing the punishment on the accused;

(b) after hearing the parties under clause (a), if the Court is of the view that Section 360 or the provisions of the Probation of Offenders Act, 1958 (20 of 1958) or any other law for the time being in force are attracted in the case of the accused, it may release the accused on probation or provide the benefit of any such law, as the case may be;

(c) after hearing the parties under clause (b), if the Court finds that minimum punishment has been provided under the law for the offence committed by the accused, it may sentence the accused to half of such minimum punishment;

(d) in case after hearing the parties under clause (b), the Court finds that the offence committed by the accused is not covered under clause (b) or clause (c), then, it may sentence the accused to one-fourth of the punishment provided or extendable, as the case may be, for such offence.

265F. Judgment of the Court. The Court shall deliver its judgment in terms of Section 265E in the open Court and the same shall be signed by the presiding officer of the Court.

265G. Finality of the judgment. The judgment delivered by the Court under Section 265G shall be final and no appeal (except the special leave petition under article 136 and writ petition under articles 226 and 227 of the Constitution) shall lie in any Court against such judgment.

265H. Power of the Court in plea bargaining. A Court shall have, for the purposes of discharging its functions under this Chapter, all the powers vested in respect of bail, trial of offences and other matters relating to the disposal of a case in such Court under this Code.

265I. Period of detention undergone by the accused to be set off against the sentence of imprisonment. The provisions of Section 428 shall apply, for setting off the period of detention undergone by the accused against the sentence of imprisonment imposed under this Chapter, in the same manner as they apply in respect of the imprisonment under other provisions of this Code.

265J. Savings. The provisions of this Chapter shall have effect notwithstanding anything inconsistent therewith contained in any other provisions of this Code and nothing in such other provisions shall be construed to constrain the meaning of any provision of this Chapter.

EXPLANATION. For the purposes of this Chapter, the expression "Public Prosecutor" has the meaning assigned to it under clause (u) of Section 2 and includes an Assistant Public Prosecutor appointed under Section 25.

265K. Statements of accused not to be used. Notwithstanding anything contained in any law for the time being in force, the statements or facts stated by an accused in an application for plea bargaining filed under Section 265B shall not be used for any other purpose except for the purpose of this Chapter.

265L. Non-application of the Chapter. Nothing in this Chapter shall apply to any juvenile or child as defined in clause (k) of Section 2 of the Juvenile Justice (Care and Protection of Children) Act, 2000.

5. Amendment of Section 292. In Section 292 of the Code of Criminal Procedure,-

(a) in sub-section 1, for the portion beginning with the words "gazetted officer" and ending with the brackets and words "(including the officer of the Controller of Stamps and Stationery)", the following shall be substituted, namely:- "officer of any Mint or of any Note Printing Press or of any Security Printing Press (including the officer of the Controller of Stamps and Stationery) or of any Forensic Department or Division of Forensic Science Laboratory or any Government Examiner of Questioned Documents or any State Examiner of Questioned Documents, as the case may be,";

(b) in sub-section (3), for the portion beginning with the words "except with" and ending with the words "as the case may be", the following shall be substituted, namely:- "except with the permission of the General Manager or any officer in charge of any Mint or of any Note Printing Press or of any Security Printing Press or of any Forensic Department or any officer in charge of the Forensic Science Laboratory or of the Government Examiner of Questioned Documents Organisation or of the State Examiner of Questioned Documents Organisation, as the case may be".

6. Amendment of Section 340. In Section 340 of the Code of Criminal Procedure, in sub-section (3), for clause (b), the following clause shall be substituted, namely:- "(b) in any other case, by the presiding officer of the Court or by such officer of the Court as the Court may authorise in writing in this behalf."

7. Amendment of the First Schedule. In the First Schedule to the Code of Criminal Procedure, under the heading "I.- OFFENCES UNDER THE INDIAN PENAL CODE,"-

(a) after the entries relating to Section 195, the following entries shall be inserted, namely:-

1 2 3 4 5 6 "195A Threatening any Imprisonment for Cognizable Non-bail-Court by person to give 7 years, or fine, able which offence false evidence or both of giving false evidence is triable. If innocent the same as for Ditto Ditto Ditto", Person is the offence. Convicted and sentenced in consequence of false evidence with death, or imprisonment for more than seven years.

(b) in the 4th column, in the entry relating to Section 196, for the word "Ditto", the word "Non- cognizable" shall be substituted'.

8. Omission of Section 25 of Act 25 of 2005. Section 25 of the Code of Criminal Procedure (Amendment) Act, 2005 shall be omitted.

CHAPTER - IV : AMENDMENT TO THE INDIAN EVIDENCE ACT, 1872

9. Amendment of Section 154 of Act 1 of 1872. In the Indian Evidence Act, 1872, Section 154 shall be numbered as sub-section (1) thereof and after sub-section (1) as so numbered, the following sub-section shall be inserted, namely:-

"(2) Nothing in this section shall disentitle the person so permitted under sub-section (1), to rely on any part of the evidence of such witness.".

❑❑❑

5

The Criminal Law Amendment Act, 1932

Act No. 23 of 1932 [19th December, 1932]

AN ACT to supplement the criminal law.

WHEREAS it is expedient to supplement the criminal law and to that end to amend the Indian Press (Emergency Powers) Act, 1931 (23 of 1931), and further to amend the Indian Criminal Law Amendment Act, 1908 (14 of 1908), for the purposes hereinafter appearing;

It is hereby enacted as follows:-

1. Short title, extent, duration and commencement.

(1) This Act may be called the Criminal Law Amendment Act, 1932.

(2) It extends to the whole of India except the territories which, immediately before the 1st November, 1956 , were comprised in Part B States.

(3) The whole of the Act except Section 7 shall come into force at once, and the State Government may, by notification in the Official Gazette direct that Section 7 shall come into force in any area on such date as may be specified in the notification.

5. Dissemination of contents of prescribed document.

(1) Whoever publishes, circulates or repeats in public any passage from a newspaper, book or other document copies whereof have been declared to be forfeited to Government under any law for the time being in force, shall be punished with imprisonment for a term which may extend to six months, or with fine, or with both.

(2) No Court shall take cognizance of an offence punishable under this section unless the State Government has certified that the passage published, circulated or repeated contains, in the opinion of the State Government, seditious or

other matter of the nature referred to in sub-section (1) of Section 99A of the Code of Criminal Procedure, 1898 (5 of 1898) or sub-section (1) of Section 4 of the Indian Press (Emergency, Powers) Act, 1931 (23 of 1931).

6. Dissemination of false rumours. *Rep. by the Criminal Law Amendment Act, 1935, s. 2.*

7. Molesting a person to prejudice of employment or business.

(1) Whoever-

(a) with intent to cause any person to abstain from doing or to do any act which such person has a right to do or to abstain from doing, obstructs or uses violence to or intimidates such person or any member of his family or person in his employ, or loiters at or near a place where such person or member or employed person resides or works or carries on business or happens to be, or persistently follows him from place to place, or interferes with any property owned or used by him or deprives him of or hinders him in the use thereof, or

(b) loiters or does any similar act at or near the place where a person carries on business, in such a way and with intent that any person may thereby be deterred from entering or approaching or dealing at such place, shall be punished with imprisonment for a term which may extend to six months, or with fine which may extend to five hundred rupees, or with both.

EXPLANATION - Encouragement of indigenous industries or advocacy of temperance, without the commission of any of the acts prohibited by this Section is not an offence under this section.

(2) No Court shall take cognizance of an offence punishable under this section except upon a report in writing of facts which constitute such offence made by a police-officer not below the rank of officer in charge of a police-station.

8. Power to order parent or guardian to pay line imposed on young person. *Rep. by the Criminal Law Amendment Act, 1935, s. 2.*

9. Procedure in offences under the Act. Notwithstanding anything contained in the Code of Criminal Procedure, 1898 (5 of 1898),

(i) no Court inferior to that of a Presidency Magistrate or Magistrate of the first class shall try any offence under this Act;

(ii) an offence punishable under Sections 5 or 7 shall be cognizable by the police; and

(iii) an offence punishable under Section 7 shall be non-bailable.

10. Power of State Government to make certain offences cognizable and non-bailable.

(1) The State Government may, by notification in the Official Gazette, declare that any offence punishable under Section 186, 188, 189, 190, 228, 295A, 298, 505, 506 or 507 of the Indian Penal Code (45 of 1860), when committed in any area specified in the notification shall, notwithstanding anything contained in the Code of Criminal Procedure, 1898 (5 of 1898), be cognizable, and thereupon

the Code of Criminal Procedure, 1898 (5 of 1898), shall, while such notification remains in force, be deemed to be amended accordingly.

(2) The State Government may, in like manner and subject to the like conditions, and with the like effect, declare that an offence punishable under Section 188 or Section 506 of the Indian Penal Code (45 of 1860) shall be non-bailable. 11th Amendment of s. 16, Act 14 of 1908 . Amendment of s. 17, Act 14 of 1908. Insertion of new ss. 17A to 17F in Act 14 of 1908. Amendmentof title and preamble of Act 23 of 1931. 11 to 14.[Amendment of s. 16, Act 14 of 1908 . Amendment of s. 17, Act 14 of 1908. Insertion of new ss. 17A to 17F in Act 14 of 1908. Amendment of title and preamble of Act 23 of 1931. *Rep. by the Repealing Act, 1938 (1 of 1938), s. 2 and Sch.*

15. Amendment of s. 1, Act 23 of 1931. *Rep. by the Criminal Law Amendment Act, 1935, s. 2.*

16. Amendment of s. 4, Act 23 of 1931. *Rep. by the Repealing Act, 1938 (1 of 1938), s. 2 and Sch.*

17. Cessation of effect of s. 62, Ordinance 10 of 1932. *Rep. by the Criminal Law Amendment Act, 1935 , s. 2.*

18. Adoption and continuance of action taken under Ordinance 10 of 1932. Anything done or any proceedings commenced in pursuance of the provisions of Chapter VI of the Special Powers Ordinance, 1932 (10 of 1932), shall, upon the commencement of this Act, be deemed to have been done or to have been commenced in pursuance of the corresponding provisions of the Indian Criminal Law Amendment Act, 1908 (45 of 1908), as amended by this Act, and shall have effect as if this Act was already in force when such thing was done or such proceedings were commenced.

19. Adoption and continuance of action taken under Act 23 of 1931 as amended by Ordinance 10 of 1932. Anything done or any proceedings commenced in pursuance of the provisions of the Indian Press (Emergency Powers) Act, 1931 (23 of 1931), as amended by Section 77 of the Special Powers Ordinance, 1932 (10 of 1932), shall, upon the commencement of this Act, be deemed to have been done or to have been commenced in pursuance of the corresponding provisions of the Indian Press (Emergency Powers) Act, 1931, as amended by this Act, and shall have effect as if this Act was already in force when such thing was done or such proceedings were commenced.

20. Trial of, and completion of trials of, offences against Ordinance 10 of 1932. Rep. by the Criminal Law Amendment Act, 1935 , s. 2.

❑❑❑

6

The Criminal Law Amendment Act, 1938

AN ACT to amend the criminal law.

WHEREAS it is expedient to supplement the criminal law by providing for the punishment of certain acts prejudicial to the recruitment of persons to serve in, and to the discipline of the, Armed Forces of the Union it is hereby enacted as follows :

1. Short title, extent and commencement.

(1) This Act may be called the Criminal Law Amendment Act, 1938.

(2) It extends to the whole of India.

(3) It shall come into force in a state on such date as the State Government may, by notification in the Official Gazette, apponting this behalf for such State.

2. Dissuasion from enlistment and instigation to mutiny or insubordination after enlistment. Whoever -

(a) with intent to affect adversely the recruitment of persons to serve in the Military, Naval or Air Forces of the Union, wilfully dissuades or attempts to dissuade the public or any person from entering any such Forces, or

(b) without dissuading or attempting to dissuade any person from entering such Forces, instigates the public or any person to do, after entering any such Force, anything which is an offence punishable as mutiny or insubordination under Section 27 of the Indian Army Act, 1911 (8 of 1911), or Sections 10 to 12 and 14 to 27 inclusive of the Indian Navy (Discipline) Act, 1934 (34 of 1934), or Sections 35 to 37 inclusive of the Indian Air force Act, 1932 (14 of 1932), as the case may be, shall be punishable with imprisonment for a term which may extend to one year, or with fine, or with both.

No person shall be proposed for any offence under this Act except with the previous sanction of the State Government.

EXCEPTION 1. The provisions of clause (a) of this section do not extend to comments on or criticism of the policy of Government in connection with the Military, Naval or Air Forces made in good faith without any intention of dissuading from enlistment.

EXCEPTION 2. The provisions of clause (a) of this section do not extend to the case in which advice is given in good faith for the benefit of the individual to whom it is given, or for the benefit of any member of his family of any of his dependents.

❑❑❑

7

The Criminal Law Amendment Act, 1961

AN ACT to supplement the criminal law.

Be it enacted by Parliament in the Twelfth Year of Republic of India as follows :

1. Short title and extent.

(1) This Act may be called the Criminal Law Amendment Act, 1961.

(2) It extends to the whole of India except the State of Jammu and Kashmir.

2. Questioning the territorial integrity or frontiers of India in a manner prejudicial to the interests of safety and security of India.

[1]**[1]**[(1) Whoever by words either spoken or written, or by signs, or by visible representation or otherwise, questions the territorial integrity or frontiers of India in a manner which is, or is likely to be, prejudicial to the interest of the safety or security of India, shall be punishable with imprisonment for a term which may extend to three years, or with fine, or with both.]

[2]**[2]**[(2) Whoever publishes a map of India, which is not in conformity with the maps of India as published by the Survey of India, shall be punishable with imprisonment, which may extend to six months, or with fine, or with both.

(3) No court shall take cognizance of an offence punishable under sub-section (2), except on a complaint made by the Government.]

3. Statements, etc., in a notified area prejudicial to maintenance of public order, etc., therein or to safety or security of India and regulation of entry of persons in such area.

(1) If the Central Government considers that in the interests of the safety or security of India in the public interests, it is necessary or expedient so to do, it may, by notification in the Official Gazette, declare any area adjoining the frontiers of

India to be a notified area; and thereupon, for so long as the notification is in force, such area shall be a notified area for the purposes to this section.

(2) Whoever makes, publishes or circulates in any notified area any statement, rumour or report which is, or is likely to be, prejudicial to the maintenance of public order or essential supplies or services in the said area or to the interests of the safety or security of India, shall be punishable with imprisonment for a term which may extend to three years, or with fine, or with both.

(3) On and after such day as may be specified in, and subject to any exemptions for which provision may be made by, a notification issued under sub-section (1), no person who was not immediately before the said day a resident in the area declared to be a notified area by the notification shall enter or attempt to enter that area or be therein except in accordance with the terms of a permit in writing granted to him by a person, not below the rank of a magistrate of the first class, specified in the said notification.

(4) Any police officer, not below the rank of sub-inspector of police, may search any person entering or attempting to enter, or being in or leaving, a notified area and any vehicle, vessel, animal or article brought in by such person, and may, for the purpose of the search, detain such person, vehicle, vessel, animal or article :

PROVIDED that no woman shall be searched in pursuance of this sub-section except by a woman authorised in this behalf by the police officer.

(5) If any person is in a notified area in contravention of the provisions of sub-section (3), then, without prejudice to any other proceedings which may be taken against him, he may be removed there from by or under the direction of any police officer on duty in the notified area, not below the rank of sub-inspector of police.

(6) If any person enters or attempts to enter a notified area or is therein in contravention of any of the provisions of sub-section (3), he shall be punishable with imprisonment for a term which may extend to one year, or with fine, or with both.

4. Power to declare certain publications forfeited and to issue search warrants for the same.

(1) Where any newspaper or book as defined in the Press and Registration of Books Act, 1867 (25 of 1867) or any other document, wherever printed, appears to the State Government to contain any matter the publication of which is punishable under Section 2 or sub-section (2) of Section 3, the State Government may, by notification in the Official Gazette, stating the grounds of its opinion, declare every copy of the issue of the newspaper containing such matter and every copy of such book or other document to be forfeited to the Government, and thereupon any police officer may seize the same wherever found and any magistrate may by warrant authorise any police officer not below the rank of sub-inspector to enter upon and search for the same in any premises where

any copy of such issue or any copy of such book or other document may be or may be reasonably suspected to be.

(2) The powers conferred by sub-section (1) on the State Government may also be exercised by the Central Government.

(3) In sub-section (1) document includes also any painting, drawing or photograph, or other visible representation.

5. Application to High Court to set aside order of forfeiture.

(1) Any person having any interest in any newspaper, book or other document in respect of which an order of forfeiture has been made under Section 4 may, within two months from the date of such order, apply to the High Court to set aside such order on the ground that the issue of the newspaper, or the book or other document in respect of which the order was made did not contain any matter of such a nature as is referred to in sub-section (1) of Section 4.

(2) The provision of [3]**[3]**[Sections 99C to 99F of the Code of Criminal Procedure, 1898 (5 of 1898),], shall apply in relation to an application under sub-section (1) as they apply in relation to an application under Section 99B of that Code and the reference in Section 99D to seditious or other matter of such a nature as is referred to in sub-section (1) of Section 99A of that Code shall be construed as reference to any matter of such a nature as is referred to in sub-section (1) of Section 4 of this Act.

(3) No order passed or action taken under Section 4 shall be called in question in any court otherwise than in accordance with the provisions of this section.

❑❑❑

8

The Drugs (Control) Act, 1950

AN ACT to provide for the control of the sale, supply and distribution of drugs.

Be it enacted by Parliament as follows:

1. Short title and extent.

(1) This Act may be called the Drugs(Control) Act, 1950.

(2) It extends to the territories which immediately before the Ist November, 1956 were comprised in Part C states.

2. Interpretation.

(1) In this Act, unless the context otherwise requires,

(a) *dealer* means a person carrying on, either personally or through any other person, the business of selling any drugs, whether wholesale or retail;

(b) *drug* means any durg as defined in Clause (b) of Section 3 of the Drugs and Cosmetics Act, 1940 (23 of 1940) in respect of which a declaration has been made under Section 3;

(c) *offer for sale* includes a reference to an intimation by a person of the price proposed by him for a sale of any drug, made by the publication of a price list, by exposing the dug for sale in association with a mark indicating price,by the furnishing of a quotation or otherwise howsoever;

(d) *producer* producer includes a manufacturer.

(1-A) As from the Ist November, 1956, any reference in this Act to the Central Government or the Chief Commissioner shall, in relation to the territories which, immediately before the Ist November 1956, were comprised in the Part C State of Ajmer or Bhopal and Vindhya Pradesh or Coorg or Kutch be construed as a reference to the State Government of Rajasthan or Madhya Pradesh or Mysore or Bombay, as the case may be.

(2) A drug shall be deemed to be in the possession of a person

(i) when it is held on behalf of that person by person or when held by that person behalf of another person;

(ii) notwithstanding that it is mortgaged to another person.

3. Drugs to which this Act applies. The Central Government may by notification in Official Gazette, declare any drug to be a drug to which this Act applies.

4. Fixing of maximum prices and maximum quantities which may be held or sold.

(1) The Chief Commissioner may,by notification in the Official Gazette, fix in respect of any drug

(a) the maximum price or rate which may be charged by a dealer or producer;

(b) the maximum quantity which may at any one time be possessed by a dealer or producer;

(c) the maximum quantity which may in any one transaction be sold to any person.

(2) The prices or rates and the quantities fixed in respect of any drug under this section may be different in different localities or for different classes of dealers or producers.

5. Restrictions on sale, etc., where maximum is fixed under Section. No dealer or producer shall

(a) sell, agree to sell, offer for sale or otherwise dispose of, to any person any drug for a price or at a rate exceeding the maximum fixed by notification under Clause(a) of sub-section (1) of Section 4;

(b) have in his possession at any one time a quantity of any drug exceeding the maximum fixed by notification under Clause (b) of sub-section (1) of Section 4; or

(c) sell, agree to sell or offer for sale to any person in any one transaction a quantity of any drug exceeding the maximum fixed by notification under Clause (c) of sub-section (1) of Section 4.

6. General limitation on quantity which may be possessed at any one time.

(1) No person shall have in his possession at any one time a greater quantity of any drug to which this section applies than the quantity necessary for his reasonable needs.

(2) This section shall apply only to such drugs as the Chief Commissioner may, by order published in the Official Gazette,specify for the purpose:

Provided that nothing contained in this section shall apply to a dealer or producer in respect of any drug sold or produced by him.

7. Duty to declare possession of excess stocks. Any person having in his possession a quantity of any drug exceeding that permitted by or under this Act shall forthwith report the fact to the Chief Commissioner or other Officer empowered in this behalf by the Chief Commissioner and shall take such action as to be storage, distribution or disposal of the excess quantity as the Chief Commissioner may direct.

8. Refusal to sell. No dealer or producer shall, unless previously authorised to do so by the Chief Commissioner, without sufficient cause refuse to sell to any person any drug within the limits as to quantity,if any,imposed by this Act.

EXPLANATION. The possibility or expectation of obtaining a higher price for a drug at a later date shall not be deemed to be a sufficient cause for the purpose of this section.

9. Cash memorandum to be given of certain sales.

(1) Every dealer or producer when selling any drug for cash shall, if the amount of the purchase in five rupees or more, in all cases, and, if the amount of the purchase is less than five rupees,when so requested by the purchaser, give to the purchaser a cash memorandum containing particulars of the transaction.

(2) The Chief Commissioner may, by notification in the Official Gazette, prescribe the particulars to be contained in any such cash memorandum.

(3) The Chief Commissioner may, be notification in the Official Gazette, exempt specified areas, classes of dealers or producers,or classes of drugs from the operation of this section.

10. Marking of prices and exhibiting list of prices and stocks.

(1) The Chief Commissioner may direct dealers or producers in general, or any dealer or producer in particular to mark any drug exposed or intended for sale with the sale prices or to exhibit on the premises a price list of drugs held for sale and the quantities of such drugs in his possession, and may further give directions as to the manner in which any such direction as aforesaid is to be carried out.

(2) No dealer shall destroy, efface or alter or cause to be destroyed, effaced or altered any label or mark affixed to a drug and indicating the price marked by a producer.

11. Obligation to state price separately on composite offer. Where a dealer or producer makes an offer to enter into a transaction for a consideration to be given as whole in respect both of a sale of any drug and of some other matter, the dealer or producer making the offer shall state in writing the price which he assigns to that drug, if he is required to do so by any person to whom the offer is made, and the offer shall be deemed for the purposes of the Act to be an offer to sell that drug at the price so stated.

12. Prohibition or regulation of the disposal of drugs. If in the opinion of the Chief Commissioner it is necessary or expedient so to do, he may be order in writing.

(a) prohibit the disposal of any drug except in such circumstances and under such conditions as may be specified in the order;

(b) direct the sale of any drug to any such dealer or class or dealers and in such quantities as may be specified in the order; and make such further orders as appear to him to be necessary or expedient in connection with any order issued under this section.

13. Penalties.

(1) Whoever contravenes any of the provisions of this Act or fails to comply with any direction made under authority conferred by this Act shall be punishable

with imprisonment for a term which may extend to three years, or with fine, or with both.

(2) A Court convicting any person of an offence punishable under this Act may order that the whole or any part of the stock of drugs in respect of which the offence was committed shall be forfeited to the Government.

(3) It shall be defence for a person charged with a contravention of any of the provisions of this section to prove that, in relation to the matter in respect of which he is charged, he acted in the course of his employment as servant or agent of another person on the instructions of his employer or of some other specified person.

14. Offences by corporations. Where a person committing an offence punishable under this Act is a company or an association or a body of persons, whether incorporated or not, every director, manager, secretary, agent or other officer or person concerned with the management thereof, shall, unless he proves that the offence was committed without his knowledge or that he has exercised all due diligence to prevent its commission, be deemed to be guilty of such offence.

15. Procedure.

(1) No person other than a police officer of or above the rank of an Inspector of Police or an officer not below the rank of an Inspector of Police authorised in this behalf by the Central Government by notification in the Official Gazette, shall investigate any offence under this Act.

(2) No prosecution for any offence punishable under this Act shall be instituted except with the previous sanction of the district Magistrate.

16. Powers of search and seizure. Any person competent to investigate any offence under this Act may search any place in which he has reason to believe that an offence under this Act has been, or in being committed, and take possession of any stock of drugs in respect of which the offence has been or is being committed and the provisions of the Code of Criminal Procedure, 1898 (5 of 1898) shall so far as may be applicable, apply to any search or seizure under this Act as they apply to any search or seizure made under the authority of a warrant issued under Section 98 of that Code.

17. Power to make rules.

(1) The Central Government may make rules to carry out the purposes of this Act.

(2) In particular, and without prejudice to the generality of forgoing power, such rules may provide for all or any of the following matters, namely :-

(a) the maintenance by dealers and producers generally, or by any dealer or producer in particular, of records of all sale and purchase transactions made by them;

(b) the furnishing of any such information as may be required with respect to the business carried on by any dealer or producer;

(c) the inspection of any books of account or other document belonging to or under the control of any dealer or producer.

18. Protection of action in good faith. No suit, prosecution or other legal proceeding shall lie against any person for anything in good faith done or intended to be done under this Act.

19. Saving of other laws. The provisions of this Act shall be in addition to, and not in derogation of, any other law for the time being inforce regulating any of the matters dealt with in this Act.

20. [* * * Repealed].

❑❑❑

9

The Economic Offences (Inapplicability of Limitation) Act, 1974

[12 OF 1974]

AN ACT to provide for the inapplicability of the provisions of Chapter XXXVI of the Code of Criminal Procedure 1973 to certain economic offences.

Be it enacted by Parliament in the Twenty fifth Year of the Republic of India as follows:

1. Short title extent and commencement.

(1) This Act may be called the Economic Offences (Inapplicability of Limitation) Act 1974.

(2) It extends to the territories to which the Code of Criminal Procedure applies.

(3) It shall come into force on the 1st day of April 1974.

2. Chapter XXXVI of the Code of Criminal Procedure 1973 not to apply to certain economic offences. Nothing in Chapter XXXVI of the Code of Criminal Procedure 1973 shall apply to -

(i) any offence punishable under any of the enactments or provisions if any thereof specified in the Schedule; or

(ii) any other offence which under the provisions of that Code may be tried along with such offence and every offence referred to in clause (i) or in clause (ii) may be taken cognizance of by the Court having jurisdiction as if the provisions of that Chapter were not enacted.

THE SCHEDULE
[Section 2]

(1) The Indian Income Tax Act, 1922 (11 of 1922).

(1A) Clause (a) of Section 63 of the Copyright Act, 1957 (14 of 1957).

(2) The Income Tax Act, 1961 (43 of 1961).

(2A) The Interest Tax Act, 1974.

(2B) The Hotel Receipts Tax Act, 1980.

(2C) The Expenditure Tax Act, 1987.

(3) The Companies (Profits) Surtax Act, 1964 (7 of 1964).

(4) The Wealth Tax Act, 1957 (27 of 1957).

(5) The Gift Tax Act, 1958 (18 of 1958).

(6) The Central Sales Tax Act, 1956 (74 of 1956).

(7) The Central Excises and Salt Act, 1944 (1 of 1944).

(8) The Medicinal and Toilet Preparations (Excise Duties) Act, 1955 (16 of 1955).

(9) The Customs Act, 1962 (52 of 1962).

(10) The Gold (Control) Act, 1968 (45 of 1968).

(11) The Imports and Exports (Control) Act, 1947 (18 of 1947).

(12) The Foreign Exchange Regulation Act, 1947 (7 of 1947).

(13) The Foreign Exchange Regulation Act, 1973 (46 of 1973).

(14) The Capital Issues (Control) Act, 1947 (29 of 1947).

(15) The Indian Stamp Act, 1899 (2 of 1899).

(16) The Emergency Risks (Goods) Insurance Act, 1962 (62 of 1962).

(17) The Emergency Risks (Factories) Insurance Act, 1962 (63 of 1962).

(18) The Emergency Risks (Goods) Insurance Act, 1971 (50 of 1971).

(19) The Emergency Risks (Undertakings) Insurance Act, 1971 (51 of 1972).

(20) The General Insurance Business (Nationalisation) Act, 1972 (57 of 1972).

(21) The Industries (Development and Regulation) Act, 1951 (65 of 1951).

❑❑❑

10

The Enforcement of Security Interest and Recovery of Debts Laws (Amendment) Act, 2004

ACT NO. 30 OF 2004 [29TH DECEMBER, 2004]

AN ACT to amend the Securitisation and Reconstruction of Financial Assets and Enforcement of Security Interest Act, 2002 and further to amend the Recovery of Debts Due to Banks and Financial Institutions Act, 1993 and the Companies Act, 1956.

BE it enacted by Parliament in the Fifty- fifth Year of the Republic of India as follows:-

CHAPTER - I : PRELIMINARY

1. Short title and commencement.

(1) This Act may be called the Enforcement of Security Interest and Recovery of Debts Laws (Amendment) Act, 2004 .

(2) Save as otherwise provided in this Act, the provisions of this Act shall be deemed to have come into force on the 11th day of November, 2004.

CHAPTER - II : AMENDMENTS TO THE SECURITISATION AND RECONSTRUCTION OF FINANCIAL ASSETS AND ENFORCEMENT OF SECURITY INTEREST ACT, 2002

2. Amendment of Section 2. In Section 2 of the Securitisation and Reconstruction of Financial Assets and Enforcement of Security Interest Act, 2002 (54 of 2002) (hereafter in this Chapter referred to as the principal Act), in sub-section 1,-

(i) after clause (h), the following clause shall be inserted, namely:- '(ha) "debt" shall have the meaning assigned to it in clause (g) of Section 2 of the Recovery of Debts Due to Banks and Financial Institutions Act, 1993 (51 of 1993);'

(ii) in clause (j), the words "in accordance with the directions or guidelines issued by the Reserve Bank" shall be omitted;

(iii) in clause (o), for the words "doubtful or loss asset, in accordance with the directions or under guidelines relating to assets classifications issued by the Reserve Bank", the following shall be substituted, namely:- "doubtful or loss asset,-

(a) in case such bank or financial institution is administered or regulated by any authority or body established, constituted or appointed by any law for the time being in force, in accordance with the directions or guidelines relating to assets classifications issued by such authority or body;

(b) in any other case, in accordance with the directions or guidelines relating to assets classifications issued by the Reserve Bank;";

(iv) in clause (u), for the words "trustee or any asset management company making investment on behalf of mutual fund or provident fund or gratuity fund or pension fund", the words, brackets and figures "trustee or securitisation company or reconstruction company which has been granted a certificate of registration under sub-section (4) of Section 3 or any asset management company making investment on behalf of mutual fund" shall be substituted;

(v) in clause (zd), for sub-clause (ii), the following sub-clause shall be substituted, namely:- "(ii) securitisation company or reconstruction company, whether acting as such or managing a trust set up by such securitisation company or reconstruction company for the securitisation or reconstruction, as the case may be; or".

3. Amendment of Section 3. In Section 3 of the principal Act, in sub-section (3), after clause (g), the following clause shall be inserted at the end, namely:- "(h) that securitisation company or reconstruction company has complied with one or more conditions specified in the guidelines issued by the Reserve Bank for the said purpose".

4. Amendment of Section 4. In Section 4 of the principal Act, in sub-section (2),-

(a) the words "rejection of application for registration or" shall be omitted;

(b) for the words "such order of rejection or cancellation", the words "such order of cancellation" shall be substituted.

5. Insertion of new Section 5A. After Section 5 of the principal Act, the following section shall be inserted, namely:-

"5A. Transfer of pending applications to any one of Debts Recovery Tribunals in certain cases.

(1) If any financial asset, of a borrower acquired by a securitisation company or reconstruction company, comprise of secured debts of more than one bank or financial institution for recovery of which such banks or financial institutions has filed applications before two or more Debts Recovery Tribunals, the securitisation company or reconstruction company may file an application to the Appellate Tribunal having jurisdiction over any of such Tribunals in which

such applications are pending for transfer of all pending applications to any one of the Debts Recovery Tribunals as it deems fit.

(2) On receipt of such application for transfer of all pending applications under sub-section (1), the Appellate Tribunal may, after giving the parties to the application an opportunity of being heard, pass an order for transfer of the pending applications to any one of the Debts Recovery Tribunals.

(3) Notwithstanding anything contained in the Recovery of Debts Due to Banks and Financial Institutions Act, 1993 (51 of 1993), any order passed by the Appellate Tribunal under sub-section (2) shall be binding on all the Debts Recovery Tribunals referred to in sub-section (1) as if such order had been passed by the Appellate Tribunal having jurisdiction on each such Debts Recovery Tribunal.

(4) Any recovery certificate, issued by the Debts Recovery Tribunal to which all the pending applications are transferred under sub-section (2), shall be executed in accordance with the provisions contained in sub-section (23) of Section 19 and other provisions of the Recovery of Debts Due to Banks and Financial Institutions Act, 1993 (51 of 1993) shall, accordingly, apply to such execution.".

6. Amendment of Section 7. In Section 7 of the principal Act,-

(i) after sub-section (2), the following sub-section shall be inserted, namely:- "(2A)

(a) The scheme for the purpose of offering security receipts under sub-section (1) or raising funds under sub-section (2), may be in the nature of a trust to be managed by the securitisation company or reconstruction company, and the securitisation company or reconstruction company shall hold the assets so acquired or the funds so raised for acquiring the assets, in trust for the benefit of the qualified institutional buyers holding the security receipts or from whom the funds are raised.

(b) The provisions of the Indian Trusts Act, 1882 (2 of 1882) shall, except in so far as they are inconsistent with the provisions of this Act, apply with respect to the trust referred to in clause (a) above.";

(ii) in sub-section (3), for the words "security receipts issued by such company", the words" security receipts issued under a scheme by such company" shall be substituted.

7. Insertion of new Section 12A. After Section 12 of the principal Act, the following section shall be inserted, namely:-

"**12A. Power of Reserve Bank to call for statements and information.** The Reserve Bank may at any time direct a securitisation company or reconstruction company to furnish it within such time as may be specified by the Reserve Bank, with such statements and information relating to the business or affairs of such securitisation company or reconstruction company (including any business or affairs with which such company is concerned) as the Reserve Bank may consider necessary or expedient to obtain for the purposes of this Act."

8. Amendment of Section 13. In Section 13 of the principal Act,-

(i) after sub-section (3), the following sub-section shall be inserted, namely:- "(3A). If, on receipt of the notice under sub-section (2), the borrower makes any representation or raises any objection, the secured creditor shall consider such representation or objection and if the secured creditor comes to the conclusion that such representation or objection is not acceptable or tenable, he shall communicate within one week of receipt of such representation or objection the reasons for non-acceptance of the representation or objection to the borrower:

PROVIDED that the reasons so communicated or the likely action of the secured creditor at the stage of communication of reasons shall not confer any right upon the borrower to prefer an application to the Debts Recovery Tribunal under Section 17 or the Court of District Judge under Section 17A.";

(ii) in sub-section (4), for clause (b), the following clause shall be substituted, namely:- "(b) take over the management of the business of the borrower including the right to transfer by way of lease, assignment or sale for realising the secured asset:

PROVIDED that the right to transfer by way of lease, assignment or sale shall be exercised only where the substantial part of the business of the borrower is held as security for the debt:

PROVIDED FURTHER that where the management of whole of the business or part of the business is severable, the secured creditor shall take over the management of such business of the borrower which is relatable to the security for the debt;".

9. Amendment of Section 15. In Section 15 of the principal Act, in sub-section 1, for the words "When the management of business of a borrower is taken over by a secured creditor", the words "brackets, letters and figures". When the management of business of a borrower is taken over by a securitisation company or reconstruction company under clause (a) of Section 9 or, as the case may be, by a secured creditor under clause (b) of sub-section (4) of Section 13" shall be substituted.

10. Amendment of Section 17. In Section 17 of the principal Act,-

(a) in sub-section (1),-

(i) for the words "may prefer an appeal", the words "may make an application along with such fee, as may be prescribed," shall be substituted and shall be deemed to have been substituted with effect from the 21st day of June, 2002;

(ii) after sub-section (1), the following proviso shall be inserted and shall be deemed to have been inserted with effect from the 21st day of June, 2002, namely:-

"PROVIDED that different fees may be prescribed for making the application by the borrower and the person other than the borrower";

(iii) after the proviso as so inserted, the following Explanation shall be inserted, namely:-

"*EXPLANATION:* For the removal of doubts, it is hereby declared that the communication of the reasons to the borrower by the secured creditor for not having accepted his representation or objection or the likely action of the secured creditor at the stage of communication of reasons to the borrower shall not entitle the person (including borrower) to make an application to the Debts Recovery Tribunal under this sub-section.";

(b) for sub-sections (2) and (3), the following sub-sections shall be substituted, namely:-

"(2) The Debts Recovery Tribunal shall consider whether any of the measures referred to in sub-section (4) of Section 13 taken by the secured creditor for enforcement of security are in accordance with the provisions of this Act and the rules made thereunder.

(3) If, the Debts Recovery Tribunal, after examining the facts and circumstances of the case and evidence produced by the parties, comes to the conclusion that any of the measures referred to in sub-section (4) of Section 13, taken by the secured creditor are not in accordance with the provisions of this Act and the rules made thereunder, and require restoration of the management of the business to the borrower or restoration of possession of the secured assets to the borrower, it may by order, declare the recourse to any one or more measures referred to in sub-section (4) of Section 13 taken by the secured creditors as invalid and restore the possession of the secured assets to the borrower or restore the management of the business to the borrower, as the case may be, and pass such order as it may consider appropriate and necessary in relation to any of the recourse taken by the secured creditor under sub-section (4) of Section 13.

(4) If, the Debts Recovery Tribunal declares the recourse taken by a secured creditor under sub-section (4) of Section 13, is in accordance with the provisions of this Act and the rules made thereunder, then, notwithstanding anything contained in any other law for the time being in force, the secured creditor shall be entitled to take recourse to one or more of the measures specified under sub-section (4) of Section 13 to recover his secured debt.

(5) Any application made under sub-section (1) shall be dealt with by the Debts Recovery Tribunal as expeditiously as possible and disposed of within sixty days from the date of such application:

PROVIDED that the Debts Recovery Tribunal may, from time to time, extend the said period for reasons to be recorded in writing, so, however, that the total period of pendency of the application with the Debts Recovery Tribunal, shall not exceed four months from the date of making of such application made under sub-section (1).

(6) If the application is not disposed of by the Debts Recovery Tribunal within the period of four months as specified in sub-section (5), any part to the application may make an application, in such form as may be prescribed,

to the Appellate Tribunal for directing the Debts Recovery Tribunal for expeditious disposal of the application pending before the Debts Recovery Tribunal and the Appellate Tribunal may, on such application, make an order for expeditious disposal of the pending application by the Debts Recovery Tribunal.

(7) Save as otherwise provided in this Act, the Debts Recovery Tribunal shall, as far as may be, dispose of the application in accordance with the provisions of the Recovery of Debts Due to Banks and Financial Institutions Act, 1993 (51 of 1993) and the rules made thereunder.".

11. Insertion of new Section 17A. After Section 17 of the principal Act, the following section shall be inserted, namely:-

"17A. Making of application to Court of District Judge in certain cases.- In the case of a borrower residing in the State of Jammu and Kashmir, the application under Section 17 shall be made to the Court of District Judge in that State having jurisdiction over the borrower which shall pass an order on such application.

EXPLANATION. For the removal of doubts, it is hereby declared that the communication of the reasons to the borrower by the secured creditor for not having accepted his representation or objection or the likely action of the secured creditor at the stage of communication of reasons shall not entitle the person (including borrower) to make an application to the Court of District Judge under this section".

12. Amendment of Section 18. In Section 18 of the principal Act,-

(a) in sub-section (1),-

(i) for the words and figures "under Section 17, may prefer an appeal", the words and figures under Section 17, may prefer an appeal along with such fee, as may be prescribed" shall be substituted and shall be deemed to have been substituted with effect from the 21st day of June, 2002;

(ii) after sub-section (1), the following proviso shall be inserted and shall be deemed to have been inserted with effect from the 21st day of June, 2002, namely:-

"PROVIDED that different fees may be prescribed for filing an appeal by the borrower or by the person other than the borrower:";

(iii) after the proviso as so inserted, the following provisos shall be inserted, namely:-

"PROVIDED FURTHER that no appeal shall be entertained unless the borrower has deposited with the Appellate Tribunal fifty per cent. of the amount of debt due from him, as claimed by the secured creditors or determined by the Debts Recovery Tribunal, whichever is less:

PROVIDED ALSO that the Appellate Tribunal may, for the reasons to be recorded in writing, reduce the amount to not less than twenty-five per cent. of debt referred to in the second proviso".

13. Insertion of new Sections 18A and 18B. After Section 18 of the principal Act, the following Sections shall be inserted, namely:-

"18A. Validation of fees levied. Any fee levied and collected for preferring, before the commencement of the Enforcement of Security Interest and Recovery of Debts Laws (Amendment) Act, 2004 , an appeal to the Debts Recovery Tribunal or the Appellate Tribunal under this Act, shall be deemed always to have been levied and collected in accordance with law as if the amendments made to Sections 17 and 18 of this Act by Sections 10 and 12 of the said Act were in force at all material times.

18B. Appeal to High Court in certain cases. Any borrower residing in the State of Jammu and Kashmir and aggrieved by any order made by the Court of District Judge under Section 17A may prefer an appeal, to the High Court having jurisdiction over such Court, within thirty days from the date of receipt of the order of the Court of District Judge:

PROVIDED that no appeal shall be preferred unless the borrower has deposited, with the Jammu and Kashmir High Court, fifty per cent of the amount of the debt due from him as claimed by the secured creditor or determined by the Court of District Judge, whichever is less:

PROVIDED FURTHER that the High Court may, for the reasons to be recorded in writing, reduce the amount to not less than twenty-five per cent of the debt referred to in the first proviso".

14. Substitution of new section for Section 19. For Section 19 of the principal Act, the following section shall be substituted, namely:-

"19. Right of borrower to receive compensation and costs in certain cases. If the Debts Recovery Tribunal or the Court of District Judge, on an application made under Section 17 or Section 17A or the Appellate Tribunal or the High Court on an appeal preferred under Section 18 or Section 18A, holds that the possession of secured assets by the secured creditor is not in accordance with the provisions of this Act and rules made thereunder and directs the secured creditors to return such secured assets to the concerned borrowers, such borrower shall be entitled to the payment of such compensation and costs as may be determined by such Tribunal or Court of District Judge or Appellate Tribunal or the High Court referred to in Section 18B.".

15. Amendment of Section 25. In Section 25 of the principal Act,-

(a) after sub-section (1), the following sub-section shall be inserted, namely:- "**(1A).** On receipt of intimation under sub-section (1), the Central Registrar shall order that a memorandum of satisfaction shall be entered in the Central Register";

(b) in sub-section (2), for the words "The Central Registrar shall, on receipt of such intimation", the words, "brackets and figures". If the concerned borrower gives an intimation to the Central Registrar for not recording the payment or satisfaction referred to in sub-section (1), the Central Registrar shall on receipt of such intimation" shall be substituted.

16. Amendment of Section 28. In Section 28 of the principal Act, for the words and figures "under Section 12", the words, figures and letter" under Section 12 or Section 12A" shall be substituted.

17. Amendment of Section 31. In Section 31 of the principal Act, in clause (g), for the words "any properties not liable to attachment", the words and brackets "any properties not liable to attachment (excluding the properties specifically charged with the debt recoverable under this Act)" shall be substituted.

18. Amendment of Section 38. In Section 38 of the principal Act, in sub-section (2), after clause (b), the following clauses shall be inserted, namely:-

"(ba) the fee for making an application to the Debts Recovery Tribunal under sub-section (1) of Section 17;

(bb) the form of making an application to the Appellate Tribunal under sub-section (6) of Section 17;

(bc) the fee for preferring an appeal to the Appellate Tribunal under sub-section (1) of Section 18;".

CHAPTER - III : AMENDMENTS TO THE RECOVERY OF DEBTS DUE TO BANKS AND FINANCIAL INSTITUTIONS ACT, 1993

19. Amendment of Section 2. In Section 2 of the Recovery of Debts Due to Banks and Financial Institutions Act, 1993 (51 of 1993) (hereafter in this Chapter referred to as the principal Act), in clause (h), after sub-clause (i), the following sub-clause shall be inserted, namely:-

"(ia) the securitisation company or reconstruction company which has obtained a certificate of registration under sub-section (4) of Section 3 of the Securitisation and Reconstruction of Financial Assets and Enforcement of Security Interest Act, 2002 (54 of 2002);".

20. Amendment of Section 19. In Section 19 of the principal Act, after sub-section 1, the following provisos shall be inserted, namely:-

"PROVIDED that the bank or financial institution may, with the permission of the Debts Recovery Tribunal, on an application made by it, withdraw the application, whether made before or after the Enforcement of Security Interest and Recovery of Debts Laws (Amendment) Act, 2004 for the purpose of taking action under the Securitisation and Reconstruction of Financial Assets and Enforcement of Security Interest Act, 2002 (54 of 2002), if no such action had been taken earlier under that Act:

PROVIDED FURTHER that any application made under the first proviso for seeking permission from the Debts Recovery Tribunal to withdraw the application made under sub-section (1) shall be dealt with by it as expeditiously as possible and disposed of within thirty days from the date of such application:

PROVIDED ALSO that in case the Debts Recovery Tribunal refuses to grant permission for withdrawal of the application filed under this sub-section, it shall pass such orders after recording the reasons therefor.".

CHAPTER - IV : AMENDMENTS TO THE COMPANIES ACT, 1956

21. Amendment of Section 4A. In Section 4A of the Companies Act, 1956 (1 of 1956) (hereafter in this Chapter referred to as the principal Act), in sub-section 1, clause (vii) shall be omitted.

22. Amendment of Section 424A. In Section 424A of the principal Act, in sub-section 1, after the second proviso, the following provisos shall be inserted, namely:-

"PROVIDED ALSO that in case any reference had been made before the Tribunal and a scheme for revival and rehabilitation submitted before the commencement of the Enforcement of Security Interest and Recovery of Debts Laws (Amendment) Act, 2004 , such reference shall abate if the secured creditors, representing three- fourth in value of the amount outstanding against financial assistance disbursed to the borrower, have taken measures to recover their secured debt under sub-section (4) of Section 13 of the Securitisation and Reconstruction of Financial Assets and Enforcement of Security Interest Act, 2002 (54 of 2002):

PROVIDED ALSO that no reference shall be made under this Section if the secured creditors representing three- fourth in value of the amount outstanding against financial assistance disbursed to the borrower have taken measures to recover their secured debt under sub-section (4) of Section 13 of the Securitisation and Reconstruction of Financial Assets and Enforcement Security Interest Act, 2002 (54 of 2002)".

CHAPTER - V : REPEAL AND SAVING

23. Repeal and saving.

(1) The Enforcement of Security Interest and Recovery of Debts Laws (Amendment) Ordinance, 2004 (5 of 2004) is hereby repealed.

(2) Notwithstanding such repeal, anything done or any action taken under the Securitisation and Reconstruction of Financial Assets and Enforcement of Security Interest Act, 2002 (54 of 2002), and the Recovery of Debts Due to Banks and Financial Institutions Act, 1993 (51 of 1993) and the Companies Act, 1956 (1 of 1956), as amended by the said Ordinance, shall be deemed to have been done or taken under the corresponding provisions of those Acts, as amended by this Act.

❑❑❑

11

The Extradition Act, 1962

ACT NO. 34 OF 1962 [15TH SEPTEMBER, 1962]

AN ACT to consolidate and amend the law relating to the extradition of fugitive criminals
1 and to provide for matters connected therewith or incidental thereto.

Be it enacted by Parliament in the Thirteenth Year of the Republic of India as follows:-

CHAPTER - I : PRELIMINARY

1. Short title, extent and commencement.

(1) This Act may be called the Extradition Act, 1962.

(2) It extends to the whole of India.

(3) It shall come into force on such date as the Central Government may, by notification in the Official Gazette, appoint.

2. Definitions. In this Act, unless the context otherwise requires,—

(a) "composite offence" means an act or conduct of a person occurred, wholly or in part, in a foreign State or in India but its effects or intended effects, taken as a whole, would constitute an extradition offence in India or in a foreign State, as the case may be;

(b) "conviction" and "convicted" do not include or refer to a conviction which under foreign law is a conviction for contumacy, but the term "person accused" includes a person so convicted for contumacy;

(c) "Extradition offence" means-

(i) in relation to a foreign State, being a treaty State, an offence provided for in the extradition treaty with that State;

(ii) in relation to a foreign State other than a treaty State an offence punishable with imprisonment for a term which shall not be less than one year under the laws of India or of a foreign State and includes a composite offence;

(d) "extradition treaty" means a treaty, agreement or arrangement made by India with a foreign State relating to the extradition of fugitive criminals, and includes any treaty, agreement or arrangement relating to the extradition of fugitive criminals made before the 15th day of August, 1947, which extends to, and is binding on, India;

(e) "foreign State" means any State outside India, and includes every constituent part, colony or dependency of such State;

(f) "fugitive criminal" means a person who is accused or convicted of an extradition offence within the jurisdiction of a foreign State and includes a person who, while in India, conspires, attempts to commit or incites or participates as an accomplice in the commission of an extradition offence in a foreign State.

(g) "magistrate" means a magistrate of the first class or a presidency magistrate;

(h) "notified order" means an order notified in the Official Gazette;

(i) "prescribed" means prescribed by rules made under this Act; and

(j) "treaty State" means a foreign State with which an extradition treaty is in operation.

3. Application of Act.

(1) The Central Government may, by notified order, direct that the provisions of this Act, other than Chapter III, shall apply to such foreign State or part thereof as may be specified in the order.

(2) The Central Government may, by the same notified order as is referred to in sub-section (1) or any subsequent notified order, restrict such application to fugitive criminals found, or suspected to be, in such part of India as may be specified in the order.

(3) Where the notified order relates to a treaty State,-

(a) it shall set out in full the extradition treaty with that State;

(b) it shall not remain in force for any period longer than that treaty; and the Central Government may, by the same or any subsequent notified order, render the application of this Act subject to such modifications, exceptions, conditions and qualifications as may be deemed expedient for implementing the treaty with that State.

(4) Where there is no extradition treaty made by India with any foreign State, the Central Government may, by notified order, treat any Convention to which India and a foreign State are parties, as an extradition treaty made by India with that foreign State providing for extradition in respect of the offences specified in that Convention.

CHAPTER - III : DOES NOT APPLY CHAPTER II EXTRADITION OF FUGITIVE CRIMINALS TO FOREIGN STATES

4. Requisition for surrender. A requisition for the surrender of a fugitive criminal of a foreign State may be made to the Central Government—

(a) by a diplomatic representative of the foreign State at Delhi; or

(b) by the Government of that foreign State communicating with the Central Government through its diplomatic representative in that State and if neither of these modes is convenient, the requisition shall be made in such other mode as is settled by arrangement made by the Government of the foreign State the Government of India.

5. Order for magisterial inquiry. Where such requisition is made, the Central Government may, if it thinks fit, issue an order to any magistrate who would have had jurisdiction to inquire into the offence if it had been an offence committed within the local limits of his jurisdiction, directing him to inquire into the case.

6. Issue of warrant for arrest. On receipt of an order of the Central Government under Section 5, the magistrate shall issue a warrant for the arrest of the fugitive criminal.

7. Procedure before magistrate.

(1) When the fugitive criminal appears or is brought before the magistrate, the magistrate shall inquire into the case in the same manner and shall have the same jurisdiction and powers, as nearly as may be, as if the case were one triable by a court of session or High Court.

(2) Without prejudice to the generality of the foregoing provisions, the magistrate shall, in particular, take such evidence as may be produced in support of the requisition of the foreign State and on behalf of the fugitive criminal, including any evidence to show that the offence of which the fugitive criminal is accused or has been convicted is an offence of political character or is not an extradition offence.

(3) If the magistrate is of opinion that a *prima facie* case is not made out in support of the requisition of the foreign State, he shall discharge the fugitive criminal.

(4) If the magistrate is of opinion that a *prima facie* case is made out in support of the requisition of the foreign State, he may commit the fugitive criminal to prison to await the orders of the Central Government, and shall report the result of his inquiry to the Central Government, and shall forward together with such report, any written statement which the fugitive criminal may desire to submit for the consideration of the Central Government.

8. Surrender of fugitive criminal. If, upon receipt of the report and statement under sub-section (4) of Section 7, the Central Government is of opinion that the fugitive criminal ought to be surrendered to the foreign State, it may issue a warrant for the custody and removal of the fugitive criminal and for his delivery at a place and to a person to be named in the warrant.

9. Power of magistrate to issue warrant of arrest in certain cases.

(1) Where it appears to any magistrate that a person within the local limits of his jurisdiction is a fugitive criminal of a foreign State he may, if he thinks fit, issue a warrant for the arrest of that person on such information and on such evidence as would, in his opinion, justify the issue of a warrant if the offence of which the person is accused or has been convicted had been committed within the local limits of his jurisdiction.

(2) The magistrate shall forthwith report the issue of a warrant under sub-section (1) to the Central Government and shall forward the information, and the evidence or certified copies thereof to that Government.

(3) A person arrested on a warrant issued under sub-section (1) shall not be detained for more than three months unless within that period the magistrate receives from the Central Government an order made with reference to such person under Section 5.

10. Receipt in evidence of exhibits, depositions and other documents and authentication thereof.

(1) In any proceedings against a fugitive criminal of a foreign State under this Chapter, exhibits and depositions (whether received or taken in the presence of the person against whom they are used or not) and copies thereof and official certificates of facts and judicial documents stating facts may, if duly authenticated, be received as evidence.

(2) Warrants, depositions or statements on oath, which purport to have been issued or taken by any court of justice outside India or copies thereof, certificates of, or judicial documents stating the facts of, conviction before any such court shall be deemed to be duly authenticated if—

(a) the warrant purports to be signed by a judge, magistrate or officer of the State or country where the same was issued or acting in or for such State or country;

(b) the depositions or statements or copies thereof purport to be certified, under the hand of a judge, magistrate or officer of the State or country where the same were taken, or acting in or for such State or country, to be the original depositions or statements or to be true copies thereof, as the case may require;

(c) the certificate of, or judicial document stating the fact of, a conviction purports to be certified by a judge, magistrate or officer of the State or country where the conviction took place or acting in or for such State;

(d) the warrants, depositions, statements, copies, certificates and judicial documents, as the case may be, are authenticated by the oath of some witness or by the official seal of a minister of the State or country where the same were issued, taken or given.

Chapter not to apply to foreign states countries to which Chapter III applies. Nothing contained in this Chapter shall apply to fugitive criminals to which Chapter III applies.

CHAPTER - III : RETURN OF FUGITIVE CRIMINALS TO FOREIGN STATES WITH EXTRADITION ARRANGEMENTS

12. Application of Chapter.

(1) This Chapter shall apply only to any such foreign state to which, by reason of an extradition arrangement entered into with that State, it may seem expedient to the Central Government to apply the same.

(2) Every such application shall be by notified order, and the Central Government may, by the same or any subsequent notified order, direct that this Chapter and Chapters I, IV and V shall, in relation to any such foreign state, apply subject to such modifications, exceptions, conditions and qualifications as it may think fit to specify in the order for the purpose of implementing the arrangement.

13. Liability of fugitive criminals from foreign states to be apprehended and returned. Where a fugitive criminal of any foreign state to which this Chapter applies is found in India, he shall be liable to be apprehended and returned in the manner provided by this Chapter to that foreign state.

14. Endorsed and provisional warrants. A fugitive criminal may be apprehended in India under an endorsed warrant or a provisional warrant.

15. Endorsed warrant for apprehension of fugitive criminal. Where a warrant for the apprehension of a fugitive criminal has been issued in any foreign state to which this Chapter applies and such fugitive criminal is, or is suspected to be, in India, the Central Government may, if satisfied that the warrant was issued by a person having lawful authority to issue the same, endorse such warrant in the manner prescribed, and the warrant so endorsed shall be sufficient authority to apprehend the person named in the warrant and to bring him before and magistrate in India.

CHAPTER - III : RETURN OF FUGITIVE CRIMINALS TO FOREIGN STATE WITH EXTRADITION ARRANGEMENTS

16. Provisional warrant for apprehension of fugitive criminal.

(1) Any magistrate may issue a provisional warrant for the apprehension of a fugitive criminal from any commonwealth country to which this Chapter applies who is, or is suspected to be, in or on his way to India, on such information and under such circumstances as would, in his opinion, justify the issue of a warrant, if the offence of which the fugitive criminal is accused or has been convicted had been committed within his jurisdiction and such warrant may be executed accordingly.

(2) A magistrate issuing a provisional warrant shall forthwith send a report of the issue of the warrant together with the information or a certified copy thereof to the Central Government, and the Central Government may, if it thinks fit, discharge the person apprehended under such warrant.

(3) A fugitive criminal apprehended on a provisional warrant may, from time to time, be remanded for such reasonable time, not exceeding seven days at any

one time, as under the circumstances seems requisite for the production of an endorsed warrant.

17. Dealing with fugitive criminal when apprehended.

(1) If the magistrate, before whom a person apprehended under this Chapter is brought, is satisfied on inquiry that the endorsed warrant for the apprehension of the fugitive criminal is duly authenticated and that the offence of which the person is accused or has been convicted in an extradition offence, the magistrate shall commit the fugitive criminal to prison to await his return and shall forthwith send to the Central Government a certificate of the committal.

(2) If on such inquiry the magistrate is of opinion that the endorsed warrant is not duly authenticated or that the offence of which such person is accused or has been convicted is not an extradition offence, the magistrate may, pending the receipt of the orders of the Central Government, detain such person in custody or release him on bail.

(3) The magistrate shall report the result of his inquiry to the Central Government and shall forward together with such report any written statement which the fugitive criminal may desire to submit for the consideration of that Government.

18. Return of fugitive criminal by warrant. The Central Government may, at any time after a fugitive criminal has been committed to prison under this Chapter.

Chapter III. Return of fugitive criminals to foreign states with extradition arrangements.

Chapter IV. Surrender or return of accused or accused or convicted persons from foreign States. a warrant for the custody and removal to the commonwealth country concerned of thc fugitivc criminal and for his delivery at a place and to a person to be named in the warrant.

CHAPTER - IV : SURRENDER OR RETURN OF ACCUSED OR CONVICTED PERSONS FROM FOREIGN STATES

20. Conveyance of accused or convicted person surrendered or returned. Any person accused or convicted of an extradition offence who is surrendered or returned by a foreign State or may, under the warrant of arrest for his surrender or return issued in such State or country, be brought into India and delivered to the proper authority to be dealt with according to law.

21. Accused or convicted person surrendered or returned by foreign State not to be tried for certain offences. Whenever any person accused or convicted of an offence, which, if committed in India would be an extradition offence, is surrendered or returned by a foreign State, such person shall not, until he has been restored or has had an opportunity of returning to that State, be tried in India for an offence other than—

(a) the extradition offence in relation to which he was surrendered or returned; or

(b) any lesser offence disclosed by the facts proved for the purposes of securing his surrender or return other than an offence in relation to which an order for his surrender or return could not be lawfully made; or

(c) the offence in respect of which the foreign State has given its consent.

CHAPTER - V : MISCELLANEOUS

22. Liability of fugitive criminals to be arrested and surrendered or returned. Every fugitive criminal of a foreign State shall, subject to the provisions of this Act, be liable to be arrested and surrendered or returned, whether the offence in respect of which the surrender or return is sought was committed before or after the commencement of this Act, and whether or not a court in India has jurisdiction to try that offence.

23. Jurisdiction as to offences committed at sea or in air. Where the offence in respect of which the surrender or return of a fugitive criminal is sought was committed on board any vessel on the high seas or any aircraft while in the air outside India or the Indian territorial waters which comes into any port or aerodrome of India, the Central Government and any magistrate having jurisdiction in such port or aerodrome may exercise the powers conferred by this Act.

24. Discharge of person apprehended if not surrendered or returned within two months. if a fugitive criminal who, in pursuance of this Act, has been committed to prison to await his surrender or return to any foreign State is not conveyed out of India within two months after such committal, the High Court, upon application made to it by or on behalf of the fugitive criminal and upon proof that reasonable notice of the intention to make such application has been given to the Central Government, may order such prisoner to be discharged unless sufficient cause is shown to the contrary.

25. Release of persons arrested on bail. In the case of a person who is a fugitive criminal arrested or detained under this Act, the provisions of the Code of Criminal Procedure, 1973 (2 of 1974) relating to bail shall apply in the same manner as they would apply if such person were accused of committing in India the offence of which he is accused or has been convicted, and in relation to such bail, the magistrate before whom the fugitive criminal is brought shall have, as far as may be, the same powers and jurisdiction as a court of session under that Code.

Abetment of extradition offences. A fugitive criminal who is accused or convicted of abetting, conspiring, attempting to commit, inciting or participating as an accomplice in the commission of any extradition offence shall be deemed for the purposes of this Act to be accused or convicted of having committed such offence and shall be liable to be arrested and surrendered accordingly.

27. Lawfulness of, and re- taking on escape from, custody under warrants. It shall be lawful for any person to whom a warrant is directed for the apprehension of a fugitive criminal to hold in custody and convey the person mentioned in the warrant to the place named in the warrant, and if such person escapes out of any custody to which he may be delivered in pursuance of such warrant, he may be re- taken as a person accused of an offence against the law of India may be re- taken upon an escape.

28. Property found on fugitive criminal. Everything found in the possession of a fugitive criminal at the time of his arrest which may be material as evidence in proving the extradition offence may be delivered up with the fugitive criminal on his surrender or return, subject to the rights, if any, of third parties with respect thereto.

29. Power of Central Government to discharge any fugitive criminal. If it appears to the Central Government that by reason of the trivial nature of the case or by reason of the application for the surrender or return of a fugitive criminal not being made in good faith or in the interests of justice or for political reasons or otherwise, it is unjust or inexpedient to surrender or return the fugitive criminal, it may, by order, at any time stay any proceedings under this Act and direct any warrant issued or endorsed under this Act to be cancelled and the person for whose arrest the warrant has been issued or endorsed to be discharged.

30. Simultaneous requisitions. If requisitions for the surrender of a fugitive criminal are received from more than one foreign State, the Central Government may, having regard to the circumstances of the case, surrender the fugitive criminal to such State or country as that Government thinks fit.

31. Restrictions on surrender.

(1) A fugitive criminal shall not be surrendered or returned to a foreign State.

- (a) if the offence in respect of which his surrender is sought is of a political character or if he proves to the satisfaction of the magistrate or court before whom he may be produced or of the Central Government that the requisition or warrant for his surrender has, in fact, been made with a view to try or punish him for an offence of a political character;
- (b) if prosecution for the offence in respect of which his surrender is sought is according to the law of that State or country barred by time;
- (c) unless provision is made by that law of the foreign State or in the extradition treaty with the foreign State that the fugitive criminal shall not be determined or tried in that State for an offence other than—
  - (i) the extradition offence in relation to which he is to be surrendered or returned;
  - (ii) any lesser offence disclosed by the facts proved for the purposes of securing his surrender or return other than an offence in relation to which an order for his surrender or return could not be lawfully made; or
  - (iii) the offence in respect of which the Central Government has given its consent;
- (d) if he has been accused of some offence in India, not being the offence for which his surrender or return is sought, or is undergoing sentence under any conviction in India until after he has been discharged, whether by acquittal or on expiration of his sentence or otherwise;
- (e) until after the expiration of fifteen days from the date of his being committed to prison by the magistrate.

(2) For the purposes of sub-section (1), the offence specified in the Schedule shall not be regarded as offences of a political character.

(3) The Central Government having regard to the extradition treaty made by India with any foreign State may, by notified order, add or omit any offence from the list given in the Schedule.

32. Sections 29 and 31 to apply without any modification thereof. Notwithstanding anything to the contrary contained in Section 3 or Section 12, the provisions of Sections 29 and 31 shall apply without any modification to every foreign State.

33. Act not to affect the Foreigners Act, 1946. Nothing in this Act shall affect the provisions of the Foreigners Act. 1946, (31 of 1946), or any order made thereunder.

34. Extra territorial jurisdiction. An extradition offence committed by any person in a foreign State shall be deemed to have been committed in India and such person shall be liable to be prosecuted in India for such offence.

34A. Prosecution on refusal to extradition. Where the Central Government is of the opinion that a fugitive criminal cannot be surrendered or returned pursuant to a request for extradition from a foreign State, it may, as it thinks fit, take steps to prosecute such fugitive criminal in India.

34B. Provisional arrest.

(1) On receipt of an urgent request from a foreign State for the immediate arrest of a fugitive criminal, the Central Government may request the Magistrate having competent jurisdiction to issue a provisional warrant for the arrest of such fugitive criminal.

(2) A fugitive criminal arrested under sub-section (1) shall be discharged upon the expiration of sixty days from the date of his arrest if no request for his surrender or return is received within the said period.

34C. Provision of life imprisonment for death penalty. Notwithstanding anything contained in any other law for the time being in force, where a fugitive criminal, who has committed an extradition offence punishable with death in India, is surrendered or returned by a foreign State on the request of the Central Government and the laws of that foreign State do not provide for a death penalty for such an offence, such fugitive criminal shall be liable for punishment of imprisonment for life only for that offence.

35. Notified orders and notifications to be laid before Parliament. Every notified order made or notification issued under this Act shall, as soon as may be after it is made or issued, be laid before each House of Parliament.

Power to make rules.

(1) The central Government may, by notification in the Official Gazette, make rules to carry out the purposes of this Act.

(2) In particular, and without prejudice to the generality of the foregoing power, such rules may provide for all or any of the following matters, namely:—

(a) the form in which a requisition for the surrender of a fugitive criminal may be made;

(b) the form in which a warrant for the apprehension of any person in a foreign state to which Chapter III applies may be made;

(c) the manner in which any warrant may be endorsed or authenticated under this Act;

(d) the removal of fugitive criminals accused or in custody under this Act and their control and maintenance until such time as they are handed over to the persons named in the warrant as entitled to receive them;

(e) the seizure and disposition of any property which is the subject of, or required for proof of, any alleged offence to which this Act applies;

(f) the form and manner in which or the channel through which a magistrate may be required to make his report to the Central Government under this Act;

(g) any other matter which has to be, or may be, prescribed.

(3) Every rule made under this section shall be laid as soon as may be after it is made before each House of Parliament while it is in session for a total period of thirty days which may be comprised in one session or in two or more successive sessions, and if, before the expiry of the session immediately following the session aforesaid, both Houses agree in making any modification in the rule or both Houses agree that the rule should not made, the rule shall thereafter have effect only in such modified form or be of no effect, as the case may be; so however that any such modification or annulment shall be without prejudice to the validity of anything previously done under that rule.

37. Repeals and savings.

(1) The Indian Extradition Act, 1903 (15 of 1903), and any law corresponding thereto in force at the commencement of this Act in the territories which, immediately before the 1st day of November, 1956 , were comprised in Part B States and the North East Frontier Agency and (Chapter V— Miscellaneous - The First Schedule. The Second Schedule) Tuensang District (Extradition) Regulation, 1961 (3 of 1961), are hereby repealed.

(2) The Extradition Acts, 1870 to 1932 and the Fugitive Offenders Act, 1881, insofar as they apply to and operate as part of the law of India, are hereby repealed.

❑❑❑

12

The Indian Extradition Act, 1903

Act No. 15 of 1903

This Act has been repealed by the Extradition Act, 1962. (34 of 1962), s. 37 (w.e.f. 5th January, 1963).

13

The Indian Partnership Act, 1932

ACT NO. 9 OF 1932 [8TH APRIL, 1932]

AN ACT to define and amend the law relating to partnership.

WHEREAS it is expedient to define and amend the law relating to partnership. It is hereby enacted as follows:

CHAPTER - I : PRELIMINARY

1. Short title, extent and commencement.

(1) This Act may be called the Indian Partnership Act, 1932.

(2) It extends to the whole of India except the State of Jammu and Kashmir.

(3) It shall come into force on the 1st day of October, 1932, except Section 69, which shall come into force on the 1st day of October, 1933.

2. Definitions. In this Act, unless there is anything repugnant in the subject or context,-

(a) an "act of a firm" means any act or omission by all the partners, or by any partner or agent of the firm which gives rise to a right enforceable by or against the firm;

(b) "business" includes every trade, occupation and profession;

(c) "prescribed" means prescribed by rules made under this Act;

(d) "third party" used in relation to a firm or to a partner therein means any person who is not a partner in the firm; and

(e) expressions used but not defined in this Act and defined in the Indian Contract Act, 1872, (9 of 1872) shall have the meanings assigned to them in that Act.

3. Application of provisions of Act 9 of 1872. The unrepealed provisions of the Indian Contract Act, 1872, (9 of 1872) save insofar as they are inconsistent with the express provisions of this Act, shall continue to apply to firms.

CHAPTER - II : THE NATURE OF PARTNERSHIP

4. Definition of "partnership", "partner" "firm" and "firm name". "Partnership" is the relation between persons who have agreed to share the profits of a business carried on by all or any of them acting for all. Persons who have entered into partnership with one another are called individually "partners" and collectively "a firm", and the name under which their business is carried on is called the "firm name".

5. Partnership not created by status. The relation of partnership arises from contract and not from status; and, in particular, the members of a Hindu undivided family carrying on a family business as such, or a Burmese Buddhist husband and wife carrying on business as such are not partners in such business.

6. Mode of determining existence of partnership. In determining whether a group of persons is or is not a firm, or whether a person is or is not a partner in a firm, regard shall be had to the real relation between the parties, as shown by all relevant facts taken together.

EXPLANATION 1. The sharing of profits or of gross returns arising from property by persons holding a joint or common interest in that property does not of itself make such persons partners.

EXPLANATION 2. The receipt by a person of a share of the profits of a business, or of a payment contingent upon the earning of profits or varying with the profits earned by a business, does not of itself make him a partner with the persons carrying on the business; and, in particular, the receipt of such share or payment-

(a) by a lender of money to persons engaged or about to engage in any business,

(b) by a servant or agent as remuneration,

(c) by the widow or child of a deceased partner, as annuity, or

(d) by a previous owner or part owner of the business, as consideration for the sale of the goodwill or share thereof, does not of itself make the receiver a partner with the persons carrying on the business.

7. Partnership at will. Where no provision is made by contract between the partners for the duration of their partnership, or for the determination of their partnership, the partnership is "partnership at will".

8. Particular partnership. A person may become a partner with another person in particular adventures or undertakings.

CHAPTER - III : RELATIONS OF PARTNERS TO ONE ANOTHER

9. General duties of partners. Partners are bound to carry on the business of the firm to the greatest common advantage, to be just and faithful to each other, and to render true accounts and full information of all things affecting the firm to any partner or his legal representative.

10. Duty to indemnify for loss caused by fraud. Every partner shall indemnify the firm for any loss caused to it by his fraud in the conduct of the business of the firm.

11. Determination of rights and duties of partners by contract between the partners.

(1) Subject to the provisions of this Act, the mutual rights and duties of the partners of a firm may be determined by contract between the partners, and such contract may be expressed or may be implied by a course of dealing. Such contract may be varied by consent of all the partners, and such consent may be expressed or may be implied by a course of dealing.

(2) **Agreements in restraint of trade.** Notwithstanding anything contained in Section 27 of the Indian Contract Act, 1872, (9 of 1872) such contracts may provide that a partner shall not carry on any business other than that of the firm while he is a partner.

12. The conduct of the business. Subject to contract between the partners-

(a) every partner has a right to take part in the conduct of the business;

(b) every partner is bound to attend diligently to his duties in the conduct of the business;

(c) any difference arising as to ordinary matters connected with the business may be decided by a majority of the partners, and every partner shall have the right to express his opinion before the matter is decided, but no change may be made in the nature of the business without the consent of all the partners; and

(d) every partner has a right to have access to and to inspect and copy any of the books of the firm.

13. Mutual rights and liabilities. Subject to contract between the partners-

(a) a partner is not entitled to receive remuneration for taking part in the conduct of the business;

(b) the partners are entitled to share equally in the profits earned, and shall contribute equally to the losses sustained by the firm;

(c) where a partner is entitled to interest on the capital subscribed by him such interest shall be payable only out of profits;

(d) a partner making, for the purposes of the business, any payment or advance beyond the amount of capital he has agreed to subscribe, is entitled to interest thereon at the rate of six per cent per annum;

(e) the firm shall indemnify a partner in respect of payments made and liabilities incurred by him-

   (i) in the ordinary and proper conduct of the business, and

   (ii) in doing such act, in an emergency, for the purpose of protecting the firm from loss, as would be done by a person of ordinary prudence, in his own case, under similar circumstances; and

(f) a partner shall indemnify the firm for any loss caused to it by his wilful neglect in the conduct of the business of the firm.

14. The property of the firm. Subject to contract between the partners, the property of the firm includes all property and rights and interests in property originally brought into the stock of the firm, or acquired, by purchase or otherwise, by or for the firm, or for the purposes and in the course of the business of the firm, and includes also the goodwill of the business. Unless the contrary intention appears, property and rights and interests in property acquired with money belonging to the firm are deemed to have been acquired for the firm.

15. Application of the property of the firm. Subject to contract between the partners, the property of the firm shall be held and used by the partners exclusively for the purposes of the business.

16. Personal profits earned by partners. Subject to contract between the partners,-

(a) if a partner derives any profit for himself from any transaction of the firm, or from the use of the property or business connection of the firm or the firm name, he shall account for that profit and pay it to the firm;

(b) if a partner carries on any business of the same nature as and competing with that of the firm, he shall account for and pay to the firm all profits made by him in that business.

17. Rights and duties of partners. Subject to contract between the partners,-

(a) after a change in the firm, where a change occurs in the constitution of a firm, the mutual rights and duties of the partners in the reconstituted firm remain the same as they were immediately before the change, as far as may be;

(b) after the expity of the term of the firm, and where a firm constituted for a fixed term continues to carry on business after the expiry of that term, the mutual rights and duties of the partners remain the same as they were before the expiry, so far as they may be consistent with the incidents of partnership at will; and

(c) where additional undertakings are carried out, where a firm constituted to carry out one or more adventures or undertakings carries out other adventures or undertakings, the mutual rights and duties of the partners in respect of the other adventures or undertakings are the same as those in respect of the original adventures or undertakings.

CHAPTER - IV : RELATIONS OF PARTNERS TO THIRD PARTIES

18. Partner to be agent of the firm. Subject to the provisions of this Act, a partner is the agent of the firm for the purposes of the business of the firm.

19. Implied authority of partner as agent of the firm.

(1) Subject to the provisions of Section 22, the act of a partner which is done to carry on, in the usual way, business of the kind carried on by the firm, binds the firm.

The authority of a partner to bind the firm conferred by this section is called his "implied authority".

(2) In the absence of any usage or custom of trade to the contrary, the implied authority of a partner does not empower him to-

(a) submit a dispute relating to the business of the firm to arbitration,

(b) open a banking account on behalf of the firm in his own name,

(c) compromise or relinquish any claim or portion of a claim by the firm,
(d) withdraw a suit or proceeding filed on behalf of the firm,
(e) admit any liability in a suit or proceeding against the firm,
(f) acquire immovable property on behalf of the firm,
(g) transfer immovable property belonging to the firm, or
(h) enter into partnership on behalf of the firm.

20. Extension and restriction of partner' s implied authority. The partners in a firm may, by contract between the partners, extend or restrict the implied authority of any partner. Notwithstanding any such restriction, any act done by a partner on behalf of the firm which falls within his implied authority binds the firm, unless the person with whom he is dealing knows of the restriction or does not know or believe that partner to be a partner.

21. Partner' s authority in an emergency. A partner has authority, in an emergency, to do all such acts for the purpose of protecting the firm from loss as would be done by a person of ordinary prudence, in his own case, acting under similar circumstances, and such acts bind the firm.

22. Mode of doing act to bind firm. In order to bind a firm, an act or instrument done or executed by a partner or other person on behalf of the firm shall be done or executed in the firm name, or in any other manner expressing or implying an intention to bind the firm.

23. Effect of admissions by a partner. An admission or representation made by a partner concerning the affairs of the firm is evidencc against the firm, if it is made in the ordinary course of business.

24. Effect of notice to acting partner. Notice to a partner who habitually acts in the business of the firm of any matter relating to the affairs of the firm operates as notice to the firm, except in the case of a fraud on the firm committed by or with the consent of that partner.

25. Liability of a partner for acts of the firm. Every partner is liable, jointly with all the other partners and also severally, for all acts of the firm done while he is a partner.

26. Liability of the firm for wrongful acts of a partner. Where, by the wrongful act or omission of a partner acting in the ordinary course of the business of a firm, or with the authority of his partners, loss or injury is caused to any third party, or any penalty is incurred, the firm is liable therefore to the same extent as the partner.

27. Liability of firm for misapplication by partners. Where-

(a) a partner acting within his apparent authority receives money or property from a third party and misapplies it, or
(b) a firm in the course of its business receives money or property from a third party, and the money or property is misapplied by any of the partners while it is in the custody of the firm, the firm is liable to make good the loss.

28. Holding out.

(1) Any one who by words spoken or written or by conduct represents himself, or knowingly permits himself to be represented, to be a partner in a firm, is liable

as a partner in that firm to any one who has on the faith of any such representation given credit to the firm, whether the person representing himself or represented to be a partner does or does not know that the representation has reached the person so giving credit.

(2) Where after a partner' s death the business is continued in the old firm name, the continued use of that name or of the deceased partner' s name as a part thereof shall not of itself make his legal representative or his estate liable for any act of the firm done after his death.

29. Rights of transferee of a partner' s interest.

(1) A transfer by a partner of his interest in the firm, either absolute or by mortgage, or by the creation by him of a charge on such interest, does not entitle the transferee, during the continuance of the firm, to interfere in the conduct of the business, or to require accounts, or to inspect the books of the firm, but entitles the transferee only to receive the share of profits of the transferring partner, and the transferee shall accept the account of profits agreed to by the partners.

(2) If the firm is dissolved or if the transferring partner ceases to be a partner, the transferee is entitled as against the remaining partners to receive the share of the assets of the firm to which the transferring partner is entitled, and, for the purpose of ascertaining that share, to an account as from the date of the dissolution.

30. Minors admitted to the benefits of partnership.

(1) A person who is a minor according to the law to which he is subject may not be a partner in a firm, but, with the consent of all the partners for the time being, he may be admitted to the benefits of partnership.

(2) Such minor has a right to such share of the property and of the profits of the firm as may be agreed upon, and he may have access to and inspect and copy any of the accounts of the firm.

(3) Such minor' s share is liable for the acts of the firm, but the minor is not personally liable for any such act.

(4) Such minor may not sue the partners for an account or payment of his share of the property or profits of the firm, save when severing his connection with the firm, and in such case the amount of his share shall be determined by a valuation made as far as possible in accordance with the rules contained in Section 48:

PROVIDED that all the partners acting together or any partner entitled to dissolve the firm upon notice to other partners may elect in such suit to dissolve the firm, and thereupon the Court shall pro- ceed with the suit as one for dissolution and for settling accounts between the partners, and the amount of the share of the minor shall be determined along with the shares of the partners.

(5) At any time within six months of his attaining majority, or of his obtaining knowledge that he had been admitted to the benefits of partnership, whichever date is later, such person may give public notice that he has elected to become

or that he has elected not to become a partner in the firm, and such notice shall determine his position as regards the firm:

PROVIDED that, if he fails to give such notice, he shall become a partner in the firm on the expiry of the said six months.

(6) Where any person has been admitted as a minor to the benefits of partnership in a firm, the burden of proving the fact that such person had no knowledge of such admission until a particular date after the expiry of six months of his attaining majority shall lie on the persons asserting that fact.

(7) Where such person becomes a partner,-

(a) his rights and liabilities as a minor continue up to the date on which he becomes a partner, but he also becomes personally liable to third parties for all acts of firm done since he was admitted to the benefits of partnurship; and

(b) his share in the property and profits of the firm shall be the share to which he was entitled as a minor.

(8) Where such person elects not to become a partner,-

(a) his rights and liabilities shall continue to be those of a minor under this section up to the date on which he gives public notice,

(b) his share shall not be liable for any acts of the firm done after the date of the notice, and

(c) he shall be entitled to sue the partners for his share of the property and profits in accordance with sub-section (4).

(9) Nothing in sub-sections (7) and (8) shall affect the provisions of Section 28.

CHAPTER - V : INCOMING AND OUTGOING PARTNERS

31. Introduction of a partner.

(1) Subject to contract between the partners and to the provisions of Section 30, no person shall be introduced as a partner into a firm without the consent of all the existing partners.

(2) Subject to the provisions of Section 30, a person who is introduced as a partner into a firm does not thereby become liable for any act of the firm done before he became a partner.

32. Retirement of a partner.

(1) A partner may retire-

(a) with the consent of all the other partners,

(b) in accordance with an express agreement by the partners, or

(c) where the partnership is at will, by giving notice in writing to all the other partners of his intention to retire.

(2) A retiring partner may be discharged from any liability to any third party for acts of the firm done before his retirement by an agreement made by him with such third party and the partners of the reconstituted firm, and such agreement

may be implied by a course of dealing between such third party and the reconstituted firm after he had knowledge of the retirement.

(3) Notwithstanding the retirement of a partner from a firm, he and the partners continue to be liable as partners to third parties for any act done by any of them which would have been an act of the firm if done before the retirement, until public notice is given of the retirement:

PROVIDED that a retired partner is not liable to any third party who deals with the firm without knowing that he was a partner.

(4) Notices under sub-section (3) may be given by the retired partner or by any partner of the reconstituted firm.

33. Expulsion of a partner.

(1) A partner may not be expelled from a firm by any majority of the partners, save in the exercise in good faith of powers conferred by contract between the partners.

(2) The provisions of sub-sections (2), (3) and (4) of Section 32 shall apply to an expelled partner as if he were a retired partner.

34. Insolvency of a partner.

(1) Where a partner in a firm is adjudicated an insolvent he ceases to be a partner on the date on which the order of adjudication is made, whether or not the firm is thereby dissolved.

(2) Where under a contract between the partners the firm is not dissolved by the adjudication of a partner as an insolvent, the estate of a partner so adjudicated is not liable for any act of the firm and the firm is not liable for any act of the insolvent, done after the date on which the order of adjudication is made.

35. Liability of estate of deceased partner. Where under a contract between the partners the firm is not dissolved by the death of a partner, the estate of a deceased partner is not liable for any act of the firm done after his death.

36. Rights of outgoing partner to carry on competing business.

(1) An outgoing partner may carry on a business competing with that of the firm and he may advertise such business, but, subject to contract to the contrary, he may not-

(a) use the firm name,

(b) represent himself as carrying on the business of the firm, or

(c) solicit the custom of persons who were dealing with the firm before he ceased to be a partner.

(2) Agreements in restraint of trade. A partner may make an agreement with his partners that on ceasing to be a partner he will not carry on any business similar to that of the firm within a specified period or within specified local limits; and, notwithstanding anything contained in Section 27 of the Indian Contract Act, 1872, (9 of 1872), such agreement shall be valid if the restrictions imposed are reasonable.

37. Right of outgoing partner in certain cases to share subsequent profits. Where any member of a firm has died or otherwise ceased to be a partner, and the surviving or continuing partners carry on the business of the firm with the property of the firm without any final settlement of accounts as between them and the outgoing partner or his estate, then, in the absence of a contract to the contrary, the outgoing partner or his estate is entitled at the option of himself or his representatives to such share of the profits made since he ceased to be a partner as may be attributable to the use of his share of the property of the firm or to interest at the rate of six per cent. per annum on the amount of his share in the property of the firm:

PROVIDED that where by contract between the partners an option is given to surviving or continuing partners to purchase the interest of a deceased or outgoing partner, and that option is duly exercised, the estate of the deceased partner, or the outgoing partner or his estate, as the case may be, is not entitled to any further or other share of profits; but if any partner assuming to act in exercise of the option does not in all material respects comply with the terms thereof, he is liable to account under the foregoing provisions of this section.

38. Revocation of continuing guarantee by change in firm. A continuing guarantee given to a firm, or to a third party in respect of the transactions of a firm, is, in the absence of agreement to the contrary, revoked as to future transactions from the date of any change in the constitution of the firm.

CHAPTER - VI : DISSOLUTION OF A FIRM

39. Dissolution of a firm. The dissolution of partnership between all the partners of a firm is called the "dissolution of the firm".

40. Dissolution by agreement. A firm may be dissolved with the consent of all the partners or in accordance with a contract between the partners.

41. Compulsory dissolution. A firm is dissolved-

(a) by the adjudication of all the partners or of all the partners but one as insolvent, or

(b) by the happening of any event which makes it unlawful for the business of the firm to be carried on or for the partners to carry it on in partnership:

PROVIDED that, where more than one separate adventure or undertaking is carried on by the firm, the illegality of one or more shall not of itself cause the dissolution of the firm in respect of its lawful adventures and undertakings.

42. Dissolution on the happening of certain contingencies. Subject to contract between the partners a firm is dissolved-

(a) if constituted for a fixed term, by the expiry of that term;

(b) if constituted to carry out one or more adventures or undertakings, by the completion thereof;

(c) by the death of a partner; and

(d) by the adjudication of a partner as an insolvent.

43. Dissolution by notice of partnership at will.

(1) Where the partnership is at will, the firm may be dissolved by any partner giving notice in writing to all the other partners of his intention to dissolve the firm.

(2) The firm is dissolved as from the date mentioned in the notice as the date of dissolution or, if no date is so mentioned, as from the date of the communication of the notice.

44. Dissolution by the Court. At the suit of a partner, the Court may dissolve a firm on any of the following grounds, namely:-

(a) that a partner has become of unsound mind, in which case the suit may be brought as well by the next friend of the partner who has become of unsound mind as by any other partner;

(b) that a partner, other than the partner suing, has become in any way permanently incapable of performing his duties as partner;

(c) that a partner, other than the partner suing, is guilty of conduct which is likely to affect prejudicially the carrying on of the business, regard being had to the nature of the business;

(d) that a partner, other than the partner suing, wilfully or persistently commits breach of agreements relating to the management of the affairs of the firm or the conduct of its business, or otherwise so conducts himself in matters relating to the business that it is not reasonably practicable for the other partners to carry on the business in partnership with him;

(e) that a partner, other than the partner suing, has in any way transferred the whole of his interest in the firm to a third party, or has allowed his share to be charged under the provisions of Rule 49 of Order XXI of the First Schedule to the Code of Civil Procedure, 1908, (5 of 1908) or has allowed it to be sold in the recovery of arrears of land- revenue or of any dues recoverable as arrears of land revenue due by the partner;

(f) that the business of the firm cannot be carried on save at a loss; or

(g) on any other ground which renders it just and equitable that the firm should be dissolved.

45. Liability for acts of partners done after dissolution.

(1) Notwithstanding the dissolution of a firm, the partners continue to be liable as such to third parties for any act done by any of them which would have been an act of the firm if done before the dissolution, until public notice is given of the dissolution:

PROVIDED that the estate of a partner who dies, or who is adjudicated an insolvent, or of a partner who, not having been known to the person dealing with the firm to be a partner, retires from the firm, is not liable under this section for acts done after the date on which he ceases to be a partner.

(2) Notices under sub-section (1) may be given by any partner.

46. Right of partners to have business wound up after dissolution. On the dissolution of a firm every partner or his representative is entitled, as against all the other partners or their representatives, to have the property of the firm applied in payment of the debts and liabilities of the firm, and to have the surplus distributed among the partners or their representatives according to their rights.

47. Continuing authority of partners for purposes of winding up. After the dissolution of a firm the authority of each partner to bind the firm, and the other mutual rights and obligations of the partners, continue notwithstanding the dissolution, so far as may be necessary to wind up the affairs of the firm and to complete transactions begun but unfinished at the time of the dissolution, but not otherwise:

PROVIDED that the firm is in no case bound by the acts of a partner who has been adjudicated insolvent; but this proviso does not affect the liability of any person who has after the adjudication represented himself or knowingly permitted himself to be represented as a partner of the insolvent.

48. Mode of settlement of accounts between partners. In settling the accounts of a firm after dissolution, the following rules shall, subject to agreement by the partners, be observed:-

(a) Losses, including deficiencies of capital, shall be paid first out of profits, next out of capital, and, lastly, if necessary, by the partners individually in the proportions in which they were entitled to share profits.

(b) The assets of the firm, including any sums contributed by the partners to make up deficiencies of capital, shall be applied in the following manner and order:-

   (i) in paying the debts of the firm to third parties;

   (ii) in paying to each partner rateably what is due to him from the firm for advances as distinguished from capital;

   (iii) in paying to each partner rateably what is due to him on account of capital; and

   (iv) the residue, if any, shall be divided among the partners in the proportions in which they were entitled to share profits.

49. Payment of firm debts and of separate debts. Where there are joint debts due from the firm, and also separate debts due from any partner, the property of the firm shall be applied in the first instance in payment of the debts of the firm, and, if there is any surplus, then the share of each partner shall be applied in payment of his separate debts or paid to him. The separate property of any partner shall be applied first in the payment of his separate debts, and the surplus (if any) in the payment of the debts of the firm.

50. Personal profits earned after dissolution. Subject to contract between the partners, the provisions of clause (a) of Section 16 shall apply to transactions by any surviving partner or by the representatives of a deceased partner, undertaken after the firm is dissolved on account of the death of a partner and before its affairs have been completely wound up:

PROVIDED that where any partner or his representative has bought the goodwill of the firm, nothing in this section shall affect his right to use the firm name.

51. Return of premium on premature dissolution. Where a partner has paid a premium on entering into partnership for a fixed term, and the firm is dissolved before the expiration of that term otherwise than by the death of a partner, he shall be entitled to repayment of the premium or of such part thereof as may be reasonable, regard being had to the terms upon which he became a partner and to the length of time during which he was a partner, unless -

(a) the dissolution is mainly due to his own misconduct, or

(b) the dissolution is in pursuance of an agreement containing no provision for the return of the premium or any part of it.

52. Rights where partnership contract is rescinded for fraud or misrepresentation. Where a contract creating partnership is rescinded on the ground of the fraud or misrepresentation of any of the parties thereto, the party entitled to rescind is, without prejudice to any other right, entitled-

(a) to a lien on, or a right of retention of, the surplus or the assets of the firm remaining after the debts of the firm have been paid, for any sum paid by him for the purchase of a share in the firm and for any capital contributed by him;

(b) to rank as a creditor of the firm in respect of any payment made by him towards the debts of the firm; and

(c) to be indemnified by the partner or partners guilty of the fraud or misrepresentation against all the debts of the firm.

53. Right to restrain from use of firm name or firm property. After a firm is dissolved, every partner or his representative may, in the absence of a contract between the partners to the contrary, restrain any other partner or his representative from carrying on a similar business in the firm name or from using any of the property of the firm for his own benefit, until the affairs of the firm have been completely wound up:

PROVIDED that where any partner or his representative has bought the goodwill of the firm, nothing in this section shall affect his right to use the firm name.

54. Agreements in restraint of trade. Partners may, upon or in anticipation of the dissolution of the firm, make an agreement that some or all of them will not carry on a business similar to that of the firm within a specified period or within specified local limits; and notwithstanding anything contained in Section 27 of the Indian Contract Act, 1872 (9 of 1872), such agreement shall be valid if the restrictions imposed are reasonable.

55. Sale of goodwill after dissolution.

(1) In settling the accounts of a firm after dissolution, the goodwill shall, subject to contract between the partners, be included in the assets, and it may be sold either separately or along with other property of the firm.

(2) **Rights of buyer and seller of goodwill.** Where the goodwill of a firm is sold after dissolution, a partner may carry on a business competing with that of the buyer and he may advertise such business, but, subject to agreement between him and the buyer, he may not-

  (a) use the firm name,

  (b) represent himself as carrying on the business of the firm, or

  (c) solicit the custom of persons who were dealing with the firm before its dissolution.

(3) **Agreements in restraint of trade.** Any partner may, upon the sale of the goodwill of a firm, make an agreement with the buyer that such partner will not carry on any business similar to that of the firm within a specified period or within

specified local limits, and, notwithstanding anything contained in Section 27 of the Indian Contract Act, 1872 (9 of 1872), such agreement shall be valid if the restrictions imposed are reasonable.

CHAPTER - VII : REGISTRATION OF FIRMS

56. Power to exempt from application of this Chapter. The State Government of any State may, by notification in the Official Gazette, direct that the provisions of this Chapter shall not apply to that State or to any part thereof specified in the notification.

57. Appointment of Registrars.

(1) The State Government may appoint Registrars of Firms for the purposes of this Act, and may define the areas within which they shall exercise their powers and perform their duties.

(2) Every Registrar shall be deemed to be a public servant within the meaning of Section 21 of the Indian Penal Code (45 of 1860).

58. Application for registration.

(1) The registration of a firm may be effected at any time by sending by post or delivering to the Registrar of the area in which any place of business of the firm is situated or proposed to be situated, a statement in the prescribed form and accompanied by the prescribed fee, stating-

- (a) the firm name,
- (b) the place or principal place of business of the firm,
- (c) the names of any other places where, the firm carries on business,
- (d) the date when each partner joined the firm,
- (e) the names in full and permanent addresses of the partners, and
- (f) the duration of the firm. The statement shall be signed by all the partners, or by their agents specially authorized in this behalf.

(2) Each person signing the statement shall also verify it in the manner prescribed.

(3) A firm name shall not contain any of the following words, namely:-

"Crown", "Emperor", "Empress", "Empire", "Imperial", "King", "Queen", "Royal", or words expressing or implying the sanction, approval or patronage of Government, except when the State Government signifies its consent to the use of such words as part of the firm name by order in writing.

59. Registration. When the Registrar is satisfied that the provisions of Section 58 have been duly complied with, he shall record an entry of the statement in a register called the Register of Firms, and shall file the statement.

60. Recording of alterations in firm name and principal place of business.

(1) When an alteration is made in the firm name or in the location of the principal place of business of a registered firm, a statement may be sent to the Registrar accompanied by the prescribed fee, specifying the alteration, and signed and verified in the manner required under Section 58.

(2) When the Registrar is satisfied that the provisions of sub-section (1) have been duly complied with, he shall amend the entry relating to the firm in the

Register of Firms in accordance with the statement, and shall file it along with the statement relating to the firm filed under Section 59.

61. Noting of closing and opening of branches. When a registered firm discontinues business at any place or begins to carry on business at any place, such place not being its principal place of business, any partner or agent of the firm may send intimation thereof to the Registrar, who shall make a note of such intimation in the entry relating to the firm in the Register of Firms, and shall file the intimation along with the statement relating to the firm filed under Section 59.

62. Noting of changes in names and addresses of partners. When any partner in a registered firm alters his name or permanent address, an intimation of the alteration may be sent by any partner or agent of the firm to the Registrar, who shall deal with it in the manner provided in Section 61.

63. Recording of changes in and dissolution of a firm.

(1) When a change occurs in the constitution of a registered firm any incoming, continuing or outgoing partner, and when a registered firm is dissolved any person who was a partner immediately before the dissolution, or the agent of any such partner or person specially authorised in this behalf, may give notice to the Registrar of such change or dissolution, specifying the date thereof; and the Registrar shall make a record of the notice in the entry relating to the firm in the Register of Firms, and shall file the notice along with the statement relating to the firm filed under Section 59.

(2) **Recording of withdrawal of a minor.** When a minor who has been admitted to the benefits of partnership in a firm attains majority and elects to become or not to become a partner, and the firm is then a registered firm, he, or his agent specially authorised in this behalf, may give notice to the Registrar that he has or has not become a partner, and the Registrar shall deal with the notice in the manner provided in sub-section (1).

64. Rectification of mistakes.

(1) The Registrar shall have power at all times to rectify any mistake in order to bring the entry in the Register of Firms relating to any firm into conformity with the documents relating to that firm filed under this Chapter.

(2) An application made by all the parties who have signed any document relating to a firm filed under this Chapter, the Registrar may rectify any mistake in such document or in the record or note thereof made in the Register of Firms.

65. Amendment of Register by order of Court. A Court deciding any matter relating to a registered firm may direct that the Registrar shall make any amendment in the entry in the Register of Firms relating to such firm which is consequential upon its decision; and the Registrar shall amend the entry accordingly.

66. Inspection of Register and filed documents.

(1) The Register of Firms shall be open to inspection by any person on payment of such fee as may be prescribed.

(2) All statements, notices and intimations filed under this Chapter shall be open to inspection, subject to such conditions and on payment of such fee as may be prescribed.

67. Grant of copies. The Registrar shall on application furnish to any person, on payment of such fee as may be prescribed, a copy, certified under his hand, of any entry or portion thereof in the Register of Firms.

68. Rules of evidence.

(1) Any statement, intimation or notice recorded or noted in the Register of Firms shall, as against any person by whom or on whose behalf such statement, intimation or notice was signed, be conclusive proof of any fact therein stated.

(2) A certified copy of an entry relating to a firm in the Register of Firms may be produced in proof of the fact of the registration of such firm, and of the contents of any statement, intimation or notice recorded or noted therein.

69. Effect of non-registration.

(1) No suit to enforce a right arising from a contract or conferred by this Act shall be instituted in any Court by or on behalf of any person suing as a partner in a firm against the firm or any person alleged to be or to have been a partner in the firm unless the firm is registered and the person suing is or has been shown in the Register of Firms as a partner in the firm.

(2) No suit to enforce a right arising from a contract shall be instituted in any Court by or on behalf of a firm against any third party unless the firm is registered and the persons suing are or have been shown in the Register of Firms as partners in the firm.

(3) The provisions of sub-sections (1) and (2) shall apply also to claim of set-off or other proceeding to enforce a right arising from contract, but shall not affect-

   (a) the enforcement of any right to sue for the dissolution of a firm or for accounts of a dissolved firm, or any right or power to realise the property of a dissolved firm, or

   (b) the powers of an official assignee, receiver or Court under the Presidency-towns Insolvency Act, 1909, (2 of 1909) or the Provincial Insolvency Act, 1920, (5 of 1920) to realise the property of an insolvent partner.

(4) This section shall not apply-

   (a) to firms or to partners in firms which have no place of business in the territories to which this Act extends, or whose places of business in the said territories are situated in areas to which, by notification under Section 56, this Chapter does not apply, or

   (b) to any suit or claim of set-off not exceeding one hundred rupees in value which, in the Presidency-towns, is not of a kind specified in Section 19 of the Presidency Small Cause Courts Act, 1882 (15 of 1882) or, outside the Presidency-towns, is not of a kind specified in the Second Schedule to the Provincial Small Cause Courts Act, 1887 (9 of 1887) or to any proceeding in execution or other proceeding incidental to or arising from any such suit or claim.

70. Penalty for furnishing false particulars. Any person who signs any statement, amending statement, notice or intimation under this Chapter containing any particular which he knows to be false or does not believe to be true, or containing particulars which he knows to be incomplete or does not believe to be complete, shall be punishable with imprisonment which may extend to three months, or with fine or with both.

71. Power to make rules.

(1) The State Government may by notification in the Official Gazette make rules prescribing the fees which shall accompany documents sent to the Registrar of Firms, or which shall be payable for the inspection of documents in the custody of the Registrar of Firms, or for copies from the Register of Firms:

PROVIDED that such fees shall not exceed the maximum fees specified in Schedule 1.

(2) The State Government may also make rules-

(a) prescribing the form of statement submitted under Section 58, and of the verification thereof;

(b) requiring statements, intimations and notices under Sections 60, 61, 62 and 63 to be in prescribed form, and prescribing the form thereof;

(c) prescribing the form of the Register of Firms, and the mode in which entries relating to firms are to be made therein, and the mode in which such entries are to be amended or notes made therein;

(d) regulating the procedure of the Registrar when disputes arise;

(e) regulating the filing of documents received by the Registrar;

(f) prescribing conditions for the inspection of original documents;

(g) regulating the grant of copies;

(h) regulating the elimination of registers and documents;

(i) providing for the maintenance and form of an index to the Register of Firms; and

(j) generally, to carry out the purposes of this Chapter.

(3) All rules made under this section shall be subject to the condition of previous publication.

(4) Every rule made by the the State Government under this section shall be laid, as soon as it is made before the State Legislature.

CHAPTER - VIII : SUPPLEMENTAL

72. Mode of giving public notice. A public notice under this Act is given-

(a) where it relates to the retirement or expulsion of a partner from a registered firm, or to the dissolution of a registered firm, or to the election to become or not to become a partner in a registered firm by a person attaining majority who was admitted as a minor to the benefits of partnership, by notice to the Registrar of Firms under section 63, and by publication in the Official Gazette and in at least one vernacular newspaper circulating in the district where the firm to which it relates has its place or principal place of business, and

(b) in any other case, by publication in the Official Gazette and in at least one vernacular newspaper circulating in the district where the firm to which it relates has its place or principal place of business.

73. Repeals. *Rep. by the Repealing Act, 1938 (1 of 1938), s. 2 and Sch.*

74. Savings. Nothing in this Act or any repeal effected thereby shall affect or be deemed to affect-

(a) any right, title, interest, obligation or liability already acquired, accrued or incurred before the commencement of this Act, or

(b) any legal proceeding or remedy in respect of any such right, title, interest, obligation or liability, or anything done or suffered before the commencement of this Act, or

(c) anything done or suffered before the commencement of this Act, or

(d) any enactment relating to partnership not expressly repealed by this Act, or

(e) any rule of insolvency relating to partnership, or

(f) any rule of law not inconsistent with this Act.

❑❑❑

14

The Indian Penal Code, 1860

ACT NO. 45 OF 1860 [6TH OCTOBER, 1860]

CHAPTER - I : INTRODUCTION

Preamble. WHEREAS it is expedient to provide a general Penal Code for 2 India;

It is enacted as follows:—

1. Title and extent of operation of the Code. This Act shall be called the Indian Penal Code, and shall extend to the whole of India except the State of Jammu and Kashmir.

2. Punishment of offences committed within India. Every person shall be liable to punishment under this Code and not otherwise for every act or omission contrary to the provisions thereof, of which he shall be guilty within India.

3. Punishment of offences committed beyond, but which by law may be tried within, India. Any person liable, by any Indian law, to be tried for an offence committed beyond India shall be dealt with according to the provisions of this Code for any act committed beyond India in the same manner as if such act had been committed within India.

4. Extension of Code to extraterritorial offences. The provisions of this Code apply also to any offence committed by—

(1) any citizen of India in any place without and beyond India;

(2) any person on any ship or aircraft registered in India wherever it may be.

EXPLANATION. In this Section the word "offence" includes every act committed outside India which, if committed in India would be punishable under this Code. Illustration A, who is a citizen of India, commits a murder in Uganda. He can be tried and convicted of murder in any place in India in which he may be found.

5. Certain laws not to be affected by this Act. Nothing in this Act shall affect the provisions of any Act for punishing mutiny and desertion of officers, soldiers, sailors or airmen in the service of the Government of India or the provision of any special or local law.

CHAPTER - II : GENERAL EXPLANATIONS

6. Definitions in the Code to be understood subject to exceptions. Throughout this Code every definition of an offence, every penal provision and every illustration of every such definition or penal provision, shall be understood subject to the exceptions contained in the Chapter entitled" General Exceptions", though those exceptions are not repeated in such definition, penal provision, or illustration.

ILLUSTRATIONS

(a) The Sections, in this Code, which contain definitions of offences, do not express that a child under seven years of age cannot commit such offences; but the definitions are to be understood subject to the general exception which provides that nothing shall be an offence which done by child under seven years of age.

(b) A, a police-officer, without warrant, apprehends Z who has committed murder. Here A is not guilty of the offence of wrongful confinement; for he was bound by law to apprehend Z, and therefore the case falls within the general exception which provides that "nothing is an offence which is done by a person who is bound by law to do it".

7. Sense of expression once explained. Every expression which is explained in any part of this Code, is used in every part of this Code in conformity with the explanation.

8. Gender. The pronoun" he" and its derivatives are used of any person, whether male or female.

9. Number. Unless the contrary appears from the context, words importing the singular number include the plural number, and words importing the plural number include the singular number.

10. "Man"- "Woman". The word "man" denotes a male human being of any age; the word "woman" denotes a female human being of any age.

11. "Person". The word "person" includes any Company or Association or body of persons, whether incorporated or not.

12. "Public". The word "public" includes any class of the public or any community.

14. "Servant of Government". The words "Servant of Government" denote any officer or servant continued, appointed or employed in India by or under the authority of Government.

18. "India". "India" means the territory of India excluding the State of Jammu and Kashmir.

19. "Judge". The word "Judge" denotes not only every person who is officially designated as a Judge, but also every person. who is empowered by law to give, in any legal proceeding, civil or criminal, a definitive judgment, or a judgment which, if not appealed against, would be definitive, or a judgment which, if confirmed by some other authority, would be definitive, or who is one of a body of persons, which body of persons is empowered by law to give such a judgment.

ILLUSTRATIONS

(a) A collector exercising jurisdiction in a suit under Act 10 of 1859, is a Judge.

(b) A Magistrate exercising jurisdiction in respect of a charge on which he has power to sentence to fine or imprisonment with or without appeal, is a Judge.

(c) A member of a panchayat which has power, under Regulation VII, 1816, of the Madras Code, to try and determine suit, is a Judge.

(d) A Magistrate exercising jurisdiction in respect of a charge on which he has power only to commit for trial to another Court, is not a Judge.

20. "Court of Justice". The words "Court of Jutsice" denote a Judge who is empowered by law to act judicially alone, or a body of Judges which is empowered by law to act judicially as a body, when such Judge or body of Judges is acting judicially. A Panchayat acting under Regulation VII, 1816, of the Madras Code, having power to try and determine suits, is a Court of Justice.

21. "Public servant". The words "public servant" denote a person falling under any of the descriptions hereinafter following, namely:— **Second.** Every Commissioned Officer in the Military, Naval or Air Forces of India; **Third.** Every Judge including any person empowered by law to discharge, whether by himself or as a member of any body of persons. any adjudicatory functions; **Fourth.** Every officer of a Court of Justice (including a liquidator, receiver or commissioner) whose duty it is, as such officer, to investigate or report on any matter of law or fact, or to make, authenticate, or keep any document, or to take charge or dispose of any property, or to execute any judicial process, or to administer any oath, or to interpret, or to preserve order in the Court, and every person specially authorized by a Court of Justice to perform any of such duties; **Fifth.** Every juryman, assessor, or member of a panchayat assisting a Court of Justice or public servant; **Sixth.** Every arbitrator or other person to whom any cause or matter has been referred for decision or report by any Court of Justice, or by any other competent public authority; **Seventh.** Every person who holds any office by virtue of which he is empowered to place or keep any person in confinement; **Eighth.** Every officer of the Government whose duty it is, as such officer, to prevent offences, to give information of offences, to bring offenders to justice, or to protect the public health, safety or convenience; **Ninth.** Every officer whose duty it is as such officer, to take, receive, keep or expend any property on behalf of the Government, or to make any survey, assessment or contract on behalf of the Government, or to execute any revenue-process, or to investigate, or to report, on any matter affecting the pecuniary interests of the Government, or to make. authenticate or keep any document relating to the pecuniary interests of the Government, or to prevent the infraction of any law for the protection of the pecuniary interests of the Government; **Tenth.** Every officer whose duty it is, as such officer, to take, receive, keep or expend any property, to make any survey or assessment or to levy any rate or tax for any secular common purpose of any village, town or district, or to make, authenticate or keep any document for the ascertaining of the rights of the people of any village, town or district;

Eleventh. Every person who holds any office in virtue of which he is empowered to prepare, publish, maintain or revise an electoral roll or to conduct an election or part of an election; **Twelfth.** Every person—

(a) in the service or pay of the Government or remunerated by fees or commission for the performance of any public duty by the Government;

(b) in the service or pay of a local authority, a corporation established by or under a Central, Provincial or State Act or a Government company as defined in Section 617 of the Companies Act, 1956 (1 of 1956).

ILLUSTRATION. A Municipal Commissioner is a public servant.

EXPLANATION 1. Persons falling under any of the above descriptions are public servants, whether appointed by the Government or not.

EXPLANATION 2. Wherever the words "public servant" occur, they shall be understood of every person who is in actual possession of the situation of a public servant, whatever legal defect there may be in his right tc hold that situation.

EXPLANATION 3. The word "election" denotes an election for the purpose of selecting members of any legislative, municipal or other public authority, of whatever character, the method of selection to which is by, or under, any law prescribed as by election.

22. "Movable property". The words "movable property" are intended to include corporeal property of every description, except land and things attached to the earth or permanently fastcncd to anything which is attached to the earth.

23. "Wrongful gain". "Wrongful gain" is gain by unlawful means of property to which the person gaining is not legally entitled. "Wrongful loss" is the loss by unlawful means of property to which the person losing it is legally entitled. A person is said to gain wrongfully when such person retains wrongfully, as well as when such person acquires wrongfully. A person is said to lose wrongfully when such person is wrongfully kept out of any property, as well as when such person is wrongfully deprived of property.

24. "Dishonestly". Whoever does anything with the intention of causing wrongful gain to one person or wrongful loss to another person, is said to do that thing" dishonestly".

25. "Fraudulently". A person is said to do a thing fraudulently if he does that thing with intent to defraud but not otherwise.

26. "Reason to believe". A person is said to have "reason to believe" a thing, if he has sufficient cause to believe that thing but not otherwise.

27. Property in possession of wife, clerk or servant. When property is in the possession of a person's wife, clerk or servant, on account of that person, it is in that person's possession within the meaning of this Code.

EXPLANATION. A person employed temporarily or on a particular occasion in the capacity of a clerk, or servant, is a clerk or servant within the meaning of this Section.

28. "Counterfeit". A person is said to "counterfeit" who causes one thing to resemble another thing, intending by means of that resemblance to practise deception, or knowing it to be likely that deception will thereby be practised. Explanation 1. It is not essential to counterfeiting that the imitation should be exact.

EXPLANATION 2. When a person causes one thing to resemble another thing, and the resemblance is such that a person might be deceived thereby, it shall be presumed, until the contrary is proved, that the person so causing the one thing to resemble the other thing intended by means of that resemblance to practise deception or knew it to be likely that deception would thereby be practised.

29. "Document". The word "document" denotes any matter expressed or described upon any substance by means of letters, figures or marks, or by more than one of those means, intended to be used, or which may be used, as evidence of that matter.

EXPLANATION 1: It is immaterial by what means or upon what substance the letters, figures or marks are formed, or whether the evidence is intended for, or may be used in, a Court of Justice, or not.

ILLUSTRATIONS. A writing expressing the terms of a contract, which may be used as evidence of the contract, is a document. A cheque upon a banker is a document. A power of attorney is a document. A map or plan which is intended to be used or which may be used as evidence, is a document. A writing containing directions or instructions is a document.

EXPLANATION 2: Whatever is expressed by means of letters, figures or marks as explained by mercantile or other usage, shall be deemed to be expressed by such letters, figures or marks within the meaning of this Section, although the same may not be actually expressed.

ILLUSTRATION. A writes his name on the back of a bill of exchange payable to his order. The meaning of the endorsement as explained by mercantile usage, is that the bill is to be paid to the holder. The endorsement is a document, and must be construed in the same manner as if the words "pay to the holder" or words to that effect had been written over the signature.

30. "Valuable security". The words "valuable security" denote a document which is, or purports to be, a document whereby any legal right is created, extended, transferred, restricted, extinguished or released, or who hereby any person acknowledges that he lies under legal liability, or has not a certain legal right.

ILLUSTRATION. A writes his name on the back of a bill of exchange. As the effect of this endorsement is to transfer the right to the bill to any person who may become the lawful holder of it, the endorsement is a "valuable security".

31. "A will". The words "a will" denote any testamentary document.

32. Words referring to acts include illegal omissions. In every part of this Code, except where a contrary intention appears from the context, words which refer to acts done extend also to illegal omissions.

33. "Act", "Omission". The word "act" denotes as well as series of acts as a single act: the word "omission" denotes as well a series of omissions as a single omission.

34. Acts done by several persons in futherance of common intention. When a criminal act is done by several persons in furtherance of the common intention of all, each of such persons is liable for that act in the same manner as if it were done by him alone.

35. When such an act is criminal by reason of its being done with a criminal knowledge or intention. Whenever an act, which is criminal only by reason of its being done with a criminal knowledge or intention, is done by several persons, each of such persons who joins in the act with such knowledge or intention is liable for the act in the same manner as if the act were done by him alone with that knowledge or intention.

36. Effect caused partly by act and partly by omission. Wherever, the causing of a certain effect, or an attempt to cause that effect, by an act or by an omission, is an offence, it is to be understood that the causing of that effect partly by an act and partly by an omission is the same offence.

ILLUSTRATION. A intentionally causes Z's death, partly by illegally omitting to give Z food, and party by beating Z. A has committed murder.

37. Co- operation by doing one of several acts constituting an offence. When an offence is committed by means of several acts, whoever intentionally co-operates in the commission of that offence by doing any one of those acts, either singly or jointly with any other person, commits that offence.

ILLUSTRATIONS.

(a) A and B agree to murder Z by severally and at different times giving him small doses of poison. A and B administer the poison according to the agreement with intent to murder Z. Z dies from the effects the several doses of poison so administered to him. Here A and B intentionally co-operate in the commission of murder and as each of them does an act by which the death is caused, they are both guilty of the offence though their acts are separate.

(b) A and B are joint jailors, and as such have the charge of Z, a prisoner, alternatively for six hours at a time. A and B, intending to cause Z's death, knowingly co-operate in causing that effect by illegally omitting, each during the time of his attendance, to furnish Z with food supplied to them for that purpose. Z dues of hunger. Both A and B are guilty of the murder of Z.

(c) A, a jailor, has the charge of Z, a prisoner. A, intending to cause Z's death, illegally omits to supply Z with food; in consequence of which Z is much reduced in strength, but the starvation is not sufficient to cause his death. A is dismissed from his office, and B succeeds him. B, without collusion or co-operation with A, illegally omits to supply Z with food, knowing that he is likely thereby to cause Z's death. Z dies of hunger. B is guilty of murder, but, as A did not co-operate with B. A is guilty only of an attempt to commit murder.

38. Persons concerned in criminal Act may be guilty of different offences. Where several persons are engaged or concerned in the commission of a criminal act, they may be guilty of different offences by means of that act.

ILLUSTRATION. A attacks Z under such circumstances of grave provocation that his killing of Z would be only culpable homicide not amounting to murder. B, having ill- will towards Z and intending to kill him, and not having been subject to the provocation, assists A in killing Z. Here, though A and B are both engaged in causing Z's death, B is guilty of murder, and A is guilty only of culpable homicide.

39. "Voluntarily". A person is said to cause an effect "voluntarily" when he causes it by means whereby he intended to cause it, or by means which, at the time of employing those means, he knew or had reason to believe to be likely to cause it.

ILLUSTRATION. A sets fire, by night, to an inhabited house in a large town, for the purpose of facilitating a robbery and thus causes the death of a person. Here, A may not have intended to cause death; and may even be sorry that death has been caused by his act; yet, if he knew that he was likely to cause death, he has caused death voluntarily.

40. "Offence". Except in the Chapters and Sections mentioned in clauses 2 and 3 of this Section, the word "offence" denotes a thing made punishable by this Code. In Chapter IV, Chapter VA and in the following Sections, namely, Sections 4, 109, 110, 112, 114, 115, 116, 117, 187, 194, 195, 203, 211, 213, 214, 221, 222, 223, 224, 225, 327, 328, 329, 330, 331, 347, 348, 388, 389 and 445, the word "offence" denotes a thing punishable under this Code, or under any special or local law as hereinafter defined. And in Sections 141, 176, 177, 201, 202, 212, 216 and 441, the word "offence" has the same meaning when the thing punishable under the special or local law is punishable under such law with imprisonment for a term of six months or upwards, whether with or without fine.

41. "Special law". A "special law" is a law applicable to a particular subject.

42. "Local law". A "local law" is a law applicable only to a particular part of India.

43. "Illegal", "Legally bound to do". The word "illegal" is applicable to everything which is an offence or which is prohibited by law, or which furnishes ground for a civil action; and a person is said to be "legally bound to do" whatever it is illegal in him to omit.

44. "Injury". The word "injury" denotes any harm whatever illegally caused to any person, in body, mind, reputation or property.

45. "Life". The word "life" denotes the life of a human being, unless the contrary appears from the context.

46. "Death". The word "death" denotes the death of a human being unless the contrary appears from the context.

47. "Animal". The word "animal" denotes any living creature, other than a human being.

48. "Vessel". The word "vessel" denotes anything made for the conveyance by water of human beings or of property.

49. "Year", "Month". Wherever the word "year" or the word "month" is used, it is to be understood that the year or the month is to be reckoned according to the British calendar.

50. "Section". The word "section" denotes one of those portions of a Chapter of this Code which are distinguished by prefixed numeral figures.

51. "Oath". The word "oath" includes a solemn affirmation substituted by law for an oath, and any declaration required or authorized by law to be made before a public servant or to be used for the purpose of proof, whether in a Court of Justice or not.

52. "Good faith". Nothing is said to be done or believed in "good faith" which is done or believed without due care and attention.

52A. "Harbour". Except in Section 157, and in Section 130 in the case in which the harbour is given by the wife or husband of the person harboured, the word "harbour" includes the supplying a person with shelter, food, drink, money, clothes, arms, ammunition or means of conveyance, or the assisting a person by any means, whether of the same kind as those enumerated in this Section or not, to evade apprehension.

CHAPTER - III : OF PUNISHMENTS

53. Punishments. The punishments to which offenders are liable under the provisions of this Code are— **First.** Death; **Secondly.** Imprisonment for life; **Fourthly.** Imprisonment, which is of two descriptions, namely:-

(1) Rigorous, that is with hard labour;

(2) Simple; **Fifthly.** Forfeiture of property; **Sixthly.** Fine.

53A. Construction of reference to transportation.

(1) Subject to the provisions of sub-section (2) and sub-section (3), any reference to "transportation for life" in any other law for the time being in force or in any instrument or order having effect by virtue of any such law or of any enactment repealed shall be construed as a reference to "imprisonment for life".

(2) In every case in which a sentence of transportation for a term has been passed before the commencement of the Code of Criminal Procedure (Amendment) Act, 1955, (26 of 1955), the offender shall be dealt with in the same manner as if sentenced to rigorous imprisonment for the same term.

(3) Any reference to transportation for a term or to transportation for any shorter term (by whatever name called) in any other law for the time being in force shall be deemed to have been omitted.

(4) Any reference to "transportation" in any other law for the time being in force shall,-

   (a) if the expression means transportation for life, be construed as a reference to imprisonment for life;

   (b) if the expression means transportation for any shorter term, be deemed to have been omitted.

54. Commutation of sentence of death. In every case in which sentence of death shall have been passed, the appropriate Government may, without the consent of the offender, commute the punishment for any other punishment provided by this Code.

55. Commutation of sentence of imprisonment for life. In every case in which sentence of imprisonment for life shall have been passed, the appropriate Government may, without the consent of the offender, commute the punishment for imprisonment of either description for a term not exceeding fourteen years.

55A. Definition of "appropriate Government". In Sections fifty-four and fifty-five the expression "appropriate Government" means,-

(a) in cases where the sentence is a sentence of death or is for an offence against any law relating to a matter to which the executive power of the Union extends, the Central Government; and

(b) in cases where the sentence (whether of death or not) is for an offence against any law relating to a matter to which the executive power of the State extends, the Government of the State within which the offender is sentenced.

56. Sentence of Europeans and Americans to penal servitude. Proviso as to sentence for term exceeding ten years but not for life. *Rep. by the Criminal Law (Removal of Racial Discriminations) Act, 1949 (17 of 1949) (w. e. f. 6-4-1949).*

57. Fractions of terms of punishment. In calculating fractions of terms of punishment, imprinsonment for life shall be reckoned as equivalent to imprisonment for twenty years.

58. Offenders sentenced to transportation how dealt with until transported. *Rep. by the Code of Criminal Procedure (Amendment) Act, 1955 (26 of 1955), s. 117 and Sch.*

59. Transportation instead of imprisonment. *Rep. by the Code of Criminal Procedure (Amendment) Act, 1955 (26 of 1955) s. 117 and Sch., (w. e. f. 1-1-1956).*

60. Sentence may be (in certain cases of imprisonment) wholly or partly rigorous or simple. In every case in which an offender is punishable with imprisonment which may be of either description, it shall be competent to the Court which sentences such offender to direct in the sentence that such imprisonment shall be wholly rigorous, or that such imprisonment shall be wholly simple or that any part of such imprisonment shall be rigorous and the rest simple.

61. Sentence of forfeiture of property. *Rep. by the Indian Penal Code (Amendment) Act, 1921 (16 of 1921), s. 4.*

62. Forfeiture of property, in respect of offenders punishable with death, transportation or imprisonment. *Rep., by s. 4 ibid.*

63. Amount of fine. Where no sum is expressed to which a fine may extend, the amount of fine to which the offender is liable is unlimited, but shall not be excessive.

64. Sentence of imprisonment for non-payment of fine. In every case of an offence punishable with imprisonment as well as fine, in which the offender is sentenced to a fine, whether with or without imprisonment, and in every case of an offence punishable with imprisonment or fine, or with fine only, in which the offender is sentenced to a fine. it shall be competent to the Court which sentences such offender to direct by the sentence that, in default of payment of the fine, the offender shall suffer imprisonment for a certain term, which imprisonment shall be in excess of any other imprisonment to which he may have been sentenced or to which he may be liable under a commutation of a sentence.

65. Limit to imprisonment for non-payment of fine, when imprisonment and fine awardable. The term for which the Court directs the offender to be imprisoned in default of payment of a fine shall not exceed one-fourth of the term of imprisonment which is the maximum fixed for the offence, if the offence be punishable with imprisonment as well as fine.

66. Description of imprisonment for non-payment of fine. The imprisonment which the Court imposes in default of payment of a fine may be of any description to which the offender might have been sentenced for the offence.

67. Imprisonment for non-payment of fine, when offence punishable with fine only. If the offence be punishable with fine only, the imprisonment which the Court imposes in default of payment of the fine shall be simple, and the term for which the Court directs the offender to be imprisoned, in default of payment of fine, shall not exceed the following scale, that is to say, for any term not exceeding two months when the amount of the fine shall not exceed fifty rupees, and for any term not exceeding four months when the amount shall not exceed one hundred rupees, and for any term not exceeding six months in any other case.

68. Imprisonment to terminate on payment of fine. The imprisonment which is imposed in default of payment of a fine shall terminate whenever that fine is either paid or levied by process of law.

69. Termination of imprisonment on payment of proportional part of fine. If, before the expiration of the term of imprisonment fixed in default of payment, such a proportion of the fine be paid or levied that the term of imprisonment suffered in default of payment is not less than proportional to the part of the fine still unpaid, the imprisonment shall terminate.

ILLUSTRATION. A is sentenced to a fine of one hundred rupees and to four months' imprisonment in default of payment. Here, if seventy-five rupees of the fine be paid or levied before the expiration of one month of the imprisonment. A will be discharged as soon as the first month has expired. If seventy-five rupees be paid or levied at the time of the expiration of the first month, or at any later time while A continues in imprisonment. A will be immediately discharged. If fifty rupees of the fine be paid or levied before the expiration of two months of the imprisonment. A will be discharged as soon as the two months are completed. If fifty rupees be paid or levied at the time of the expiration of those two months, or at any later time while A continues in imprisonment, A will be immediately discharged.

70. Fine leviable within six years, or during imprisonment. Death not to discharge property from liability. The fine, or any part thereof which remains unpaid, may be levied at any time within six years after the passing of the sentence, and if, under the sentence, the offender be liable to imprisonment for a longer period than six years, then at any time previous to the expiration of that period; and the death of the offender does not discharge from the liability any property which would, after his death, be legally liable for his debts.

71. Limit of punishment of offence made up of several offences. Where anything which is an offence is made up of parts, any of which parts is itself an offence, the offender shall not be punished with the punishment of more than one of such his offences, unless it be so expressly provided. Where anything is an offence falling within two or more separate definitions of any law in force for the time being by which offences are defined or punished, or where several acts, of which one or more than one would by itself or themselves constitute an offence, constitute, when combined, a different offence, the offender shall not be punished with a more severe punishment than the Court which tries him could award for any one of such offences.

ILLUSTRATIONS -

(a) A gives Z fifty strokes with a stick. Here A may have committed the offence of voluntarily causing hurt to Z by the whole beating, and also by each of the blows which make up the whole beating. If A were liable to punishment for every blow, he might be imprisoned for fifty years, one for each blow. But he is liable only to one punishment for the whole beating.

(b) But, if, while A is beating Z, Y interferes, and A intentionally strikes Y, here, as the blow given to Y is no part of the act whereby A voluntarily causes hurt to Z, A is liable to one punishment for voluntarily causing hurt to Z, and to another for the blow given to Y.

72. Punishment of person guilty of one of several offences, the judgment stating that it is doubtful of which. In all cases in which judgment is given that a person is guilty of one of several offences specified in the judgment, but that it is doubtful of which of these offences he is guilty, the offender shall be punished for the offence for which the lowest punishment is provided if the same punishment is not provided for all.

73. Solitary confinement. Whenever any person is convicted of an offence for which under this Code the Court has power to sentence him to rigorous imprisonment, the Court may, by its sentence, order that the offender shall be kept in solitary confinement for any portion or portions of the imprisonment to which he is sentenced, not exceeding three months in the whole, according to the following scale, that is to say - a time not exceeding one month if the term of imprisonment shall not exceed six months: a time not exceeding two months if the term of imprisonment shall exceed six months and shall not exceed one year: a time not exceeding three months if the term of imprisonment shall exceed one year.

74. Limit of solitary confinement. In executing a sentence of solitary confinement, such confinement shall in no case exceed fourteen days at a time, with intervals between the periods of solitary confinement of not less duration than such periods; and when the imprisonment awarded shall exceed three months, the solitary confinement shall not exceed seven days in any one month of the whole imprisonment awarded, with intervals between the periods of solitary confinement of not less duration than such periods.

75. Enhanced punishment for certain offences under Chapter XII or Chapter XVII after previous conviction. Whoever, having been convicted,-

(a) by a Court in India, of an offence punishable under Chapter XII or Chapter XVII of this Code with imprisonment of either description for a term of three years or upwards, shall be guilty of any offence punishable under either of those Chapters with like imprisonment for the like term, shall be subject for every such subsequent offence to imprisonment for life or to imprisonment of either description for a term which may extend to ten years.

CHAPTER - IV : GENERAL EXCEPTIONS

76. Act done by a person bound, or by mistake of fact believing himself bound, by law. Nothing is an offence which is done by a person who is, or who by reason of a mistake of fact and not by reason of a mistake of law in good faith believes himself to be, bound by law to do it.

ILLUSTRATIONS -

(a) A, a soldier, fires on a mob by the order of his superior officer, in conformity with the commands of the law. A has committed no offence.

(b) A, an officer of a Court of Justice, being ordered by that Court to arrest Y, and after due enquiry, believing Z to be Y, arrests Z. A has committed no offence.

77. Act of Judge when acting judicially. Nothing is an offence which is done by a Judge when acting judicially in the exercise of any power which is, or which in good faith he believes to be, given to him by law.

78. Act done pursuant to the judgment or order of Court. Nothing which is done in pursuance of, or which is warranted by the judgment or order of, a Court of Justice, if done whilst such judgment or order remains in force, is an offence, notwithstanding the Court may have had no jurisdiction to pass such judgment or order, provided the person doing the act in good faith believes that the Court had such jurisdiction.

79. Act done by a person justified, or by mistake of fact believing himself, justified, by law. Nothing is an offence which is done by any person who is justified by law, or who by reason of a mistake of fact and not by reason of a mistake of law in good faith, believes himself to be justified by law, in doing it.

ILLUSTRATION. A sees Z commit what appears to A to be a murder. A, in the exercise, to the best of his judgment exerted in good faith, of the power which the law gives to all persons of apprehending murderers in the fact, seizes Z, in order to bring Z before the proper authorities. A has committed no offence, though it may turn out that Z was acting in self-defence.

80. Accident in doing a lawful act. Nothing is an offence which is done by accident or misfortune, and without any criminal intention or knowledge in the doing of a lawful act in a lawful manner by lawful means and with proper care and caution.

ILLUSTRATION. A is at work with a hatchet; the head flies off and kills a man who is standing by. Here, if there was no want of proper caution on the part of A, his act is excusable and not an offence.

81. Act likely to cause harm, but done without criminal intent, and to prevent other harm. Nothing is an offence merely by reason of its being done with the knowledge that it is likely to cause harm, if it be done without any criminal intention to cause harm, and in good faith for the purpose of preventing or avoiding other harm to person or property.

EXPLANATION - It is a question of fact in such a case whether the harm to be prevented or avoided was of such a nature and so imminent as to justify or excuse the risk of doing the act with the knowledge that it was likely to cause harm.

ILLUSTRATIONS.

(a) A, the captain of a steam vessel, suddenly and without any fault or negligence on his part, finds himself in such a position that, before he can stop his vessel, he must inevitably run down a boat B, with twenty or thirty passengers on board, unless he changes the course of his vessel, and that, by changing his course, he must incur risk of running down a boat C with only two passengers on board, which he may possibly clear. Here, if A alters his course without any intention to run down the boat C and in good faith for the purpose of avoiding the danger to the passengers in the boat B, he is not guilty of an offence, though he may run down the boat C by doing an which he knew was likely to cause that effect, if it be found as a matter of fact that the danger which he intended to avoid was such as to excuse him in incurring the risk of running down C.

(b) A, in a great fire, pulls down houses in order to prevent the conflagration from spreading. He does this with the intention in good faith of saving human life or property. Here, if it be found that the harm to be prevented was of such a nature and so imminent as to excuse A's act, A is not guilty of the offence.

82. Act of a child under seven years of age. Nothing is an offence which is done by a child under seven years of age.

83. Act of a child above seven and under twelve of immature understanding. Nothing is an offence which is done by a child above seven years of age and under twelve, who has not attained sufficient maturity of understanding to judge of the nature and consequences of his conduct on that occasion.

84. Act of a person of unsound mind. Nothing is an offence which is done by a person who, at the time of doing it, by reason of unsoundness of mind, is incapable of knowing the nature of the act, or that he is doing what is either wrong or contrary to law.

85. Act of a person incapable of judgment by reason of intoxication caused against his will. Nothing is an offence which is done by a person who, at the time of doing it is, by reason of intoxication, incapable of knowing the nature of the act, or that he is doing what is either wrong, or contrary to law:

PROVIDED that the thing which intoxicated him was administered to him without his knowledge or against his will.

86. Offence requiring a particular intent or knowledge committed by one who is intoxicated. In cases where an act done is not an offence unless done with a particular knowledge or intent, a person who does the act in a state of intoxication shall be liable to be dealt with as if he had the same knowledge as he would have had if he had not been intoxicated, unless the thing which intoxicated him was administered to him without his knowledge or against his will.

87. Act not intended and not known to be likely to cause death or grievous hurt, done by consent. Nothing which is not intended to cause death, or grievous hurt, and which is not known by the doer to be likely to cause death or grievous hurt, is an offence by reason of any harm which it may cause, or be intended by the doer to cause, to any person, above eighteen years of age, who has given consent, whether express or implied, to suffer that harm; or by reason of any harm which it may be known by the doer to be likely to cause to any such person who has consented to take the risk of that harm.

ILLUSTRATION. A and Z agree to fence with each other for amusement. This agreement implies the consent of each to suffer any harm which, in the course of such fencing, may be caused without foul play; and if A, while playing fairly, hurts Z, A commits no offence.

88. Act not intended to cause death, done by consent in good faith for person's benefit. Nothing, which is not intented to cause death, is an offence by reason of any harm which it may cause, or be intended by the doer to cause, or be known by the doer to be likely to cause, to any person for whose benefit it is done in good faith, and who has given a consent, whether express or implied to suffer that harm, or to take the risk of that harm.

ILLUSTRATION. A, a surgeon, knowing that a particular operation is likely to cause the death of Z, who suffers under the painful complaint, but not intending to cause Z's death, and intending, in good faith, Z's benefit, performs that operation on Z, with Z's consent. A has committed no offence.

89. Act done in good faith for benefit of child or insane person, by or by consent of guardian. Nothing which is done in good faith for the benefit of a person under twelve years of age, or of unsound mind, by or by consent, either express or implied, of the guardian or other person having lawful charge of that person, is an offence by reason of any harm which it may cause, or be intended by the doer to cause or be known by the doer to be likely to cause to that person: Provided-

Provisos. First. That this exception shall not extend to the intentional causing of death, or to the attempting to cause death; **Secondly.** That this exception shall not extend to the doing of anything which the person doing it knows to be likely to cause death, for any purpose other than the preventing of death or grievous hurt, or the curing of any grievous disease or infirmity; **Thirdly.** That this exception shall not extend to the voluntary causing of grievous hurt, or to the attempting to cause grievous hurt, unless it be for the purpose of preventing death or grievous hurt, or the curing of any grievous disease or infirmity; **Fourthly.** That this exception shall not extend to the abetment of any offence, to the committing of which offence it would not extend.

ILLUSTRATION. A, in good faith, for his child's benefit without his child's consent, has his child cut for the stone by a surgeon knowing it to be likely that the operation will cause the child's death, but not intending to cause the child's death. A is within the exception, in as much as his object was the cure of the child.

90. Consent known to be given under fear or misconception. A consent is not such a consent as is intended by any Section of this Code, if the consent is given by a person under fear of injury, or under a misconception of fact, and if the person doing the act knows, or has reason to believe, that the consent was given in consequence of such fear or misconception; or

Consent of insane person - if the consent is given by a person who, from unsoundness of mind, or intoxication, is unable to understand the nature and consequence of that to which he gives his consent; or

Consent of child - unless the contrary appears from the context, if the consent is given by a person who is under twelve years of age.

91. Exclusion of acts which are offences independently of harm cause. The exceptions in Sections 87, 88 and 89 do not extend to acts which are offences independently of any harm which they may cause, or be intended to cause, or be known to be likely to cause, to the person giving the consent, or on whose behalf the consent is given. Illustration Causing miscarriage (unless caused in good faith for the purpose of saving the life of the woman) is offence inexpediently of any harm which it may cause or be intended to cause to the woman. Therefore, it is not an offence "by reason of such harm"; and the consent of the woman or of her guardian to the causing of such miscarriage does not justify the act.

92. Act done in good faith for benefit of a person without consent. Nothing is an offence by reason of any harm which it may causes to a person for whose benefit it is done in good faith, even without that person's consent, if the circumstances are such that it is impossible for that person to signify consent, or if that person is incapable of giving consent, and has no guardian or other person in lawful charge of him from whom it is possible to obtain consent in time for the thing to be done with benefit:

> *PROVIDED - **Provisos. First.** That this exception shall not extend to the intentional causing of death or the attempting to cause death; **Secondly.** That this exception shall not extend to the doing of anything which the person doing it knows to be likely to cause death, for any purpose other than the preventing of death or grievous hurt, or the curing of any grievous disease or infirmity; **Thirdly.** That this exception shall not extend to the voluntary causing of hurt, or to the attempting to cause hurt, for any purpose other than the preventing of death or hurt; **Fourthly.** That this exception shall not extend to the abetment of any offence, to the committing of which offence it would not extend.*

ILLUSTRATIONS.

(a) Z is thrown from his horse, and is insensible. A, a surgeon, finds that Z requires to be trepanned. A, not intending Z's death, but in good faith, for Z's benefit, performs the trepan before Z recovers his power of judging for himself. A has committed no offence.

(b) Z is carried off by a tiger. A fires at the tiger knowing it to be likely that the shot may kill Z, but not intending to kill Z, and in good faith intending Z's benefit. A's ball gives Z a mortal wound. A has committed no offence.

(c) A, a surgeon, sees a child suffer an accident which is likely to prove fatal unless an operation be immediately performed. There is no time to apply to the child's guardian. A performs the operation in spite of the entreaties of the child, intending, in good faith, the child's benefit. A has committed no offence.

(d) A is in a house which is on fire, with Z, a child. People below hold out a blanket. A drops the child, from the house-top, knowing it to be likely that the fall may kill the child, but not intending to kill the child, and intending, in good faith, the child's benefit. Here, even if the child is killed by the fall, A has committed no offence.

EXPLANATION - Mere pecuniary benefit is not benefit within the meaning of Sections 88, 89 and 92.

93. Communication made in good faith. No communication made in good faith is an offence by reason of any harm to the person to whom it is made, if it is made for the benefit of that person.

ILLUSTRATION. A, a surgeon, in good faith, communicates to a patient his opinion that he cannot live. The patient dies in consequence of the shock. A has committed no offence, though he knew it to be likely that the communication might cause the patient's death.

94. Act to which a person is compelled by threats. Except murder, and offences against the State punishable with death, nothing is an offence which is done by a person who is compelled to do it by threats, which, at the time of doing it, reasonnably cause the apprehension that instant death to that person will otherwise be the consequence:

> *PROVIDED the person doing the act did not of his own accord, or from a reasonable apprehension of harm to himself short of instant death, place himself in the situation by which he became subject to such constraint.*

EXPLANATION 1. A person who, of his own accord, or by reason of a threat of being beaten, joins a gang of dacoits, knowing their character. is not entitled to the benefit of this exception, on the ground of his having been compelled by his associates to do anything that is an offence by law.

EXPLANTION 2. A person seized by a gang of dacoits, and forced, by threat of instant death, to do a thing which is an offence by law; for example, a smith compelled to take his tools and to force the door of a house for the dacoits to enter and plunder it, is entitled to the benefit of this exception.

95. Act causing slight harm. Nothing is an offence by reason that it causes, or that it is intended to cause, or that it is known to be likely to cause, any harm, if that harm is so slight that no person of ordinary sense and temper would complain of such harm of the Right of Private Defence.

96. Things done in private defence. Nothing is an offence which is done in the exercise of the right of private defence.

97. Right of private defence of the body and of property. Every person has a right, subject to the restrictions contained in Section 99, to defend- **First.** His own body, and the body of any other person, against any offence affecting the human body; **Secondly.** The property, whether movable or immovable, of himself or of any other person, against any act which is an offence falling under the defintion of theft, robbery, mischief or criminal trespass, or which is an attempt to commit theft, robbery, mischief or criminal trespass.

98. Right of private defence against the act of a person of unsound mind, etc. When an act which would otherwise be a certain offence, is not that offence, by reason of the youth, the want of maturity of understanding, the unsoundness of mind or the intoxication of the person doing that act, or by reason of any misconception on the part of that person, every person has the same right of private defence against that act which he would have if the act were that offence.

ILLUSTRATIONS.

(a) Z, under the influence of madness, attempts to kill A; Z is guilty of no offence. But A has the same right of private defence which he would have if Z were sane.

(b) A enters by night a house which he is legally entitled to enter. Z, in good faith, taking A for a house-breaker, attacks A. Here Z, by attacking A under this misconception, commits no offence. But A has the same right of private defence against Z, which he would have if Z were not acting under that misconception.

99. Acts against which there is no right of private defence. There is no right of private defence against an act which does not reasonably cause the apprehension of death or of grievous hurt, if done, or attempted to be done, by a public servant acting in good faith under colour of his office, though that act may not be strictly justifiable by law. There is no right of private defence against an act which does not reasonably cause the apprehension of death or of grievous hurt, if done, or attempted to be done, by the direction of a public servant acting in good faith under colour of his office though that direction may not be strictly justifiable by law. There is no right of private defence in cases in which there is time to have recourse to protection of the public authorities. Extent to which the right may be exercised. The right of private defence in no case extends to the inflicting of more harm than it is necessary to inflict for the purpose of defence.

EXPLANATION 1. A person is not deprived of the right of private defence against an act done, or attempted to be done, by a public servant, as such, unless he knows or has reason to believe, that the person doing the act is such public servant.

EXPLANATION 2. A person is not deprived of the right of private defence against an act done, or attempted to be done, by the direction of a public servant, unless he knows, or has reason to believe, that the person doing the act is acting by such direction, or unless such person states the authority under which he acts, or if he has authority in writing, unless he produces such authority, if demanded.

100. When the right of private defence of the body extends to causing death. The right of private defence of the body extends, under the restrictions mentioned in the last preceding Section, to the voluntary causing of death or of any other harm to the assailant, if the offence which occasions the exercise of the right be of any of the descriptions hereinafter enumerated, namely:- **First.** Such an assault as may reasonably cause the apprehension that death will otherwise be the consequence of such assault; **Secondly.** Such an assault as may reasonably cause the apprehension that grievous hurt will otherwise be the consequence of such assault; **Thirdly.** An assault with the intention of committing rape; **Fourthly.** An assault with the intention of gratifying unnatural lust; **Fifthly.** An assault with the intention of kidnapping or abducting; **Sixthly.** An assault with the intention of wrongfully confining a person, under circumstances which may reasonably cause him to apprehend that he will be unable to have recourse to the public authorities for his release.

101. When such right extends to causing any harm other than death. If the offence be not of any of the descriptions enumerated in the last preceding Section, the right of private defence of the body does not extend to the voluntary causing of death to the assailant, but does extend, under the restrictions mentioned in Section 99, to the voluntary causing to the assailant of any harm other than death.

102. Commencement and continuance of the right of private defence of the body. The right of private defence of the body commences as soon as a reasonable apprehension of danger to the body arises from an attempt or threat to commit the offence though the offence may not have been committed; and it continues as long as such apprehension of danger to the body continues.

103. When the right of private defence of property extends to causing death. The right of private defence of property extends, under the restrictions mentioned in Section 99, to the voluntary causing of death or of any other harm to the wrong-doer, if the offence, the committing of which, or the attempting to commit which, occasions the exercise of the right, be an offence of any of the descriptions hereinafter enumerated, namely:- **First.** Robbery; **Secondly.** House-breaking by night; **Thirdly.** Mischief by fire committed on any building, tent or vessel, which building, tent or vessel is used as a human dwelling, or as a place for the custody of property; **Fourthly.** Theft, mischief, or house-trespass, under such circumstances as may reasonably cause apprehension that death or grievous hurt will be the consequence, if such right of private defence is not exercised.

104. When such right to causing any harm other than death. If the offence, the committing of which, or the attempting to commit which occasions the exercise of the right of private defence, be theft, mischief, or criminal trespass, not of any of the descriptions enumerated in the last preceding Section, that right does not extend to the voluntary causing of death, but does extend, subject to the restrictions mentioned in Section 99, to the voluntary causing to the wrong-doer of any harm other than death.

105. Commencement and continuance of the right of private defence of property. The right of private defence of property commences when a reasonable apprehension of danger to the property commences. The right of private defence of property against theft continues till the offender has effected his retreat with the property or either the assistance of the public authorities is obtained, or the property has been recovered. The right of private defence of property against robbery continues as long as the offender causes or attempts to cause to any person death or hurt or wrongful restraint or as long as the fear of instant death or of instant hurt or of instant personal restraint continues. The right of private defence of property against criminal trespass or mischief continues as long as the offender continues in the commission of criminal trespass or mischief. The right of private defence of property against house-breaking by night continues as long as the house- trespass which has been begun by such house-breaking continues.

106. Right of private defence against deadly assault when there is risk of harm to innocent person. If in the exercise of the right of private defence against an assault which reasonably causes the apprehension of death, the defender be so situated that he cannot effectually exercise that right without risk of harm to an innocent person, his right of private defence extends to the running of that risk.

ILLUSTRATION. A is attacked by a mob who attempt to murder him. He cannot effectually exercise his right of private defence without firing on the mob, and he cannot fire without risk of harming young children who are mingled with the mob. A commits no offence if by so firing he harms any of the children.

CHAPTER - V : OF ABETMENT

107. Abetment of a thing. A person abets the doing of a thing, who- **First.** Instigates any person to do that thing; or **Secondly.** Engages with one or more other person or persons in any conspiracy for the doing of that thing, if an act or illegal omission takes place in pursuance of that conspiracy, and in order to the doing of that thing; or **Thirdly.** Intentionally aids, by any act or illegal omission, the doing of that thing.

EXPLANATION 1. A person who, by wilful misrepresentation, or by wilful concealment of a material fact which he is bound to disclose, voluntarily causes or procures, or attempts to cause or procure, a thing to be done, is said to instigate the doing of that thing.

ILLUSTRATION. A, a public officer, is authorized by a warrant from a Court of Justice to apprehend Z, B, knowing that fact and also that C is not Z, wilfully represents to A that C is Z, and thereby intentionally causes A to apprehend C. Here B abets by instigation the apprehension of C.

EXPLANATION 2. Whoever, either prior to or at the time of the commission of an act, does anything in order to facilitate the commission of that act, and thereby facilitates the commission, thereof, is said to aid the doing of that act.

108. Abettor. A person abets an offence, who abets either the commission of an offence, or the commission of an act which would be an offence, if committed by a person capable by law of committing an offence with the same intention or knowledge as that of the abettor.

EXPLANATION 1. The abetment of the illegal omission of an act may amount to an offence although the abettor may not himself be bound to do that act.

EXPLANATION 2. To constitute the offence of abetment it is not necessary that the act abetted should be committed, or that the effect requisite to constitute the offence should be caused. Illustrations

(a) A instigates B to murder C. B refuses to do so. A is guilty of abetting B to commit murder.

(b) A instigates B to murder D. B in pursuance of the instigation stabs D. D recovers from the wound. A is guilty of instigating B to commit murder.

EXPLANATION 3. It is not necessary that the person abetted should be capable by law of committing an offence, or that he should have the same guilty intention or knowledge as that of the abettor, or any guilty intention or knowledge.

ILLUSTRATIONS.

(a) A, with a guilty intention, abets a child or a lunatic to commit an act which would be an offence, if committed by a person capable by law of committing an offence, and having the same intention as A. Here A, whether the act be committed or not, is guilty of abetting an offence.

(b) A, with the intention of murdering Z, instigates B, a child under seven years of age, to do an act which causes Z's death. B, in consequence of the abetment, does the act in the absence of A and thereby causes Z's death. Here, though B was not capable by law of committing an offence, A is liable to be punished in the same manner as if B had been capable by law of committing an offence, and had committed murder, and he is, therefore, subject to the punishment of death.

(c) A instigates B to set fire to a dwelling-house. B, in consequence of the unsoundness of his mind, being incapable of knowing the nature of the act, or that he is doing what is wrong or contrary to law, sets fire to the house in consequence of A's instigation. B has committed no offence, but A is guilty of abetting the offence of setting fire to a dwelling-house, and is liable to the punishment provided for that offence.

(d) A, intending to cause a theft to be committed, instigates B to take property belonging to Z out of Z's possession. A induces B to believe that the property belongs to A. B takes the property out of Z's possession, in good faith, believing it to be A's property. B, acting under this misconception, does not take dishonestly, and therefore does not commit theft. But A is guilty of abetting theft, and is liable to the same punishment as if B had committed theft.

EXPLANATION 4. The abetment of an offence being an offence, the abetment of such an abetment is also an offence.

ILLUSTRATION. A instigates B to instigate C to murder Z. B accordingly instigates C to murder Z, and C commits that offence in consequence of B's instigation. B is liable to be punished for his offence with the punishment for murder; and, as A instigated B to commit the offence, A is also liable to the same punishment.

EXPLANATION 5. It is not necessary to the commission of the offence of abetment by conspiracy that the abettor should concert the offence with the person who commits it. It is sufficient if he engages in the conspiracy in pursuance of which the offence is committed.

ILLUSTRATION. A concerts with B a plan for poisoning Z. It is agreed that A shall administer the poison. B then explains the plan to C mentioning that a third person is to administer the poison, but without mentioning A's name. C agrees to procure the poison, and procures and delivers it to B for the purpose of its being used in the manner explained. A administers the poison; Z dies in consequence. Here, though A and C have not conspired together, yet C has been engaged in the conspiracy in pursuance of which Z has been murdered. C has therefore committed the offence defined in this Section and is liable to the punishment for murder.

108A. Abetment in India of offences outside India. A person abets an offence within the meaning of this Code who, in India, abets the commission of any act without and beyond India which would constitute an offence if committed in India.

ILLUSTRATION. A, in India, instigates B, a foreigner in Goa, to commit a murder in Goa, A is guilty of abetting murder.

109. Punishment of abetment if the act abetted is committed in consequence and where no express provision is made for its punishment. Whoever abets any offence shall, if the act abetted is committed in consequence of the abetment, and no express provision is made by this Code for the punishment of such abetment, be punished with the punishment provided for the offence.

EXPLANATION. An act or offence is said to be committed in consequence of abetment, when it is committed in consequence of the instigation, or in pursuance of the conspiracy, or with the aid which constitutes the abetment.

ILLUSTRATIONS.

(a) A offers a bribe to B, a public servant, as a reward for showing A some favour in the exercise of B's official functions. B accepts the bribe. A has abetted the offence defined in Section 161.

(b) A instigates B to give false evidence. B, in consequence of the instigation, commits that offence. A is guilty of abetting that offence, and is liable to the same punishment as B.

(c) A and B conspire to poison Z. A, in pursuance of the conspiracy, procures the poison and delivers it to B in order that he may administer it to Z. B, in pursuance of the conspiracy, administers the poison to Z in A's absence and thereby causes Z's death. Here B is guilty of murder. A is guilty of abetting that offence by conspiracy, and is liable to the punishment for murder.

110. Punishment of abetment if person abetted does act with different intention from that of abettor. Whoever abets the commission of an offence shall, if the person abetted does the act with a different intention or knowledge from that of the abettor, be punished with the punishment provided for the offence which would have been committed if the act had been done with the intention or knowledge of the abettor and with no other.

111. Liability of abettor when one act abetted and different act done. When an Act is abetted and a different act is done, the abettor is liable for the act done, in the same manner and to the same extent as if he had directly abetted it:

> *PROVIDED the act done was a probable consequence of the abetment, and was committed under the influence of the instigation, or with the aid or in pursuance of the conspiracy which constituted the abetment.*

ILLUSTRATIONS.

(a) A instigates a child to put poison into the food of Z, and gives him poison for that purpose. The child, in consequence of the instigation, by mistake puts the poison into the food of Y, which is by the side of that of Z. Here if the child was acting under the influence of A's instigation, and the act done was under the circumstances a probable consequence of the abetment, A is liable in the same manner and to the same extent as if he had instigated the child to put the poison into the food of Y.

(b) A instigates B to burn Z's house. B sets fire to the house and at the same time commits theft of property there. A, though guilty of abetting the burning of the house, is not guilty of abetting the theft; for the theft was a distinct act, and not a probable consequence of the burning.

(c) A instigates B and C to break into an inhabited house at midnight for the purpose of robbery, and provides them with arms for that purpose. B and C break into the house, and being resisted by Z, one of the inmates, murder Z. Here, if that murder was the probable consequence of the abetment, A is liable to the punishment provided for murder.

112. Abettor when liable to cumulative punishment for act abetted and for act done. If the act for which the abettor is liable under the last preceding Section is committed in addition to the act abetted, and constitute a distinct offence, the abettor is liable to punishment for each of the offences.

ILLUSTRATION. A instigates B to resist by force a distress made by a public servant. B, in consequence resists that distress. In offering the resistance, B voluntarily causes grievous hurt to the officer executing the distress. As B has committed both the offence of resisting the distress, and the offence of voluntarily causing grievous hurt, B is liable to punishment for both these offences; and, if A knew that B was likely voluntarily to cause grievous hurt in resisting the distress A will also be liable to punishment for each of the offences.

113. Liability of abettor for an effect caused by the act abetted different from that intended by the abettor. When an act is abetted with the intention on the part of the abettor of causing a particular effect, and an act for which the abettor is liable in consequence of the abetment, causes a different effect from that intended by the abettor, the abettor is liable for the effect caused, in the same manner and to the same extent as if he had abetted the act with the intention of causing that effect, provided he knew that the act abetted was likely to cause that effect.

ILLUSTRATION. A instigates B to cause grievous hurt to Z. B, in consequence of the instigation, causes grievous hurt to Z. Z dies in consequence. Here, if A knew that the grievous hurt abetted was likely to cause death, A is liable to be punished with the punishment provided for murder.

114. Abettor present when offence is committed. Whenever any person who if absent would be liable to be punished as an abettor, is present when the act or offence for which he would be punishable in consequence of the abetment is committed, he shall be deemed to have committed such act or offence.

115. Abetment of offence punishable with death or imprisonment for life - if offence not committed. Whoever abets the commission of an offence punishable with death or imprisonment for life, shall, if that offence be not committed in consequence of the abetment, and no express provision is made by this Code for the punishment of such abetment, be punished with imprisonment of either description for a term which may extend to seven years, and shall also be liable to fine: if act causing harm be done in consequence, if act causing harm be done in consequence and if any act for which the abettor is liable in consequence of the abetment, and which causes hurt to any person, is done, the abettor shall be liable to imprisonment of either description for a term which may extend to fourteen years, and shall also be liable to fine.

ILLUSTRATION. A instigates B to murder Z. The offence is not committed. If B had murdered Z, he would have been subject to the punishment of death or imprisonment for life. Therefore, A is liable to imprisonment for a term which may extend to seven years and also to a fine; and, if any hurt be done to Z in consequence of the abetment, he will be liable to imprisonment for a term which may extend to fourteen years, and to fine.

116. Abetment of offence punishable with imprisonment— if offence be not committed. Whoever abets an offence punishable with imprisonment shall, if that offence be not committed in consequence of the abetment, and no express provision is made by this Code for the punishment of such abetment, be punished with imprisonment of any description provided for that offence for a term which may extend to one- fourth part of the longest term provided for that offence; or with such fine as is provided for that offence, or with both; if abettor or person abetted be a public servant whose duty it is to prevent offence and if the abettor or the person abetted is a public servant, whose duty it is to prevent the commission of such offence, the abettor shall be punished with imprisonment of any description provided for that offence, for a term which may extend to one-half of the longest term provided for that offence, or with such fine as is provided for the offence, or with both.

ILLUSTRATIONS

(a) A offers a bribe to B, a public servant, as a reward for showing. A some favour in the exercise of B's official functions. B refuses to accept the bribe. A is punishable under this Section.

(b) A instigates B to give false evidence. Here, if B does not give false evidence, A has nevertheless committed the offence defined in this Section, and is punishable accordingly.

(c) A, a police-officer, whose duty it is to prevent robbery, abets the commission of robbery. Here, though the robbery be not committed, A is liable to one-half of the longest term of imprisonment provided for that offence, and also to fine.

(d) B abets the commission of a robbery by A, a police-officer, whose duty it is to prevent that offence. Here though the robbery be not committed, B is liable to one-half of the longest term of imprisonment provided for the offence of robbery, and also to fine.

117. Abetting commission of offence by the public or by more than ten persons. Whoever abets the commission of an offence by the public generally or by any number or class of persons exceeding ten, shall be punished with imprisonment of either description for a term which may extend to three years, or with fine, or with both.

Illustration. A affixes in a public place a placard instigating a sect consisting of more than ten members to meet at a certain time and place, for the purpose of attacking the members of an adverse sect, while engaged in a procession. A has committed the offence defined in this Section.

118. Concealing design to commit offence punishable with death or imprisonment for life. Whoever intending to facilitate or knowing it to be likely that he will thereby facilitate the commission of an offence punishable with death or imprisonment for life, voluntarily conceals, by any act or illegal omission, the existence of a design to commit such offence or makes any representation which he knows to be false respecting such design, if offence be committed- if offence be not committed shall, if that offence be committed, be punished with imprisonment of either description for a term which may extend to seven years, or, if the offence of not committed, with imprisonment of either description, for a term which may extend to three years; and in either case shall also be liable to fine.

ILLUSTRATION. A, knowing that dacoity is about to be committed at B, falsely informs the Magistrate that a dacoity is about to be committed at C, a place in an opposite direction, and thereby misleads the Magistrate with intent to facilitate the commission of the offence. The dacoity is committed at B in pursuance of the design. A is punishable under this Section.

119. Public servant concealing design to commit offence which it is his duty to prevent. Whoever, being a public servant intending to facilitate or knowing it to be likely that he will thereby facilitate the commission of an offence which it is his duty as such public servant to prevent, voluntarily conceals, by any act or illegal omission, the existence of a design to commit such offence, or makes any representation which he knows to be false respecting such design, if offence be committed - shall be punished with imprisonment of any description provided for the offence, for a term which may extend to one-half of the longest term of such imprisonment, or with such fine as is provided for that offence, or with both; if offence be punishable with death, etc. if offence be punishable with death, etc. or, if the offence be punishable with death or imprisonment for life, with imprisonment of either description for a term which may extend to ten years; if offence be not committed. if offence be not committed or, if the offence be not committed, shall be punished with imprisonment of any description provided for the offence for a term which may extend to one-fourth part of the longest term of such imprisonment or with such fine as is provided for the offence, or with both.

ILLUSTRATION. A, an officer of police, being legally bound to give information of all designs to commit robbery which may come to his knowledge, and knowing that B designs to commit robbery, omits to give such information, with intent to facilitate the commission of that offence. Here A has by an illegal omission concealed the existence of B's design and is liable to punishment according to the provision of this Section.

120. Concealing design to commit offence punishable with imprisonment. Whoever, intending to facilitate or knowing it to be likely that he will thereby facilitate the commission of an offence punishable with imprisonment, voluntarily conceals, by any act or illegal omission, the existence of a design to commit such offence, or makes any representation which he knows to be false respecting such design, if offence be committed- if offence be not committed. if offence be committed- if offence be not committed— shall, if the offence be committed, be punished with imprisonment of the description provided for the offence, for a term which may extend to one-fourth, and, if the offence be not committed, to one-eight, of the longest term of such imprisonment, or with such fine as is provided for the offence, or with both.

CHAPTER - V (A) : CRIMINAL CONSPIRACY

120A. Definition of criminal conspiracy. When two or more persons agree to do, or cause to be done,-

(1) an illegal act, or

(2) an act which is not illegal by illegal means, such an agreement is designated a criminal conspiracy:

PROVIDED that no agreement except an agreement to commit an offence shall amount to a criminal conspiracy unless some act besides the agreement is done by one or more parties to such agreement in pursuance thereof.

EXPLANATION. It is immaterial whether the illegal act is the ultimate object of such agreement, or is merely incidental to that object.

120B. Punishment of criminal conspiracy.

(1) Whoever is a party to a criminal conspiracy to commit an offence punishable with death, imprisonment for life or rigorous imprisonment for a term of two years or upwards, shall, where no express provision is made in this Code for the punishment of such a conspiracy, be punished in the same manner as if he had abetted such offence.

(2) Whoever is a party to a criminal conspiracy other than a criminal conspiracy to commit an offence punishable as aforesaid shall be punished with imprisonment of either description for a term not exceeding six months, or with fine or with both.

CHAPTER - VI : OF OFFENCES AGAINST THE STATE

121. Waging, or attempting to wage war, against the Government of India. Whoever wages war against the Government of India, or attempts to wage such war, or abets the waging of such war, shall be punished with death, or imprisonment for life and shall also be liable to fine.

ILLUSTRATION. A joins an insurrection against the Government of India. A has committed the offence defined in this Section.

121A. Conspiracy to commit offences punishable by Section 121. Whoever within or without India conspires to commit any of the offences punishable by Section 121, or conspires to overawe, by means of criminal force or the show of criminal force, the Central Government or any State Government, shall be punished with imprisonment for life, or with imprisonment of either description which may extend to ten years, and shall also be liable to fine.

EXPLANATION. To constitute a conspiracy under this Section, it is not necessary that any act or illegal omission shall take place in pursuance thereof.

122. Collecting arms, etc., with intention of waging war against the Government of India. Whoever collects men, arms or ammunition or otherwise prepares to wage war with the intention of either waging or being prepared to wage war against the Government of India, shall be punished with imprisonment for life or imprisonment of either description for a term not exceeding ten years, and shall also be liable to fine.

123. Concealing with intent to facilitate design to wage war. Whoever, by any act, or by any illegal omission, conceals the existence of a design to wage war against the Government of India, intending by such concealment to facilitate, or knowing it to be likely that such concealment will facilitate, the waging of such war, shall be punished with imprisonment of either description for a term which may extend to ten years, and shall also be liable to fine.

124. Assaulting President, Governor, etc., with intent to compel or restrain the exercise of any lawful power. Whoever, with the intention of inducing or compelling the President of India, or Governor of any State, to exercise or refrain from exercising in any manner any of the lawful powers of such President or Governor, assaults or wrongfully restrains, or attempts wrongfully to restrain, or overawes, by means of criminal force or the show of criminal force, or attempts so to overawe, such President or Governor, shall be punished with imprisonment of either description for a term which may extend to seven years, and shall also be liable to fine.

124A. Sedition. Whoever by words, either spoken or written, or by signs, or by visible representation, or otherwise, brings or attempts to bring into hatred or contempt, or excites or attempts to excite disaffection towards, the Government established by law in India, a shall be punished with imprisonment for life, to which fine may be added, or with imprisonment which may extend to three years, to which fine may be added, or with fine.

EXPLANATION 1. The expression "disaffection" includes disloyalty and all feelings of enmity.

EXPLANATION 2. Comments expressing disapprobation of the measures of the Government with a view to obtain their alteration by lawful means, without exciting or attempting to excite hatred, contempt or disaffection, do not constitute an offence under this Section.

EXPLANATION 3. Comments expressing disapprobation of the administrative or other action of the Government without exciting or attempting to excite hatred, contempt or disaffection, do not constitute an offence under this Section.

125. Waging war against any Asiatic Power in alliance with the Government of India. Whoever wages war against the Government of any Asiatic Power in alliance or at peace with the Government of India or attempts to wage such war, or abets the waging of such war, shall be punished with imprisonment for life, to which fine may be added, or with imprisonment of either description for a term which may extend to seven years, to which fine may be added, or with fine.

126. Committing depredation on territories of Power at peace with the Government of India. Whoever commits depredation, or makes preparations to commit depredation, on the territories of any Power in alliance or at peace with the Government of India, shall be punished with imprisonment of either description for a term which may extend to seven years, and shall also be liable to fine and to forfeiture of any property used or intended to be used in committing such depredation, or acquired by such depredation.

127. Receiving property taken by war or depredation mentioned in Sections 125 and 126. Whoever receives any property knowing the same to have been taken in the commission of any of the offences mentioned in Sections 125 and 126, shall be punished with imprisonment of either description for a term which may extend to seven years, and shall also be liable to fine and to forfeiture of the property so received.

128. Public servant voluntarily allowing prisoner of state or war to escape. Whoever, being a public servant and having the custody of any State prisoner or prisoner of war, voluntarily allows such prisoner to escape from any place in which such prisoner is confined, shall be punished with imprisonment for life, or imprisonment of either description for a term which may extend to ten years, and shall also be liable to fine.

129. Public servant negligently suffering such prisoner to escape. Whoever, being a public servant and having the custody of any State prisoner or prisoner of war, negligently suffers such prisoner to escape from any place of confinement in which such prisoner is confined, shall be punished with simple imprisonment for a term which may extend to three years, and shall also be liable to fine.

130. Aiding escape of, rescuing or harbouring such prisoner. Whoever knowingly aids or assists any State prisoner or prisoner of war in escaping from lawful custody, or rescues or attempts to rescue any such prisoner, or harbours or conceals any such prisoner who has escaped from lawful custody, or offers or attempts to offer any resistance to the recapture of such prisoner shall be punished with imprisonment for life, or with imprisonment of either description for a term which may extend to ten years, and shall also be liable to fine.

EXPLANATION. A State prisoner or prisoner of war, who is permitted to be at large on his parole within certain limits in India, is said to escape from lawful custody if he goes beyond the limits within which he is allowed to be at large.

CHAPTER - VII : OF OFFENCES RELATING TO THE ARMY, NAVY AND AIR FORCE

131. Abetting mutiny, or attempting to seduce a soldier, sailor or airman from his duty. Whoever abets the committing of mutiny by an officer, soldier, sailor or airman, in the Army, Navy or Air Force of the Government of India or attempts to seduce any such officer, soldier, sailor or airman from his allegiance or his duty, shall be punished with imprisonment for life, or with imprisonment of either description for a term which may extend to ten years, and shall also be liable to fine.

EXPLANATION. In this Section the words "officer", "soldier", "sailor" and "airman" include any person subject to the Army Act, the Army Act, 1950 (46 of 1950), the Naval Discipline Act, the Indian Navy (Discipline) Act, 1934 (34 of 1934), the Air Force Act or the Air Force Act, 1950 (45 of 1950), as the case may be.

132. Abetment of mutiny, if mutiny is committed in consequence thereof. Whoever abets the committing of mutiny by an officer, soldier, sailor or airman, in the Army, Navy or Air Force of the Government of India, shall, if mutiny be committed in consequence of that abetment, be punished with death or with imprisonment for life, or imprisonment of either description for a term which may extend to ten years, and shall also be liable to fine.

133. Abetment of assault by soldier, sailor or airman on his superior officer, when in execution of his office. Whoever abets an assault by an officer, soldier, sailor or airman, in the Army, Navy or Air Force of the Government of India, on any superior officer being in the execution of his office, shall be punished with imprisonment of either description for a term which may extend to three years, and shall also be liable to fine.

134. Abetment of such assault, if the assault committed. Whoever abets an assault by an officer, soldier, sailor or airman, in the Army, Navy or Air Force of the Government of India, on any superior officer being in the execution of his office, shall, if such assault be committed in consequence of that abetment be punished with imprisonment of either description for a term which may extend to seven years, and shall also be liable to fine.

135. Abetment of desertion of soldier, sailor or airman. Whoever, abets the desertion of any officer, soldier, sailor or airman, in the Army, Navy or Air Force of the Government of India, shall be punished with imprisonment of either description for a term which may extend to two years, or with fine, or with both.

136. Harbouring deserter. Whoever, except as hereinafter excepted, knowing or having reason to believe that an officer, soldier, sailor or airman, in the Army, Navy or Air Force of the Government of India, has deserted, harbours such officer, soldier, sailor or airman, shall be punished with imprisonment of either description for a term which may extend to two years, or with fine or with both.

Exception. This provision does not extend to the case in which the harbour is given by a wife to her husband.

137. Deserter concealed on board merchant vessel through negligence of master. The master or person in charge of a merchant vessel, on board of which any deserter from the Army, Navy or Air Force of the Government of India is concealed, shall, though ignorant of such concealment, be liable to a penalty not exceeding five hundred rupees, if he might have known of such concealment but for some neglect of his duty as such master or person in charge, or but for some want of discipline on board of the vessel.

138. Abetment of act of insubordination by soldier, sailor or airman. Whoever abets what he knows to be an act of insubordination by an officer, soldier, sailor or airman, in the Army, Navy or air Force, of the Government of India, shall, if such act of insubordination be committed in consequence of that abetment, be punished with imprisonment of either description for a term which may extend to six months, or with fine, or with both.

138A. Application of foregoing Sections to the Indian Marine Service.

139. Persons subject to certain Acts. No person subject to the Army Act, the Army Act, 1950 (46 of 1950), the Naval Discipline Act, the Indian Navy (Discipline) Act, 1934 (34 of 1934), the Air Force Act or the Air Force Act, 1950 (45 of 1950), is subject to punishment under this Code for any of the offences defined in this Chapter.

140. Wearing garb or carrying token used by soldier, sailor or airman. Whoever, not being a soldier, sailor or airman in the Military, Naval or Air service of the Government of India, wears any garb or carries any token resembling any garb or token used by such a soldier, sailor or airman with the intention that it may be believed that he is such a soldier, sailor or airman, shall be punished with imprisonment of either description for a term which may extend to three months, or with fine which may extend to five hundred rupees, or with both.

CHAPTER - VIII : OF OFFENCES AGAINST THE PUBLIC TRANQUILLITY

141. Unlawful assembly. An assembly of five or more persons is designated an "unlawful assembly", if the common object of the persons composing that assembly is- **First.** To overawe by criminal force, or show of criminal force, the Central or any State Government or Parliament or the Legislature of any State, or any public servant in the exercise of the lawful power of such public servant; or **Second.** To resist the execution of any law, or of any legal process; or **Third.** To commit any mischief or criminal trespass, or other offence; or **Fourth.** By means of criminal force, or show of criminal force, to any person to take or obtain possession of any property, or to deprive any person of the enjoyment of a right of way, or of the use of water or other incorporeal right of which he is in possession or enjoyment, or to enforce any right or supposed right; or **Fifth.** By means of criminal force, or show of criminal force, to compel any person to do what he is not legally bound to do, or to omit to do what he is legally entitled to do.

EXPLANATION. An assembly which was not unlawful when it assembled, may subsequently become an unlawful assembly.

142. Being member of unlawful assembly. Whoever, being aware of facts which render any assembly an unlawful assembly, intentionally joins that assembly, or continues in it, is said to be a member of an unlawful assembly.

143. Punishment. Whoever is a member of an unlawful assembly, shall be punished with imprisonment of either description for a term which may extend to six months, or with fine, or with both.

144. Joining unlawful assembly armed with deadly weapon. Whoever, being armed with any deadly weapon, or with anything which, used as a weapon of offence, is likely to cause death, is a member of an unlawful assembly, shall be punished with imprisonment of either description for a term which may extend to two years, or with fine, or with both.

145. Joining or continuing in unlawful assembly, knowing it has been commanded to disperse. Whoever joins or continues in an unlawful assembly, knowing that such unlawful assembly has been commanded in the manner prescribed by law to disperse, shall be punished with imprisonment of either description for a term which may extent to two years, or with fine, or with both.

146. Rioting. Whenever force or violence is used by an unlawful assembly, or by any member thereof, in prosecution of the common object of such assembly, every member of such assembly is guilty of the offence of rioting.

147. Punishment for rioting. Whoever is guilty of rioting, shall be punished with imprisonment of either description for a term which may extend to two years, or with fine, or with both.

148. Rioting, armed with deadly weapon. Whoever is guilty of rioting, being armed with a deadly weapon or with anything which, used as a weapon of offence, is likely to cause death, shall be punished with imprisonment of either description for a term which may extend to three years, or with fine, or with both.

149. Every member of unlawful assembly guilty of offence committed in prosecution of common object. If an offence is committed by any member of an unlawful assembly in prosecution of the common object of that assembly, or such as the members of that assembly knew to be likely to be committed in prosecution of that object, every person who, at the time of the committing of that offence, is a member of the same assembly, is guilty of that offence.

150. Hiring, or conniving at hiring, of persons to join unlawful assembly. Whoever hires or engages, or employes, or promotes, or connives at the hiring, engagement or employment of any person to join or become a member of any unlawful assembly, shall be punishable as a member of such unlawful assembly, and for any offence which may be committed by any such person as a member of such unlawful assembly in pursuance of such hiring, engagement or employment, in the same manner as if he had been a member of such unlawful assembly, or himself had committed such offence.

151. Knowingly joining or continuing in assembly of five or more persons after it has been commanded to disperse. Whoever knowingly joins or continues in any assembly of five or more persons likely to cause a disturbance of the public peace, after such assembly has been lawfully commanded to disperse, shall be punished with imprisonment of either description for a term which may extend to six months, or with fine, or with both.

EXPLANATION. If the assembly is an unlawful assembly within the meaning of Section 141, the offender will be punishable under Section 145.

152. Assaulting or obstructing public servant when suppressing riot, etc. Whoever assaults or threatens to assault, or obstructs or attempts to obstruct, any public servant in the discharge of his duty as such public servant, in endeavouring to disperse an unlawful assembly, or to suppress a riot or affray, or uses, or threatens, or attempts to use criminal force to such public servant, shall be punished with imprisonment of either description for a term which may extend to three years, or with fine, or with both.

153. Want only giving provocation with intent to cause riot - if rioting be committed: if not committed. Whoever malignantly, or wantonly by doing anything which is illegal, gives provocation to any person intending or knowing it to be likely that such provocation will cause the offence of rioting to be committed, shall, if the offence of rioting be committed in consequence of such provocation, be punished with imprisonment of either description for a term which may extend to one year, or with fine, or with both, and if the offence of rioting be not committed, with imprisonment of either description for a term which may extend to six months, or with fine, or with both.

153A. Promoting enmity between different groups on ground of religion, race, place of birth, residence, language, etc., and doing acts prejudicial to maintenance of harmony.

(1) Whoever-

(a) by words, either spoken or written, or by signs or by visible representations or otherwise, promotes or attempts to promote, on grounds of religion, race, place of birth, residence, language, caste or community or any other ground whatsoever, disharmony or feelings of enmity, hatred or ill-will between different religious, racials, language or regional groups or castes or communities, or

(b) commits any act which is prejudicial to the maintenance of harmony between different religious, racial, language or regional groups or castes or communities, and which disturbs or is likely to disturb the public tranquillity, or

(c) organizes any exercise, movement, drill or other similar activity intending that the participants in such activity shall use or be trained to use criminal force or violence or knowing it to be likely that the participants in such activity will use or be trained to use criminal force or violence, or participates in such activity intending to use or be trained to use criminal force or violence or knowing it to be likely that the participants in such activity will use or be trained to use criminal force or violence, against any religious, racial, language or regional group or caste or community and such activity for any reason whatsoever causes or is likely to cause fear or alarm or a feeling of insecurity amongst members of such religious, racial, language or regional group or caste or community, shall be punished with imprisonment which may extend to three years, or with fine, or with both.

(2) Offence committed in place of worship, etc. Whoever commits an offence specified in sub-section (1) in any place of worship or in any assembly engaged in the performance of religious worship or religious ceremonies, shall be punished with imprisonment which may extend to five years and shall also be liable to fine.

153B. Imputations, assertions prejudicial to national integration.

(1) Whoever, by words either spoken or written or by signs or by visible representations or otherwise,-

(a) makes or publishes any imputation that any class of persons cannot, by reason of their being members of any religious, racial, language or regional group or caste or community, bear true faith and allegiance to the Constitution of India as by law established or uphold the sovereignty and integrity of India, or

(b) asserts, counsels, advises, propagates or publishes that any class of persons by reason of their being members of any religious, racial, language or regional group or caste or community be denied, or deprived of their rights as citizens of India, or

(c) makes or publishes and assertion, counsel, plea or appeal concerning the obligation of any class of persons, by reason of their being members of any religious, racial, language or regional group or caste or community, and such assertion, counsel, plea or appeal causes or is likely to cause disharmony or feelings of enmity or hatred or ill-will between such members and other persons, shall be punished with imprisonment which may extend to three years, or with fine, or with both.

(2) Whoever commits an offence specified in sub-section (1), in any place of worship or in any assembly engaged in the performance of religious worship or religious ceremonies, shall be punished with imprisonment which may extend to five years and shall also be liable to fine.

154. Owner or occupier of land on which an unlawful assembly is held. Whenever any unlawful assembly or riot takes place, the owner or occupier of the land upon which such unlawful assembly is held, or such riot is committed, and any person having or claiming an interest in such land, shall be punishable with fine not exceeding one thousand rupees, if he or his agent or manager, knowing that such offence is being or has been committed, or having reason to believe it is likely to be committed, do not give the earliest notice thereof in his or their power to the principal officer at the nearest police- station, and do not, in the case of his or their having reason to believe that it was about to be committed, use all lawful means in his or their power to prevent it and, in the event of its taking place, do not use all lawful means in his or their power to disperse or suppress the riot or unlawful assembly.

155. Liability of person for whose benefit riot is committed. Whenever a riot is committed for the benefit or on behalf of any person who is the owner or occupier of any land respecting which such riot takes place or who claims any interest in such land, or in the subject of any dispute which gave rise to the riot, or who has accepted or derived any benefit therefrom, such person shall be punishable with fine, if he or his agent or manager, having reason to believe that such riot was likely to be committed or that the unlawful assembly by which such riot was committed was likely to be held, shall not respectively use all lawful means in his or their power to prevent such assembly or riot from taking place, and for suppressing and dispersing the same.

156. Liability of agent of owner or occupier for whose benefit riot is committed. Whenever a riot is committed for the benefit or on behalf of any person who is the owner or occupier of any land respecting which such riot takes place, or who claims any interest in such land, or in the subject of any dispute which gave rise to the riot, or who has accepted or derived any benefit therefrom, the agent or manager of such person shall be punishable with fine, if such agent or manager, having reason to believe that such riot was likely to be committed, or that the unlawful assembly by which such riot was committed was likely to be held, shall not use all lawful means in his power to prevent such riot or assembly from taking place and for suppressing and dispersing the same.

157. Harbouring persons hired for an unlawful assembly. Whoever harbours, receives or assembles, in any house or premises in his occupation or charge, or under his control any persons knowing that such persons have been hired, engaged or employed, or are about to be hired, engaged or employed, to join or become members of an unlawful assembly, shall be punished with imprisonment of either description for a term which may extend to six months, or with fine, or with both.

158. Being hired to take part in an unlawful assembly or riot. Whoever is engaged, or hired, or offers or attempts to be hired or engaged, to do or assist in doing any of the acts specified in Section 141, shall be punished with imprisonment of either description for a term which may extend to six months, or with fine, or with both or to go armed and whoever, being so engaged or hired as aforesaid, goes armed, or engages or offers to go armed, with any deadly weapon or with anything which used as a weapon of offence is likely to cause death, shall be punished with imprisonment of either description for a term which may extend to two years, or with fine, or with both.

159. Affray. When two or more persons, by fighting in a public place, disturb the public peace, they are said to "commit an affray".

160. Punishment for committing affray. Whoever commits an affray, shall be punished with imprisonment of either description for a term which may extend to one month, or with fine which may extend to one hundred rupees, or with both.

CHAPTER - IX : OF OFFENCES BY OR RELATING TO PUBLIC SERVANTS 161 to 165A

161 to 165A. Rep. by the Prevention of Corruption Act, 1988 (49 of 1988), s. 31.

166. Public servant disobeying law, with intent to cause injury to any person. Whoever, being a public servant, knowingly disobeys any direction of the law as to the way in which he is to conduct himself as such public servant, intending to cause, or knowing it to be likely that he will, by such disobedience, cause injury to any person, shall be punished with simple imprisonment for a term which may extend to one year, or with fine, or with both.

IIIUSTRATION. A, being an officer directed by law to take property in execution, in order to satisfy a decree pronounced in Z's favour by a Court of Justice, knowingly disobeys that direction of law, with the knowledge that he is likely thereby to cause injury to Z. A has committed the offence defined in this Section.

167. Public servant framing an incorrect document with intent to cause injury. Whoever, being a public servant, and being, as such public servant, charged with the preparation or translation of any document, frames or translates that document in a manner which he knows or believes to be incorrect, intending thereby to cause or knowing it to be likely that he may thereby cause injury to any person, shall be punished with imprisonment of either description for a term which may extend to three years, or with fine, or with both.

168. Public servant unlawfully engaging in trade. Whoever, being a public servant, and being legally bound as such public servant not to engages in trade, engages in trade, shall be punished with simple imprisonment for a term which may extend to one year, or with fine, or with both.

169. Public servant unlawfully buying or bidding for property. Whoever, being a public servant, and being legally bound as such public servant, not to purchase or bid for certain property, purchases or bids for that property, either in his own name or in the name of another, or jointly, or in shares with others, shall be punished with simple imprisonment for a term which may extend to two years, or with fine, or with both; and the property, if purchased, shall be confiscated.

170. Personating a public servant. Whoever pretends to hold any particular office as public servant, knowing that he does not hold such office or falsely personates any other person holding such office, and in such assumed character does or attempts to do any act under colour of such office, shall be punished with imprisonment of either description for a term which may extend to two years, or with fine, or with both.

171. Wearing garb or carrying token used by public servant with fraudulent intent. Whoever, not belonging to a certain class of public servants, wears any garb or carries any token resembling any garb or token used by that class of public servants, with the intention that it may be believed, or with the knowledge that it is likely to be believed, that he belongs to that class of public servants, shall be punished with imprisonment of either description, for a term which may extend to three months, or with fine which may extend to two hundred rupees, or with both.

CHAPTER - IXA : OF OFFENCES RELATING TO ELECTIONS

171A. "Candidate", "Electoral right" defined. For the purposes of this Chapter-

(a) "candidate" means a person who has been nominated as a candidate at any election;

(b) "electoral right" means the right of a person to stand, or not to stand as, or to withdraw from being, a candidate or to vote or refrain from voting at an election.

171B. Bribery.

(1) Whoever-

(i) gives a gratification to any person with the object of inducing him or any other person to exercise any electoral right or of rewarding any person for having exercised any such right; or

(ii) accepts either for himself or for any other person any gratification as a reward for exercising any such right or for inducing or attempting to induce any other person to exercise any such right, commits the offence of bribery:

PROVIDED that a declaration of public policy or a promise of public action shall not be an offence under this Section.

(2) A person who offers, or agrees to give, or offers or attempts to procure, a gratification shall be deemed to give a gratification.

(3) A person who obtains or agrees to accept or attempts to obtain a gratification shall be deemed to accept a gratification, and a person who accepts a gratification as a motive for doing what he does not intend to do, or as a reward

for doing what he has not done, shall be deemed to have accepted the gratification as a reward.

171C. Undue influence at elections.

(1) Whoever voluntarily interferes or attempts to interfere with the free exercise of any electoral right commits the offence of undue influence at an election.

(2) Without prejudice to the generality of the provisions of sub-section (1), whoever-

(a) threatens any candidate or voter, or any person in whom a candidate or voter is interested, with injury of any kind, or

(b) induces or attempts to induce a candidate or voter to believe that he or any person in whom he is interested will become or will be rendered an object of Divine displeasure or of spiritual censure, shall be deemed to interfere with the free exercise of the electoral right of such candidate or voter, within the meaning of sub-section (1).

(3) A declaration of public policy or a promise of public action, or the mere exercise or a legal right without intent to interfere with an electoral right, shall not be deemed to be interference within the meaning of this Section.

171D. Personation at elections. Whoever at an election applies for a voting paper on votes in the name of any other person, whether living or dead, or in a fictitious name, or who having voted once at such election applies at the same election for a voting paper in his own name, and whoever abets, procures or attempts to procure the voting by any person in any such way, commits the offence of personation at an election.

171E. Punishment for bribery. Whoever commits the offence of bribery shall be punished with imprisonment of either description for a term which may extend to one year, or with fine, or with both:

PROVIDED that bribery by treating shall be punished with fine only.

EXPLANATION. "Treating" means that form of bribery where the gratification consists in food, drink, entertainment, or provision.

171F. Punishment for undue influence or personation at an election. Whoever commits the offence of undue influence or personation at an election shall be punished with imprisonment of either description for a term which may extend to one year or with fine, or with both.

171G. False statement in connection with an election. Whoever with intent to affect the result of an election makes or publishes any statement purporting to be a statement of fact which is false and which he either knows or believes to be false or does not believe to be true, in relation to the personal character or conduct of any candidate shall be punished with fine.

171H. Illegal payments in connection with an election. Whoever without the general or special authority in writing of a candidate incurs or authorizes expenses on account of the holding of any public meeting, or upon any advertisement, circular or publication, or in any other way whatsoever for the purpose of promoting or procuring the election of such candidate, shall be punished with fine which may extend to five hundred rupees:

PROVIDED that if any person having incurred any such expenses not exceeding the amount of ten rupees without authority obtains within ten days from the date on which such expenses were incurred the approval in writing of the candidate, he shall be deemed to have incurred such expenses with the authority of the candidate.

171-I. Failure to keep election accounts. Whoever being required by any law for the time being in force or any rule having the force of law to keep accounts of expenses incurred at or in connection with an election fails to keep such accounts shall be punished with fine which may extend to five hundred rupees.

CHAPTER - X : OF CONTEMPTS OF THE LAWFUL AUTHORITY OF PUBLIC SERVANTS

172. Absconding to avoid service of summons or other proceeding. Whoever absconds in order to avoid being served with a summons, notice or order proceeding from any public servant legally competent, as such public servant, to issue such summons, notice or order, shall be punished with simple imprisonment for a term which may extend to one month, or with fine which may extend to five hundred rupees, or with both; or, if the summons or notice or order is to attend in person or by agent, or to produce a document in a Court of Justice, with simple imprisonment for a term which may extend to six months, or with fine which may extend to one thousand rupees, or with both.

173. Preventing service of summons or other proceeding, or preventing publication thereof. Whoever in any manner intentionally prevents the serving on himself, or on any other person, of any summons, notice or order proceeding from any public servant legally competent, such public servant, to issue such summons, notice or order, or intentionally prevents the lawful affixing to any place of any such summons, notice or order, or intentionally removes any such summons, notice or order from any place to which it is lawfully affixed, or intentionally prevents the lawful making of any proclamation, under the authority of any public servant legally competent, as such public servant, to direct such proclamation to be made, shall be punished with simple imprisonment for a term which may extend to one month, or with fine which may extend to five hundred rupees, or with both; or, if the summons, notice, order or proclamation is to attend in person or by agent, or to produce a document in a Court of Justice, with simple imprisonment for a term which may extend to six months, or with fine which may extend to one thousand rupees, or with both.

174. Non- attendance in obedience to an order from public servant. Whoever, being legally bound to attend in person or by an agent at a certain place and time in obedience to a summons, notice, order, or proclamation proceeding from any public servant legally competent, as such public servant, to issue the same, intentionally omits to attend at that place or time, or departs from the place where he is bound to attend before the time at which it is lawful for him to depart, shall be punished with simple imprisonment for a term which may extend to one month, or with fine which may extend to five hundred rupees, or with both; or, if the summons, notice, order or proclamation is to attend in person or by agent in a Court of Justice, with simple imprisonment for a term which may extend to six months, or with fine which may extend to one thousand rupees, or with both.

ILLUSTRATIONS.

(a) A, being legally bound to appear before the High Court at Calcutta, in obedience to a subpoena issuing from that Court, intentionally omits to appear. A has committed the offence defined in this Section.

(b) A, being legally bound to appear before a District Judge, as a witness, in obedience to a summons issued by that District Judge intentionally omits to appear. A has committed the offence defined in this Section.

175. Omission to produce document to public servant by person legally bound to produce it. Whoever, being legally bound to produce or deliver up any document to any public servant, as such, intentionally omits so to produce or deliver up the same, shall be punished with simple imprisonment for a term which may extend to one month, or with fine which may extend to five hundred rupees, or with both; or, if the document is to be produced or delivered up to a Court of Justice, with simple imprisonment for a term which may extend to six months, or with fine which may extend to one thousand rupees, or with both.

ILLUSTRATION. A, being legally bound to produce a document before a District Court, intentionally omits to produce the same. A has committed the offence defined in this Section.

176. Omission to give notice or information to public servant by person legally bound to give it. Whoever, being legally bound to give any notice or to furnish information on any subject to any public servant, as such, intentionally omits to give such notice or to furnish such information in the manner and at the time required by law, shall be punished with simple imprisonment for a term which may extend to one month, or with fine which may extend to five hundred rupees, or with both; or, if the notice or information required to be given respects the commission of an offence, or is required for the purpose of preventing the commission of an offence, or in order to the apprehension of an offender, with simple imprisonment for a term which may extend to six months, or with fine which may extend to one thousand rupees, or with both; or, if the notice or information required to be given is required by an order passed under sub-section (1) of Section 565 of the Code of Criminal Procedure, 1898 (5 of 1898), with imprisonment of either description for a term which may extend to six months, or with fine which may extend to one thousand rupees, or with both.

177. Furnishing false information. Whoever, being legally bound to furnish information on any subject to any public servant, as such, furnishes, as true, information on the subject which he knows or has reason to believe to be false shall be punished with simple imprisonment for a term which may extend to six months, or with fine which may extend to one thousand rupees, or with both; or, if the information which he is legally bound to give respects the commission of an offence, or is required for the purpose of preventing the commission of an offence, or in order to the apprehension of an offender, with imprisonment of either description for a term which may extend to two years, or with fine, or with both.

ILLUSTRATIONS.

(a) A, a landholder, knowing of the commission of a murder within the limits of his estate, wilfully misinforms the Magistrate of the district that the death has occurred by accident in consequence of the bite of a snake. A is guilty of the offence defined in this Section.

(b) A, a village watchman, knowing that a considerable body of strangers has passed through his village in order to commit a dacoity in the house of Z, a wealthy merchant residing in a neighbouring place, and being bound under clause 5, Section VII, Regulation III, 1821, of the Bengal Code, to give early and punctual information of the above fact to the officer of the nearest police station, wilfully misinforms the police officer that a body of suspicious characters passed through the village with a view to commit dacoity in a certain distant place in a different direction. Here A is guilty of the offence defined in the latter part of this Section.

EXPLANATION. In Section 176 and in this Section the word "offence" includes any act committed at any place out of India, which, if committed in India, would be punishable under any of the following Sections, namely, 302, 304, 382, 392, 393, 394, 395, 396, 397, 398, 399, 402, 435, 436, 449, 450, 457, 458, 459 and 460; and the word "offender" includes any person who is alleged to have been guilty of any such act.

178. Refusing oath or affirmation when duly required by public servant to make it. Whoever refuses to bind himself by an oath or affirmation to state the truth, when required so to bind himself by a public servant legally competent to require that he shall so bind himself, shall be punished with simple imprisonment for a term which may extend to six months, or with fine which may extend to one thousand rupees, or with both.

179. Refusing to answer public servant authorized to question. Whoever, being legally bound to state the truth on any subject to any public servant, refuses to answer any question demanded of him touching that subject by such public servant in the exercise of the legal powers of such public servant, shall be punished with simple imprisonment for a term which may extend to six months, or with fine which may extend to one thousand rupees, or with both.

180. Refusing to sign statement. Whoever refuses to sign any statement made by him, when required to sign that statement by a public servant legally competent to require that he shall sign that statement, shall be punished with simple imprisonment for a term which may extend to three months, or with fine which may extend to five hundred rupees, or with both.

181. False statement on oath or affirmation to public servant or person authorized to administer an oath or affirmation. Whoever, being legally bound by an oath or affirmation to state the truth on any subject to any public servant or other person authorized by law to administer such oath or affirmation, makes, to such public servant or other person as aforesaid, touching that subject, any statement which is false, and which he either knows or believes to be false or does not believe to be true, shall be punished with imprisonment of either description for a term which may extend to three years, and shall also be liable to fine.

182. False information, with intent to cause public servant to use his lawful power to the injury of another person. Whoever gives to any public servant any information which he knows or believes to be false, intending thereby to cause, or knowing it to be likely that he will thereby cause such public servant-

(a) to do or omit anything which such public servant ought not to do or omit if the true state of facts respecting which such information is given were known by him, or

(b) to use the lawful power of such public servant to the injury or annoyance of any person, shall be punished with imprisonment of either description for a term which may extend to six months, or with fine which may extend to one thousand rupees, or with both.

ILLUSTRATIONS.

(a) A informs a Magistrate that Z, a police-officer, subordinate to such Magistrate, has been guilty of neglect of duty or misconduct, knowing such information to be false, and knowing it to be likely that the information will cause the Magistrate to dismiss Z. A has committed the offence defined in this Section.

(b) A falsely informs a public servant that Z has contraband salt in a secret place, knowing such information to be false, and knowing that it is likely that the consequence of the information will be a search of Z's premises, attended with annoyance to Z. A has committed the offence defined in this Section.

(c) A falsely informs a policeman that he has been assaulted and robbed in the neighbourhood of a particular village. He does not mention the name of any person as one of his assailants, but knows it to be likely that in consequence of this information the police will make enquiries and institute searches in the village to the annoyance of the villagers or some of them. A has committed an offence under this Section.

183. Resistance to the taking of property by the lawful authority of a public servant. Whoever offers any resistance to the taking of any property by the lawful authority of any public servant, knowing or having reason to believe that he is such public servant, shall be punished with imprisonment of either description for a term which may extend to six months, or with fine which may extend to one thousand rupees, or with both.

184. Obstructing sale of property offered for sale by authority of public servant. Whoever intentionally obstructs any sale of property offered for sale by the lawful authority of any public servant, as such, shall be punished with imprisonment of either description for a term which may extend to one month, or with fine which may extend to five hundred rupees, or with both.

185. Illegal purchase or bid for property offered for sale by authority of public servant. Whoever, at any sale of property held by the lawful authority of a public servant, as such, purchases or bids for any property on account of any person, whether himself or any other, whom he knows to be under a legal incapacity to purchase that property at that sale, or bids for such property not intending to perform the obligations under which he lays himself by such bidding, shall be punished with imprisonment of either description for a term which may extend to one month, or with fine which may extend to two hundred rupees, or with both.

186. Obstructing public servant in discharge of public functions. Whoever voluntarily obstructs any public servant in the discharge of his public functions, shall be punished with imprisonment of either description for a term which may extend to three months, or with fine which may extend to five hundred rupees, or with both.

187. Omission to assist public servant when bound by law to give assistance. Whoever, being bound by law to render or furnish assistance to any public servant in the execution of his public duty, intentionally omits to give such assistance, shall be punished with simple imprisonment for a term which may extend to one month, or with fine which may extend to two hundred rupees, or with both; and if such assistance be demanded of him by a public servant legally competent to make such demand for the purposes of executing any process lawfully issued by a Court of Justice, or of preventing the commission of an offence, or suppressing a riot, or affray, or of apprehending a person charged with or guilty of an offence, or of having escaped from lawful custody, shall be punished with simple imprisonment for a term which may extend to six months, or with fine which may extend to five hundred rupees, or with both.

188. Disobedience to order duly promulgated by public servant. Whoever, knowing that, by an order promulgated by a public servant lawfully empowered to promulgate such order, he is directed to abstain from a certain act, or to take certain order with certain property in his possession or under his management, disobeys such direction, shall, if such disobedience causes or tends to cause obstruction, annoyance or injury, or risk of obstruction, annoyance or injury, to any persons lawfully employed, be punished with simple imprisonment for a term which may extend to one month or with fine which may extend to two hundred rupees, or with both and if such disobedience causes or tends to cause danger to human life, health or safety, or causes or tends to cause a riot or affray, shall be punished with imprisonment of either description for a term which may extend to six months, or with fine which may extend to one thousand rupees, or with both.

EXPLANATION. It is not necessary that the offender should intend to produce harm, or contemplate his disobedience as likely to produce harm. It is sufficient that he knows of the order which he disobeys, and that his disobedience produces, or is likely to produce, harm.

ILLUSTRATION. An order is promulgated by a public servant lawfully empowered to promulgated such order, directing that a religious procession shall not pass down a certain street. A knowingly disobeys the order, and thereby causes danger of riot. A has committed the offence defined in this Section.

189. Threat of injury to public servant. Whoever holds out any threat of injury to any public servant, or to any person in whom he believes that public servant to be interested, for the purpose of inducing that public servant to do any act, or to forbear or delay to do any act, connected with the exercise of the public functions of such public servant, shall be punished with imprisonment of either description for a term which may extend to two years, or with fine, or with both.

190. Threat of injury to induce person to refrain from applying for protection to public servant. Whoever holds out any threat of injury to any person for the purpose of inducing that person to refrain or desist from making a legal application for protection against any injury to any public servant legally empowered as such to give such protection, or to cause such protection to be given, shall be punished with imprisonment of either description for a term which may extend to one year, or with fine, or with both.

CHAPTER - XI : OF FALSE EVIDENCE AND OFFENCES AGAINST PUBLIC JUSTICE

191. Giving false evidence. Whoever, being legally bound by an oath or by an express provision of law to state the truth, or being bound by law to make a declaration upon any subject, makes any statement which is false, and which he either knows or believes to be false or does not believe to be true, is said to give false evidence.

EXPLANATION 1. A statement is within the meaning of this Section whether it is made verbally or otherwise.

EXPLANATION 2. A false statement as to the belief of the person attesting is within the meaning of this Section, and a person may be guilty of giving false evidence by stating that he believes a thing which he does not believe, as well as by stating that he knows a thing which he does not know.

ILLUSTRATIONS.

(a) A, in support of a just claim which B has against Z for one thousand rupees, falsely swears on a trial that he heard Z admit the justice of B's claim. A has given false evidence.

(b) A, being bound by an oath to state the truth, states that he believes a certain signature to be the handwriting of Z, when he does not believe it to be the handwriting of Z. Here A states that which he knows to be false, and therefore gives false evidence.

(c) A, knowing the general character of Z's handwriting, states that he believes a certain signature to be the handwriting of Z; A in good faith believing it to be so. Here A's statement is merely as to his belief, and is true as to his belief, and therefore, although the signature may not be the handwriting of Z, A has not given false evidence.

(d) A, being bound by an oath to state the truth, states that he knows that Z was at a particular place on a particular day, not knowing anything upon the subject. A gives false evidence whether Z was at that place on the day named or not.

(e) A, an interpreter or translator, gives or certifies as a true interpretation or translation of a statement or document, which he is bound by oath to interpret or translate truly, that which is not and which he does not believe to be a true interpretation or translation. A has given false evidence.

192. Fabricating false evidence. Whoever causes any circumstance to exist or makes any false entry in any book or record, or makes any document containing a false statement, intending that such circumstance, false entry or false statement may appear in evidence in a judicial proceeding, or in a proceeding taken by law before a public servant as such, or before an arbitrator, and that such circumstance, false entry or false statement, so appearing in evidence, may cause any person who in such proceeding is to form an opinion upon the evidence, to entertain an erroneous opinion touching any point material to the result of such proceeding is said "to fabricate false evidence".

ILLUSTRATIONS.

(a) A puts jewels into a box belonging to Z, with the intention that they may be found in that box, and that this circumstance may cause Z to be convicted of theft. A has fabricated false evidence.

(b) A makes a false entry in his shop-book for the purpose of using it as corroborative evidence in a Court of Justice. A has fabricated false evidence.

(c) A, with the intention of causing Z to be convicted of a criminal conspiracy, writes a letter in imitation of Z's handwriting, purporting to be addressed to an accomplice in such criminal conspiracy, and puts the letter in a place which he knows that the officers of the police are likely to search. A has fabricated false evidence.

193. Punishment for false evidence. Whoever intentionally gives false evidence in any of a judicial proceeding, or fabricates false evidence for the purpose of being used in any stage of a judicial proceeding, shall be punished with imprisonment of either description for a term which may extend to seven years, and shall also be liable to fine; and whoever intentionally gives or fabricates false evidence in any other case, shall be punished with imprisonment of either description for a term which may extend to three years, and shall also be liable to fine.

EXPLANATION 1. A trial before a Court- martial is a judicial proceeding.

EXPLANATION 2. An investigation directed by law preliminary to a proceeding before a Court of Justice, is a stage of a judicial proceeding, though that investigation may not take place before a Court of Justice. Illustration A, in an enquiry before a Magistrate for the purpose of ascertaining whether Z ought to be committed for trial, makes on oath a statement which he knows to be false. As this enquiry is a stage of a judicial proceeding, A as given false evidence.

EXPLANATION 3. An investigation directed by a Court of Justice according to law, and conducted under the authority of a Court of Justice, is a stage of a judicial proceeding, though that investigation may not take place before a Court of Justice. Illustration A, in an enquiry before an officer deputed by a Court of Justice to ascertain on the spot the boundaries of land, makes on oath a statement which he knows to be false. As this enquiry is a stage of a judicial proceeding, A has given false evidence.

194. Giving or fabricating false evidence with intent to procure conviction of capital offence. Whoever gives or fabricates false evidence, intending thereby to cause, or knowing it to be likely that he will thereby cause, any person to be convicted of an offence which is capital by the laws for the time being in force in India shall be punished with imprisonment for life, or with rigorous imprisonment for a term which may extend to ten years, and shall also be liable to fine; and if an innocent person be convicted and executed in consequence of such false evidence, the person who gives such false evidence shall be punished either with death or the punishment hereinbefore described.

195. Giving or fabricating false evidence with intent to procure conviction of offence punishable with imprisonment for life or imprisonment. Whoever gives or fabricates false evidence intending thereby to cause, or knowing it to be likely that he will thereby cause, any person to be convicted of an offence which by the law for the time being in force in India is not capital, but punishable with imprisonment for life, or imprisonment for a term of seven years or upwards, shall be punished as a person convicted of that offence would be liable to be punished.

ILLUSTRATION. A gives false evidence before a Court of Justice, intending thereby to cause Z to be convicted of a dacoity. The punishment of dacoity is imprisonment for life, or rigorous imprisonment for a term which may extend to ten years, with or without fine. A, therefore, is liable to imprisonment for life or imprisonment, with or without fine.

196. Using evidence known to be false. Whoever corruptly uses or attempts to use as true or genuine evidence any evidence which he knows to be false or fabricated, shall be punished in the same manner as if he gave or fabricated false evidence.

197. Issuing or signing false certificate. Whoever issues or signs any certificate required by law to be given or signed, or relating to any fact of which such certificate is by law admissible in evidence, knowing or believing that such certificate is false in any material point, shall be punished in the same manner as if he gave false evidence.

198. Using as true a certificate known to be false. Whoever corruptly uses or attempts to use any such certificate as a true certificate, knowing the same to be false in any material point, shall be punished in the same manner as if he gave false evidence.

199. False statement made in declaration which is by law receivable as evidence. Whoever, in any declaration made or subscribed by him, which declaration any Court of Justice, or any public servant or other person, is bound or authorized by law to receive as evidence of any fact, makes any statement which is false, and which he either knows or believes to be false or does not believe to be true, touching any point material to the object for which the declaration is made or used, shall be punished in the same manner as if he gave false evidence.

200. Using as true such declaration knowing it to be flase. Whoever corruptly uses or attempts to use as true any such declaration, knowing the same to be false in any material point, shall be punished in the same manner as if he gave false evidence.

EXPLANATION. A declaration which is inadmissible merely upon the ground of some informality, is a declaration within the meaning of Sections 199 and 200.

201. Causing disappearance of evidence of offence, or giving false information to screen offender. Whoever, knowing or having reason to believe that an offence has been committed, causes any evidence of the commission of that offence to disappear, with the intention of screening the offender from legal punishment, or with that intention gives any information respecting the offence which he knows or believes to be false, if a capital offence; if a capital offence, shall, if the offence which he knows or believes to have been committed is punishable with death, be punished with imprisonment of either description for a term which may extend to seven years, and shall also be liable to fine; if punishable with imprisonment for life; if punishable with imprisonment for life. and if the offence is punishable with imprisonment for life, or with imprisonment which may extend to ten years, shall be punished with imprisonment of either description for a term which may extend to three years, and shall also be liable to fine; if punishable with less than ten years' imprisonment and if the offence is punishable with imprisonment for any term not extending to ten years, shall be punished with imprisonment of the description provided for the offence, for a term which may extend to one-fourth part of the longest term of the imprisonment provided for the offence, or with fine, or with both.

ILLUSTRATION. A, knowing that B has murdered Z, assists B to hide the body with the intention of screening B from punishment. A is liable to imprisonment of either description for seven years, and also to fine.

202. Intentional omission to give information of offence by person bound to inform. Whoever, knowing or having reason to believe that an offence has been committed, intentionally omits to give any information respecting that offence which he is legally bound to give, shall be punished with imprisonment of either description for a term which may extend to six months, or with fine, or with both.

203. Giving false information respecting an offence committed. Whoever, knowing or having reason to believe that an offence has been committed, gives any information respecting that offence which he knows or believes to be false, shall be punished with imprisonment of either description for a term which may extend to two years, or with fine, or with both.

EXPLANATION. In Sections 201 and 202 and in this Section the word "offence" includes any act committed at any place out of India, which, if committed in India, would be punishable under any of the following Sections, namely, 302, 304, 382, 392, 393, 394, 395, 396, 397, 398, 399, 402, 435, 436, 449, 450, 457, 458, 459 and 460.

204. Destruction of document to prevent its production as evidence. Whoever secretes or destroys any document which he may be lawfully compelled to produce as evidence in a Court of Justice, or in any proceeding lawfully held before a public servant, as such, or obliterates or renders illegible the whole or any part of such document with the intention of preventing the same from being produced or used as evidence before such Court or public servant as aforesaid, or after he shall have been lawfully summoned or required to produce the same for that purpose, shall be punished with imprisonment of either description for a term which may extend to two years, or with fine, or with both.

205. False personation for purpose of act or proceeding in suit or prosecution. Whoever falsely personates another, and in such assumed character makes any admission or statement, or confesses judgment, or causes any process to be issued or becomes bail or security, or does any other act in any suit or criminal prosecution, shall be punished with imprisonment of either description for a term which may extend to three years, or with fine, or with both.

206. Fraudulent removal or concealment of property to prevent its seizure as forfeited or in execution. Whoever fraudulently removes, conceals, transfers or delivers to any person any property or any interest therein, intending thereby to prevent that property or interest therein from being taken as a forfeiture or in satisfaction of a fine, under a sentence which has been pronounced, or which he knows to be likely to be pronounced, by a Court of Justice or other competent authority, or from being taken in execution of a decree or order which has been made, or which he knows to be likely to be made by a Court of Justice in a civil suit, shall be punished with imprisonment of either description for a term which may extend to two years, or with fine, or with both.

207. Fraudulent claim to property to prevent its seizure as forfeited or in execution. Whoever fraudulently accepts, receives or claims any property or any interest therein, knowing that he has no right or rightful claim to such property or interest, or practices any deception touching any right to any property or any interest therein, intending thereby to prevent that property or interest therein from being taken as a forfeiture or in satisfaction of a fine, under a sentence which has been pronounced, or which he knows to be likely to be pronounced by a Court of Justice or other competent authority, or from being taken in execution of a decree or order which has been made, or which he knows to be likely to be made by a Court of Justice in a civil suit, shall be punished with imprisonment of either description for a term which may extend to two years, or with fine, or with both.

208. Fraudulently suffering decree for sum not due. Whoever fraudulently causes or suffers a decree or order to be passed against him at the suit of any person for a sum not due or for a larger sum than is due to such person or for any property or interest in property to which such person is not entitled, or fraudulently causes or suffers a decree or order to be executed against him after it has been satisfied, or for anything in respect of which it has been satisfied, shall be punished with imprisonment of either description for a term which may extend to two years, or with fine, or with both.

ILLUSTRATION. A institutes a suit against Z. Z, knowing that A is likely to obtain a decree against him, fraudulently suffers a judgment to pass against him for a larger amount at the suit of B, who has no just claim against him, in order that B, either on his own account or for the benefit of Z, may share in the proceeds of any sale of Z's property which may be made under A's decree. Z has committed an offence under this Section.

209. Dishonesty making false claim in Court. Whoever fraudulently or dishonestly, or with intent to injure or annoy any person, makes in a Court of Justice any claim which he knows to be false, shall be punished with imprisonment of either description for a term which may extend to two years, and shall also be liable to fine.

210. Fraudulently obtaining decree for sum not due. Whoever fraudulently obtains a decree or order against any person for a sum not due, or for a larger sum than is due or for any property or interest in property to which he is not entitled, or fraudulently causes a decree or order to be executed against any person after it has been satisfied or for anything in respect of which it has been satisfied, or fraudulently suffers or permits any such act to be done in his name, shall be punished with imprisonment of either description for a term which may extend to two years, or with fine, or with both.

211. False charge of offence made with intent to injure. Whoever, with intent to cause injury to any person, institutes or causes to be instituted any criminal proceeding against that person, or falsely charges any person with having committed an offence, knowing that there is no just or lawful ground for such proceeding or charge against that person, shall be punished with imprisonment of either description for a term which may extend to two years, or with fine, or with both; and if such criminal proceeding be instituted on a false charge of an offence punishable with death imprisonment for life, or imprisonment for seven years or upwards, shall be punishable with imprisonment of either description for a term which may extend to seven years, and shall also be liable to fine.

212. Harbouring offender. Whenever an offence has been committed, whoever harbours or conceals a person whom he knows or has reason to believe to be the offender, with the intention of screening him from legal punishment, if a capital offence; if a capital offence shall, if the offence is punishable with death, be punished with imprisonment of either description for a term which may extend to five years, and shall also be liable to fine; if punishable with imprisonment for life, or with imprisonment and if the offence is punishable with imprisonment for life, or with imprisonment which may extend to ten years, shall be punished with imprisonment of either description for a term which may extend to three years, and shall also be liable to fine; and if the offence is punishable with imprisonment which may extend to one year, and not to ten years, shall be punished with imprisonment of the description provided for the offence for a term which may extend to one-fourth part of the longest term of imprisonment provided for the offence, or with fine, or with both.

"Offence" in this Section includes any act committed at any place out of India, which, if committed in India, would be punishable under any of the following Sections, namely, 302, 304, 382, 392, 393, 394, 395, 396, 397, 398, 399, 402, 435, 436, 449, 450, 457, 458, 459 and 460; and every such act shall, for the purposes of this Section, be deemed to be punishable as if the accused person had been guilty of it in India.

Exception. This provision shall not extend to any case in which the harbour or concealment is by the husband or wife of the offender.

ILLUSTRATION. A, knowing that B has committed dacoity, knowingly conceals B in order to screen him from legal punishment. Here, as B is liable to imprisonment for life, A is liable to imprisonment of either description for a term not exceeding three years, and is also liable to fine.

213. Taking gift, etc., to screen an offender from punishment. Whoever accepts or attempts to obtain, or agrees to accept, any gratification for himself or any other person, or any restitution of property to himself or any other person, in consideration of his concealing an offence or of his screening any person from legal punishment for any offence, or of his not proceeding against any person for the purpose of bringing him to legal punishment, if a capital offence is punishable with death, be punished with imprisonment of either description for a term which may extend to seven years, and shall also be liable to fine; if punishable with imprisonment for life, or with imprisonment which may extend to ten years, shall be punished with imprisonment of either description for a term which may extend to three years, and shall also be liable to fine; and if the offence is punishable with imprisonment not extending to ten years, shall be punished with imprisonment of the description provided for the offence for a term which may extend to one fourth part of the longest term of imprisonment provided for the offence, or with fine, or with both.

214. Offering gift or restoration of property in consideration of screening offender. Whoever gives or causes, or offers or agrees to give or cause, any gratification to any person, or restores or causes the restoration of any property to any person, in consideration of that person's concealing an offence, or of his screening any person from legal punishment for any offence, or of his not proceeding against any person for the purpose of bringing him to legal punishment, if a capital offence; if a capital offence shall, if the offence is punishable with death, be punished with imprisonment of either description for a term which may extend to seven years, and shall also be liable to fine; if punishable with imprisonment for life, or with imprisonment which may extend to ten years, shall be punished with imprisonment of either description for a term which may extend to three years, and shall also be liable to fine.

Exception. The provisions of Sections 213 and 214 do not extend to any case in which the offence may lawfully be compounded.

215. Taking gift to help to recover stolen property, etc. Whoever takes or agrees or consents to take any gratification under pretence or on account of helping any person to recover any movable property of which he shall have been deprived by any offence punishable under this Code, shall, unless he uses all means in his power to cause the offender to be apprehended and convicted of the offence, be punished with imprisonment of either description for a term which may extend to two years, or with fine, or with both.

216. Harbouring offender who has escaped from custody or whose apprehension has been ordered. Whenever any person convicted of or charged with an offence, being in lawful custody for that offence, escapes from such custody, or whenever a public servant, in the exercise of the lawful powers of such public servant, orders a certain person to be apprehended for an offence, whoever, knowing of such escape or order for apprehension, harbours or conceals that person with the intention of preventing him from being apprehended, shall be punished in the manner following, that is to say, if a capital offence — if the offence for which the person was in custody or is ordered to be apprehended is punishable with death, he shall be punished with imprisonment of either description for a term which may extend to seven years, and shall also be liable to fine; if punishable with imprisonment for life, or with imprisonment. if punishable with imprisonment for life, or with imprisonment - if the offence is punishable with imprisonment for life or imprisonment for ten years, he shall be punished with imprisonment of either description for a term which may extend to three years, with or without fine; and if the offence is punishable with imprisonment which may extend to one year and not to ten years, he shall be punished with imprisonment of the description provided for the offence for a term which may extend to one- fourth part of the longest term of the imprisonment provided for such offence or with fine, or with both. "Offence" in this Section includes also any act or omission of which a person is alleged to have been guilty out of India, which, if he had been guilty of it in India, would have been punishable as an offence, and for which he is, under any law relating to extradition, or otherwise liable to be apprehended or detained in custody in India, and every such act or omission shall, for the purposes of this Section, be deemed to be punishable as if the accused person had been guilty of it in India.

Exception. The provision does not extend to the case in which the harbour or concealment is by the husband or wife of the person to be apprehended.

216A. Penalty for harbouring robbers or dacoits. Whoever, knowing or having reason to believe that any persons are about to commit or have recently committed robbery or dacoity, harbours them or any of them, with the intention of facilitating the commission of such robbery or dacoity or of screening them or any of them from punishment, shall be punished with rigorous imprisonment for a term which may extend to seven years, and shall also be liable to fine.

EXPLANATION. For the purposes of this Section it is immaterial whether the robbery or dacoity is intended to be committed, or has been committed, within or without India.

Exception. This provision does not extend to the case in which the harbour is by the husband or wife of the offender.

216B. Definition of "harbour" in Sections 212, 216 and 216A. *Rep. by the Indian Penal Code (Amendment) Act, 1942 (8 of 1942), s. 3.*

217. Public servant disobeying direction of law with intent to save person from punishment or property from forfeiture. Whoever, being a public servant, knowingly disobeys any direction of the law as to the way in which he is to conduct himself as such public servant, intending thereby to save, or knowing it to be likely that he will thereby save, any person from legal punishment, or subject him to a less punishment than that to which he is liable, or with intent to save, or knowing that he is likely thereby to save, any property from forfeiture or any charge to which it is liable by law, shall be punished with imprisonment of either description for a term which may extend to two years, or with fine, or with both.

218. Public servant framing incorrect record or writing with intent to save person from punishment or property from forfeiture. Whoever, being a public servant, and being as such public servant, charged with the preparation of any record or other writing, frames that record or writing in a manner which he knows to be incorrect, with intent to cause, or knowing it to be likely that he will thereby cause, loss or injury to the public or to any person, or with intent thereby to save, or knowing it to be likely that he will thereby save, any person from legal punishment, or with intent to save, or knowing that he is likely thereby to save, any property from forfeiture or other charge to which it is liable by law, shall be punished with imprisonment of either description for a term which may extend to three years, or with fine, or with both.

219. Public servant in judicial proceeding corruptly making report, etc., contrary to law. Whoever, being a public servant, corruptly or maliciously makes or pronounces in any stage of a judicial proceeding, any report, order, verdict, or decision which he knows to be contrary to law, shall be punished with imprisonment of either description for a term which may extend to seven years, or with fine, or with both.

220. Commitment for trial or confinement by person having authority who knows that he is acting contrary to law. Whoever, being in any office which gives him legal authority to commit persons for trial or to confinement, or to keep persons in confinement, corruptly or maliciously commits any person for trial or to confinement, or keeps any person in confinement, in the exercise of that authority, knowing that in so doing he is acting contrary to law, shall be punished with imprisonment of either description for a term which may extend to seven years, or with fine, or with both.

221. Intentional omission to apprehend on the part of public servant bound to apprehend. Whoever, being a pubic servant, legally bound as such public servant to apprehend or to keep in confinement any person charged with or liable to be apprehended for an offence, intentionally omits to apprehend such person, or intentionally suffers such person to escape, or intentionally aids such person in escaping or attempting to escape from such confinement, shall be punished as follows, that is to say: with imprisonment of either description for a term which may extend to seven years, with or without fine, if the person in confinement, or who ought to have been apprehended, was charged with, or liable to be apprehended for, an offence punishable with death; or with imprisonment of either description for a term which may extend to three years, with or without fine, if the person in confinement, or who ought to have been apprehended, was charged with, or liable to be apprehended for, an offence punishable with imprisonment for life or imprisonment for a term which may extend to ten years; or with imprisonment of either description for a term which may extend to two years, with or without fine, if the person in confinement, or who ought to have been apprehended, was charged with, or liable to be apprehended for, an offence punishable with imprisonment for a term less than ten years.

222. Intentional omission to apprehend on the part of public servant bound to apprehend person under sentence or lawfully committed. Whoever, being a public servant, legally bound as such public servant to apprehend or to keep in confinement any person under sentence of a Court of Justice for any offence or lawfully committed to custody, intentionally omits to apprehend such person, or intentionally suffers such person to escape or intentionally aids such person in escaping or attempting to escape from such confinement, shall be punished as follows, that is to say: with imprisonment for life or with imprisonment of either description for a term which may extend to fourteen years, with or without fine, if the person in confinement, or who ought to have been apprehended, is under sentence of death; or with imprisonment of either description for a term which may extend to seven years, with or without fine, if the person in confinement, or who, ought to have been apprehended, is subject, by a sentence of a Court of Justice, or by virtue of a commutation of such sentence, to imprisonment for life or imprisonment for a term of ten years or upwards; or with imprisonment of either description for a term which may extend to three years, or with fine, or with both, if the person in confinement, or who ought to have been apprehended is subject, by a sentence of a Court of Justice, to imprisonment for a term not extending to ten years or if the person was lawfully committed to custody.

223. Escape from confinement or custody negligently suffered by public servant. Whoever, being a public servant legally bound as such public servant to keep in confinement any person charged with or convicted of any offence or lawfully committed to custody, negligently suffers such person to escape from confinement, shall be punished with simple imprisonment for a term which may extend to two years, or with fine, or with both.

224. Resistance or obstruction by a person to his lawful apprehension. Whoever intentionally offers any resistance or illegal obstruction to the lawful apprehension of himself for any offence with which he is charged or of which he has been convicted, or escapes or attempts to escape from any custody in which he is lawfully detained for any such offence, shall be punished with imprisonment of either description for a term which may extend to two years, or with fine, or with both.

Explanation. The punishment in this Section is in addition to the punishment for which the person to be apprehended or detained in custody was liable for the offence with which he was charged, or of which he was convicted.

225. Resistance or obstruction to lawful apprehension of another person. Whoever intentionally offers any resistance or illegal obstruction to the lawful apprehension of any other person for an offence, or rescues or attempts to rescue any other person from any custody in which that person is lawfully detained for an offence, shall be punished with imprisonment of either description for a term which may extend to two years, or with fine, or with both; or, if the person to be apprehended, or the person rescued or attempted to be rescued, is charged with or liable to be apprehended for an offence punishable with imprisonment for life or imprisonment for a term which may extend to ten years, shall be punished with imprisonment of either description for a term which may extend to three years, and shall also be liable to fine; or, if the person to be apprehended or rescued, or attempted to be rescued, is charged with or liable to be apprehended for an offence punishable with death, shall be punished with imprisonment of either description for a term which may extend to seven years, and shall also be liable to fine; or, if the person to be apprehended or rescued, or attempted to be rescued, is liable under the sentence of a Court of Justice, or by virtue of a commutation of such a sentence, to imprisonment for life, or imprisonment, for a term of ten years or upwards, shall be punished with imprisonment of either description for a term which may extend to seven years, and shall also be liable to fine; or, if the person to be apprehended or rescued, or attempted to be rescued, is under sentence of death, shall be punished with imprisonment for life or imprisonment of either description for a term not exceeding ten years, and shall also be liable to fine.

225A. Omission to apprehend, or sufferance of escape, on part of public servant, in cases not otherwise, provided for. Whoever, being a public servant legally bound as such public servant to apprehend, or to keep in confinement, any person in any case not provided for in Section 221, Section 222 or Section 223, or in any other law for the time being in force, omits to apprehend that person or suffers him to escape from confinement, shall be punished-

(a) if he does so intentionally, with imprisonment of either description for a term which may extend to three years, or with fine or with both; and

(b) if he does so negligently, with simple imprisonment for a term which may extend to two years, or with fine, or with both.

225B. Resistance or obstruction to lawful apprehension, or escape or rescue in cases not otherwise provided for. Whoever, in any case not provided for in Section 224 or Section 225 or in any other law for the time being in force, intentionally offers any resistance or illegal obstruction to the lawful apprehension of himself or of any other person, or escapes or attempts to escape from any custody in which he is lawfully detained, or rescues or attempts to rescue any other person from any custody in which that person is lawfully detained, shall be punished with imprisonment of either description for a term which may extend to six months, or with fine, or with both.

226. Unlawful return from transportation. *Rep. by the Code of Criminal Procedure (Amendment) Act, 1955 (26 of 1955), s. 117 and Sch.*

227. Violation of condition of remission of punishment. Whoever, having accepted any conditional remission of punishment, knowingly violates any condition on which such remission was granted, shall be punished with the punishment to which he was originally sentenced, if he has already suffered no part of that punishment, and if he has suffered any part of that punishment, then with so much of that punishment as he has not already suffered.

228. Intentional insult or interruption to public servant sitting in judicial proceeding. Whoever intentionally offers any insult, or causes any interruption to any public servant, while such public servant is sitting in any stage of a judicial proceeding, shall be punished with simple imprisonment for a term which may extend to six months, or with fine which may extend to one thousand rupees, or with both.

228A. Disclosure of identity of the victim of certain offences, etc.

(1) Whoever prints or publishes the name or any matter which may make known the identity of any person against whom an offence under Section 376, Section 376A, Section 376B, Section 376C or Section 376D is alleged or found to have been committed (hereafter in this Section referred to as the victim) shall be punished with imprisonment of either description for a term which may extend to two years and shall also be liable to fine.

(2) Nothing in sub-section (1) extends to any printing or publication of the name or any matter which may make known the identity of the victim if such printing or publication is-

(a) by or under the order in writing of the officer-in-charge of the police station or the police officer making the investigation into such offence acting in good faith for the purposes of such investigation; or

(b) by, or with the authorisation in writing of, the victim; or

(c) where the victim is dead or minor or of unsound mind, by, or with the authorisation in writing of, the next- of- kin of the victim: Provided that no such authorisation shall be given by the next-of-kin to anybody other than the chairman or the secretary, by whatever name called, of any recognised welfare institution or organisation.

EXPLANATION. For the purposes of this sub-section," recognised welfare institution or organisation" means a social welfare institution or organisation recognised in this behalf by the Central or State Government.

(3) Whoever prints or publishes any matter in relation to any proceeding before a court with respect to an offence referred to in sub-section (1) without the previous permission of such court shall be punished with imprisonment of either description for a term which may extend to two years and shall also be liable to fine.

EXPLANATION. The printing or publication of the judgment of any High Court or the Supreme Court does not amount to an offence within the meaning of this Section.

229. Personation of a juror or assessor. Whoever, by personation or otherwise, shall intentionally cause, or knowingly suffer himself to be returned, empanelled or sworn as a juryman or assessor in any case in which he knows that he is not entitled by law to be so returned, empanelled or sworn, or knowing himself to have been so returned, empanelled or sworn contrary to law, shall voluntarily serve on such jury or as such assessor, shall be punished with imprisonment of either description for a term which may extend to two years, or with fine, or with both.

CHAPTER - XII : OF OFFENCES RELATING TO COIN AND GOVERNMENT STAMPS

230. "Coin" defined. Coin is metal used for the time being as money, and stamped and issued by the authority of some State or Sovereign Power in order to be so used. Indian coin is metal stamped and issued by the authority of the Government of India in order to be used as money; and metal which has been so stamped and issued shall continue to be Indian coin for the purposes of this Chapter, notwithstanding that it may have ceased to be used as money.

ILLUSTRATIONS.

(a) Cowries are not coin.

(b) Lumps of unstamped copper, though used as money, are not coin.

(c) Medals are not coin, inasmuch as they are not intended to be used as money.

(d) The coin denominated as the Company's rupee is Indian coin.

(e) The "Farukhabad rupee", which was formerly used as money under the authority of the Government of India, is Indian coin although it is no longer so used.

231. Counterfeiting coin. Whoever counterfeits or knowingly performs any part of the process of counterfeiting coin, shall be punished with imprisonment of either description for a term which may extend to seven years, and shall also be liable to fine.

EXPLANATION. A person commits this offence who intending to practise deception, or knowing it to be likely that deception will thereby be practised, causes a genuine coin to appear like a different coin.

232. Counterfeiting Indian coin. Whoever counterfeits, or knowingly performs any part of the process of counterfeiting Indian coin, shall be punished with imprisonment for life, or with imprisonment of either description for a term which may extend to ten years, and shall also be liable to fine.

233. Making or selling instrument for counterfeiting coin. Whoever makes or mends, or performs any part of the process of making or mending, or buys, sells or disposes of, any die or instrument, for the purpose of being used, or knowing or having reason to believe that it is intended to be used, for the purpose of counterfeiting coin, shall be punished with imprisonment of either description for a term which may extended to three years, and shall also be liable to fine.

234. Making or selling instrument for counterfeiting Indian coin. Whoever makes or mends, or performs any part of the process of making or mending or buys, sells or disposes of, any die or instrument, for the purpose of being used, or knowing or having reason to believe that it is intended to be used, for the purpose of counterfeiting Indian coin, shall be punished with imprisonment of either description for a term which may extend to seven years, and shall also be liable to fine.

235. Possession of instrument or material for the purpose of using the same for counterfeiting coin. Whoever is in possession of any instrument or material, for the purpose of using the same for counterfeiting coin, or knowing or having reason to believe that the same is intended to be used for that purpose, shall be punished with imprisonment of either description for a term which may extend to three years, and shall also be liable to fine; and if the coin to be counterfeited is Indian coin, shall be punished with imprisonment of either description for a term which may extend to ten years, and shall also be liable to fine.

236. Abetting in India the counterfeiting out of India of coin. Whoever, being within India abets the counterfeiting of coin out of India shall be punished in the same manner as if he abetted the counterfeiting of such coin within India.

237. Import or export of counterfeit coin. Whoever imports into India, or exports therefrom, any counterfeit coin, knowingly or having reason to believe that the same is counterfeit, shall be punished with imprisonment of either description for a term which may extend to three years, and shall also be liable to fine.

238. Import or export of counterfeits of the Indian coin. Whoever imports into India, or exports therefrom, any counterfeit coin, which he knows or has reason to believe to be a counterfeit of Indian coin, shall be punished with Imprisonment for life, or with imprisonment of either description for a term which may extend to ten years, and shall also be liable to fine.

239. Delivery of coin possessed with knowledge that it is counterfeit. Whoever, having any counterfeit coin, which at the time when he became possessed of it, he knew to be counterfeit, fraudulently or with intent that fraud may be committed, delivers the same to any persons or attempts to induce any person to receive it, shall be punished with imprisonment of either description for a term which may extend to five years, and shall also be liable to fine.

240. Delivery of Indian coin, possessed with knowledge that it is counterfeit. Whoever having any counterfeit coin, which is a counterfeit of Indian coin, and which, at the time when he became possessed of it, he knew to be a counterfeit of Indian coin, fraudulently or with intent that fraud may be committed, delivers the same to any person, or attempts to induce any person to receive it, shall be punished with imprisonment of either description for a term which may extend to ten years, and shall also be liable to fine.

241. Delivery of coin as genuine, which, when first possessed, the deliverer did not know to be counterfeit. Whoever delivers to any other person as genuine, or attempts to induce any other person to receive as genuine, any counterfeit coin which he knows to be counterfeit, but which he did not know to be counterfeit at the time when he took it into his possession, shall be punished with imprisonment of either description for a term which may extend to two years, or with fine to an amount which may extend to ten times the value of the coin counterfeited, or with both.

ILLUSTRATION. A, a coiner, delivers counterfeit Company's rupees to his accomplice B, for the purpose of uttering them. B sells the rupees to C, another utterer, who buys them knowing them to be counterfeit. C pays away the rupees for goods to D, who receives them, not knowing them to be counterfeit. D, after receiving the rupees, discovers that they are counterfeit and pays them away as if they were good. Here D is punishable only under this Section, but B and C are punishable under Section 239 or 240, as the case may be.

242. Possession of counterfeit coin by person who knew it to be counterfeit when he became possessed thereof. Whoever, fraudulently or with intent that fraud may be committed, is in possession of counterfeit coin, having known at the time when he became possessed thereof that such coin was counterfeit, shall be punished with imprisonment of either description for a term which may extend to three years, and shall also be liable to fine.

243. Possession of Indian coin by person who knew it to be counterfeit when he became possessed thereof. Whoever, fraudulently or with intent that fraud may be committed, is in possession of counterfeit coin, which is a counterfeit of Indian coin, having known at the time when he became possessed of it that it was counterfeit, shall be punished with imprisonment of either description for a term which may extend to seven years, and shall also be liable to fine.

244. Person employed in mint causing coin to be of different weight or composition from that fixed by law. Whoever, being employed in any mint lawfully established in India, does any act, or omits what he is legally bound to do, with the intention of causing any coin issued from that mint to be of a different weight or composition from the weight or composition fixed by law, shall be punished with imprisonment of either description for a term which may extend to seven years, and shall also be liable to fine.

245. Unlawfully taking coining instrument from mint. Whoever, without lawful authority, takes out of any mint, lawfully established in India, any coining tool or instrument, shall be punished with imprisonment of either description for a term which may extend to seven years, and shall also be liable to fine.

246. Fraudulently or dishonestly diminishing weight or altering composition of coin. Whoever, fraudulently or dishonestly performs on any coin any operation which diminishes the weight or alters the composition of that coin, shall be punished with imprisonment of either description for a term which may extend to three years, and shall also be liable to fine.

EXPLANATION. A person who scoops out part of the coin and puts anything else into the cavity alters the composition of the coin.

247. Fraudulently or dishonestly diminishing weight or altering composition of Indian coin. Whoever fraudulently or dishonestly performs on any Indian coin any operation which diminishes the weight or alters the composition of that coin, shall be punished with imprisonment of either description for a term which may extend to seven years, and shall also be liable to fine.

248. Altering appearance of coin with intent that it shall pass as coin of different description. Whoever performs on any coin any operation which alters the appearance of that coin, with the intention that the said coin shall pass as a coin of a different description, shall be punished with imprisonment of either description for a term which may extend to three years, and shall also be liable to fine.

249. Altering appearance of Indian coin with intent that it shall pass as coin of different description. Whoever performs on any Indian coin any operation which alters the appearance of that coin, with the intention that the said coin shall pass as a coin of a different description, shall be punished with imprisonment of either description for a term which may extend to seven years, and shall also be liable to fine.

250. Delivery of coin possessed with knowledge that it is altered. Whoever, having coin in his possession with respect to which the offence defined in Section 246 or 248 has been committed, and having known at the time when he became possessed of such coin that such offence had been committed with respect to it, fraudulently or with intent that fraud may be committed, delivers such coin to any other person, or attempts to induce any other person to receive the same, shall be punished with imprisonment of either description for a term which may extend to five years, and shall also be liable to fine.

251. Delivery of Indian coin, possessed with knowledge that it is altered. Whoever, having coin in his possession with respect to which the offence defined in Section 247 or 249 has been committed, and having known at the time when he became possessed of such coin that such offence had been committed with respect to it, fraudulently or with intent that fraud may be committed, delivers such coin to any other person, or attempts to induce any other person to receive the same, shall be punished with imprisonment of either description for a term which may extend to ten years, and shall also be liable to fine.

252. Possession of coin by person who knew it to be altered when he became possessed thereof. Whoever fraudulently or with intent that fraud may be committed, is in possession of coin with respect to which the offence defined in either of the Sections 246 or 248 has been committed having known at the time of becoming possessed thereof that such offence had been committed with respect to such coin, shall be punished with imprisonment of either description for a term which may extend to three years, and shall also be liable to fine.

253. Possession of Indian coin by person who knew it to be altered when he became possessed thereof. Whoever fraudulently or with intent that fraud may be committed, is in possession of coin with respect to which the offence defined in either of the Sections 247 or 249 has been committed having known at the time of becoming possessed thereof, that such offence had been committed with respect to such coin, shall be punished with imprisonment of either description for a term which may extend to five years, and shall also be liable to fine.

254. Delivery of coin as genuine which, when first possessed, the deliverer did not know to be altered. Whoever delivers to any other person as genuine or as a coin of a different description from what it is, or attempts to induce any person to receive as genuine, or as a different coin from what it is, any coin in respect of which he knows that any such operation as that mentioned in Sections 246, 247, 248 or 249 has been performed, but in respect of which he did not, at the time when he took it into his possession, know that such operation had been performed, shall be punished with imprisonment of either description for a term which may extend to two years or with fine to an amount which may extend to ten times the value of the coin for which the altered coin is passed, or attempted to be passed.

255. Counterfeiting Government stamp. Whoever counterfeits, or knowingly performs any part of the process of counterfeiting, any stamp issued by Government for the purpose of revenue shall be punished with imprisonment for life or with imprisonment of either description for a term which may extend to ten years, and shall also be liable to fine.

EXPLANATION. A person commits this offence who counterfeits by causing a genuine stamps of one denomination to appear like a genuine stamp of a different denomination.

256. Having possession of instrument or material for counterfeiting Government stamp. Whoever has in his possession any instrument or material for the purpose of being used, or knowing or having reason to believe that it is intended to be used, for the purpose of counterfeiting any stamp issued by Government for the purpose of revenue, shall be punished with imprisonment of either description for a term which may extend to seven years, and shall also be liable to fine.

257. Making or selling instrument for counterfeiting Government stamp. Whoever makes or performs any part of the process of making, or buys, or sells, or disposes of, any instrument for the purpose of being used, or knowing or having reason to believe that it is intended to be used, for the purpose of counterfeiting any stamp issued by Government for the purpose of revenue, shall be punished with imprisonment of either description for a term which may extend to seven years, and shall also be liable to fine.

258. Sale of counterfeit Government stamp. Whoever sells, or offers for sale, any stamp which he knows or has reason to believe to be a counterfeit of any stamp issued by Government for the purpose of revenue, shall be punished with imprisonment of either description for a term which may extend to seven years, and shall also be liable to fine.

259. Having possession of counterfeit Government stamp. Whoever has in his possession any stamp which he knows to be a counterfeit of any stamp issued by Government for the purpose of revenue, intending to use, or dispose of the same as a genuine stamp, or in order that it may be used as a genuine stamp, shall be punished with imprisonment of either description for a term which may extend to seven years, and shall also be liable to fine.

260. Using as genuine a Government stamp known to be counterfeit. Whoever uses as genuine any stamp, knowing it to be a counterfeit of any stamp issued by Government for the purpose of revenue, shall be punished with imprisonment of either description for a term which may extend to seven years, or with fine, or with both.

261. Effacing writing from substance bearing Government stamp, or removing from document a stamp used for it, with intent to cause loss to Government. Whoever, fraudulently or with intent to cause loss to the Government, removes or effaces from any substance, bearing any stamp issued by Government for the purpose of revenue, any writing or document for which such stamp has been used, or removes from any writing or document a stamp which has been used for such writing or document, in order that such stamp may be used for a different writing or document, shall be punished with imprisonment of either description for a term which may extend to three years, or with fine, or with both.

262. Using Government stamp known to have been before used. Whoever, fraudulently or with intent to cause loss to the Government, uses for any purpose a stamp issued by Government for the purpose of revenue, which he knows to have been before used, shall be punished with imprisonment of either description for a term which may extend to two years, or with fine, or with both.

263. Erasure of mark denoting that stamp has been used. Whoever, fraudulently or with intent to cause loss to Government, erases or removes from a stamp issued by Government for the purpose of revenue, any mark, put or impressed upon such stamp for the purpose of denoting that the same has been used, or knowingly has in his possession or sells or disposes of any such stamp from which such mark has been erased or removed, or sells or disposes of any such stamp which he knows to have been used, shall be punished with imprisonment of either description for a term which may extend to three years, or with fine, or with both.

263A. Prohibition of fictitious stamps.

(1) Whoever-

(a) makes, knowingly utters, deals in or sells any fictitious stamp, or knowingly uses for any postal purpose any fictitious stamp; or

(b) has in his possession, without lawful excuse, any fictitious stamp; or

(c) makes or, without lawful excuse, has in his possession any die, plate, instrument or materials for making any fictitious stamp, shall be punished with fine which may extend to two hundred rupees.

(2) Any such stamp, die, plate, instrument or materials in the possession of any person for making any fictitious stamp may be seized and, if seized shall be forfeited.

(3) In this Section "fictitious stamp" means any stamp falsely purporting to be issued by Government for the purpose of denoting a rate of postage, or any facsimile or imitation or representation, whether on paper or otherwise, of any stamp issued by Government for that purpose.

(4) In this Section and also in Sections 255 to 263, both inclusive, the word "Government", when used in connection with, or in reference to, any stamp issued for the purpose of denoting a rate of postage, shall, notwithstanding anything in Section 17, be deemed to include the person or persons authorized by law to administer executive Government in any part of India, and also in any part of Her Majesty's dominions or in any foreign country.

CHAPTER - XIII : OF OFFENCES RELATING TO WEIGHTS AND MEASURES

264. Fraudulent use of false instrument for weighing. Whoever, fraudulently uses any instrument for weighing which he knows to be false, shall be punished with imprisonment of either description for a term which may extend to one year, or with fine, or with both.

265. Fraudulent use of false weight or measure. Whoever, fraudulently uses any false weight or false measure of length or capacity, or fraudulently uses any weight or any measure of length or capacity as a different weight or measure from what it is, shall be punished with imprisonment of either description for a term which may extend to one year, or with fine, or with both.

266. Being in possession of false weight or measure. Whoever is in possession of any instrument for weighing, or of any weight, or of any measure of length or capacity, which he knows to be false, intending that the same may be fraudulently used, shall be punished with imprisonment of either description for a term which may extend to one year, or with fine, or with both.

267. Making or selling false weight or measure. Whoever makes, sells or disposes of any instrument for weighing, or any weight, or any measure of length or capacity which he knows to be false, in order that the same may be used as true, or knowing that the same is likely to be used as true, shall be punished with imprisonment of either description for a term which may extend to one year, or with fine, or with both.

CHAPTER - XIV : OF OFFENCES AFFECTING THE PUBLIC HEALTH, SAFETY, CONVENIENCE, DECENCY AND MORALS

268. Public nuisance. A person is guilty of a public nuisance who does any act or is guilty of an illegal omission which causes any common injury, danger or annoyance to the public or to the people in general who dwell or occupy property in the vicinity, or which must necessarily cause injury, obstruction, danger or annoyance to persons who may have occasion to use any public right. A common nuisance is not excused on the ground that it causes some convenience or advantage.

269. Negligent act likely to spread infection of disease dangerous to life. Whoever unlawfully or negligently does any act which is, and which he knows or has reason to believe to be, likely to spread the infection of any disease dangerous to life, shall be punished with imprisonment of either description for a term which may extend to six months, or with fine, or with both.

270. Malignant act likely to spread infection of disease dangerous to life. Whoever malignantly does any act which is, and which he knows or has reason to believe to be, likely to spread the infection of any disease dangerous to life, shall be punished with imprisonment of either description for a term which may extend to two years, or with fine, or with both.

271. Disobedience to quarantine rule. Whoever knowingly disobeys any rule made and promulgated by the Government for putting any vessel into a state of quarantine, or for regulating the intercourse of vessels in a state of quarantine with the shore or with other vessels, for regulating the intercourse between places where an infectious disease prevails and other places, shall be punished with imprisonment of either description for a term which may extend to six months, or with fine, or with both.

272. Adulteration of food or drink intended for sale. Whoever adulterates any article of food or drink, so as to make such article noxious as food or drink, intending to sell such article as food or drink, or knowing it to be likely that the same will be sold as food or drink, shall be punished with imprisonment of either description for a term which may extend to six months, or with fine which may extend to one thousand rupees, or with both.

273. Sale of noxious food or drink. Whoever sells, or offers or exposes for sale, as food or drink, any article which has been rendered or has become noxious, or is in a state unfit for food or drink, knowing or having reason to believe that the same is noxious as food or drink, shall be punished with imprisonment of either description for a term which may extend to six months, or with fine which may extend to one thousand rupees, or with both.

274. Adulteration of drugs. Whoever adulterates any drug or medical preparation in such a manner as to lessen the efficacy or change the operation of such drug or medical preparation, or to make it noxious, intending that it shall be sold or used for, or knowing it to be likely that it will be sold or used for, any medicinal purpose, as it had not undergone such adulteration, shall be punished with imprisonment of either description for a term which may extend to six months, or with fine which may extend to one thousand rupees, or with both.

275. Sale of adulterated drugs. Whoever, knowing any drug or medical preparation to have been adulterated in such a manner as to lessen its efficacy, to change its operation, or to render it noxious, sells the same, or offers or exposes it for sale, or issues it from any dispensary for medicinal purposes as unadulterated, or causes it to be used for medicinal purposes by any person not knowing of the adulteration, shall be punished with imprisonment of either description for a term which may extend to six months, or with fine which may extend to one thousand rupees, or with both.

276. Sale of drug as a different drug or preparation. Whoever knowingly sells, or offers or exposes for sale, or issues from a dispensary for medicinal purposes, any drug or medical preparation, as a different drug or medical preparation, shall be punished with imprisonment of either description for a term which may extend to six months, or with fine which may extend to one thousand rupees, or with both.

277. Fouling water of public spring or reservoir. Whoever voluntarily corrupts or fouls the water of any public spring or reservoir, so as to render it less fit for the purpose for which it is ordinarily used, shall be punished with imprisonment of either description for a term which may extend to three months, or with fine which may extend to five hundred rupees, or with both.

278. Making atmosphere noxious to health. Whoever voluntarily vitiates the atmosphere in any place so as to make it noxious to the health of persons in general dwelling or carrying on business in the neighbourhood or passing along a public way, shall be punished with fine which may extend to five hundred rupees.

279. Rash driving or riding on a public way. Whoever drives any vehicle, or rides, on any public way in a manner so rash or negligent as to endanger human life, or to be likely to cause hurt or injury to any other person, shall be punished with imprisonment of either description for a term which may extend to six months, or with fine which may extend to one thousand rupees, or with both.

280. Rash navigation of vessel. Whoever navigates any vessel in a manner so rash or negligent as to endanger human life, or to be likely to cause hurt or injury to any other person, shall be punished with imprisonment of either description for a term which may extend to six months, or with fine which may extend to one thousand rupees, or with both.

281. Exhibition of false light, mark or buoy. Whoever exhibits any false light, mark or buoy, intending or knowing it to be likely that such exhibition will mislead any navigator, shall be punished with imprisonment of either description for a term which may extend to seven years, or with fine, or with both.

282. Conveying person by water for hire in unsafe or overloaded vessel. Whoever knowingly or negligently conveys, or causes to be conveyed for hire, any person by water in any vessel, when that vessel is in such a state or so loaded as to endanger the life of that person, shall be punished with imprisonment of either description for a term which may extend to six months, or with fine which may extend to one thousand rupees, or with both.

283. Danger or obstruction in public way or line of navigation. Whoever, by doing any act, or by omitting to take order with any property in his possession or under his charge, causes danger, obstruction or injury to any person in any public way or public line of navigation, shall be punished, with fine which may extend to two hundred rupees.

284. Negligent conduct with respect to poisonous substance. Whoever does, with any poisonous substance, any act in a manner so rash or negligent as to endanger human life, or to be likely to cause hurt or injury to any person, or knowingly or negligently omits to take such order with any poisonous substance in his possession as is sufficient to guard against probable danger to human life from such poisonous substance, shall be punished with imprisonment of either description for a term which may extend to six months, or with fine which may extend to one thousand rupees, or with both.

285. Negligent conduct with respect to fire or combustible matter. Whoever does, with fire or any combustible matter, any act so rashly or negligently as to endanger human life, or to be likely to cause hurt or injury to any other person, or knowingly or negligently omits to take such order with any fire or any combustible matter in his possession as is sufficient to guard against any probable danger to human life from such fire or combustible matter, shall be punished with imprisonment of either description for a term which may extend to six months, or with fine which may extend to one thousand rupees, or with both.

286. Negligent conduct with respect to explosive substance. Whoever does, with any explosive substance, any act so rashly or negligently as to endanger human life, or to be likely to cause hurt or injury to any other person, or knowingly or negligently omits to take such order with any explosive substance in his possession as is sufficient to guard against any probable danger to human life from that substance, shall be punished with imprisonment of either description for a term which may extend to six months, or with fine which may extend to one thousand rupees, or with both.

287. Negligent conduct with respect to machinery. Whoever does, with any machinery, any act so rashly or negligently as to endanger human life or to be likely to cause hurt or injury to any other person, or knowingly or negligently omits to take such order with any machinery in his possession or under his care as is sufficient to guard against any probable danger to human life from such machinery, shall be punished with imprisonment of either description for a term which may extend to six months, or with fine which may extend to one thousand rupees, or with both.

288. Negligent conduct with respect to pulling down or repairing buildings. Whoever, in pulling down or repairing any building, knowingly or negligently omits to take such order with that building as is sufficient to guard against any probable danger to human life from the fall of that building, or of any part thereof, shall be punished with imprisonment of either description for a term which may extend to six months, or with fine which may extend to one thousand rupees, or with both.

289. Negligent conduct with respect to animal. Whoever knowingly or negligently omits to take such order with any animal in his possession as is sufficient to guard against any probable danger to human life, or any probable danger of grievous hurt from such animal, shall be punished with imprisonment of either description for a term which may extend to six months, or with fine which may extend to one thousand rupees, or with both.

290. Punishment for public nuisance in cases not otherwise provided for. Whoever commits a public nuisance in any case not otherwise punishable by this Code, shall be punished with fine which may extend to two hundred rupees.

291. Continuance of nuisance after injunction to discontinue. Whoever repeats or continues a public nuisance, having been enjoined by any public servant who has lawful authority to issue such injunction not to repeat or continue such nuisance, shall be punished with simple imprisonment for a term which may extend to six months, or with fine, or with both.

292. Sale, etc., of obscene books, etc.

(1) For the purposes of sub-section (2), a book, pamphlet, paper, writing, drawing, painting representation, figure or any other object, shall be deemed to be obscene if it is lascivious or appeals to the prurient interest or if its effect, or (where it comprises two or more distinct items) the effect of any one of its items, is, if taken as a whole, such as to tend to deprave and corrupt persons who are likely, having regard to all relevant circumstances, to read, see or hear the matter contained or embodied in it.

(2) Whoever-

(a) sells, lets to hire, distributes, publicly exhibits or in any manner puts into circulation, or for purposes of sale, hire, distribution, public exhibition or circulation, makes, reduces or has in his possession any obscene book, pamphlet, paper, drawing, painting, representation or figure or any other obscene object whatsoever; or

(b) imports, exports or conveys any obscene object for any of the purposes aforesaid, or knowing or having reason to believe that such object will be sold, let to hire, distributed or publicly exhibited or in any manner put into circulation; or

(c) takes part in or receives profits from any business in the course of which he knows or has reason to believe that any such obscene objects are, for any of the purposes aforesaid, made, produced, purchased, kept, imported, exported, conveyed, publicly exhibited or in any manner put into circulation; or

(d) advertises or makes known by any means whatsoever that any person is engaged or is ready to engage in any act which is an offence under this Section, or that any such obscene object can be procured from or through any person; or

(e) offers or attempts to do any act which is an offence under this Section, shall be punished on first conviction with imprisonment of either description for a term which may extend to two years, and with fine which may extend to two thousand rupees, and, in the event of a second or subsequent conviction, with imprisonment of either description for a term which may extend to five years, and also with fine which may extend to five thousand rupees.

Exception. This Section does not extend to-

(a) any book, pamphlet, paper, writing, drawing, painting, representation or figure-

(i) the publication of which is proved to be justified as being for the public good on the ground that such book, pamphlet, paper, writing, drawing, painting, representation or figure is in the interest of science, literature, art or learning or other objects of general concern; or

(ii) which is kept or used bona fide for religious purposes;

(b) any representation sculptured, engraved, painted or otherwise represented on or in-

(i) any ancient monument within the meaning of the Ancient Monuments and Archaeological Sites and Remains Act, 1958 (24 of 1958); or

(ii) any temple, or on any car used for the conveyance of idols, or kept or used for any religious purpose.

293. Sale, etc., of obscene objects to young person. Whoever sells, lets to hire, distributes, exhibits or circulates to any person under the age of twenty years any such obscene object as is referred to in the last preceding Section, or offers or attempts so to do, shall be punished on first conviction with imprisonment of either description for a term which may extend to three years, and with fine which may extend to two thousand rupees, and, in the event of a second or subsequent conviction, with imprisonment of either description for a term which may extend to seven years, and also with fine which may extend to five thousand rupees.

294. Obscene acts and songs. Whoever, to the annoyance of others,

(a) does any obscene act in any public place, or

(b) sings, recites or utters any obscene song, ballad or words, in or near any public place, shall be punished with imprisonment of either description for a term which may extend to three months, or with fine, or with both.

294A. Keeping lottery office. Whoever keeps any office or place for the purpose of drawing any lottery not being a State lottery or a lottery authorised by the State Government, shall be punished with imprisonment of either description for a term which may extend to six months, or with fine, or with both. And whoever publishes any proposal to pay any sum, or to deliver any goods, or to do or forbear doing anything for the benefit of any person, on any event or contingency relative or applicable to the drawing of any ticket, lot, number or figure in any such lottery shall be punished with fine which may extend to one thousand rupees.

CHAPTER - XV : OF OFFENCES RELATING TO RELIGION

295. Injuring or defiling place of worship, with intent to insult the religion of any class. Whoever destroys, damages or defiles any place of worship, or any object held sacred by any class of persons with the intention of thereby insulting the religion of any class of persons or with the knowledge that any class of persons is likely to consider such destruction, damage or defilement as an insult to their religion, shall be punished with imprisonment of either description for a term which may extend to two years, or with fine, or with both.

295A. Deliberate and malicious acts intended to outrage religious feelings of any class by insulting its religion or religious beliefs. Whoever, with deliberate and malicious intention of outraging the religious feelings of any class of citizens of India, by words, either spoken or written, or by signs or by visible representations or otherwise insults or attempts to insult the religion or the religious beliefs of that class, shall be punished with imprisonment of either description for a term which may extend to three years, or with fine, or with both.

296. Disturbing religious assembly. Whoever voluntarily causes disturbance to any assembly lawfully engaged in the performance of religious worship, or religious ceremonies, shall be punished with imprisonment of either description for a term which may extend to one year, or with fine, or with both.

297. Trespassing on burial places, etc. Whoever, with the intention of wounding the feelings of any person, or of insulting the religion of any person, or with the knowledge that the feelings of any person are likely to be wounded, or that the religion of any person is likely to be insulted thereby, commits any trespass in any place of worship or on any place of sepulture, or any place set apart for the performance of funeral rites or as a depository for the remains of the dead, or offers any indignity to any human corpse, or causes disturbance to any persons assembled for the performance of funeral ceremonies, shall be punished with imprisonment of either description for a term which may extend to one year, or with fine, or with both.

298. Uttering words, etc., with deliberate intent to wound religious feelings. Whoever, with the deliberate intention of wounding the religious feelings of any person, utters any word or makes any sound in the hearing of that person or makes any gesture in the sight of that person or places any object in the sight of that person, shall be punished with imprisonment of either description for a term which may extend to one year, or with fine, or with both offences affecting life.

CHAPTER - XVI : OF OFFENCES AFFECTING THE HUMAN BODY Of

299. Culpable homicide. Whoever causes death by doing an act with the intention of causing death, or with the intention of causing such bodily injury as is likely to cause death, or with the knowledge that he is likely by such act to cause death, commits the offence of culpable homicide.

ILLUSTRATIONS.

(a) A lays sticks and turf over a pit, with the intention of thereby causing death, or with the knowledge that death is likely to be thereby caused. Z, believing the ground to be firm, treads on it, falls in and is killed. A has committed the offence of culpable homicide.

(b) A knows Z to be behind a bush. B does not know it. A, intending to cause, or knowing it to be likely to cause Z's death, induces B to fire at the bush. B fires and kills Z. Here B may be guilty of no offence; but A has committed the offence of culpable homicide.

(c) A, by shooting at a fowl with intent to kill and steal it, kills B, who is behind a bush; A not knowing that he was there. Here, although A was doing an unlawful act, he was not guilty of culpable homicide, as he did not intend to kill B or to cause death by doing an act that he knew was likely to cause death.

EXPLANATION 1. A person who causes bodily injury to another who is labouring under a disorder, disease or bodily infirmity, and thereby accelerates the death of that other, shall be deemed to have caused his death.

EXPLANATION 2. Where death is caused by bodily injury, the person who causes such bodily injury shall be deemed to have caused the death, although by resorting to proper remedies and skilful treatment the death might have been prevented.

EXPLANATION 3. The causing of the death of a child in the mother's womb is not homicide. But it may amount to culpable homicide to cause the death of a living child, if any part of that child has been brought forth, though the child may not have breathed or been completely born.

300. Murder. Except in the cases hereinafter excepted, culpable homicide is murder, if the act by which the death is caused is done with the intention of causing death, or-

Secondly. If it is done with the intention of causing such bodily injury as the offender knows to be likely to cause the death of the person to whom the harm is caused. or-

Thirdly.- If it is done with the intention of causing bodily injury to any person and the bodily injury intended to be inflicted is sufficient in the ordinary course of nature to cause death, or-

Fourthly. If the person committing the act knows that it is so imminently dangerous that it must, in all probability, cause death, or such bodily injury as is likely to cause death, and commits such act without any excuse for incurring the risk of causing death or such injury as aforesaid.

ILLUSTRATIONS.

(a) A shoots Z with the intention of killing him. Z dies in consequence. A commits murder.

(b) A, knowing that Z is labouring under such a disease that a blow is likely to cause his death, strikes him with the intention of causing bodily injury. Z dies in consequence of the blow. A is guilty of murder, although the blow might not have been sufficient in the ordinary course of nature to cause the death of a person in a sound state of health. But if A, not knowing that Z is labouring under any disease, gives him such a blow as would not in the ordinary course of nature kill a person in a sound state of health, here A, although he may intend to cause bodily injury, is not guilty of murder, if he did not intend to cause death, or such bodily injury as in the ordinary course of nature would cause death.

(c) A intentionally gives Z a sword-cut or club-wound sufficient to cause the death of a man in the ordinary course of nature. Z dies in consequence. Here A is guilty of murder, although he may not have intended to cause Z's death.

(d) A without any excuse fires a loaded cannon into a crowd of persons and kills one of them. A is guilty of murder, although he may not have had a premeditated design to kill any particular individual.

Exception 1. When culpable homicide is not murder.- Culpable homicide is not murder if the offender, whilst deprived of the power of self-control by grave and sudden provocation, causes the death of the person who gave the provocation or causes the death of any other person by mistake or accident. The above exception is subject to the following provisos:- **Firstly.** That the provocation is not sought or voluntarily provoked by the offender as an excuse for killing or doing harm to any person. **Secondly.** That the provocation is not given by anything done in obedience to the law, or by a public servant in the lawful exercise of the powers of such public servant. **Thirdly.** That the provocation is not given by anything done in the lawful exercise of the right of private defence.

EXPLANATION. Whether the provocation was grave and sudden enough to prevent the offence from amounting to murder is a question of fact.

ILLUSTRATIONS.

(a) A, under the influence of passion excited by a provocation given by Z, intentionally kills Y, Z's child. This is murder, inasmuch as the provocation was not given by the child, and the death of the child was not caused by accident or misfortune in doing an act caused by the provocation.

(b) Y gives grave and sudden provocation to A. A, on this provocation, fires a pistol at Y, neither intending nor knowing himself to be likely to kill Z, who is near him, but out of sight. A kills Z. Here A has not committed murder, but merely culpable homicide.

(c) A is lawfully arrested by Z, a bailiff. A is excited to sudden and violent passion by the arrest, and kills Z. This is murder, inasmuch as the provocation was given by a thing done by a public servant in the exercise of his powers.

(d) A appears as a witness before Z, a Magistrate. Z says that he does not believe a word of A's deposition, and that A has perjured himself. A is moved to sudden passion by these words, and kills Z. This is murder.

(e) A attempts to pull Z's nose. Z, in the exercise of the right of private defence, lays hold of A to prevent him from doing so. A is moved to sudden and violent passion in consequence, and kills Z. This is murder, inasmuch as the provocation was giving by a thing done in the exercise of the right of private defence.

(f) Z strikes B. B is by this provocation excited to violent rage. A, a bystander, intending to take advantage of B's rage, and to cause him to kill Z, puts a knife into B's hand for that purpose. B kills Z with the knife. Here B may have committed only culpable homicide, but A is guilty of murder.

Exception 2. Culpable homicide is not murder if the offender in the exercise in good faith of the right of private defence or person or property, exceeds the power given to him by law and causes the death of the person against whom he is exercising such right of defence without premeditation, and without any intention of doing more harm than is necessary for the purpose of such defence.

ILLUSTRATION. Z attempts to horsewhip A, not in such a manner as to cause grievous hurt to A. A draws out a pistol. Z persists in the assault. A believing in good faith that he can by no other means prevent himself from being horsewhipped, shoots Z dead. A has not committed murder, but only culpable homicide.

Exception 3. Culpable homicide is not murder if the offender, being a public servant or aiding a public servant acting for the advancement of public justice, exceeds the powers given to him by law, and causes death by doing an act which he, in good faith, believes to be lawful and necessary for the due discharge of his duty as such public servant and without ill-will towards the person whose death is caused.

Exception 4. Culpable homicide is not murder if it is committed without premeditation in a sudden fight in the heat of passion upon a sudden quarrel and without the offender s having taken undue advantage or acted in a cruel or unusual manner.

EXPLANATION. It is immaterial in such cases which party offers the provocation or commits the first assault.

Exception 5. Culpable homicide is not murder when the person whose death is caused, being above the age of eighteen years, suffers death or takes the risk of death with his own consent.

ILLUSTRATION. A, by instigation, voluntarily causes Z, a person under eighteen years of age, to commit suicide. Here, on account of Z's youth, he was incapable of giving consent to his own death; A has therefore abetted murder.

301. Culpable homicide by causing death of person other than person whose death was intended. If a person, by doing anything which he intends or knows to be likely to cause death, commits culpable homicide by causing the death of any person, whose death he neither intends nor knows himself to be likely to cause, the culpable homicide committed by the offender is of the description of which it would have been if he had caused the death of the person whose death he intended or knew himself to he likely to cause.

302. Punishment for murder. Whoever commits murder shall be punished with death, or imprisonment for life, and shall also be liable to fine.

303. Punishment for murder by life-convict. Whoever, being under sentence of imprisonment for life, commits murder, shall be punished with death.

304. Punishment for culpable homicide not amounting to murder. Whoever commits culpable homicide not amounting to murder shall be punished with imprisonment for life, or imprisonment of either description for a term which may extend to ten years, and shall also be liable to fine, if the act by which the death is caused is done with the intention of causing death or of causing such bodily injury as is likely to cause death; or with imprisonment of either description for a term which may extend to ten years, or with fine, or with both, if the act is done with the knowledge that it is likely to cause death, but without any intention to cause death, or to cause such bodily injury as is likely to cause death.

304A. Causing death by negligence. Whoever causes the death of any person by doing any rash or negligent act not amounting to culpable homicide shall be punished with imprisonment of either description for a term which may extend to two years, or with fine, or with both.

304B. Dowry death.

(1) Where the death of a woman is caused by any burns or bodily injury or occurs otherwise than under normal circumstances within seven years of her marriage and it is shown that soon before her death she was subjected to cruelty or harassment by her husband or any relative of her husband for, or in

connection with, any demand for dowry, such death shall be called "dowry death", and such husband or relative shall be deemed to have caused her death.

EXPLANATION. For the purposes of this sub-section, "dowry" shall have the same meaning as in Section 2 of the Dowry Prohibition Act, 1961 (28 of 1961).

(2) Whoever commits dowry death shall be punished with imprisonment for a term which shall not be less than seven years but which may extend to imprisonment for life.

305. Abetment of suicide of child or insane person. If any person under eighteen years of age, any insane person, any delirious person, any idiot, or any person in a state of intoxication commits suicide, whoever abets the commission of such suicide, shall be punished with death or imprisonment for life, or imprisonment for a term not exceeding ten years, and shall also be liable to fine.

306. Abetment of suicide. If any person commits suicide, whoever abets the commission of such suicide, shall be punished with imprisonment of either description for a term which may extend to ten years, and shall also be liable to fine.

307. Attempt to murder. Whoever does any act with such intention or knowledge, and under such circumstances that, if he by that act caused death, he would be guilty of murder, shall be punished with imprisonment of either description for a term which may extend to ten years, and shall also be liable to fine; and, if hurt is caused to any person by such act, the offender shall be liable either to imprisonment for life, or to such punishment as is hereinbefore mentioned.

Attempts by life-convicts. When any person offending under this Section is under sentence of imprisonment for life, he may, if hurt is caused, be punished with death.

ILLUSTRATIONS.

(a) A shoots at Z with intention to kill him, under such circumstances that, if death ensued A would be guilty of murder. A is liable to punishment under this Section

(b) A, with the intention of causing the death of a child of tender years, exposes it in a desert place A has committed the offence defined by this Section, though the death of the child does not ensue.

(c) A, intending to murder Z, buys a gun and loads it. A has not yet committed the offence. A fires the gun at Z. He has committed the offence defined in this Section, and, if by such firing he wounds Z, he is liable to the punishment provided by the latter part of the first paragraph of this Section.

(d) A, intending to murder Z by poison, purchases poison and mixes the same with food which remains in A's keeping; A has not yet committed the offence in this Section. A places the food on Z's table or delivers it to Z's servants to place it on Z's table. A has committed the offence defined in this Section.

308. Attempt to commit culpable homicide. Whoever does any act with such intention or knowledge and under such circumstances that, if he by that act caused death, he would be guilty of culpable homicide not amounting to murder, shall be punished with imprisonment of either description for a term which may extend to three years, or with fine, or with both; and, if hurt is caused to any person by such act, shall be punished with imprisonment of either description for a term which may extend to seven years, or with fine, or with both.

ILLUSTRATION. A, on grave and sudden provocation, fires a pistol at Z, under such circumstances that if he there by caused death he would be guilty of culpable homicide not amounting to murder. A has committed the offence defined in this Section.

309. Attempt to commit suicide. Whoever attempts to commit suicide and does any act towards the commission of such offence, shall be punished with simple imprisonment for a term which may extend to one year or with fine, or with both.

310. Thug. Whoever, at any time after the passing of this Act, shall have been habitually associated with any other or others for the purpose of committing robbery or child-stealing by means of or accompanied with murder, is a thug.

311. Punishment. Whoever is a thug, shall be punished with imprisonment for life, and shall also be liable to fine. Of the causing of miscarriage, of injuries to unborn children, of the exposure of infants, and of the concealment of births.

312. Causing miscarraige. Whoever voluntarily causes a woman with child to miscarry, shall if such miscarriage be not caused in good faith for the purpose of saving the life of the woman, be punished with imprisonment of either description for a term which may extend to three years, or with fine, or with both; and, if the woman be quick with child, shall be punished with imprisonment of either description for a term which may extend to seven years, and shall also be liable to fine.

EXPLANATION. A woman who causes herself to miscarry, is within the meaning of this Section.

313. Causing miscarriage without woman's consent. Whoever commits the offence defined in the last preceding Section without the consent of the woman, whether the woman is quick with child or not, shall be punished with imprisonment for life, or with imprisonment of either description for a term which may extend to ten years, and shall also be liable to fine.

314. Death caused by act done with intent to cause miscarriage. Whoever, with intent to cause the miscarriage of a woman with child, does any act which causes the death of such woman, shall be punished with imprisonment of either description for a term which may extend to ten years, and shall also be liable to fine; if act done without woman's consent. if act done without woman's consent and if the act is done without the consent of the woman, shall be punished either with imprisonment for life, or with the punishment above mentioned.

EXPLANATION. It is not essential to this offence that the offender should know that the act is likely to cause death.

315. Act done with intent to prevent child being born alive or to cause it to die after birth. Whoever before the birth of any child does any act with the intention of thereby preventing that child from being born alive or causing it to die after its birth, and does by such act prevent that child from being born alive, or causes it to die after its birth, shall, if such act be not caused in good faith for the purpose of saving the life of the mother, be punished with imprisonment of either description for a term which may extend to ten years, or with fine, or with both.

316. Causing death of quick unborn child by act amounting to culpable homicide. Whoever does any act under such circumstances, that if he thereby caused death he would be guilty of culpable homicide, and does by such act cause the death of a quick unborn child, shall be punished with imprisonment of either description for a term which may extend to ten years, and shall also be liable to fine.

ILLUSTRATION. A, knowing that he is likely to cause the death of a pregnant woman, does an act which, if it caused the death of the woman, would amount to culpable homicide. The woman is injured, but does not die; but the death of an unborn quick child with which she is pregnant is thereby caused. A is guilty of the offence defined in this Section.

317. Exposure and abandonment of child under twelve years, by parent or person having care of it. Whoever being the father or mother of a child under the age of twelve years, or having the care of such child, shall expose or leave such child in any place with the intention of wholly abandoning such child, shall be punished with imprisonment of either description for a term which may extend to seven years, or with fine, or with both.

EXPLANATION. This Section is not intended to prevent the trial of the offender for murder or culpable homicide, as the case may be, if the child die in consequence of the exposure.

318. Concealment of birth by secret disposal of dead body. Whoever, by secretly burying or otherwise disposing of the dead body of a child whether such child die before or after or during its birth, intentionally conceals or endeavours to conceal the birth of such child, shall be punished with imprisonment of either description for a term which may extend to two years, or with fine, or with both.

319. Hurt. Whoever causes bodily pain, disease or infirmity to any person is said to cause hurt.

320. Grievous hurt. The following kinds of hurt only are designated as "grievous":- **First.-** Emasculation. **Secondly.** Permanent privation of the sight of either eye. **Thirdly.** Permanent privation of the hearing of either ear. **Fourthly.** Privation of any member or joint. **Fifthly.** Destruction or permanent impairing of the powers of any member or joint. **Sixthly.** Permanent disfiguration of the head or face. **Seventhly.** Fracture or dislocation of a bone or tooth. **Eighthly.** Any hurt which endangers life or which causes the sufferer to be during the space of twenty days in severe bodily pain, or unable to follow his ordinary pursuits.

321. Voluntarily causing hurt. Whoever does any act with the intention of thereby causing hurt to any person, or with the knowledge that he is likely thereby to cause hurt to any person, and does thereby cause hurt to any person, is said "voluntarily to cause hurt".

322. Voluntarily causing grievous hurt. Whoever voluntarily causes hurt, if the hurt which he intends to cause or knows himself to be likely to cause is grievous hurt, and if the hurt which he causes is grievous hurt, is said "voluntarily to cause grievous hurt".

EXPLANATION. A person is not said voluntarily to cause grievous hurt except when he both causes grievous hurt and intends or knows himself to be likely to cause grievous hurt.

But he is said voluntarily to cause grievous hurt, if intending or knowing himself to be likely to cause grievous hurt of one kind, he actually causes grievous hurt of another kind.

ILLUSTRATION. A, intending of knowing himself to be likely permanently to disfigure Z's face, gives Z a blow which does not permanently disfigure Z's face, but which causes Z to suffer severe bodily pain for the space of twenty days. A has voluntarily caused grievous hurt.

323. Punishment for voluntarily causing hurt. Whoever, except in the case provided for by Section 334, voluntarily causes hurt, shall be punished with imprisonment of either description for a term which may extend to one year, or with fine which may extend to one thousand rupees, or with both.

324. Voluntarily causing hurt by dangerous weapons or means. Whoever, except in the case provided for by Section 334, voluntarily causes hurt by means of any instrument for shooting, stabbing or cutting, or any instrument which, used as a weapon of offence, is likely to cause death, or by means of fire or any heated substance, or by means of any poison or any corrosive substance, or by means of any explosive substance or by means of any substance which it is deleterious to the human body to inhale, to swallow, or to receive into the blood, or by means of any animal, shall be punished with imprisonment of either description for a term which may extend to three years, or with fine, or with both.

325. Punishment for voluntarily causing grievous hurt. Whoever, except in the case provided for by Section 335, voluntarily causes grievous hurt, shall be punished with imprisonment of either description for a term which may extend to seven years, and shall also be liable to fine.

326. Voluntarily causing grievous hurt by dangerous weapons or means. Whoever, except in the case provided for by Section 335, voluntarily causes grievous hurt by means of any instrument for shooting, stabbing or cutting, or any instrument which, used as a weapon of offence, is likely to cause death, or by means of fire or any heated substance, or by means of any poison or any corrosive substance, or by means of any explosive substance, or by means of any substance which it is deleterious to the human body to inhale, to swallow, or to receive into the blood, or by means of any animal, shall be punished with imprisonment for life, or with imprisonment of either description for a term which may extend to ten years, and shall also be liable to fine.

327. Voluntarily causing hurt to extort property, or to constrain to an illegal to an act. Whoever voluntarily causes hurt, for the purpose of extorting from the sufferer, or from any person interested in the sufferer, any property or valuable security, or of constraining the sufferer or any person interested in such sufferer to do anything which is illegal or which may facilitate the commission of an offence, shall be punished with imprisonment of either description for a term which may extend to ten years, and shall also be liable to fine.

328. Causing hurt by means of poison, etc., with intent to commit and offence. Whoever administers to or causes to be taken by any person any poison or any stupefying, intoxicating or unwholesome drug, or other thing with intent to cause hurt to such person, or with intent to commit or to facilitate the commission of an offence or knowing it to be likely that he will thereby cause hurt, shall be punished with imprisonment of either description for a term which may extend to ten years, and shall also be liable to fine.

329. Voluntarily causing grievous hurt to extort property, or to constrain to an illegal act. Whoever voluntarily causes grievous hurt for the purpose of extorting from the sufferer or from any person interested in the sufferer any property or valuable security, or of constraining the sufferer or any person interested in such sufferer to do anything that is illegal or which may facilitate the commission of an offence, shall be punished with imprisonment for life, or imprisonment of either description for a term which may extend to ten years, and shall also be liable to fine.

331. Voluntarily causing grievous hurt to extort confession, or to compel restoration of property. Whoever voluntarily causes grievous hurt for the purpose of extorting from the sufferer or from any person interested in the sufferer any confession or any information which may lead to the detection of an offence or misconduct, or for the purpose of constraining the sufferer or any person interested in the sufferer to restore or to cause the restoration of any property or valuable security, or to satisfy any claim or demand or to give information which may lead to the restoration of any property or valuable security shall be punished with imprisonment of either description for a term which may extend to ten years, and shall also be liable to fine.

332. Voluntarily causing hurt to deter public servant from his duty. Whoever voluntarily causes hurt to any person being a public servant in the discharge of his duty as such public servant, or with intent to prevent or deter that person or any other public servant from discharging his duty as such public servant, or in consequence of anything done or attempted to be done by that person in the lawful discharge of his duty as such public servant, shall be punished with imprisonment of either description for a term which may extend to three years, or with fine, or with both.

333. Voluntarily causing grievous hurt to deter public servant from his duty. Whoever voluntarily causes grievous hurt to any person being a public servant in the discharge of his duty as such public servant, or with intent to prevent or deter that person or any other public servant from discharging his duty as such public servant, or in consequence of anything done or attempted to be done by that person in the lawful discharge of his duty as such public servant, shall be punished with imprisonment of either description for a term which may extend to ten years, and shall also be liable to fine.

334. Voluntarily causing hurt on provocation. Whoever voluntarily causes hurt on grave and sudden provocation, if he neither intends nor knows himself to be likely to cause hurt to any person other than the person who gave the provocation, shall be punished with imprisonment of either description for a term which may extend to one month, or with fine which may extend to five hundred rupees, or with both.

335. Voluntarily causing grievous hurt on provocation. Whoever voluntarily causes grievous hurt on grave and sudden provocation, if he neither intends nor knows himself to be likely to cause grievous hurt to any person other than the person who gave the provocation shall be punished with imprisonment of either description for a term which may extend to four years, or with fine which may extend to two thousand rupees, or with both.

EXPLANATION. The last two Sections are subject to the same provisos as Exception 1, Section 300.

336. Act endangering life or personal safety of others. Whoever does any act so rashly or negligently as to endanger human life or the personal safety others, shall be punished with imprisonment of either description for a term which may extend to three months or with fine which may extend to two hundred and fifty rupees, or with both.

337. Causing hurt by act endangering life or personal safety of others. Whoever causes hurt to any person by doing any act so rashly or negligently as to endanger human life, or the personal safety of others, shall be punished with imprisonment of either description for a term which may extend to six months, or with fine which may extend to five hundred rupees, or with both.

338. Causing grievous hurt by act endangering life or personal safety of others. Whoever causes grievous hurt to any person by doing any act so rashly or negligently as to endanger human life, or the personal safety of others, shall be punished with imprisonment of either description for a term which may extend to two years, or with fine which may extend to one thousand rupees, or with both. Of wrongful restraint and wrongful confinement

339. Wrongful restraint. Whoever voluntarily obstructs any person so as to prevent that person from proceeding in any direction in which that person has a right to proceed, is said wrongfully to restrain that person.

Exception. The obstruction of a private way over land or water which a person in good faith believes himself to have a lawful right to obstruct, is not an offence within the meaning of this Section.

ILLUSTRATION. A obstructs a path along which Z has a right to pass. A not believing in good faith that he has a right to stop the path. Z is thereby prevented from passing. A wrongfully restrains Z.

340. Wrongful confinement. Whoever wrongfully restrains any person in such a manner as to prevent that person from proceeding beyond certain circumscribing limits, is said "wrongfully to confine" that person.

ILLUSTRATIONS.

(a) A causes Z to go within a walled space, and locks Z. Z is thus prevented from proceeding in any direction beyond the circumscribing line of wall. A wrongfully confines Z.

(b) A places men with firearms at the outlets of a building, and tells Z that they will fire at Z if Z attempts leave the building. A wrongfully confines Z.

341. Punishment for wrongful restraint. Whoever wrongfully restrains any person shall be punished with simple imprisonment for a term which may extend to one month, or with fine which may extend to five hundred rupees, or with both.

342. Punishment for wrongful confinement. Whoever wrongfully confines any person shall be punished with simple imprisonment of either description for a term which may extend to one year, or with fine which may extend to one thousand rupees, or with both.

343. Wrongful confinement for three or more days. Whoever wrongfully confines any person for three days or more, shall be punished with imprisonment of either description for a term which may extend to two years, or with fine, or with both.

344. Wrongful confinement for ten or more days. Whoever wrongfully confines any person for ten days, or more, shall be punished with imprisonment of either description for a term which may extend to three years, and shall also be liable to fine.

345. Wrongful confinement of person for whose liberation writ has been issued. Whoever keeps any person in wrongful confinement, knowing that a writ for the liberation of that person has been duly issued, shall be punished with imprisonment of either description for a term which may extend to two years in addition to any term of imprisonment to which he may be liable under any other Section of this Chapter.

346. Wrongful confinement in secret. Whoever wrongfully confines any person in such manner as to indicate an intention that the confinement of such person may not be known to any person interested in the person so confined, or to any public servant, or that the place of such confinement may not be known to or discovered by any such person or public servant as hereinbefore mentioned, shall be punished with imprisonment of either description for a term which may extend to two years in addition to any other punishment to which he may be liable for such wrongful confinement.

347. Wrongful confinement to extort property, or constrain to illegal act. Whoever wrongfully confines any person for the purpose of extorting from the person confined, or from any person interested in the person confined, any property or valuable security or of constraining the person confined or any person interested in such person to do anything illegal or to give any information which may facilitate the commission of an offence, shall be punished with imprisonment of either description for a term which may extend to three years, and shall also be liable to fine.

348. Wrongful confinement to extort confession, or compel restoration of property. Whoever wrongfully confines any person for the purpose of extorting from the person confined or any person interested in the person confined any confession or any information which may lead to the detection of an offence or misconduct, or for the purpose of constraining the person confined or any person interested in the person confined to restore or to cause the restoration of any property or valuable security or to satisfy any claim or demand, or to give information which may lead to the restoration of any property or valuable security, shall be punished with imprisonment of either description for a term which may extend to three years, and shall also be liable to fine. Of criminal force and assault.

349. Force. A person is said to use force to another if he causes motion, change of motion, or cessation of motion to that other, or if he causes to any substance such motion, or change of motion, or cessation of motion as brings that substance into contact with any part of that other's body, or with anything which that other is wearing or carrying, or with anything so situated that such contact affects that other's sense of feeling:

> *PROVIDED that the person causing the motion, or change of motion, or cessation of motion, causes that motion, change of motion, or cessation of motion in one of the three ways hereinafter described:* ***First.****- By his own bodily power.* ***Secondly.****- By disposing any substance in such a manner that the motion or change or cessation of motion takes place without any further act on his part, or on the part of any other person.* ***Thirdly.****- By inducing any animal to move, to change its motion, or to cease to move.*

350. Criminal force. Whoever intentionally uses force to any person, without that person's consent, in order to the committing of any offence, or intending by the use of such force to cause, or knowing it to be likely that by the use of such force he will cause injury, fear or annoyance to the person to whom the force is used, is said to use criminal force to that other.

ILLUSTRATIONS.

(a) Z is sitting in a moored boat on a river. A unfastens the moorings, and thus intentionally causes the boat to drift down the stream. Here A intentionally causes motion to Z, and he does this by disposing substances in such a manner that the motion is produced without any other action on any person's part. A has therefore intentionally used force to Z; and if he has done so without Z's consent, in order to the committing of any offence, or intending or knowing it to be likely that this use of force will cause injury, fear or annoyance to Z, A has used criminal force to Z.

(b) Z is riding in a chariot. A lashes Z's horses and thereby causes them to quicken their pace. Here A has caused change of motion to Z by inducing the animals to change their motion. A has therefore used force to Z; and if A has done this without Z's consent, intending or knowing it to be likely that he may thereby injure, frighten or annoy Z, A has used criminal force to Z.

(c) Z is riding in a palanquin. A, intending to rob Z, seizes the pole and stops the palanquin. Here A has caused cessation of motion to Z, and he has done this by his own bodily power. A has therefore used force to Z; and as A has acted thus intentionally, without Z's consent, in order to the commission of an offence. A has used criminal force to Z.

(d) A intentionally pushes against Z in the street. Here A has by his own bodily power moved his own person so as to bring it into contact with Z. He has therefore intentionally used force to Z; and if he has done so without Z's consent, intending or knowing it to be likely that he may thereby injure, frighten or annoy Z, he has used criminal force to Z.

(e) A throws a stone, intending or knowing it to be likely that the stone will be thus brought into contact with Z, or with Z's clothes, or with something carried by Z, or that it will strike water, and dash up the water against Z's clothes or something carried by Z. Here, if the throwing of the stone produce the effect of causing any substance to come into contact with Z, or Z's clothes, A has used force to Z, and if he did so without Z's consent, intending thereby to injure, frighten or annoy Z, he has used criminal force to Z.

(f) A intentionally pulls up a Woman's veil. Here A intentionally uses force to her, and if he does so without her consent intending or knowing it to be likely that he may thereby injure, frighten or annoy her, he has used criminal force to her.

(g) Z is bathing. A pours into the bath water which he knows to be boiling. Here A intentionally by his own bodily power causes such motion in the boiling water as brings that water into contact with Z, or with other water so situated that such contact must affect Z's sense of feeling, A has therefore intentionally used force to Z; and if he has done this without Z's consent intending or knowing it to be likely that he may thereby cause injury, fear or annoyance to Z, A has used criminal force.

(h) A incites a dog to spring upon Z, without Z's consent. Here, if A intends to cause injury, fear or annoyance to Z, he uses criminal force to Z.

351. Assault. Whoever makes any gesture, or any preparation intending or knowing it to be likely that such gesture or preparation will cause any person present to apprehend that he who makes that gesture or preparation is about to use criminal force to that person, is said to commit an assault.

EXPLANATION. Mere words do not amount to an assault. But the words which a person uses may give to his gestures or preparation such a meaning as may make those gestures or preparations amount to an assault.

ILLUSTRATIONS.

(a) A shakes his fist at Z, intending or knowing it to be likely that he may thereby cause Z to believe that A is about to strike Z. A has committed an assault.

(b) A begins to unloose the muzzle of a ferocious dog, intending or knowing it to be likely that he may thereby cause Z to believe that he is about to cause the dog to attack Z. A has committed an assault upon Z.

(c) A takes up a stick, saying to Z, "I will give you a beating". Here, though the words used by A could in no case amount to an assault, and though the mere gesture, unaccompanied by any other circumstances, might not amount to an assault, the gesture explained by the words may amount to an assault.

352. Punishment for assault or criminal force otherwise than on grave provocation. Whoever assaults or uses criminal force to any person otherwise than on grave and sudden provocation given by that person, shall be punished with imprisonment of either description for a term which may extend to three months, or with fine which may extend to five hundred rupees, or with both. Explanation.- Grave and sudden provocation will not mitigate the punishment for an offence under this Section, if the provocation is sought or voluntarily provoked by the offender as an excuse for the offence, or if the provocation is given by anything done in obedience to the law, or by a public servant, in the lawful exercise of the powers of such public servant, or if the provocation is given by anything done in the lawful exercise of the right of private defence. Whether the provocation was grave and sudden enough to mitigate the offence, is a question of fact.

353. Assault or criminal force to deter public servant from discharge of his duty. Whoever assaults or uses criminal force to any person being a public servant in the execution of his duty as such public servant, or with intent to prevent or deter that person from discharging his duty as such public servant, or in consequence of anything done or attempted to be done by such person to the lawful discharge of his duty as such public servant, shall be punished with imprisonment of either description for a term which may extend to two years, or with fine, or with both.

354. Assault or criminal force to woman with intent to outrage her modesty. Whoever assaults or uses criminal force to any woman, intending to outrage or knowing it to be likely that he will there by outrage her modesty, shall be punished with imprisonment of either description for a term which may extend to two years, or with fine, or with both.

355. Assault or criminal force with intent to dishonour person, otherwise than on grave provocation. Whoever assaults or uses criminal force to any person, intending thereby to dishonour that person, otherwise than on grave and sudden provocation given by that person, shall be punished with imprisonment of either description for a term which may extend to two years, or with fine, or with both.

356. Assault or criminal force in attempt to commit theft of property carried by a person. Whoever assaults or uses criminal force to any person, in attempting to commit theft on any property which that person is then wearing or carrying shall be punished with imprisonment of either description for a term which may extend to two years, or with fine, or with both.

357. Assault or criminal force in attempt wrongfully to confine a person. Whoever assaults or uses criminal force to any person, in attempting wrongfully to confine that person, shall be punished with imprisonment of either description for a term which may extend to one year, or with fine which may extend to one thousand rupees, or with both.

358. Assault or criminal force on grave provocation. Whoever assaults or uses criminal force to any person on grave and sudden provocation given by that person, shall be punished with simple imprisonment for a term which may extend to one month, or with fine which may extend to two hundred rupees, or with both.

EXPLANATION. The last Section is subject to the same explanation as Section 352. Of kidnapping, abduction, slavery and forced labour

359. Kidnapping. Kidnapping is of two kinds: kidnapping from India, and kidnapping from lawful guardianship.

360. Kidnapping from India. Whoever conveys any person beyond the limits of India without the consent of that person, or of some person legally authorized to consent on behalf of that person, is said to kidnap that person from India.

361. Kidnapping from lawful guardianship. Whoever takes or entices any minor under sixteen years of age if a male, or under eighteen years of age if a female, or any person of unsound mind, out of the keeping of the lawful guardian of such minor or person of unsound mind, without the consent of such guardian, is said to kidnap such minor or person from lawful guardianship.

EXPLANATION. The words “lawful guardian” in this Section include any person lawfully entrusted with the care or custody of such minor or other person.

Exception. This Section does not extend to the act of any person who in good faith believes himself to be the father of an illegitimate child, or who in good faith believes himself to be entitled to the lawful custody of such child, unless such act is committed for an immoral or unlawful purpose.

362. Abduction. Whoever by force compels, or by any deceitful means induces any person to go from any place, is said to abduct that person.

363. Punishment for kidnapping. Whoever kidnaps any person from India or from lawful guardianship, shall be punished with imprisonment of either description for a term which may extend to seven years, and shall also be liable to fine.

363A. Kidnapping or maiming a minor for purposes of begging.

(1) Whoever kidnaps any minor or, not being the lawful guardian of a minor, obtains the custody of the minor, in order that such minor may be employed or used for the purposes of begging shall be punishable with imprisonment of either description for a term which may extend to ten years, and shall also be liable to fine.

(2) Whoever maims any minor in order that such minor may be employed or used for the purposes of begging shall be punishable with imprisonment for life, and shall also be liable to fine.

(3) Where any person, not being the lawful guardian of a minor, employs or uses such minor for the purposes of begging, it shall be presumed, unless the contrary is proved, that he kidnapped or otherwise obtained the custody of that minor in order that the minor might be employed or used for the purposes of begging.

(4) In this Section,-

(a) " begging" means-

(i) soliciting or receiving alms in a public place, whether under the pretence of singing, dancing, fortune-telling, performing tricks or selling articles or otherwise;

(ii) entering on any private premises for the purpose of soliciting or receiving alms;

(iii) exposing or exhibiting, with the object of obtaining or extorting alms, any sore, wound, injury, deformity or disease, whether of himself or of any other person or of an animal;

(iv) using a minor as an exhibit for the purpose of soliciting or receiving alms;

(b) " minor" means-

(i) in the case of a male, a person under sixteen years of age; and

(ii) in the case of a female, a person under eighteen years of age.

364. Kidnapping or abducting in order to murder. Whoever kidnaps or abducts any person in order that such person may be murdered or may be so disposed of as to be put in danger of being murdered, shall be punished with imprisonment for life or rigorous imprisonment for a term which may extend to ten years, and shall also be liable to fine.

IIIUSTRATIONS.

(a) A kidnaps Z from India, intending or knowing it to be likely that Z may be sacrificed to an idol. A has committed the offence defined in this Section.

(b) A forcibly carries or entices B away from his home in order that B may be murdered. A has committed the offence defined in this Section.

364A. Kidnapping for ransom, etc. Whoever kidnaps or abducts any person or keeps a person in detention after such kidnapping or abduction, and threatens to cause death or hurt to such person, or by his conduct gives rise to a reasonable appreension that such person may be put to death or hurt, or causes hurt or death to such person in order to compel the Government or any foreign State or international inter-governmental organisation or any other person to do or abstain from doing any act or to pay a ransom, shall be punishable with death or imprisonment for life, and shall also be liable to fine.

365. Kidnapping or abducting with intent secretly and wrongfully to confine person. Whoever kidnaps or abducts any person with intent to cause that person to be secretly and wrongfully confined, shall be punished with imprisonment of either description for a term which may extend to seven years, and shall also be liable to fine.

366. Kidnapping, abducting or inducing woman to compel her marriage, etc. Whoever kidnaps or abducts any woman with intent that she may be compelled, or knowing it to be likely that she will be compelled, to marry any person against her will, or in order that she may be forced or seduced to illicit intercourse, or knowing it to be likely that she will be forced or seduced to illicit intercourse, shall be punished with imprisonment of either description for a term which may extend to ten years, and shall also be liable to fine; and whoever, by means of criminal intimidation as defined in this Code or of abuse of authority or any other method of compulsion, induces any woman to go from any place with intent that she may be, or knowing that it is likely that she will be, forced or seduced to illicit intercourse with another person shall also be punishable as aforesaid.

366A. Procuration of minor girl. Whoever, by any means whatsoever, induces any minor girl under the age of eighteen years to go from any place or to do any act with intent that such girl may be, or knowing that it is likely that she will be, forced or seduced to illicit intercourse with another person shall be punishable with imprisonment which may extend to ten years, and shall also be liable to fine.

366B. Importation of girl from foreign country. Whoever imports into India from any country outside India or from the State of Jammu and Kashmir any girl under the age of twenty-one years with intent that she may be, or knowing it to be likely that she will be, forced or seduced to illicit intercourse with another person, shall be punishable with imprisonment which may extend to ten years, and shall also be liable to fine.

367. Kidnapping or abducting in order to subject person to grievous hurt, slavery, etc. Whoever kidnaps or abducts any person in order that such person may be subjected, or may be so disposed of as to be put in danger of being subjected to grievous hurt, or slavery, or to the unnatural lust of any person, or knowing it to be likely that such person will be so subjected or disposed of, shall be punished with imprisonment of either description for a term which may extend to ten years, and shall also be liable to fine.

368. Wrongfully concealing or keeping in confinement, kidnapped or abducted person. Whoever, knowing that any person has been kidnapped or has been abducted, wrongfully conceals or confines such person, shall be punished in the same manner as if he had kidnapped or abducted such person with the same intention or knowledge, or for the same purpose as that with or for which he conceals or detains such person in confinement.

369. Kidnapping or abducting child under ten years with intent to steal from its person. Whoever kidnaps or abducts any child under the age of ten years with the intention of taking dishonestly any movable property from the person of such child, shall be punished with imprisonment of either description for a term which may extend to seven years, and shall also be liable to fine.

370. Buying or disposing of any person as a slave. Whoever imports, exports, removes, buys, sells or disposes of any person as a slave, or accepts, receives or detains against his will any person as a slave, shall be punished with imprisonment of either description for a term which may extend to seven years, and shall also be liable to fine.

371. Habitual dealing in slaves. Whoever habitually imports, exports, removes, buys, sells traffics or deals in slaves, shall be punished with imprisonment for life, or with imprisonment of either description for a term not exceeding ten years, and shall also be liable to fine.

372. Selling minor for purposes of prostitution, etc. Whoever sells, lets to hire, or otherwise disposes of any person under the age of eighteen years with intent that such person shall at any age be employed or used for the purpose of prostitution or illicit intercourse with any person or for any unlawful and immoral purpose, or knowing it to be likely that such person will at any age be employed or used for any such purpose, shall be punished with imprisonment of either description for a term which may extend to ten years, and shall also be liable to fine.

EXPLANATION I. When a female under the age of eighteen years is sold, let for hire, or otherwise disposed of to a prostitute or to any person who keeps or manages a brothel, the person so disposing of such female shall, until the contrary is proved, be presumed to have disposed of her with the intent that she shall be used for the purpose of prostitution.

EXPLANATION II. For the purposes of this Section "illicit intercourse" means sexual intercourse between persons not united by marriage, or by any union or tie which though not amounting to a marriage, is recognised by the personal law or custom of the community to which they belong or, where they belong to different communities, of both such communities, as constituting between them a quasi- marital relation.

373. Buying minor for purposes of prostitution, etc. Whoever buys, hires or otherwise obtains possession of any person under the age of eighteen years with intent that such person shall at any age be employed or used for the purpose of prostitution or illicit intercourse with any person or for any unlawful and immoral purpose, or knowing it to be likely that such person will at any age be employed or used for any such purpose, shall be punished with imprisonment of either description for a term which may extend to ten years, and shall also be liable to fine.

EXPLANATION I. Any prostitute or any person keeping or managing a brothel, who buys, hires or otherwise obtains possession of a female under the age of eighteen years shall, until the contrary is proved, be presumed to have obtained possession of such female with the intent that she shall be used for the purpose of prostitution.

EXPLANATION II. "Illicit intercourse" has the same meaning as in Section 372.

374. Unlawful compulsory labour. Whoever unlawfully compels any person to labour against the will of that person, shall be punished with imprisonment of either description for a term which may extend to one year, or with fine, or with both.

Sexual Offences

375. Rape. A man is said to commit "rape" who, except in the case hereinafter excepted, has sexual intercourse with a woman under circumstances falling under any of the six following descriptions:- **Firstly.** Against her will. **Secondly.** Without her consent. **Thirdly.** With her consent, when her consent has been obtained by putting her or any person in whom she is interested in fear of death or of hurt. **Fourthly.** With her consent, when the man knows that he is not her husband, and that her consent is given because she believes that he is another man to whom she is or believes herself to be lawfully married. **Fifthly.** With her consent, when, at the time of giving such consent, by reason of unsoundness of mind or intoxication or the administration by him personally or through another of any stupefying or unwholesome substance, she is unable to understand the nature and consequences of that to which she gives consent. **Sixthly.** With or without her consent, when she is under sixteen years of age.

EXPLANATION. Penetration is sufficient to constitute the sexual intercourse necessary to the offence of rape.

Exception. Sexual intercourse by a man with his own wife, the wife not being under fifteen years of age, is not rape.

376. Punishment for rape.

(1) Whoever, except in the cases provided for by sub-section (2), commits rape shall be punished with imprisonment of either description for a term which shall not be less than seven years but which may be for life or for a term which may extend to ten years and shall also be liable to fine unless the woman raped is his own wife and is not under twelve years of age, in which case, he shall be punished with imprisonment of either description for a term which may extend to two years or with fine or with both:

PROVIDED that the court may, for adequate and special reasons to be mentioned in the judgment, impose a sentence of imprisonment for a term of less than seven years.

(2) Whoever,-

- (a) being a police officer commits rape-
    - (i) within the limits of the police station to which he is appointed; or
    - (ii) in the premises of any station house whether or not situated in the police station to which he is appointed; or
    - (iii) on a woman in his custody or in the custody of a police officer subordinate to him; or
- (b) being a public servant, takes advantage of his official position and commits rape on a woman in his custody as such public servant or in the custody of a public servant subordinate to him; or
- (c) being on the management or on the staff of a jail, remand home or other place of custody established by or under any law for the time being in force or of a women's or children's institution takes advantage of his official position and commits rape on any inmate of such jail, remand home, place or institution; or
- (d) being on the management or on the staff of a hospital, takes advantage of his official position and commits rape on a woman in that hospital; or
- (e) commits rape on a woman knowing her to be pregnant; or

(f) commits rape on a woman when she is under twelve years of age; or

(g) commits gang rape, shall be punished with rigorous imprisonment for a term which shall not be less than ten years but which may be for life and shall also be liable to fine:

PROVIDED that the court may, for adequate and special reasons to be mentioned in the judgment, impose a sentence of imprisonment of either description for a term of less than ten years.

EXPLANATION 1. Where a women's is raped by one or more in a group of persons acting in furtherance of their common intention, each of the persons shall be deemed to have committed gang rape within the meaning of this sub-section.

EXPLANATION 2. "Women's or children's institution" means an institution, whether called and orphanage or a home for neglected women or children or a widows' home or by any other name, which is established and maintained for the reception and care of women or children.

EXPLANATION 3. "Hospital" means the precincts of the hospital and includes the precincts of any institution for the reception and treatment of persons during convalescence or of persons requiring medical attention or rehabilitation.

376A. Intercourse by a man with his wife during separation. Whoever has sexual intercourse with his own wife, who is living separately from him under a decree of separation or under any custom or usage without her consent shall be punished with imprisonment of either description for a term which may extend to two years and shall also bc liablc to finc.

376B. Intercourse by public servant with woman in his custody. Whoever, being a public servant, takes advantage of his official position and induces or seduces, any woman, who is in his custody as such public servant or in the custody of a public servant subordinate to him, to have sexual intercourse with him, such sexual intercourse not amounting to the offence of rape, shall be punished with imprisonment of either description for a term which may extend to five years and shall also be liable to fine.

376C. Intercourse by superintendent of jail, remand home, etc. Whoever, being the superintendent or manager of a jail, remand home or other place of custody established by or under any law for the time being in force or of a women's or children's institution takes advantage of his official position and induces or seduces any female inmate of such jail, remand home, place or institution to have sexual intercourse with him, such sexual intercourse not amounting to the offence of rape, shall be punished with imprisonment of either description for a term which may extend to five years and shall also be liable to fine.

Explanation 1. "Superintendent" in relation to a jail, remand home or other place of custody or a women's or children's institution, includes a person holding any other office in such jail, remand home, place or institution by virtue of which he can exercise any authority or control over its inmates.

Explanation 2. The expression "women's or children's institution" shall have the same meaning as in Explanation 2 to sub-section (2) of Section 376.

376D. Intercourse by any member of the management or staff of a hospital with any woman in that hospital. Whoever, being on the management of a hospital or being on the staff of a hospital takes advantage of his position and has sexual intercourse with any woman in that hospital, such sexual intercourse not amounting to the offence of rape, shall be punished with imprisonment of either description for a term which may extend to five years and shall also be liable to fine.

EXPLANATION. The expression "hospital" shall have the same meaning as in Explanation 3 to sub-section (2) of Section 376.

Of Unnatural Offences

377. Unnatural offences. Whoever voluntarily has carnal intercourse against the order of nature with any man, woman or animal, shall be punished with imprisonment for life, or with imprisonment of either description for a term which may extend to ten years, and shall also be liable to fine.

EXPLANATION. Penetration is sufficient to constitute the carnal intercourse necessary to the offence described in this Section.

CHAPTER - XVII : OF OFFENCES AGAINST PROPERTY OF THEFT

378. Theft. Whoever, intending to take dishonestly any movable property out of the possession of any person without that person's consent, moves that property in order to such taking, is said to commit theft.

EXPLANATION 1. A thing so long as it is attached to the earth, not being movable property, is not the subject of theft; but it becomes capable of being the subject of theft as soon as it is severed from the earth.

EXPLANATION 2. A moving effected by the same act which effects the severance may be a theft.

EXPLANATION 3. A person is said to cause a thing to move by removing an obstacle which prevented it from moving or by separating it from any other thing, as well as by actually moving it.

EXPLANATION 4. A person, who by any means causes an animal to move, is said to move that animal, and to move everything which, in consequence of the motion so caused, is moved by that animal.

EXPLANATION 5. The consent mentioned in the definition may be express or implied, and may be given either by the person in possession, or by any person having for that purpose authority either express or implied.

ILLUSTRATIONS.

(a) A cuts down a tree on Z's ground, with the intention of dishonestly taking the tree out of Z's possession without Z's consent. Here, as soon as A has severed the tree in order to such taking, he has committed theft.

(b) A puts a bait for dogs in his pocket, and thus induces Z's dog to follow it. Here, if A's intention be dishonestly to take the dog out of Z's possession without Z's consent, A has committed theft as soon as Z's dog has begun to follow A.

(c) A meets a bullock carrying a box of treasure. He drives the bullock in a certain direction, in order that he may dishonestly take the treasure. As soon as the bullock begins to move, A has committed theft of the treasure.

(d) A being Z's servant, and entrusted by Z with the care of Z's plate, dishonestly runs away with the plate, without Z's consent. A has committed theft.

(e) Z, going on a journey, entrusts his plate to A, the keeper of a warehouse, till Z shall return. A carries the plate to a goldsmith and sells it. Here the plate was not in Z's possession. It could not therefore be taken out of Z's possession, and A has not committed theft, though he may have committed criminal breach of trust.

(f) A finds a ring belonging to Z on a table in the house which Z occupies. Here the ring is in Z's possession, and if A dishonestly removes it, A commits theft.

(g) A finds a ring lying on the high-road, not in the possession of any person. A, by taking it, commits no theft, though he may commit criminal misappropriation of property.

(h) A sees a ring belonging to Z lying on a table in Z's house. Not venturing to misappropriate the ring immediately for fear of search and detection, A hides the ring in a place where it is highly improbable that it will ever be found by Z, with the intention of taking the ring from the hiding place and selling it when the loss is forgotten. Here A, at the time of first moving the ring, commits theft.

(i) A delivers his watch to Z, a jeweller, to be regulated. Z carries it to his shop. A, not owing to the jeweller any debt for which the jeweller might lawfully detain the watch as a security, enters the shop openly, takes his watch by force out of Z's hand, and carries it away. Here A, though he may have committed criminal trespass and assault, has not committed theft, inasmuch as what he did was not done dishonestly.

(j) If A owes money to Z for repairing the watch, and if Z retains the watch lawfully as a security for the debt, and A takes the watch out of Z's possession, with the intention of depriving Z of the property as a security for his debt, he commits theft, inasmuch as he takes it dishonestly.

(k) Again, if A, having pawned his watch to Z, takes it out of Z's possession without Z's consent, not having paid what he borrowed on the watch, he commits theft, though the watch is his own property inasmuch as he takes it dishonestly.

(l) A takes an article belonging to Z out of Z's possession without Z's consent, with the intention of keeping it until he obtains money from Z as a reward for its restoration. Here A takes dishonestly; A has therefor committed theft.

(m) A, being on friendly terms with Z, goes into Z's library in Z's absence, and takes away a book without Z's express consent for the purpose merely of reading it, and with the intention of returning it. Here, it is probable that A may have conceived that he had Z's implied consent to use Z's book. If this was A's impression, A has not committed theft.

(n) A asks charity from Z's wife. She gives A money, food and clothes, which A knows to belong to Z her husband. Here it is probable that A may conceive that

Z's wife is authorized to give away alms. If this was A's impression, A has not committed theft.

(o) A is the paramour of Z's wife. She gives a valuable property, which A knows to belong to her husband Z, and to be such property as she has not authority from Z to give. If A takes the property dishonestly, he commits theft.

(p) A, in good faith, believing property belonging to Z to be A's own property, takes that property out of B's possession. Here, as A does not take dishonestly, he does not commit theft.

379. Punishment for theft. Whoever commits theft shall be punished with imprisonment of either description for a term which may extend to three years, or with fine, or with both.

380. Theft in dwelling house, etc. Whoever commits theft in any building, tent or vessel, which building, tent or vessel is used as a human dwelling, or used for the custody of property, shall be punished with imprisonment of either description for a term which may extend to seven years, and shall also be liable to fine.

381. Theft by clerk or servant of property in possession of master. Whoever, being a clerk or servant, or being employed in the capacity of a clerk or servant, commits theft in respect of any property in the possession of his master or employer, shall be punished with imprisonment of either description for a term which may extend to seven years, and shall also be liable to fine.

382. Theft after preparation made for causing death, hurt or restraint in order to the committing of the theft. Whoever commits theft, having made preparation for causing death, or hurt, or restraint, or fear of death, or of hurt, or of restraint, to any person, in order to the committing of such theft, or in order to the effecting of his escape after the committing of such theft or in order to the retaining of property taken by such theft, shall be punished with rigorous imprisonment for a term which may extend to ten years, and shall also be liable to fine.

ILLUSTRATIONS.

(a) A commits theft on property in Z's possession; and, while committing this theft, he has a loaded pistol under his garment, having provided this pistol for the purpose of hurting Z in case Z should resist. A has committed the offence defined in this Section.

(b) A picks Z's pocket, having posted several of his companions near him, in order that they may restrain Z, if Z should perceive what is passing and should resist, or should attempt to apprehend A. A has committed the offence defined in this Section.

383. Extortion. Whoever intentionally puts any person in fear of any injury to that person, or to any other, and thereby dishonestly induces the person so put in fear to deliver to any person any property, or valuable security or anything signed or sealed which may be converted into a valuable security, commits "extortion".

ILLUSTRATIONS.

(a) A threatens to publish a defamatory libel concerning Z unless Z gives him money. He thus induces Z to give him money. A has committed extortion.

(b) A threatens Z that he will keep Z's child in worngful confinement, unless Z will sign and deliver to A a promissory note binding Z to pay certain monies to A to Z signs and delivers the note. A has committed extortion.

(c) A threatens to send club-men to plough up Z's field unless Z will sign and deliver to B a bond binding Z under a penalty to deliver certain produce to B, and thereby induces Z to sign and deliver the bond. A has committed extortion.

(d) A, by putting Z in fear of grievous hurt, dishonestly induces Z to sign or affix his seal to a blank paper and deliver it to A. Z signs and delivers the paper to A. Here, as the paper so signed may be converted into a valuable security A has committed extortion.

384. Punishment for extortion. Whoever commits extortion shall be punished with imprisonment of either description for a term which may extend to three years, or with fine, or with both.

385. Putting person in fear of injury in order to commit extortion. Whoever, in order to the committing of extortion, puts any person in fear, or attempts to put any person in fear, of any injury, shall be punished with imprisonment of either description for a term which may extend to two years, or with fine, or with both.

386. Extortion by putting a person in fear of death or grievous hurt. Whoever commits extortion by putting any person in fear of death or of grievous hurt to that person or to any other, shall be punished with imprisonment of either description for a term which may extend to ten years, and shall also be liable to fine.

387. Putting person in fear of death or of grievous hurt, in order to commit extortion. Whoever in order to the committing of extortion, puts or attempts to put any person in fear of death or of grievous hurt to that person or to any other, shall be punished with imprisonment of either description for a term which may extend to seven years, and shall also be liable to fine.

388. Extortion by threat of accusation of an offence punishable with death or imprisonment for life, etc. Whoever commits extortion by putting any person in fear of an accusation against that person or any other, of having committed or attempted to commit any offence punishable with death, or with imprisonment for life, or with imprisonment for a term which may extend to ten years, or of having attempted to induce any other person to commit such offence, shall be punished with imprisonment of either description for a term which may extend to ten years, and shall also be liable to fine; and, if the offence be one punishable under Section 377 of this Code, may be punished with imprisonment for life.

389. Putting person in fear or accusation of offence, in order to commit extortion. Whoever, in order to the committing of extortion, puts or attempts to put any person in fear of an accusation, against that person or any other, of having committed, or attempted to commit, an offence punishable with death or with imprisonment for life, or with imprisonment for a term which may extend to ten years, shall be punished with imprisonment of either description for a term which may extend to ten years, and shall also be liable to fine; and, if the offence be punishable under Section 377 of this Code, may be punished with imprisonment for life.

Of Robbery and Dacoity

390. Robbery. In all robbery there is either theft or extortion. When theft is robbery. Theft is "robbery" if, in order to the committing of the theft, or in committing the theft, or in carrying away or attempting to carry away property obtained by the theft, the offender, for that end, voluntarily causes or attempts to cause to any person death or hurt or wrongful restraint, or fear of instant death or of instant hurt, or of instant wrongful restraint. When extortion is robbery. Extortion is "robbery" if the offender, at the time of committing the extortion, is in the presence of the person put in fear, and commits the extortion by putting that person in fear of instant death, of instant hurt, or of instant wrongful restraint to that person or to some other person, and, by so putting in fear, induces the person, so put in fear then and there to deliver up the thing extorted.

Explanation. The offender is said to be present if he is sufficiently near to put the other person in fear of instant death, of instant hurt, or of instant wrongful restraint.

Illustrations

(a) A holds Z down, and fraudulently takes Z's money and jewels from Z's clothes, without Z's consent. Here A has committed theft, and, in order to the committing of that theft, has voluntarily caused wrongful restraint to Z. A has therefore committed robbery.

(b) A meets Z on the high road, shows a pistol, and demands Z's purse. Z, in consequence, surrenders his purse. Here A has extorted the purse from Z by putting him in fear of instant hurt, and being at the time of committing the extortion in his presence. A has therefore committed robbery.

(c) A meets Z and Z's child on the high road. A takes the child, and threatens to filing it down a precipice, unless Z delivers his purse. Z, in consequence, delivers his purse. Here A has extorted the purse from Z, by causing Z to be in fear of instant hurt to the child who is there present. A has therefore committed robbery on Z.

(d) A obtains property from Z by saying- "Your child is in the hands of my gang, and will be put to death unless you send us ten thousand rupees". This is extortion, and punishable as such: but it is not robbery, unless Z is put in fear of the instant death of his child.

391. Dacoity. When five or more persons conjointly commit or attempt to commit a robbery, or where the whole number of persons conjointly committing or attempting to commit a robbery, and persons present and aiding such commission or attempt, amount to five or more, every person so committing, attempting or aiding, is said to commit "dacoity".

392. Punishment for robbery. Whoever commits robbery shall be punished with rigorous imprisonment for a term which may extend to ten years, and shall also be liable to fine; and, if the robbery be committed on the highway between sunset and sunrise, the imprisonment may be extended to fourteen years.

393. Attempt to commit robbery. Whoever attempts to commit robbery shall be punished with rigorous imprisonment for a term which may extend to seven years, and shall also be liable to fine.

394. Voluntarily causing hurt in committing robbery. If any person, in committing or in attempting to commit robbery, voluntarily causes hurt, such person, and any other person jointly concerned in committing or attempting to commit such robbery, shall be punished with imprisonment for life, or with rigorous imprisonment for a term which may extend to ten years, and shall also be liable to fine.

395. Punishment for dacoity. Whoever commits dacoity shall be punished with imprisonment for life, or with rigorous imprisonment for a term which may extend to ten years, and shall also be liable to fine.

396. Dacoity with murder. If any one of five or more persons, who are conjointly committing dacoity, commits murder in so committing dacoity, every one of those persons shall be punished with death, or imprisonment for life, or rigorous imprisonment for a term which may extend to ten years, and shall also be liable to fine.

397. Robbery or dacoity, with attempt to cause death or grievous hurt. If, at the time of committing robbery or dacoity, the offender uses any deadly weapon, or causes grievous hurt to any person, so attempts to cause death or grievous hurt to any person, the imprisonment with which such offender shall be punished shall not be less than seven years.

398. Attempt to commit robbery or dacoity when armed with deadly weapon. If, at the time of attempting to commit robbery or dacoity, the offender is armed with any deadly weapon, the imprisonment with which such offender shall be punished shall not be less than seven years.

399. Making preparation to commit dacoity. Whoever makes any preparation for committing dacoity, shall be punished with rigorous imprisonment for a term which may extend to ten years, and shall also be liable to fine.

400. Punishment for belonging to gang of dacoits. Whoever, at any time after the passing of this Act, shall belong to a gang of persons associated for the purpose of habitually committing dacoity, shall be punished with imprisonment for life, or with rigorous imprisonment for a term which may extend to ten years, and shall also be liable to fine.

401. Punishment for belonging to gang of thieves. Whoever, at any time after the passing of this Act, shall belong to any wandering or other gang of persons associated for the purpose of habitually committing theft or robbery, and not being a gang of thugs or dacoits, shall be punished with rigorous imprisonment for a term which may extend to seven years, and shall also be liable to fine.

402. Assembling for purpose of committing dacoity. Whoever, at any time after the passing of this Act, shall be one of five or more persons assembled for the purpose of committing dacoity, shall be punished with rigorous imprisonment for a term which may extend to seven years, and shall also be liable to fine.

403. Dishonest misappropriation of property. Whoever dishonestly misappropriates or converts to his own use any movable property, shall be punished with imprisonment of either description for a term which may extend to two years, or with fine, or with both.

ILLUSTRATIONS.

(a) A takes property belonging to Z out of Z's possession in good faith, believing, at the time when he takes it, that the property belongs to himself. A is not guilty of theft; but if A, after discovering his mistake, dishonestly appropriates the property to his own use, he is guilty of an offence under this Section.

(b) A, being on friendly terms with Z, goes into Z's library in Z's absence and takes away a book without Z's express consent. Here, if A was under the impression that he had Z's implied consent to take the book for the purpose of reading it, A has not committed theft. But, if A afterwards sells the book for his own benefit, he is guilty of an offence under this Section.

(c) A and B being joint owners of a horse, A takes the horse out of B's possession, intending to use it. Here as A has a right to use the horse, he does not dishonestly misappropriate it. But, if A sells the horse and appropriates the whole proceeds to his own use, he is guilty of an offence under this Section.

EXPLANATION 1. A dishonest misappropriation for a time only is a misappropriation with the meaning of this Section.

ILLUSTRATION. A finds a Government promissory note belonging to Z, bearing a blank endorsement. A, knowing that the note belongs to Z, pledges it with a banker as a security or a loan, intending at a future time to restore it to Z. A has committed an offence under this Section.

EXPLANATION 2. A person who finds property not in the possession of any other person, and such property for the purpose of protecting it for, or of restoring it to, the owner, does not take or misappropriate it dishonestly, and is not guilty of an offence; but he is guilty of the offence above defined, if he appropriates it to his own use, when he knows or has the means of discovering the owner, or before he has used reasonable means to discover and give notice to the owner and has kept the property a reasonable time to enable the owner to claim it. What are reasonable means or what is a reasonable time in such a case, is a question of fact. It is not necessary that the finder should know who is the owner of the property, or that any particular person is the owner of it: it is sufficient if, at the time of appropriating it, he does not believe it to be his own property, or in good faith believe that the real owner cannot be found.

ILLUSTRATIONS.

(a) A finds a rupee on the high-road, not knowing to whom the rupee belong, A picks up the rupee. Here A has not committed the offence defined in this Section.

(b) A finds a letter on the road, containing a bank note. From the direction and contents of the letter he learns to whom the note belongs. He appropriates the note. He is guilty of an offence under this Section.

(c) A finds a cheque payable to bearer. He can form no conjecture as to the person who has lost the cheque. But the name of the person, who has drawn the cheque, appears. A knows that this person can direct him to the person in whose favour the cheque was drawn. A appropriates the cheque without attempting to discover the owner. He is guilty of an offence under this Section.

(d) A sees Z drop his purse with money in it. A pick up the purse with the intention of restoring it to Z, but afterwards appropriates it to his own use. A has committed an offence under this Section.

(e) A finds a purse with money, not knowing to whom it belongs; he afterwards discovers that it belongs to Z, and appropriates it to his own use. A is guilty of an offence under this Section.

(f) A finds a valuable ring, not knowing to whom it belongs. A sells it immediately without attempting to discover the owner. A is guilty of an offence under this Section.

404. Dishonest misappropriation of property possessed by deceased person at the time of his death. Whoever dishonestly misappropriates or converts to his own use property, knowing that such property was in the possession of a deceased person at the time of that person's decease, and has not since been in the possession of any person legally entitled to such possession, shall be punished with imprisonment of either description for a term which may extend to three years, and shall also be liable to fine, and if the offender at the time of such person's decease was employed by him as a clerk or servant, the imprisonment may extend to seven years.

ILLUSTRATION. Z dies in possession of furniture and money. His servant A, before the money comes into the possession of any person entitled to such possession, dishonestly misappropriates it. A has committed the offence defined in this Section.

405. Criminal breach of trust. Whoever, being in any manner entrusted with property, or with any dominion over property, dishonestly misappropriates or converts to his own use that property, or dishonestly uses or disposes of that property in violation of any direction of law prescribing the mode in which such trust is to be discharged, or of any legal contract, express or implied, which he has made touching the discharge of such trust, or wilfully suffers any other person so to do, commits "criminal breach of trust".

EXPLANATION 1. A person, being an employer of an establishment whether exempted under Section 17 of the Employees' Provident Funds and Miscellaneous Provisions Act, 1952 (19 of 1952) or not who deducts the employees' contribution from the wages payable to the employee for credit to a Provident Fund or Family Pension Fund established by any law for the time being in force, shall be deemed to have been entrusted with the amount of the contribution so deducted by him and if he makes default in the payment of such contribution to the said Fund in violation of the said law shall be deemed to have dishonestly used the amount of the said contribution in violation of a direction of law as aforesaid.

EXPLANATION 2. A person, being an employer, who deducts the employees contribution from the wages payable to the employee for credit to the Employees' State Insurance Fund held and administered by the Employees' State Insurance Corporation established under the Employees' State Insurance Act, 1948 (34 of 1948), shall be deemed to have been entrusted with the amount of the contribution so deducted by him and if he makes default in the payment of such contribution to the said Fund in violation of the said Act, shall be deemed to have dishonestly used the amount of the said contribution in violation of a direction of law as aforesaid.

ILLUSTRATIONS.

(a) A, being executor to the will of a deceased person, dishonestly disobeys the law which directs him to divide the effects according to the will, and appropriates them to his own use. A has committed criminal breach of trust.

(b) A is a warehouse-keeper, Z, going on a journey, entrusts his furniture to A, under a contract that it shall be returned on payment of a stipulated sum for warehouse-room. A dishonestly sells the goods. A has committed criminal breach of trust.

(c) A, residing in Calcutta, is agent for Z, residing at Delhi. There is an express or implied contract between A and Z, that all sums remitted by Z to A shall be invested by A, according to Z's direction. Z remits a lakh of rupees to A, with directions to A to invest the same in Company's paper. A dishonestly disobeys the directions and employs the money in his own business. A has committed criminal breach of trust.

(d) But if A, in the last illustration, not dishonestly but in good faith, believing that it will be more for Z's advantage to hold shares in the Bank of Bengal, disobeys Z's directions, and buys shares in the Bank of Bengal, for Z, instead of buying Company's paper, here, thought Z should suffer loss, and should be entitled to bring a civil action against A, on account of that loss, yet A, not having acted dishonestly, has not committed criminal breach of trust.

(e) A, a revenue-officer, is entrusted with public money and is either directed by law, or bound by a contract, express or implied, with the Government, to pay into a certain treasury all the public money which he holds. A dishonestly appropriates the money. A has committed criminal breach of trust.

(f) A, a carrier, is entrusted by Z with property to be carried by land or by water. A dishonestly misappropriates the property. A has committed criminal breach of trust.

406. Punishment for criminal breach of trust. Whoever commits criminal breach of trust shall be punished with imprisonment of either description for a term which may extend to three years, or with fine, or with both.

407. Criminal breach of trust by carrier, etc. Whoever, being entrusted with property as a carrier, wharfinger or warehouse-keeper, commits criminal breach of trust, in respect of such property, shall be punished with imprisonment of either description for a term which may extend to seven years, and shall also be liable to fine.

408. Criminal breach of trust by clerk or servant. Whoever, being a clerk or servant or employed as a clerk or servant, and being in any manner entrusted in such capacity with property, or with any dominion over property, commits criminal breach of trust in respect of that property, shall be punished with imprisonment of either description for a term which may extend to seven years, and shall also be liable to fine.

409. Criminal breach of trust by public servant, or by banker, merchant or agent. Whoever, being in any manner entrusted with property, or with any dominion over property in his capacity of a public servant or in the way of his business as a banker, merchant, factor, broker, attorney or agent, commits criminal breach of trust in respect of that property, shall be punished with imprisonment for life, or with imprisonment of either description for a term which may extend to ten years, and shall also be liable to fine.

OF THE RECEIVING OF STOLEN PROPERTY

410. Stolen property. Property, the possession whereof has been transferred by theft, or by extortion, or by robbery, and property which has been criminally misappropriated or in respect of which criminal breach of trust has been committed, is designated as "stolen property", whether the transfer has been made, or the misappropriation or breach of trust has been committed, within or without India. But, if such property subsequently comes into the possession of a person legally entitled to the possession thereof, it then ceases to be stolen property.

411. Dishonestly receiving stolen property. Whoever dishonestly receives or retains any stolen property, knowing or having reason to believe the same to be stolen property, shall be punished with imprisonment of either description for a term which may extend to three years, or with fine, or with both.

412. Dishonestly receiving property stolen in the commission of a dacoity. Whoever dishonestly receives or retains any stolen property, the possession whereof he knows or has reason to believe to have been transferred by the commission of dacoity, or dishonestly receives from a person, whom he knows or has reason to believe to belong or to have belonged to a gang of dacoits, property which he knows or has reason to believe to have been stolen, shall be punished with imprisonment for life, or with rigorous imprisonment for a term which may extend to ten years, and shall also be liable to fine.

413. Habitually dealing in stolen property. Whoever habitually receives or deals in property which he knows or has reason to believe to be stolen property, shall be punished with imprisonment for life, or with imprisonment of either description for a term which may extend to ten years, and shall also be liable to fine.

414. Assisting in concealment of stolen property. Whoever voluntarily assists in concealing or disposing of or making away with property which he knows or has reason to believe to be stolen property, shall be punished with imprisonment of either description for a term which may extend to three years, or with fine, or with both.

415. Cheating. Whoever, by deceiving any person, fraudulently or dishonestly induces the person so deceived to deliver any property to any person, or to consent that any person shall retain any property, or intentionally induces the person so deceived to do or omit to do anything which he would not do or omit if he were not so deceived, and which act or omission causes or is likely to cause damage or harm to that person in body, mind, reputation or property, is said to "cheat".

EXPLANATION. A dishonest concealment of facts is a deception within the meaning of this Section.

ILLUSTRATIONS.

(a) A, by falsely pretending to be in the Civil Service, intentionally deceives Z, and thus dishonestly induces Z to let him have on credit goods for which he does not mean to pay. A cheats.

(b) A, by putting a counterfeit mark on an article, intentionally deceives Z into a belief that this article was made by a certain celebrated manufacturer, and thus dishonestly induces Z to buy and pay for the article. A cheats.

(c) A, by exhibiting to Z a false sample of an article intentionally deceives Z into believing that the article corresponds with the sample, and thereby dishonestly induces Z to buy and pay for the article. A cheats.

(d) A, by tendering in payment for an article a bill on a house with which A keeps no money, and by which A expects that the bill will be dishonoured, intentionally deceives Z, and thereby dishonestly induces Z to deliver the article, intending not to pay for it. A cheats.

(e) A, by pledging as diamond articles which he knows are not diamonds, intentionally deceives Z, and thereby dishonestly induces Z to lend money. A cheats.

(f) A Intentionally deceives Z into a belief that A means to repay any money that Z may lend to him and thereby dishonestly induces Z to lend him money, A not intending to repay it. A cheats.

(g) A intentionally deceives Z into a belief that A means to deliver to Z a certain quantity of indigo plant which he does not intend to deliver, and thereby dishonestly induces Z to advance money upon the faith of such delivery. A cheats; but if A, at the time of obtaining the money, intends to deliver the indigo plant, and afterwards breaks his contract and does not deliver it, he does not cheat, but is liable only to a civil action for breach of contract.

(h) A intentionally deceives Z into a belief that A has performed A's part of a contract made with Z, which he has not performed, and thereby dishonestly induces Z to pay money. A cheats.

(i) A sells and conveys an estate to B. A, knowing that in consequence of such sale he has no right to the property, sells or mortgages the same to Z, without disclosing the fact of the previous sale and conveyance to B, and receives the purchase or mortgage money from Z. A cheats.

416. Cheating by personation. A person is said to "cheat by personation" if he cheats by pretending to be some other person, or by knowingly substituting one person for or another, or representing that he or any other person is a person other than he or such other person really is.

EXPLANATION. The offence is committed whether the individual personated is a real or imaginary person.

ILLUSTRATIONS.

(a) A cheats, by pretending to be a certain rich banker of the same name. A cheats by personation.

(b) A cheats by pretending to be B, a person who is deceased. A cheats by personation.

417. Punishment for cheating. Whoever cheats shall be punished with imprisonment of either description for a term which may extend to one year, or with fine, or with both.

418. Cheating with knowledge that wrongful loss may ensue to person whose interest offender is bound to protect. Whoever cheats with the knowledge that he is likely thereby to cause wrongful loss to a person whose interest in the transaction to which the cheating relates, he was bound either by law, or by legal contract, to protect, shall be punished with imprisonment of either description for a term which may extend to three years, or with fine, or with both.

419. Punishment for cheating by personation. Whoever cheats by personation shall be punished with imprisonment of either description for a term which may extend to three years, or with fine, or with both.

420. Cheating and dishonestly inducing delivery of property. Whoever cheats and thereby dishonestly induces the person deceived to deliver any property to any person, or to make, alter or destroy the whole or any part of a valuable security, or anything which is signed or sealed, and which is capable of being converted into a valuable security, shall be punished with imprisonment of either description for a term which may extend to seven years, and shall also be liable to fine.

421. Dishonest or fraudulent removal or concealment of property to prevent distribution among creditors. Whoever dishonestly or fraudulently removes, conceals or delivers to any person, or transfers or causes to be transferred to any person, without adequate consideration, any property, intending thereby to prevent, or knowing it to be likely that he will thereby prevent the distribution of that property according to law among his creditors or the creditors of any other person, shall be punished with imprisonment of either description for a term which may extend to two years, or with fine, or with both.

422. Dishonestly or fraudulently preventing debt being available for creditors. Whoever dishonestly or fraudulently prevents any debt or demand due to himself or to any other person from being made available according to law for payment of his debts or the debts of such other person, shall be punished with imprisonment of either description for a term which may extend to two years, or with fine, or with both.

423. Dishonest or fraudulent execution of deed of transfer containing false statement of consideration. Whoever dishonestly or fraudulently signs, executes or becomes a party to any deed or instrument which purports to transfer or subject to any charge any property, or any interest therein, and which contains any false statement relating to the consideration for such transfer or charge, or relating to the person or persons for whose use or benefit it is really intended to operate, shall be punished with imprisonment of either description for a term which may extend to two years, or with fine, or with both.

424. Dishonest or fraudulent removal or concealment of property. Whoever dishonestly or fraudulently conceals or removes any property of himself or any other person, or dishonestly or fraudulently assists in the concealment or removal thereof, or dishonestly releases any demand or claim to which he is entitled, shall be punished with imprisonment of either description for a term which may extend to two years, or with fine, or with both.

425. Mischief. Whoever with intent to cause, or knowing that he is likely to cause, wrongful loss or damage to the public or to any person, causes the destruction of any property, or any such change in any property or in the situation thereof as destroys or diminishes its value or utility, or affects it injuriously, commits “mischief”.

EXPLANATION 1. It is not essential to the offence of mischief that the offender should intend to cause loss or damage to the owner of the property injured or destroyed. It is sufficient if he intends to cause, or knows that he is likely to cause, wrongful loss or damage to any person by injuring any property, whether it belongs to that person or not.

EXPLANATION 2. Mischief may be committed by an act affecting property belonging to the person who commits the act, or to that person and others jointly.

ILLUSTRATIONS.

(a) A voluntarily burns a valuable security belonging to Z intending to cause wrongful loss to Z. A has committed mischief.

(b) A introduces water in to an ice- house belonging to Z and thus causes the ice to melt, intending wrongful loss to Z. A has committed mischief.

(c) A voluntarily throws into a river a ring belonging to Z, with the intention of there by causing wrongful loss to Z. A has committed mischief.

(d) A, knowing that his effects are about to be taken in execution in order to satisfy a debt due from him to Z, destroys those effects, with the intention of thereby preventing Z from obtaining satisfaction of the debt, and of thus causing damage to Z. A has committed mischief.

(e) A having insured a ship, voluntarily causes the same to be cast away, with the intention of causing damage to the underwriters. A has committed mischief.

(f) A causes a ship to be cast away, intending thereby to cause damage to Z who has lent money on bottomry on the ship. A has committed mischief.

(g) A, having joint property with Z in a horse, shoots the horse, intending thereby to cause wrongful loss to Z. A has committed mischief.

(h) A causes cattle to enter upon a field belonging to Z, intending to cause and knowing that he is likely to cause damage to Z's crop. A has committed mischief.

426. Punishment for mischief. Whoever commits mischief shall be punished with imprisonment of either description for a term which may extend to three months, or with fine, or with both.

427. Mischief causing damage to the amount of fifty rupees. Whoever commits mischief and thereby causes loss or damage to the amount of fifty rupees or upwards, shall be punished with imprisonment of either description for a term which may extend to two years, or with fine, or with both.

428. Mischief by killing or maiming animal of the value of ten rupees. Whoever commits mischief by killing, poisoning, maiming or rendering useless any animals or animal of the value of the ten rupees or upwards, shall be punished with imprisonment of either description for a term which may extend to two years, or with fine, or with both.

429. Mischief by killing or maiming cattle, etc., of any value or any animal of the value of fifty rupees. Whoever commits mischief by killing, poisoning, maiming or rendering useless, any elephant, camel, horse, mule, buffalo, bull, cow or ox, whatever may be the value thereof, of any other animal of the value of fifty rupees or upwards, shall be punished with imprisonment or either description for a term which may extend to five years, or with fine, or with both.

430. Mischief by injury to works of irrigation or by wrongfully diverting water. Whoever commits mischief by doing any act which causes, or which he knows to be likely to cause, a diminution of the supply of water for agricultural purposes, or for food or drink for human beings or for animals which are property, or for cleanliness or for carrying on any manufacture, shall be punished with imprisonment of either description for a term which may extend to five years, or with fine, or with both.

431. Mischief by injury to public road, bridge, river or channel. Whoever commits mischief by doing any act which renders or which he knows to be likely to render any public road, bridge, navigable river or navigable channel, natural or artificial, impassable or less safe for travelling or conveying property, shall be punished with imprisonment of either description for a term which may extend to five years, or with fine, or with both.

432. Mischief by causing inundation or obstruction to public drainage attended with damage. Whoever commits mischief by doing any act which causes or which he knows to be likely to cause an inundation or an obstruction to any public drainage attended with injury or damage, shall be punished with imprisonment of either description for a term which may extend to five years, or with fine, or with both.

433. Mischief by destroying, moving or rendering less useful a light-house or sea-mark. Whoever commits mischief by destroying or moving any light-house or other light used as a sea-mark, or any sea- mark or buoy or other thing placed as a guide for navigators, or by any act which renders any such light-house, sea-mark, buoy or other such thing as aforesaid less useful as a guide for navigators, shall be punished with imprisonment of either description for a term which may extend to seven years, or with fine, or with both.

434. Mischief by destroying or moving, etc., a land- mark fixed by public authority. Whoever commits mischief by destroying or moving any land- mark fixed by the authority of a public servant, or by any act which renders such land- mark less useful as such, shall be punished with imprisonment of either description for a term which may extend to one year, or with fine, or with both.

435. Mischief by fire or explosive substance with intent to cause damage to amount of one hundred or (in case of agricultural produce) ten rupees. Whoever commits mischief by fire or any explosive substance intending to cause, or knowing it to be likely that he will thereby cause, damage to any property to the amount of one hundred rupees or upwards or (where the property is agricultural produce) ten rupees or upwards, shall be punished with imprisonment of either description for a term which may extend to seven years and shall also be liable to fine.

436. Mischief by fire or explosive substance with intent to destroy house, etc. Whoever commits mischief by fire or any explosive substance, intending to cause, or knowing it to be likely that he will thereby cause, the destruction of any building which is ordinarily used as a place of worship or as a human dwelling or as a place for the custody of property, shall be punished with imprisonment for life, or with imprisonment of either description for a term which may extend to ten years, and shall also be liable to fine.

437. Mischief with intent to destroy or make unsafe a decked vessel or one of twenty tons burden. Whoever commits mischief to any decked vessel or any vessel of a burden of twenty tons or upwards, intending to destroy or render unsafe, or knowing it to be likely that he will thereby destroy or render unsafe, that vessel, shall be punished with imprisonment of either description for a term which may extend to ten years, and shall also be liable to fine.

438. Punishment for the mischief described in Section 437 committed by fire or explosive substance. Whoever commits, or attempts to commit, by fire or any explosive substance, such mischief as is described in the last preceding Section, shall be punished with imprisonment for life, or with imprisonment of either description for a term which may extend to ten years, and shall also be liable to fine.

439. Punishment for intentionally running vessel aground or ashore with intent to commit theft, etc. Whoever intentionally runs any vessel aground or ashore, intending to commit theft of any property contained therein or to dishonestly misappropriate any such property, or with intent that such theft or misappropriation of property may be committed, shall be punished with imprisonment of either description for a term which may extend to ten years, and shall also be liable to fine.

440. Mischief committed after preparation made for causing death or hurt. Whoever commits mischief, having made preparation for causing to any person death, or hurt, or wrongful restraint, or fear of death, or hurt, or of wrongful restraint, shall be punished with imprisonment of either description for a term which may extend to five years, and shall also be liable to fine.

441. Criminal trespass. Whoever enters into or upon property in the possession of another with intent to commit an offence or to intimidate, insult or annoy any person in possession of such property, or having lawfully entered into or upon such property, unlawfully remains therewith intent thereby to intimidate, insult or annoy any such person, or with intent to commit an offence, is said to commit" criminal trespass".

442. House- trespass. Whoever commits criminal trespass by entering into or remaining in any building, tent or vessel used as a human dwelling or any building used as a place for worship, or as a place for the custody of property, is said to commit "house-trespass".

EXPLANATION. The introduction of any part of the criminal trespasser's body is entering sufficient to constitute house-trespass.

443. Lurking house-trespass. Whoever commits house-trespass having taken precautions to conceal such house-trespass from some person who has a right to exclude or eject the trespasser from the building, tent or vessel which is the subject of the trespass, is said to commit "lurking house-trespass".

444. Lurking house-trespass by night. Whoever commits lurking house- trespass after sunset and before sunrise, is said to commit "lurking house-trespass by night".

445. House-breaking. A person is said to commit "house-breaking" who commits house-trespass if he effects his entrance into the house or any part of it in any of the six ways hereinafter described; or if, being in the house or any part of it for the purpose of committing an offence, or having committed an offence therein, he quits the house or any part of it in any of it in such six ways, that is to say:- **First.** If he enters or quits through a passage made by himself, or by any abettor of the house- trespass, in order to the committing of the house-trespass. **Secondly.** If he enters or quits through any passage not intended by any person, other than himself or an abettor of the offence, for human entrance; or through any passage to which he has obtained access by scaling or climbing over any wall or building. **Thirdly.** If he enters or quits through any passage which he or any abettor of the house-trespass has opened, in order to the committing of the house-trespass by any means by which that passage was not intended by the occupier of the house to be opened. **Fourthly.** If he enters or quits by opening any lock in order to the committing of the house- trespass, or in order to the quitting of the house after a house-trespass. **Fifthly.** If he effects his entrance or departure by using criminal force or committing an assault, or by threatening any person with assault. **Sixthly.** If he enters or quits by any passage which he knows to have been fastened against such entrance or departure, and to have been unfastened by himself or by an abettor of the house-trespass.

EXPLANATION. Any out-house or building occupied with a house, and between which and such house there is an immediate internal communication, is part of the house within the meaning of this Section.

ILLUSTRATIONS.

(a) A commits house-trespass by making a hole through the wall of Z's house, and putting his hand through the aperture. This is house-breaking.

(b) A commits house-trespass by creeping into a ship at a port-hole between decks. This is house-breaking.

(c) A commits house-trespass by entering Z's house through a window. This is house-breaking.

(d) A commits house-trespass by entering Z's house through the door, having opened a door which was fastened. This is house-breaking.

(e) A commits house-trespass by entering Z's house through the door, having lifted a latch by putting a wire through a hole in the door. This is house-breaking.

(f) A finds the key of Z's house door, which Z had lost, and commits house trespass by entering Z's house, having opened the door with that key. This is house-breaking.

(g) Z is standing in his doorway. A forces a passage by knocking Z down, and commits house-trespass by entering the house. This is house-breaking.

(h) Z, the door-keeper of Y, is standing in Y's doorway. A commits house-trespass by entering the house, having deterred Z from opposing him by threatening to beat him. This is house-breaking.

446. House-breaking by night. Whoever commits house-breaking after sunset and before sunrise, is said to commit "house-breaking by night".

447. Punishment for criminal trespass. Whoever commits criminal trespass shall be punished with imprisonment of either description for a term which may extend to three months, or with fine which may extend to five hundred rupees, or with both.

448. Punishment for house-trespass. Whoever commits house-trespass shall be punished with imprisonment of either description for a term which may extend to one year, or with fine which may extend to one thousand rupees, or with both.

449. House-trespass in order to commit offence punishable with death. Whoever commits house-trespass in order to the committing of any offence punishable with death, shall be punished with imprisonment for life, or with rigorous imprisonment for a term not exceeding ten years, and shall also be liable to fine.

450. House-trespass in order to commit offence punishable with imprisonment for life. Whoever commits house-trespass in order to the committing of any offence punishable with imprisonment for life, shall be punished with imprisonment of either description for a term not exceeding ten years, and shall also be liable to fine.

451. House-trespass in order to commit offence punishable with imprisonment. Whoever commits house-trespass in order to the committing of any offence punishable with imprisonment, shall be punished with imprisonment of either description for a term which may extend to two years, and shall also be liable to fine; and if the offence intended to be committed is theft, the term of the imprisonment may be extended to seven years.

452. House-trespass alter preparation for hurt, assault or wrongful restraint. Whoever commits house-trespass, having made preparation for causing hurt to any person or for assaulting any person, or for wrongfully restraining any person, or for putting and person in fear of hurt, or of assault, or of wrongful restraint, shall be punished with imprisonment of either description for a term which may extend to seven years, and shall also be liable to fine.

453. Punishment for lurking house-trespass or house-breaking. Whoever commits lurking house-trespass or house-breaking, shall be punished with imprisonment of either description for a term which may extend to two years, and shall also be liable to fine.

454. Lurking house-trespass or house-breaking in order to commit offence punishable with imprisonment. Whoever commits lurking house-trespass or house-breaking, in order to the committing of any offence punishable with imprisonment, shall be punished with imprisonment of either description for a term which may extend to three years, and shall also be liable to fine; and if the offence intended to be committed is theft, the term of the imprisonment may be extended to ten years.

455. Lurking house-trespass or house-breaking after preparation for hurt, assault or wrongful restraint. Whoever commits lurking house-trespass, or house-breaking, having made preparation for causing hurt to any person, or for assaulting any person, or for wrongfully restraining any person, or for putting any person in fear of hurt or of assault or of wrongful restraint, shall be punished with imprisonment of either description or a term which may extend to ten years, and shall also be liable to fine.

456. Punishment for lurking house-trespass or house-breaking by night. Whoever commits lurking house-trespass by night, or house-breaking by night, shall be punished with imprisonment of either description for a term which may extend to three years, and shall also be liable to fine.

457. Lurking house-trespass or house-breaking by night in order to commit offence punishable with imprisonment. Whoever commits lurking house-trespass by night, or house-breaking by night in order to the committing of any offence punishable with imprisonment, shall be punished with imprisonment of either description for a term which may extend to five years, and shall also be liable to fine; and, if the offence intended to be committed is theft, the term of the imprisonment may be extended to fourteen years.

458. Lurking house-trespass or house-breaking by night after preparation for hurt, assault, or wrongful restraint. Whoever commits lurking house-trespass by night, or house-breaking by night, having made preparation for causing hurt to any person or for assaulting any person, or for wrongfully restraining any person, or for putting any person in fear of hurt, or of assault, or of wrongful restraint, shall be punished with imprisonment of either description for a term which may extend to fourteen years, and shall also be liable to fine.

459. Grievous hurt caused whilst committing lurking house-trespass or house-breaking. Whoever, whilst committing lurking house-trespass or house-breaking, causes grievous hurt to any person or attempts to cause death or grievous hurt to any person, shall be punished with imprisonment for life, or imprisonment of either description for a term which may extend to ten years, and shall also be liable to fine.

460. All persons jointly concerned in lurking house-trespass or house-breaking by night punishable where death or grievous hurt caused by one of them. If at the time of the committing of lurking house-trespass by night or house-breaking by night, any person guilty of such offence shall voluntarily cause or attempt to cause death or grievous hurt to any person, every person jointly concerned in committing such lurkking house-trespass by night or house-breaking by night, shall be punished with imprisonment for life, or with imprisonment of either description for a term which may extend to ten years, and shall also be liable to fine.

461. Dishonestly breaking open receptacle containing property. Whoever dishonestly or with intent to commit mischief, breaks open or unfastens any closed receptacle which contains or which he believes to contain property, shall be punished with imprisonment of either description for a term which may extend to two years, or with fine, or with both.

462. Punishment for same offence when committed by person entrusted with custody. Whoever, being entrusted with any closed receptacle which contains or which he believes to contain property without having authority to open the same, dishonestly, or with intent to commit mischief, breaks open or unfastens that receptacle, shall be punished with imprisonment of either description for a term which may extend to three years, or with fine, or with both.

CHAPTER -XVIII : OF OFFENCES RELATING TO DOCUMENTS AND TO PROPERTY MARKS

463. Forgery. Whoever makes any false document or part of a document with intent to cause damage or injury, to the public or to any person, or to support any claim or title, or to cause any person to part with property, or to enter into any express or implied contract, or with intent to commit fraud or that fraud may be committed, commits forgery.

464. Making a false document. A person is said to make a false document. **First.** Who dishonestly or fraudulently makes, signs, seals or executes a document or part of a document, or makes any mark denoting the execution of a document, with the intention of causing it to be believed that such document or part of a document was made, signed, sealed or executed by or by the authority of a person by whom or by whose authority he knows that it was not made, signed, sealed or executed, or at a time at which he knows that it was not made, signed, sealed or executed; or **Secondly.** Who, without lawful authority, dishonestly or fraudulently, by cancellation or otherwise, alters a document in any material part thereof, after it has been made or executed either by himself or by any other person, whether such person be living or dead at the time of such alteration; or **Thirdly.** Who dishonestly or fraudulently causes any person to sign, seal, execute or alter a document, knowing that such person by reason of unsoundness of mind or intoxication cannot, or that by reason of deception practised upon him, he does not know the contents of the document or the nature of the alteration.

ILLUSTRATIONS.

(a) A has a letter of credit upon B for rupees 10, 000, written by Z. A, in order to defraud B, adds cipher to the 10, 000, and makes the sum 1, 00, 000 intending that it may be believed by B that Z so wrote the letter. A has committed forgery.

(b) A without Z's authority, affixes Z's seal to a document purporting to be a conveyance of an estate from Z to A, with the intention of selling the estate to B and thereby of obtaining from B the purchase-money. A has committed forgery.

(c) A picks up a cheque on a banker signed by B, payable to bearer, but without any sum having been inserted in the cheque. A fraudulently fills up the cheque by inserting the sum of ten thousand rupees. A commits forgery.

(d) A leaves with B, his agent, a cheque on a banker, signed by A, without inserting the sum payable and authorizes B to fill up the cheque by inserting a sum not exceeding ten thousand rupees for the purpose of making certain payments. B fraudulently fills up the cheque by inserting the sum of twenty thousand rupees. B commits forgery.

(e) A draws a bill of exchange on himself in the name of B without B's authority, intending to discount it as a genuine bill with a banker and intending to take up the bill on its maturity. Here, as A draws the bill with intent to deceive the banker by leading him to suppose that he had the security of B, and thereby to discount the bill, A is guilty of forgery.

(f) Z's will contains these words- "I direct that all my remaining property be equally divided between A, B and C." A dishonestly scratches out B's name, intending that it may be believed that the whole was left to himself and C. A has committed forgery.

(g) A endorses a Government promissory note and makes it payable to Z for his order by writing on the bill the words" Pay to Z or his order" and signing the endorsement. B dishonestly erases the words" Pay to Z or his order", and thereby converts the special endorsement into a blank endorsement. B commits forgery.

(h) A sells and conveys an estate to Z. A afterwards, in order to defraud Z of his estate, executes a conveyance of the same estate to B, dated six months earlier than the date of the conveyance to Z, intending it to be believed that he had conveyed the estate to B before he conveyed it to Z. A has committed forgery.

(i) Z dictates his will to A. A intentionally writes down a different legatee named by Z, and by representing to Z that he has prepared the will according to his instructions, induces Z to sign the will. A has committed forgery.

(j) A writes a letter and signs it with B's name without B's authority, certifying that A is a man of good character and in distressed circumstances from unforeseen misfortune, intending by means of such letter to obtain alms from Z and other persons. Here, as A made a false document in order to induce Z to part with property. A has committed forgery.

(k) A without B's authority writes a letter and signs it in B's name certifying to A's character, intending thereby to obtain employment under Z. A has committed forgery inasmuch as he intended to deceive Z by the forged certificate, and thereby to induce Z to enter into an express or implied contract for service.

EXPLANATION I. A man's signature of his own name may amount to forgery.

ILLUSTRATIONS.

(a) A signs his own name to a bill of exchange, intending that it may be believed that the bill was drawn by another person of the same name. A has committed forgery.

(b) A writes the word "accepted" on a piece of paper and signs it with Z's name, in order that B may afterwards write on the paper a bill of exchange drawn by B upon Z, and negotiate the bills as though it had been accepted by Z. A is guilty of forgery; and if B, knowing the fact, draws the bill upon the paper pursuant to A's intention, B is also guilty of forgery.

(c) A picks up a bill of exchange payable to the order of a different person of the same name. A endorses the bill in his own name, intending to cause it to be believed that it was endorsed by the person to whose order it was payable; here A has committed forgery.

(d) A purchases an estate sold under execution of a decree against B. B, after the seizure of the estate, in collusion with Z, executes a lease of the estate to Z at a nominal rent and for a long period and dates the lease six months prior to the seizure, with intent to defraud A, and to cause it to be believed that the lease was granted before the seizure. B, though he executes the lease in his own name, commits forgery by antedating it.

(e) A, a trader, in anticipation of insolvency, lodges effects with B for A's benefit, and with intent to defraud his creditors; and in order to give a colour to the transaction, writes a promissory note binding himself to pay to B a sum for value received, and antedates the note, intending that it may be believed to have been made before A was on the point of insolvency. A has committed forgery under the first head of the definition.

EXPLANATION 2. The making of a false document in the name of a fictitious person, intending it to be believed that the document was made by real person, or in the name of a deceased person, intending it to be believed that the document was made by the person in his lifetime, may amount to forgery.

ILLUSTRATION. A draws a bill of exchange upon a fictitious person, and fraudulently accepts the bill in the name of such fictitious person with intent to negotiate it. A commits forgery.

465. Punishment for forgery. Whoever commits forgery shall be punished with imprisonment of either description for a term which may extend to two years, or with fine, or with both.

466. Forgery of record of Court or of public register, etc. Whoever forges a document, purporting to be a record or proceeding of or in a Court of Justice, or a register of birth, baptism, marriage or burial, or a register kept by a public servant as such, or a certificate or document purporting to be made by a public servant in his official capacity, or an authority to institute or defend a suit, or to take any proceedings therein, or to confess judgment, or a power of attorney, shall be punished with imprisonment of either description for a term which may extend to seven years, and shall also be liable to fine.

467. Forgery of valuable security, will, etc. Whoever forges a document which purports to be a valuable security or a will, or an authority to adopt a son, or which purports to give authority to any person to make or transfer any valuable security, or to receive the principal, interest or dividends thereon, or to receive or deliver any money, movable property, or valuable security, or any document purporting to be an acquittance or receipt acknowledging the payment of money, or an acquittance or receipt for the delivery of any movable property or valuable security, shall be punished with imprisonment for life, or with imprisonment of either description for a term which may extend to ten years, and shall also be liable to fine.

468. Forgery for purpose of cheating. Whoever commits forgery, intending that the document forged shall be used for the purpose of cheating, shall be punished with imprisonment of either description for a term which may extend to seven years, and shall also be liable to fine.

469. Forgery for purpose of harming reputation. Whoever commits forgery, intending that the document forged shall harm the reputation of any party, or knowing that it is likely to be used for that purpose, shall be punished with imprisonment of either description for a term which may extend to three years, and shall also be liable to fine.

470. Forged document. A false document made wholly or in part by forgery is designated "a forged document".

471. Using as genuine a forged document. Whoever fraudulently or dishonestly uses as genuine any document which he knows or has reason to believe to be a forged document, shall be punished in the same manner as if he had forged such document.

472. Making or possessing counterfeit seal, etc., with intent to commit forgery punishable under Section 467. Whoever makes or counterfeits any seal, plate or other instrument for making an impression, intending that the same shall be used for the purpose of committing any forgery which would be punishable under Section 467 of this Code, or, with such intent, has in his possession any such seal, plate or other instrument, knowing the same to be counterfeit, shall be punishable with imprisonment for life, or with imprisonment of either description for a term which may extend to seven years, and shall also be liable to fine.

473. Making or possessing counterfeit seal, etc., with intent to commit forgery punishable otherwise. Whoever makes or counterfeits any seal, plate or other instrument for making an impression, intending that the same shall be used for the purpose of committing any forgery which would be punishable under any Section of this Chapter other than Section 467, or, with such intent, has in his possession any such seal, plate or other instrument, knowing the same to be counterfeit, shall be punished with imprisonment of either description for a term which may extend to seven years, and shall also be liable to fine.

474. Having possession of document described in Section 466 or 467, knowing it to be forged and intending to use it genuine. Whoever has in his possession any document, knowing the same to be forged, and intending that the same shall fraudulently or dishonestly be used as genuine, shall, if the document is one of the description mentioned in Section 466 of this Code, be punished with imprisonment of either description for a term which may extend to seven years, and shall also be liable to fine; and if the document is one of the description mentioned in Section 467, shall be punished with imprisonment for life, or with imprisonment of either description, for a term which may extend to seven years, and shall also be liable to fine.

475. Counterfeiting device or mark used for authenticating documents described in Section 467, or possessing counterfeit marked material. Whoever counterfeits upon, or in the substance of, any material, any device or mark used for the purpose of authenticating any document described in Section 467 of this Code, intending that such device or mark shall be used for the purpose of giving the appearance of authenticity to any document then forged or thereafter to be forged on such material, or who, with such intent, has in his possession any material upon or in the substance of which any such device or mark has been counterfeited, shall be punished with imprisonment for life, or with imprisonment of either description for a term which may extend to seven years, and shall also be liable to fine.

476. Counterfeiting device or mark used for authenticating documents other than those described in Section 467, or possessing counterfeit marked material. Whoever counterfeits upon, or in the substance of, any material, any device or mark used for the purpose of authenticating any document other than the documents described in Section 467 of this Code, intending that such device or mark shall be used for the purpose of giving the appearance of authenticity to any document then forged or thereafter to be forged on such material, or who with such intent, has in his possession any material upon or in the substance of which any such device or mark has been counterfeited, shall be punished with imprisonment of either description for a term which may extend to seven years, and shall also be liable to fine.

477. Fraudulent cancellation, destruction, etc., of will, authority to adopt, or valuable security. Whoever fraudulently or dishonestly, or with intent to cause damage or injury to the public or to any person, cancels, destroys or defaces, or attempts to cancel, destroy or deface, or secretes or attempts to secrete any document which is or purports to be a will, or an authority to adopt a son, or any valuable security, or commits mischief in respect of such document, shall be punished with imprisonment for life, or with imprisonment of either description for a term which may extend to seven years, and shall also be liable to fine.

477A. Falsification of accounts. Whoever, being a clerk, officer or servant, or employed or acting in the capacity of a clerk, officer or servant, wilfully, and with intent to defraud, destroys, alters, mutilates or falsifies any book, paper, writing, valuable security or account which belongs to or is in the possession of his employer, or has been received by him for or on behalf of his employer, or wilfully, and with intent to defraud, makes or abets the making of any false entry in, or omits or alters or abets the omission or alteration of any material particular from or in any such book, paper, writing, valuable security or account, shall be punished with imprisonment of either description for a term which may extend to seven years, or with fine, or with both.

EXPLANATION. It shall be sufficient in any charge under this Section to allege a general intent to defraud without naming any particular person intended to be defrauded or specifying any particular sum of money intended to be the subject of the fraud, or any particular day on which the offence was committed.

Of Property and Other Marks

478. Trade Mark. Rep. by the Trade and Merchandise Marks Act, 1958 (43 of 1958), s. 135 and Sch. (w.e.f. 25-11-1959).

479. Property mark. A mark used for denoting that movable property belongs to a particular person is called a property mark.

480. Using a false trade mark. Rep. by the Trade and Merchandise Marks Act, 1958 (43 of 1958), s. 135 and Sch. (w.e.f. 25-11-1959).

481. Using a false property mark. Whoever marks any movable property or goods or any case, package or other receptacle containing movable property or goods, or uses any case, package or other receptacle having any mark thereon, in a manner reasonably calculated to cause it to be believed that the property or goods so marked, or any property or goods contained in any such receptacle so marked, belong to a person to whom they do not belong, is said to use a false property mark.

482. Punishment for using a false property mark. Whoever uses any false property mark shall, unless he proves that he acted without intent to defraud, be punished with imprisonment of either description for a term which may extend to one year, or with fine, or with both.

483. Counterfeiting a property mark used by another. Whoever counterfeits any property mark used by any other person shall be punished with imprisonment of either description for a term which may extend to two years, or with fine, or with both.

484. Counterfeiting a mark used by a public servant. Whoever counterfeits any property mark used by a public servant, or any mark used by a public servant to denote that any property has been manufactured by a particular person or at a particular time or place, or that the property is of a particular quality or has passed through a particular office, or that it is entitled to any exemption, or uses as genuine any such mark knowing the same to be counterfeit, shall be punished with imprisonment of either description for a term which may extend to three years, and shall also be liable to fine.

485. Making or possession of any instrument for counterfeiting a property mark. Whoever makes or has in his possession any die, plate or other instrument for the purpose of counterfeiting a proper mark, or has in his possession a property mark for the purpose of denoting that any goods belong to a person to whom they do not belong, shall be punished with imprisonment of either description for a term which may extend to three years, or with fine, or with both.

486. Selling goods marked with a counterfeit property mark. Whoever sells, or exposes, or has in possession for sale, any goods or things with a counterfeit property mark affixed to or impressed upon the same or to or upon any case, package or other receptacle in which such goods are contained, shall, unless he proves-

(a) that, having taken all reasonable precautions against committing an offence against this Section, he had at the time of the commission of the alleged offence no reason to suspect the genuineness of the mark, and

(b) that, on demand made by or on behalf of the prosecutor, he gave all the information in his power with respect to the persons from whom he obtained such goods or things, or

(c) that otherwise he had acted innocently, be punished with imprisonment of either description for a term which may extend to one year, or with fine, or with both.

487. Making a false mark upon any receptacle containing goods. Whoever makes any false mark upon any case, package or other receptacle containing goods, in a manner reasonably calculated to cause any public servant or any other person to believe that such receptacle contains goods which it does not contain or that it does not contain goods which it does contain, or that the goods contained in such receptacle are of a nature or quality different from the real nature or quality thereof, shall, unless he proves that he acted without intent to defraud, be punished with imprisonment of either description for a term which may extend to three years, or with fine, or with both.

488. Punishment for making use of any such false mark. Whoever makes use of any such false mark in any manner prohibited by the last foregoing Section shall, unless he proves that he acted without intent to defraud, be punished as if he had committed an offence against that Section.

489. Tampering with property mark with intent to cause injury. Whoever removes, destroys, defaces or adds to any property mark, intending or knowing it to be likely that he may thereby cause injury to any person, shall be punished with imprisonment of either description for a term which may extend to one year, or with fine, or with both. Of currency-notes and bank-notes

489A. Counterfeiting currency-notes or bank-notes. Whoever counterfeits, or knowingly performs any part of the process of counterfeiting, any currency-note or bank-note, shall be punished with imprisonment for life, or with imprisonment of either description for a term which may extend to ten years, and shall also be liable to fine.

EXPLANATION. For the purposes of this Section and of Sections 489B, 489C, 489D and 489E, the expression" bank-note" means a promissory note or engagement for the payment of money to bearer on demand issued by any person carrying on the business of banking in any part of the world, or issued by or under the authority of any State or Sovereign Power, and intended to be used as equivalent to, or as a substitute for money.

489B. Using as genuine, forged or counterfeit currency-notes or bank-notes. Whoever sells to, or buys or receives from, any other person, or otherwise traffics in or uses as genuine, any forged or counterfeit currency-note or bank-note, knowing or having reason to believe the same to be forged or counterfeit, shall be punished with imprisonment for life, or with imprisonment of either description for a term which may extend to ten years, and shall also be liable to fine.

489C. Possession of forged or counterfeit currency-notes or bank-notes. Whoever has in his possession any forged or counterfeit currency-note or bank-note, knowing or having reason to believe the same to be forged or counterfeit and intending to use the same as genuine or that it may be used as genuine, shall be punished with imprisonment of either description for a term which may extend to seven years, or with fine, or with both.

489D. Making or possessing instruments or materials for forging or counterfeiting currency notes or bank-notes. Whoever makes, or performs any part of the process of making, or buys of sells or disposes of, or has in his possession, any machinery, instrument of material for the purpose of being used, or knowing or having reason to believe that it is intended to be used, for forging or counterfeiting any currency-note or bank-note, shall be punished with 1 imprisonment for life, or with imprisonment of either description for a term which may extend to ten years, and shall also be liable to fine.

489E. Making or using documents resembling currency-notes or bank-notes.

(1) Whoever makes, or causes to be made, or uses for any purpose whatsoever, or delivers to any person, any document purporting to be, or in any way resembling, or so nearly resembling as to be calculated to deceive, any currency-note or bank-note shall be punished with fine which may extend to one hundred rupees.

(2) If any person, whose name appears on a document the making of which is an offence under sub-section (1), refuses, without lawful excuse, to disclose to a police-officer on being so required the name and address of the person by whom it was printed or otherwise made, he shall be punished with fine which may extend to two hundred rupees.

(3) Where the name of any person appears on any document in respect of which any person is charged with an offence under sub-section (1) or on any other document used or distributed in connection with that document it may, until the contrary is proved, be presumed that that person caused the document to be made.

CHAPTER -XIX : OF THE CRIMINAL BREACH OF CONTRACTS OF SERVICE

490. Breach of contract of service during voyage or journey. *Rep. by the Workmen's Breach of Contract (Repealing) Act, 1925 (3 of 1925), s. 2 and Sch.*

491. Breach of contract to attend on and supply wants of helpless person. Whoever, being bound by a lawful contract to attend on or to supply the wants of any person who, by reason of youth, or of unsoundness of mind, or of a disease or bodily weakness, is helpless or incapable of providing for his own safety or of supplying his own wants, voluntarily omits so to do, shall be punished with imprisonment of either description for a term which may extend to three months, or with fine which may extend to two hundred rupees, or with both.

492. Breach of contract to serve at distant place to which servant is conveyed at master's expense. *Rep. by the Workmen's Breach of Contract (Repealing) Act, 1925 (3 of 1925), s. 2 and Sch.*

CHAPTER -XX : OF OFFENCES RELATING TO MARRIAGE

493. Cohabitation caused by a man deceitfully inducing a belief of lawful marriage. Every man who by deceit causes any woman who is not lawfully married to him to believe that she is lawfully married to him and to cohabit or have sexual intercourse with him in that belief, shall be punished with imprisonment of either description for a term which may extend to ten years, and shall also be liable to fine.

494. Marrying again during lifetime of husband or wife. Whoever, having a husband or wife living, marries in any case in which such marriage is void by reason of its taking place during the life of such husband or wife, shall be punished with imprisonment of either description for a term which may extend to seven years, and shall also be liable to fine.

Exception. This Section does not extend to any person whose marriage with such husband or wife has been declared void by a Court of competent jurisdiction, nor to any person who contracts a marriage during the life of a former husband or wife, if such husband or wife, at the time of the subsequent marriage, shall have been continually absent from such person for the space of seven years, and shall not have been heard of by such person as being alive within that time provided the person contracting such subsequent marriage shall, before such marriage takes place, inform the person with whom such marriage is contracted of the real state of facts so far as the same are within his or her knowledge.

495. Same offence with concealment of former marriage from person with whom subsequent marriage is contracted. Whoever commits the offence defined in the last preceding Section having concealed from the person with whom the subsequent marriage is contracted, the fact of the former marriage, shall be punished with imprisonment of either description for a term which may extend to ten years, and shall also be liable to fine.

496. Marriage ceremony fraudulently gone through without lawful marriage. Whoever, dishonestly or with a fraudulent intention, goes through the ceremony of being married, knowing that he is not thereby lawfully married, shall be punished with imprisonment of either description for a term which may extend to seven years, and shall also be liable to fine.

497. Adultery. Whoever has sexual intercourse with a person who is and whom he knows or has reason to believe to be the wife of another man, without the consent or connivance of that man, such sexual intercourse not amounting to the offence of rape, is guilty of the offence of adultery, and shall be punished with imprisonment of either description for a term which may extend to five years, or with fine, or with both. In such case the wife shall not be punishable as an abettor.

498. Enticing or taking away or detaining with criminal intent a married woman. Whoever takes or entices away any woman who is and whom he knows or has reason to believe to be the wife of any other man, from that man, or from any person having the care of her on behalf of that man, with intent that she may have illicit intercourse with any person, or conceals or detains with that intent any such woman, shall be punished with imprisonment of either description for a term which may extend to two years, or with fine, or with both.

CHAPTER -XXA : OF CRUELTY BY HUSBAND OR RELATIVES OF HUSBAND

498A. Husband or relative of husband of a woman subjecting her to cruelty. Whoever, being the husband or the relative of the husband of a woman, subjects such woman to cruelty shall be punished with imprisonment for a term which may extend to three years and shall also be liable to fine.

EXPLANATION. For the purposes of this Section, "cruelty" means-

(a) any wilful conduct which is of such a nature as is likely to drive the woman to commit suicide or to cause grave injury or danger to life, limb or health (whether mental or physical) of the woman; or

(b) harassment of the woman where such harassment is with a view to coercing her or any person related to her to meet any unlawful demand for any property or valuable security or is on account of failure by her or any person related to her to meet such demand.

CHAPTER -XXI : OF DEFAMATION

499. Defamation. Whoever by words either spoken or intended to be read, or by signs or by visible representations, makes or publishes any imputation concerning any person intending to harm, or knowing or having reason to believe that such imputation will harm, the reputation of such person, is said, except in the cases hereinafter excepted, to defame that person.

EXPLANATION 1. It may amount to defamation to impute anything to a deceased person, if the imputation would harm the reputation of that person if living, and is intended to be hurtful to the feelings of his family or other near relatives.

EXPLANATION 2. It may amount to defamation to make an imputation concerning a company or an association or collection of persons as such.

EXPLANATION 3. An imputation in the form of an alternative or expressed ironically, may amount to defamation.

EXPLANATION 4. No imputation is said to harm a person's reputation, unless that imputation directly or indirectly, in the estimation of others, lowers the moral or intellectual character of that person, or lowers the character of that person in respect of his caste or of his calling, or lowers the credit of that person, or causes it to be believed that the body of that person is in a lothsome state, or in a state generally considered as disgraceful.

ILLUSTRATIONS.

(a) A says- "Z is an honest man; he never stole B's watch", intending to cause it to be believed that Z did steal B's watch. This is defamation, unless it fall within one of the exceptions.

(b) A is asked who stole B's watch. A points to Z, intending to cause it to be believed that Z stole B's watch. This is defamation, unless it fall within one of the exceptions.

(c) A draws a picture of Z running away with B's watch, intending it to be believed that Z stole B's watch. This is defamation, unless it fall within one of the exceptions.

First Exception. Imputation of truth which public good requires to be made or published. It is not defamation to impute anything which is true concerning any person, if it be for the public good that the imputation should be made or published. Whether or not it is for the public good is a question of fact.

Second Exception. Public conduct of public servants.-It is not defamation to express in good faith any opinion whatever respecting the conduct of a public servant in the discharge of his public functions, or respecting his character, so far as his character appears in that conduct, and no further.

Third Exception. Conduct of any person touching any public question.-It is not defamation to express in good faith any opinion whatever respecting the conduct of any person touching any public question, and respecting his character, so far as his character appears in that conduct, and no further.

ILLUSTRATION. It is not defamation in A to express in good faith any opinion whatever respecting Z's conduct in petitioning Government on a public question, in signing a requisition for a meeting on a public question, in presiding or attending at such meeting, in forming or joining any society which invites the public support, in voting or canvassing for a particular candidate for any situation in the efficient discharge of the duties of which the public is interested.

Fourth Exception. Publication of reports of proceedings of courts-It is not defamation to publish a substantially true report of the proceedings of a Court of Justice, or of the result of any such proceedings.

EXPLANATION. A Justice of the Peace or other officer holding an enquiry in open Court preliminary to a trial in a Court of Justice, is a Court within the meaning of the above Section.

Fifth Exception. Merits of case decided in Court or conduct of witnesses and others concerned. It is not defamation to express in good faith any opinion whatever respecting the merits of any case, civil or criminal, which has been decided by a Court of Justice, or respecting the conduct of any person as a party, witness or agent, in any such case, or respecting the character of such person, as far as his character appears in that conduct, and no further.

ILLUSTRATIONS.

(a) A says- "I think Z's evidence on that trial is so contradictory that he must be stupid or dishonest." A is within this exception if he says this in good faith, inasmuch as the opinion which he expresses respects Z's character as it appears in Z's conduct as a witness, and no farther.

(b) But if A says- "I do not believe what Z asserted at that trial because I know him to be a man without veracity"; A is not within this exception, inasmuch as the opinion which expresses of Z's character, is an opinion not founded on Z's conduct as a witness.

Sixth Exception. Merits of public performance.-It is not defamation to express in good faith any opinion respecting the merits of any performance which its author has submitted to the judgment of the public, or respecting the character of the author so far as his character appears in such performance, and no farther.

EXPLANATION. A performance may be submitted to the judgment of the public expressly or by acts on the part of the author which imply such submission to the judgment of the public.

ILLUSTRATIONS.

(a) A person who publishes a book, submits that book to the judgment of the public.

(b) A person who makes a speech in public, submits that speech to the judgment of the public.

(c) An actor or singer who appears on a public stage, submits his acting or singing to the judgment of the public.

(d) A says of a book published by Z-"Z's book is foolish; Z must be a weak man. Z's book is indecent; Z must be a man of impure mind." A is within the exception, if he says this in good faith, inasmuch as the opinion which he expresses of Z respects Z's character only so far as it appears in Z's book, and no further.

(e) But if A says-"I am not surprised that Z's book is foolish and indecent, for he is a weak man and a libertine." A is not within this exception, inasmuch as the opinion which he expresses of Z's character is an opinion not founded on Z's book.

Seventh Exception. Censure passed in good faith by person having lawful authority over another. It is not defamation in a person having over another any authority, either conferred by law or arising out of a lawful contract made with that other, to pass in good faith any censure on the conduct of that other in matters to which such lawful authority relates.

ILLUSTRATION. A Judge censuring in good faith the conduct of a witness, or of an officer of the Court; a head of a department censuring in good faith those who are under his orders; a parent censuring in good faith a child in the presence of other children; a schoolmaster, whose authority is derived from a parent, censuring in good faith a pupil in the presence of other pupils; a master censuring a servant in good faith for remissness in service; a banker censuring in good faith the cashier of his bank for the conduct of such cashier as such cashier-are within this exception.

Eighth Exception. Accusation preferred in good faith to authorised person.-It is not defamation to prefer in good faith an accusation against any person to any of those who have lawful authority over that person with respect to the subject-matter of accusation.

ILLUSTRATION. If A in good faith accuses Z before a Magistrate; if A in good faith complains of the conduct of Z, a servant, to Z's master; if A in good faith complains of the conduct of Z, a child, to Z's father-A is within this exception.

Ninth Exception. Imputation made in good faith by person for protection of his or other's interests. It is not defamation to make an imputation on the character of another provided that the imputation be made in good faith for the protection of the interest of the person making it, or of any other person, or for the public good.

ILLUSTRATIONS.

(a) A, a shopkeeper, says to B, who manages his business-"Sell nothing to Z unless he pays you ready money, for I have no opinion of his honesty." A is within the exception, if he has made this imputation on Z in good faith for the protection of his own interests.

(b) A, a Magistrate, in making a report to his own superior officer, casts an imputation on the character of Z. Here, if the imputation is made in good faith, and for the public good, A is within the exception.

Tenth Exception. Caution intended for good of person to whom conveyed or for public good. It is not defamation to convey a caution, in good faith, to one person against another, provided that such caution be intended for the good of the person to whom it is conveyed, or of some person in whom that person is interested, or for the public good.

500. Punishment for defamation. Whoever defames another shall be punished with simple imprisonment for a term which may extend to two years, or with fine, or with both.

501. Printing or engraving matter known to be defamatory. Whoever prints or engraves any matter, knowing or having good reason to believe that such matter is defamatory of any person, shall be punished with simple imprisonment for a term which may extend to two years, or with fine, or with both.

502. Sale of printed or engraved substance containing defamatory matter. Whoever sells or offers for sale any printed or engraved substance containing defamatory matter, knowing that it contains such matter, shall be punished with simple imprisonment for a term which may extend to two years, or with fine, or with both.

CHAPTER -XXII : OF CRIMINAL INTIMIDATION, INSULT AND ANNOYANCE

503. Criminal intimidation. Whoever threatens another with any injury to his person, reputation or property, or to the person or reputation of any one in whom that person is interested, with intent to cause alarm to that person, or to cause that person to do any act which he is not legally bound to do, or to omit to do any act which that person is legally entitled to do, as the means of avoiding the execution of such threat, commits criminal intimidation.

EXPLANATION. A threat to injure the reputation of any deceased person in whom the person threatened is interested, is within this Section.

ILLUSTRATION. A, for the purpose of inducing B to resist from prosecuting a civil suit, threatens to burn B's house. A is guilty of criminal intimidation.

504. Intentional insult with intent to provoke breach of the peace. Whoever intentionally insults, and thereby gives provocation to any person, intending or knowing it to be likely that such provocation will cause him to break the public peace, or to commit any other offence, shall be punished with imprisonment of either description for a term which may extend to two years, or with fine, or with both.

505. Statements conducing public mischief.

(1) Whoever makes, publishes or circulates any statement, rumour or report,-

(a) with intent to cause, or which is likely to cause, any officer, soldier, sailor or airman in the Army, Navy or Air Force of India to mutiny or otherwise disregard or fail in his duty as such; or

(b) with intent to cause, or which is likely to cause, fear or alarm to the public, or to any Section of the public whereby any person may be induced to commit an offence against the State or against the public tranquility; or The words "or in the Royal Indian Marine" occurring after the word "Majesty" were rep. by Act 35 of 1934.

(c) with intent to incite, or which is likely to incite, any class or community of persons to commit any offence against any other class or community, shall be punished with imprisonment which may extend to three years, or with fine, or with both.

(2) Statements creating or promoting enmity, hatred or ill-will between classes. Whoever makes, publishes or circulates any statement or report containing rumour or alarming news with intent to create or promote, or which is likely to create or promote, on grounds of religion, race, place of birth, residence, language, caste or community or any other ground whatsoever, feelings of enmity, hatred or ill-will between different religious, racial, language or regional groups or castes or communities, shall be punished with imprisonment which may extend to three years, or with fine, or with both.

(3) Offence under sub-section (2) committed in place of worship, etc. Whoever commits an offence specified in sub-section (2) in any place of worship or in any assembly engaged in the performance of religious worship or religious ceremonies, shall be punished with imprisonment which may extend to five years and shall also be liable to fine.

Exception. It does not amount to an offence, within the meaning of this Section, when the person making, publishing or circulating any such statement, rumour or report, has reasonable grounds for believing that such statement, rumour or report is true and makes, publishes or circulates it in good faith and without any such intent as aforesaid.

506. Punishment for criminal intimidation. Whoever commits the offence of criminal intimidation shall be punished with imprisonment of either description for a term which may extend to two years, or with fine, or with both; If threat be to cause death or grievous hurt, etc. and if the threat be to cause death or grievous hurt, or to cause the destruction of any property by fire, or to cause an offence punishable with death or imprisonment for life, of with imprisonment for a term which may extend to seven years, or to impute unchastity to a woman, shall be punished with imprisonment of either description for a term which may extend to seven years, or with fine, or with both.

507. Criminal intimidation by an anonymous communication. Whoever commits the offence of criminal intimidation by an anonymous communication, or having taken precaution to conceal the name or abode of the person from whom the threat comes, shall be punished with imprisonment of either description for a term which may extend to two years, in addition to the punishment provided for the offence by the last preceding Section.

508. Act caused by inducing person to believe that he will be rendered an object of the Divine displeasure. Whoever voluntarily causes or attempts to cause any person to do anything which that person is not legally bound to do, or to omit to do anything which he is legally entitled to do, by inducing or attempting to induce that person to believe that he or any person in whom he is interested will become or will be rendered by some act of the offender an object of Divine displeasure if he does not do the thing which it is the object of the offender to cause him to do, or if he does the thing which it is the object of the offender to cause him to omit, shall be punished with imprisonment of either description for a term which may extend to one year, or with fine, or with both.

ILLUSTRATIONS.

(a) A sits dhurna at Z's door with the intention of causing it to be believed that, by so sitting, he renders Z an object of Divine displeasure. A has committed the offence defined in this Section.

(b) A threatens Z that, unless Z performs a certain act, A will kill one of A's own children, under such circumstances that the killing would be believed to render Z an object of Divine displeasure. A has committed the offence defined in this Section.

509. Word, gesture or act intended to insult the modesty of a woman. Whoever, intending to insult the modesty of any woman, utters any word, makes any sound or gesture, or exhibits any object, intending that such word or sound shall be heard, or that such gesture or object shall be seen, by such woman, or intrudes upon the privacy of such woman, shall be punished with simple imprisonment for a term which may extend to one year, or with fine, or with both.

510. Misconduct in public by a drunken person. Whoever, in a state of intoxication, appears in any public place, or in any place which it is a trespass in him to enter, and there conducts himself in such a manner as to cause annoyance to any person, shall be punished with simple imprisonment for a term which may extend to twenty-four hours, or with fine which may extend to ten rupees, or with both.

CHAPTER -XXIII : OF ATTEMPTS TO COMMIT OFFENCES

511. Punishment for attempting to commit offences punishable with imprisonment for life or other imprisonment. Whoever attempts to commit an offence punishable by this Code with imprisonment for life or imprisonment, or to cause such an offence to be committed, and in such attempt does any act towards the commission of the offence, shall, where no express provision is made by this Code for the punishment of such attempt, be punished with imprisonment of any description provided for the offence, for a term which may extend to one-half of the imprisonment for life or, as the case may be, one-half of the longest term of imprisonment provided for that offence, or with such fine as is provided for the offence, or with both.

ILLUSTRATIONS.

(a) A makes an attempt to steal some jewels by breaking open a box, and finds after so opening the box, that there is no jewel in it. He has done an act towards the commission of theft, and therefore is guilty under this Section.

(b) A makes an attempt to pick the pocket of Z by thrusting his hand into Z's pocket. A fails in the attempt in consequence of Z's having nothing in his pocket. A is guilty under this Section.

❑❑❑

15

The Juvenile Justice (Care and Protection of Children) Act, 2000

ACT NO. 56 OF 2000 [30TH DECEMBER, 2000]

AN ACT to consolidate and amend the law relating to juveniles in conflict with law and children in need of care and protection, by providing for proper care, protection and treatment by catering to their development needs, and by adopting a child friendly approach in the adjudication and disposition of matters in the best interest of children and for their ultimate rehabilitation through various institutions established under this enactment.

WHEREAS the Constitution has, in several provisions, including clause (3) of article 15, clauses (e) and (f) of article 39, articles 45 and 47, impose on the State a primary responsibility of ensuring that all the needs of children are met and that their basic human rights are fully protected;

AND WHEREAS, the General Assembly of the United Nations has adopted the Convention on the Rights of the Child on the 20th November, 1989;

AND WHEREAS, the Convention on the Rights of the Child has prescribed a set of standards to be adhered to by all State parties in securing the best interests of the child;

AND WHEREAS, the Convention on the Rights of the Child emphasis social reintegration of child victims, to the extent possible, without resorting to judicial proceedings;

AND WHEREAS, the Government of India has ratified the Convention on the 11th December, 1992.

AND WHEREAS, it is expedient to re-enact the existing law relating to juveniles bearing in mind the standards prescribed in the Convention on the Rights of the Child, the United Nations Standard Minimum Rules for the Administration of Juvenile Justice, 1985 (the

Beijing Rules), the United Nations Rules for the Protection of Juveniles Deprived of their Liberty (1990), and all other relevant international instruments.

Be it enacted by Parliament in the Fifty-first Year of the Republic of India as follows:-

CHAPTER - I : PRELIMINARY

1. Short title, extent and commencement.

(1) This Act may be called the Juvenile Justice (Care and Protection of Children) Act, 2000.

(2) It extends to the whole of India except the State of Jammu and Kashmir.

(3) It shall come into force on such date as the Central Government may, by notification in the Official Gazette, appoint.

2. Definitions. In this Act, unless the context otherwise requires,-

(a) "advisory board" means a Central or a State Advisory Board or a district and city level advisory board, as the case may be, constituted under Section 62;

(b) "begging" means-

  (i) soliciting or receiving alms in a public place or entering into any private premises for the purpose of soliciting or receiving alms, whether under any pretence;

  (ii) exposing or exhibiting with the object of obtaining or extorting alms, any sore, wound, injury, deformity or disease, whether of himself or of any other person or of an animal;

(c) "Board" means a Juvenile Justice Board constituted under Section 4;

(d) "child in need of care and protection" means a child-

  (i) who is found without any home or settled place or abode and without any ostensible means of subsistence,

  (ii) who resides with a person (whether a guardian of the child or not) and such person-

    (a) has threatened to kill or injure the child and there is a reasonable likelihood of the threat being carried out, or

    (b) has killed, abused or neglected some other child or children and there is a reasonable likelihood of the child in question being killed, abused or neglected by that person,

  (iii) who is mentally or physically challenged or ill children or children suffering from terminal diseases or incurable diseases having no one to support or look after,

  (iv) who has a parent or guardian and such parent or guardian is unfit or incapacitated to exercise control over the child,

  (v) who does not have parent and no one is willing to take care of or whose parents have abandoned him or who is missing and run away child and whose parents cannot be found after reasonable inquiry,

(vi) who is being or is likely to be grossly abused, tortured or exploited for the purpose of sexual abuse or illegal acts,

(vii) who is found vulnerable and is likely to be inducted into drug abuse or trafficking,

(viii) who is being or is likely to be abused for unconscionable gains,

(ix) who is victim of any armed conflict, civil commotion or natural calamity;

(e) "children' s home" means an institution established by a State Government or by voluntary organisation and certified by that Government under Section 34;

(f) "Committee" means a Child Welfare Committee constituted under Section 29;

(g) "competent authority" means in relation to children in need of care and protection a Committee and in relation to juveniles in conflict with law a Board;

(h) "fit institution" means a governmental or a registered non-governmental organisation or a voluntary organisation prepared to own the responsibility of a child and such organisation is found fit by the competent authority;

(i) "fit person" means a person, being a social worker or any other person, who is prepared to own the responsibility of a child and is found fit by the competent authority to receive and take care of the child;

(j) "guardian", in relation to a child, means his natural guardian or any other person having the actual charge or control over the child and recognised by the competent authority as a guardian in course of proceedings before that authority;

(k) "juvenile" or "child" means a person who has not completed eighteenth year of age;

(l) "juvenile in conflict with law" means a juvenile who is alleged to have committed an offence;

(m) "local authority" means Panchayats at the village and Zila Parishad at the district level and shall also include a Municipal Committee or Corporation or a Cantonment Board or such other body legally entitled to function as local authority by the Government;

(n) "narcotic drug" and "psychotropic substance" shall have the meanings respectively assigned to them in the Narcotic Drugs and Psychotropic Substances Act, 1985 (61 of 1985);

(o) "observation home" means a home established by a State Government or by a voluntary organisation and certified by that State Government under Section 8 as an observation home for the juvenile in conflict with law;

(p) "offence" means an offence punishable under any law for the time being in force;

(q) "place of safety" means any place or institution (not being a police lock-up or jail), the person incharge of which is willing temporarily to receive and take care of the juvenile and which, in the opinion of the competent authority, may be a place of safety for the juvenile;

(r) "prescribed" means prescribed by rules made under this Act;

(s) "probation officer" means an officer appointed by the State Government as a probation officer under the Probation of Offenders Act, 1958 (20 of 1958);

(t) "public place" shall have the meaning assigned to it in the Immoral Traffic (Prevention) Act, 1956 (104 of 1956);

(u) "shelter home" means a home or a drop-in-centre set up under Section 37;

(v) "special home" means an institution established by a State Government or by a voluntary organisation and certified by that Government under Section 9;

(w) "special juvenile police unit" means a unit of the police force of a State designated for handling of juveniles or children under Section 63;

(x) "State Government", in relation to a Union territory, means the Administrator of that Union territory appointed by the President under article 239 of the Constitution;

(y) all words and expressions used but not defined in this Act and defined in the Code of Criminal Procedure, 1973 (2 of 1974), shall have the meanings respectively assigned to them in that Code.

3. Continuation of inquiry in respect of juvenile who has ceased to be a juvenile. Where an inquiry has been initiated against a juvenile in conflict with law or a child in need of care and protection and during the course of such inquiry the juvenile or the child ceases to be such, then, notwithstanding anything contained in this Act or in any other law for the time being in force, the inquiry may be continued and orders may be made in respect of such person as if such person had continued to be a juven le or a child.

CHAPTER - II : JUVENILE IN CONFLICT WITH LAW

4. Juvenile Justice Board.

(1) Notwithstanding anything contained in the Code of Criminal Procedure, 1973 (2 of 1974), the State Government may, by notification in the Official Gazette, constitute for a district or a group of districts specified in the notification, one or more Juvenile Justice Boards for exercising the powers and discharging the duties conferred or imposed on such Boards in relation to juveniles in conflict with law under this Act.

(2) A Board shall consist of a Metropolitan Magistrate or a Judicial Magistrate of the first class, as the case may be, and two social workers of whom at least one shall be a woman, forming a Bench and every such Bench shall have the powers conferred by he Code of Criminal Procedure, 1973 (2 of 1974), on a Metropolitan Magistrate or, as the case may be, a Judicial Magistrate of the first class and the Magistrate on the Board shall be designated as the principal Magistrate.

(3) No Magistrate shall be appointed as a member of the Board unless he has special knowledge or training in child psychology or child welfare and no social worker shall be appointed as a member of the Board unless he has been actively involved in health education, or welfare activities pertaining to children for at least seven years.

(4) The term of office of the members of the Board and the manner in which such member may resign shall be such as may be prescribed.

(5) The appointment of any member of the Board may be terminated after holding inquiry, by the State Government, if-

(i) he has been found guilty of misuse of power vested under this Act,

(ii) he has been convicted of an offence involving moral turpitude, and such conviction has not been reversed or he has not been granted full pardon in respect of such offence,

(iii) he fails to attend the proceedings of the Board for consecutive three months without any valid reason or he fails to attend less than three-fourth of the sittings in a year.

5. Procedure, etc., in relation to Board.

(1) The Board shall meet at such times and shall observe such rules of procedure in regard to the transaction of business at its meetings, as may be prescribed.

(2) A child in conflict with law may be produced before an individual member of the Board, when the Board is not sitting.

(3) A Board may act notwithstanding the absence of any member of the Board, and no order made by the Board shall be invalid by reason only of the absence of any member during any stage of proceedings:

PROVIDED that there shall be at least two members including the principal Magistrate present at the time of final disposal of the case.

(4) In the event of any difference of opinion among the members of the Board in the interim or final disposition, the opinion of the majority shall prevail, but where there is no such majority, the opinion of the principal Magistrate shall prevail.

6. Powers of Juvenile Justice Board.

(1) Where a Board has been constituted for any district or a group of districts, such Board shall, notwithstanding anything contained in any other law for the time being in force but save as otherwise expressly provided in this Act, have power to deal exclusively with all proceedings under this Act relating to juvenile in conflict with law.

(2) The powers conferred on the Board by or under this Act may also be exercised by the High Court and the Court of Session, when the proceeding comes before them in appeal, revision or otherwise.

7. Procedure to be followed by a Magistrate not empowered under the Act.

(1) When any Magistrate not empowered to exercise the powers of a Board under this Act is of the opinion that a person brought before him under any of the provisions of this Act (other than for the purpose of giving evidence), is a juvenile or the child, he shall without any delay record such opinion and forward the juvenile or the child and the record of the proceeding to the competent authority having jurisdiction over the proceeding.

(2) The competent authority to which the proceeding is forwarded under sub-section (1) shall hold the inquiry as if the juvenile or the child had originally been brought before it.

8. Observation homes.

(1) Any State Government may establish and maintain either by itself or under an agreement with voluntary organisations, observation homes in every district or a group of districts, as may be required for the temporary reception of any juvenile in conflict with law during the dependency of any inquiry regarding them under this Act.

(2) Where the State Government is of opinion that any institution other than a home established or maintained under sub-section (1), is fit for the temporary reception of juvenile in conflict with law during the dependency of any inquiry regarding them under this Act, it may certify such institution as an observation home for the purposes of this Act.

(3) The State Government may, by rules made under this Act, provide for the management of observation homes, including the standards and various types of services to be provided by them for rehabilitation and social integration of a juvenile, and the circumstances under which, and the manner in which, the certification of an observation home may be granted or withdrawn.

(4) Every juvenile who is not placed under the charge of parent or guardian and is sent to an observation home shall be initially kept in a reception unit of the observation home for preliminary inquiries, care and classification for juveniles according to his age group, such as seven to twelve years, twelve to sixteen years and sixteen to eighteen years, giving due considerations to physical and mental status and degree of the offence committed, for further induction into observation home.

9. Special homes.

(1) Any State Government may establish and maintain either by itself or under an agreement with voluntary organisations, special homes in every district or a group of districts, as may be required for reception and rehabilitation of juvenile in conflict with law under this Act.

(2) Where the State Government is of opinion that any institution other than a home established or maintained under sub-section (1), is fit for the reception of juvenile in conflict with law to be sent there under this Act, it may certify such institution as a special home for the purposes of this Act.

(3) The State Government may, by rules made under this Act, provide for the management of special homes, including the standards and various types of services to be provided by them which are necessary for re-socialisation of a juvenile, and the circumstances under which, and the manner in which, the certification of a special home may be granted or withdrawn.

(4) The rules made under sub-section (3) may also provide for the classification and separation of juvenile in conflict with law on the basis of age and the nature of offences committed by them and his mental and physical status.

10. Apprehension of juvenile in conflict with law.

(1) As soon as a juvenile in conflict with law is apprehended by police, he shall be placed under the charge of the special juvenile police unit or the designated police officer who shall immediately report the matter to a member of the Board.

(2) The State Government may make rules consistent with this Act,-

(i) to provide for persons through whom (including registered voluntary organisations) any juvenile in conflict with law may be produced before the Board;

(ii) to provide the manner in which such juvenile may be sent to an observation home.

11. Control of custodian over juvenile. Any person in whose charge a juvenile is placed in pursuance of this Act shall, while the order is in force have the control over the juvenile as he would have if he were his parents, and shall be responsible for his maintenance, and the juvenile shall continue in his charge for the period stated by competent authority, notwithstanding that he is claimed by his parents or any other person.

12. Bail of juvenile.

(1) When any person accused of a bailable or non-bailable offence, and apparently a juvenile, is arrested or detained or appears or is brought before a Board, such person shall, notwithstanding anything contained in the Code of Criminal Procedure, 1973 (2 of 1974) or in any other law for the time being in force, be released on bail with or without surety but he shall not be so released if there appear reasonable grounds for believing that the release is likely to bring him into association with any known criminal or expose him to moral, physical or psychological danger or that his release would defeat the ends of justice.

(2) When such person having been arrested is not released on bail under sub-section (1) by the officer incharge of the police station, such officer shall cause him to be kept only in an observation home in the prescribed manner until he can be brought before a Board.

(3) When such person is not released on bail under sub-section (1) by the Board it shall, instead of committing him to prison, make an order sending him to an observation home or a place of safety for such period during the dependency of the inquiry regarding him as may be specified in the order.

13. Information to parent, guardian or probation officer. Where a juvenile is arrested, the officer incharge of the police station or the special juvenile police unit to which the juvenile is brought shall, as soon as may be after the arrest, inform-

(a) the parent or guardian of the juvenile, if he can be found of such arrest and direct him to be present at the Board before which the juvenile will appear; and

(b) the probation officer of such arrest to enable him to obtain information regarding the antecedents and family background of the juvenile and other material circumstances likely to be of assistance to the Board for making the inquiry.

14. Inquiry by Board regarding juvenile. Where a juvenile having been charged with the offence is produced before a Board, the Board shall hold the inquiry in accordance with the provisions of this Act and may make such order in relation to the juvenile s it deems fit:

> *PROVIDED that an inquiry under this Section shall be completed within a period of four months from the date of its commencement, unless the period is extended by the Board having regard to the circumstances of the case and in special cases after recording the reasons in writing for such extension.*

15. Order that may be passed regarding juvenile.

(1) Where a Board is satisfied on inquiry that a juvenile has committed an offence, then, notwithstanding anything to the contrary contained in any other law for the time being in force, the Board may, if it thinks so fit -

(a) allow the juvenile to go home after advice or admonition following appropriate inquiry against and counselling to the parent or the guardian and the juvenile;

(b) direct the juvenile to participate in group counselling and similar activities;

(c) order the juvenile to perform community service;

(d) order the parent of the juvenile or the juvenile himself to pay a fine, if he is over fourteen years of age and earns money;

(e) direct the juvenile to be released on probation of good conduct and placed under the care of any parent, guardian or other fit person, on such parent, guardian or other fit person executing a bond, with or without surety, as the Board may require, for the good behaviour and well-being of the juvenile for any period not exceeding three years;

(f) direct the juvenile to be released on probation of good conduct and placed under the care of any fit institution for the good behaviour and well-being of the juvenile for any period not exceeding three years;

(g) make an order directing the juvenile to be sent to a special home,-

(i) in the case of juvenile, over seventeen years but less than eighteen years of age for a period of not less than two years;

(ii) in case of any other juvenile for the period until he ceases to be a juvenile:

> *PROVIDED that the Board may, if it is satisfied that having regard to the nature of the offence and the circumstances of the case it is expedient so to do, for reasons to be recorded, reduce the period of stay to such period as it thinks fit.*

(2) The Board shall obtain the social investigation report on juvenile either through a probation officer or a recognised voluntary organisation or otherwise, and shall take into consideration the findings of such report before passing an order.

(3) Where an order under clause (d), clause (e) or clause (f) of sub-section (1) is made, the Board may, if it is of opinion that in the interests of the juvenile and of the public, it is expedient so to do, in addition make an order that the juvenile in conflict with law shall remain under the supervision of a probation officer named in the order during such period, not exceeding three years as may be

specified therein, and may in such supervision order impose such conditions as it deems necessary for he due supervision of the juvenile in conflict with law:

PROVIDED that if at any time afterwards it appears to the Board on receiving a report from the probation officer or otherwise, that the juvenile in conflict with law has not been of good behaviour during the period of supervision or that the fit institute on under whose care the juvenile was placed is no longer able or willing to ensure the good behaviour and well-being of the juvenile it may, after making such inquiry as it deems fit, order the juvenile in conflict with law to be sent to a special home.

(4) The Board shall while making a supervision order under sub-section (3), explain to the juvenile and the parent, guardian or other fit person or fit institution, as the case may be, under whose care the juvenile has been placed, the terms and conditions of the order and shall forthwith furnish one copy of the supervision order to the juvenile, the parent, guardian or other fit person or fit institution, as the case may be, the sureties, if any, and the probation officer.

16. Order that may not be passed against juvenile.

(1) Notwithstanding anything to the contrary contained in any other law for the time being in force, no juvenile in conflict with law shall be sentenced to death or life imprisonment, or committed to prison in default of payment of fine or in default of furnishing security:

PROVIDED that where a juvenile who has attained the age of sixteen years has committed an offence and the Board is satisfied that the offence committed is of so serious in nature or that his conduct and behaviour have been such that it would not be in his interest or in the interest of other juvenile in a special home to send him to such special home and that none of the other measures provided under this Act is suitable or sufficient, the Board may order the juvenile in conflict with law to be kept in such place of safety and in such manner as it thinks fit and shall report the case for the order of the State Government.

(2) On receipt of a report from a Board under sub-section (1), the State Government may make such arrangement in respect of the juvenile as it deems proper and may order such juvenile to be kept under protective custody at such place and on such conditions as it thinks fit:

PROVIDED that the period of detention so ordered shall not exceed the maximum period of imprisonment to which the juvenile could have been sentenced for the offence committed.

17. Proceeding under Chapter VIII of the Code of Criminal Procedure not competent against juvenile. Notwithstanding anything to the contrary contained in the Code of Criminal Procedure, 1973 (2 of 1974) no proceeding shall be instituted and no order shall be passed against the juvenile under Chapter VIII of the said Code.

18. No joint proceeding of juvenile and person not a juvenile.

(1) Notwithstanding anything contained in Section 223 of the Code of Criminal Procedure, 1973 (2 of 1974) or in any other law for the time offence together with a person who is not a juvenile being in force, no juvenile shall be charged with or tried for any.

(2) If a juvenile is accused of an offence for which under Section 223 of the Code of Criminal Procedure, 1973 (2 of 1974) or any other law for the time being in force, such juvenile and any person who is not a juvenile would, but for the prohibition contained in sub-section (1), have been charged and tried together, the Board taking cognizance of that offence shall direct separate trials of the juvenile and the other person.

19. Removal of disqualification attaching to conviction.

(1) Notwithstanding anything contained in any other law, a juvenile who has committed an offence and has been dealt with under the provisions of this Act shall not suffer disqualification, if any, attaching to a conviction of an offence under such law.

(2) The Board shall make an order directing that the relevant records of such conviction shall be removed after the expiry of the period of appeal or a reasonable period as prescribed under the rules, as the case may be.

20. Special provision in respect of pending cases. Notwithstanding anything contained in this Act, all proceedings in respect of a juvenile pending in any court in any area on the date on which this Act comes into force in that area, shall be continued in that court as if this Act had not been passed and if the court finds that the juvenile has committed an offence, it shall record such finding and instead of passing any sentence in respect of the juvenile, forward the juvenile to the Board which shall pass orders in respect of that juvenile in accordance with the provisions of this Act as if it had been satisfied on inquiry under this Act that a juvenile has committed the offence.

21. Prohibition of publication of name, etc., of juvenile involved in any proceeding under the Act.

(1) No report in any newspaper, magazine, news-sheet or visual media of any inquiry regarding a juvenile in conflict with law under this Act shall disclose the name, address or school or any other particulars calculated to lead to the identification of the juvenile nor shall any picture of any such juvenile be published:

PROVIDED that for reasons to be recorded in writing the authority holding the inquiry may permit such disclosure, if in its opinion such disclosure is in the interest of the juvenile.

(2) Any person contravening the provisions of sub-section (1) shall be punishable with fine, which may extend to one thousand rupees.

22. Provision in respect of escaped juvenile. Notwithstanding anything to the contrary contained in any other law for the time being in force, any police officer may take charge without warrant of a juvenile in conflict with law who has escaped from a special home or an observation home or from the care of a person under whom he was placed under this Act, and shall be sent back to the special home or the observation home or that person, as the case may be; and no proceeding shall be instituted in respect of the juvenile by reason of such escape, but the special home, or the observation home or the person may, after giving the information to the Board which passed the order in respect of the juvenile, take such steps in respect of the juvenile as may be deemed necessary under the provisions of this Act.

23. Punishment for cruelty to juvenile or child. Whoever, having the actual charge of or control over, a juvenile or the child, assaults, abandons, exposes or wilfully neglects the juvenile or causes or procures him to be assaulted, abandoned, exposed or neglected in a manner likely to cause such juvenile or the child unnecessary mental or physical suffering shall be punishable with imprisonment for a term which may extend to six months, or fine, or with both.

24. Employment of juvenile or child for begging.

(1) Whoever, employs or uses any juvenile or the child for the purpose or causes any juvenile to beg shall be punishable with imprisonment for a term which may extend to three years and shall also be liable to fine.

(2) Whoever, having the actual charge of, or control over, a juvenile or the child abets the commission of the offence punishable under sub-section (1), shall be punishable with imprisonment for a term which may extend to one year and shall also be liable to fine.

25. Penalty for giving intoxicating drug or psychotropic substance to juvenile or child. Whoever gives, or causes to be given, to any juvenile or the child any intoxicating liquor in a public place or any narcotic drug or psychotropic substance except upon the order of duly qualified medical practitioner or in case of sickness shall be punishable with imprisonment for a term which may extend to three years and shall also be liable to fine.

26. Exploitation of juvenile or child employee. Whoever ostensibly procures a juvenile or the child for the purpose of any hazardous employment keeps him in bondage and withholds his earnings or uses such earning for his own purposes shall be punishable with imprisonment for a term which may extend to three years and shall also be liable to fine.

27. Special offences. The offences punishable under Sections 23, 24, 25 and 26 shall be cognizable.

28. Alternative punishment. Where an act or omission constitute an offence punishable under this Act and also under any other Central or State Act, then, notwithstanding anything contained in any law for the time being in force, the offender found guilty of such offences shall be liable to punishment only under such Act as provides for punishment which is greater in degree.

CHAPTER - III : CHILD IN NEED OF CARE AND PROTECTION

29. Child Welfare Committee.

(1) The State Government may, by notification in Official Gazette, constitute for every district or group of districts, specified in the notification, one or more Child Welfare Committees for exercising the powers and discharge the duties conferred on such Committees in relation to child in need of care and protection under this Act.

(2) The Committee shall consist of a Chairperson and four other members as the State Government may think fit to appoint, of whom at least one shall be a woman and another, an expert on matters concerning children.

(3) The qualifications of the Chairperson and the members, and the tenure for which they may be appointed shall be such as may be prescribed.

(4) The appointment of any member of the Committee may be terminated, after holding inquiry, by the State Government, if-

(i) he has been found guilty of misuse of power vested under this Act;

(ii) he has been convicted of an offence involving moral turpitude, and such conviction has not been reversed or he has not been granted full pardon in respect of such offence;

(iii) he fails to attend the proceedings of the Committee for consecutive three months without any valid reason or he fails to attend less than three-fourth of the sittings in a year.

(5) The Committee shall function as a Bench of Magistrates and shall have the powers conferred by the Code of Criminal Procedure, 1973 (2 of 1974) on a Metropolitan Magistrate or, as the case may be, a Judicial Magistrate of the first class.

30. Procedure, etc., in relation to Committee.

(1) The Committee shall meet at such times and shall observe such rules of procedure in regard to the transaction of business at its meetings, as may be prescribed.

(2) A child in need of care and protection may be produced before an individual member for being placed in safe custody or otherwise when the Committee is not in session.

(3) In the event of any difference of opinion among the members of the Committee at the time of any interim decision, the opinion of the majority shall prevail but where there is no such majority the opinion of the Chairperson shall prevail.

(4) Subject to the provisions of sub-section (1), the Committee may act, notwithstanding the absence of any member of the Committee, and no order made by the Committee shall be invalid by reason only of the absence of any member during any stage of the proceeding.

31. Powers of Committee.

(1) The Committee shall have the final authority to dispose of cases for the care, protection, treatment, development and rehabilitation of the children as well as to provide for their basic needs and protection of human right.

(2) Where a Committee has been constituted for any area, such Committee shall, notwithstanding anything contained in any other law for the time being in force but save as otherwise expressly provided in this Act, have the power to deal exclusively with all proceedings under this Act relating to children in need of care and protection.

32. Production before Committee.

(1) Any child in need of care and protection may be produced before the Committee by one of the following persons-

(i) any police officer or special juvenile police unit or a designated police officer;

(ii) any public servant;

(iii) child line, a registered voluntary organisation or by such other voluntary organisation or an agency as may be recognised by the State Government;

(iv) any social worker or a public spirited citizen authorised by the State Government; or

(v) by the child himself.

(2) The State Government may make rules consistent with this Act to provide for the manner of making the report to the police and to the Committee and the manner of sending and entrusting the child to children's home pending the inquiry.

33. Inquiry.

(1) On receipt of a report under Section 32, the Committee or any police officer or special juvenile police unit or the designated police officer shall hold an inquiry in the prescribed or agency as mentioned in sub-section (1) of Section 32, may pass an order to send the child to the children' s home for speedy inquiry by a social worker or child welfare officer manner and the Committee, on its own or on the report from any person.

(2) The inquiry under this Section shall be completed within four months of the receipt of the order or within such shorter period as may be fixed by the Committee:

PROVIDED that the time for the submission of the inquiry report may be extended by such period as the Committee may, having regard to the circumstances and for the reasons recorded in writing, determine.

(3) After the completion of the inquiry if the Committee is of the opinion that the said child has no family or ostensible support, it may allow the child to remain in the children' s home or shelter home till suitable rehabilitation is found for him or till he attains the age of eighteen years.

34. Children's homes.

(1) The State Government may establish and maintain either by itself or in association with the voluntary organisations, children' s homes, in every district or group of districts, as the case may be, for the reception of child in need of care and protection during the dependency of any inquiry and subsequently for their care, treatment, education, training, development and rehabilitation.

(2) The State Government may, by rules made under this Act, provide for the management of children' s homes including the standards and the nature of services to be provided by them, and the circumstances under which, and the manner in which, the certification of a children's home or recognition to a voluntary organisation may be granted or withdrawn.

35. Inspection.

(1) The State Government may appoint inspection committees for the children's homes (hereinafter referred to as the inspection committees) for the State, a

district and city, as the case may be, for such period and for such purposes as ma be prescribed.

(2) The inspection committee of a State, district or of a city shall consist of such number of representatives from the State Government, local authority, Committee, voluntary organisations and such other medical experts and social workers as may be prescribed.

36. Social auditing. The Central Government or State Government may monitor and evaluate the functioning of the Children' s homes at such period and through such persons and institutions as may be specified by that Government.

37. Shelter homes.

(1) The State Government may recognise, reputed and capable voluntary organisations and provide them assistance to set up and administer as many shelter homes for juveniles or children as may be required.

(2) The shelter homes referred in sub-section (1) shall function as drop-in-centres for the children in the need of urgent support who have been brought to such homes through such persons as are referred to in sub-section (1) of Section 32.

(3) As far as possible, the shelter homes shall have such facilities as may be prescribed by the rules.

38. Transfer.

(1) If during the inquiry it is found that the child hails from the place outside the jurisdiction of the Committee, the Committee shall order the transfer of the child to the competent child authority having jurisdiction over the place of residence of the child.

(2) Such juvenile or the child shall be escorted by the staff of the home in which he is lodged originally.

(3) The State Government may make rules to provide for the travelling allowance to be paid to the child.

39. Restoration.

(1) Restoration of and protection to a child shall be the prime objective of any children' s home or the shelter home.

(2) The children' s home or a shelter home, as the case may be, shall take such steps as are considered necessary for the restoration of and protection to a child deprived of his family environment temporarily or permanently where such child is under the are and protection of a children' s home or a shelter home, as the case may be.

(3) The Committee shall have the powers to restore any child in need of care and protection to his parent, guardian, fit person or fit institution, as the case may be, and give them suitable directions.

EXPLANATION. For the purposes of this Section "restoration of child" means restoration to -

(a) parents;

(b) adopted parents;

(c) foster parents.

CHAPTER - IV : REHABILITATION AND SOCIAL REINTEGRATION

40. Process of rehabilitation and social reintegration. The rehabilitation and social reintegration of a child shall begin during the stay of the child in a children's home or special home and the rehabilitation and social reintegration of children shall be carried out alternatively by (i) adoption, (ii) foster care, (iii) sponsorship, and (iv) sending the child to an after-care organisation.

41. Adoption.

(1) The primary responsibility for providing care and protection to children shall be that of his family.

(2) Adoption shall be resorted to for the rehabilitation of such children as are orphaned, abandoned, neglected and abused through institutional and non-institutional methods.

(3) In keeping with the provisions of the various guidelines for adoption issued from time to time by the State Government, the Board shall be empowered to give children in adoption and carry out such investigations as are required for giving children in adoption in accordance with the guidelines issued by the State Government from time to time in this regard.

(4) The children's homes or the State Government run institutions for orphans shall be recognised as an adoption agencies both for scrutiny and placement of such children for adoption in accordance with the guidelines issued under sub-section (3).

(5) No child shall be offered for adoption-

(a) until two members of the Committee declare the child legally free for placement in the case of abandoned children,

(b) till the two months period for reconsideration by the parent is over in the case of surrendered children, and

(c) without his consent in the case of a child who can understand and express his consent.

(6) The Board may allow a child to be given in adoption-

(a) to a single parent, and

(b) to parents to adopt a child of same sex irrespecitve of the number of living biological sons or daughters.

42. Foster care.

(1) The foster care may be used for temporary placement of those infants who are ultimately to be given for adoption.

(2) In foster care, the child may be placed in another family for a short or extended period of time, depending upon the circumstances where the child' s own parent usually visit regularly and eventually after the rehabilitation, where the children may return to their own homes.

(3) The State Government may make rules for the purposes of carrying out the scheme of foster care programme of children.

43. Sponsorship.

(1) The sponsorship programme may provide supplementary support to families, to children' s homes and to special homes to meet medical, nutritional, educational and other needs of the children with a view to improving their quality of life.

(2) The State Government may make rules for the purposes of carrying out various schemes of sponsorship of children, such as individual to individual sponsorship, group sponsorship or community sponsorship.

44. After-care organization. The State Government may, by rules made under this Act, provide-

(a) for the establishment or recognition of after-care organisations and the functions that may be performed by them under this Act;

(b) for a scheme of after-care programme to be followed by such after-care organisations for the purpose of taking care of juveniles or the children after they leave special homes, children homes and for the purpose of enabling them to lead an honest, industrious and useful life;

(c) for the preparation or submission of a report by the probation officer or any other officer appointed by that Government in respect of each juvenile or the child prior to his discharge from a special home, children' s home, regarding the necessity and nature of after-care of such juvenile or of a child, the period of such after-care, supervision thereof and for the submission of report by the probation officer or any other officer appointed for the purpose, on the progress of each juvenile or the child;

(d) for the standards and the nature of services to be maintained by such after-care organisations;

(e) for such other matters as may be necessary for the purpose of carrying out the scheme of after-care programme for the juvenile or the child: Provided that any rule made under this Section shall not provide for such juvenile or child to stay in the after-care organisation for more than three years:

PROVIDED FURTHER that a juvenile or child over seventeen years of age but less than eighteen years of age would stay in the after-care organisation till he attains the age of twenty years.

45. Linkages and co-ordination. The State Government may make rules to ensure effective linkages between various governmental, non-governmental, corporate and other community agencies for facilitating the rehabilitation and social reintegration of the child.

CHAPTER - V : MISCELLANEOUS

46. Attendance of parent or guardian of juvenile or child. Any competent authority before which a juvenile or the child is brought under any of the provisions of this Act, may, whenever it so thinks fit, require any parent or guardian having the actual charge of or control over the juvenile or the child to be present at any proceeding in respect of the juvenile or the child.

47. Dispensing with attendance of juvenile or child. If, at any stage during the course of an inquiry, a competent authority is satisfied that the attendance of the juvenile or the child is not essential for the purpose of inquiry, the competent authority may dispense with his attendance and proceed with the inquiry in the absence of the juvenile or the child.

48. Committal to approved place or juvenile or child suffering from dangerous diseases and his future disposal.

(1) When a juvenile or the child who has been brought before a competent authority under this Act, is found to be suffering from a disease requiring prolonged medical treatment or physical or mental complaint that will respond to treatment, the competent authority may send the juvenile or the child to any place recognised to be an approved place in accordance with the rules made under this Act or such period as it may think necessary for the required treatment.

(2) Where a juvenile or the child is found to be suffering from leprosy, sexually transmitted disease, Hepatitis B, open cases of Tuberculosis and such other diseases or is of unsound mind, he shall be dealt with separately through various specialised referral services or under the relevant laws as such.

49. Presumption and determination of age.

(1) Where it appears to a competent authority that person brought before it under any of the provisions of this Act (otherwise than for the purpose of giving evidence) is a juvenile or the child, the competent authority shall make due inquiry so as to the age of that person and for that purpose shall take such evidence as may be necessary (but not an affidavit) and shall record a finding whether the person is a juvenile or the child or not, stating his age as nearly as may be.

(2) No order of a competent authority shall be deemed to have become invalid merely by any subsequent proof that the person in respect of whom the order has been made is not a juvenile or the child, and the age recorded by the competent authority to be the age of person so brought before it, shall for the purpose of this Act, be deemed to be the true age of that person.

50. Sending a juvenile or child outside jurisdiction. In the case of a juvenile or the child, whose ordinary place of residence lies outside the jurisdiction of the competent authority before which he is brought, the competent authority may, if satisfied after due inquiry that it is expedient so to do, send the juvenile or the child back to a relative or other person who is fit and willing to receive him at his ordinary place of residence and exercise proper care and control jurisdiction of the competent authority; and the competent authority exercising jurisdiction over the place to which the juvenile or the child is sent shall in respect of any matter arising subsequently have the s over him, notwithstanding that such place of residence is outside the me powers in relation to the juvenile or the child as if the original order had been passed by itself.

51. Reports to be treated as confidential. The report of the probation officer or social worker considered by the competent authority shall be treated as confidential:

PROVIDED that the competent authority may, if it so thinks fit, communicate the substance thereof to the juvenile or the child or his parent or guardian and may give such juvenile or the child, parent or guardian an opportunity of producing such evidence as may be relevant to the matter stated in the report.

52. Appeals.

(1) Subject to the provisions of this Section, any person aggrieved by an order made by a competent authority under this Act may, within thirty days from the date of such order, prefer an appeal to the Court of Session:

PROVIDED that the Court of Session may entertain the appeal after the expiry of the said period of thirty days if it is satisfied that the appellant was prevented by sufficient cause from filing the appeal in time.

(2) No appeal shall lie from-

(a) any order of acquittal made by the Board in respect of a juvenile alleged to have committed an offence; or

(b) any order made by a Committee in respect of a finding that a person is not a neglected juvenile.

(3) No second appeal shall lie from any order of the Court of Session passed in appeal under this Section.

53. Revision. The High Court may, at any time, either of its own motion or on an application received in this behalf, call for the record of any proceeding in which any competent authority or Court of Session has passed an order for the purpose of satisfying itself as to the legality or propriety of any such order and may pass such order in relation thereto as it thinks fit:

PROVIDED that the High Court shall not pass an order under this Section prejudicial to any person without giving him a reasonable opportunity of being heard.

54. Procedure in inquiries, appeals and revision proceedings.

(1) Save as otherwise expressly provided by this Act, a competent authority while holding any inquiry under any of the provisions of this Act, shall follow such procedure as may be prescribed and subject thereto, shall follow, as far as may be, the procedure laid down in the Code of Criminal Procedure, 1973 (2 of 1974) for trials in summons cases.

(2) Save as otherwise expressly provided by or under this Act, the procedure to be followed in hearing appeals or revision proceedings under this Act shall be, as far as practicable, in accordance with the provisions of the Code of Criminal Procedure, 1973 (2 of 1974).

55. Power to amend orders.

(1) Without prejudice to the provisions for appeal and revision under this Act, any competent authority may, on an application received in this behalf, amend any order as to the institution to which a juvenile or the child is to be sent or as to the person under whose care or supervision a juvenile or the child is to be placed under this Act:

PROVIDED that there shall be at least two members and the parties or its defence present during the course of hearing for passing an amendment in relation to any of its order.

(2) Clerical mistakes in orders passed by a competent authority or errors arising therein from any accidental slip or omission may, at any time, be corrected by the competent authority either on its own motion or on an application received in this behalf.

56. Power of competent authority to discharge and transfer juvenile or child. The competent authority or the local authority may, notwithstanding anything contained in this Act, at any time, order a child in need of care and protection or a juvenile in conflict with law to be discharged or transferred from one children' s home or special home to another, as the case may be, keeping in view the best interest of the child or the juvenile, and his natural place of stay, either absolutely or on such condition as it may think fit to impose:

PROVIDED that the total period of stay of the juvenile or the child in a children' s home or a special home or a fit institution or under a fit person shall not be increased by such transfer.

57. Transfer between children' s homes, under the Act, and juvenile homes, of like nature in different parts of India. The State Government or the local authority may direct any child or the juvenile to be transferred from any children's home or special home outside the State to any other children's home, special home or institution of a like nature with the prior intimation to the local Committee or the Board, as the case may be, and such order shall be deemed to be operative for the competent authority of the area to which the child or the juvenile is sent.

58. Transfer of juvenile or child of unsound mind or suffering from leprosy or addicted to drugs. Where it appears to the competent authority that any juvenile or the child kept in a special home or a children' s home or shelter home or in an institution in pursuance of this Act, is suffering from leprosy or is of unsound mind or is addicted to any narcotic drug or psychotropic substance, the competent authority may order his removal to a leper asylum or mental hospital or treatment centre for drug addict or to a place of safety for being kept therefor such period not exceeding the period for which he is required to be kept under the order of the competent authority or for such further period as may be certified by the medical officer necessary for the roper treatment of the juvenile or the child.

59. Release and absence of juvenile or child on placement.

(1) When a juvenile or the child is kept in a children's home or special home and on a report of a probation officer or social worker or of Government or a voluntary organisation, as the case may be, the competent authority may consider, the release of such juvenile or the child permitting him to live with his parent or guardian or under the supervision of any authorised person named in the order, willing to receive and take charge of the juvenile or the child to educate and train him for some useful trade or calling or to look after him for rehabilitation.

(2) The competent authority may also permit leave of absence to any juvenile or the child, to allow him, on special occasions like examination, marriage of

relatives, death of kith and kin or the accident or serious illness of parent or any emergency of like nature, to go on leave under supervision, for maximum seven days, excluding the time taken in journey.

(3) Where a permission has been revoked or forfeited and the juvenile or the child refuses or fails to return to the home concerned or juvenile to which he was directed so to return, the Board may, if necessary, cause him to be taken charge of and to be taken back to the concerned home.

(4) The time during which a juvenile or the child is absent from a concerned home in pursuance of such permission granted under this Section shall be deemed to be part of the time for which he is liable to be kept in the special home:

PROVIDED that when a juvenile has failed to return to the special home on the permission being revoked or forfeited, the time which elapses after his failure so to return shall be excluded in computing the time during which he is liable to be kept in the institution.

60. Contribution by parents.

(1) The competent authority which makes an order for sending a juvenile or the child to a children's home or to a special home or placing the juvenile under the care of a fit person or fit institution may make an order requiring the parent or other person liable to maintain the juvenile or the child to contribute to his maintenance, if able to do so, in the prescribed manner according to income.

(2) The competent authority may direct, if necessary, the payment to be made to poor parent or guardian by the Superintendent or the Project Manager of the home to pay such expenses for the journey of the inmate or parent or guardian or both, from the home to his ordinary place of residence at the time of sending the juvenile as may be prescribed.

61. Fund.

(1) The State Government or local authority may create a Fund under such name as it thinks fit for the welfare and rehabilitation of the juvenile or the child dealt with under this Act.

(2) There shall be credited to the Fund such voluntary donations, contributions or subscriptions as may be made by any individual or organisation.

(3) The Fund created under sub-section (1) shall be administered by the State advisory board in such manner and for such purposes as may be prescribed.

62. Central, State, district and city advisory boards.

(1) The Central Government or a State Government may constitute a Central or a State advisory board, as the case may be, to advise that Government on matter relating to the establishment and maintenance of the homes, mobilisation of resources, provision of facilities for education, training and rehabilitation of child in need of care and protection and juvenile in conflict with law and co-ordination among the various official and non-official agencies concerned.

(2) The Central or State advisory board shall consist of such persons as the Central Government or the State Government, as the case may be, may think fit and

shall include eminent social workers, representatives of voluntary organisation in the field of child welfare corporate sector, academicians, medical professionals and the concerned Department of the State Government.

(3) The district or city level inspection committee constituted under Section 35 of this Act shall also function as the district or city advisory boards.

63. Special juvenile police unit.

(1) In order to enable the police officers who frequently or exclusively deal with juveniles or are primarily engaged in the prevention of juvenile crime or handling of more effectively, they shall be specially instructed and trained. The juveniles or children under this Act to perform their functions.

(2) In every police station at least one officer with aptitude and appropriate training and orientation may be designated as the 'juvenile or the child welfare officer' who will handle the juvenile or the child in co-ordination with the police.

(3) Special juvenile police unit, of which all police officers designated as above, to handle juveniles or children will be members, may be created in every district and city to co-ordinate and to upgrade the police treatment of the juveniles and the children.

64. Juvenile in conflict with law undergoing sentence at commencement of this Act. In any area in which this Act is brought into force, the State Government or the local authority may direct that a juvenile in conflict with law who is undergoing any sentence of imprisonment at the commencement of this Act, shall, in lieu of undergoing such sentence, be sent to a special home or be kept in fit institution in such manner as the State Government or the local authority thinks fit for the remainder of the period of the sentence; and the provisions of this Act shall apply to the juvenile as if he had been ordered by the Board to be sent to such special home or institution or, as the case may be, ordered to be kept under protective care under sub-section (2) of Section 16 of this Act.

65. Procedure in respect of bonds. Provisions of Chapter XXXIII of the Code of Criminal Procedure, 1973 (2 of 1974) shall, as far as may be, apply to bonds taken under this Act.

66. Delegation of powers. The State Government may, by the general order, direct that any power exercisable by it under this Act shall, in such circumstances and under such conditions, if any, as may be prescribed in the order, be exercisable also by an officer subordinate to that Government or the local authority.

67. Protection of action taken in good faith. No suit or legal proceedings shall lie against the State Government or voluntary organisation running the home or any officer and the staff appointed in pursuance of this Act in respect of anything which is in good faith done or intended to be done in pursuance of this Act or of any rules or order made thereunder.

68. Power to make rules.

(1) The State Government may, by notification in the Official Gazette, make rules to carry out the purposes of this Act.

(2) In particular, and without prejudice to the generality of the foregoing powers, such rules may provide for all or any of the following matters, namely:-

(i) the term of office of the members of the Board and the manner in which such member may resign under sub-section (4) of Section 4;

(ii) the time of the meetings of the Board and the rules of procedure in regard to the transaction of business at its meeting under sub-section (1) of Section 5;

(iii) the management of observation homes including the standards and various types of services to be provided by them and the circumstances in which and the manner in which, the certification of the observation home may be granted or withdrawn and such there matters as are referred to in Section 8;

(iv) the management of special homes including the standards and various types of services to be provided by them and the circumstances in which and the manner in which, the certification of the special referred to in Section 9; home may be granted or withdrawn and such other matters as are

(v) persons to whom any juvenile in conflict with law may be produced before the Board and the manner of sending such juvenile, to an observation home under sub-section (2) of Section 10;

(vi) matters relating to removal of disqualification attaching to conviction of a juvenile under Section 19;

(vii) the qualifications of the Chairperson and members, and the tenure for which they may be appointed under sub-section (3) of Section 29;

(viii) the time of the meetings of the Committee and the rules of procedure in regard to the transaction of business at its meeting under sub-section (1) of Section 30;

(ix) the manner of making the report to the police and to the Committee and the manner of sending and entrusting the child to children' s home pending the inquiry under sub-section (2) of Section 32;

(x) the management of children's homes including the standards and nature of services to be provided by them, and the manner in which certification of a children's home or recognition to a voluntary organisation may be granted or withdrawn under sub-section (2) of Section 34;

(xi) appointment of inspection committees for children' s homes, their tenure and purposes for which inspection committees may be appointed and such other matters as are referred to in Section 35;

(xii) facilities to be provided by the shelter homes under sub-section (3) of Section 37;

(xiii) for carrying out the scheme of foster care programme of children under sub-section (3) of Section 42;

(xiv) for carrying out various schemes of sponsorship of children under sub-section (2) of Section 43;

(xv) matters relating to after-care organisation under Section 44;

(xvi) for ensuring effective linkages between various agencies for facilitating rehabilitation and social integration of the child under Section 45;

(xvii) the purposes and the manner in which the Fund shall be administered under sub-section (3) of Section 61;

(xviii) any other matter which is required to be, or may be, prescribed.

(3) Every rule made by a State Government under this Act shall be laid, as soon as may be after it is made, before the Legislature of that State.

69. Repeal and savings.

(1) The Juvenile Justice Act, 1986 (53 of 1986) is hereby repealed.

(2) Notwithstanding such repeal, anything done or any action taken under the said Act shall be deemed to have been done or taken under the corresponding provisions of this Act.

70. Power to remove difficulties.

(1) If any difficulty arises in giving effect to the provisions of this Act, the Central Government may, by order, not inconsistent with the provisions of this Act, remove the difficulty:

PROVIDED that no such order shall be made after the expiry of the period of two years from the commencement of this Act.

(2) However, order made under the Section shall be laid, as soon as may be after it is made, before each House of Parliament.

❑❑❑

16

The Juvenile Justice (Care and Protection of Children) Amendment Act, 2006

ACT NO. 33 OF 2006 [22ND AUGUST, 2006]

AN ACT to amend the Juvenile Justice (Care and Protection of Children) Act, 2000.

Be it enacted by Parliament in the Fifty-seventh Year of the Republic of India as follows:

1. Short title. This Act may be called the Juvenile Justice (Care and Protection of Children) Amendment Act, 2006.

2. Amendment of long title. In the Juvenile Justice (Care and Protection of Children) Act, 2000 (hereinafter referred to as the principal Act), in the long title, for the words through various institutions established under this enactment, the words and for matters connected therewith or incidental thereto shall be substituted.

3. Amendment of Section 1. In Section 1 of the principal Act,

(i) in the marginal heading, for the words and commencement, the words, commencement and application shall be substituted;

(ii) after sub-section (3), the following sub-section shall be inserted, namely: (4) Notwithstanding anything contained in any other law for the time being in force, the provisions of this Act shall apply to all cases involving detention, prosecution, penalty or sentence of imprisonment of juveniles in conflict with law under such other law.

4. Amendment of Section 2. In Section 2 of the principal Act,

(i) after clause (a), the following clause shall be inserted, namely:

(aa) adoption means the process through which the adopted child is permanently separated from his biological parents and become the legitimate child of his adoptive parents with all the rights, privileges and responsibilities that are attached to the relationship;

(ii) in clause (d),

(I) after sub-clause (i), the following sub-clause shall be inserted, namely:

(ia) who is found begging, or who is either a street child or a working child;

(II) in sub-clause (v), after the word abandoned, the words or surrendered shall be inserted;

(iii) in clause (h), for the words competent authority, the words State Government on the recommendation of the competent authority shall be substituted;

(iv) for clause (l), the following clause shall be substituted, namely:

(l) juvenile in conflict with law means a juvenile who is alleged to have committed an offence and has not completed eighteenth year of age as on the date of commission of such offence;;

(v) clause (m) shall be omitted.

5. Omission of certain expressions. Throughout the principal Act, the words local authority, or local authority and or the local authority, wherever they occur, shall be omitted.

6. Amendment of Section 4. In Section 4 of the principal Act, in sub-section (1), for the words by notification in the Official Gazette, constitute for a district or a group of districts specified in the notification, the words within a period of one year from the date of commencement of the Juvenile Justice (Care and Protection of Children) Amendment Act, 2006 , by notification in the Official Gazette, constitute for every district shall be substituted.

7. Amendment of Section 6. In Section 6 of the principal Act, in sub-section 1, the words or a group of districts shall be omitted.

8. Insertion of new Section 7A. After Section 7 of the principal Act, the following Section shall be inserted, namely:

7A. Procedure to be followed when claim of juvenility is raised before any court.

(1) Whenever a claim of juvenility is raised before any court or a court is of the opinion that an accused person was a juvenile on the date of commission of the offence, the court shall make an inquiry, take such evidence as may be necessary (but not an affidavit) so as to determine the age of such person, and shall record a finding whether the person is a juvenile or a child or not, stating his age as nearly as may be:

PROVIDED that a claim of juvenility may be raised before any court and it shall be recognised at any stage, even after final disposal of the case, and such claim shall be determined in terms of the provisions contained in this Act and the rules made thereunder, even if the juvenile has ceased to be so on or before the date of commencement of this Act.

(2) If the court finds a person to be a juvenile on the date of commission of the offence under sub-section (1), it shall forward the juvenile to the Board for passing appropriate order, and the sentence if any, passed by a court shall be deemed to have no effect.

9. Amendment of Section 10. In Section 10 of the principal Act, for sub-section 1, the following sub-section shall be substituted, namely:

(1) As soon as a juvenile in conflict with law is apprehended by police, he shall be placed under the charge of the special juvenile police unit or the designated police officer, who shall produce the juvenile before the Board without any loss of time but within a period of twenty-four hours of his apprehension excluding the time necessary for the journey, from the place where the juvenile was apprehended, to the Board:

PROVIDED that in no case, a juvenile in conflict with law shall be placed in a police lockup or lodged in a jail..

10. Amendment of Section 12. In Section 12 of the principal Act, in sub-section 1, after the words with or without surety, the words or placed under the supervision of a Probation Officer or under the care of any fit institution or fit person shall be inserted.

11. Amendment of Section 14. Section 14 of the principal Act shall be renumbered as sub-section -

(1) thereof, and after sub-section (1) as so renumbered, the following sub-section shall be inserted, namely:

(2) The Chief Judicial Magistrate or the Chief Metropolitan Magistrate shall review the pendency of cases of the Board at every six months, and shall direct the Board to increase the frequency of its sittings or may cause the constitution of additional Boards.

12. Amendment of Section 15. In Section 15 of the principal Act, in sub-section 1, for clause (g), the following clause shall be substituted, namely:

(g) make an order directing the juvenile to be sent to a special home for a period of three years:

PROVIDED that the Board may, if it is satisfied that having regard to the nature of the offence and the circumstances of the case, it is expedient so to do, for reasons to be recorded, reduce the period of stay to such period as it thinks fit."

13. Amendment of Section 16. In Section 16 of the principal Act,

(i) in sub-section (1), for the words or life imprisonment, the words or imprisonment for any term which may extend to imprisonment for life shall be substituted;

(ii) in sub-section (2), for the proviso, the following proviso shall be substituted, namely:

PROVIDED that the period of detention so ordered shall not exceed in any case the maximum period provided under Section 15 of this Act.

14. Amendment of Section 20. In Section 20 of the principal Act, the following proviso and Explanation shall be inserted, namely:

PROVIDED that the Board may, for any adequate and special reason to be mentioned in the order, review the case and pass appropriate order in the interest of such juvenile.

EXPLANATION. In all pending cases including trial, revision, appeal or any other criminal proceedings in respect of a juvenile in conflict with law, in any court, the determination of juvenility of such a juvenile shall be in terms of clause (l) of Section 2, even if the juvenile ceases to be so on or before the date of commencement of this Act and the provisions of this Act shall apply as if the said provisions had been in force, for all purposes and at all material times when the alleged offence was committed.

15. Substitution of new Section for Section 21. For Section 21 of the principal Act, the following Section shall be substituted, namely:

21. Prohibition of publication of name, etc., of juvenile in conflict with law or child in need of care and protection involved in any proceeding under the Act.

(1) No report in any newspaper, magazine, news-sheet or visual media of any inquiry regarding a juvenile in conflict with law or a child in need of care and protection under this Act shall disclose the name, address or school or any other particulars calculated to lead to the identification of the juvenile or child nor shall any picture of any such juvenile or child be published:

PROVIDED that for reasons to be recorded in writing, the authority holding the inquiry may permit such disclosure, if in its opinion such disclosure is in the interest of the juvenile or the child.

(2) Any person who contravenes the provisions of sub-section (1), shall be liable to a penalty which may extend to twenty-five thousand rupees.

16. Amendment of Section 29. In Section 29 of the principal Act, in sub-section 1, for the words by notification in Official Gazette, constitute for every district, or group of districts specified in the notification, the words within a period of one year from the date of commencement of the Juvenile Justice (Care and Protection of Children) Amendment Act, 2006 , by notification in the Official Gazette, constitute for every district shall be substituted.

17. Amendment of Section 32. In Section 32 of the principal Act,

(a) in sub-section (1),

(i) in clause (iv), the words authorised by the State Government shall be omitted;

(ii) the following proviso shall be inserted at the end, namely:

PROVIDED that the child shall be produced before the Committee without any loss of time but within a period of twenty-four hours excluding the time necessary for the journey.;

(b) in sub-section (2), the words to the police and shall be omitted.

18. Amendment of Section 33. In Section 33 of the principal Act,

(a) in sub-section (1), the words or any police officer or special juvenile police unit or the designated police officer shall be omitted;

(b) for sub-section (3), the following sub-sections shall be substituted, namely:

(3) The State Government shall review the pendency of cases of the Committee at every six months, and shall direct the Committee to increase the frequency of its sittings or may cause the constitution of additional Committees.

(4) After the completion of the inquiry, if, the Committee is of the opinion

that the said child has no family or ostensible support or is in continued need of care and protection, it may allow the child to remain in the children home or shelter home till suitable rehabilitation is found for him or till he attains the age of eighteen years.

19. Amendment of Section 34. In Section 34 of the principal Act, after sub-section (2), the following sub-section shall be inserted, namely:

(3) Without prejudice to anything contained in any other law for the time being in force, all institutions, whether State Government run or those run by voluntary organisations for children in need of care and protection shall, within a period of six months from the date of commencement of the Juvenile Justice (Care and Protection of Children) Amendment Act, 2006, be registered under this Act in such manner as may be prescribed.

20. Amendment of Section 39. In Section 39 of the principal Act, for the Explanation, the following Explanation shall be substituted, namely:

EXPLANATION. For the purposes of this Section restoration of and protection of a child means restoration to -

(a) parents;

(b) adopted parents;

(c) foster parents;

(d) guardian;

(e) fit person;

(f) fit institution.

21. Amendment of Section 39. In Section 41 of the principal Act,

(i) for sub-sections (2), (3) and (4), the following sub-sections shall be substituted, namely:

(2) Adoption shall be resorted to for the rehabilitation of the children who are orphan, abandoned or surrendered through such mechanism as may be prescribed.

(3) In keeping with the provisions of the various guidelines for adoption issued from time to time, by the State Government, or the Central Adoption Resource Agency and notified by the Central Government, children may be given in adoption by a court after satisfying itself regarding the investigations having been carried out, as are required for giving such children in adoption.

(4) The State Government shall recognise one or more of its institutions or voluntary organisations in each district as specialised adoption agencies in such manner as may be prescribed for the placement of orphan, abandoned or surrendered children for adoption in accordance with the guidelines notified under sub-section (3):

PROVIDED that the children' s homes and the institutions run by the State Government or a voluntary organisation for children in need of care and protection, who are orphan, abandoned or surrendered, shall ensure that these children are declared free for adoption by the Committee and all such cases shall be referred to the adoption agency in that district for placement of such children in adoption in accordance with the guidelines notified under sub-section (3);

(ii) for sub-section (6), the following sub-section shall be substituted, namely:

(6) The court may allow a child to be given in adoption -

(a) to a person irrespective of marital status; or

(b) to parents to adopt a child of same sex irrespective of the number of living biological sons or daughters; or

(c) to childless couples.

22. Substitution of new Section for Section 57. For Section 57 of the principal Act, the following Section shall be substituted, namely:

Transfer between children's homes under the act, and juvenile homes of like nature in different parts of India. The State Government may direct any child or the juvenile to be transferred from any children home or special home within the State to any other children home, special home or institution of a like nature or to such institutions outside the State in consultation with the concerned State Government and with the prior intimation to the Committee or the Board, as the case may be, and such order shall be deemed to be operative for the competent authority of the area to which the child or the juvenile is sent.

23. Amendment of Section 59. In Section 59 of the principal Act, in sub-section (2), for the words for maximum seven days, the words for a period generally not exceeding seven days shall be substituted.

24. Insertion of new Section 62A. After Section 62 of the principal Act, the following Section shall be inserted, namely:

62A. Constitution of Child Protection Unit responsible for implementation of the Act. Every State Government shall constitute a Child Protection Unit for the State and, such Units for every District, consisting of such officers and other employees as may be appointed by that Government, to take up matters relating to children in need of care and protection and juveniles in conflict with law with a view to ensure the implementation of this Act including the establishment and maintenance of homes, notification of competent authorities in relation to these children and their rehabilitation and co-ordination with various official and non-official agencies concerned.

25. Amendment of Section 64. In Section 64 of the principal Act,

(i) for the words may direct, the words shall direct shall be substituted;

(ii) the following proviso and Explanation shall be inserted, namely:

PROVIDED that the State Government, or as the case may be the Board, may, for any adequate and special reason to be recorded in writing, review the case of a juvenile in conflict with law undergoing a sentence of imprisonment, who has ceased to be so on or before the commencement of this Act, and pass appropriate order in the interest of such juvenile.

EXPLANATION. In all cases where a juvenile in conflict with law is undergoing a sentence of imprisonment at any stage on the date of commencement of this Act, his case including the issue of juvenility, shall be deemed to be decided in terms of clause (l) of Section 2 and other provisions contained in this Act and the rules made thereunder, irrespective of the fact that he ceases to be a juvenile on or before such date and accordingly he shall be sent to the special home or a fit institution, as the case may be, for the remainder of the period of the sentence but such sentence shall not in any case exceed the maximum period provided in Section 15 of this Act."

26. Amendment of Section 68. In Section 68 of the principal Act,

(a) in sub-section (1), the following proviso shall be inserted, namely:

PROVIDED that the Central Government may, frame model rules in respect of all or any of the matters with respect to which the State Government may make rules under this Section, and where any such model rules have been framed in respect of any such matter, they shall apply to the State until the rules in respect of that matter is made by the State Government and while making any such rules, so far as is practicable, they conform to such model rules;

(b) in sub-section (2),

(i) in clause (x), after the words, letter and brackets sub-section (2), the following words, letter and brackets shall be inserted, namely: and the manner of registration of institutions under sub-section (3);

(ii) after clause (xii), the following clause shall be inserted, namely:

(xiia) rehabilitation mechanism to be resorted to in adoption under sub-section (2), notification of guidelines under sub-section (3) and the manner of recognition of specialised adoption agencies under sub-section (4) of Section 41;

(c) sub-section (3) shall be re-numbered as sub-section (4) thereof, and before sub-section (4) as so re-numbered, the following sub-section shall be inserted namely:

(3) Every rule made by the Central Government under this Act shall be laid, as soon as may be after it is made, before each House of Parliament, while it is in session, for a total period of thirty days which may be comprised in one session or in two or more successive sessions, and if, before the expiry of the session immediately following the session or the successive sessions aforesaid, both Houses agree in making any modification in the rule or both Houses agree that the rule should not be made, the rule shall thereafter have effect only in such modified form or be of no effect, as the case may be; so, however, that any such modification or annulment shall be without prejudice to the validity of anything previously done under that rule.

❑❑❑

17

The Narcotic Drugs and Psychotropic Substances (Amendment) Act, 2001

Act No. 9 of 2001 [9th May, 2001]

AN ACT further to amend the Narcotic Drugs and Psychotropic Substances Act, 1985.

Be it enacted by Parliament in the Fifty-second Year of the Republic of India as follows:-

1. Short title and commencement.

(1) This Act may be called the Narcotic Drugs and Psychotropic Substances (Amendment) Act, 2001.

(2) It shall come into force on such date as the Central Government may, by notification in the Official Gazette, appoint; and different dates may be appointed for different provisions of this Act, and any reference in any provision to the commencement of this Act shall be construed as a reference to the coming into force of that provision.

2. Amendment of Section 1. In the Narcotic Drugs and Psychotropic Substances Act, 1985 (61 of 1985) (hereinafter referred to as the principal Act), in Section 1, in sub-section (2), after the words "whole of India", the following shall be inserted, namely:- "and it applies also-

(a) to all citizens of India outside India;

(b) to all persons on ships and aircrafts registered in India, wherever they may be".

3. Amendment of Section 2. In Section 2 of the principal Act,-

(a) for clause (i), the following clause shall be substituted, namely:- '(i) "addict" means a person who has dependence on any narcotic drug or psychotropic substance';

(b) clause (viia) shall be relettered as clause (viid) and before clause (viid) as so relettered, the following clauses shall be inserted, namely:- '(viia) "commercial quantity", in relation to narcotic drugs and psychotropic substances, means any quantity greater than the quantity specified by the Central Government by notification in the Official Gazette;

(viib) "controlled delivery" means the technique of allowing illicit or suspect consignments of narcotic drugs, psychotropic substances, controlled substances or substances substituted for them to pass out of, or through or into the territory of India with the knowledge and under the supervision of an officer empowered in this behalf or duly authorised under Section 50A with a view to identifying the persons involved in the commission of an offence under this Act;

(viic) "corresponding law" means any law corresponding to the provisions of this Act';

(c) after clause (xxiii), the following clause shall be inserted, namely:- '(xxiiia) "small quantity", in relation to narcotic drugs and psychotropic substances, means any quantity lesser than the quantity specified by the Central Government by notification in the Official Gazette'.

4. Amendment of Section 7A. In Section 7A of the principal Act, for sub-sections (2) and (3), the following sub-sections shall be substituted, namely:-

"(2) The Fund shall be applied by the Central Government to meet the expenditure incurred in connection with the measures taken for-

(a) combating illicit traffic in narcotic drugs, psychotropic substances or controlled substances;

(b) controlling the abuse of narcotic drugs and psychotropic substances;

(c) identifying, treating, rehabilitating addicts;

(d) preventing drug abuse;

(e) educating public against drug abuse; and

(f) supplying drugs to addicts where such supply is a medical necessity.

(3) The Central Government may constitute a Governing Body as it thinks fit to advise that Government and to sanction money out of the said Fund subject to the limit notified by the Central Government in the Official Gazette.".

5. Insertion of new Section 8A. After Section 8 of the principal Act, the following Section shall be inserted, namely:-

"8A. Prohibition of certain activities relating to property derived from offence. No person shall-

(a) convert or transfer any property knowing that such property is derived from an offence committed under this Act or under any other corresponding law of any other country or from an act of participation in such offence, for the purpose of concealing or disguising the illicit origin of the property or to assist any person in the commission of an offence or to evade the legal consequences; or

(b) conceal or disguise the true nature, source, location, disposition of any property knowing that such property is derived from an offence committed under this Act or under any other corresponding law of any other country; or

(c) knowingly acquire, possess or use any property which was derived from an offence committed under this Act or under any other corresponding law of any other country.'.

6. Substitution of new Sections for Sections 15 to 18. For Sections 15 to 18 of the principal Act, the following Sections shall be substituted, namely:-

"15. Punishment for contravention in relation to poppy straw. Whoever, in contravention of any provisions of this Act or any rule or order made or condition of a licence granted thereunder, produces, possesses, transports, imports inter-state, exports inter-state, sells, purchases, uses or omits to warehouse poppy straw or removes or does any act in respect of warehoused poppy straw shall be punishable,-

(a) where the contravention involves small quantity, with rigorous imprisonment for a term which may extend to six months, or with fine which may extend to ten thousand rupees, or with both;

(b) where the contravention involves quantity lesser than commercial quantity but greater than small quantity, with rigorous imprisonment for a term which may extend to ten years, and with fine which may extend to one lakh rupees;

(c) where the contravention involves commercial quantity, with rigorous imprisonment for a term which shall not be less than ten years but which may extend to twenty years, and shall also be liable to fine which shall not be less than one lakh rupees but which may extend to two lakh rupees:

PROVIDED that the court may, for reasons to be recorded in the judgment, impose a fine exceeding two lakh rupees.

16. Punishment for contravention in relation to coca plant and coca leaves. Whoever, in contravention of any provision of this Act or any rule or order made or condition of licence granted thereunder, cultivates any coca plant or gathers any portion of a coca plant or produces, possesses, sells, purchases, transports, imports inter-state, exports inter-state or uses coca leaves shall be punishable with rigorous imprisonment for a term which may extend to ten years, and with fine which may extend to one lakh rupees.

17. Punishment for contravention in relation to prepared opium. Whoever, in contravention of any provision of this Act or any rule or order made or condition of licence granted thereunder, manufactures, possesses, sells, purchases, transports, imports inter-state, exports inter-state or uses prepared opium shall be punishable-

(a) where the contravention involves small quantity, with rigorous imprisonment for a term which may extend to six months, or with fine which may extend to ten thousand rupees, or with both; or

(b) where the contravention involves quantity lesser than commercial quantity but greater than small quantity, with rigorous imprisonment for a term which may extend to ten years, and with fine which may extend to one lakh rupees; or

(c) where the contravention involves commercial quantity, with rigorous imprisonment for a term which shall not be less than ten years but which may extend to twenty years, and shall also be liable to fine which shall not be less than one lakh rupees but which may extend to two lakh rupees:

PROVIDED that the court may, for reasons to be recorded in the judgment, impose a fine exceeding two lakh rupees.

18. Punishment for contravention in relation to opium poppy and opium. Whoever, in contravention of any provision of this Act or any rule or order made or condition of licence granted thereunder, cultivates the opium poppy or produces, manufactures, possesses, sells, purchases, transports, imports inter-state, exports inter-state or uses opium shall be punishable,-

(a) where the contravention involves small quantity, with rigorous imprisonment for a term which may extend to six months, or with fine which may extend to ten thousand rupees, or with both;

(b) where the contravention involves commercial quantity, with rigorous imprisonment for a term which shall not be less than ten years but which may extend to twenty years, and shall also be liable to fine which shall not be less than one lakh rupees which may extend to two lakh rupees:

PROVIDED that the court may, for reasons to be recorded in the judgment, impose a fine exceeding two lakh rupees;

(c) in any other case, with rigorous imprisonment which may extend to ten years and with fine which may extend to one lakh rupees."

7. Amendment of Section 20. In Section 20 of the principal Act, in clause (b), for sub-clauses (i) and (ii), the following sub-clauses shall be substituted, namely:-

"(i) where such contravention relates to clause (a) with rigorous imprisonment for a term which may extend to ten years, and shall also be liable to fine which may extend to one lakh rupees; and (ii) where such contravention relates to sub-clause (b),-

(A) and involves small quantity, with rigorous imprisonment for a term which may extend to six months, or with fine which may extend to ten thousand rupees, or with both;

(B) and involves quantity lesser than commercial quantity but greater than small quantity, with rigorous imprisonment for a term which may extend to ten years, and with fine which may extend to one lakh rupees;

(C) and involves commercial quantity, with rigorous imprisonment for a term which shall not be less than ten years which may extend to twenty years and shall also be liable to fine which shall not be less than one lakh rupees but which may extend to two lakh rupees:

PROVIDED that the court may, for reasons to be recorded in the judgment, impose a fine exceeding two lakh rupees.".

8. Substitution of new Sections for Sections 21 to 23. For Sections 21 to 23 of the principal Act, the following Sections shall be substituted, namely:-

"21. Punishment for contravention in relation to manufactured drugs and preparations. Whoever, in contravention of any provision of this Act or any rule or order made or condition of licence granted thereunder, manufactures, possesses, sells, purchases, transports, imports inter-state, exports inter-state or uses any manufactured drug or any preparation containing any manufactured drug shall be punishable :-

(a) where the contravention involves small quantity, with rigorous imprisonment for a term which may extend to six months, or with fine which may extend to ten thousand rupees, or with both;

(b) where the contravention involves quantity, lesser than commercial quantity but greater than small quantity, with rigorous imprisonment for a term which may extend to ten years, and with fine which may extend to one lakh rupees;

(c) where the contravention involves commercial quantity, with rigorous imprisonment for a term which shall not be less than ten years but which may extend to twenty years, and shall also be liable to fine which shall not be less than one lakh rupees but which may extend to two lakh rupees:

PROVIDED that the court may, for reasons to be recorded in the judgment, impose a fine exceeding two lakh rupees.

22. Punishment for contravention in relation to psychotropic substances. Whoever, in contravention of any provision of this Act or any rule or order made or condition of licence granted thereunder, manufacturers, possesses, sells, purchases, transports, imports inter-state, exports inter-state or uses any psychotropic substance shall be punishable,-

(a) where the contravention involves small quantity, with rigorous imprisonment for a term which may extend to six months, or with fine which may extend to ten thousand rupees, or with both;

(b) where the contravention involves quantity, lesser than commercial quantity but greater than small quantity, with rigorous imprisonment for a term which may extend to ten years, and with fine which may extend to one lakh rupees;

(c) where the contravention involves commercial quantity, with rigorous imprisonment for a term which shall not be less than ten years but which may extend to twenty years, and shall also be liable to fine which shall not be less than one lakh rupees but which may extend to two lakh rupees:

PROVIDED that the court may, for reasons to be recorded in the judgment, impose a fine exceeding two lakh rupees.

23. Punishment for illegal import into India, export from India or transhipment of narcotic drugs and psychotropic substances. Whoever, in contravention of any provision of this Act or any rule or order made or condition of licence or permit granted or certificate or authorisation issued thereunder, imports into India or exports from India or transships any narcotic drug or psychotropic substance shall be punishable,-

(a) where the contravention involves small quantity, with rigorous imprisonment for a term which may extend to six months, or with fine which may extend to ten thousand rupees, or with both;

(b) where the contravention involves quantity, lesser than commercial quantity but greater than small quantity, with rigorous imprisonment for a term which may extend to ten years, and with fine which may extend to one lakh rupees;

(c) where the contravention involves commercial quantity, with rigorous imprisonment for a term which shall not be less than ten years but which may extend to twenty years, and shall also be liable to fine which shall not be less than one lakh rupees but which may extend to two lakh rupees:

PROVIDED that the court may, for reasons to be recorded in the judgment, impose a fine exceeding two lakh rupees.".

9. Substitution of new Section for Section 25. For Section 25 of the principal Act, the following Section shall be substituted, namely:-

"25. Punishment for allowing premises, etc., to be used for commission of an offence. Whoever, being the owner or occupier or having the control or use of any house, room, enclosure, space, place, animal or conveyance, knowingly permits it to be used for the commission by any other person of an offence punishable under any provision of this Act, shall be punishable with the punishment provided for that offence."

10. Substitution of new Section for Section 27. For Section 27 of the principal Act, the following Section shall be substituted, namely:-

"27. Punishment for consumption of any narcotic drug or psychotropic substance. Whoever consumes any narcotic drug or psychotropic substance shall be punishable,-

(a) where the narcotic drug or psychotropic substance consumed is cocaine, morphine, diacetyl-morphine or any other narcotic drug or any psychotropic substance as may be specified in this behalf by the Central Government by notification in the Official Gazette, with rigorous imprisonment for a term which may extend to one year, or with fine which may extend to twenty thousand rupees, or with both; and

(b) where the narcotic drug or psychotropic substance consumed is other than those specified in or under clause (a), with imprisonment for a term which may extend to six months, or with fine which may extend to ten thousand rupees, or with both.".

11. Amendment of Section 30. In Section 30 of the principal Act, for the words, figures and brackets" Section 15 to Section 25 (both inclusive) and from the circumstances of the case", the words, figures and letter" Sections 19, 24 and 27A and for offences involving commercial quantity of any narcotic drug or psychotropic substance and from the circumstances of the case" shall be substituted.

12. Substitution of new Section for Section 31. For Section 31 of the principal Act, the following Section shall be substituted, namely:-

"31. Enhanced punishment for offences after previous conviction.

(1) If any person who has been convicted of the commission of, or attempt to commit, or abetment of, or criminal conspiracy to commit, any of the offences punishable under this Act is subsequently convicted of the commission of, or

attempt to commit, or abetment of, or criminal conspiracy to commit, an offence punishable under this Act with the same amount of punishment shall be punished for the second and every subsequent offence with rigorous imprisonment for a term which may extend to one-half of the maximum term of imprisonment, and also be liable to fine which shall extend to one-half of the maximum amount of fine.

(2) Where the person referred to in sub-section (1) is liable to be punished with a minimum term of imprisonment and to a minimum amount of fine, the minimum punishment for such person shall be one-half of the minimum term of imprisonment and one-half of the minimum amount of fine:

PROVIDED that the court may, for reasons to be recorded in the judgment, impose a fine exceeding the fine for which a person is liable.

(3) Where any person is convicted by a competent court of criminal jurisdiction outside India under any corresponding law, such person, in respect of such conviction, shall be dealt with for the purposes of sub-sections (1) and (2) as if he had been convicted by a court in India.".

13. Amendment of Section 31A. In Section 31A of the principal Act,-

(a) in sub-section (1),-

(i) for the words, figures, brackets and letter "Section 15 to Section 25 (both inclusive) or Section 27A", the words, figures and letter "Section 19, Section 24, Section 27A and for offences involving commercial quantity of any narcotic drug or psychotropic substance" shall be substituted;

(ii) in sub-clause (a), in the Table, in column (2), against entry (viii), for the figures and word "1, 500 grams", the words "lesser of the quantity between the quantities given against the respective narcotic drugs or psychotropic substances mentioned above forming part of the mixture" shall be substituted;

(b) in sub-section (2), for the words, figures, brackets and letter "Section 15 to Section 25 (both inclusive), Section 27A, Section 28 or Section 29", the words, figures and letter "Section 19, Section 24 or Section 27A and for offences involving commercial quantity of any narcotic drug or psychotropic substance" shall be substituted.

14. Insertion of new Section 32B. After Section 32A of the principal Act, the following Section shall be inserted, namely:-

"32B. Factors to be taken into account for imposing higher than the minimum punishment. Where a minimum term of imprisonment or amount of fine is prescribed for any offence committed under this Act, the court may, in addition to such factors as it may deem fit, take into account the following factors for imposing a punishment higher than the minimum term of imprisonment or amount of fine, namely:-

(a) the use or threat of use of violence or arms by the offender;

(b) the fact that the offender holds a public office and that he has taken advantage of that office in committing the offence;

(c) the fact that the minors are affected by the offence or the minors are used for the commission of an offence;

(d) the fact that the offence is committed in an educational institution or social service facility or in the immediate vicinity of such institution or faculty or in other place to which school children and students resort for educational, sports and social activities;

(e) the fact that the offender belongs to organised international or any other criminal group which is involved in the commission of the offence; and

(f) the fact that the offender is involved in other illegal activities facilitated by commission of the offence."

15. Substitution of new Section for Section 36A. For Section 36A of the principal Act, the following Section shall be substituted, namely:-

"36A. Offences triable by Special Courts.

(1) Notwithstanding anything contained in the Code of Criminal Procedure, 1973 (2 of 1974) -

(a) all offences under this Act which are punishable with imprisonment for a term of more than three years shall be triable only by the Special Court constituted for the area in which the offence has been committed or where there are more Special Courts than one for such area, by such one of them as may be specified in this behalf by the Government;

(b) where a person accused of or suspected of the commission of an offence under this Act is forwarded to a Magistrate under sub-section (2) or sub-section (2A) of Section 167 of the Code of Criminal Procedure, 1973 (2 of 1974), such Magistrate may authorise the detention of such person in such custody as he thinks fit for a period not exceeding fifteen days in the whole where such Magistrate is a Judicial Magistrate and seven days in the whole where such Magistrate is an Executive Magistrate:

PROVIDED that in cases which are triable by the Special Court where such Magistrate considers-

(i) when such person is forwarded to him as aforesaid; or

(ii) upon or at any time before the expiry of the period of detention authorised by him, that the detention of such person is unnecessary, he shall order such person to be forwarded to the Special Court having jurisdiction;

(c) the Special Court may exercise, in relation to the person forwarded to it under clause (b), the same power which a Magistrate having jurisdiction to try a case may exercise under Section 167 of the Code of Criminal Procedure, 1973 (2 of 1974), in relation to an accused person in such case who has been forwarded to him under that Section;

(d) a Special Court may, upon perusal of police report of the facts constituting an offence under this Act or upon complaint made by an officer of the

Central Government or a State Government authorised in this behalf, take cognizance of that offence without the accused being committed to it for trial.

(2) When trying an offence under this Act, a Special Court may also try an offence other than an offence under this Act with which the accused may, under the Code of Criminal Procedure, 1973 (2 of 1974), be charged at the same trial.

(3) Nothing contained in this Section shall be deemed to affect the special powers of the High Court regarding bail under Section 439 of the Code of Criminal Procedure, 1973 (2 of 1974), and the High Court may exercise such powers including the power under clause (b) of sub-section (1) of that Section as if the reference to "Magistrate" in that Section included also a reference to a "Special Court" constituted under Section 36.

(4) In respect of persons accused of an offence punishable under Section 19 or Section 24 or Section 27A or for offences involving commercial quantity the references in sub-section (2) of Section 167 of the Code of Criminal Procedure, 1973 (2 of 1974) thereof to "ninety days", where they occur, shall be construed as reference to "one hundred and eighty days":

PROVIDED that, if it is not possible to complete the investigation within the said period of one hundred and eighty days, the Special Court may extend the said period up to one year on the report of the Public Prosecutor indicating the progress of the investigation and the specific reasons for the detention of the accused beyond the said period of one hundred and eighty days.

(5) Notwithstanding anything contained in the Code of Criminal Procedure, 1973 (2 of 1974), the offences punishable under this Act with imprisonment for a term of not more than three years may be tried summarily'.

16. Substitution of new Section for Section 36D. For Section 36D of the principal Act, the following Section shall be substituted, namely:-

"36D. Transitional provisions.

(1) Any offence committed under this Act on or after the commencement of the Narcotic Drugs and Psychotropic Substances (Amendment) Act, 1988 (2 of 1989), which is triable by a Special Court shall, until a Special Court is constituted under Section 36, notwithstanding anything contained in the Code of Criminal Procedure, 1973 (2 of 1974), be tried by a Court of Session.

(2) Where any proceedings in relation to any offence committed under this Act on or after the commencement of the Narcotic Drugs and Psychotropic Substances (Amendment) Act, 1988 (2 of 1989) are pending before a Court of Session, then, notwithstanding anything contained in sub-section (1), such proceeding shall be heard and disposed of by the Court of Session:

PROVIDED that nothing contained in this sub-section shall affect the power of the High Court under Section 407 of the Code of Criminal Procedure, 1973 (2 of 1974) to transfer any case or class of cases taken cognizance by a Court of Session under sub-section (1)."

17. Amendment of Section 37. In Section 37 of the principal Act, in sub-section 1, in clause (b), for the words "a term of imprisonment of five years or more under this Act", the words, figures and letter "offences under Section 19 or Section 24 or Section 27A and also for offences involving commercial quantity" shall be substituted.

18. Amendment of Section 39. In Section 39 of the principal Act, in sub-section 1, after the words and figures "under Section 27", the words "or for offences relating to small quantity of any narcotic drug or psychotropic substance" shall be inserted.

19. Substitution of new Sections for Section 41 to 43. For Sections 41 to 43 of the principal Act, the following Sections shall be substituted, namely:-

"41. Power to issue warrant and authorisation.

(1) A Metropolitan Magistrate or a Magistrate of the first class or any Magistrate of the second class specially empowered by the State Government in this behalf, may issue a warrant for the arrest of any person whom he has reason to believe to have committed any offence punishable under this Act, or for the search, whether by day or by night, of any building, conveyance or place in which he has reason to believe any narcotic drug or psychotropic substance or controlled substance in respect of which an offence punishable under this Act has been committed or any document or other article which may furnish evidence of the commission of such offence or any illegally acquired property or any document or other article which may furnish evidence of holding any illegally acquired property which is liable for seizure or freezing or forfeiture under Chapter VA of this Act is kept or concealed.

(2) Any such officer of Gazetted rank of the departments of central excise, narcotics, customs, revenue, intelligence or any other department of the Central Government including the para-military forces or the armed forces as is empowered in this behalf by general or special order by the Central Government, or any such officer of the revenue, drugs control, excise, police or any other department of a State Government as if empowered in this behalf by general or special order of the State Government if he has reason to believe from personal knowledge or information given by any person and taken in writing that any person has committed an offence punishable under this Act or that any narcotic drug or psychotropic substance or controlled substance in respect of which any offence under this Act has been committed or any document or other article which may furnish evidence of the commission of such offence or any illegally acquired property or any document or other article which may furnish evidence of holding any illegally acquired property which is liable for seizure or freezing or forfeiture under Chapter VA of this Act is kept or concealed in any building, conveyance or place, may authorise any officer subordinate to him but superior in rank to a peon, sepoy or a constable to arrest such a person or search a building, conveyance or place whether by day or by night or himself arrest such a person or search a building, conveyance or place.

(3) The officer to whom a warrant under sub-section (1) is addressed and the officer who authorised the arrest or search or the officer who is so authorised under sub-section (2) shall have all the powers of an officer acting under Section 42.

42. Power of entry, search, seizure and arrest without warrant or authorisation.

(1) Any such officer (being an officer superior in rank to a peon, sepoy or constable) of the departments of central excise, narcotics, customs, revenue, intelligence or any other department of the Central Government including para-military or armed forces as is empowered in this behalf by general or special order by the Central Government, or any such officer (being an officer superior in rank to a peon, sepoy or constable) of the revenue, drugs control, excise, police or any other department of a State Government as is empowered in this behalf by general knowledge or information given by any person and taken down in writing that any narcotic drug, or psychotropic substance, or controlled substance in respect of which an offence punishable under this Act has been committed or any document or other article which may furnish evidence of the commission of such offence or any illegally acquired property or any document or other article which may furnish evidence of holding any illegally acquired property which is liable for seizure or freezing or forfeiture under Chapter VA of this Act is kept or concealed in any building, conveyance or enclosed place, may between sunrise and subset -

- (a) enter into and search any such building, conveyance or place;
- (b) in case of resistance, break open any door and remove any obstacle to such entry;
- (c) seize such drug or substance and all materials used in the manufacture thereof and any other article and any animal or conveyance which he has reason to believe to be liable to confiscation under this Act and any document or other article which he has reason to believe may furnish evidence of the commission of any offence punishable under this Act or furnish evidence of holding any illegally acquired property which is liable for seizure or freezing or forfeiture under Chapter VA of this Act; and
- (d) detail and search, and, if he thinks proper, arrest any person whom he has reason to believe to have committed any offence punishable under this Act:

PROVIDED that if such officer has reason to believe that a search warrant or authorisation cannot be obtained without affording opportunity for the concealment of evidence or facility for the escape of an offender, he may enter and search such building, conveyance or enclosed place at any time between sunset and sunrise after recording the grounds of his belief.

(2) Where an officer takes down any information in writing under sub-section (1) or records grounds for his belief under the proviso thereto, he shall within seventy-two hours send a copy thereof to his immediate official superior.

43. Power of seizure and arrest in public place. Any officer of any of the departments mentioned in Section 42 may-

(a) seize in any public place or in transit, any narcotic drug or psychotropic substance or controlled substance in respect of which he has reason to believe an offence punishable under this Act has been committed, and, along with such drug or substance, any animal or conveyance or article liable to confiscation under this Act, any document or other article which he has reason to believe may furnish evidence of the commission of an offence punishable under this Act or any document or other article which may furnish evidence of holding any illegally acquired property which is liable for seizure or freezing or forfeiture under Chapter VA of this Act;

(b) detain and search any person whom he has reason to believe to have committed an offence punishable under this Act, and if such person has any narcotic drug or psychotropic substance or controlled substance in his possession and such possession appears to him to be unlawful, arrest him and any other person in his company.

EXPLANATION. For the purposes of this Section, the expression "public place" includes any public conveyance, hotel, shop, or other place intended for use by, or accessible to, the public.'.

20. Amendment of Section 44. In Section 44 of the principal Act, after the words "psychotropic substance", the words "or controlled substance" shall be inserted.

21. Amendment of Section 49. In Section 49 of the principal Act, after sub-section (4), the following sub-sections shall be inserted, namely:-

"(5) When an officer duly authorised under Section 42 has reason to believe that it is not possible to take the person to be searched to the nearest Gazetted Officer or Magistrate without the possibility of the person to be searched parting with possession of any narcotic drug or psychotropic substance, or controlled substance or article or document, he may, instead of taking such person to the nearest Gazetted Officer or Magistrate, proceed to search the person as provided under Section 100 of the Code of Criminal Procedure, 1973 (2 of 1974).

(6) After a search is conducted under sub-section (5), the officer shall record the reasons for such belief which necessitated such search and within seventy-two hours send a copy thereof to his immediate official superior."

23. Insertion of new Section 50A. After Section 50 of the principal Act, the following Section shall be inserted, namely:-

"50A. Power to undertake controlled delivery. The Director General of Narcotics Control Bureau constituted under sub-section (3) of Section 4 or any other officer authorised by him in this behalf, may, notwithstanding anything contained in this Act, undertake controlled delivery of any consignment to-

(a) any destination in India;

(b) a foreign country, in consultation with the competent authority of such foreign country to which such consignment is destined, in such manner as may be prescribed."

24. Amendment of Section 53. In Section 53 of the principal Act,-

(a) in sub-section (1), for the words "or Border Security Force", the words "or any other department of the Central Government including para-military forces or armed forces" shall be substituted;

(b) in sub-section (2), after the word "excise", the words "or any other department" shall be inserted.

25. Substitution of new Section for Section 54. For Section 54 of the principal Act, the following Section shall be substituted, namely:-

"**54. Presumption from possession of illicit articles.** In trials under this Act, it may be presumed, unless and until the contrary is proved, that the accused has committed an offence under this Act in respect of-

(a) any narcotic drug or psychotropic substance or controlled substance;

(b) any opium poppy, cannabis plant or coca plant growing on any land which he has cultivated;

(c) any apparatus specially designed or any group of utensils specially adopted for the manufacture of any narcotic drug or psychotropic substance or controlled substance; or

(d) any materials which have undergone any process towards the manufacture of a narcotic drug or psychotropic substance or controlled substance, or any residue left of the materials from which any narcotic drug or psychotropic substance or controlled substance has been manufactured, for the possession of which he fails to account satisfactorily."

26. Amendment of Section 60. In Section 60 of the principal Act,-

(a) for sub-section (1), the following sub-section shall be substituted, namely:-"(1) Whenever any offence punishable under this Act has been committed, the narcotic drug, psychotropic substance, controlled substance, opium poppy, coca plant, cannabis plant, materials, apparatus and utensils in respect of which or by means of which such offence has been committed, shall be liable to confiscation.";

(b) in sub-sections (2) and (3), after the words "psychotropic substance", wherever they occur, the words "or controlled substances" shall be inserted.

27. Amendment of Section 61. In Section 61 of the principal Act, for the words "narcotic drug or psychotropic substance", the words "narcotic drug, psychotropic substance or controlled substance" shall be substituted.

28. Amendment of Section 62. In Section 62 of the principal Act, for the words "narcotic drug or psychotropic substance", the words "narcotic drug, psychotropic substance or controlled substance" shall be substituted.

29. Amendment of Section 63. In Section 63 of the principal Act,-

(a) in sub-section (2), in the second proviso, after the words "psychotropic substance", the words "controlled substance" shall be inserted;

(b) sub-section (3) shall be omitted.

30. Substitution of new Section for Section 64A. For Section 64A of the principal Act, the following Section shall be substituted, namely:-

"**64A. Immunity from prosecution to addicts volunteering for treatment.** Any addict, who is charged with an offence punishable under Section 27 or with offences involving small quantity of narcotic drugs or psychotropic substances, who voluntarily seeks to undergo medical treatment for de-addiction from a hospital or an institution maintained or recognised by the Government or a local authority and undergoes such treatment shall not be liable to prosecution under Section 27 or under any other Section for offences involving small quantity of narcotic drugs or psychotropic substances:

> *PROVIDED that the said immunity from prosecution may be withdrawn if the addict does not undergo the complete treatment for de-addiction.".*

31. Amendment of Section 68A. In Section 68A of the principal Act, in sub-section (2),-

(i) in clause (a), for the word "five", the word "ten" shall be substituted;

(ii) after clause (c), the following clause shall be inserted, namely:- "(cc) every person who has been arrested or against whom a warrant or authorisation of arrest has been issued for the commission of an offence punishable under this Act with imprisonment for a term of ten years or more, and every person who has been arrested or against whom a warrant or authorisation of arrest has been issued for the commission of a similar offence under any corresponding law of any other country;"

(iii) in clauses (d), (e) and (f), after the word, brackets and letter "clause (c)", the words, brackets and letters "or clause (cc)" shall be inserted.

32. Amendment of Section 68B. In Section 68B of the principal Act, in clause (g), in sub-clause (i), for the words "illicit traffic", the words "the contravention of any provisions of this Act" shall be substituted.

33. Amendment of Section 68C. In Section 68C of the principal Act, in sub-section (2), for the proviso, the following proviso shall be substituted, namely:-

> *"PROVIDED that no property shall be forfeited under this Chapter if such property was acquired, by a person to whom this Act applies, before a period of six years from the date he was arrested or against whom a warrant or authorisation of arrest has been issued for the commission of an offence punishable under this Act or from the date the order or detention was issued, as the case may be."*

34. Amendment of Section 68E. In Section 68E of the principal Act, for sub-section 1, the following sub-section shall be substituted, namely:-"(1) Every officer empowered under Section 53 and every officer-in-charge of a police station shall, on receipt of information is satisfied that any person to whom this Chapter applies holds any illegally acquired property, he may, after recording reasons for doing so, proceed to take all steps necessary for tracing and identifying such property."

36. Amendment of Section 68-I. In Section 68-I of the principal Act, after sub-section (3), the following proviso shall be inserted, at the end, namely:-

> *"PROVIDED that no illegally acquired property of any person who is referred to in clause (cc) of sub-section (2) of Section 68A or relative of a person referred to in that clause or associate of a person referred to in that clause or holder of any property which was at any time previously held by a person referred to in that clause shall stand forfeited."*

37. Amendment of Section 68-O. In Section 68-O of the principal Act, in sub-section (1), for the words "Any person aggrieved by an order of the competent authority", the words, brakets, figures and letter "Any officer referred to in sub-section (1)of Section 68E or any person aggrieved by an order of the competent authority" shall be substituted.

38. Insertion of new Section 68Z. After Section 68Y of the principal Act, the following Section shall be inserted, namely:-

"68Z. Release of property in certain cases.

(1) Where the detention order of a detenu is set aside or withdrawn, properties seized or frozen under this Chapter shall stand released.

(2) Where any person referred to in clause (a) or clause (b) or clause (cc) of sub-section (2) of Section 68A has been acquitted or discharged from the charges under this Act or any other corresponding law of any other country and the acquittal was not appealed against or when appealed against, the appeal was disposed of as a consequence of which such property could not be forfeited or warrant of arrest or authorisation of arrest issued against such person has been withdrawn, then, property seized or frozen under this Chapter shall stand released."

39. Amendment of Section 76. In Section 76 of the principal Act, in sub-section (2), after clause (c), the following clause shall be inserted, namely:-"(ca) the manner in which" controlled delivery" under Section 50A is to be undertaken."

40. Amendment of Section 77. In Section 77 of the principal Act, for the portion beginning with the words "Every rule made under this Act" and ending with "shall be laid, as soon as may be, after it is made or issued", the following shall be substituted, namely:- "Every rule made under this Act by the Central Government and every notification or order issued under clause (viia), clause (xi), clause (xxiiia) of Section 2, Section 3, Section 7A, Section 9A and clause (a) of Section 27 shall be laid, as soon as may be, after it is made or issued".

41. Application of this Act to pending cases.

(1) Notwithstanding anything contained in sub-section (2) of Section 1, all cases pending before the courts or under investigation at the commencement of this Act shall be disposed of in accordance with the provisions of the principal Act as amended by this Act and accordingly, any person found guilty of any offence punishable under the principal Act, as it stood immediately before such commencement, shall be liable for a punishment which is lesser than the punishment for which he is otherwise liable at the date of the commission of such offence:

PROVIDED that nothing in this Section shall apply to cases pending in appeal.

(2) For the removal of doubts, it is hereby declared that no act or omission on the part of any person shall be punishable as an offence which would not have been so punishable if this Act has not come into force.

❑❑❑

18

The Narcotic Drugs and Psychotropic Substances Act, 1985

Act No. 61 of 1985 [16th September, 1985]

AN ACT to consolidate and amend the law relating to narcotic drugs, to make stringent provisions for the control and regulation of operations relating to narcotic drugs and psychotropic substances 1 to provide for the forfeiture of property derived from, or used in, illicit traffic in narcotic drugs and psychotropic substances, to implement the provisions of the International Conventions on Narcotic Drugs and Psychotropic Substances and for matters connected therewith.

Be it enacted by Parliament in the Thirty-sixth Year of the Republic of India as follows:—

CHAPTER - I : PRELIMINARY

1. Short title, extent and commencement.

(1) This Act may be called the Narcotic Drugs and Psychotropic Substances Act, 1985.

(2) It extends to the whole of India.

(3) It shall come into force on such date as the Central Government may, by notification in the Official Gazette, appoint, and different dates may be appointed for different provisions of this Act and for different States and any reference in any such provision to the commencement of this Act shall be construed in relation to any State as a reference to the coming into force of that provision in that State.

2. Definitions. In this Act, unless the context otherwise requires,—

(i) "addict" means a person addicted to any narcotic drug or psychotropic substance;

(ii) "Board" means the Central Board of Excise and Customs constituted under the Central Boards of Revenue Act, 1963 (54 of 1963),

(iii) "cannabis (hemp)" means—

(a) charas, that is, the separated resin, in whatever form, whether crude or purified, obtained from the cannabis plant and also includes concentrated preparation and resin known as hashish oil or liquid hashish;

(b) ganja, that is, the flowering or fruiting tops of the cannabis plant (excluding the seeds and leaves when not accompanied by the tops), by whatever name they may be known or designated; and any mixture, with or without any neutral material, of any of the above forms of cannabis or any drink prepared therefrom;

(iv) "cannabis plant" means any plant of the genus cannabis;

(v) "coca derivative" means—

(a) crude cocaine, that is, any extract of coca leaf which can be used, directly or indirectly, for the manufacture of cocaine;

(b) ecgonine and all the derivatives of ecgonine from which it can be recovered;

(c) cocaine, that is, methyl ester of benzoyl-ecgonine and its salts; and

(d) all preparations containing more than 0.1 percent of cocaine;

(vi) "coca leaf" means—

(a) the leaf of the coca plant except a leaf from which all ecgonine, cocaine and any other ecgonine alkaloids have been removed;

(b) any mixture thereof with or without any neutral material, out does not include any preparation containing not more than 0.1 percent of cocaine;

(vii) "coca plant" means the plant of any species of the genus Frythroxylon;

(viia) "controlled substance" means any substance which the Central Government may, having regard to the available information as to its possible use in the production or manufacture of narcotic drugs or psychotropic substances or to the provisions of any International Convention, by notification in the Official Gazette, declare to be a controlled substance,

(viii) "conveyance" means a conveyance of any description whatsoever and includes any aircraft, vehicle or vessel;

(viiia) "illicit traffic", in relation to narcotic drugs and psychotropic substances, means—

(i) cultivating any coca plant or gathering any portion of caca plant;

(ii) cultivating the opium poppy or any cannabis plant;

(iii) engaging in the production, manufacture, possession, sale, purchase, transportation, warehousing, concealment, use or consumption, import inter-state, export inter-state, import into India, export from India or transhipment, of narcotic drugs or psychotropic substances;

(iv) dealing in any activities in narcotic drugs or psychotropic substances other than those referred to in sub-clauses (i) to (ii); or

(v) handling or letting out any premises for the carrying on of any of the activities referred to in sub-clauses (i) to (iv), other than those permitted under this Act, or any rule or order made, or any condition of any licence, term or authorisation issued, thereunder, and includes—

(1) financing, directly or indirectly, any of the aforementioned activities;

(2) abetting or conspiring in the furtherance of or in support of doing any of the aforementioned activities; and

(3) harbouring persons engaged in any of the aforementioned activities;'

(ix) "International Convention" means—

(a) the Single Convention on Narcotic Drugs, 1961 adopted by the United Nations Conference at New York in March, 1961 ;

(b) the Protocol, amending the Convention mentioned in sub-clause (a), adopted by the United Nations Conference at Geneva in March, 1972 ;

(c) the Convention on Psychotropic Substances, 1971 adopted by the United Nations Conference at Vienna in February, 1971 ; and

(d) any other international convention, or protocol or other instrument amending an international convention, relating to narcotic drugs or psychotropic substances which may be ratified or acceded to by India after the commencement of this Act;

(x) "manufacture", in relation to narcotic drugs or psychotropic substances, includes—

(1) all processes other than production by which such drugs or substances may be obtained;

(2) refining of such drugs or substances;

(3) transformation of such drugs or substances; and

(4) making of preparation (otherwise than in a pharmacy on prescription) with or containing such drugs or substances;

(xi) "manufactured drug" means—

(a) all coca derivatives, medicinal cannabis, opium derivatives and poppy straw concentrate;

(b) any other narcotic substance or preparation which the Central Government may, having regard to the available information as to its nature or to a decision, if any, under any International Convention, by notification in the Official Gazette, declare not to be a manufactured drug;

(xii) "medicinal cannabis", that is, medicinal hemp, means any extract or tincture of cannabis (hemp);

(xiii) "Narcotics Commissioner" means the Narcotics Commissioner appointed under Section 5;

(xiv) "narcotic drug" means coca leaf, cannabis (hemp), opium, popy straw and includes all manufactured drugs;

(xv) "opium" means—

(a) the coagulated juice of the opium poppy; and

(b) any mixture, with or without any neutral material, of the coagulated juice of the opium poppy, but does not include any preparation containing not more than 0.2 percent of morphine;

(xvi) "opium derivative" means—

(a) medicinal opium, that is, opium which has undergone the processes necessary to adapt it for medicinal use in accordance with the requirements of the Indian Pharmacopoeia or any other pharmacopoeia notified in this behalf by the Central Government, whether in powder form or granulated or otherwise or mixed with neutral materials;

(b) prepared opium, that is, any product of opium obtained by any series of operations designed to transform opium into an extract suitable for smoking and the dross or other residue remaining after opium is smoked;

(c) phenanthrene alkaloids, namely, morphine, codeine, thebaine and their salts;

(d) diacetylmorphine, that is, the alkaloid also known as dia-morphine or heroin and its salts; and

(e) all preparations containing more than 0.2 percent of morphine or containing any diacetylmorphine;

(xvii) "opium poppy" means—

(a) the plant of the species Papaver somniferum L; and

(b) the plant of any other species of Papaver from which opium or any phenanthrene alkaloid can be extracted and which the Central Government may, by notification in the Official Gazette, declare to be opium poppy for the purposes of this Act;

(xviii) "poppy straw" means all parts (except the seeds) of the opium poppy after harvesting whether in their original form or cut, crushed or powdered and whether or not juice has been extracted therefrom;

(xix) "poppy straw concentrate" means the material arising when poppy straw has entered into a process for the concentration of its alkaloids;

(xx) "preparation", in relation to a narcotic drug or psychotropic substance, means any one or more such drugs or substances in dosage form or any solution or mixture, in whatever physical state, containing one or more such drugs or substances;

(xxi) "Prescribed" means prescribed by rules made under this Act;

(xxii) "production" means separation of opium, poppy straw, coca leaves or cannabis from the plants from which they are obtained;

(xxiii) "Psychotropic substance" means any substance, natural or synthetic, or any natural material or any salt or preparation of such substance or material included in the list of psychotropic substances specified in the Schedule;

(xxiv) "to import inter-state" means to bring into a State or Union territory in India from another State or Union territory in India;

(xxv) "to import into India", with its grammatical variations and cognate expressions, means to bring into India from a place outside India and includes the bringing into any port or airport or place in India of a narcotic drug or a psychotropic substance intended to be taken out of India without being removed from the vessel, aircraft, vehicle or any other conveyance in which it is being carried.

EXPLANATION. For the purposes of this clause and clause (xxvi)," India" includes the territorial waters of India;

(xxvi) "to export from India", with its grammatical variations and cognate expressions, means to take out of India to a place outside India;

(xxvii) "to export inter-state" means to take out of a State or Union territory in India to another State or Union territory in India;

(xxviii) "to transport" means to take from one place to another within the same State or Union territory;

(xxviia) "use" in relation to narcotic drugs and psychotropic substances, means any kind of use except personal consumption;

(xxix) Words and expressions used herein and not defined but defined in the Code of Criminal Procedure, 1973 (2 of 1973) have the meanings respectively assigned to them in that Code.

EXPLANATION: For the purposes of clauses (v), (vi), (xv) and (xvi) the percentages in the case of liquid preparations shall be calculated on the basis that a preparation containing one per cent. of a substance means a preparation in which one gram of substance, if solid, or one mililitre of substance, if liquid, is contained in every one hundred mililitre of the preparation and so on in proportion for any greater or less percentage:

PROVIDED that the Central Government may, having regard to the developments in the field of methods of calculating percentages in liquid preparations prescribe, by rules, any other basis which it may deem appropriate for such calculation.

3. Power to add to or omit from the list of psychotropic substances. The Central Government may, if satisfied that it is necessary or expedient so to do on the basis of—

(a) the information and evidence which has become available to it with respect to the nature and effects of, and the abuse or the scope for abuse of, any substance (natural or synthetic) or natural material or any salt or preparation of such substance or material; and

(b) the modifications or provisions (if any) which have been made to, or in, any International Convention with respect to such substance, natural material or salt or preparation of such substance or material, by notification in the Official Gazette, add to, or, as the case may be, omit from, the list of psychotropic substances specified in the Schedule such substance or natural material or salt or preparation of such substance or material.

CHAPTER - II : AUTHORITIES AND OFFICERS

4. Central Government to take measures for preventing and combating abuse of and illicit traffic in narcotic drugs, etc.

(1) Subject to the provisions of this Act, the Central Government shall take all such measures as it deems necessary or expedient for the purpose of preventing and combating abuse of narcotic drugs and psychotropic substances and the illicit traffic therein.

(2) In particular and without prejudice to the generality of the provisions of sub-section (1), the measures which the Central Government may take under that sub-section include measures with respect to all or any of the following matters, namely:—

(a) coordination of actions by various officers, State Governments and other authorities—

(i) under this Act, or

(ii) under any other law for the time being in force in connection with the enforcement of the provisions of this Act;

(b) obligations under the International Conventions;

(c) assistance to the concerned authorities in foreign countries and concerned international organisations with a view to facilitating coordination and universal action for prevention and suppression of illicit traffic in narcotic drugs and psychotropic substances;

(d) identification, treatment, education, after care, rehabilitation and social re-integration of addicts;

(e) such other matters as the Central Government deems necessary or expedient for the purpose of securing the effective implementation of the provisions of this Act and preventing and combating the abuse of narcotic drugs and psychotropic substances and illicit traffic therein.

(3) The Central Government may, if it considers it necessary or expedient so to do for the purposes of this Act, by order, published in the Official Gazette, constitute an authority or a hierarchy of authorities by such name or names as may be specified in the order for the purpose of exercising such of the powers and functions of the Central Government under this Act and for taking measures with respect to such of the matters referred to in sub-section (2) as may be mentioned in the order, and subject to the supervision and control of the Central Government and the provisions of such order, such authority or authorities may exercise the powers and take the measures so mentioned in the order as

if such authority or authorities had been empowered by this Act to exercise those powers and take such measures.

5. Officers of Central Government.

(1) Without prejudice to the provisions of sub-section (3) of Section 4, the Central Government shall appoint a Narcotics Commissioner and may also appoint such other officers with such designations as it thinks fit for the purposes of this Act.

(2) The Narcotics Commissioner shall, either by himself or through officers subordinate to him, exercise all powers and perform all functions relating to the superintendence of the cultivation of the opium poppy and production of opium and shall also exercise and perform such other powers and functions as may be entrusted to him by the Central Government.

(3) The officers appointed under sub-section (1) shall be subject to the general control and direction of the Central Government, or, if so directed by that Government, also of the Board or any other authority or officer.

6. The Narcotic Drugs and Psychotropic Substances Consultative Committee.

(1) The Central Government may constitute, by notification in the Official Gazette, an advisory committee to be called "The Narcotic Drugs and Psychotropic Substances Consultative Committee" (hereafter in this Section referred to as the Committee) to advise the Central Government on such matters relating to the administration of this Act as are referred to it by that Government from time to time.

(2) The Committee shall consist of a Chairman and such other members, not exceeding twenty, as may be appointed by the Central Government.

(3) The Committee shall meet when required to do so by the Central Government and shall have power to regulate its own procedure.

(4) The Committee may, if it deems it necessary so to do for the efficient discharge of any of its functions, constitute one or more sub-committees and may appoint to any such sub-committee, whether generally or for the consideration of any particular matter, any person (including a non-official) who is not a member of the Committee.

(5) The term of office of, the manner of filling casual vacancies in the offices of and the allowances, if any, payable to, the Chairman and other members of the Committee, and the conditions and restrictions subject to which the Committee may appoint a person who is not a member of the Committee as a member of any of its sub-committees, shall be such as may be prescribed by rules made by the Central Government.

7. Officers of State Government.

(1) The State Government may appoint such officers with such designations as it thinks fit for the purposes of this Act.

(2) The officers appointed under sub-section (1) shall be subject to the general control and direction of the State Government, or, if so directed by that Government, also of any other authority or officer.

CHAPTER - IIA : NATIONAL FUND FOR CONTROL OF DRUG ABUSE

7A. National Fund for Control of Drug Abuse.

(1) The Central Government may, by notification in the Official Gazette, constitute a Fund to be called the National Fund for Control of Drug Abuse (hereafter in this Chapter referred to as the Fund) and there shall be credited thereto—

- (a) an amount which the Central Government may, after due appropriation made by Parliament by law in this behalf, provide;
- (b) the sale proceeds of any property forfeited under Chapter VA;
- (c) any grants that may be made by any person or institution;
- (d) any income from investment of the amounts credited to the Fund under the aforesaid provisions.

(2) The Fund shall be applied by the Central Government to meet the expenditure incurred in connection with the measures taken for combating illicit traffic in, or controlling abuse of, narcotic drugs and psychotropic substances for all or any of the purposes specified in sub-section (1) of Section 71.

(3) The Central Government may constitute a Governing Body as it thinks fit to advise that Government in regard to the application of the Fund.

(4) The Governing Body shall consist of a Chairman (not below the rank of an Additional Secretary to the Central Government) and such other members not exceeding six as the Central Government may appoint.

(5) The Governing Body shall have the power to regulate its own procedure.

7B. The Central Government shall, as soon as may be, after the end of each financial year, cause to be published in the Official Gazette, a report giving an account of the activities financed under Section 7A during the financial year, together with a statement of accounts.

CHAPTER - III : PROHIBITION, CONTROL AND REGULATION

8. Prohibition of certain operations. No person shall—

- (a) cultivate any coca plant or gather any portion of coca plant; or
- (b) cultivate the opium poppy or any cannabis plant; or
- (c) produce, manufacture, possess, sell, purchase, transport, warehouse, use, consume, import inter-state, export inter-state, import into India, export from India or tranship any narcotic drug or psychotropic substance, except for medical or scientific purposes and in the manner and to the extent provided by the provisions of this Act or the rules or orders made thereunder and in a case where any such provision, imposes any requirement by way of licence, permit or authorisation also in accordance with the terms and conditions of such licence, permit or authorisation:

PROVIDED that, and subject to the other provisions of this Act and the rules made thereunder, the prohibition against the cultivation of the cannabis plant for the production of ganja or the production, possession, use, consumption, purchase, sale, transport, warehousing, import inter-state and export inter-state of ganja for any purpose other than medical and scientific purpose shall take effect only from the date which the Central Government may, by notification in the Official Gazette, specify in this behalf. Provided further that nothing in this Section shall apply to the export of poppy straw for decorative purposes.

9. Power of Central Government to permit, control and regulate.

(1) Subject to the provisions of Section 8, the Central Government may, by rules—

(a) permit and regulate—

(i) the cultivation, or gathering of any portion (such cultivation or gathering being only on account of the Central Government) of coca plant, or the production, possession, sale, purchase, transport, import inter-state, export inter-state, use or consumption of coca leaves.

(ii) the cultivation (such cultivation being only on account of Central Government) of the opium poppy;

(iii) the production and manufacture of opium and production of poppy straw;

(iv) the sale of opium and opium derivatives from the Central Government factories for export from India or sale to State Government or to manufacturing chemists;

(v) the manufacture of manufactured drugs (other than prepared opium) but not including manufacture of medicinal opium or any preparation containing any manufactured drug from materials which the maker is lawfully entitled to possess;

(vi) the manufacture, possession, transport, import inter-state, export inter-state, sale, purchase, consumption or use of psychotropic substances;

(vii) the import into India and export from India and transhipment of narcotic drugs and psychotropic substances;

(b) prescribe any other matter requisite to render effective the control of the Central Government over any of the matters specified in clause (a).

(2) In particular and without prejudice to the generality of the foregoing power, such rules may—

(a) empower the Central Government to fix from time to time the limits within which licences may be given for the cultivation of the opium poppy;

(b) require that all opium, the produce of land cultivated with the opium poppy, shall be delivered by the cultivators to the officers authorised in this behalf by the Central Government;

(c) prescribe the forms and conditions of licences for cultivation of the opium poppy and for production and manufacture of opium; the fees that may be charged therefore; the authorities by which such licences may be granted, withheld, refused or cancelled and the authorities before which appeals against the orders of withholding, refusal or cancellation of licences shall lie;

(d) prescribe that opium shall be weighed, examined and classified according to its quality and consistence by the officers authorised in this behalf by the Central Government in the presence of the cultivator at the time of delivery by the cultivator;

(e) empower the Central Government to fix from time to time the price to be paid to the cultivators for the opium delivered;

(f) provide for the weighment, examination and classification, according to the quality and consistence, of the opium received at the factory and the deductions from or additions (if any) to the standard price to be made in accordance with the result of such examination; and the authorities by which the decisions with regard to the weighment, examination, classification, deductions or additions shall be made and the authorities before which appeals against such decisions shall lie;

(g) require that opium delivered by a cultivator, if found as a result of examination in the Central Government factory to be adulterated, may be confiscated by the officers authorised in this behalf;

(h) prescribe the forms and conditions of licences for the manufacture of manufactured drugs, the authorities by which such licences may be granted and the fees that may be charged therefore;

(i) prescribe the forms and conditions of licences or permits for the manufacture, possession, transport, import inter-state, export inter-state, sale, purchase, consumption or use of psychotropic substances, the authorities by which such licences or permits may be granted and the fees that may be charged therefor;

(j) prescribe the ports and other places at which any kind of narcotic drugs or psychotropic substances may be imported into India or exported from India or transhipped; the forms and conditions of certificates, authorisations or permits, as the case may be, for such import, export or transhipment; the authorities by which such certificates, authorisations or permits may be granted and the fees that may be charged therefor.

9A. Power to control and regulate controlled substances.

(1) If the Central Government is of the opinion that, having regard to the use of any controlled substance in the production or manufacture of any narcotic drug or psychotropic substance, it is necessary or expedient so to do in the public interest, it may, by order, provide for regulating or prohibiting the production, manufacture, supply and distribution thereof and trade and commerce therein.

(2) Without prejudice to the generality of the power conferred by sub-section (1), an order made thereunder may provide for regulating by licences, permits or otherwise, the production, manufacture, possession, transport, import inter-

state, export inter-state, sale, purchase, consumption, use, storage, distribution, disposal or acquisition of any controlled substance."

10. Power of State Government to permit, control and regulate.

(1) Subject to the provisions of Section 8, the State Government may, by rules—

(a) permit and regulate—

(i) the possession, transport, import inter-state, export inter-state, warehousing, sale, purchase, consumption and use of poppy straw;

(ii) the possession, transport, import inter-state, export inter-state, sale, purchase, consumption and use of opium;

(iii) the cultivation of any cannabis plant, production, manufacture, possession, transport, import inter-state, export inter-state, sale, purchase, consumption or use of cannabis (excluding charas);

(iv) the manufacture of medicinal opium or any preparation containing any manufactured drug from materials which the maker is lawfully entitled to possess;

(v) the possession, transport, purchase, sale, import inter-state, export inter-state, use or consumption of manufactured drugs other than prepared opium and of coca leaf and any preparation containing any manufactured drug;

(vi) the manufacture and possession of prepared opium from opium lawfully possessed by an addict registered with the State Government on medical advice for his personal consumption:

PROVIDED that save insofar as may be expressly provided in the rules made under sub-clauses (iv) and (v), nothing in Section 8 shall apply to the import inter-state, export inter-state, transport, possession, purchase, sale, use or consumption of manufactured drugs which are the property and in the possession of the Government:

PROVIDED FURTHER that such drugs as are referred to in the preceding proviso shall not be sold or otherwise delivered to any person who, under the rules made by the State Government under the aforesaid sub-clauses, is not entitled to their possession;

(b) prescribe any other matter requisite to render effective the control of the State Government over any of the matters specified in clause (a).

(2) In particular and without prejudice to the generality of the foregoing power, such rules may—

(a) empower the State Government to declare any place to be a warehouse wherein it shall be the duty of the owners to deposit all such poppy straw as is legally imported inter-state and is intended for export inter-state or export from India; to regulate the safe custody of such poppy straw warehoused and the removal of such poppy straw for sale or export inter-state or export from India; to levy fees for such warehousing and to prescribe the manner in which and the period after which the poppy straw warehoused shall be disposed of in default of payment of fees;

(b) provide that the limits within which licences may be given for the cultivation of any cannabis plant shall be fixed from time to time by or under the orders of the State Government;

(c) provide that only the cultivators licenced by the prescribed authority of the State Government shall be authorised to engage in cultivation of any cannabis plant;

(d) require that all cannabis, the produce of land cultivated with cannabis plant, shall be delivered by the cultivators to the officers of the State Government authorised in this behalf;

(e) empower the State Government to fix from time to time, the price to be paid to the cultivators for the cannabis delivered;

(f) prescribe the forms and conditions of licences or permits for the purposes specified in sub-clauses (i) to (vi) of clause (a) of sub-section (1) and the authorities by which such licences or permits may be granted and the fees that may be charged therefor.

11. Narcotic drugs and psychotropic substances, etc., not liable to distress or attachment. Notwithstanding anything to the contrary contained in any law or contract, no narcotic drug, psychotropic substance, coca plant, the opium poppy or cannabis plant shall be liable to be distrained or attached by any person for the recovery of any money under any order or decree of any court or authority or otherwise.

12. Restrictions over external dealings in narcotic drugs and psychotropic substances. No person shall engage in or control any trade whereby a narcotic drug or psychotropic substance is obtained outside India and supplied to any person outside India save with the previous authorisation of the Central Government and subject to such conditions as may be imposed by that Government in this behalf.

13. Special provisions relating to coca plant and coca leaves for use in the preparation of flavouring agent. Notwithstanding anything contained in Section 8, the Central Government may permit, with or without conditions, and on behalf of Government, the cultivation of any coca plant or gathering of any portion thereof or the production, possession, sale, purchase, transport, import inter-state, export inter-state or import into India of coca leaves for use in the preparation of any flavouring agent which shall not contain any alkaloid and to the extent necessary for such use.

14. Special provision relating to cannabis. Notwithstanding anything contained in Section 8, Government may, by general or special order and subject to such conditions as may be specified in such order, allow cultivation of any cannabis plant for industrial purposes only of obtaining fibre or seed or for horticultural purposes.

CHAPTER -IV : OFFENCES AND PENALTIES

15. Punishment for contravention in relation to poppy straw. Whoever, in contravention of any provision of this Act or any rule or order made or condition of a licence granted thereunder, produce, possesses, transports, imports inter-state, exports inter-state, sells, purchases, uses or omits to warehouse poppy straw or removes or does any act in respect of warehoused poppy straw, shall be punishable with rigorous imprisonment for a term which shall not be less than ten years but which may extend to twenty years and shall also be liable to fine which shall not be less than one lakh rupees but which may extend to two lakh rupees:

PROVIDED that the court may, for reasons to be recorded in the judgment, impose a fine exceeding two lakh rupees.

16. Punishment for contravention in relation to coca plant and coca leaves. Whoever, in contravention of any provision of this Act or any rule or order made or condition of licence granted thereunder, cultivates any coca plant or gathers any portion of a coca plant or produces, possesses, sells, purchases, transports, imports inter-state, exports inter-state or uses coca leaves, shall be punishable with rigorous imprisonment for a term which shall not be less than ten years but which may extend to twenty years and shall also be liable to fine which shall not be less than one lakh rupees but which may extend to two lakh rupees:

PROVIDED that the court may, for reasons to be recorded in the judgment, impose a fine exceeding two lakh rupees.

17. Punishment for contravention in relation to prepared opium. Whoever, in contravention of any provision of this Act or any rule or order made or condition of licence granted thereunder manufactures, possesses, sells, purchases, transports, imports inter-state, exports inter-state or uses prepared opium shall be punishable with rigorous imprisonment for a term which shall not be less than ten years but which may extend to twenty years and shall also be liable to fine which shall not be less than one lakh rupees but which may extend to two lakh rupees:

PROVIDED that the court may, for reasons to be recorded in the judgment, impose a fine exceeding two lakh rupees.

18. Punishment for contravention in relation to opium poppy and opium. Whoever, in contravention of any provision of this Act, or any rule or order made or condition of licence granted thereunder cultivates the opium poppy or produces, manufactures, possesses, sells, purchases, transports, imports inter-state, exports inter-state or uses opium shall be punishable with rigorous imprisonment for a term which shall not be less than ten years but which may extend to twenty years and shall also be liable to fine which shall not be less than one lakh rupees but which may extend to two lakh rupees:

PROVIDED that the court may, for reasons to be recorded in the judgment, impose a fine exceeding two lakh rupees.

19. Punishment for embezzlement of opium by cultivator. Any cultivator licensed to cultivate the opium poppy on account of the Central Government who embezzles or otherwise illegally disposes of the opium produced or any part thereof, shall be punishable with rigorous imprisonment for a term which shall not be less than ten years but which may extend to twenty years and shall also be liable to fine which shall not be less than one lakh rupees but which may extend to two lakh rupees:

PROVIDED that the court may, for reasons to be recorded in the judgment, impose a fine exceeding two lakh rupees.

20. Punishment for contravention in relation to cannabis plant and cannabis. Whoever, in contravention of any provision of this Act or any rule or order made or condition of licence granted thereunder :-

(a) cultivates any cannabis plant; or

(b) produces, manufactures, possesses, sells, purchases, transports, imports inter-state, exports inter-state or uses cannabis, shall be punishable,—

(i) where such contravention relates to ganja or the cultivation of cannabis plant, with rigorous imprisonment for a term which may extend to five years and shall also be liable to fine which may extend to fifty thousand rupees;

(ii) where such contravention relates to cannabis other than ganja, with rigorous imprisonment for a term which shall not be less than ten years but which may extend to twenty years and shall also be liable to fine which shall not be less than one lakh rupees and which may extend to two lakh rupees:

PROVIDED that the court may, for reasons to be recorded in the judgment, impose a fine exceeding two lakh rupees.

21. Punishment for contravention in relation to manufactured drugs and preparations. Whoever, in contravention of any provision of this Act, or any rule or order made or condition of licence granted thereunder manufactures, possesses, sells, purchases, transports, imports inter-state, exports inter-state or uses any manufactured drug or any preparation containing any manufactured drug shall be punishable with rigorous imprisonment for a term which shall not be less than ten years but which may extend to twenty years and shall also be liable to fine which shall not be less then one lakh rupees but which may extend to two lakh rupees:

PROVIDED that the court may, for reasons to be recorded in the judgment, impose a fine exceeding two lakh rupees.

22. Punishment for contravention in relation to psychotropic substances. Whoever, in contravention of any provision of this Act or any rule or order made or condition of licence granted thereunder, manufactures, possesses, sells, purchases, transports, imports inter-state, exports inter-state, or uses any psychotropic substance shall be punishable with rigorous imprisonment for a term which shall not be less than ten years but which may extend to twenty years and shall also be liable to fine which shall not be less than one lakh rupees but which may extend to two lakh rupees:

PROVIDED that the court may, for reasons to be recorded in the judgment, impose a fine exceeding two lakh rupees.

23. Punishment for illegal import into India, export from India or transhipment of narcotic drugs and psychotropic substances. Whoever, in contravention of any provision of this Act or any rule or order made or condition of licence or permit granted or certificate or authorisation issued thereunder, imports into India or exports from India or transships any narcotic drug or psychotropic substance shall be punishable with rigorous imprisonment for a term which shall not be less than ten years but which may extend to twenty years and shall also be liable to fine which shall not be less than one lakh rupees but may extend to two lakh rupees:

PROVIDED that the court may, for reasons to be recorded in the judgement, impose a fine exceeding two lakh rupees.

24. Punishment for external dealings in narcotic drugs and psychotropic substances in contravention of Section 12. Whoever engages in or controls any trade whereby a narcotic drug or a psychotropic substance is obtained outside India and supplied to any person outside India without the previous authorisation of the Central Government or otherwise than in accordance with the condition (if any) of such authorisation granted under Section 12, shall be punishable with rigorous imprisonment for a term which shall not be less than ten years but which may extend to twenty years and shall also be liable to fine which shall not be less than one lakh rupees but may extend to two lakh rupees:

PROVIDED that the court may, for reasons to be recorded in the judgment, impose a fine exceeding two lakh rupees.

25. Punishment for allowing premises, etc., to be used for commission of an offence. Whoever, being the owner or occupier or having the control or use of any house, room, enclosure, space, place, animal or conveyance, knowingly permits it to be used for the commission by any other person of an offence punishable under any provision of this Act, shall be punishable with rigorous imprisonment for a term which shall not be less than ten years but which may extend to twenty years and shall also be liable to fine which shall not be less than one lakh rupees but which may extend to two lakh rupees:

PROVIDED that the court may, for reasons to be recorded in the judgment, impose a fine exceeding two lakh rupees.

25A. Punishment for contravention of orders made under Section 9A, if any person contravenes an order made under Section 9A. He shall be punishable with rigorous imprisonment for a term which may extend to ten years and shall also be liable to fine which may extend to one lakh rupees:

PROVIDED that the court may, for reasons to be recorded in the judgment, impose a fine exceeding one lakh rupees."

Punishment for certain acts by licensee or his servants. If the holder of any licence permit or authorisation granted under this Act or any rule or order made thereunder or any person in his employ and acting on his behalf—

(a) omits, without any reasonable cause, to maintain accounts or to submit any return in accordance with the provisions of this Act, or any rule made thereunder,

(b) fails to produce without any reasonable cause such licence, permit or authorisation on demand of any officer authorised by the Central Government or State Government in this behalf;

(c) keeps any accounts or makes any statement which is false or which he knows or has reason to believe to be incorrect; or

(d) wilfully and knowingly does any act in breach of any of the conditions of licence, permit or authorisation for which a penalty is not prescribed elsewhere in this Act, he shall be punishable with imprisonment for a term which may extend to three years or with fine or with both.

27. Punishment for illegal possession in small quantity for personal, consumption of any narcotic drug or psychotropic substance or consumption of such drug or substance.

(1) Whoever, in contravention of any provision of this Act, or any rule or order made or permit issued thereunder, possesses in a small quantity, any narcotic drug or psychotropic substance, which is proved to have been intended for his personal consumption and not for sale or distribution, or consumes any narcotic drug or psychotropic substance, shall, notwithstanding anything contained in this Chapter, be punishable,—

(a) where the narcotic drug or psychotropic substance possessed or consumed is cocaine, morphine, diacetyl-morphine or any other narcotic drug or any psychotropic substance as may be specified in this behalf by the Central Government, by notification in the Official Gazette, with imprisonment for a term which may extend to one year or with fine or with both; and

(b) where the narcotic drug or psychotropic substance possessed or consumed is other than those specified in or under clause (a), with imprisonment for a term which may extend to six months or with fine or with both.

EXPLANATION. (1) For the purposes of this Section "small quantity" means such quantity as may be specified by the Central Government by notification in the Official Gazette.

(2) Where a person is shown to have been in possession of a small quantity of a narcotic drug or psychotropic substance, the burden of proving that it was intended for the personal consumption of such person and not for sale or distribution, shall lie on such person.

27A. Punishment for financing illicit traffic and harbouring offenders. Whoever indulges in financing, directly or indirectly, any of the activities specified in sub-clauses (i) to (v) of clause (viiia) of Section 2 or harbours any person engaged in any of the aforementioned activities, shall be punishable with rigorous imprisonment for a term which shall not be less than ten years but which may extend to twenty years and shall also be liable to fine which shall not be less than one lakh rupees but which may extend to two lakh rupees:

PROVIDED that the court may, for reasons to be recorded in the judgment impose a fine exceeding two lakh rupees.

28. Punishment for attempts to commit offences. Whoever attempts to commit any offence punishable under this Chapter or to cause such offence to be committed and in such attempt does any act towards the commission of the offence shall be punishable with the punishment provided for the offence.

29. Punishment for abetment and criminal conspiracy.

(1) Whoever abets, or is a party to a criminal conspiracy to commit, an offence punishable under this Chapter, shall, whether such offence be or be not committed in consequence of such abetment or in pursuance of such criminal conspiracy, and notwithstanding anything contained in Section 116 of the Indian Penal Code (45 of 1860) be punishable with the punishment provided for the offence.

A person abets, or is a party to a criminal conspiracy to commit, an offence, within the meaning of this Section, who, in India, abets or is a party to the criminal conspiracy to the commission of any act in a place without and beyond India which—

(a) would constitute an offence if committed within India; or

(b) under the laws of such place, is an offence relating to narcotic drugs or psychotropic substances having all the legal conditions required to constituted it such an offence the same as or analogous to the legal conditions required to constituted it an offence punishable under this Chapter, if committed within India.

30. Preparation. If any person makes preparation to do or omits to do anything which constitutes an offence punishable under any of the provisions of Section 15 to Section 25 (both inclusive) and from the circumstances of the case it may be reasonably inferred that he was determined to carry out his intention to commit the offence but had been prevented by circumstances independent of his will, he shall be punishable with rigorous imprisonment for a term which shall not be less than one-half of the minimum term (if any), but which may extend to one-half of the maximum term, of imprisonment with which he would have been punishable in the event of his having committed such offence, and also with fine which shall not be less than one-half of the minimum amount (if any), of fine with which he would have been punishable, but which may extend to one-half of the maximum amount of fine with which he would have ordinarily (that is to say in the absence of special reasons) been punishable, in the event aforesaid:

PROVIDED that the court may, for reasons to be recorded in the Judgment, impose a higher fine.

31. Enhanced punishment for certain offences after previous conviction.

(1) If any person who has been convicted of the commission of, or attempt to commit, or abetment of, or criminal conspiracy to commit, any of the offences punishable under Section 15 to Section 25 (both inclusive) is subsequently convicted of the commission of, or attempt to commit, or abetment of, or criminal conspiracy to commit, an offence punishable under—

(a) section 15 to Section 19, clause (ii) of Section 20 and Section 21 to Section 25 (both inclusive), he shall be punished for the second and every subsequent offence with rigorous imprisonment for a term which shall not be less than fifteen years but which may extend to thirty years and shall also be liable to fine which shall not be less than one lakh fifty thousand rupees but which may extend to three lakh rupees;

(b) clause (i) of Section 20, he shall be punished for the second and every subsequent offence for a term which may extend to ten years and shall also be liable to fine which may extend to one lakh rupees:

PROVIDED that the court may, for reasons to be recorded in the judgment, impose -

(i) in a case falling under clause (a), a fine exceeding three lakh rupees; and

(ii) in a case falling under clause (b), a fine exceeding one lakh rupees.

(2) Where any person is convicted by a competent court of criminal jurisdiction outside India under any law corresponding to the provisions of Section 15 to Section 25 (both inclusive), Section 28 and Section 29, such person, in respect of such conviction, shall be dealt with for the purposes of sub-section (1) as if he had been convicted by a court in India.

31A. Death penalty for certain offences after previous conviction.

(1) Notwithstanding anything contained in Section 31, if any person who has been convicted of the commission of, or attempt to commit, or abetment of, or criminal conspiracy to commit, any of the offences punishable under Section 15 to Section 25 (both inclusive) or Section 27A, is subsequently convicted of the commission of, or attempt to commit, or abetment of, or criminal conspiracy to commit, an offence relating to,—

(a) engaging in the production, manufacture, possession, transportation, import into India, export from India or transshipment, of the narcotic drugs or psychotropic substances specified under column (1) of the Table below and involving the quantity which is equal to or more than the quantity indicated against each such drug or substance, as specified in column (2) of the said Table;

TABLE

Particulars of narcotic drugs	**Quantity psychotropic substances**
(i) Opium	10 kgs.
(ii) Morphine	1 kg.
(iii) Heroin	1 kg.
(iv) Codeine	1 kg.
(v) Thebaine	1 kg.
(vi) Cocaine	500 grams
(vii) Hashish	20 kgs.
(viii) Any mixture with or without any neutral material of any of the above drugs	1,500 grams
(ix) LSD, LSD-25-N, N-Diethyllysergamide (d-lysergic acid diethylamide)	500 grams
(x) THC (Tetrahydrocannabinols), the following isomers: 6a (10a), 6a (7), 7, 8, 9, 10, 9 and their stereochemical variants	500 grams

(xi) Methamphetamine-2-amino-l-Phenylpropane 1,500 gram

(xii) Methaqualone 2-Methyl-3-o-tolyl-4-(3H)-quinazolinone 1,500 gram

(xiii) Amphetamine-2-amino-1-phenylpropane 1,500 gram

(xiv) Salts and preparations of the Psychotropic substances mentioned in (ix) to (xiii) 1,500 gram;

(b) financing, directly or indirectly, any of the activities specified in clause (a), shall be punishable with death.

(2) Where any person is convicted by a competent court of criminal jurisdiction outside India under any law corresponding to the provisions of Section 15 to Section 25 (both inclusive), Section 27A, Section 28 or Section 29, such person, in respect of such conviction, shall be dealt with for the purposes of sub-section (1) as if he had been convicted by a court in India."

32. Punishment for offence for which no punishment is provided. Whoever contravenes any provision of this Act or any rule or order made, or any condition of any licence, permit or authorisation issued thereunder for which no punishment is separately provided in this Chapter, shall be punishable with imprisonment for a term which may extend to six months, or with fine, or with both.

32A. No suspension, remission or commutation in any sentence awarded under this Act. Notwithstanding anything contained in the Code of Criminal Procedure, 1973 (2 of 1974), or any other law for the time being in force but subject to the provisions of Section 33, no sentence awarded under this Act (other than Section 27) shall be suspended or remitted or commuted.

33. Application of Section 360 of the Code of Criminal Procedure, 1973 and of the Probation of Offenders Act, 1958. Nothing contained in Section 360 of the Code of Criminal Procedure, 1973 (2 of 1974) or in the Probation of Offenders Act, 1958 (20 of 1958) shall apply to a person convicted of an offence under this Act unless such person is under eighteen years of age or that the offence for which such person is convicted is punishable under Section 26 or Section 27.

34. Security for abstaining from commission of offence.

(1) Whenever any person is convicted of an offence punishable under any provision of Chapter IV and the court convicting him is of opinion that it is necessary to require such person to execute a bond for abstaining from the commission of any offence under this Act, the court may, at the time of passing sentence on such person, order him to execute a bond for a sum proportionate to his means, with or without sureties, for abstaining from commission of any offence under Chapter IV during such period not exceeding three years as it thinks fit to fix.

(2) The bond shall be in such form as may be prescribed by the Central Government and the provisions of the Code of Criminal Procedure, 1973 (2 of 1974), shall, insofar as they are applicable, apply to all matters connected with such bond as if it were a bond to keep the peace ordered to be executed under Section 106 of that Code.

(3) If the conviction is set aside on appeal or otherwise, the bond so executed shall become void.

(4) An order under this Section may also be made by an appellate court or by the High Court or Sessions Judge when exercising the powers of revision.

35. Presumption of culpable mental state.

(1) In any prosecution for an offence under this Act which requires a culpable mental state of the accused, the court shall presume the existence of such mental state but it shall be a defence for the accused to prove the fact that he had no such mental state with respect to the act charged as an offence in that prosecution.

EXPLANATION: In this Section "culpable mental state" includes intention motive, knowledge of a fact and belief in, or reason to believe, a fact.

For the purpose of this Section, a fact is said to be proved only when the court believes it to exist beyond a reasonable doubt and not merely when its existence is established by a preponderance of probability.

36. Constitution of Special Court.

(1) The Government may, for the purpose of providing speedy trial of the offences under this Act, by notification in the Official Gazette, constitute as many Specified in the notification.

(2) A Special Court shall consist of a single Judge who shall be appointed by the Government with the concurrence of the Chief Justice of the High Court. Explanation.— In this sub-section, "High Court" means the High Court of the State in which the Sessions Judge or the Additional Sessions Judge of a Special Court was working immediately before his appointment as such Judge.

(3) A person shall not be qualified for appointment as a Judge of a Special Court unless he is, immediately before such appointment, a Sessions Judge or an Additional Sessions Judge.

36A. Offences triable by Special Courts.

(1) Notwithstanding anything contained in the Code of Criminal Procedure, 1973 (2 of 1974),—

(a) all offences under this Act shall be triable only be the Special Court constituted for the area in which the offence has been committed or where there are more Special Courts than one for such area, by such one of them as may be specified in this behalf by the Government;

(b) where a person accused of or suspected of the commission of an offence under this Act is forwarded to a Magistrate under sub-section (2A) of Section 167 of the Code of Criminal Procedure, 1973 (2 of 1974), such Magistrate may authorise the detention of such person in such custody as he thinks fit for a period not exceeding fifteen days in the whole where such Magistrate is a Judicial Magistrate and seven days in the whole where such Magistrate is an Executive Magistrate:

PROVIDED that where such Magistrate considers—

(i) when such person is forwarded to him as aforesaid; or

(ii) upon or at any time before the expiry of the period of detention authorised by him, that the detention of such person is unnecessary, he shall order such person to be forwarded to the Special Court having jurisdiction;

(c) the Special Court may exercise, in relation to the person forwarded to it under clause (b), the same power which a Magistrate having jurisdiction to try a case may exercise under Section 167 of the Code of Criminal Procedure, 1973 (2 of 1974), in relation to an accused person in such case who has been forwarded to him under that Section;

(d) a Special Court may, upon a perusal of police report of the facts constituting an offence under this Act or upon a complaint made by an officer of the Central Government or a State Government authorised in this behalf, take cognizance of that offence without the accused being committed to it for trial.

(2) When trying an offence under this Act, a Special Court may also try an offence other than an offence under this Act, with which the accused may, under the Code of Criminal Procedure, 1973 (2 of 1974) be charged at the same trial.

(3) Nothing contained in this Section shall be deemed to affect the special powers of the High Court regarding bail under Section 439 of the Code of Criminal Procedure, 1973 (2 of 1974), and the High Court may exercise such powers including the power under clause (b) of sub-section (1) of that Section as if the reference to "Magistrate" in that Section included also a reference to a" Special Court" constituted under Section 36.

36B. Appeal and revision. The High Court may exercise, so for as may be applicable, all the powers conferred by Chapters XXIX and XXX of the Code of Criminal Procedure, 1973 (12 of 1986) on a High Court, as if a Special Court within the local limits of the jurisdiction of the High Court were a Court of Session trying cases within the local limits of the jurisdiction of the High Court.

36C. Application of Code to proceedings before a Special Court. Save as otherwise provided in this Act, the provisions of the Code of Criminal Procedure, 1973 (12 of 1974), (including the provisions as to bail and bonds) shall apply to the proceedings before a Special Court and for the purposes of the said provisions the Special Court shall be deemed to be a Court of Session and the person conducting a prosecution before a Special Court, shall be deemed to be a Public Prosecutor.

36D. Transitional provisions.

(1) Any offence committed under this Act on or after the commencement of the narcotic Drugs and Psychotropic Substances (Amendment) Act, 1988 (46 of 1988), until a Special Court is constituted under Section 36, shall, notwithstanding anything contained in the Code of Criminal Procedure, 1973 (12 of 1974), be tried by a Court of Session:

PROVIDED that offences punishable under Sections 26, 27 and 32 may be tried summarily.

(2) Nothing in sub-section (1) shall be construed to require the transfer to a Special Court of any proceedings in relation to an offence taken cognizance of by a

Court of Session under the said sub-section (1) and the same shall be heard and disposed of by the Court of Session.

37. Offences to be cognizable and non-bailable.

(1) Notwithstanding anything contained in the Code of Criminal Procedure, 1973 (2 of 1974),

(a) every offence punishable under this Act shall be cognizable;

(b) no person accused of an offence punishable for a term of imprisonment of five years or more under this Act shall be released on bail or on his own bond unless—

(i) the Public Prosecutor has been given an opportunity to oppose the application for such release, and

(ii) where the Public Prosecutor opposes the application the court is satisfied that there are reasonable grounds for believing that he is not guilty of such offence and that he is not likely to commit any offence while on bail.

(2) The limitations on granting of bail specified in clause (b) of sub-section (1) are in addition to the limitations under the Code of Criminal Procedure, 1973 (12 of 1974), or any other law for the time being in force on granting of bail.

38. Offences by companies.

(1) Where an offence under Chapter IV has been committed by a company, every person, who, at the time the offence was committed was in charge of, and was responsible to, the company for the conduct of the business of the company as well as the company, shall be deemed to be guilty of the offence and shall be liable to be proceeded against and punished accordingly:

PROVIDED that nothing contained in this sub-section shall render any such person liable to any punishment if he proves that the offence was committed without his knowledge or that he had exercised all due diligence to prevent the commission of such offence.

(2) Notwithstanding anything contained in sub-section (1), where any offence under Chapter IV has been committed by a company and it is proved that the offence has been committed with the consent or connivance of, or is attributable to any neglect on the part of, any director, manager, secretary or other officer of the company, such director, manager, secretary or other officer shall be deemed to be guilty of that offence and shall be liable to be proceeded against and punished accordingly.

EXPLANATION. For the purposes of this Section,—

(a) "company" means any body corporate and includes a firm or other association of individuals; and

(b) "director", in relation to a firm, means a partner in the firm.

39. Power of court to release certain offenders on probation.

(1) When any addict is found guilty of an offence punishable under Section 27 and if the court by which he is found guilty is of the opinion, regard being had to

the age, character, antecedents or physical or mental condition of the offender, that it is expedient so to do, then, notwithstanding anything contained in this Act or any other law for the time being in force, the court may, instead of sentencing him at once to any imprisonment, with his consent, direct that he be released for undergoing medical treatment for de-toxification or de-addiction from a hospital or an institution maintained or recognised by Government and on his entering into a bond in the form prescribed by the Central Government, with or without sureties, to appear and furnish before the court within a period not exceeding one year, a report regarding the result of his medical treatment and, in the meantime, to abstain from the commission of any offence under Chapter IV.

If it appears to the court, having regard to the report regarding the result of the medical treatment furnished under sub-section (1), that it is expedient so to do, the court may direct the release of the offender after due admonition on his entering into a bond in the form prescribed by the Central Government, with or without sureties, for abstaining from the commission of any offence under Chapter IV during such period not exceeding three years as the court may deem fit to specify or on his failure so to abstain, to appear before the court and receive sentence when called upon during such period.

40. Power of court to publish names, place of business, etc., of certain offenders.

(1) Where any person is convicted of any of the offences punishable under Section 15 to Section 25 (both inclusive), Section 28, Section 29 or Section 30, it shall be competent for the court convicting the person to cause the name and place of business or residence of such person, nature of the contravention, the fact that the person has been so convicted and such other particulars as the court may consider to be appropriate in the circumstances of the case, to be published at the expense of such person in such newspapers or in such manner as the court may direct.

(2) No publication under sub-section (1) shall be made until the period for preferring an appeal against the orders of the court has expired without any appeal having been preferred, or such appeal, having been preferred, has been disposed of.

(3) The expenses of any publication under sub-section (1) shall be recoverable from the convicted person as if it were a fine imposed by the court.

CHAPTER - V : PROCEDURE

41. Power to issue warrant and authorisation.

(1) A Metropolitan Magistrate or a Magistrate of the first class or any Magistrate of the second class specially empowered by the State Government in this behalf, may issue a warrant for the arrest of any person whom he has reason to believe to have committed any offence punishable under Chapter IV, or for the search, whether by day or by night, of any building, conveyance or place in which he has reason to believe any narcotic drug or psychotropic substance in respect of which an offence punishable under Chapter IV has been committed or any document

or other article which may furnish evidence of the commission of such offence is kept or concealed.

(2) Any such officer of gazetted rank of the departments of central excise, narcotics, customs, revenue intelligence or any other department of the Central Government or of the Border Security Force as is empowered in this behalf by general or special order by the Central Government, or any such officer of the revenue, drugs control, excise, police or any other department of a State Government as is empowered in this behalf by general or special order of the State Government, if he has reason to believe from personal knowledge or information given by any person and taken in writing that any person has committed an offence punishable under Chapter IV or that any narcotic drug, or psychotropic substance in respect of which any offence punishable under Chapter IV has been committed or any document or other article which may furnish evidence of the commission of such offence has been kept or concealed in any building, conveyance or place, may authorise any officer subordinate to him but superior in rank to a peon, sepoy, or a constable, to arrest such a person or search a building, conveyance or place whether by day or by nigh or himself arrest a person or search a building, conveyance or place.

(3) The officer to whom a warrant under sub-section (1) is addressed and the officer who authorised the arrest or search or the officer who is so authorised under sub-section (2) shall have all the powers of an officer acting under Section 42.

42. Power of entry, search, seizure and arrest without warrant or authorisation.

(1) Any such officer (being an officer superior in rank to a peon, sepoy or constable) of thc dcpartmcnts of ccntral cxcisc, narcotics, customs, rcvcnuc intclligence or any other department of the Central Government or of the Border Security Force as is embowered in this behalf by general or special order by the Central Government, or any such officer (being an officer superior in rank to a peon, sepoy or constable) of the revenue, drugs control, excise, police or any other department of a State Government as is empowered in this behalf by general or special order of the State Government, if he has reason to believe from personal knowledge or information given by any person and taken down in writing, that any narcotic drug, or psychotropic substance, in respect of which an offence punishable under Chapter IV has been committed or any document or other article which may furnish evidence of the commission of such offence is kept or concealed in any building, conveyance or enclosed place, may, between sunrise and sunset,—

(a) enter into and search any such building, conveyance or place;

(b) in case of resistance, break open any door and remove any obstacle to such entry;

(c) seize such drug or substance and all materials used in the manufacture thereof and any other article and any animal or conveyance which he has reason to believe to be liable to confiscation under this Act and any document or other article which he has reason to believe may furnish evidence of the commission of any offence punishable under Chapter IV relating to such drug or substance:

PROVIDED that if such officer has reason to believe that a search warrant or authorisation cannot be obtained without affording opportunity for the concealment of evidence or facility for the escape of an offender, he may enter and search such building, conveyance or enclosed place at any time between sunset and sunrise after recording the grounds of his belief.

(2) Where an officer takes down any information in writing under sub-section (1) or records grounds for his belief under the proviso thereto, he shall forthwith send a copy thereof to his immediate official superior.

43. Power of seizure and arrest in public places. Any officer of any of the departments mentioned in Section 42 may—

(a) seize, in any public place or in transit, any narcotic drug or psychotropic substance in respect of which he has reason to believe an offence punishable under Chapter IV has been committed, and, along with such drug or substance, any animal or conveyance or article liable to confiscation under this Act, and any document or other article which he has reason to believe may furnish evidence of the commission of an offence punishable under Chapter IV relating to such drug or substance;

(b) detain and search any person whom he has reason to believe to have committed an offence punishable under Chapter IV, and, if such person has any narcotic drug or psychotropic substance in his possession and such possession appears to him to be unlawful, arrest him and any other person in his company.

EXPLANATION. For the purposes of this Section, the expression" public place" includes any public conveyance, hotel, shop, or other place intended for use by, or accessible to the public.

44. Power of entry, search, seizure and arrest in offences relating to coca plant, opium poppy and cannabis plant. The provisions of Sections 41, 42 and 43, shall so far as may be, apply in relation to the offence punishable under Chapter IV and relating to coca plant, the opium poppy or cannabis plant and for this purpose references in those Sections to narcotic drugs, or psychotropic substance, shall be construed as including references to coca plant, the opium poppy and cannabis plant.

45. Procedure where seizure of goods liable to confiscation not practicable. Where it is not practicable to seize any goods (including standing crop) which are liable to confiscation under this Act, any officer duly authorised under Section 42 may serve on the owner or person in possession of the goods, an order that he shall not remove, part with or otherwise deal with the goods except with the previous permission of such officer.

46. Duty of land holder to give information of illegal cultivation. Every holder of land shall give immediate information to any officer of the Police or of any of the departments mentioned in Section 42 of all the opium poppy, cannabis plant or coca plant which may be illegally cultivated within his land and every such holder of land who knowingly neglects to give such information, shall be liable to punishment.

47. Duty of certain officers to give information of illegal cultivation. Every officer of the Government and every panch, sarpanch and other village officer of whatever description shall give immediate information to any officer of the Police or of any of the departments mentioned in Section 42 when it may come to his knowledge that any land has been illegally cultivated with the opium poppy, cannabis plant or coca plant, and every such officer of the Government, panch, sarpanch and other village officer who neglects to give such information shall be liable to punishment.

48. Power of attachment of crop illegally cultivated. Any Metropolitan Magistrate, Judicial Magistrate of the first class or any Magistrate specially empowered in this behalf by the State Government or any officer of a gazetted rank empowered under Section 42 may order attachment of any opium poppy, cannabis plant or coca plant which he has reason to believe to have been illegally cultivated and while doing so may pass such order (including an order to destroy the crop) as he thinks fit.

49. Power to stop and search conveyance. Any officer authorised under Section 42, may, if he has reason to suspect that any animal or conveyance is, or is about to be, used for the transport of any narcotic drug or psychotropic substance, in respect of which he suspects that any provision of this Act has been, or is being, or is about to be, contravened at any time, stop such animal or conveyance, or, in the case of an aircraft, compel it to land and -

(a) rummage and search the conveyance or part thereof;

(b) examine and search any goods on the animal or in the conveyance;

(c) if it becomes necessary to stop the animal or the conveyance, he may use all lawful means for stopping it, and where such means fail, the animal or the conveyance may be fired upon.

50. Conditions under which search of persons shall be conducted.

(1) When any officer duly authorised under Section 42 is about to search any person under the provisions of Section 41, Section 42 or Section 43, he shall, if such person so requires, take such person without unnecessary delay to nearest Gazetted Officer of any of the departments mentioned in Section 42 or to the nearest Magistrate.

(2) If such requisition is made, the officer may detain the person until he can bring him before the Gazetted Officer or the Magistrate referred to in sub-section (1).

(3) The Gazetted Officer or the Magistrate before whom any such person is brought shall, if he sees no reasonable ground for search, forthwith discharge the person but otherwise shall direct that search be made.

(4) No female shall be searched by anyone excepting a female.

51. Provisions of the code of Criminal Procedure, 1973 to apply to warrants, arrests, searches and seizures. The provisions of the Code of Criminal Procedure, 1973 (2 of 1974) shall apply, insofar as they are not inconsistent with the provisions of this Act, to all warrants issued and arrests, searches and seizures made under this Act.

52. Disposal of persons arrested and articles seized.

(1) Any officer arresting a person under Section 41, Section 42, Section 43 or Section 44 shall, as soon as may be, inform him of the grounds for such arrest.

(2) Every person arrested and article seized under warrant issued under sub-section (1) of Section 41 shall be forwarded without unnecessary delay to the Magistrate by whom the warrant was issued.

(3) Every person arrested and article seized under sub-section (2) of Section 41, Section 42, Section 43 or Section 44 shall be forwarded without unnecessary delay to—

(a) the officer-in-charge of the nearest police station, or

(b) the officer empowered under Section 53.

(4) The authority or officer to whom any person or article is forwarded under sub-section (2) or sub-section (3) shall, with all convenient dispatch, take such measures as may be necessary for the disposal according to law of such person or article.

52A. Disposal of seized narcotic drugs and psychotropic substances.

(1) The Central Government may, having regard to the hazardous nature of any narcotic drugs or psychotropic substances, their vulnerability to theft, substitution, constraints of proper storage space or any other relevant considerations, by notification published in the Official Gazette, specify such narcotic drugs or psychotropic substances or class of narcotic drugs or class of psycho-tropic substances which shall, as soon as may be after their seizure, be disposed of by such officer and in such manner as that Government may, from time, determine after following the procedure hereinafter specified.

(2) Where any narcotic drug or psychotropic substance has been seized and forwarded to the officer-in-charge of the nearest police station or to the officer empowered under Section 53, the officer referred to in sub-section (1) shall prepare an inventory of such narcotic drugs or psychotropic substances containing such details relating to their description, quality, quantity, mode of packing, marks, numbers or such other identifying particulars of the narcotic drugs or psychotropic substances or the packing in which they are packed, country of origin and other particulars as the officer referred to in sub-section (1) may consider relevant to the identity of the narcotic drugs or psychotropic substances in any proceedings under this Act and make an application, to any Magistrate for the purpose of—

(a) certifying the correctness of the inventory so prepared; or

(b) taking, in the presence of such magistrate, photographs of such drugs or substances and certifying such photographs as true; or

(c) allowing to draw representative samples of such drugs or substances, in the presence of such magistrate and certifying the correctness of any list of samples so drawn.

(3) Where an application is made under sub-section (2), the Magistrate shall, as soon as may be, allow the application.

(4) Notwithstanding anything contained in the Indian Evidence Act, 1872 (1 of 1972), or the Code of Criminal Procedure, 1973 (2 of 1974), every court trying an offence under this Act, shall treat the inventory, the photographs of narcotic

drugs or psychotropic substances and any list of samples drawn under sub-section (2) and certified by the Magistrate, as primary evidence in respect of such offence.

53. Power to invest officers of certain departments with powers of an officer-in-charge of a police station.

(1) The Central Government, after consultation with the State Government, may, by notification published in the Official Gazette, invest any officer of the department of central excise, narcotics, customs, revenue intelligence or Border Security Force or any class of such officers with the powers of an officer-in-charge of a police station for the investigation of the offences under this Act.

(2) The State Government may, by notification published in the Official Gazette, invest any officer of the department of drugs control, revenue or excise or any class of such officers with the powers of an officer-in-charge of a police station for the investigation of offences under this Act.

53A. Relevancy of statements under certain circumstances.

(1) A statement made and signed by a person before any officer empowered under Section 53 for the investigation of offences, during the course of any inquiry or proceedings by such officer, shall be relevant for the purpose of proving, in any prosecution for an offence under this Act, the truth of the facts which it contains,—

(a) when the person who made the statement is dead or cannot be found, or is incapable of giving evidence or is kept out of the way by the adverse party, or whose presence cannot be obtained without an amount of delay or expense which, under the circumstances of the case, the court considers unreasonable; or

(b) when the person who made the statement is examined as a witness in the case before the court and the court is of the opinion that, having regard to the circumstances of the case, the statement should be admitted in evidence in the interest of justice.

(2) The provisions of sub-section (1) shall, so far as may be, apply in relation to any proceedings under this Act or the rules or orders made thereunder, other than a proceeding before a court, as they apply in relation to a proceeding before a court.

54. Presumption from possession of illicit articles. In trials under this Act, it may be presumed, unless and until the contrary is proved, that the accused has committed an offence under Chapter IV in respect of—

(a) any narcotic drug or psychotropic substance;

(b) any opium poppy, cannabis plant or coca plant growing on any land which he has cultivated;

(c) any apparatus specially designed or any group of utensils specially adopted for the manufacture of any narcotic drug or psychotropic substance; or

(d) any materials which have undergone any process towards the manufacture of a narcotic drug or psychotropic substance, or any residue left of the materials from which any narcotic drug or psychotropic substance has been manufactured, for the possession of which he fails to account satisfactorily.

55. Police to take charge of articles seized and delivered. An officer-in-charge of a police station shall take charge of and keep in safe custody, pending the orders of the Magistrate, all articles seized under this Act within the local area of that police station and which may be delivered to him, and shall allow any officer who may accompany such articles to the police station or who may be deputed for the purpose, to affix his seal to such articles or to take samples of and from them and all samples so taken shall also be sealed with a seal of the officer-in-charge of the police station.

56. Obligation of officers to assist each other. All officers of the several departments mentioned in Section 42 shall, upon notice given or request made, be legally bound to assist each other in carrying out the provisions of this Act.

57. Report of arrest and seizure. Whenever any person makes any arrest or seizure under this Act, he shall, within forty-eight hours next after such arrest or seizure, make a full report of all the particulars of such arrest or seizure to his immediate official superior.

58. Punishment for vexatious entry, search, seizure or arrest.

(1) Any person empowered under Section 42 or Section 43 or Section 44 who—

(a) without reasonable ground of suspicion enters or searches, or causes to be entered or searched, any building, conveyance or place;

(b) vexatiously and unnecessarily seizes the property of any person on the pretence of seizing or searching for any narcotic drug or psychotropic substance or other article liable to be confiscated under this Act, or of seizing any document or other article liable to be seized under Section 42, Section 43 or Section 44; or

(c) vexatiously and unnecessarily detains, searches or arrests any person, shall be punishable with imprisonment for a term which may extend to six months or with fine which may extend to one thousand rupees, or with both.

(2) Any person wilfully and maliciously giving false information and so causing an arrest or a search being made under this Act shall be punishable with imprisonment for a term which may extend to two years or with fine or with both.

59. Failure of officer in duty or his connivance at the contravention of the provisions of this Act.

(1) Any officer, on whom any duty has been imposed by or under this Act and who ceases or refuses to perform or withdraws himself from the duties of his official superior or has other lawful excuse for so doing, be punishable with imprisonment for a term which may extend to one year or with fine or with both.

(2) Any officer on whom any duty has been imposed by or under this Act or any person who has been given the custody of—

(a) any addict; or

(b) any other person who has been charged with an offence under this Act, and who wilfully aids in, or connives at, the contravention of any provision of this Act or any rule or order made thereunder, shall be punishable with rigorous imprisonment for a term which shall not be less than ten years but which may extend to twenty years, and shall also be liable to fine which shall not be less than one lakh rupees but which may extend to two lakh rupees.

EXPLANATION: For the purposes of this sub-section, the expression" officer" includes any person employed in a hospital or institution maintained or recognised by the Government or a local authority under Section 64A for providing de-addiction treatment.

(3) No court shall take cognizance of any offence under sub-section (1) or sub-section (2) except on a complaint in writing made with the previous sanction of the Central Government, or as the case may be, the State Government.

60. Liability of illicit drugs, substances, plants, articles and conveyances to confiscation.

(1) Whenever any offence punishable under Chapter IV has been committed, the narcotic drug, psychotropic substance, the opium poppy, coca plant, cannabis plant, materials, apparatus and utensils in respect of which or by means of which such offence has been committed, shall be liable to confiscation.

(2) Any narcotic drug or psychotropic substance lawfully produced, imported inter-state, exported inter-state, imported into India, transported, manufactured, possessed, used, purchased or sold along with, or in addition to, any narcotic drug or psychotropic substance which is liable to confiscation under sub-section (1) and thc rcccptaclcs, packagcs and covcrings in which any narcotic drug or psychotropic substance, materials, apparatus or utensils liable to confiscation under sub-section (1) is found, and the other contents, if any, of such receptacles or packages shall likewise be liable to confiscation.

(3) Any animal or conveyance used in carrying any narcotic drug or psychotropic substance, or any article liable to confiscation under sub-section (1) or sub-section (2) shall be liable to confiscation, unless the owner of the animal or conveyance proves that it was so used without the knowledge or connivance of the owner himself, his agent, if any, and the person-in-charge of the animal or conveyance and that each of them had taken all reasonable precautions against such use.

61. Confiscation of goods used for concealing illicit drugs or substances. Any goods used for concealing any narcotic drug or psychotropic substance which is liable to confiscation under this Act shall also be liable to confiscation.

EXPLANATION: In this Section "goods" does not include conveyance as a means of transport.

62. Confiscation of sale proceeds of illicit drugs or substances. Where any narcotic drug or psychotropic substance is sold by a person having knowledge or reason to believe that the drug or substance is liable to confiscation under this Act, the sale proceeds thereof shall also be liable to confiscation.

63. Procedure in making confiscations.

(1) In the trial of offences under this Act, whether the accused is convicted or acquitted or discharged, the court shall decide whether any article or thing seized under this Act is liable to confiscation under Section 60 or Section 61 or Section 62 and, if it decides that the article is so liable, it may order confiscation accordingly.

(2) Where any article or thing seized under this Act appears to be liable to confiscation under Section 60 or Section 61 or Section 62, but the person who committed the offence in connection therewith is not known or cannot be found; the court may inquire into and decide such liability, and may order confiscation accordingly:

PROVIDED that no order of confiscation of an article or thing shall be made until the expiry of one month from the date of seizure, or without hearing any person who may claim any right thereto and the evidence, if any, which he produces in respect of his claim:

PROVIDED FURTHER that if any such article or thing, other than a narcotic drug, psychotropic substance, the opium poppy, coca plant or cannabis plant is liable to speedy and natural decay, or if the court is of opinion that its sale would be for the benefit of its owner, it may at any time direct it to be sold; and the provisions of this sub-section shall, as nearly as may be practicable, apply to the net proceeds of the sale.

(3) Any person not convicted who claims any right to property which has been confiscated under this Section may appeal to the Court of Session against the order of confiscation.

64. Power to tender immunity from prosecution.

(1) The Central Government or the State Government may, if it is of opinion (the reasons for such opinion being recorded in writing) that with a view to obtaining the evidence of any person appearing to have been directly or indirectly concerned in or privy to the contravention of any of provisions of this Act or of any rule or order made thereunder it is necessary or expedient so to do, tender to such person immunity from prosecution for any offence under this Act or under the Indian Penal Code (45 of 1860) or under any other Central Act or State Act, as the case may be, for the time being in force, on condition of his making a full and true disclosure of the whole circumstances relating to such contravention.

(2) A tender of immunity made to, and accepted by, the person concerned, shall, to the extent to which the immunity extends, render him immune from prosecution for any offence in respect of which the tender was made.

(3) If it appears to the Central Government or, as the case may be, the State Government, that any person to whom immunity has been tendered under this Section has not complied with the conditions on which the tender was made or is wilfully concealing anything or is giving false evidence, the Central Government or, as the case may be, the State Government, may record a finding to that effect and thereupon the immunity shall be deemed to have been withdrawn and such person may be tried for the offence in respect of

which the tender of immunity was made or for any other offence of which he appears to have been guilty in connection with the same matter.

64A. Immunity from prosecution to addicts volunteering for treatment. Any addict, who is not charged with any offence punishable under Sections 15 to 25 (both inclusive) or Section 27A, who voluntarily seeks to undergo medical treatment for de-toxification or de-addiction from a hospital or an institution maintained or recognised by the Government or a local authority and undergoes such treatment shall not be liable to prosecution under Section 27 once in his lifetime:

PROVIDED that the said immunity from prosecution may be withdrawn if the addict does not undergo the complete treatment for detoxification or de-addiction."

66. Presumption as to documents in certain cases. Where any document—

(i) is produced or furnished by any person or has been seized from the custody or control of any person, in either case, under this Act or under any other law, or

(ii) has been received from any place outside India (duly authenticated by such authority or person and in such manner as may be prescribed by the Central Government) in the course of investigation of any offence under this Act alleged to have been committed by a person, and such document is tendered in any prosecution under this Act in evidence against him, or against him and any other person who is tried jointly with him, the court shall—

(a) presume, unless the contrary is proved, that the signature and every other part of such document which purports to be in the handwriting of any particular person or which the court may reasonably assume to have been signed by, or to be in the handwriting of, any particular person, is in that person's handwriting; and in the case of a document executed or attested, that it was executed or attested by the person by whom it purports to have been so executed or attested;

(b) admit the document in evidence, notwithstanding that it is not duly stamped, if such document is otherwise admissible in evidence;

(c) examine any person acquainted with the facts and circumcontrary is proved, the truth of the contents of such document.

67. Power to call for information, etc. Any officer referred to in Section 42 who is authorised in this behalf by the Central Government or a State Government may, during the course of any enquiry in connection with the contravention of any provision of this Act, -

(a) call for information from any person for the purpose of satisfying himself whether there has been any contravention of the provisions of this Act or any rule or order made thereunder;

(b) require any person to produce or deliver any document or thing useful or relevant to the enquiry;

(c) examine any person acquainted with the facts and circumstances of the case.

68. Information as to commission of offences. No officer acting in exercise of powers vested in him under any provision of this Act or any rule or order made thereunder shall be compelled to say whence he got any information as to the commission of any offence.

CHAPTER - VA : FORFEITURE OF PROPERTY DERIVED FROM, OR USED IN, ILLICIT TRAFFIC

68A. Application.

(1) The provisions of this Chapter shall apply only to the persons specified in sub-section (2).

(2) The persons referred to in sub-section (1) are the following, namely:-

(a) every person who has been convicted of an offence punishable under this Act with imprisonment for a term of five years or more;

(b) every person who has been convicted of a similar offence by a competent court of criminal jurisdiction outside India;

(c) every person in respect of whom an order of detention has been made under the Prevention of Ilicit Traffic in Narcotic Drugs and Psychotropic Substances Act, 1988 (46 of 1988), or under the Jammu and Kashmir Prevention of Ilicit Traffic in Narcotic Drugs and Psychotropic Substances Act, 1988:

PROVIDED that such order of detention has not been revoked on the report of the Advisory Board constituted under the said Acts or such order of detention has not been set aside by a court of competent jurisdiction;

(d) every person who is a relative of a person referred to in clause (a) or clause (b) or clause (c);

(e) every associate of a person referred to in clause (a) or clause (b) or clause (c);

(f) any holder (hereafter in this clause referred to as the "present holder") of any property which was at any time previously held by a person referred to in clause (a) or clause (b) or clause (c) unless the present holder or, as the case may be, any one who held such property after such person and before the present holder, is or was a transferee in good faith for adequate consideration.

68B. Definitions. In this Chapter, unless the context otherwise requires,—

(a) "Appellate Tribunal" means the Appellate Tribunal for Forfeited Property constituted under Section 68N;

(b) "associate" in relation to a person whose property is liable to be forfeited under this Chapter, means—

(i) any individual who had been or is residing in the residential premises (including out-houses) of such person;

(ii) any individual who had been or is managing the affairs or keeping the accounts of such person;

(iii) any association of persons, body of individuals, partnership firm, or private company within the meaning of the Companies Act, 1956 (1 of 1956), of which such person had been or is a member, partner or director;

(iv) any individual who had been or is a member, partner or director of an association of persons, body of individuals, partnership firm or private company referred to in sub-clause (iii) at any time when such person had been or is a member, partner or director of such association, body, partnership firm or private company;

(v) any person, who had been or is managing the affairs, or keeping the accounts, of any association of persons, body of individuals, partnership firm or private company referred to in sub-clause (iii);

(vi) the trustee of any trust, where,—

(1) the trust has been created by such person; or

(2) the value of the assets contributed by such person (including the value of the assets, if any, contributed by him earlier) to the trust amounts, on the date on which contribution is made, to not less than twenty per cent. of the value of the assets of the trust on that date;

(vii) where the competent authority, for reasons to be recorded in writing, considers that any properties of such person are held on his behalf by any other person, such other person;

(c) "competent authority" means an officer of the Central Government authorised by it under Section 68D;

(d) "concealment" means the concealment or disguise of the nature, source, disposition, movement or ownership of property and includes the movement or conversion of such property by electronic transmission or by any other means;

(e) "freezing" means temporarily prohibiting the transfer, conversion, disposition or movement of property by an order issued under Section 68F;

(f) "identifying" includes establishment of proof that the property was derived from, or used in, the illicit traffic;

(g) "illegally acquired property", in relation to any person to whom this Chapter applies, means,—

(i) any property acquired by such person, whether before or after the commencement of this Chapter, wholly or partly out of or by means of any income, earnings or assets derived or obtained from or attributable to illicit traffic; or

(ii) any property acquired by such person, whether before or after the commencement of this Chapter, for a consideration, or by any means wholly or partly traceable to any property referred to in sub-clause (i) or the income or earning from such property, and includes—

(A) any property held by such person which would have been, in relation to any previous holder thereof, illegally acquired property under this clause if such previous holder had not ceased to hold it, unless such person or any other person who held the property at any time after such previous holder or, where there are two or more such previous holders, the last of such previous holders is or was a transferee in good faith for adequate consideration;

(B) any property acquired by such person, whether before or after the commencement of this Chapter, for a consideration, or by any means, wholly or partly traceable to any property falling under item (A), or the income or earnings therefrom;

(h) "property" means property and assets of every description, whether corporeal or incorporeal, movable or immovable, tangible or intangible and deeds and instruments evidencing title to, or interest in, such property or assets, derived from, or used in, the illicit traffic;

(i) " relative" means—

(1) spouse of the person;

(2) brother or sister of the person;

(3) brother or sister of the spouse of the person;

(4) any lineal ascendant or descendant of the person;

(5) any lineal ascendant or descendant of the spouse of the person;

(6) spouse of a person referred to in sub-clause (2), sub-clause (3), sub-clause (4) or sub-clause (5);

(7) any lineal descendant of a person referred to in sub-clause (2) or sub-clause (3);

(j) "tracing" means determining the nature, source, disposition, movement, title or ownership of property;

(k) "trust" includes any other legal obligation.

68C. Prohibition of holding illegally acquired property.

(1) As from the commencement of this Chapter, it shall not be lawful for any person to whom this Chapter applies to hold any illegally acquired property either by himself or through any other person on his behalf.

(2) Where any person holds any illegally acquired property in contravention of the provisions of sub-section (1), such property shall be liable to be forfeited to the Central Government in accordance with the provisions of this Chapter:

PROVIDED that no property shall be forfeited under this Chapter if such property was acquired by a person to whom this Act applies before a period of six years from the date on which he was charged for an offence relating to illicit traffic.

68D. Competent authority.

(1) The Central Government may, by order published in the Official Gazette, authorise any Collector of Customs or Collector of Central Excise or Commissioner of Income-tax or any other officer of the Central Government of equivalent rank to perform the functions of the competent authority under this Chapter.

(2) The competent authorities shall perform their functions in respect of such persons or classes of persons as the Central Government may, by order, direct.

68E. Identifying illegally acquired property.

(1) Every officer empowered under Section 53 and every officer-in-charge of a police station, shall, on receipt of information that any person to whom this Chapter applies has been charged with any offence punishable under this Act, whether committed in India or outside, proceed to take all steps necessary for tracing and identifying any property illegally acquired by such person.

(2) The steps referred to in sub-section (1) may include any inquiry, investigation or survey in respect of any person, place, property, assets, documents, books of account in any bank or public financial institution or any other relevant matters.

(3) Any inquiry, investigation or survey referred to in sub-section (2) shall be carried out by an officer mentioned in sub-section (1) in accordance with such directions or guidelines as the competent authority may make or issue in this behalf.

68F. Seizure or freezing of illegally acquired property.

(1) Where any officer conducting an inquiry or investigation under Section 68E has reason to believe that any property in relation to which such inquiry or investigation is being conducted is an illegally acquired property and such property is likely to be concealed, transferred or dealt with in any manner which will result in frustrating any proceeding relating to forfeiture of such property under this Chapter, he may make an order for seizing such property and where it is not practicable to seize such property, he may make an order that such property shall not be transferred or otherwise dealt with, except with the prior permission of the officer making such order, or of the competent authority and a copy of such order shall be served on the person concerned:

PROVIDED that the competent authority shall be duly informed of any order made under this sub-section and a copy of such an order shall be sent to the competent authority within forty-eight hours of its being made.

(2) Any order made under sub-section (1) shall have no effect unless the said order is confirmed by an order of the competent authority within a period of thirty days of its being made.

EXPLANATION. For the purposes of this Section, "transfer of property" means any disposition, conveyance, assignment, settlement, delivery, payment or other alienation of property and, without limiting the generality of the foregoing, includes—

(a) the creation of a trust in property;

(b) the grant or creation of any lease, mortgage, charge, easement, licence, power, partnership or interest in property;

(c) the exercise of a power of appointment of property vested in any person, not the owner of the property, to determine its disposition in favour of any person other than the donee of the power; and

(d) any transaction entered into by any person with intent thereby to diminish directly or indirectly the value of his own property and to increase the value of the property of any other person.

68G. Management of properties seize or forfeited under this Chapter.

(1) The Central Government may, by order published in the Official Gazette, appoint as many of its officers (not below the rank of a Joint secretary to the Government) as it thinks fit, to perform the functions of an Administrator.

(2) The Administrator appointed under sub-section (1) shall receive and manage the property in relation to which an order has been made under sub-section (1) of Section 68F or under Section 68I in such manner and subject to such conditions as may be prescribed.

(3) The Administrator shall also take such measures, as the Central Government may direct, to dispose of the property which is forfeited to the Central Government.

68H. Notice of forfeiture of property.

(1) If, having regard to the value of the properties held by any person to whom this Chapter applies, either by himself or through any other person on his behalf, his known sources of income, earnings or assets, and any other information or material available to it as a result of a report from any officer making an investigation under Section 68E or otherwise, the competent authority has reason to believe (the reasons for such belief to be recorded in writing) that all or any of such properties are illegally acquired properties, it may serve a notice upon such person (hereinafter referred to as the person affected) calling upon him within a period of thirty days specified in the notice to indicate the sources of his income, earnings or assets, out of which or by means of which he has acquired such property, the evidence on which he relies and other relevant information and particulars, and to show cause why all or any of such properties, as the case may be, should not be declared to be illegally acquired properties and forfeited to the Central Government under this Chapter.

(2) Where a notice under sub-section (1) to any person specifies any property as being held on behalf of such person by any other person, a copy of the notice shall also be served upon such other person.

68I. Forfeiture of property in certain cases.

(1) The competent authority may, after considering the explanation, if any, to the show-cause notice issued under Section 68H, and the materials available before it and after giving to the person affected (and in a case where the person affected holds any property specified in the notice through any other person, to such other person also) a reasonable opportunity of being heard, by order, record a finding whether all or any of the properties in question are illegally acquired properties:

PROVIDED that if the person affected (and in a case where the person affected holds any property specified in the notice through any other person such other person also) does not appear before the competent authority or represent his case before it within a period of thirty days specified in the show-cause notice, the competent authority may proceed to record a finding under this sub-section exparte on the basis of evidence available before it.

(2) Where the competent authority is satisfied that some of the properties referred to in the show-cause notice are illegally acquired properties but is not able to identify specifically such properties, then, it shall be lawful for the competent authority to specify the properties which, to the best of its judgment, are illegally acquired properties and record a finding accordingly under sub-section (1).

(3) Where the competent authority records a finding under this Section to the effect that any property is illegally acquired property, it shall declare that such property shall, subject to the provisions of this Chapter, stand forfeited to the Central Government free from all encumbrances.

(4) Where any shares in a company stand forfeited to the Central Government under this Chapter, then, the company shall, notwithstanding anything contained in the Companies Act, 1956 (1 of 1956) or the articles of association of the company, forthwith register the Central Government as the transferee of such shares.

68J. Burden of proof. In any proceedings under this Chapter, the burden of proving that any property specified in the notice served under Section 68H is not illegally acquired property shall be on the person affected.

68K. Fine in lieu of forfeiture.

(1) Where the competent authority makes a declaration that any property stands forfeited to the Central Government under Section 68I and it is a case where the source of only a part of the illegally acquired property has not been proved to the satisfaction of the competent authority, it shall make an order giving an option to the person affected to pay, in lieu of forfeiture, a fine equal to the market value of such part.

(2) Before making an order imposing a fine under sub-section (1), the person affected shall be given a reasonable opportunity of being heard.

(3) Where the person affected pays the fine due under sub-section (1), within such time as may be allowed in that behalf, the competent authority may, by order, revoke the declaration of forfeiture under Section 68I and thereupon such property shall stand released.

68L. Procedure in relation to certain trust properties. In the case of any person referred to in sub-clause (vi) of clause (b) of Section 68B, if the competent authority, on the basis of the information and materials available to it, has reason to believe (the reasons for such belief to be recorded in writing) that any property held in trust is illegally acquired property, it may serve a notice upon the author of the trust or, as the case may be, the contributor of the assets out of or by means of which such property was acquired by the trust and the trustees, calling upon them within a period of thirty days specified in the notice, to explain the source of money or other assets out of or by means of which such property was acquired or, as the case may be, the source of money or other assets which were contributed to the trust for acquiring such property and thereupon such notice shall be deemed to be a notice served under Section 68H and all the other provisions of this Chapter shall apply accordingly.

EXPLANATION: For the purposes of this Section" illegally acquired property", in relation to any property held in trust, includes—

(i) any property which if it had continued to be held by the author of the trust or the contributor of such property to the trust would have been illegally acquired property in relation to such author or contributor;

(ii) any property acquired by the trust out of any contributions made by any person which would have been illegally acquired property in relation to such person had such person acquired such property out of such contributions.

68M. Certain transfers to be null and void. Where after the making of an order under sub-section (1) of Section 68F or the issue of a notice under Section 68H or under Section 68L, any property referred to in the said order or notice is transferred by any mode whatsoever such transfer shall, for the purposes of the proceedings under this Chapter, be ignored and if such property is subsequently forfeited to the Central Government under Section 68I, then, the transfer of such property shall be deemed to be null and void.

68N. Constitution of Appellate Tribunal.

(1) The Central Government may, by notification in the Official Gazette, constitute an Appellate Tribunal to be called the Appellate Tribunal for Forfeited Property consisting of a Chairman and such number of other members (being officers of the Central Government not below the rank of a Joint Secretary to the Government) as the Central Government thinks fit, to be appointed by that Government for hearing appeals against the orders made under Section 68F, Section 68I, sub-section (1) of Section 68K of Section 68L.

(2) The Chairman of the Appellate Tribunal shall be a person who is or has been or is qualified to be a Judge of the Supreme Court or of a High Court.

(3) The terms and conditions of service of the Chairman and other members shall be such as may be prescribed.

68O. Appeals.

(1) Any person aggrieved by an order of the competent authority made under Section 68F, Section 68I, sub-section (1) of Section 68K or Section 68L, may, within forty-five days from the date on which the order is served on him, prefer an appeal to the Appellate Tribunal:

PROVIDED that the Appellate Tribunal may entertain an appeal after the said period of forty-five days, but not after sixty days, from the date aforesaid if it is satisfied that the appellant was prevented by sufficient cause from filling the appeal in time.

(2) On receipt of an appeal under sub-section (1), the Appellate Tribunal may, after giving an opportunity to the appellant to be heard, if he so desires, and after making such further inquiry as it deems fit, confirm, modify or set aside the order appealed against.

(3) The powers and functions of the Appellate Tribunal may be exercised and discharged by Benches consisting of three members and constituted by the Chairman of the Appellate Tribunal.

(4) Notwithstanding anything contained in sub-section (3), where the Chairman considers it necessary so to do for the expeditious disposal of appeals under this Section, he may constitute a Bench of two members and a Bench so constituted may exercise and discharge the powers and functions of the Appellate Tribunal:

PROVIDED that if the members of a Bench so constituted differ on any point or points, they shall state the point or points on which they differ and refer the same to a third member (to be specified by the Chairman) for hearing of such point or points and such point or points shall be decided according to the opinion of that member.

(5) The Appellate Tribunal may regulate its own procedure.

(6) On application to the Appellate Tribunal and on payment of the prescribed fee, the Tribunal may allow a party to any appeal or any person authorised in his behalf by such party to inspect at any time during office hours, any relevant records and registers of the Tribunal and obtain a certified copy of any part thereof.

68P. Notice or order not to be invalid for error in description. No notice issued or served, no declaration made, and no order passed, under this Chapter shall be deemed to be invalid by reason of any reason of any error in the description of the property or person mentioned therein if such property or person is identifiable from the description so mentioned.

68Q. Bar of jurisdiction. No order passed or declaration made under this Chapter shall be appeal able except as provided there and no civil court shall have jurisdiction in respect of any matter which the Appellate Tribunal or any competent authority is empowered by or under this Chapter to determine, and no injunction shall be granted by any court or other authority in respect of any action taken of any action taken or to be taken in pursuance of any power conferred by or under this Chapter.

68R. Competent authority and Appellate Tribunal to have powers of civil court. The competent authority and the Appellate Tribunal shall have all the powers of a civil court while trying a suit under the Code of Civil Procedure, 1908, in respect of the following matters, namely:-

(a) summoning and enforcing the attendance of any person and examining him on oath;

(b) requiring the discovery and production of documents;

(c) receiving evidence on affidavits;

(d) requisitioning any public record or copy thereof from any court or office;

(e) issuing commissions for examination of witnesses or documents;

(f) any other matter which may be prescribed.

68S. Information to competent authority.

(1) Notwithstanding anything contained in any other law, the competent authority shall have power to require any officer or authority of the Central Government or a State Government or a local authority to furnish information in relation to such persons, points or matters as in the opinion of the competent authority will be useful for, or relevant to, the purpose of this Chapter.

(2) Every officer referred to in Section 68T may furnish suo motu any information available with him to the competent authority if in the opinion of the officer such information will be useful to the competent authority for the purposes of this Chapter.

68T. Certain officers to assist Administrator, competent authority and Appellate Tribunal. For the purposes of any proceedings under this Chapter, the following officers are hereby empowered and required to assists the Administrator appointed under Section 68G, competent authority and the Appellate Tribunal, namely:—

(a) officers of the Narcotics Control Bureau;

(b) officers of the Customs Department;

(c) officers of the Central Excise Department;

(d) officers of the Income-tax Department;

(e) officers of enforcement appointed under the Foreign Exchange Regulation Act, 1973 (46 of 1973);

(f) officers of police;

(g) officers of the Narcotics Department;

(h) officers of the Central Economic Intelligence Bureau;

(i) officers of the Directorate of Revenue Intelligence Bureau;

(j) such other officers of the Central or State Government as are specified by the Central Government in this behalf by notification in the Official Gazette.

68U. Power to take possession.

(1) Where any property has been declared to be forfeited to the Central Government under this Chapter, or where the person affected has failed to pay the fine due under sub-section (1) of Section 68K within the time allowed therefore under sub-section (3) of that Section, the competent authority may order the person affected as well as any other person who may be in possession of the property to surrender or deliver possession thereof to the Administrator appointed under Section 68G or to any person duly authorised by him in this behalf within thirty days of the service of the order.

(2) If any person refuses or fails to comply with an order made under sub-section (1), the Administrator may take possession of the property and may for that purpose use such force as may be necessary.

(3) Notwithstanding anything contained in sub-section (2), the Administrator may, for the purpose of taking possession of any property referred to in sub-section (1), requisition the service of any police officer to assist him and it shall be the duty of such officer to comply with such requisition.

68V. Rectification of mistakes. With a view to rectifying any mistakes apparent from record, the competent authority or the Appellate Tribunal, as the case may be, may amend any order made by it within a period of one year from the date of the order.

PROVIDED that if any such amendment is likely to affect any person prejudicially, it shall not be made without giving to such person a reasonable opportunity of being heard.

68W. Findings under other laws not conclusive for proceedings under this Chapter. No finding of any officer or authority under any other law shall be conclusive for the purposes of any proceedings under this Chapter.

68X. Service of notices and orders. Any notice or order issued or made under this Chapter shall be served-

(a) by tendering the notice or order or sending it by registered post to the person for whom it is intended or to his agent;

(b) if the notice or order cannot be served in the manner provided in clause (a), by affixing it on a conspicuous place in the property in relation to which the notice or order is issued or made or on some conspicuous part of the premises in which the person for whom it is intended is known to have last resided or carried on business or personally worked for gain.

68Y. Punishment for acquiring property in relation to which property in relation to which proceedings have this taken, been under Chapter. Any person who knowingly acquired, by any mode whatsoever, any property in relation to which proceedings are pending under this Chapter shall be punishable with imprisonment for a term which may extend to five years and with fine which may extend to 'fifty thousand rupees'.

CHAPTER -VI : MISCELLANEOUS

69. Protection of action taken in good faith. No suit, prosecution or other legal proceeding shall lie against the Central Government or a State Government or any officer of the Central Government or of the State Government or any other person exercising any powers or discharging any functions or performing any duties under this Act, for anything in good faith done or intended to be done under this Act or any rule or order made thereunder.

70. Central Government and State Government to have regard to international conventions while making rules. Wherever under this Act the Central Government or the State Government has been empowered to make rules, the Central Government or the State Government, as the case may be, subject to other provisions of this Act, may while making the rules have regard to the provisions of the Single Convention on Narcotic Drugs, 1961, the Protocol of 1972 amending the said Convention and of the Convention on Psychotropic Substances, 1971 to which India is a party and to the provisions of any other international convention relating to narcotic drugs or psychotropic substances to which India may become a party.

71. Power of Government to establish centre for identification, treatment, etc., of addicts and for supply of narcotic drug and psychotropic substances.

(1) The Government may, in its discretion, establish as many centres as it thinks fit for identification, treatment, education, after-care, rehabilitation, social re-integration of addicts and for supply, subject to such conditions and in such manner as may be prescribed, by the concerned Government of any narcotic drugs and psychotropic substances to the addicts registered with the Government and to others where such supply is a medical necessity.

(2) The Government may make rules consistent with this Act providing for the establishment, appointment, maintenance, management and superintendence of, and for supply of narcotic drugs and psychotropic substances from the centres referred to in sub-section (1) and for the appointment, training, powers, duties and persons employed in such centres.

72. Recovery of sums due to Government.

(1) In respect of any licence fee or other sum of any kind payable to the Central Government or to the State Government under any of the provisions of this Act or of any rule or order made thereunder, the officer of the Central Government or the State Government, as the case may be, who is empowered to require the payment of such sum, may deduct the amount of such sum from any money owing to the person from whom such sum may be recoverable or due or may recover such amount or sum by attachment and sale of the goods belonging to such persons and if the amount of the same is not so recovered, the same may be recovered from the person or from his surety (if any) as if it were an arrears of land revenue.

(2) When any person, in compliance with any rule made under this Act, gives a bond (other than a bond under Section 34 and Section 39) for the performance of any act, or for his abstention from any act, such performance or abstention shall be deemed to be a public duty within the meaning of Section 74 of the Indian Contract Act, 1872 (9 of 1872); and upon breach of the conditions of such bond by him, the whole sum named therein as the amount to be paid in case of such breach may be recovered from him or from his surety (if any) as if it were an arrears of land revenue.

73. Bar of jurisdiction. No civil court shall entertain any suit or proceeding against any decision made or order passed by any officer or authority under this Act or under any rule made thereunder on any of the following matters, namely:-

(a) withholding, refusal or cancellation of any licence for the cultivation of the opium poppy;

(b) weighment, examination and classification according to the quality and consistence of opium and any deductions from, or addition to, the standard price made in accordance with such examination;

(c) confiscation of opium found to be adulterated with any foreign substance.

74. Transitional provisions. Every officer or other employee of the Government exercising or performing, immediately before the commencement of this Act, any powers or duties with respect to any matters provided for in this Act, shall on such commencement, be deemed to have been appointed under the relevant provisions of this Act to the same post and with the same designation as he was holding immediately before such commencement.

74A. Power of Central Government to give directions. The Central Government may give such directions as it may deem necessary to a State Government regarding the carrying into execution of the provisions of this Act, and the State Government shall comply with such directions.

75. Power to delegate.

(1) The Central Government may, by notification in the Official Gazette, delegate, subject to such conditions and limitations as may be specified in the notification, such of its powers and functions under this Act (except the power to make rules) as it may deem necessary or expedient, to the Board or any other authority or the Narcotics Commissioner.

(2) The State Government may, by notification in the Official Gazette, delegate, subject to such conditions and limitations as may be specified in the notification, such of its powers and functions under this Act (except the power to make rules) as it may deem necessary or expedient, to any authority or officer of that Government.

76. Power of Central Government to make rules.

(1) Subject to the other provisions of this Act, the Central Government may, by notification in the Official Gazette, make rules for carrying out the purposes of this Act.

(2) Without prejudice to the generality of the foregoing power, such rules may provide for all or any of the following matters, namely:—

(a) the method by which percentages in the case of liquid preparations shall be calculated for the purposes of clauses (v), (vi) (xiv) and (xv) of Section 2;

(b) the form of bond to keep the peace to be executed under Section 34;

(c) the form of bond to be executed for release of an addict convict for medical treatment under sub-section (1) of Section 39 and the bond to be executed by such convict before his release after due admonition under sub-section (2) of that Section;

(d) the authority or the person by whom and the manner in which a document received from any place outside India shall be authenticated under clause (ii) of Section 66;

(da) the manner in which and the conditions subject to which properties shall be managed by the Administrator under sub-section (2) of Section 68G;

(db) the terms and conditions of service of the Chairman and other members of the Appellate Tribunal under sub-section (3) of Section 68N;

(dc) the fees which shall be paid for the inspection of the records and registers of the Appellate Tribunal or for obtaining the certified copy of any part thereof under sub-section (6) of Section 68-O;

(dd) the powers of a civil court that may be exercised by the competent authority and the Appellate Tribunal under clause (f) of Section 68R;

(de) the disposal of all articles or things confiscated under this Act;

(df) the drawing of samples and testing and analysis of such samples;

(dg) the rewards to be paid to the officers, informers and other persons;

(e) the conditions and the manner in which narcotic drugs and psychotropic substances may be supplied for medical necessity to the addicts registered with the Central Government and to others under sub-section (1) of Section 71;

(f) the establishment, appointment, maintenance, management and superintendence of centres established by the Central Government under sub-section (1) of Section 71 and appointment, training, powers and duties of persons employed in such centres;

(g) the term of office of, the manner of filling casual vacancies of, and the allowances payable to, the Chairman and members of the Narcotic Drugs and Psychotropic Substances Consultative Committee and the conditions and restrictions subject to which a non-member may be appointed to a sub-committee under sub-section (5) of Section 6;

(h) any other matter which is to be, or may be, prescribed Rules and Notifications to be laid before Parliament. Every rule made under this Act by the Central Government and every notification issued under clause (xi) of Section 2, Section 3 and clause (a) of, and Explanation (1) to, Section 27 shall be laid, as soon as may be, after it is made or issued, before each House of Parliament while it is in session, for a total period of thirty days which may be comprised in one session or in two or more successive sessions, and if, before the expiry of the session immediately following the session or the successive sessions aforesaid, both Houses agree in making any modification in the rule or notification or both Houses agree that the rule or notification should not be made or issued, the rule or the notification shall thereafter have effect only in such modified form or be of no effect, as the case may be; so, however, that any such modification or annulment shall be without prejudice to the validity of anything previously done under that rule or notification.

78. Power of State Government to make rules.

(1) Subject to the other provisions of this Act, the State Government may, by notification in the Official Gazette, make rules for carrying out the purposes of this Act.

(2) Without prejudice to the generality of the foregoing power, such rules may provide for all or any of the following matters, namely:—

(a) the conditions and the manner in which narcotic drugs and psychotropic substances shall be supplied for medical necessity to the addicts registered with the State Government and others under sub-section (1) of Section 71;

(b) the establishment, appointment, maintenance, management, superintendence of centres established under sub-section (1) of Section 71 and appointment, training, powers and duties of persons employed in such centres;

(c) any other matter which is to be, or may be, prescribed.

(3) Every rule made by a State Government under this Act shall be laid, as soon as may be after it is made, before the Legislature of that State.

79. Application of the Customs Act, 1962. All prohibitions and restrictions imposed by or under this Act on the import into India, the export from India and transhipment of narcotic drugs and psychotropic substances shall be deemed to be prohibitions and restrictions imposed by or under the Customs Act, 1962 (52 of 1962) and the provisions of that Act shall apply accordingly:

PROVIDED that, where the doing of anything is an offence punishable under that Act and under this Act, nothing in that Act or in this Section shall prevent the offender from being punished under this Act.

80. Application of the Drugs and Cosmetics Act, 1940 not barred. The provisions of this Act or the rules made thereunder shall be in addition to, and not in derogation of, the Drugs and Cosmetics Act, 1940 (23 of 1940) or the rules made thereunder.

81. Saving of State and special laws. Nothing in this Act or in the rules made thereunder shall affect the validity of any Provincial Act or an Act of any State Legislature for the time being in force, or of any rule made thereunder which imposes any restriction or provides for a punishment not imposed by or provided for under this Act or imposes a restriction or provides for a punishment greater in degree than a corresponding restriction imposed by or a corresponding punishment provided for by or under this Act for the cultivation of cannabis plant or consumption of, or traffic in, any narcotic drug or psychotropic substance within India.

82. Repeal and savings.

(1) The Opium Act, 1857 (13 of 1857), the Opium Act, 1878 (1 of 1878) and the Dangerous Drugs Act, 1930 (2 of 1930) are hereby repealed.

(2) Notwithstanding such repeal, anything done or any action taken or purported to have been done or taken under any of the enactments repealed by sub-section (1) shall, insofar as it is not inconsistent with the provisions of this Act, be deemed to have been done or taken under the corresponding provisions of this Act.

83. Power to remove difficulties.

(1) If any difficulty arises in giving effect to the provisions of this Act, the Central Government may, by published in the Official Gazette, make such provisions not inconsistent with the provisions of this Act as appear to it to be necessary or expedient for removing the difficulty:

PROVIDED that no such order shall be made after the expiry of a period of three years from the date on which this Act receives the assent of the President.

(2) Every order made under this Section shall, as soon as may be after it is made, be laid before the Houses of Parliament.

❑❑❑

19

The Prevention of Blackmarketing and Maintenance of Supplies of Essential Commodities Act, 1980

(7 OF 1980) [12TH FEBRUARY, 1980]

AN ACT to provide for detention in certain cases for the purpose of prevention of blackmarketing and maintenance of supplies of commodities essential to the community and for matters connected therewith.

Be it enacted by Parliament in the Thirty-first Year of the Republic of India as follows:—

1. Short title, extent and commencement.

(1) This Act may be called the Prevention of Blackmarketing and Maintenance of Supplies of Essential Commodities Act, 1980.

(2) It extends to the whole of India except the State of Jammu and Kashmir.

(3) It shall be deemed to have come into force on the 5th day of October, 1979.

2. Definitions. In this Act, unless the context otherwise requires,

(a) "appropriate Government" means, as respects a detention order made by the Central Government or by an officer of the Central Government or person detained under such order, the Central Government, and as respects a detention order made by a State Government or by an officer of a State Government or as respects a person detained under such order, the State Government;

(b) "detention order" means an order made under Section 3;

(c) "State Government", in relation to a Union Territory, means the administrator thereof.

3. Power to make orders detaining certain persons.

(1) The Central Government or a State Government or any officer of the Central Government, not below the rank of a Joint Secretary to that Government specially empowered for the purposes of this Section by that Government, or any officer of a State Government, not below the rank of a Secretary to that Government specially empowered for the purposes of this Section by that Government, may, if satisfied, with respect to any person that with a view to preventing him from acting in any manner prejudicial to the maintenance of supplies of the commodities essential to the community it is necessary so to do, make an order directing that such person be detained.

EXPLANATION: For the purposes of this sub-section, the expression "acting in any manner prejudicial to the maintenance of supplies of commodities essential to the community" means -

(a) committing or instigating any person to commit any offence punishable under the Essential Commodities Act, 1955 (10 of 1955) or under any other law for the time being in force relating to the control of the production, supply or distribution of, or trade and commerce in, any commodity essential to the community; or

(b) dealing in any commodity –

(i) which is an essential commodity as defined in the Essential Commodities Act, 1955 (10 of 1955), or

(ii) with respect to which provisions have been made in any such other law as is referred to in clause (a), with a view to making gain in any manner which may directly or indirectly defeat or tend to defeat the provisions of that Act or other law aforesaid.

(2) Any of the following officers, namely –

(a) District Magistrates;

(b) Commissioners of Police, wherever they have been appointed, may also, if satisfied as provided in sub-section (1), exercise the powers conferred by the said sub-section.

(3) When any order is made under this Section by an officer mentioned in sub-section (2), he shall forthwith report the fact to the State Government to which he is subordinate together with the grounds on which the order has been made and such other particulars as in his opinion have a bearing on the matter, and no such order shall remain in force for more than twelve days after the making thereof unless in the meantime it has been approved by the State Government:

PROVIDED that where under Section 8 the grounds of detention are communicated by the authority making the order after five days but not later than ten days from the date of detention, this sub-section shall apply subject to the modification that for the words "twelve days", the words "fifteen days" shall be substituted.

(4) When any order is made or approved by the State Government under this Section or when any order is made under this Section by an officer of the State

Government not below the rank of Secretary to that Government specially empowered under sub-section (1), the State Government shall, within seven days, report the fact to the Central Government together with the grounds on which the order has been made and such other particulars as, in the opinion of the State Government, have a bearing on the necessity for the order.

4. Execution of detention orders. A detention order may be executed at any place in India in the manner provided for the execution of warrants of arrest under the Code of Criminal Procedure, 1973 (2 of 1974).

5. Power to regulate place and conditions of detention. Every person in respect of whom a detention order has been made shall be liable—

(a) to be detained in such place and under such conditions, including conditions as to maintenance, discipline and punishment for breaches of discipline, as the appropriate Government may, by general or special order, specify; and

(b) to be removed from one place of detention to another place of detention, whether within the same State or in another State, by order of the appropriate Government:

PROVIDED that no order shall be made by a State Government under clause (b) for the removal of a person from one State to another State except with the consent of the Government of that other State.

6. Detention orders not to be invalid or inoperative on certain grounds. No detention order shall be invalid or inoperative merely by reason –

(a) that the person to be detained thereunder is outside the limits of the territorial jurisdiction of the Government or officer making the order, or

(b) that the place of detention of such person is outside the said limits.

7. Powers in relation to absconding persons.

(1) If the appropriate Government or an officer mentioned in sub-section (2) of Section 3, as the case may be has reason to believe that a person in respect of whom a detention order has been made has absconded or is concealing himself so that the order cannot be executed, that Government or officer may—

(a) make a report in writing of the fact to a Metropolitan Magistrate or a Judicial Magistrate of the First Class having jurisdiction in the place where the said person ordinarily resides; and thereupon the provisions of Section 82, 83, 84 and 85 of the Code of Criminal Procedure, 1973 (2 of 1974), shall apply in respect of the said person and his property as if the order directing that he be detained were a warrant issued by the Magistrate;

(b) by order notified in the Official Gazette direct the said person to appear before such officer, at such place and within such period as may be specified in the order; and if the said person fails to comply with such direction he shall, unless he proves that it was not possible for him to comply therewith and that he had, within the period specified in the order, informed the officer mentioned in the order, of the reason which rendered compliance therewith impossible and of his whereabouts, be punishable with imprisonment for a term which may extend to one year or with fine or with both.

(2) Notwithstanding anything contained in the Code of Criminal Procedure, 1973 (2 of 1974), every offence under clause (b) of sub-section (1) shall be cognizable.

8. Grounds of order of detention to be disclosed to person affected by the order.

(1) When a person is detained in pursuance of a detention order, the authority making the order shall, as soon as may be, but ordinarily not later than five days and in exceptional circumstances and for reasons to be recorded in writing, not later than ten days from the date of detention, communicate to him the grounds on which the order has been made and shall afford him the earliest opportunity of making a representation against the order to the appropriate Government.

(2) Nothing in sub-section (l) shall require the authority to disclose facts which it considers to be against the public interest to disclose.

9. Constitution of Advisory Boards.

(1) The Central Government and each State Government shall, whenever necessary, constitute one or more Advisory Boards for the purposes of this Act.

(2) Every such Board shall consist of three persons who are, or have been or are qualified to be appointed as, Judges of a High Court, and such persons shall be appointed by the appropriate Government.

(3) The appropriate Government shall appoint one of the members of the Advisory Board who is, or has been, a Judge of a High Court to be its Chairman, and in the case of a Union Territory, the appointment to the Advisory Board of any person who is a Judge of the High Court of a State shall be with the previous approval of the State Government concerned.

10. Reference to Advisory Boards. Save as otherwise expressly provided in this Act, in every case where a detention order has been made under this Act, the appropriate Government shall, within three weeks from the date of detention of a person under the order, place before the Advisory Board constituted by it under Section 9, the grounds on which the order has been made and the representation, if any, made by the person affected by the order and in case where the order has been made by an officer referred to in sub-section (2) of Section 3, also the report by such officer under sub-section (3), of that Section.

11. Procedure of Advisory Boards.

(1) The Advisory Board shall, after considering the materials placed before it and, after calling for such further information as it may deem necessary from the appropriate Government or from any person called for the purpose through the appropriate Government or from the person concerned, and if, in any particular case, it considers it essential so to do or if the person concerned desires to be heard, after hearing him in person, submit its report to the appropriate Government within seven weeks from the date of detention of the person concerned.

(2) The report of Advisory Board shall specify in separate part thereof the opinion of the Advisory Board as to whether or not there is sufficient cause for the detention of the person concerned.

(3) When there is a difference of opinion among the members forming the Advisory Board, the opinion of the majority of such members shall be deemed to be the opinion of the Board.

(4) Nothing in this Section shall entitle any person against whom a detention order has been made to appear by any legal practitioner in any matter connected with the reference to the Advisory Board, and the proceedings of the Advisory Board, and its report, excepting that part of the report in which the opinion of the Advisory Board is specified, shall be confidential.

12. Action upon the report of Advisory Board.

(1) In any case where the Advisory Board has reported that there is, in its opinion, sufficient cause for the detention of a person, the appropriate Government may confirm the detention order and continue the detention of the person concerned for such period as it thinks fit.

(2) In any case where the Advisory Board has reported that there is, in its opinion, no sufficient cause for the detention of the person concerned, the appropriate Government shall revoke the detention order and cause the person to be released forthwith.

13. Maximum period of detention.

(1) The maximum period for which any person may be detained in pursuance of any detention order which has been confirmed under Section 12, shall be six months from the date of detention:

PROVIDED that nothing contained in this Section shall affect the power of the appropriate Government to revoke or modify the detention order at any earlier time.

14. Revocation of detention orders.

(1) Without prejudice to the provisions of Section 21 of the General Clauses Act, 1897 (10 of 1897), a detention order may, at any time, be revoked or modified

(a) notwithstanding that the order has been made by an officer of the State Government, by that State Government or by the Central Government;

(b) notwithstanding that the order has been made by an officer of the Central Government or by a State Government, by the Central Government.

(2) The revocation or expiry of a detention order shall not bar the making of a fresh detention order under Section 3 against the same person in any case where fresh facts have arisen after the date of revocation or expiry on which the Central Government or a State Government or an officer, as the case may be, is satisfied that such an order should be made.

15. Temporary release of persons detained.

(1) The appropriate Government may, at any time, direct that any person detained in pursuance of a detention order may be released for any specified period

either without conditions or upon such conditions specified in the direction as the person accepts, and may, at any time, cancel his release.

(2) In directing the release of any person under sub-section (1), the appropriate Government may require him to enter into a bond with or without sureties for the due observance of the conditions specified in the direction.

(3) Any person released under sub-section (1) shall surrender himself at the time and place, and to the authority, specified in the order directing his release or cancelling his release, as the case may be.

(4) If any person fails without sufficient cause to surrender himself in the manner specified in sub-section (3), he shall be punishable with imprisonment for a term which may extend to two years or with fine, or with both.

(5) If any person released under sub-section (1) fails to fulfil any of the conditions imposed upon him under the said sub-section or in the bond entered into by him, the bond shall be declared to be forfeited and any person bound thereby shall be liable to pay the penalty thereof.

16. Protection of action taken in good faith. No suit or other legal proceeding shall lie against the Central Government or a State Government, and no suit, prosecution or other legal proceeding shall lie against any person, for any thing in good faith done or intended to be done in pursuance of this Act.

17. Repeal and saving.

(1) The Prevention of Blackmarketing and Maintenance of Supplies of Essential Commodities Ordinance, 1979 (10 of 1979), is hereby repealed.

(2) Nothwithstanding such repeal anything done or any action taken under the Ordinance so repealed shall be deemed to have been done or taken under the corresponding provisions of this Act.

LIST OF COMMODITIES DECLARED ESSENTIAL UNDER THE ESSENTIAL COMMODITIES ACT, 1955
(As on 15.12.2004)

Declared under Clause (a) of Section 2 of the Act

1. Cattle fodder, including oilcakes and other concentrates.
2. Coal, including coke and other derivatives.
3. Component parts and accessories of automobiles.
4. Cotton and woollen textiles.
5. Drugs.
6. Foodstuffs, including edible oilseeds and oils.
7. Iron and Steel, including manufactured products of Iron & Steel.
8. Paper, including newsprint, paperboard and strawboard.
9. Petroleum and Petroleum products.
10. Raw Cotton, either ginned or unginned and cotton seed.
11. Raw Jute.

Declared as essential through notifications under sub-clause (xi) of clause (a) of Section 2 of the E. C. Act

12. Jute textiles.
13. Fertilizer, whether inorganic, organic or mixed.
14. Yarn made wholly from cotton.
15. (i) seeds of food crops and seeds of fruits and vegetables,
    (ii) seeds of cattle fodder and
    (iii) jute seeds.

❑❑❑

20

The Prevention of Corruption Act, 1988

CHAPTER - I : PRELIMINARY

1. Short title and extent.

(1) This Act may be called the Prevention of Corruption Act, 1988.

(2) If extends to the whole of India except the State of Jammu and Kashmir and it applies also to all citizens of India outside India.

2. Definitions. In this Act, unless the context otherwise, requires,—

(a) "election" means any election, by whatever means held under any law for the purpose of selecting members of Parliament or of any Legislature, local authority or other public authority;

(b) "public duty" means a duty in the discharge of which the State, the public or the community at large has an interest;

EXPLANATION. In this clausen "State" includes a corporation established by or under a Central, Provincial or State Act, or an authority or a body owned or controlled or aided by the Government or a Government company as defined in Section 617 of the Companies Act, 1956 (1 of 1956);

(c) "public servant" means—

(i) any person in the service or pay of the Government or remunerated by the Government by fees or commission for the performance of any public duty;

(ii) any person in the service or pay of a local authority;

(iii) any person in the service or pay of a corporation evidence by or under a Central, Provincial or State Act, or an authority or a body owned or controlled or aided by the Government or a Government company as defined in Section 617 of the Companies Act, 1956 (1 of 1956);

(iv) any Judge, including any person empowered by law to discharge, whether by himself or as a member of any body of persons, any adjudicatory functions;

(v) any person authorised by a court of justice to perform any duty, in connection with the administration of justice, including a liquidator, receiver or commission appointed by such court;

(vi) any arbitrator or other person to whom any cause or matter has been referred for decision or report by a court of justice or by a competent public authority;

(vii) any person who holds an office by virtue of which he is empowered to prepare, publish, maintain or revise an electoral roll or to conduct an election or part of an election;

(viii) any person who holds an office by virtue of which he is authorised or required to perform any public duty;

(ix) any person who is the president, secretary or other office-bearer of a registered co-operative society engaged in agriculture, industry, trade or banking, receiving or having received any financial aid from the Central Government or a State Government or from any corporation established by or under a Central, Provincial or State Act, or any authority or body owned or controlled or aided by the Government or a Government company as defined in Section 617 of the Companies Act, 1956 (1 of 1956);

(x) any person who is a chairman, member or employee of any Service Commission or Board, by whatever name called, or a member of any selection committee appointed by such Commission or Board for the conduct of any examination or making any selection on behalf of such Commission or Board;

(xi) any person who is a Vice-Chancellor or member of any governing body, professor, reader, lecturer or any other teacher or employee, by whatever designation called, of any University and any person whose services have been availed of by a University or any other public authority in connection with holding or conducting examinations;

(xii) any person who is an office-bearer or an employee of an educational, scientific, social, cultural or other institution, in whatever manner established, receiving or having received any financial assistance from the Central Government or any State Government, or local or other public authority.

EXPLANATION 1: Persons falling under any of the above sub-clauses are public servants, whether appointed by the Government or not.

EXPLANATION 2: Wherever the words" public servant" occur, they shall be understood of every person who is in actual possession of the situation of a public servant, whatever legal defect there may be in his right to hold that situation.

3. Power to appoint special Judges.

(1) The Central Government or the State Government may, by notification in the Official Gazette, appoint as many special Judges as may be necessary for such area or areas or for such case or group of cases as may be specified in the notification to try the following offences, namely:—

(a) any offence punishable under this Act; and

(b) any conspiracy to commit or any attempt to commit or any abetment of any of the offences specified in clause (a).

(2) A person shall not be qualified for appointment as a special Judge under this Act unless he is or has been a Sessions Judge or an Additional Sessions Judge or an Assistant Sessions Judge under the Code of Criminal Procedure, 1973 (2 of 1974).

4. Cases triable by special Judges.

(1) Notwithstanding anything contained in the Code of Criminal Procedure, 1973 (2 of 1974), or in any other law for the time being in force, the offences specified in sub-section (1) of Section 3 shall be tried by special Judges only.

(2) Every offence specified in sub-section (1) of Section 3 shall be tried by the special Judge for the area within which it was committed, or, as the case may be, by the special Judge appointed for the case, or where there are more special Judges than one for such area, by such one of them as may be specified in this behalf by the Central Government.

(3) When trying any case, a special Judge may also try any offence, other than an offence specified in Section 3, with which the accused may, under the Code of Criminal Procedure, 1973 (2 of 1974), be charged at the same trial.

(4) Notwithstanding anything contained in the Code of Criminal Procedure, 1973 (2 of 1974), a special Judge shall, as far as practicable, hold the trial of an offence on day-to-day basis.

5. Procedure and powers of special Judge.

(1) A special Judge may take cognizance of offences without the accused being committed to him for trial and, in trying the accused persons, shall follow the procedure prescribed by the Code of Criminal Procedure, 1973 (2 of 1974), for the trial of warrant case by Magistrates.

(2) A special Judge may, with a view to obtaining the evidence of any person supposed to have been directly or indirectly concerned in, or privy to, an offence, tender a pardon to such person on condition of his making a full and true disclosure of the whole circumstances within his knowledge relating to the offence and to every other person concerned, whether as principal or abettor, in the commission thereof and any pardon so tendered shall, for the purposes of sub-sections (1) to (5) of Section 308 of the Code of Criminal Procedure, 1973 (2 of 1974), be deemed to have been tendered under Section 307 of that Code.

(3) Save as provided in sub-section (1) or sub-section (2), the provisions of the Code of Criminal Procedure, 1973 (2 of 1974), shall, so far as they are not inconsistent with this Act, apply to the proceedings before a special Judge; and for the purposes of the said provisions, the Court of the special Judge shall be deemed to be a Court of Session and the person conducting a prosecution before a special Judge shall be deemed to be a public prosecutor.

(4) In particular and without prejudice to the generality of the provisions contained in sub-section (3), the provisions of Sections 326 and 457 of the Code of Criminal Procedure, 1973 (2 of 1974), shall, so far as may be, apply to the proceedings before a special Judge and for the purposes of the said provisions, a special Judge shall be deemed to be a Magistrate.

(5) A special Judge may pass upon any person convicted by him any sentence authorised by law for the punishment of the offence of which such person is convicted.

(6) A special Judge, while trying an offence punishable, under this Act, shall exercise all the powers and functions exercisable by a District Judge under the Criminal Law Amendment Ordinance, 1944. (Ord. 38 of 1944)

6. Power to try summarily.

(1) Where a special Judge tries any offence specified in sub-section (1) of Section 3, alleged to have been committed by a public servant in relation to the contravention of any special order referred to in sub-section (1) of Section 12A of the Essential Commodities Act, 1955 (10 of 1955) or of an order referred to in clause (a) of sub-section (2) of that Section, them, notwithstanding anything contained in sub-section (1) of Section 5 of this Act or Section 260 of the Code of Criminal Procedure, 1973 (2 of 1974), the special Judge shall try the offence in a summary way, and the provisions of Sections 262 to 265 (both inclusive) of the said Code shall, as far as may be, apply to such trial:

PROVIDED that, in the case of any conviction in a summary trial under this Section, it shall be lawful for the special Judge to pass a sentence of imprisonment for a term not exceeding one year:

PROVIDED FURTHER that when at the commencement of, or in the course of, a summary trial under this Section, it appears to the special Judge that the nature of the case is such that a sentence of imprisonment for a term exceeding one year may have to be passed or that it is, for any other reason, undesirable to try the case summarily, the special Judge shall, after hearing the parties, record an order to that effect and thereafter recall any witnesses who may have been examined and proceed to hear or re-hear the case in accordance with the procedure prescribed by the said Code for the trial of warrant cases by Magistrates.

(2) Notwithstanding anything to the contrary contained in this Act or in the Code of Criminal Procedure, 1973 (2 of 1974), there shall be no appeal by a convicted person in any case tried summarily under this Section in which the special Judge passes a sentence of imprisonment not exceeding one month, and of fine not exceeding two thousand rupees whether or not any order under Section

452 of the said Code is made in addition to such sentence, but an appeal shall lie where any sentence in excess of the aforesaid limits is passed by the special Judge.

CHAPTER -III : OFFENCES AND PENALTIES

7. Public servant taking gratification other than legal remuneration in respect of an official Act. Whoever, being, or expecting to be a public servant, accepts or obtains or agrees to accept or attempts to obtain from any person, for himself or for any other person, any gratification whatever, other than legal remuneration, as a motive or reward for doing or forbearing to do any official act or for showing or forbearing to show, in the exercise of his official functions, favour or disfavour to any person or for rendering or attempting to render any service or disservice to any person, with the Central Government or any State Government or Parliament or the Legislature of any State or with any local authority, corporation or Government company referred to in clause (c) of Section 2, or with any public servant, whether named or otherwise, shall be punishable with imprisonment which shall be not less than six months but which may extend to five years and shall also be liable to fine.

EXPLANATIONS.

(a) ***"Expecting to be a public servant."*** If a person not expecting to be in office obtains a gratification by deceiving others into a belief that he is about to be in office, and that he will when serve them, be may be guilty of cheating, but he is not guilty of the offence defined in this Section.

(b) ***"Gratification."*** The word "gratification" is not restricted to pecuniary gratifications or to gratifications estimable in money.

(c) ***"Legal remuneration."*** The words "legal remuneration" are not restricted to remuneration which a public servant can lawfully demand, but include all remuneration which he is permitted by the Government or the organisation, which he serves, to accept.

(d) ***"A motive or reward for doing."*** A person who receives a gratification as a motive or reward for doing what he does not intend or is not in a position to do, or has not done, comes within this expression.

(e) Where a public servant induces a person erroneously to believe that his influence with the Government has obtained a title for that person and thus induces that person to give the public servant, money or any other gratification as a reward for this service, the public servant has committed an offence under this Section.

8. Taking gratification, in order, by corrupt or illegal means, to influence public servant. Whoever accepts or obtains, or agrees to accept, or attempts to obtain, from any person, for himself or for any other person, any gratification whatever as a motive or reward for including, by corrupt or illegal means, any public servant, whether named or otherwise, to do or to forbear to do any official act, or in the exercise of the official functions of such public servant to show favour or disfavour to any person, or to render or attempt to render any service or disservice to any person with the Central Government or any State

Government or Parliament or the Legislature of any State or with any local authority, corporation or Government company referred to i.. clause (c) of Section 2, or with any public servant, whether named or otherwise, shall be punishable with imprisonment for a term which shall be not less than six months but which may extend to five years and shall also be liable to fine.

9. Taking gratification, for exercise of personal influence with public servant. Whoever accepts or obtains, or agrees to accept, or attempts to obtain, from any person, for himself or for any other person, any gratification whatever as a motive or reward for including, by the exercise of personal influence, any public servant, whether named or otherwise, to do or to forbear to do any official act, or in the exercise of the official functions of such public servant to show favour or disfavour to any person, or to render or attempt to render any service or disservice to any person with the Central Government or any State Government or Parliament or the Legislature of any State or with any local authority, corporation or Government company referred to in clause (c) of Section 2, or with any public servant, whether named or otherwise, shall be punishable with imprisonment for a term which shall be not less than six months but which may extend to five years and shall also be liable to fine.

10. Punishment for abetment by public servant of offences defined in Section 8 or 9. Whoever, being a public servant, in respect of whom either of the offences defined in Section 8 or Section 9 is committed, abets the offence, whether or not that offence is committed in consequence of that abetment, shall be punishable with imprisonment for a term which shall be not less than six months but which may extend to five years and shall also be liable to fine.

11. Public servant obtaining valuable thing without consideration from person concerned in proceeding or business transacted by such public servant. Whoever, being a public servant, accept or obtains or agrees to accept or attempts to obtain for himself, or for any other person, any valuable thing without consideration, or for a consideration which he knows to be inadequate, from any person whom he knows to have been, or to be, or to be likely to be concerned in any proceeding or business transacted or about to be transacted by such public servant, or having any connection with the official functions of himself or of any public servant to whom he is subordinate, or from any person whom he knows to be interested in or related to the person so concerned, shall be punishable with imprisonment for a term which shall be not less than six months but which may extend to five years and shall also be liable to fine.

12. Punishment for abetment of offences defined in Section 7 or Section 11. Whoever abets any offence punishable under Section 7 or Section 11 whether or not that offence is committed in consequence of that abetment, shall be punishable with imprisonment for a term which shall be not less than six months but which may extend to five years and shall also be liable to five.

13. Criminal, misconduct by a public servant.

(1) A public servant is said to commit the offence of criminal misconduct.-

(a) if he habitually accepts or obtained or agrees to accept or attempts to obtain from any person for himself or for any other person for himself or for any other person any gratification other than legal remuneration as a motive or reward such as is mentioned in Section 7; or

(b) if he habitually accepts or obtains or agrees to accept or attempts to obtain for himself or for any other person, any valuable thing without consideration or for a consideration which he knows to be inadequate from any person whom he knows to have been, or to be, or to be likely to be concerned in any proceedings or business transacted or about to be transacted by him, or having any connection with the official functions of himself or of any public servant to whom he is subordinate, or from any person whom he knows to be interested in or related to the person so concerned; or

(c) if he dishonestly or fraudulently misappropriates or otherwise converts for his own use any property entrusted to him or under his control as a public servant or allows any other person so to do; or

(d) if he,—

(i) by corrupt or illegal means, obtains for himself or for any other person any valuable thing or pecuniary advantage; or

(ii) by abusing his position as a public servant, obtains for himself or for any other person any valuable thing or pecuniary advantage; or

(iii) while holding office as a public servant, obtains for any person any valuable thing or pecuniary advantage without any public, interest; or

(e) if he or any person on his behalf, is in possession or has, at any time during the period of his office, been in possession for which the public servant cannot satisfactorily account, of pecuniary resources or property disproportionate to his known sources of income.

EXPLANATION. For the purposes of this Section, "known sources of income" means income received from any lawful source and such receipt has been intimated in accordance with the provisions of any law, rules or orders for the time being applicable to a public servant.

(2) Any public servant who commits criminal misconduct shall be punishable with imprisonment for a term which shall be not less than one year but which may extend to seven years and shall also be liable to fine.

14. Habitual committing of offence under Sections 8, 9 and 12. Whoever habitually commits—

(a) an offence punishable under Section 8 or Section 9; or

(b) an offence punishable under Section 12 shall be punishable with imprisonment for a term which shall be not less than two years but which may extend to seven years and shall also be liable to fine.

15. Punishment for attempt. Whoever attempts to commit an offence referred to in clause (c) or clause (d) of sub-section (1) of Section 13 shall be punishable with imprisonment for a term which may extend to three years and with fine.

16. Matters to be taken into consideration for fixing fine. Where a sentence of fine is imposed under sub-section (2) of Section 13 or Section 14, the court in fixing the amount of the fine shall take into consideration the amount or the value of the property, if any, which the accused person has obtained by committing the offence or where the conviction is for an offence referred to in clause (e) of sub-section (1) of Section 13, the pecuniary resources or property referred to in that clause for which the accused person is unable to account satisfactorily.

CHAPTER - IV : INVESTIGATIONS INTO CASES UNDER THE ACT

17. Persons authorised to investigate. Notwithstanding anything contained in the Code of Criminal Procedure, 1973 (2 of 1974), no police officer below the rank,—

(a) in the case of the Delhi Special Police Establishment, of an Inspector of Police;

(b) in the metropolitan areas of Bombay, Calcutta, Madras and Ahmedabad and in any other metropolitan area notified as such under sub-section (1) of Section 8 of the Code of Criminal Procedure, 1973 (2 of 1974), of an Assistant Commissioner of Police;

(c) elsewhere, of a Deputy Superintendent of Police or a police officer of equivalent, rank, shall investigate any offence punishable under this Act without the order of a Metropolitan Magistrate or a Magistrate of the first class, as the case may be, or make any arrest therefore without a warrant:

PROVIDED that if a police officer not below the rank of an Inspector of Police is authorised by the State Government in this behalf by general or special order, he may also investigate any such offence without the order of a metropolitan Magistrate or a Magistrate of the first class, as the case may be, or make arrest therefore without a warrant.

18. Power to inspect bankers books. If from information received or otherwise, a police officer has reason to suspect the commission of an offence which he is empowered to investigate under Section 17 and considers that for the purpose of investigation or inquiry into such offence, it is necessary to inspect any bankers' books, then, notwithstanding anything contained in any law for the time being in force, he may inspect any bankers' books insofar as they relate to the accounts of the persons suspected to have committed that offence or of any other person suspected to be holding money on behalf of such person, and take or cause to be taken certified copies of the relevant entries therefrom, and the bank concerned shall be bound to assist the police officer in the exercise of his powers under this Section:

PROVIDED that no power under this Section in relation to the accounts of any person shall be exercised by a police officer below the rank of a Superintendent of Police, unless he is specially authorised in this behalf by a police officer of or above the rank of a Superintendent of Police.

EXPLANATION. In this Section, the expressions "bank" and "bankers' books" shall have the meanings respectively assigned to them in the Bankers' Books Evidence Act, 1891 (18 of 1891).

CHAPTER - V : SANCTION FOR PROSECUTION AND OTHER MISCELLANEOUS PROVISIONS

19. Previous sanction necessary for prosecution.

(1) No court shall take cognizance of an offence punishable under Sections 7, 10, 11, 13 and 15 alleged to have been committed by a public servant, except with the previous sanction,—

- (a) in the case of a person who is employed in connection with the affairs of the Union and is not removable from his office save by or with the sanction of the Central Government, of that Government;
- (b) in the case of a person who is employed in connection with the affairs of a State and is not removable from his office save by or with the sanction of the State Government, of that Government;
- (c) in the case of any other person, of the authority competent to remove him from his office.

(2) Where for any reason whatsoever any doubt arises as to whether the previous sanction as required under sub-section (1) should be given by the Central Government or the State Government or any other authority, such sanction shall be given by that Government or authority which would have been competent to remove the public servant from his office at the time when the offence was alleged to have been committed.

(3) Notwithstanding anything contained in the Code of Criminal Procedure, 1973 (2 of 1974),—

- (a) no finding, sentence or order passed by a special Judge shall be reversed or altered by a Court in appeal, confirmation or revision on the ground of the absence of, or any error, omission or irregularity in, the sanction required under sub-section (1), unless in the opinion of that court, a failure of justice has in fact been occasioned thereby;
- (b) no court shall stay the proceedings under this Act on the ground of any error, omission or irregularity in the sanction granted by the authority, unless it is satisfied that such error, omission or irregularity has resulted in a failure of justice;
- (c) no court shall stay the proceedings under this Act on any other ground and no court shall exercise the powers of revision in relation to any interlocutory order passed in any inquiry, trial, appeal or other proceedings.

(4) In determining under sub-section (3) whether the absence of, or any error, omission or irregularity in, such sanction has occasioned or resulted in a failure of justice the court shall have regard to the fact whether the objection could and should have been raised at any earlier stage in the proceedings.

EXPLANATION: For the purposes of this Section,—

- (a) sanction includes competency of the authority to grant sanction;
- (b) a sanction required for prosecution includes reference to any requirement that the prosecution shall be at the instance of a specified authority or

with the sanction of a specified person or any requirement of a similar nature.

20. Presumption where public servant accepts gratification other than legal remuneration.

(1) Where, in any trial of an offence punishable under Section 7 or Section 11 or clause (a) or clause (b) or sub-section (1) of Section 13 it is proved that an accused person has accepted or obtained or has agreed to accept or attempted to obtain for himself, or for any other person, any gratification (other than legal remuneration) or any valuable thing from any person, it shall be presumed, unless the contrary is proved, that he accepted or obtained or agreed to accept or attempted to obtain that gratification or that valuable thing, as the case may be, as a motive or reward such as is mentioned in Section 7 or, as the case may be, without consideration or for a consideration which he knows to be inadequate.

(2) Where in any trial of an offence punishable under Section 12 or under clause (b) of Section 14, it is proved that any gratification (other than legal remuneration) or any valuable thing has been given or offered to be given or attempted to be given by an accused person, it shall be presumed, unless the contrary is proved, that he gave or offered to give or attempted to give that gratification or that valuable thing, as the case may be, as a motive or reward such as is mentioned in Section 7, or, as the case may be, without consideration or for a consideration which he knows to be inadequate.

(3) Notwithstanding anything contained in sub-sections (1) and (2), the court may decline to draw the presumption referred to in either of the said sub-sections, if the gratification or thing aforesaid is, in its opinion, so trivial that no inference of corruption may fairly be drawn.

21. Accused to be a competent witness. Any person charged with an offence punishable under this Act, shall be a competent witness for the defence and may give evidence on oath in disproof of the charges made against him or any person charged together with him at the same trial:

PROVIDED that—

(a) he shall not be called as a witness except at his own request;

(b) his failure to give evidence shall not be made the subject of any comment by the prosecution or give rise to any presumption against himself or any person charged together with him at the same trial;

(c) he shall not be asked, and if asked shall not be required to answer, any question tending to show that he has committed or been convicted of any offence other than the offence with which he is charged, or is of bad character, unless—

(i) the proof that he has committed or been convicted of such offence is admissible evidence to show that he is guilty of the offence with which he is charged, or

(ii) he has personally or by his pleader asked any question of any witness for the prosecution with a view to establish his own good character, or has given evidence of

his good character, or the nature or conduct of the defence is such as to involve imputations on the character of the prosecutor or of any witness for the prosecution, or

(iii) he has given evidence against any other person charged with the same offence.

22. The Code of Criminal Procedure, 1973, to apply subject certain modifications. The provisions of the Code of Criminal Procedure, 1973 (2 of 1974), shall in their application to any proceeding in relation to an offence punishable under this Act have effect as if,—

(a) in sub-section (1) of Section 243, for the words "The accused shall then be called upon", the words "The accused shall then be required to give in writing at once or within such time as the Court may allow, a list of the persons (if any) whom he proposes to examine as his witnesses and of the documents (if any) on which he proposes to rely and he shall then be called upon" had been substituted;

(b) in sub-section (2) of Section 309, after the third proviso, the following proviso had been inserted, namely:—

"*PROVIDED ALSO that the proceeding shall not be adjourned or postponed merely on the ground that an application under Section 397 has been made by a party to the proceeding*";

(c) after sub-section (2) of Section 317, the following sub-section had been inserted, namely:—" (3) Notwithstanding anything contained in sub-section (1) or Section (2), the Judge may, if he thinks fit and for reasons to be recorded by him, proceed with inquiry or trial in the absence of the accused or his pleader and record the evidence of any witness subject to the right of the accused to recall the witness for cross-examination.';

(d) in sub-section (1) of Section 397, before the Explanation, the following proviso had been inserted, namely:—

"*PROVIDED that where the powers under this Section are exercised by a Court on an application made by a party to such proceedings, the Court shall not ordinarily call for the record of the proceedings:—*

(a) without giving the other party an opportunity of showing cause why the record should not be called for; or

(b) if it is satisfied that an examination of the record of the proceedings may be made from the certified copies.".

23. Particulars in a charge in relation to an offence under Section 13(C). Notwithstanding anything contained in the Code of Criminal Procedure, 1973 (2 of 1974), when an accused is charged with an offence under clause (c) of sub-section (1) of Section 13, it shall be sufficient to describe in the charge the property in respect of which the offence is alleged to have been committed and the dates between which the offence is alleged to have been committed, without specifying particular items or exact dates, and the charge so framed shall be deemed to be a charge of one offence within the meaning of Section 219 of the said Code;

PROVIDED that the time included between the first and last of such dates shall not exceed one year.

24. Statement by bribe giver not to subject him to prosecution. Notwithstanding anything contained in any law for the time being in force, a statement made by a person in any proceeding against a public servant for an offence under Sections 7 to 11 or under Section 13 or Section 15, that he offered or agreed to offer any gratification (other than legal remuneration) or any valuable thing to the public servant, shall not subject such person to a prosecution under Section 12.

25. Military, Naval and Air Force or other law not to be affected.

(1) Nothing in this Act shall affect the jurisdiction exercisable by, or the procedure applicable to, any court or other authority under the Army Act, 1950 (45 of 1950), the Air Force Act, 1950 (46 of 1950), the Navy Act, 1957 (62 of 1957), the Border Security Force Act, 1968 (47 of 1968), the Coast Guard Act, 1978 (30 of 1978) and the National Security Guard Act, 1986 (47 of 1986).

(2) For the removal of doubts, it is hereby declared that for the purposes of any such law as is referred to in sub-section (1), the court of a special Judge shall be deemed to be a court of ordinary criminal justice.

26. Special Judges appointed under Act 46 of 1952 to be special Judges appointed under this Act. Every special Judge appointed under the Criminal Law Amendment Act, 1952, for any area or areas and is holding office on the commencement of this Act shall be deemed to be a special Judge appointed under Section 3 of this Act for that area or areas and, accordingly, on and from such commencement, every such Judge shall continue to deal with all the proceedings pending before him on such commencement in accordance with the provisions of this Act.

27. Appeal and revision. Subject to the provisions of this Act, the High Court may exercise, so far as they may be applicable, all the powers of appeal and revision conferred by the Code of Criminal Procedure, 1973 (2 of 1974) on a High Court as if the court of the special Judge were a court of Session trying cases within the local limits of the High Court.

28. Act to be in addition to any other law. The provisions of this Act shall be in addition to, and not in derogation of, any other law for the time being in force, and nothing contained herein shall exempt any public servant from any proceeding which might, apart from this Act, be instituted against him.

29. Amendment of Ordinance 38 of 1944. In the Criminal Law Amendment Ordinance, 1944 -

(a) in sub-section (1) of Section 3, sub-section (1) of Section 9, clause (a) of Section 10, sub-section (1) of Section 11 and sub-section (1) of Section 13, for the words "State Government", wherever they occur, the words "State Government or, as the case may be, the Central Government" shall be substituted;

(b) in Section 10, in clause (a), for the words "three months", the words "one year" shall be substituted;

(c) in the Schedule,—

    (i) paragraph 1 shall be omitted;

    (ii) in paragraphs 2 and 4 —

(a) after the words "a local authority", the words and figures "or a corporation established by or under a Central, Provincial or State Act, or an authority or a body owned or controlled or aided by Government or a Government company as defined in Section 617 of the Companies Act, 1956 (1 of 1956) or a society aided by such corporation, authority, body or Government company" shall be inserted;

(b) after the words "or authority", the words "or corporation or body or Government company or society" shall be inserted;

(iii) for paragraph 4A, the following paragraph shall be substituted, namely: **"4A.** An offence punishable under the Prevention of Corruption Act, 1988";

(iv) in paragraph 5, for the words and figures "items 2, 3 and 4", the words, figures and letter "items 2, 3, 4 and 4A" shall be substituted.

30. Repeal and saving.

(1) The Prevention of Corruption Act, 1947 (2 of 1947) and the Criminal Law Amendment Act, 1952 (46 of 1952) are hereby repealed.

(2) Notwithstanding such repeal, but without prejudice to the application of Section 6 of the General Clauses Act, 1897 (10 of 1897), anything done or any action taken or purported to have been done or taken under or in pursuance of the Acts so repealed shall, insofar as it is not inconsistent with the provisions of this Act, be deemed to have been done or taken under or in pursuance of the corresponding provision of this Act.

31. Omission of certain Sections of Act 45 of 1860. Sections 161 to 165A (both inclusive) of the Indian Penal Code shall be omitted, and Section 6 of the General Clauses Act, 1897 (10 of 1897), shall apply to such omission as if the said Sections had been repealed by a Central Act.

❑❑❑

21

The Prevention of Cruelty to Animals Act, 1960

(59 OF 1960) (26TH DECEMBER, 1960)

AN ACT to prevent the infliction of unnecessary pain or suffering on animals and for that purpose to amend the law relating to the prevention of cruelty to animals.

Be it enacted by Parliament in the Eleventh year of the Republic of India as follows:

CHAPTER - I : PRELIMINARY

1. Short title, extent and commencement.

(1) This Act may be called the Prevention of Cruelty to Animals Act, 1960.

(2) It extends to the whole of India except the State of Jammu and Kashmir.

(3) It shall come into force on such date as the Central Government may, by notification in the official Gazette, appoint, and different dates may be appointed for different States and for the different provisions companied in this Act.

2. Definitions. In this Act, unless the context otherwise requires,

(a) "animal" means any living creature other than a human being,

[(b) "Board" means the Board established under Section 4 and as reconstituted from time to time under Section 5A]

(c) "captive animal" means any animal (not being a domestic animal) which is in capacity or confinement, whether permanent or temporary, or which is subjected to any appliance of contrivance for the purpose of hindering or preventing its escape from captivity or confinement or which is pinioned or which is or appears to be maimed;

(i). "domestic animal" means any animal which is tamed or which has been or is being sufficiently tamed to serve some purpose for the use of man or which, although it neither has been nor is intended to be so tamed, is or has become in fact wholly or partly tamed,

(e) "local authority" means a municipal committee, district board or other authority for the time being invested by law with the control and administration of any matters within a specified local area;

(f) "owner", used with reference to an animal, includes not only the owner but also any other person for the time being in possession or custody of the animal, whether with or without the consent of the owner.

(g) "phooka" or "doom dev" includes any process of introducing air or any substance into the female organ of a milch animal with the object of drawing off from the animal any secretion of milk;

(h) "prescribed" means prescribed by Rules made under this Act;

(i) "street" includes any way, road, lane, square, court, alley, passage or open space, whether a thoroughfare or not to which the public have access.

3. Duties of persons having charge of animals. It shall be the duty of every person having the care or charge of any animal to take all reasonable measures to ensure the well-being of such animal and to prevent the infliction upon such animal of unnecessary pain or suffering.

CHAPTER - II : (ANIMAL WELFARE BOARD OF INDIA)

4. Establishment of Animal Welfare Board of India.

(1) For the promotion of animal welfare generally and for the purpose of protecting animals from being subjected to unnecessary pain or suffering, in particular, there shall be established by the Central Government, as soon as may be after the commencement of this Act, a Board to be called the (Animal Board of India)

(2) The Board, shall be a body corporate having perpetual succession and a common seal with power, subject to the provisions of this Act, to acquire, hold and dispose of property and may by its name sue and be sued.

5. Constitution of the Board.

(1) The Board shall consist of the following persons, namely:

(a) the Inspector General of Forests, Government of India, *ex-officio*,

(b) the Animal Husbandry Commissioner to the Government of India, *ex-officio*;

(ba) two persons to represent respectively the Ministries of the Central Government dealing with Home Affairs and Education, to be appointed by the Central Government;

(bb) one person to represent the Indian Board for Wild Life, to be appointed by the Central Government;

(bc) three persons who, in the opinion of the Central Government, are or have been actively engaged in animal welfare work and are well-known humanitarians, to be nominated by the Central Government;)

(c) one person to represent such association of veterinary practitioners as in the opinion of the Central Government ought to be represented on the Board, to be elected by that association in the prescribed manner;

(d) two persons to represent practitioners of modern and indigenous systems of medicine, to be nominated by the Central Government;

[(e) one person to represent each of such two municipal corporations as in the opinion of the Central Government ought to be represented on the Board, to be elected by each of the said corporations in the prescribed manner;

(f) one person to represent each of such three organisations actively interested in animal welfare as in the opinion of the Central Government ought to be represented on the Board, to be chosen by each of the said organisations in the prescribed manner;

(g) one person to represent each of such three societies dealing with prevention of cruelty to animal as in the opinion of the Central Government ought to be represented on the Board, to be chosen, in the prescribed manner;

(h) three persons to be nominated by the Central Government;

(i) six Members of Parliament, four to be elected by the House of the People (Lok Sabha) and two by the Council of States (Rajya Sabha).

(2) Any of the persons referred to in clause (a) or [clause (b) or clause (ba) or clause (bb) of sub-section (1) may depute any other person to attend any of the meetings of the Board.

[(3) The Central Government shall nominate one of the members of the Board to be its Chairman and another member of the Board to be its Vice-Chairman].

5A. Reconstitution of the Board.

[(1) In order that the Chairman and other members of the Board hold office till the same date and that their terms of off ice come to an end on the same date, the Central Government may, by notification in the Official Gazette, reconstitute, as soon as may be after the Prevention of Cruelty to Animals (Amendment) Act, 1982 comes into force of the Board.

(2) The Board as reconstituted under sub-section (1) shall be reconstituted from time to time on the expiration of every third year, from the date of its reconstitution under sub-section (1).

(3) There shall be included amongst the members of the Board reconstituted under sub-section (1), all persons who immediately before the date on which such reconstitution is to take effect, are Members of the Board but such persons shall hold office only for the unexpired portion of the term for which they would have held office if such reconstitution had not been made and the vacancies arising as a result of their ceasing to be Members of the Board shall be filled up

as casual vacancies for the remaining period of the term of the Board as so reconstituted:

PROVIDED that nothing in this sub-section shall apply in relation to any person who ceases to be member of the Board by virute of the amendment made in sub-section (1) of Section 5 by sub-clause (ii) of clause (a) of Section 5 of the Prevention of Cruelty to Animals (Amendement) Act, 1982).

6. Term of off ice and conditions of service of Members of the Board.

(1) The term for which the Board may be reconstituted under Section 5A shall be three years from the date of the reconstitution and the Chairman and other Members of the Board as so reconstituted shall hold office till the expiry of the term for which the Board has been so reconstituted.

(2) Notwithstanding anything contained in sub-section (1):

(a) the term of office of an *ex-officio* Member shall continue so long as he holds the office by virtue of which he is such a Member;

(b) the term of office of a Member elected or chosen under clause (c), clause (e), clause (g), clause (h) or clause (i) of Section 5 to represent anybody of persons shall come to an end as soon as he ceases to be a Member of the body which elected him or in respect of which he was chosen;

(c) the term of office of a Member appointed, nominated, elected or chosen to fill a casual vacancy shall continue for the remainder of the term of office of the Member in whose place he is appointed, nominated, elected or chosen;

(d) the Central Government may, at any time, remove for reasons to be recorded in writing a member from office after giving him a reasonable opportunity of showing cause against the proposed removal and any vacancy caused by such removal shall be treated as casual vacancy for the purpose of clause (c).

(3) 'The members of the Board shall receive such allowance, if any, as the Board may, subject to the previous approval of the Central Government, provided by regulations made in this behalf,

(4) No act done or proceeding taken by the Board shall be questioned on the ground merely of the existence of any vacancy in, or defect in the constitution of the Board and in particular, and without prejudice to the generality of the foregoing, during the period intervening between the expiry of the term for which the Board has been reconstituted under Section 5A and its further reconstitution under that Section, the *ex-officio* members of the Board shall discharge all the powers and function of the Board)

7. Secretary and other employees of the Board.

(1) The Central Government shall appoint the Secretary of the Board.

(2) Subject to such rules as may be made by the Central Government in this behalf, the Board may appoint such number of other officers and employees as

may be necessary for the exercise of its powers and the discharge of its functions and may determine the terms and conditions of service of such officers and other employees by regulations made by it with the previous approval of the Central Government.

8. Funds of the Board. The funds of the Board shall consist of grants made to it from time to time by the Government and of contributions, subscriptions, bequests, gifts and the like made to it by any local authority or by any other person.

9. Functions of the Board. The functions of the Board shall be Board-

(a) to keep the law in force in, India for the prevention of cruelty to animals under constant study and advise the Government on the amendments to be undertaken in any such law from time to time;

(b) to advise the Central Government on the making of rules under this Act with a view to preventing unnecessary pain or suffering to animals generally, and more particularly when they are being transported from one place to another or when they are used as performing animals or when they are kept in captivity or confinement;

(c) to advise the Government or any local authority or other person on improvements in the design of vehicles so as to lessen the burden on draught animals;

(d) to take all such steps as the Board may think fit for (amelioration of animals) by encouraging or providing for, the construction of sheds, water-troughs and the like and by providing for veterinary assistance to animals;

(e) to advise the Government or any local authority or other person in the design of slaughter-houses or the maintenance of slaughter houses or in connection with slaughter of animals so that unnecessary pain or suffering, whether physical or mental, is eliminated in the pre-slaughter stages as far as possible, and animals are killed; wherever necessary, in as humane a manner as possible;

(f) to take all such steps as the Board may think fit to ensure that unwanted animals are destroyed by local authorities, whenever it is necessary to do so, either instantaneously or after being rendered insensible to pain or suffering.

(g) to encourage by the grant of financial assistance or otherwise, 12(the formation or establishment of pinjrapoles, rescue homes, animal shelters, sanctuaries and the like) where animals and birds may find a shelter when they have become old and useless or when they need protection;

(h) to co-operate with, and co-ordinate the work of, associations or bodies established for the purpose of preventing unnecessary pain or suffering to animals or for the protection of animals and birds;

(i) to give financial and other assistance to animal welfare organisations functioning in any local area or to encourage the formation of animal welfare organisations in any local area which shall work under the general supervision and guidance of the Board;

(j) to advise the Government on matters relating to the medical care and attention which may be provided in animal hospital, and to give financial and other assistance to animal hospitals whenever the Board thinks it necessary to do so;

(k) to impart education in relation to the humane treatment of animals and to encourage the formation of public opinion against the infliction of unnecessary pain or suffering to animals and for the promotion of animal welfare by means of lectures, books, posters, cinematographic exhibitions and the like;

(l) to advise the Government on any matter connected with animal welfare or the prevention of infliction of unnecessary pain or suffering on animals.

10. Power of Board to make regulations. The Board may, subject to the previous approval of the Central Government, make such regulations as it may think fit for the administration of its affairs and for carrying out its functions.

CHAPTER - III : CRUELTY TO ANIMALS GENERALLY

11. Treating animals cruelly.

(1) If any person

(a) beats, kicks, over-rides, over-drives, over-loads, tortures or otherwise treats any animal so as to subject it to unnecessary pain or suffering or causes, or being the owner permits, any animal to be so treated; or

(b) (employs in any work or labour or for any purpose any animal which, by reason of its age or any disease) infirmity; wound, sore or other cause, is unfit to be so employed or, being the owner, permits any such unfit animal to be employed; or

(c) wilfully and unreasonably administers any injurious drug or injurious substance to (any animal) or wilfully and unreasonably causes or attempts to cause any such drug or substance to be taken by (any animal;) or

(d) conveys or carries, whether in or upon any vehicle or not, any animal in such a manner or position as to subject it to unnecessary pain or suffering; or

(e) keeps or confines any animal in any cage or other receptacle which does not measure sufficiently in height, length and breadth to permit the animal a reasonable opportunity for movement; or

(f) keeps for an unreasonable time any animal chained or tethered upon an unreasonably short or unreasonably heavy chain or cord; or

(g) being the owner, neglects to exercise or cause to be exercised reasonably any dog habitually chained up or kept in close confinement; or

(h) being the owner of (any animal) fails to provide such animal with sufficient food, drink or shelter; or

(i) without reasonable cause, abandons any animal in circumstances which tender it likely that it will suffer pain by reason of starvation thirst; or

(j) wilfully permits any animal, of which he is the owner, to go at large in any street, while the animal is affected with contagious or infectious disease or, without reasonable excuse permits any diseased or disabled animal, of which he is the owner, to die in any street; or

(k) offers for sale or without reasonable cause, has in his possession any animal which is suffering pain by reason of mutilation, starvation, thirst, overcrowding or other illtreatment; or

[(1) mutilates any animal or kills any animal (including stray dogs) by using the method of strychnine injections, in the heart or in any other unnecessarily cruel manner or;]

[(m) solely with a view to providing entertainment

(i) confines or causes to be confined any animal (including tying of an animal as a bait in a tiger or other sanctuary) so as to make it an object or prey for any other animal; or

(n) [xxxx] organises, keeps uses or acts in the management or, any place for animal fighting or for the purpose of baiting any animal or permits or offers any place to be so used or receives money for the admission of any other person to any place kept or used for any such purposes; or

(o) promotes or takes part in any shooting match or competition wherein animals are released from captivity for the purpose of such shooting:

he shall be punishable (in the case of a first offence, with fine which shall not be less than ten rupees but which may extend to fifty rupees and in the case of a second or subsequent offence committed within three years of the previous offence, with fine which shall not be less than twenty-five rupees but which may extend, to one hundred rupees or with imprisonment for a term which may extend, to three months, or with both.]

(2) For the purposes of Section (1) an owner shall be deemed to have committed an offence if he has failed to exercise reasonable care and supervision with a view to the prevention of such offence:

PROVIDED that where an owner is convicted permitting cruelty by reason only of having failed to exercise such care and supervision, he shall not be liable to imprisonment without the option of a fine.

(3) Nothing in this Section shall apply to -

(a) the dehorning of cattle, or the castration or branding or noseroping of any animal in the prescribed manner; or

(b) the destruction of stray dogs in lethal chambers [by such other methods as may be prescribed] or

(c) the extermination or destruction of any animal under the authority of any law for the time being in force; or

(d) any matter dealt with in Chapter IV; or

(e) the commission or omission of any act in the course of the destruction or the preparation for destruction of any animal as food for mankind unless such destruction or preparation was accompanied by the infliction of unnecessary pain or suffering.

12. Penalty for practising phooka or doom dev. If any persons upon any cow or other milch animal the operation called practising phooka or [doom dev or any other operation (including injection of any or doom dev. substance) to improve lactation which is injurious to the health of the animal] or permits such operation being performed upon any such animal in his possession or under his control, he shall be punishable with fine which may extend to one thousand rupees, or with imprisonment for a term which may extend to two years, or with both, and the animal on which the operation was performed shall be forfeited to the Government.

13. 'Destruction of suffering animals'.

(1) Where the owner of an animal is convicted of an offence under Section 11, it shall be lawful for the court, if the court is satisfied that it would be cruel to keep the animal alive, to direct that the animal be destroyed and to assign the animals to any suitable person for that purpose, and the person to whom such animal is so assigned shall as soon as possible, destroy such animal or cause such animal to be destroyed in his presence without unnecessary suffering, and any reasonable expense incurred in destroying the animal may be ordered by the court, if the court is satisfied that it would be cruel to keep the animal alive, to direct that the animal be destroyed and to assign the animal to any reasonable expense incurred in destroying the animal may be ordered by the court to be recovered from the owner as if it were a fine:

PROVIDED that unless the owner assents thereto, no order shall be made under this Section except upon the evidence of a veterinary officer in charge of the area.

(2) When any magistrate, commissioner of police or district superintendent of police has reason to believe that an offence under Section 11 has been committed in respect of any animal, he may direct the immediate destruction of the animal, if in his opinion, it would be cruel to keep the animal alive.

(3) Any police officer above the rank of a constable or any person authorised by the State Government in this behalf who finds any animal so diseased or so severely injured or in such a physical condition that in his opinion it cannot be removed without cruelty, may, if the owner is absent or refuses his consent to the destruction of the animal, forth with summon the veterinary officer-in-charge of the area in which the animal is found, and if the veterinary officer certifies that the animal is mortally injured or so severely injured or in such a physical condition that it would be cruel to keep it alive, the police officer or the person authorised, as the case may be, may, after obtaining orders from a magistrate, destroy the animal injured or cause it to be destroyed; (in such manner as may be prescribed)

(4) No appeal shall lie from any order of a magistrate for the destruction of an animal.

CHAPTER - IV : EXPERIMENTATION OF ANIMALS

14. Experiments on animals. Nothing contained in this Act shall render unlawful the performance of experiments (including) experiments involving operations) on animals for the purpose of advancement by new discovery of physiological knowledge or of knowledge which will be useful for saving or for prolonging life or alleviating suffering or for combating any disease, whether of human beings, animals or plants.

15. Committee for control and supervision of experiments on animals.

(1) If at any time, on the advice of the Board, the Central Government is of opinion that it is necessary so to do for the purpose of controlling "and supervising experiments on animals it may be notification in the Official Gazette Constitute a Committee consisting of such number of officials and non-officials, as it may think fit to appoint thereto.

(2) The Central Government shall nominate one of the Members of the Committee to be its Chairman.

(3) The Committee shall have power to regulate its own Procedure in relation to the performance of its duties.

(4) The funds of the Committee shall consist of grants made to it from time to time by the Government and of contributions, donations, subscriptions, bequests, gifts and the like made to it by any person.

[**15A. Sub-Committee.**

(1) The Committee may constitute as many sub-committees as it thinks fit for exercising any power or discharging any duty of the Committee or for inquiring into or reporting and advising on any matter which the Committee may refer.

(2) A sub-committee shall consist exclusively of the Members of the Committee]

16. Staff of the Committee. Subject to the control of the Central Government, the Committee may committee appoint such number of officers and other employees as may be necessary to enable it to exercise ills powers and perform its duties and may determine the remuneration and other terms and conditions of service of such officers and other employees.

17. Duties of the Committee and power of the Committee to make rules relating to experiments on animals.

(1) It shall be the duty of the Committee to take all such measures as may be necessary to ensure that animals are not subjected to unnecessary pain or suffering before, during or after the performance of experiments on them, and for the purpose it may, by notification in the Gazette of India and subject to the condition of previous publication, make such rules as it may think fit in animals relation to the conduct of such experiments.

[(lA) In particular, and without prejudice to the generality to the foregoing power, such rules may provide for the following matters namely:

(a) the registration of persons or institutions carrying on experiments on animals;

(b) the reports and other information which shall be forwarded to the Committee by persons and institutions carrying on experiments or, animals.]

(2) In particular, and without prejudice to the generality of the foregoing power, rules made by the Committee shall be designed to secure the following objects, namely:

(a) that in cases where experiments are performed in any institution, the responsibility therefore is placed on the person in charge of the institution and that, in cases where experiments are performed outside an institution by individuals, the individuals, are performed outside an institution by individuals, the individuals, are qualified in that behalf and the experiments are performed on their full responsibility;

(b) that experiments are performed with due care and humanity and that as far as possible experiments involving operations are performed under the influence of some anaesthetic of sufficient power to prevent the animals feeling pain;

(c) that animals which, in the course of experiments under the influence of anaesthetics, are so injured that their recovery would involve serious suffering, are ordinarily destroyed while still insensible;

(d) that experiments on animals are avoided wherever it is possible to do so; as for example; in medical schools, hospitals, colleges and the like, if other teaching devices such as books, models, films and the like, may equally suffice;

(e) that experiments on larger animals are avoided when it is possible to achieve the same results by experiments upon small laboratory animals like guinea-pigs, rabbits, frogs and rats;

(f) that, as far as possible, experiments are not performed merely for the purpose of acquiring manual skill;

(g) that animals intended for the performance of experiments are properly looked after both before and after experiments;

(h) that suitable records are maintained with respect to experiments performed on animals.

(3) In making any rules under this Section, the Committee shall be guided by such directions as the Central Government (consistently with the objects for which the Committee is set up) may give to it, and the Central Government is hereby authorised to give such direction.

(4) All rules made by the Committee shall be binding on all individuals performing experiments outside institutions and on persons incharge of institutions in which experiments are performed.

18. Power of entry and inspection. For the purpose of ensuring that the rules made by it are being complied and with the Committee may authorise any of its officers or any other person in writing to inspect any institution or place where experiments are being carried on and report to it as a result of such inspection, and any officer or person so authorised may-

(a) enter at any time considered reasonable by him and inspect any institution or place in which experiments on animals are being carried on; and

(b) require any person to produce any record kept by him with respect to experiments on animals.

19. Power to prohibit experiments on animals. If the Committee is satisfied, on the report of any officer or other person made to it as a result of any inspection under Section 18 or otherwise that the rules made by it under Section 17 are not being animals the Committee may, after giving an opportunity to the person or institution carrying on experiments on animals; the Committee may, after giving an opportunity to the person or institution of being heard in the matter, by order, prohibit the person or institution from carrying on any such experiments either for a specified period or indefinitely, or may allow the person or institution to carry on such experiments subject to such special conditions as the Committee may think fit to impose.

20. Penalties. If any person-

(a) contravenes any order made by the Committee under Section 19; or

(b) commits a breach of any condition imposed by the Committee under that Section:

he shall be punishable with fine which may extend to two hundred rupees, and, when the contravention or breach of condition has taken place in any institution the person incharge of the institution shall be deemed to be guilty of the offence and shall be punishable accordingly.

CHAPTER - V : PERFORMING ANIMALS

21. "Exhibit" and "train" defined. In this Chapter, "exhibit" means exhibit or any entertainment to which the public are admitted through sale of tickets, and "train" means train for the purpose of any such exhibition, and the expressions "exhibitor" and "trainer" have respectively the corresponding meanings.

22. Restriction on exhibition and training of performing animals. No person shall exhibit or train

(i) any performing animal unless he is registered in accordance with the provisions of this Chapter;

(ii) as a performing animal, any animal which the Central Government may, by notification in the Official Gazette, specify as an animal which shall not be exhibited or trained as a performing animal.

23. Procedure for registration.

(1) Every person desirous of exhibiting or training any performing animal shall, on making an application in the prescribed form to the prescribed authority and on payment of the prescribed fee, be registered under this Act unless he is a person who, by reason of an order made by the court under this Chapter, is not entitled to be so registered.

(2) An application for registration under this Chapter shall contain such particulars as to the animals and as to the general nature of the performances in which

the animals are to be exhibited or for which they are to be trained as may be prescribed, and the particulars so given shall be entered in the register maintained by the prescribed authority.

(3) The prescribed authority shall give to every person whose name appears on the register kept by them, a certificate of registration in the prescribed form containing the particulars entered in the register.

(4) Every register kept under this Chapter shall at all reasonable times be open for inspection on payment of the prescribed fee, and any person shall, on payment of the prescribed fee, be entitled to obtain copies thereof or make extracts therefrom.

(5) Any person whose name is entered in the register shall, subject to the provisions of any order made under this Act by any court, be entitled, on making an application for the purpose, to have the particulars entered in the register with respect to him varied, and where any such particulars are so varied, the existing certificate shall be cancelled and a new certificate issued.

24. Power of court to prohibit or restrict exhibition and training of performing animals.

(1) Where it is proved to the satisfaction of any magistrate on a complaint made by a police officer or an officer authorised in writing by the prescribed authority referred to in Section 23, that the training or exhibition of any performing animals has been accompanied by unnecessary pain or suffering and should be prohibited or allowed only subject to conditions, the court may make an order against the person in respect of whom the complaint is made, prohibiting the training or exhibition or imposing such conditions in relation thereto, as may be specified by the order.

(2) Any court by which an order is made under this Section, shall cause a copy of the order to be sent, as soon as may be after the order is made, to the prescribed authority by which the person against whom the order is made is registered, and shall cause the particulars of the order to be endorsed upon the certificate field by the person, and that person shall produce his certificate on being so required by the court for the purposes of endorsement, and the prescribed authority to which a copy of an order is sent under his Section shall enter the particulars of the order in that register;

25. Power to enter premises.

(1) Any person authorised in writing by the prescribed authority referred to in Section 23 and any police officer not below the rank of a sub-inspector may

   (a) enter at all reasonable times and inspect any premises in which any performing animals are being trained or exhibited or kept for training or exhibition, and any such animals found therein; and

   (b) require any person who, he has reason to believe is a trainer or exhibitor of performing animals to produce his certificate of registration.

(2) No person or police officer referred to in sub-section (1) shall be entitled under this Section to go on or behind the stage during a public performance of performing animals.

26. Offences. If any person -

(a) not being registered under this chapter, exhibits or trains any performing animal; or

(b) being registered under the Act, exhibits or trains any performing animal with respect to which or in a manner with respect to which, he is not registered; or

(c) exhibits or trains as a performing animal, any animal which is not to be used for the purpose by reason of a notification issued under clause (ii) of Section 22; or

(d) obstructs or wilfully delays any person or police officer referred to in Section 25 in the exercise of powers under this Act as to entry and inspection; or

(e) conceals any animal with a view to avoiding such inspection; or

(f) being a person registered under ‘the Act, on being duly required in pursuance of this Act to produce his certificate under this Act, fails without reasonable excuse so to do; or

(g) applies to be registered under this Act when not entitled to be so registered,

he shall be punishable on conviction with fine which may extend to five hundred rupees or with imprisonment which may extend to three months, or with both.

27. Exemptions. Nothing contained in this Chapter shall apply to -

(a) the training of animals for bonafide military or police purpose or the exhibition of any animals so trained; or

(b) any animals kept in any zoological garden or by any society or association which has for its principal object the exhibition of animals for educational or scientific purposes.

CHAPTER - VI : MISCELLANEOUS

28. Saving as respects manner of killing prescribed by religion. Nothing contained in this Act shall render it an offence to kill any animal in a manner required by the religion of any community.

29. Power of court to deprive person convicted of ownership of animal.

(1) If the owner of any animal is found guilty of any offence under this Act, the Court upon his conviction thereof, may, if it thinks fit, in addition to any other punishment make an order that the animal with respect to which the offence was committed shall be forfeited to Government and may, further, make such order as to the disposal of the animal as it thinks fit under the circumstances.

(2) No order under sub-section (1) shall be made unless it is shown by evidence as to a previous conviction under this Act or as to the character of the owner or otherwise as to the treatment of the animal that the animal if left with the owner, is likely to be exposed to further cruelty.

(3) without prejudice to the provision contained in sub-section (1), the court may also order that a person convicted of an offence under this Act shall, either permanently or during such period as is fixed by the order, be prohibited from having the custody of any animal of any kind whatsoever, or as the court thinks fit of any animal of any kind or species specified in the order.

(4) No order under sub-section (3) shall be made unless

(a) it is shown by evidence as to a previous conviction or as to the character of the said person or otherwise as to the treatment of the animal in relation to which he has been convicted that an animal in the custody of the said person is likely to be exposed to cruelty;

(b) it is stated in the complaint upon which the conviction was made that it is the intention of the complaint upon the conviction of the accused to request that an order be made as aforesaid and

(c) the offence for which the conviction was made was committed in an area in which under the law for the time being in force a licence is necessary for the keeping of any such animal as that in respect of which the conviction was made.

(5) Notwithstanding anything to the contrary contained in any law for the time being in force, any person in respect of whom an order is made under sub-section (3) shall have no right to the custody of any animal contrary to the provisions of the order, and if he contravenes the provisions oil any order, he shall be punishable with fine which may extend to one hundred rupees, or with imprisonment for a term which may extend to three months, or with both.

(6) Any court which has made an order under sub-section (3) may at any time, either on its own motion or on application made to it in this behalf, rescind or modify such order.

30. Presumptions as to guilt in certain cases. If any person is charged with the offences of killing a goat, cow or its to guilt in progeny contrary to the provisions of clause (1) of sub-section (1) or Section 11, and it is proved that such person had in his possession, at the time the offence is alleged to have been committed, the skin of any such animal as is referred to in this Section with any the skin of any such animal as is referred to in this Section with any part of the skin of the head attached thereto, it shall be presumed until the contrary is proved that such animal was killed in a cruel manner.

31. Cognizability of offences. Notwithstanding anything contained in the Code or Criminal Procedure, 1898, (5 of 1898) an offence punishable under clause (1) or clause (n) or clause, (o) of sub-section (1) of Section 11 or under Section 12 shall be a cognizable offence within the meaning of that code.

32. Powers of search and seizure.

(1) If a police officer not below the rank of sub-inspector, or any person authorised by the State Government in this behalf has reason to believe that an offence under clause (1) of sub-section (1) of Section 11 in respect of any such animal as is referred to in Section 30 is being, or that any person has in his possession

the skin of any such animal with any part of the skin of the head attached thereto, he, may enter and search such place or any place in which he has reason to believe any such skin to be, and may seize such skin or any article or thing used or intended to be used in the commission of such offence.

(2) If a police officer not below the rank of sub-inspector, or any person authorised by the State Government in this behalf, has reason to believe that phooka or (doom dev or any other operation of the nature referred to in Section 12) has just been or is being, performed on any animal within the limits of his jurisdiction, he may enter any place in which he has reason to believe such animal to be, and may seize the animal and produce it for examination by the veterinary officer incharge of the area in which the animal is seized.

33. Search warrants.

(1) If a magistrate of the first or second class or a presidency magistrate or a commissioner of police or district superintendent of police, upon information in writing; and after such inquiry as he thinks necessary, has reason to believe that an offence under this Act is being, or is about to be, or has been committed in any place, he may either himself enter and search or by his warrant authorise any police officer not below the rank of sub-inspector to enter and search the place.

(2) The provisions of the Code of Criminal Procedure, 1898, relating to searches shall so far as those provision can be made applicable, apply to searches under this Act.

34. General Power of seizure for examination. Any police officer above the rank of a constable or any person authorised seizure for by the State Government in this behalf, who has reason to believe that examination an offence against this Act has been or is being, committed in respect of any animal, may, if in his opinion the circumstances so require, seize the animal and produce the same for examination by the nearest magistrate or by such veterinary officer as may be prescribed; and such police officer or authorised person may, when seizing the animal, require the person in charge thereof to accompany it to the place of examination.

35. Treatment and care of animals.

(1) The State Government, may by general or special order appoint infirmaries for the treatment and care of animals in respect of which offences against this Act have been committed, and may authorise the detention therein of any animal pending its production before a magistrate.

(2) The magistrate before whom a prosecution for an offence against this Act has been instituted may direct that the animals concerned shall be treated and cared for in an infirmary, until it is fit to perform its usual work or is otherwise fit for discharge, or that it shall be sent to a pinjrapole, or if the veterinary officer in charge of the area in which the animal is found or such a veterinary officer as may be authorised in this behalf by rules made under this Act certifies that it is incurable or cannot be removed without cruelty, that it shall be destroyed.

(3) An animal sent for care and treatment to an infirmary shall not, unless the magistrate directs that it shall be sent to a pinjrapole or that it shall be destroyed, be released from such place except upon a certificate of its fitness for discharge issued by the veterinary officer in charge of the area in which the infirmary is situated or such other veterinary officer as may be authorised in this behalf by rules made under this Act.

(4) The cost of transporting the animal to an infirmary or pinjrapole and of its maintenance and treatment in an infirmary, shall be payable by the district magistrate, or, in presidency-towns, by the commissioner of police:

PROVIDED that when the magistrate so orders on account of the poverty of the owner of the animal, no charge shall be payable for the treatment of the animal.

(5) Any amount payable by an owner of an animal under sub-section (4) may be recovered in the same manner as an arrear of land revenue.

(6) If the owner refuses or neglects to remove the animal within such time as a magistrate may specify, the magistrate may direct that the animal be sold and that the proceeds of the same be applied to the payment of such cost.

(7) The surplus, if any, of the proceeds of such sale shall, on application made by the owner within two months from the date of the sale be paid to him.

36. Limitation of prosecutions. A prosecution for an offence against this Act shall not be instituted after prosecutions the expiration of three months from the date of the commission of the offence.

37. Delegation of powers. The Central Government may, by notification in the Official Gazette, direct that all or any of the powers exercisable by it under this Act, may, subject to such conditions as it may think fit to impose, be also exercisable by any State Government.

38. Power to make rules.

(1) The Central Government may, by notification in the Official Gazette, and subject to the condition of previous publication, make rules to carry out the purposes of this Act.

(2) In particular and without prejudice to the generality of the foregoing power, the Central Government may make rules providing for all or any of the following matters, namely:-

(a) the terms and conditions of service of members of the Board, the allowances payable to them and the manner in which they may exercise their power and discharge their functions;

(b) the maximum load (including any load occasioned by the weight of passengers) to be carried or drawn by any animal;

(c) the conditions to be observed for preventing the over crowding of animals;

(d) the period during which, and the hours between which, any class of animals shall not be used for draught purposes;

(e) prohibiting the use of any bit or harness involving cruelty to animals;

(f) requiring persons carrying on the business of a farrier to be licensed and registered by such authority as may be prescribed and levying a fee for the purpose;

(g) the precautions to be taken in the capture of animals for purpose of sale, export or for any other purpose, and the different appliances or devices that may alone be used for the purpose; and the licensing of such capture and the levying of fees for such licenses;

(h) the precautions to be taken in the transport of animals, whether by rail, road, inland waterway, sea or air and the manner in which and the cages or other receptacles in which they may be so transported;

(i) requiring persons owning or in charge of premises in which animals are kept or milked to register such premises, to comply with such conditions as may be laid down in relation to the boundary walls or surrounding if such premises, to permit their inspection for the purpose of ascertaining whether any offence under this Act is being, or has been, committed therein and to expose in such premises copies of Section 12 in a language or language commonly understood in the locality;

(j) the form in which applications for registration under Chapter V may be made, the particulars to be contained therein, the fees payable for such registration and the authorities to whom such applications may be made;

(k) the purpose to which fines realized under this Act may by applied, including such purposes as the maintenance of infirmaries, pinjrapoles and veterinary hospitals;

(l) any other matter which has to be, or may be, prescribed.

(3) If any person contravenes, or abets the contravention of, any rules made under this Section, he shall be punishable with fine which may extend to one hundred rupees, or with imprisonment for a term which may extend to three months, or with both.

(4) Every rule made by the Central Government under this Section shall be laid as soon as may be after it is made, before each House of Parliament while it is in session for a total period of thirty days which may be comprised in one session or in two successive sessions, and if, before the expiry of the session in which it is so laid or the session immediately following, both Houses agree in making any modification in the rule, or both Houses agree that the rule should not be made, the rule shall thereafter have effect only in such modified form or be of no effect, as the case may, be, so however that such modification or annulment shall be without prejudice to the validity of anything previously done under that rule.

[**38A. Rules and regulations to be laid before Parliament.** Every rule made by the Central Government or by the Committee constituted under Section 15 and every regulation made. by the Board shall be laid, as soon as may be after it is made, before each House of Parliament, while it is in session, for a total period of thirty days which may be comprised in one session or in two or more successive sessions, and if, before the expiry of the session immediately following the session or the successive sessions aforesaid, both Houses agree in making any modification in the rule or regulation, as the case may be, should not be made the rule or regulation shall there after have effect only in such modified form or be of no effect, as the case may be; so, however, that any such modification or annulment shall be without prejudice to the validity of anything previously done under that rule or regulation.]

39. Persons authorised under Section 34 to be public servants. Every person authorised by the State Government under Section 34 shall be deemed to be a public servant within the meaning of Section 21 of the Indian Penal code.

40. Indemnity. No suit, prosecution or other legal proceeding shall lie against any person who is, or who is deemed to be a public servant within the meaning of Section 21 of the Indian Penal Code in respect of anything in good faith done or intended to be done under this Act.

41. Repeal of Act 11 of 1890. Where in pursuance of a notification under subsection (3) of Section 1 of 1890 any provision of this Act comes into force in any State, any provision of the Prevention of Cruelty to Animals Act, 1890, which corresponds to the provision so coming into force, shall thereupon stand repealed.

ANNEXURE

Notifications under Section 1 (3) of the Act bringing it into force in specified States and Union Territories.

1. (a) Chapters I and II came into force in the States of Assam, Andhra Pradesh, Bihar, Gujarat, Kerala, Chennai (Tamil Nadu), Maharashtra, Madhya Pradesh, Mysore (Karnataka), Orissa, Uttar Pradesh and West Bengal and the Union Territories of Delhi, Manipur and Tripura on the 1st September, 1961, vide Notification No. 9-2/61 L.D dated 25th August, 1951/Bhadra, 1883 of Government of India, Ministry of Food and Agriculture (Department of Agriculture).

(b) Chapter IV came into force in the States of Assam, Andhra Pradesh, Bihar, Gujarat, Kerala, Chennai (Tamil Nadu), Maharashtra, Madhya Pradesh, Mysore (Karnataka), Orissa, Rajasthan, Uttar Pradesh and West Bengal and in the Union Territories of Delhi, Himachal Pradesh, Manipur and Tripura on the 15 July, 1963, vide Notification No. 19-12/63-LD dated 11th July 1963/20th Asadha, 1885 (S.E) of Government of India, Ministry of Food and Agriculture (Department of Agriculture).

(c) Chapters III and IV came into force in the States of Assam, Andhra Pradesh, Bihar, Gujarat, Kerala, Chennai (Tamil Nadu), Maharashtra, Madhya Pradesh, Mysore (Karnataka), Orissa, Uttar Pradesh and West Bengal and the Union Territories of Delhi, Himachal Pradesh, Manipur and Tripura on the 20th November, 1963, vide Notification No. 9-24/62-LD dated 29th October, 1963/ 7th Kartika 1885 (S.E.) of Government of India, Ministry of Food and Agriculture (Department of Agriculture);

(d) Chapters III and VI came into force in West Bengal on the 1st June, 1975, vide Notification No. 21-2/74-LDI dated 28th May, 1975 of Government of India, Ministry of Agriculture and Irrigation (Department of Agriculture);

(e) The whole Act came into force in the State of Punjab and the Union Territory of Andaman and Nicobar Islands on the 1st April, 1961 vide Notification No. 9-2/61-LD of the Ministry of Food and Agriculture;

(f) Chapters I and II came into force in the then Union Territory of Himachal Pradesh on the 2nd October, 1961, vide Notification No. 9-2/61 LP of the Ministry of Food and Agriculture;

(g) Chapters I and II came into force on the 26th January, 1962 in the State of Rajasthan vide Notification No. 9-2/61-LD. of the Ministry of Food and Agriculture;

(h) Chapter V came into force in all the States and Union Territories (except Jammu & Kashmir) on 24th May 1977, vide Notification No. 14-22/76-LDI dated 24th May 1977 of Government of India, Ministry of Agriculture and Irrigation (Department of Agriculture).

❑❑❑

22

The Prevention of Food Adulteration (Extension to Kohima and Mokokchung Districts) Repeal Act, 2002

Act No. 66 of 2002 [18th December, 2002]

AN ACT to repeal the Prevention of Food Adulteration (Extension to Kohima and Mokokchung Districts) Act, 1972.

Be it enacted by Parliament in the Fifty-third Year of the Republic of India as follows:-

1. Short title. This Act may be called the Prevention of Food Adulteration (Extension to Kohima and Mokokchung Districts) Repeal Act, 2002.

2. Repeal of Act 24 of 1972. The Prevention of Food Adulteration (Extension to Kohima and Mokokchung Districts) Act, 1972, is hereby repealed.

❑❑❑

23

The Prevention of Food Adulteration Act, 1954

Act No. 37 of 1954 [29th September, 1954]

AN ACT to make provision for the prevention of adulteration of food.

Be it enacted by Parliament in the Fifth Year of the Republic of India as follows:-

1. Short title, extent and commencement.

(1) This Act may be called the Prevention of Food Adulteration Act, 1954.

(2) It extends to the whole of India.

(3) It shall come into force on such date as the Central Government may, by notification in the Official Gazette, appoint.

2. Definition. In this Act unless the context otherwise requires,

(i) "adulterant" means any material which is or could be employed for the purposes of adulteration;

(ia) "adulterated"— an article of food shall be deemed to be adulterated-

(a) if a article sold by vendor is not of the nature, substance or quality demanded by the purchaser and is to his prejudice, or is not of the nature, substance or quality which it purports or is represented to be;

(b) if the article contains any other substance which affects, or if the article is so processed as to affect, injuriously the nature, substance or quality thereof;

(c) if any inferior or cheaper substance has been substituted wholly or in part for the article so as to affect injuriously the nature, substance or quality thereof;

(d) if any constituant of the article has been wholly or in part abstracted so as to affect injuriously the nature, substance or quality thereof;

(e) if the article has been prepared, packed or kept under insanitary conditions whereby it has become contaminated or injurious to health;

(f) if the article consists wholly or, in part of any filthy putrid, [1][rotten, decomposed or diseased animal or vegetable substance or is insect-infested or is otherwise unfit for human consumption;

(g) if the article is obtained from a diseased animal;

(h) if the article contains any poisonous or other ingredient which renders it injurious to health;

(i) if the container of the article is composed, whether wholly or in part, of any poisonous or deleterious substance which renders its contents injurious to health;

(j) if any colouring matter other than that prescribed in respect thereof is present in the article, or if the amounts of the prescribed colouring matter which is present in the article are not within the prescribed limits of variability;

(k) if the article contains any prohibited preservative or permitted preservative in excess of the prescribed limits;

(l) if the quality or purity of the article falls below the prescribed standard or its constituents are present in quantities not within the prescribed limits of variability which renders it injurious to health;

(m) if the quality or purity of the article fall below the prescribed standard or its constituents are present in quantities not within the prescribed limits of variability but which does not render it injurious to health:

PROVIDED that, where the quality or purity of the article, being primary food, has fallen below the prescribed standards or its constituents are present in quantities not within the prescribed limits of variability, in either case, solely due to natural causes and beyond the control of human agency, then, such article shall not be deemed to be adulterated within the meaning of this sub-clause.

EXPLANATION. Where two or more articles of primary food are together and the resultant article of food - (a) is stored, sold or distributed under a name which denotes the ingredients thereof; and (b) is not injurious to health, then, such resultant article shall not be deemed to be adulterated within the meaning of this clause;

(ii) "Central Food Laboratory" means any laboratory or institute established or specified under Section 4;

(iii) "Committee" means the centre committee of food standarads constituted under Section 3.

(iv) "Director of Central Food Laboratory" means the pasear appointed by the Central Government by notification in the Official Gazette as the Director of the Central Food Laboratory and includes any person appointed by the Central Government in like manner to perform all or any of the functions of the Director under this Act:

PROVIDED that no person who has any financial interest in the manufacture, import or sale of any article of food shall be appointed to be a Director under this clause;

(v) "food" means any article used as food or drink for human consumption other than drugs and water and includes-

(a) any article which ordinarly enters into, or is used in the composition or preparation of, human food,

(b) any flavouring matter or condiments, and

(c) any other article which the Central Government may, having regard to its use, nature, substance or quality, declare, by notification in the Official Gazette, as food for the purposes of this Act;

(vi) "Food (Health) Authority" means the Director of Medical and Health Services or the Chief Officer-in-charge of Health administration in a State, by whatever designation he is known, and includes any officer empowered by the Central Government or the State Government, by notification in the Official Gazette, to exercise the powers and perform the duties of the Food (Health) Authority under this Act with respect to such local area as may be specified in the notification;

(vii) "local area" means any area, whether urban or rural, declared by the Central Government or the State Government, by notification in the Official Gazette, to be a local area for the purposes of this Act;

(viii) "local authority" means in the case of

(1) a local area which is-

(a) a municipality, the municipal board or municipal corporation;

(b) a cantonment, the cantonment authority;

(c) a notified area, the notified area committee;

(2) any other local area, such authority as may be prescribed by the Central Government or the State Government] under this Act;

(viii a) "Local (Health) Authority", in relation to a local area, means the officer appointed by the Central Government or the State Government, by notification in the Official Gazette, to be in charge of Health, administration in such area with such designation as may be specified therein;

(viii b) "manufacture" includes any process incidental or ancillary to the manufacture of an article of food;

(ix) "misbranded" - an article of food shall be deemed to be misbranded-

(a) if it is an imitation of, or is a substitute for, or resembles in a manner likely to deceive, another article of food under the name of which it is sold, and is not plainly and conspicuously labelled so as to indicate its true character;

(b) any place or country;

(c) if it is sold by a name which belong to another article of food;

(d) if it is so coloured, flavoured or seated powdered or polished that the fact that the article is damaged is concealed or if the article is made to appear better or of greater value than it really is;

(e) if false claims are made for each upon the label or otherwise;

(f) if, when sold in packages which have been sealed or prepared by or at the instance of the manufacturer or producer and which bear his name and address, the contents of each package are not conspicuously and correctly stated on the outside thereof within the limits of variability prescribed under this Act;

(g) if the package containing it, or the label on the package bears any statement, design or device regarding the ingredients or the substances contained therein, which is false or misleading in any material particulars; or if the package is otherwise deceptive with respect to its contents;

(h) if the package, containing it, or the lake on the package bears the name of a fictitious individual or company as the manufacturer or producer of the article;

(i) if it purports to be, or is represented as being, for special dietary uses, unless its label bears such information as may be prescribed concerning its vitamin, mineral, or other dietary properties in order sufficiently to inform its purchaser as to its value for such uses;

(j) if it contains any artificial flavouring artificial colouring or chemical preservative, without a declaratory label stating that fact, or in contravention of the requirements of this Act or rules made thereunder;

(k) if it is not labelled in accordance with the requirements of this Act or rules made thereunder;

(x) "package" means a box, bottle, casket, tin, barrel, case, receptacle, sack, bag, wrapper or other thing in which an article of food is placed or packed;

(xi) "premises" include any shop, stall, or place where any article of food is sold or manufactured or stored for sale;

(xii) "prescribed" means prescribed by rules made under this Act;

(xiia) "primary food" means any article of food, being a produce of agriculture or horticulture in its natural form,

(xiii) "sale" with grammatical varitation and cognate expressions, means the sale of any article of food, whether for cash or on credit or by way of exchange and whether by wholesale or retail, for human consumption or use, or for analysis, and includes an agreement for sale, an offer for sale, the exposing for sale or having in possession for sale of any such article, and includes also an attempt to sell any such article;

(xiv) "sample" means a sample of any article of food taken under the provisions of this Act or of any rules made thereunder;

(xv) the words "unwholesome" and "noxious" when used in relation to an article of food mean respectively that the article is harmful to health or repugnant to human use.

2A. Rule of construction. Any reference in this Act to a law which is not in force in the State of Jammu and Kashmir shall, in relation to that State, be construed as a reference to the corresponding law, if any, in force in that State.

3. Central Committee for Food Standards and Central Food Laboratory.

(1) The Central Committee for Food Standards. The Central Government shall, as soon as may be after the commencement of this Act, constitute a Committee called the Central Committee for Food Standards to advise the Central Government and the State Governments on matters arising out of the administration of this Act and to carry out the other functions assigned to it under this Act.

(2) The Committee shall consist of the following members, namely:

(a) the Director-General, Health Services, *ex-officio*, who shall be the Chairman;

(b) the Director of the Central Food Laboratory or, in a case where more than one Central Food Laboratory is established, the Directors of such Laboratories, *ex-officio*;

(c) two experts nominated by the Central Government;

(d) one representative each of the Departments of Food and Agriculture in the Central Ministry of Food and Agriculture and one representative each of the Central Ministries of Commerce, Defence, Industry and Supply and Railways, nominated by the Central Government;

(e) one representative each nominated by the Government of each State;

(f) two representatives nominated by the Central Government to represent the Union territories;

(g) one representative each, nominated by the Central Government, to represent the agricultural, commercial and industrial interests;

(gg) five representatives nominated by the Central Government to represent the consumers' interest one of whom shall be from the hotel industry;

(h) one representative of the medical profession nominated by the Indian Council of Medical Research;

(i) one representative nominated by the Indian Standards Institution referred to in clause (e) of Section 2 of the Indian Standards Institution' (Certification of Marks) Act, 1952 (36 of 1952).

(3) The members of the Committee referred to in clauses (c), (d), (e), (f), (g), (gg), (h) and (i) of sub-section (2) shall, unless their seats become vacant earlier by resignation, death or otherwise, be entitled to hold office for three years and shall be eligible for renomination.

(4) The functions of the Committee may be exercised notwithstanding any vacancy therein.

(5) The Committee may appoint such and so many sub-committees as it deems fit and may appoint to them persons who are not members of the Committee to exercise such powers and perform such duties as may, subject to such conditions, if any, as the Committee may impose, be delegated to them by the Committee.

(6) The Committee may, subject to the previous approval of the Central Government, make bye-laws for the purpose of regulating its own procedure and the transaction of its business.

3A. Appointment of Secretary and other staff.

(1) The Central Government shall appoint a Secretary to the Committee who shall, under the control and direction of the Committee, exercise such powers and perform such duties as may be prescribed or as may be delegated to him by the Committee.

(2) The Central Government shall provide the Committee with such clerical and other staff as that Government considers necessary.

4. Central Food Laboratory.

(1) The Central Government shall, by notification in the Official Gazette, establish one or more Central Food Laboratory or Laboratories to carry out the functions entrusted to the Central Food Laboratory by this Act or any rules made under this Act:

PROVIDED that the Central Government may, by notification in the Official Gazette, also specify any laboratory or institute as a Central Food Laboratory for the purposes of this Act.

(2) The Central Government may, after constitution with the committee, make rules prescribing-

(a) the functions of a Central Food Laboratory and the local area or areas within which such functions may be carried out;

(b) the procedure for the submission to the said Laboratory of samples of articles of food for analysis or tests, the forms of the Laboratory' s reports thereon and the fees payable in respect of such reports;

(c) such other matters as may be necessary or expedient to enable the said Laboratory to carry out its functions.

GENERAL PROVISIONS AS TO FOOD

5. Prohibition of import of certain articles of food. No person shall import into India-

(i) any adulterated food;

(ii) any misbranded food;

(iii) any article of food for the import of which a licence is prescribed, except in accordance with the conditions of the licence; and

(iv) any article of food in contravention of any other provision of this Act or of any rule made thereunder.

6. Application of law relating to sea customs and powers of Customs officers.

(1) The law for the time being in force relating to sea custom and to goods, the import of which is prohibited by Section 18 of the Sea Customs Act, 1878 (8 of 1878) shall, subject to the provisions of Section 16 of this Act, apply in respect of articles of food, the import of which is prohibited under Section 5 of this Act, and officers of Customs and officers empowered under that Act to perform the duties imposed thereby on a Customs Collector and other officers of Customs shall have the same powers in respect of such articles of food as they have for the time being in respect of such goods as aforesaid.

(2) without prejudice to the provisions of sub-section (1) the Customs Collector, or any officer of the Government authorised by the Central Government in this behalf, may detain any imported package which he suspects to contain any article of food the import of which is prohibited under Section 5 of this Act and shall forthwith report such detention to the Director of the Central Food Laboratory and, if required by him, forward the package or send samples of any suspected article of food found therein to the said Laboratory.

7. Prohibition of manufacture, sale, etc., of certain articles of food. No person shall himself or by any person on his behalf manufacture for sale, or store, sell or distribute-

(i) any adulterated food;

(ii) any misbranded food;

(iii) any article of food for the sale of which a licence is prescribed, except in accordance with the conditions of the licence;

(iv) any article of food the sale of which is for the time being prohibited by the Food (Health) Authority [1][in the interest of public health;

(v) any article of food in contravention of any other provision of this Act or of any rule made thereunder; or

(vi) any adulterant.

EXPLANATION. For the purposes of this Section, a person shall be deemed to store any adulterated food or misbranded food or any article of food referred to in clause (iii) or clause (iv) or clause (v) if he stores such food for the manufacture therefrom of any article of food for sale.

ANALYSIS OF FOOD

8. Public Analysis. The Central Government or the State Government may, by notification in the Official Gazette, appoint such persons as it thinks fit, having the prescribed qualifications to be public analysts for such local areas as may be assigned to them by the Central Government or the State Government, as the case may be:

PROVIDED that no person who has any financial interest in the manufacture, import or sale of any article of food shall be appointed to be a public analyst under this Section: Provided further that different public analysts may be appointed for different articles of food.

9. Food Inspectors.

(1) The Central Government or the State Government may, by notification in the

Official Gazette, appoint such persons as it thinks fit, having the prescribed qualifications to be food inspectors for such local areas as may be assigned to them by the Central Government or the State Government, as the case may be:

PROVIDED that no person who has any financial interest in the manufacture, import or sale of any article of food shall be appointed to be a food inspector under this Section.

(2) Every food inspector shall be deemed to be a public servant within the meaning of Section 21 of the Indian Penal Code (45 of 1860) and shall be officially subordinate to such authority as the Government appointing him, may specify in this behalf.

10. Powers of food inspectors.

(1) A food inspector shall have power-

(a) to take samples of any article of food from-

(i) any person selling such article;

(ii) any person who is in the course as convenying, delivering or preparing to deliver such article to a purchaser or consignee;

(iii) consignee after delivery of any such article to him; and

(b) to send such sample for analysis to the public analyst for the local area within which such sample has been taken;

(c) with the previous approval of the Local (Health) Authority having jurisdiction in the local area concerned, or with the previous approval of the Food (Health) Authority, to prohibit the sale of any article of food in the interest of public health.

EXPLANATION. for the purposes of sub clause (iii) of clause (a)," consignee" does not include a person who purchases or receives any article of food for his own consumption;

(2) Any food inspector may enter and inspect any place where any article of food is manufactured, or stored for sale, or stored for the manufacture of any other article of food for sale, or exposed or exhibited for sale or where any adulterant is manufactured or kept, and take samples of such article of food or adulterant for analysis:

PROVIDED that no sample of any article of food, being primary food, shall be taken under this sub-section if it is not intended for sale as such food.

(3) Where any sample is taken under clause (a) of sub-section (1) or sub-section (2), its cost calculated at the rate at which the article is usually sold to the public shall be paid to the person from whom it is taken.

(4) if any article intended for food appears to any food inspector to be adulterated or misbranded, he may seize and carry away or keep in the safe custody of the vendor such article in order that it may be dealt with as hereinafter provided and he shall, in either case, take a sample of such article and submit the same for analysis to a public analyst:

PROVIDED that where the food inspector keeps such article in the safe custody of the vendor he may require the vendor to execute a bond for a sum of money equal to the value of such article with one or more sureties as the food inspector deems fit and the vendor shall execute the bond accordingly.

(4A) Where any article of food seized under sub-section (4) is of a perishable nature and the Local (Health) Authority is satisfied that such article of food is so deteriorated that it is unfit for human consumption, the said Authority may, after giving notice in writing to the vendor, cause the same to be destroyed.

(5) The power conferred by this Section includes power to break open any package in which any article of food may be contained or to break open the door of any premises where any article of food may be kept for sale:

PROVIDED that the power to break open the package or door shall be exercised only after the owner or any other person in charge of the package or, as the case may be, in occupation of the premises, if he is present therein, refuses to open the package or door on being called upon to do so, and in either case after recording the reasons for doing so: Provided further that the food inspector shall, in exercising the powers of entry upon, and inspection of any place under this Section, follow, as far as may be, the provisions of the Code of Criminal Procedure, 1973] (2 of 1974), relating to the search or inspection of a place by a police officer executing a search warrant issued under that Code.

(6) any adulterant found in the possession of a manufacturer or distributor of, or dealer in, any article of food or in any of the premises occupied by him as such and for the possession of which he is unable to account to the satisfaction of the food inspector, and any books of account or other documents found in his possession or control and which would be useful for, or relevant to, any investigation or proceeding under this Act, may be seized by the food inspector and a sample of such adulterant submitted for analysis to a public analyst:

PROVIDED that no such books of account or other documents shall be seized by the food inspector except with the previous approval of the authority to which he is officially subordinate.

(7) Where the food inspector takes any action under clause (a) of sub-section (1), sub-section (2), sub-section (4) or sub-section (6), he shall, call one or more persons to be present at the time when such action is taken and take his or their signatures.

(7A) Where any books of account or other documents are seized under sub-section (6), the food inspector shall, within a period not exceeding thirty days from the date of seizure, return the same to the person from whom they were seized after copies thereof or extracts therefrom as certified by that person in such manner as may be prescribed have been taken:

PROVIDED that where such person refuses to so certify, and a prosecution has been instituted against him under this Act, such books of account or other documents shall be returned to him only after copies thereof or extracts therefrom as certified by the court have been taken.

(7B) When any adulterant is seized under sub-section (6) the burden of proving that such adulterant is not meant for purposes of adulteration shall be on the person from whose possession such adulterant was seized.

(8) Any food inspector may exercise the powers of a police officer under Section 42 of the Code of Criminal Procedure, 1973] (2 of 1973) for the purpose of ascertaining the true name and residence of the person from whom a sample is taken or an article of food is seized.

(9) Any food inspector exercising powers under this Act or under the rules made thereunder who-

(a) vexatiously and without any reasonable grounds of suspicion seizes any article of food [2][or adulterant; or

(b) commits any other act to the injury of any person without having reason to believe that such act is necessary for the execution of his duty; shall be guilty of an offence under this Act and shall be punishable for such offence with fine which shall not be less than five hundred rupees but which may extend to one thousand rupees.

11. Procedure to be followed by food inspectors.

(1) When a food inspector takes a sample of food for analysis, he shall-

(a) give notice in writing then and there of his intention to have it so analysed to the person from whom he has taken the sample and to the person, if any, whose name, address and other particulars have been disclosed under Section 14A;

(b) except in special cases provided by rules under this Act, divide the sample then and there into three parts and mark and seal or fasten up each part in such a manner as its nature permits and take the signature or thumb impression of the person from whom the sample has been taken in such place and in such manner as may be prescribed:

PROVIDED that where such person refuses to sign or put his thumb impression the food inspector shall call upon one or more witnesses and take his or their signatures or thumb impressions, as the case may be, in lieu of the signature or thumb impression of such person;

(c) (i) send one of the parts for analysis to the public analyst under intimation to the Local (Health) Authority; and (ii) Send the remaining two parts to the Local (Health) Authority for the purposes of sub-section (2) of this Section and sub-sections (2A) and (2E) of Section 13.

(2) Where the part of the sample sent to the public analyst under sub-clause (i) of clause (c) of sub-section (1) is lost or damaged, the Local (Health) Authority shall, on a requisition made to it by the public analyst or the food inspector despatch one of the parts of the sample sent to it under sub-clause (ii) of the said clause (c) to the public analyst for analysis.

(3) When a sample of any article of food or adulterant is taken under sub-section (1) or sub-section (2) of Section 10 the food inspector shall, by the immediately succeeding working day, send a sample of the article of food or adulterant or both, as the case may be, in accordance with the rules prescribed for sampling to the public analyst for the local area concerned.

(4) An article of food seized under sub-section (4) of Section 10, unless destroyed under sub-section (4A) of that Section, and any adulterant seized under sub-section (6) of that Section shall be produced before a magistrate as soon as possible and in any case not later than seven days after the receipt of the report of the public analyst:

PROVIDED that if an application is made to the magistrate in this behalf by the person from whom any article of food has been seized, the magistrate shall by order in writing direct the food inspector to produce such article before him within such time as may be specified in the order.

(5) If it appears to the magistrate on taking such evidence as he may deem necessary-

(a) that the article of food produced before him under sub-section (4) is adulterated or misbranded, he may order it-

(i) to be forfieted to the Central Government, the State Government or the local authority, as the case may be; or

(ii) to be destroyed at the cost of the owner or the person from whom it was seized so as to prevent its being used as human food; or

(iii) to be so disposed of as to prevent its being for sale or used for food under its, again exposed deceptive name; or

(iv) to be returned to the owner, on his executing a bond with or without sureties, for being sold under its appropriate name or, where the magistrate is satisfied that the article of food is capable of being made to conform to prescribed standards for human consumption after reprocessing, for being sold after reprocessing under the supervision of such officer as may be specified in the order;

(b) that the adulterant seized under sub-section 6 of Section 10 and produced before him is apparently of a kind which may be employed for purposes of adulteration and for the possession of which the manufacturer, distributor or dealer, as the case may be, is unable to account satisfactorily, he may order it to be forfeited to the Central Government, the State Government or the local authority, as the case may be.

(6) If it appears to the magistrate that any such-

(a) article of food is not adulterated; or

(b) adulterant which is purported to be an adulterant is not an adulterant. the person from whose possession the article of food or adulterant was taken shall be entitled to have it restored to him and it shall be in the discretion of the magistrate to award such person from such fund as the State Government may direct in this behalf, such compensation not exceeding the actual loss which he has sustained as the magistrate may think proper.

12. Purchaser may have food analysed. Nothing contained in this Act shall be held to prevent a purchaser of any article of food other than a food inspector or a recognised consumer association, whether the purchaser is a member of that association or not, from having such article analysed by the public analyst on payment of such fees as may be prescribed and from receiving from the public analyst a report of his analysis.

PROVIDED that such purchaser or recognised consumer association shall, inform the vendor at the time of purchase of his or its intention] to have such article so analysed; provided further that the provisions of sub-section (1), sub-section (2) and sub-section (3) of Section 11 shall, as far as may be, apply to a purchaser of article of food or recognised consumer association who or which intends to have such article so anaylsis. as they apply to a food inspector who takes a sample of food for analysis:

PROVIDED ALSO that if the report of the public analyst shows that the article of food is adulterated, the purchaser or recognised consumer association shall be intitled to get refund of the fees paid by him or it, under this Section.

EXPLANATION. For the purposes of this Section and Section 20, "recognised consumer association" means a voluntary consumer association registered under the Companies Act, 1956 or under any other law for the time being inforce.

13. Report of public analyst.

(1) The public ayalyst shall deliver, in such form as may be prescribed, a report to the Local (Health) Authority of the result of the analysis of any article of food submitted to him for analysis.

(2) On receipt of the report of the result of the analysis under sub-section (1) to the effect that the article of food is adulterated, the Local (Health) Authority shall, after the institution of prosecution against the person from whom the sample of the article of food was taken and the person, if any, whose name, address and other particulars have been disclosed under Section 14A, forward, in such manner as may be prescribed, a copy of the report of the result of the analysis to such person or persons, as the case may be, informing such person or persons that if it is so desired, either or both of them may make an application to the court within a period of ten days from the date of receipt of the copy of the report to get the sample of the article of food kept by the Local (Health) Authority analysed by the Central Food Laboratory.

(2A) When an application is made to the court under sub-section (2), the court shall require the Local (Health) Authority to forward the part or parts of the sample kept by the said Authority and upon such requisition being made, the said Authority shall forward the part or parts of the sample to the court within a period of five days from the date of receipt of such requisition.

(2B) On receipt of the part or parts of the sample from the Local (Health) Authority under sub-section (2A), the court shall first ascertain that the mark and seal or fastening as provided in clause (b) of sub-section (1) of Section 11 are intact and the signature or thumb impression, as the case may be, is not tampered with, and despatch the part or, as the case may be, one of the parts of the sample under its own seal to the Director of the Central Food Laboratory who shall thereupon send a certificate to the court in the prescribed form within one month from the date of receipt of the part of the sample specifying the result of the analysis.

(2C) Where two Parts of the sample have been sent to the court and only one part of the sample has been sent by the court to the Director of the Central Food Laboratory under sub-section (2B), the court shall, as soon as practicable, return the remaining part to the Local (Health) Authority and that Authority shall destroy that part after the certificate from the Director of the Central Food Laboratory has been received by the court:

PROVIDED that where the part of the sample sent by the court to the Director of the Central Food Laboratory is lost or damaged, the court shall require the Local (Health) Authority to forward the part of the sample, if any, retained by it to the court and on receipt thereof, the court shall proceed in the manner provided in sub-section (2B).

(2D) Until the receipt of the certificate of the result of the analysis from the Director of the Central Food Laboratory, the court shall not continue with the proceedings pending before it in relation to the prosecution.

(2E) If, after considering the report, if any, of the food inspector or otherwise, the Local (Health) Authority is of the opinion that the report delivered by the public analyst under sub-section (1) is erroneous, the said Authority shall forward one of the parts of the sample kept by it to any other public analyst for analysis and if the report of the result of the analysis of that part of the sample by that other public analyist is to eh effect that the article of food is is adulterated, the provisions of sub-sections (2) to and shall, so far as may be, apply.

(3) The certificate issued by the Director of the Central Food Laboratory under sub-section (2B) shall supersede the report given by the public analyst under sub-section (1).

(4) Where a certificate attained from the Director of the Central Food Laboratory under sub-section (2B)] is produced in any proceeding under this Act, or under Sections 272 to 276 of the Indian Penal Code (45 of 1860), it shall not be necessary in such proceeding to produce any part of the sample of food taken for analysis.

(5) any decuments purparting to be a report signed by a public analyst, unless it has been superseded under sub-section (3), or any document purporting to be a certificate signed by the Director of the Central Food Laboratory, may be used as evidence of the facts stated therein in any proceeding under this Act or under Sections 272 to 276 of the Indian Penal Code: (45 of 1860).

PROVIDED that any document purporting to be a certificate signed by the Director of the Central Food Laboratory not being a certificate with respect to the analysis of the part of the sample of any article of food referred to in the proviso to sub-section (1A) of Section 16 shall be final and conclusive evidence of the facts stated therein.

EXPLANATION. In this Section, and in clause (f) of sub-section (1) of Section 16, "Director of the Central Food Laboratory" shall include the officer for the time being in charge of any Food Laboratory (by whatever designation he is known) recognised by the Central Government for the purposes of this Section.

MISCELLANEOUS

14. Manufacturers, distributors and dealers to give warranty. No manufacturer or distributor of, or dealer in, any article of food shall sell such article to any vendor unless he also gives a warranty in writing in the prescribed form about the nature and quality of such article to the vendor:

PROVIDED that a bill, cash memorandum or invoice in respect of the sale of any article of food given by a manufacturer or distributor of, or dealer in, such article to the vendor thereof shall be deemed to be a warranty given by such manufacturer distributor or dealer under this Section.

Explanation. In this Section, in sub-section (2) of Section 19 and in Section 20A, the expression "distributor" shall include a commission agent.

14A. Vendor to disclose the name, etc., of the person from whom the articles of food was purchased. Every vendor of an article of food shall, if so required, disclose to the food inspector the name, address and other particulars of the person from whom he purchased the article of food.

15. Notification of food poisoning. The Central Government or the State Government] may, by notification in the Official Gazette, require medical practitioners carrying on their profession in any local area specified in the notification to report all occurrences of food poisoning coming within their cognizance to such officer as may be specified in the notification.

16. Penalties. Subject to the provisions of sub-section (1A), if any person -

(a) whether by himself or by any other person on his behalf, imports into India or manufactures for sale, or stores, sells or distributes any article of food -

(i) where is adulterated with the meaning of sub-clause (m) of clause (ia) of Section 2 or misbranded within the meaning of clause (ix) of that Section or the sale of which is prohibited under any provision of this Act or any rule made thereunder or by an order of the Food (Health) Authority;

(ii) other than an article of food refered to in sub-clause (i), in contravention of any of the provisions of this Act or of any rule made thereunder; or

(b) whether by himself or by any other person on his behalf, imports into India or manufactures for sale, or stores, sells or distributes any adulterant which is not injurious to health; or

(c) prevents a food inspector from taking a sample as authorised by this Act; or

(d) prevents a food inspector from exercising any other power conferred on him by or under this Act; or

(e) being a manufacturer of an article of food, has in his possession, or in any of the premises occupied by him, any adulterant which is not injurious to health; or

(f) uses any report or certificate of a test or analysis made by the Director of the Central Food Laboratory or by a public analyst or any extract thereof for the purpose of advertising any article of food; or

(g) whether by himself or by any other person on his behalf, gives to the vendor a false warranty in writing in respect of any article of food sold by him, he shall, in addition to the penalty to which he may be liable under the provisions of Section 6, be punishable with imprisonment for a term which shall not be less than six months but which may extend to three years, and with fine which shall not be less than one thousand rupees;

PROVIDED that-

(i) if the offence is under sub-clause (i), of clause (a) and is with respect to an article of food, being primary food, which is adulterated due to human agency or is with respect to an article of food which is misbranded within the meaning of sub-clause (k) of clause (ix) of Section 2; or

(ii) if the offence is under sub-clause (ii) of clause (a), but not being an offence with respect to the contravention of any rule made under clause (a) or clause (g) of sub-section (1A) of Section 23 or under clause (b) of sub-section (2) of Section 24, the court may, for any adequate and special reasons to be mentioned in the judgement, impose a sentence of imprisonment for a term which shall not be less than three months but which may extend to two years, and with fine which shall not be less than five hundred rupees.

PROVIDED FURTHER that if the offence is under sub-clause (ii) of clause (a) and is with respect to the contravention of any rule made under (a) or clause (g) of sub-section (1A) of Section 23 or under clause (b) of sub-section (2) of Section 24, the court may, for any adequate and special reasons to be mentioned in the judgment, impose a sentence of imprisonment for a term which may extend to three months and with fine which may extend to five hundred rupees.

(1A) If any person whether by himself or by any other person on his behalf, imports into India or manufactures for sale, or stores, sells or distributes,-

(i) any article of food which is adulterated within the meaning of any of the sub-clauses (e) to (1) (both inclusive) of clause (ia) of Section 2; or

(ii) any adulterant which is injurious to health, he shall, in addition to the penalty to which he may be liable under the provisions of Section 6, be punishable with imprisonment for a term which shall not be less than one year but which may extend to six years and with fine which shall not be less than two thousand rupees:

PROVIDED that if such article of food or adulterant, when consumed by any person is likely to cause his death or is likely to cause such harm on his body as would amount to grievous hurt within the meaning of Section 320 of the Indian Penal Code (45 of 1860), he shall be punishable with imprisonment for a term which shall not be less than three years but which may extend to term of life and with fine which shall not be less than five thousand rupees.

(1AA) If any person in whose safe custody any article of food has been kept under sub-section (4) of Section 10, tampers or in any other manner interferes with such, article, he shall be punishable with imprisonment for a term which shall not be less than six months but which may extend to two years and with fine which shall not be less than one thousand rupees.

(1B) If any person in whose safe custody any article of food has been kept under sub-section (4) of Section 10, sells or distributes such article which is found by the magistrate before whom it is produced to be adulterated within the meaning of sub-clause (h) of clause (ia) of Section 2 and which, when consumed by any person, is likely to cause his death or is likely to cause such harm on his body as would amount to grievous hurt within the meaning of Section 320 of the Indian Penal Code (45 of 1860), then, notwithstanding anything contained in sub-section (1AA), he shall be punishable with imprisonm-ent for a term which shall not be less than three years but which may extend to term of life and with fine which shall not be less than five thousand rupees.

(1C) If any person contravenes the provisions of Section 14 or Section 14A, he shall be punishable with imprisonment for a term which may extend to six months and with fine which shall not be less than five hundred rupees.

(1D) If any person convicted of an offence under this Act commits a like offence afterwards, then, without prejudice to the provisions of sub-section (2), the court, before which the second or subsequent conviction takes place, may order the cancellation of the licence, if any, granted to him under this Act and thereupon such licence shall, notwithstanding anything contained in this Act, or in the rules made thereunder, stand cancelled.

(2) If any person convicted of an offence under this Act commits a like offence afterwards it shall be lawful for the court before which the second or subsequent conviction takes place to cause the offender' s name and place of residence, the offence and the penalty imposed to be published at the offender's expense in such newspapers or in such other manner as the court may direct. The expenses of such publication shall be deemed to be part of the cost attending the conviction and shall be recoverable in the same manner as a fine.

16A. Power of court to try cases summarily. Notwithstanding anything contained in the Code of Criminal Procedure, 1973 (2 of 1974), all offences under sub-section (1) of Section 16 shall be 2 tried in a summary way by a Judicial Magistrate of the first class specially empowered in this behalf by the State Government or by a Metropolitan Magistrate and the provisions of Sections 262 to 265 (both inclusive) of the said Code shall, as far as may be, apply to such trial:

PROVIDED that in the case of any conviction in a summary trial under this Section, it shall be lawful for the Magistrate to pass a sentence of imprisonment for a term not exceeding one year:

PROVIDED FURTHER that when at the commencement of, or in the course of, a summary trial under this Section, it appears to the Magistrate that the nature of the case is such that a sentence of imprisonment for a term exceeding one year may have to be passed or that it is, for any other reason, undesirable to try the case summarily, the Magistrate shall after hearing the parties, record an order to that effect and thereafter recall any witness who may have been examined and proceed to hear or rehear the case in the manner provided by the said Code.

17. Offences by companies.

(1) Where an offence under this Act has been committed by a company-

(a) (i) the person, if any, who has been nominated under sub-section (2) to be in charge of, and responsible to, the company for the conduct of the business of the company (hereafter in this Section referred to as the person responsible); or (ii) where no person has been so nominated, every person who at the time the offence was committed was in charge of, and was responsible to, the company for the conduct of the business of the company; and

(b) the company, shall be deemed to be guilty of the offence and shall be liable to be proceeded against and punished accordingly:

PROVIDED that nothing contained in this sub-section shall render any such person liable to any punishment provided in this Act if he proves that the offence was committed without his knowledge and that he exercised all due diligence to prevent the commission of such offence.

(2) Any company may, by order in writing, authorise any of its directors or managers (such manager being employed mainly in a managerial or supervisory capacity) to exercise all such powers and take all such steps as may be necessary or expedient to prevent the commission by the company of any offence under this Act and may give notice to the Local (Health) Authority, in such form and in such manner as may be prescribed, that it has nominated such director or manager as the person responsible, along with the written consent of such director or manager for being so nominated.

EXPLANATION. Where a company has different establishments or branches or different units in any establishment or branch, different persons may be nominated under this sub-section in relation to different establishments or branches or units and the person nominated in relation to any establishment, branch or unit shall be deemed to be the person responsible in respect of such establishment, branch or unit.

(3) The person nominated under sub-section (2) shall, until-

(i) further notice cancelling such nomination is received from the company by the Local (Health) Authority; or

(ii) he ceases to be a director or, as the case may be, manager of the company; or

(iii) he makes a request in writing to the Local (Health) Authority, under intimation to the company, to cancel the nomination, which request shall be complied with by the Local (Health) Authority, whichever is the earliest, continue to be the person responsible:

PROVIDED that where such person ceases to be a director or, as the case may be, manager of the company, he shall intimate the fact of such cesser to the Local (Health) Authority:

PROVIDED FURTHER that where such person makes a request under clause (iii), the Local (Health) Authority shall not cancel such nomination with effect from a date earlier than the date on which the request is made.

(4) Notwithstanding anything contained in the foregoing sub-sections, where an

offence under this Act has been committed by a company and it is proved that the offence has been committed with the consent or connivance of, or is attributable to, any neglect on the part of, any director, manager, secretary or other officer of the company, [not being a person nominated under sub-section (2) such director, manager, secretary or other officer shall also be deemed to be guilty of that offence and shall be liable to be proceeded against and punished accordingly.

EXPLANATION. For the purposes of this Section-

(a) "company" means any body corporate and includes a firm or other association of individuals;

(b) "director", in relation to a firm, means a partner in the firm; and

(c) "manager", in relation to a company engaged in hotel industry, includes the person in charge of the catering department of any hotel managed or run by it.

18. Forfeiture of property. Where any person has been convicted under this Act for the contravention of any of the provisions of this Act or of any rule thereunder, the article of food in respect of which the contravention has been committed may be forfeited to the Government:

PROVIDED that where the court is satisfied that the article of food is capable of being made to conform to prescribed standards for human consumption after reprocessing, the court may order the article of food to be returned to the owner, on his executing a bond with or without sureties, for being sold, subject to the other provisions of this Act, after reprocessing under the supervision of such officer as may be specified therein.

19. Sale of any adulterated or misbranded article of food a allege mearly that vendor was ignorant of the nature. under this Act.

(1) It shall be no defence in a prosecution for an offence pertaining to food to allege merely substance or quality of the food sold by him or that the purchaser having purchased any article for analysis was not prejudiced by the sale.

(2) A vendor shall not be deemed to have committed an offence pertaining to the sale of any adulterated or misbranded article of food if he proves-

(a) that be purchased the article of food-

(i) in a case where a license is prescribed for the sale thereof, from a duly licensed manufacturer, distributor or dealer;

(ii) in any other case, from any manufacturer, distributor or dealer, with a written warranty in the prescribed form; and

(b) that the article of food while in his possession was properly stored and that he sold it in the same state as he purchased it.

(3) Any person by whom a warranty as is referred to in Section 14 is alleged to have been given shall be entitled to appear at the hearing and give evidence.

20. Cognizance and trial of offences.

(1) No prosecution for an offence under this Act, not being an offence under Section 14 or Section 14A, shall be instituted except by, or with the written consent of,

the Central Government or the State Government or a person authorised in this behalf, by general or special order, by the Central Government or the State Government :

PROVIDED that a prosecution for an offence under this Act may be instituted by a purchaser or recognised consumer association referred to in Section 12, if he or it produces in court a copy of the report of the public analyst along with the complaint.

(2) No court inferier to that of a Metropolitan Magistrate or a Judicial Magistrate of the first class shall try any offence under this Act.

(3) Notwithstanding anything contained in the Code of Criminal Procedure, 1973, an offence punishable under sub-section (1AA) of Section 16 shall be cognizable and non-bailable (of 1974).

20A. Power of court to implead manufacturer, etc. Where at any time during the trial of any offence under this Act alleged to have been committed by any person, not being the manufacturer, distributor or dealer of any article of food, the court is satisfied, on the evidence adduced before it, that such manufacturer, distributor or dealer is also concerned with that offence, then, the court may, notwithstanding anything contained in sub-section (3) of Section 319 of the Code of Criminal Proceedure, 1973 (2 of 1974)], or in section 20 proceed against him as though a prosecution had been instituted against him under Section 20.

20AA. Application of the Probation of Offenders Act, 1958 and Section 360 of the Code of Criminal Procedure 1973. Nothing contained in the Probation of Offenders Act, 1958 (20 of 1958) or Section 360 of the Code of Criminal Procedure, 1973 (2 of 1974), shall apply to a person convicted of an offence under this Act unless that person is under eighteen years of age].

21. Magistrate' s power to impose enhanced penalties. Notwithstanding anything contained in Section 29 of the Code of Criminal Procedure, 1973 (2 of 1974), it shall be lawful for any Metropolitan Magistrate or any Judicial Magistrate of the first class to pass any sentence authorised by this Act, except a sentence of imprisonment for life or for a term exceeding six years, in excess of his powers under the said Section.

22. Protection of action taken in good faith. No suit, prosecution or other legal proceedings shall lie against any person for anything which is in good faith done or intended to be done under this Act.

22A. Power of Central Government to give directions. The Central Government may give such directions as it may deem necessary to a State Government regarding the carrying into execution of all or any of the provisions of this Act and the State Government shall comply with such directions.

23. Power of the Central Government to make rules.

(1) The Central Government may, after consultation with the Committee and after previous publication by notification in the Official Gazette, make rules to carry out the provisions of this Act:

PROVIDED that consultation with the Committee may be dispensed with if the Central Government is of the opinion that circumstances have arisen which render it necessary to make rules without such consultation, but, in such a case, the Committee shall be consulted within six months of the making of the rules and the Central Government shall take into consideration any suggestions which the Committee may make in relation to the amendment of the said rules.

(1A) In particular and without prejudice to the generality of the foregoing power, such rules may provide for all or any of the following matters, namely:-

(a) specifying the articles of food or classes of food for the import of which a licence is required and prescribing the form and conditions of such licence, the authority empowered to issue the same, the fees payable therefor, the deposit of any sum as security for the performance of the conditions of the licence and the circumstances under which such licence or security may be cancelled or forfeited;

(b) defining the standards of quality for, and fixing the limits of variability permissible in respect of, any article of food;

(c) laying down special provisions for imposing rigorous control over the production, distribution and sale of any article or class of articles of food which the Central Government may, by notification in the Official Gazette, specify in this behalf including registration of the premises where they are manutactured, maintenance of the premises in a sanitary condition and maintenance of the healthy state of human beings associated with the production, distribution and sale of such article or class of articles;

(d) restricting the packing and labelling of any article of food and the design of any such package or label with a view to preventing the public or the purchaser being deceived or misled is to the character, quality or quantity of the article or to preventing adulteration;

(e) defining the qualifications, powers and duties of food inspectors and public analysts;

(ee) defining the laboratories where samples of articles of food or adulterants may be analysed by public analysis under this Act;

(f) prohibiting the sale or defining the conditions of sale of any substance which may be injurious to health when used as food or restricting in any manner its use as an ingredient in the manufacture of any article of food or regulating by the issue of licences the manufacture or sale of any article of food;

(g) defining the conditions of sale or conditions for licence of sale of any article of food in the interest of public health;

(h) specifying the manner in which containers for samples of food purchased for analysis shall be sealed up or fastened up;

(hh) defining the methods of analysis;

(i) specifying a list of permissible preservatives, other than common salt and sugar, which alone shall be used in preserved fruits, vegetables or their products or any other article of food as well as the maximum amounts of each preservative;

(j) specifying the colouring matter and the maximum quantities thereof which may be used in any article of food;

(k) providing for the exemption from this Act or of any requirements contained therein and subject to such conditions, if any, as may be specified, of any article or class of articles of food;

(l) prohibiting or regulating the manufacture, transport or sale of any article known to be used as an adulterant of food;

(m) prohibiting or regulating-

(i) addition of any water, or other diluent or adulterant to any article of food;

(ii) the abstraction and igredient from any article of food;

(iii) the sale of any article of food to which such addition or from which such attraction has been made or which has been otherwise artificially treated;

(iv) the mixing of two or more articles of food which are similar in nature or appearance;

(n) providing for the destruction of such articles of food as are not in accordance with the provisions of this Act or of the rules made thereunder.

(2) Every rule made by the Central Government under this Act shall be laid as soon as may be after it is made before each House of Parliament while it is session for a total period of thirty days which may be comprised in one session or in two or more successive sessions, and if, before the expiry of the session immediately following the session or the successive sessions aforesaid, both Houses agree in making any modification in the rule or both Houses agree that the rule should not be made, the rule shall thereafter have effect only in such modified form or be of no effect, as the case may be; so, however, that any such modification or annulment shall be without prejudice to the validity of anything previously done under that rule.

24. Power of the State Government to make rules.

(1) The State Government may, after consultation with the Committee and subject to the condition of previous publication, make rules for the purpose of giving effect to the provisions of this Act in matters not falling within the purview of Section 23.

(2) In particular, and without prejudice to the generality of the foregoing power, such rules may-

(a) define the powers and duties of the Food (Health) Authority, Local Authority and Local (Health) Authority under this Act;

(b) prescribe the forms of licences for the manufacture for sale, for the storage, for the sale and for the distribution of articles of food or any specified article of food or class of articles of food, the form of application for such licences, the conditions subject to which such licences may be issued, the authority empowered to issue the same, the fees payable therefor, the deposit of any sum as security for the performance of the conditions of the licences and the circumstances under which such licences or security may be suspended, cancelled or forfeited;

(c) direct a fee to be paid for analysing any article of food or for any matter for which a fee may be prescribed under this Act;

(d) direct that the whole or any part of the fines imposed under this Act shall be paid to a local authority on realisation;

(e) provide for the delegation of the powers and functions conferred by this Act on the State Government or the Food (Health) Authority to subordinate authorities or to local authorities.

(3) All rules made by the State Governments under this Act shall, as soon as possible after they are made, be laid before the respective State Legislatures.

25. Repeal and saving.

(1) If, immediately before the commencement of this Act, there is in force in any State to which this Act extends any law corresponding to this Act that corresponding law shall upon such commencement stand repealed.

(2) Notwithstanding the repeal by this Act of any corresponding law, all rules, regulations and bye-laws relating to the prevention of adulteration of food, made under such corresponding law and in force immediately before the commencement of this Act shall, except where and so far as they are inconsistent with or repugnant to the provisions of this Act, continue in force until altered, amended or repealed by rules made under this Act. In Section 25 of the principal Act, in its application to the State of Jammu and Kashmir, after sub-section (2), the following sub-section shall be inserted, namely:-

(3) (a) References to the commencement of this Act in this Section shall be construed as references to the commencement of the Prevention of Food Adulteration (Amendment) Act, 1971.

(b) For the avoidance of doubt, it is hereby declared that the the provisions of sub-section (2) shall be without prejudice to the provisions contained in Section 6 of the General Clauses Act, 1897 which shall also apply to the repeal of the corresponding law in force in the State of Jammu and Kashmir as if such corresponding law had been an enactment."

❑❑❑

24

The Prevention of Illicit Traffic in Narcotic Drugs and Psychotropic Substances Act, 1988

ACT NO. 46 OF 1988 [6TH SEPTEMBER, 1988]

1. Short title, extent and commencement.

(1) This Act may be called the Prevention of Illicit Traffic in Narcotic Drugs and Psychotropic Substances Act, 1988.

(2) It extends to the whole of India except the State of Jammu and Kashmir.

(3) It shall be deemed to have come into force on the 4th day of July, 1988.

2. Definitions. In this Act, unless the context otherwise requires,

(a) "appropriate Government" means, as respects a detention order made by the Central Government or by an officer of the Central Government, or a person detained under such order, the Central Government, and as respects a detention order made by a State Government or by an officer of a State Government, or a person detained under such order, the State Government;

(b) "customs airport" means any airport appointed under clause (a) of Section 7 of the Customs Act, 1962 (52 of 1962) to be a customs airport;

(c) "detention order" means an order made under Section 3;

(d) "foreigner" has the same meaning as in the Foreigners Act, 1946 (31 of 1946);

(e) "illicit traffic", in relation to narcotic drugs and psychotropic substances, means—

(i) cultivating any coca plant or gathering any portion of coca plant;

(ii) cultivating the opium poppy or any cannabis plant;

(iii) engaging in the production, manufacture, possession, sale, purchase, transportation, warehousing, concealment, use or consumption, import inter-state, export inter-state, import into India, export from India or transhipment, or narcotic drugs or psychotropic substances;

(iv) dealing in any activities in narcotic drugs or psychotropic substances other than those provided in sub-clauses (i) to (iii); or

(v) handling or letting any premises for the carrying on of any of the activities referred to in sub-clauses (i) to (iv), other than those permitted under the Narcotic Drugs and Psychotropic Substances Act, 1985, (61 of 1985), or any rule or order made, or any condition of any licence, term or authorisation issued, thereunder and includes—

(1) financing, directly or indirectly, any of the aforementioned activities;

(2) abetting or conspiring in the furtherance of or in support of doing any of the aforementioned activities; and

(3) harbouring persons engaged in any of the aforementioned activities;

(f) "Indian customs waters" has the same meaning as in clause (28) of Section 2 of the Customs Act, 1962 (52 of 1962);

(g) "State Government", in relation to a Union territory, means the Administrator thereof;

(h) words and expressions used herein but not defined, and defined in the Narcotic Drugs and Psychotropic Substances Act, 1985 (61 of 1985), have the meanings respectively assigned to them in that Act.

3. Power to make orders detaining certain persons.

(1) The Central Government or a State Government, or any officer of the Central Government, not below the rank of a Joint Secretary to that Government, specially empowered for the purposes of this Section by that Government, or any officer of a State Government, not below the rank of a Secretary to that Government, specially empowered for the purposes of this Section by that Government, may if satisfied, with respect to any person (including a foreigner) that, with a view to preventing him from engaging in illicit in narcotic drugs and psychotropic substances, it is necessary so to do, make an order directing that such person be detained.

(2) When any order of detention is made by a State Government or by an officer empowered by a State Government, the State Government shall, within ten days, forward to the Central Government a report in respect of the order.

(3) For the purposes of clause (5) of article 22 of the Constitution, the communication to a person detained in pursuance of a detention order of the grounds on which the order has been made shall be made as soon as may be after the detention, but ordinarily not later than five days, and in exceptional circumstances and for reasons to be recorded in writing not later than fifteen days, from the date of detention.

4. Execution of detention orders. A detention order may be executed at any place in India in the manner provided for the execution of warrants of arrest under the Code of Criminal Procedure, 1973 (2 of 1974).

5. Power to regulate place and conditions of detention. Every person in respect of whom a detention order has been made shall be liable—

(a) to be detained in such place and under such conditions including conditions as to maintenance, interviews or communication with others, discipline and punishment for breaches of discipline, as the appropriate Government may, by general or special order, specify; and

(b) to be removed from one place of detention to another place of detention, whether within the same State or in another State by order of the appropriate Government:

PROVIDED that no order shall be made by a State Government under clause (b) for the removal of a person from one State to another State except with the consent of the Government of that other State.

6. Grounds of detention severable. Where a person has been detained in pursuance of an order of detention under sub-section -

(1) of Section 3 which has been made on two or more grounds, such order of detention shall be deemed to have been made separately on each of such grounds and accordingly —

(a) such order shall not be deemed to be invalid or inoperative merely because one or some of the grounds is or are—

(i) vague,

(ii) non-existent,

(iii) not relevant,

(iv) not connected or not proximately connected with such person, or

(v) invalid for any other reason whatsoever, and it is not therefore possible to hold that the Government or officer making such order would have been satisfied as provided in sub-section (1) of Section 3 with reference to the remaining ground or grounds and made the order of detention;

(b) the Government or officer making the order of detention shall be deemed to have made the order of detention under the said sub-section (1) after being satisfied as provided in that sub-section with reference to the remaining ground or grounds.

7. Detention. Orders not to be invalid or inoperative on certain grounds. No detention order shall be invalid or inoperative merely by reason—

(a) that the person to be detained thereunder is outside the limits of the territorial jurisdiction of the Government or the officer making the order of detention; or

(b) that the place of detention of such person is outside the said limits.

8. Powers in relation to absconding persons.

(1) If the appropriate Government has reason to believe that a person in respect

of whom a detention order has been made has absconded or is concealing himself so that the order cannot be executed, that Government may—

(a) make a report in writing of the fact to a Metropolitan Magistrate or a Magistrate of the first class having jurisdiction in the place where the said person ordinarily resides; and thereupon the provisions of Sections 82, 83, 84 and 85 of the Code of Criminal Procedure, 1973 (2 of 1974) shall apply in respect of the said person and his property as if the order directing that he be detained were a warrant issued by the Magistrate;

(b) by order notified in the Official Gazette direct the said person to appear before such officer, at such place and within such period as may be specified in the order; and if the said person fails to comply with such direction, he shall, he proves that it was not possible for him to comply therewith and that he had, within the period specified in the order, informed the officer mentioned in the order of the reason which rendered compliance therewith impossible and of his whereabouts, be punishable with imprisonment for a term which may extend to one year, or with fine, or with both.

(2) Notwithstanding anything contained in the Code of Criminal Procedure, 1973, (2 of 1974) every offence under clause (b) of sub-section (1) shall be cognizable.

9. Advisory Boards. For the purposes of sub-clause (a) of clause (4) and sub-clause (c) of clause (7) of article 22 of the Constitution,—

(a) the Central Government and each State Government shall, whenever necessary, constitute one or more Advisory Boards each of which shall consist of a Chairman and two other persons possessing the qualifications specified in sub-clause (a) of clause (4) of article 22 of the Constitution;

(b) save as otherwise provided in Section 10, the appropriate Government shall, within five weeks from the date of detention of a person under a detention order, make a reference in respect thereof to the Advisory Board constituted under clause (a) to enable the Advisory Board to make the report under sub-clause (a) of clause (4) of article 22 of the Constitution;

(c) the Advisory Board to which a reference is made under clause (b) shall after considering the reference and the materials placed before it and after calling for such further information as it may deem necessary from the appropriate Government or from any person called for the purpose through the appropriate Government or from the person concerned, and if, in any particular case, it considers it essential so to do or if the person concerned desires to be heard in person, after hearing him in person, prepare its report specifying in a separate paragraph thereof its opinion as to whether or not there is sufficient cause for the detention of the person concerned and submit the same within eleven weeks from the date of detention of the person concerned;

(d) When there is a difference of opinion among the members forming the Advisory Board, the opinion of the majority of such members shall be deemed to be the opinion of the Board;

(e) a person against whom an order of detention has been made under this Act shall not be entitled to appear by any legal practitioner in any matter connected with the reference to the Advisory Board and the proceedings of the Advisory Board and its report, excepting that part of the report in which the opinion of the Advisory Board is specified, shall be confidential;

(f) in every case where the Advisory Board has reported that there is in its opinion sufficient cause for the detention of a person, the appropriate Government may confirm the detention order and continue the detention of the person concerned for such period as it thinks fit and in every case where the Advisory Board has reported that there is in its opinion no sufficient cause for the detention of the person concerned, the appropriate Government shall revoke the detention order and cause the person to be released forthwith.

10. Cases in which and circumstances under which persons may be detained for periods longer than three months without obtaining the opinion of Advisory Board.

(1) Notwithstanding anything contained in this Act, any person (including a foreigner) in respect of whom an order of detention is made under this Act at any time before the 31st day of July, 1996, may be detained without obtaining, in accordance with the provisions of sub-clause (a) of clause (4) of article 22 of the Constitution, the opinion of an Advisory Board for a period longer than three months but not exceeding six months from the date of his detention, where the order of detention has been made against such person with a view to preventing him from engaging in illicit traffic in narcotic drugs and psychotropic substances, and the Central Government or any officer of the Central Government, not below the rank of an Additional Secretary to that Government, specially empowered for the purposes of this Section by that Government, is satisfied that such person engages or is likely to engage in illicit traffic in narcotic drugs and psychotropic substances into, out of, through or within any area highly vulnerable to such illicit traffic and makes a declaration to that effect within five weeks of the detention of such person.

EXPLANATION 1. In this sub-section, "area highly vulnerable to such illicit traffic" means—

- (i) the India customs waters;
- (ii) the customs airports;
- (iii) the metropolitan cities of Bombay, Calcutta, Delhi, Madras and the city of Varanasi;
- (iv) the inland area one hundred kilometres in width from the coast of India falling within the territories of the States of Andhra Pradesh, Goa, Gujarat, Karnataka, Kerala, Maharashtra, Orissa, Tamil Nadu and West Bengal and the Union territories of Daman and Diu and Pondicherry;
- (v) the inland area one hundred kilometres in width from—
  - (a) the India-Pakistan border in the States of Gujarat, Punjab and Rajasthan;

(b) the India-Nepal border in the States of Bihar, Sikkim, Uttar Pradesh and West Bengal;

(c) the India-Burma border in the States of Arunachal Pradesh, Manipur, Mizoram and Nagaland;

(d) the India-Bangladesh border in the States of Assam, Meghalaya, Tripura and West Bengal;

(e) the India-Bhutan border in the States of Arunanchal Pradesh, Assam, Sikkim and West Bengal;

(vi) such other area or customs station, as the Central Government may, having regard to the vulnerability or such area or customs station, as the case may be, to illicit traffic, by notification in the Official Gazette, specify in this behalf.

EXPLANATION 2. For the purposes of Explanation 1, "customs station" has the same meaning as in clause (13) of Section 2 of the Customs Act, 1962. (52 of 1962)

(2) In the case of any person detained under a detention order to which the provisions of sub-section (1) apply, Section 9 shall have effect subject to the following modifications, namely:—

(i) in clause (b), for clause (b), for the words "shall, within five weeks", the words "shall, within four months and two weeks" shall be substituted;

(ii) in clause (c),—

(a) for the words "the detention of the person concerned", the words "the continued detention of the person concerned" shall be substituted;

(b) for the words "eleven weeks", the words "five months and three weeks" shall be substituted;

(iii) in clause (f), for the words "for the detention", at both the places where they occur, the words "for the continued detention" shall be substituted.

11. Maximum period of detention. The maximum period for which any person may be detained in pursuance of any detention order to which the provisions of Section 10 do not apply and which has been confirmed under clause (f) of Section 9 shall be one year from the date of detention, and the maximum period for which any person may be detained in pursuance of any detention order to which the provisions of Section 10 apply and which has been confirmed under clause (f) of Section 9, read with sub-section (2) of Section 10, shall be two years from the date of detention:

PROVIDED that nothing contained in this Section shall affect the power of appropriate Government in either case to revoke or modify the detention order at any earlier time.

12. Revocation of detention orders.

(1) Without prejudice to the provisions of Section 21 of the General Clauses Act, 1897, a detention order may, at any time, be revoked or modified—

(a) notwithstanding that the order has been made by an officer of a State Government, by that State Government or by the Central Government;

(b) notwithstanding that the order has been made by an officer of the Central

Government or by a State Government, by the Central Government.

(2) The revocation of a detention order shall not bar the making of another detention order under Section 3 against the same person.

13. Temporary release of persons detained.

(1) The Central Government may, at any time, direct that any person detained in pursuance of a detention order made by that Government or by an officer subordinate to that Government or by a State Government or by an officer subordinate to a State Government, may be released for any specified period either without conditions or upon such conditions specified in the direction as that person accepts, and may, at any time, cancel his release.

(2) A State Government may, at any time, direct that any person detained in pursuance of a detention order made by that Government or by an officer subordinate to that Government may be released for any specified period either without conditions or upon such conditions specified in the direction as the person accepts, and may, at any time, cancel his release.

(3) In directing the release of any person under sub-section (1) or sub-section (2), the Government directing the release may require him to enter into a bond with sureties for the due observance of the conditions specified in the direction.

(4) Any person released under sub-section (1) or sub-section (2) shall surrender himself at the time and place, and to the authority, specified in the order directing his release, or cancelling his release, as the case may be.

(5) If any person fails without sufficient cause to surrender himself in the manner specified in sub-section (4), he shall be punishable with imprisonment for a term which may extend to two years, or with fine, or with both.

(6) If any person released under sub-section (1) or sub-section (2) fails to fulfil any of the conditions imposed upon him under the said sub-section or in the bond entered into by him, the bond shall be declared to be forfeited and any person bound thereby shall be liable to pay the penalty thereof.

(7) Notwithstanding anything contained in any other law and save as otherwise provided in this Section, no person against whom a detention order made under this Act is in force shall be released whether on bail or bail bond or otherwise.

14. Protection of action taken in good faith. No suit or other legal proceeding shall lie against the Central Government or a State Government and no suit, prosecution or other legal proceeding shall lie against any person for anything in good faith done or intended to be done in pursuance of this Act.

15. Amendment of Act 52 of 1974. In Section 3 of the Conservation of Foreign Exchange and Prevention of Smuggling Activities Act, 1974 to sub-section (1), the following proviso shall be added, namely:—

> *"PROVIDED that no order of detention shall be made on any of the grounds specified in this sub-section on which an order of detention may be made under Section 3 of the Prevention of Illicit Traffic in Narcotic Drugs and Psychotropic Substances Act, 1988 (J. and K. Ordinance 1 of 1988) or under Section 3 of the Jammu and Kashmir Prevention of Illicit Traffic in Narcotic Drugs and Psychotropic Substances Ordinance, 1988.".*

16. Repeal and saving.

(1) The Prevention of Illicit Traffic in Narcotic Drugs and Psychotropic Substances Ordinance, 1988 (Ord. 7 of 1988), is hereby repealed.

(2) Notwithstanding such repeal, anything done or any action taken under the said Ordinance shall be deemed to have been done or taken under the corresponding provisions of this Act.

❑❑❑

25

The Prevention of Insults to National Honour (Amendment) Act, 2003

Act No. 31 of 2003 [8th May, 2003]

AN ACT to amend the Prevention of Insults to National Honour Act, 1971.

Be it enacted by Parliament in the Fifty-fourth Year of the Republic of India as follows:-

1. Short title. This Act may be called the Prevention of Insults to National Honour (Amendment) Act, 2003.

2. Amendment of Section 2. In Section 2 of the Prevention of Insults to National Honour Act, 1971 (69 of 1971) (hereinafter referred to as the principal Act),-

- (a) for the words otherwise brings, "the words" otherwise shows disrespect to or "brings" shall be substituted;
- (b) after Explanation 3, the following Explanation shall be inserted, namely:-'

  EXPLANATION 4. The disrespect to the Indian National Flag means and includes-

  - (a) a gross affront or indignity offered to the Indian National Flag; or
  - (b) dipping the Indian National Flag in salute to any person or thing; or
  - (c) flying the Indian National Flag at half-mast except on occasions on which the Indian National Flag is flown at half-mast on public buildings in accordance with the instructions issued by the Government; or
  - (d) using the Indian National Flag as a drapery in any form whatsoever except in State Funerals or armed forces or other para-military forces funerals; or
  - (e) using the Indian National Flag as a portion of costume or uniform of any description or embroidering or printing it on cushions, handkerchiefs, napkins or any dress material; or

(f) putting any kind of inscription upon the Indian National Flag; or

(g) using the Indian National Flag as a receptacle for receiving, delivering or carrying anything except flower petals before the Indian National Flag is unfurled as a part of celebrations on special occasions including the Republic Day or the Independence Day; or

(h) using the Indian National Flag as covering for a statute or a monument or a speaker' s desk or a speaker' s platform; or

(i) allowing the Indian National Flag to touch the ground or the floor or trail in water intentionally; or

(j) draping the Indian National Flag over the hood, top and sides or back or on a vehicle, train, boat or an aircraft or any other similar object; or

(k) using the Indian National Flag as a covering for a building; or

(l) intentionally displaying the Indian National Flag with the "saffron" down.'

3. Insertion of new Section 3A. After Section 3 of the principal Act, the following Section shall be inserted, namely:-

"**3A. Enhanced penalty on second and subsequent convictions.** Whoever, having already been convicted of an offence under Section 2 or Section 3, is again convicted of any such offence shall be punishable for the second and for every subsequent offence, with imprisonment for a term which shall not be less than one year".

❑❑❑

26

The Prevention of Insults to National Honour Act, 1971

Act No. 69 of 1971 [23rd December, 1971]

AN ACT to prevent insults to national honour.

Be it enacted by Parliament in the Twenty- second Year of the Republic of India as follows:-

1. Short title and extent.

(1) This Act may be called the Prevention of Insults to National Honour Act, 1971.

(2) It extends to the whole of India.

2. Insult to Indian National Flag and Constitution of India. Whoever, in any public place or in any other place within public view burns, mutilates, defaces, defiles, disfigures, destroys, tramples upon or otherwise brings into contempt (whether by words, either spoken or written, or by acts) the Indian National Flag or the Constitution of India or any part thereof, shall be punished with imprisonment for a term which may extend to three years, or with fine, or with both.

EXPLANATION 1. Comments expressing disapprobation or criticism of the Constitution or of the Indian National Flag or of any measures of the Government with a view to obtain an amendment of the Constitution of India or an alteration of the Indian National Flag by lawful means do not constitute an offence under this section.

EXPLANATION 2. The expression "Indian National Flag" includes any picture, painting, drawing or photograph, or other visible re- presentation of the Indian National Flag, or of any part or parts thereof, made of any substance or represented on any substance.

EXPLANATION 3. The expression "public place" means any place intended for use by, or accessible to, the public and includes any public conveyance.

3. Prevention of singing of Indian National Anthem, etc. Whoever intentionally prevents the singing of the Indian National Anthem or causes disturbance to any assembly engaged in such singing shall be punished with imprisonment for a term which may extend to three years, or with fine, or with both.

❑❑❑

27

The Prisoners (Attendance in Courts) Act, 1955

Act No. 32 of 1955 [20th September, 1955]

AN ACT to provide for the attendance in courts of persons confined in prisons for obtaining their evidence or for answering a criminal charge.

Be it enacted by Parliament in the Sixth Year of the Republic of India as follows:—

1. Short title, extent and commencement.

(1) This Act may be called the Prisoners (Attendance in Courts) Act, 1955.

(2) It extends to the whole of India except the State of Jammu and Kashmir.

(3) It shall come into force on such date' as the Central Government may, by notification in the Official Gazette, appoint.

2. Definitions. In this Act,-

(a) "confinement in a prison" references to confinement in a prison, by whatever form of words, include references to confinement or detention in a prison under any law providing for preventive detention,

(b) "prison" includes-

(i) any place which has been declared by the State Government, by general or special order, to be a subsidiary jail; and

(ii) any reformatory, Borstal institution or other institution of a like nature;

(c) "State Government", in relation to a Union territory, means the administrator thereof.

3. Power of courts to require appearance of prisoners to give evidence or answer a charge.

(1) Any civil or criminal court may, if it thinks that the evidence of any person confined in any prison is material in any matter pending before it, make an

order in the form set forth in the First Schedule, directed to the officer in charge of the prison:

PROVIDED that no civil court shall make an order under this sub-section in respect of a person confined in a prison situated outside the State in which the court is held.

(2) Any criminal court may, if a charge of an offence against a person confined in any prison is made or pending before it, make an order in the form set forth in the Second Schedule, directed to the officer in charge of the prison.

(3) No order made under this Section by a civil court which is subordinate to a district judge shall have effect unless it is countersigned by the district judge; and no order made under this Section by a criminal court which is inferior to the court of a magistrate of the first class shall have effect unless it is countersigned by the district magistrate to whom that court is subordinate or within the local limits of whose jurisdiction that court is situate.

(4) For the purposes of sub-section (3), a court of small causes outside a presidency town or the city of Hyderabad shall be deemed to be subordinate to the district judge within the local limits of whose jurisdiction such court is situate.

4. Power of State Government to exempt certain persons from operation of Section 3.

(1) The State Government may, having regard to the matters specified in sub-section (2), by general or special order, direct that any person or class of persons shall not be removed from the prison in which he or they may be confined, and thereupon so long as any such order remains in force, the provisions of Section 3 shall not apply to such person or class of persons.

(2) Before making an order under sub-section (1), the State Government shall have regard to the following matters, namely:-

(a) the nature of the offence for which or the grounds on which the confinement has been ordered in respect of the person or class of persons;

(b) the likelihood of the disturbance of public order if the person or class of persons is allowed to be removed from the prison;

(c) the public interest, generally.

5. Prisoners to be brought up. Upon delivery of any order made under Section 3 to the officer in charge of the prison in which the person named therein is confined, that officer shall cause him to be taken to the court in which his attendance is required, so as to be present in the court at the time in such order mentioned, and shall cause him to be detained in custody in or near the court until he has been examined or until the judge.

6. Officer in change of prison when to abstain from carrying out order. Where the person in respect of whom an order is made under Section 3-

(a) is, in accordance with the rules made in this behalf, declared to be unfit to be removed from the prison where he is confined by reason of sickness or other infirmity; or

(b) is under committal for trial; or

(c) is under remand pending trial or pending a preliminary investigation; or

(d) is in custody for a period which would expire before the expiration of the time required for removing him under this Act and for taking hint back to the prison in which he is confined; the officer in charge of the prison shall abstain from carrying out the order and shall send to the court from which the order had been issued a statement of reasons for so abstaining:

PROVIDED that such officer as aforesaid shall not so abstain where-

(i) the order has been made by a criminal court; and

(ii) the person named in the order is confined under committal for trial or under remand pending trial or pending a preliminary investigation and is not declared in accordance with the rules made in this behalf to be unfit to be removed from the prison where he is confined by reason of sickness or other infirmity; and

(iii) the place, where the evidence of the person named in the order is required, is not more than five miles distant from the prison in which he is confined.

7. Commissions for examination of prisoners. In any of the following cases, that is to say,-

(a) where it appears to any civil court that the evidence of a person confined in a prison is material in any matter pending before it and that the attendance of such person in court cannot be secured by reason of the provisions of Section 6 or of an order under Section 4 or of the district judge declining under sub-. Section (3) of Section 3 to countersign an order for removal; or

(b) where it appears to any civil Court as aforesaid that the evidence of a person confined in a prison which is situated outside the State in which, or is more than fifty miles distant from the place at which, such court is held is material in any such matter; the court may, if it thinks fit, issue a commission under the provisions of the Code of Civil Procedure, 1908, (5 of 1908) for the examination of the person in the prison in which he is confined.

8. Certain provisions of the Code of Criminal Procedure and the Code of Civil Procedure to apply. Save as otherwise provided in this Act and any rules made thereunder, the provisions of the Code of Civil Procedure, 1908, (5 of 1908) and the Code of Criminal Procedure, 1898, (5 of 1898) as the case may be, shall, so far as may be, apply in relation to the examination on commission or otherwise of any person confined in a prison as they apply in relation to the examination on commission of any other person.

9. Power to make rules.

(1) The State Government may, by notification in the Official Gazette, make rules for carrying out the purposes of this Act.

(2) In particular and without prejudice to the generality of the foregoing power, such rules may provide for-

(a) the procedure for obtaining the countersignature of an order made under Section 3;

(b) the authority by whom and the manner in which a declaration that a person confined in prison is unfit to be removed therefrom, may be made;

(c) the conditions, including payment of costs and charges, subject to which an order made under Section 3 by a civil court may be executed;

(d) the manner in which a process directed against any person confined in a prison issued from any court may be served upon him;

(e) the escort of persons confined in a prison to and from courts in which their attendance is required and for their custody during the period of such attendance;

(f) the amount to be allowed for the costs and charges of such escort; and

(g) the guidance of officers in all other matters connected with the enforcement of this Act.

10. Repeal.

(1) Part IX of the Prisoners Act, 1900 (3 of 1900) and the First and Second Schedules to the said Act are hereby repealed.

(2) If immediately before the commencement of this Act, there is in force in any Part B State to which this Act extends any law corresponding to the provisions of this Act, that law shall, insofar as it relates to matters dealt with in this Act, stand repealed on such commencement:

PROVIDED that anything done or any action taken under any such law shall be deemed to have been done or taken under the corresponding provisions of this Act and shall continue to have effect accordingly, unless and until superseded by anything done or any action taken under this Act.

❑❑❑

28

The Prisoners Act, 1900

(Act III of 1900) [2 February 1900]

AN ACT to consolidate the law relating to prisoners confined by order of a Court.

WHEREAS it is expedient to consolidate the law relating to prisoners confined by order of a Court;

It is hereby enacted as follows:-

PART - I : PRELIMINARY

1. Short title and extent.

(1) This Act may be called the Prisoners Act, 1900;

(2) It extends to the whole of Pakistan.

(3) * * * * * * * * * * * *

2. Definitions. In this Act, unless there is anything repugnant in the subject or context,—

(a) "Court" includes a Coroner and any officer lawfully exercising civil, criminal or revenue jurisdiction; and

(b) "prison" includes any place which has been declared by the Provincial Government, by general or special order, to be a subsidiary jail.

PART - II : GENERAL

3. Officers incharge of prisons to detain persons duly committed to their custody. The officer incharge of a prison shall receive and detain all persons duly committed to his custody, under this Act or otherwise, by any Court, according to the exigency of any writ, warrant or order by which such person has been committed, or until such person is discharged or removed in due course of law.

4. Officers incharge of prisons to return writs, etc., after execution or discharge. The officer incharge of a prison shall forthwith, after the execution of every such writ, order or warrant as aforesaid other than a warrant of commitment for trial, or after the discharge of the person committed thereby, return such writ, order or warrant to the Court by which the same was issued or made, together with a certificate, endorsed thereon and signed by him, showing how the same has been executed, or why the person committed thereby has been discharged from custody before the execution thereof.

PART - III : PRISONERS IN THE PRESIDENCY-TOWNS

Omitted by the Adaptation of Central Acts and Ordinances Order, 1949 (G.G.O. 4 of 1949), Schedule.

PART - IV : EXECUTION OF SENTENCES

14. References in this Part to prisons, etc., to be construed as referring also to Reformatory Schools. In this Part all references to prisons or to imprisonment or confinement shall be construed as referring also to Reformatory Schools or to detention therein.

15. Power for officers incharge of prisons to give effect to sentences of certain Courts.

(1) Officers in charge of prisons may give effect to any sentence or order or warrant for the detention of any person passed or issued—

(a) by any court or tribunal acting, whether within or without the Provinces, under the general or special authority of the Federal Government, or of any Provincial Government, or of the Government of Burma or of any Court or tribunal which was before the twenty-third day of March, 1956, acting under the general or special authority of Her Majesty, or of the Crown Representative; or

(b) by any Court or tribunal in any Acceding State—

(i) if the presiding Judge, or if the Court or tribunal consists of two or more Judges, at least one of the Judges, is an officer of the Government authorised to sit as such Judge by the State or the Ruler thereof or by the Federal Government or the Crown Representative, and

(ii) if the reception, detention or imprisonment in any provinces of persons sentenced by any such Court or tribunal has been authorised by general or special order by the Provincial Government; or

(c) by any other Court or tribunal in any Acceding State, with the previous sanction of the Provincial Government in the case of each such sentence, order or warrant:

PROVIDED that effect shall not be given to any sentence or order or warrant for detention passed or issued by any Court or tribunal in Burma without the previous sanction of the Provincial Government concerned.

(2) Where a Court or tribunal of such a Ruler or State has passed a sentence which cannot be executed without the concurrence of an officer of the Government and such sentence has been considered on the merits and confirmed by any such officer specially authorised in that behalf, such sentence, and any order or warrant issued in pursuance thereof, shall be deemed to be the sentence, order or warrant of a Court or tribunal acting under the authority of the Federal Government or the Crown Representative.

16. Warrant of officer of such Court to be sufficient authority. A warrant under the official signature of an officer of such Court or tribunal as is referred to in Section 15 shall be sufficient authority for holding any person in confinement, or for sending any person for transportation, in pursuance of the sentence passed upon him.

17. Procedure where officer incharge of prison doubts the legality of warrant sent to him for execution under this Part.

(1) Where an officer incharge of a prison doubts the legality of a warrant or order sent to him for execution under this Part, or the competency of the person whose official seal or signature is affixed thereto to pass the sentence and issue the warrant or order, he shall refer the matter to the Provincial Government, by whose order on the case he and all other public officers shall be guided as to the future disposal of the prisoner.

(2) Pending a reference made under sub-section (1), the prisoner shall be detained in such manner and with such restrictions or mitigations as may be specified in the warrant or order.

18. Execution in the Provinces, etc., of certain capital sentences not ordinarily executable there.

(1) Where a Court established by the authority of the Federal Government exercising, in or with respect to territory beyond the limits of the Provinces, jurisdiction which the Government has in such territory,—

(a) has sentenced any person to death; and

(b) being of opinion that such sentence should, by reason of there being in such territory no secure place for the confinement of such person or no suitable appliances for his execution in a decent and humane manner, be executed in the Provinces, has issued its warrant for the execution of such sentence to the officer-in-charge of a prison in the Provinces, such officer shall, on receipt of the warrant, cause the execution to be carried out at such place as may be prescribed therein in the same manner and subject to the same conditions in all respects as if it were a warrant duly issued under the provisions of Section 381 of the Code of Criminal Procedure, 1898.

(2) The prisons of which the officers incharge are to execute sentences under any such warrants as aforesaid shall in each Province be such as the Provincial Government may, by general or special order, direct.

(3) A Court shall be deemed, for the purposes of this Section, to be a Court established by the Federal Government if the presiding Judge, or if the Court consists of two or more Judges, at least one of the Judges, is an officer of the Government authorised to act as such Judge by any Acceding State or the Ruler thereof or the Federal Government:

PROVIDED that every warrant issued under this sub-section by any such tribunal shall, if the tribunal consists of more than one Judge, be signed by a Judge who is an officer of the Government authorised as aforesaid.

PART - V : PERSONS UNDER SENTENCE OF PENAL SERVITUDE

Omitted by the Criminal Law (Extinction of Discriminatory Privileges Act, 1949) (II of 1950), Schedule.

PART - VI : REMOVAL OF PRISONERS

28. References in this Part to prisons, etc., to be construed as referring also to Reformatory Schools. In this Part, all references to prisons or to imprisonment or confinement shall be construed as referring also to Reformatory Schools or to detention therein.

29. Removal of prisoners.

(1) The Provincial Government may, by general or special order, provide for the removal of any prisoner confined in a prison—

(a) under sentence of death, or

(b) under, or in lieu of, a sentence of imprisonment or transportation, or

(c) in default of payment of a fine,

(d) in default of giving security for keeping the peace or for maintaining good behaviour,

(e) unconvicted criminal prisoners, to any other prison in the province, or, with the consent of the Provincial Government concerned, to any prison in the other Province, or, with the consent of the Central Government to any prison maintained by it or under its authority in any part of Pakistan.

(2) Subject to the orders, and under the control of the Provincial Government the Director of Prisons may, in the like manner provide for the removal of any prisoner confined as aforesaid in a prison situate in the area for which he is appointed to any of the prison in such area.

(3) The Central Government may, by general or special order, provide for the removal of any prisoner or class of prisoners confined in any prison to any other prison in Pakistan maintained by or under the authority of the Central Government or of a Provincial Government with the consent of the Provincial Government concerned.

30. Lunatic prisoners how to be dealt with.

(1) Where it appears to the Provincial Government that any person detained or imprisoned under any order or sentence of any Court is of unsound mind, the

Provincial Government may, by a warrant setting forth the grounds of belief that the person is of unsound mind, order his removal to a lunatic asylum or other place of safe custody within the province, there to be kept and treated as the Provincial Government directs during the remainder of the term for which he has been ordered or sentenced to be detained or imprisoned, or if on the expiration of that term it is certified by a medical officer that it is necessary for the safety of the prisoner or others that he should be further detained under medical care or treatment, then until he is discharged according to law.

(2) Where it appears to the Provincial Government that the prisoner has become of sound mind, the Provincial Government shall, by a warrant directed to the person having charge of the prisoner, if still liable to be kept in custody, remand him to the prison from which he was removed, or to another prison within the Province, or, if the prisoner is no longer liable to be kept in custody, order him to be discharged.

(3) The provisions of Section 9 of the Lunatic Asylums Act, 1858, shall apply to every person confined in a lunatic asylum under sub-section (1) after the expiration of the term for which he was ordered or sentenced to be detained or imprisoned; and the time during which a prisoner is confined in a lunatic asylum under that sub-section shall be reckoned as part of the term of detention or imprisonment which he may have been ordered or sentenced by the Court to undergo.

(4) In any case in which the Provincial Government is competent under sub-section (1) to order the removal of a prisoner to a lunatic asylum or other place of safe custody within the Province, the Provincial Government may order his removal to any such asylum or place within the other Province or within any Acceding State by agreement with the Provincial Government of such other Province or with such State or the Ruler thereof, as the case may be; and the provisions of this Section respecting the custody, detention remand and discharge of a prisoner removed under sub-section (1) shall, so far as they can be made applicable, apply to a prisoner removed under this sub-section.

31. Removal of prisoners from territories under one Local Government to territories under another. Repealed by the Amending Act, 1903 (1 of 1903), section 4 and Schedule III.

PART - VII : PERSONS UNDER SENTENCE OF TRANSPORTATION

32. Appointment of places for confinement of persons under sentence of transportation and removal thereto.

(1) The Provincial Government may appoint places within the Province to which persons under sentence of transportation shall be sent; and the Provincial Government, or some officer duly authorised in this behalf by the Provincial Government, shall give orders for the removal of such persons to the places so appointed, except when sentence of transportation is passed on a person already undergoing transportation under a sentence previously passed for another offence.

(2) In any case in which the Provincial Government is competent under sub-section (1) to appoint places within the Provinces and to order the removal thereto of persons under sentence of transportation, the Provincial Government may appoint such places in the other Province by agreement with the Provincial Government of that Province and may by like agreement give orders or duly authorise some officer to give orders for the removal thereto of such persons.

PART - VIII : DISCHARGE OF PRISONERS

33. Release, on recognizance, by order of High Court, of prisoner recommended for pardon. A High Court, may, in any case in which it has recommended to the President the granting of a free pardon to any prisoner, permit him to be at liberty on his own recognizance.

PART - IX : PROVISIONS FOR REQUIRING THE ATTENDANCE OF PRISONERS AND OBTAINING THEIR EVIDENCE

ATTENDANCE OF PRISONERS IN COURT

34. References in this Part to prisons, etc. to be construed as referring also to Reformatory Schools. In this Part, all references to prisons or to imprisonment or confinement shall be construed as referring also to Reformatory Schools or to detention therein.

35. Power for Civil Courts to require appearance of prisoner to give evidence. Subject to the provisions of Section 39, any Civil Court may, if it thinks that the evidence of any person confined in any prison within the local limits of its appellate jurisdiction, if it is a High Court, or, if it is not a High Court, then within the local limits of the appellate jurisdiction of the High Court to which it is subordinate, is material in any matter pending before it, make an order in the form set forth in the first schedule, directed to the officer incharge of the prison.

36. District Judge in certain cases to countersign orders made under Section 35.

(1) Where an order under Section 35 is made in any civil matter pending—

- (a) in a Court subordinate to the District Judge, or
- (b) in a Court of Small Causes,

  it shall not be forwarded to the officer to whom it is directed, or acted upon by him, until it has been submitted to, and countersigned by,—

  - (i) the District Judge to which the Court is subordinate, or
  - (ii) the District Judge within the local limits of whose jurisdiction the Court of Small Causes is situate.

(2) Every order submitted to the District Judge under sub-section (1) shall be accompanied by a statement, under the hand of the Judge of the subordinate Court or Court of Small Causes, as the case may be, of the facts which in his opinion render the order necessary, and the District Judge may, after considering such statement, decline to countersign the order.

37. Power for certain Criminal Courts to require attendance of prisoner to give evidence or answer to charge. Subject to the provisions of Section 39, any Criminal

Court may, if it thinks that the evidence of any person confined in any prison within the local limits of its appellate jurisdiction, if it is a High Court, or, if it is not a High Court, then within the local limits of the appellate jurisdiction of the High Court to which it is subordinate, is material in any matter pending before it, or if a charge of an offence against such person is made or pending, make an order in the form set forth in the first or second schedule, as the case may be, directed to the officer incharge of the prison:

> *PROVIDED that if such Criminal Court is inferior to the Court of a Magistrate of the first class, the order shall be submitted to, and countersigned by, the Sessions Judge to whose Court such Criminal Court is subordinate or within the local limits of whose jurisdiction such Criminal Court is situated.*

38. Order to be transmitted through Magistrate of the district or sub-division in which person is confined. Where any person, for whose attendance an order as in this Part provided is made, is confined in any district other than that in which the Court making or countersigning the order is situate, the order shall be sent by the Court by which it is made or countersigned to the Sessions Judge or Magistrate within the local limits of whose jurisdiction the person is confined, and that Court shall cause it to be delivered to the officer incharge of the prison in which the person is confined.

39. Procedure where removal is desired of person confined more than one hundred miles from place where evidence is required.

(1) Where a person is confined in a prison more than one hundred miles distant from the place where any Court, subordinate to a High Court, in which his evidence is required, is held, the Judge or presiding officer of the Court in which the evidence is so required shall, if he thinks that such person should be removed under this Part for the purpose of giving evidence in such Court, and if the prison is within the local limits of the appellate jurisdiction of the High Court to which such Court is subordinate, apply in writing to the High Court, and the High Court may, if it thinks fit, make an order in the form set forth in the first schedule, directed to the officer incharge of the prison.

(2) The High Court making an order under sub-section (1) shall send it to the Sessions Judge or Magistrate within the local limits of whose jurisdiction the person named therein is confined, and such Court shall cause it to be delivered to the officer incharge of the prison in which the person is confined.

40. Persons confined beyond limits of appellate jurisdiction of High Court. Where a person is confined in a prison beyond the local limits of the appellate jurisdiction of a High Court, any Judge of such Court may, if he thinks that such person should be removed under this Part for the purpose of answering a charge of an offence or of giving evidence in any criminal matter in such Court or in any Court subordinate thereto; apply in writing to the Provincial Government of the territories within which the prison is situate, and the Provincial Government may, direct that the person be so removed, subject to such rules regulating the escort of prisoners as the Provincial Government may prescribe.

41. Prisoner to be brought up. Upon delivery of any order under this Part to the officer incharge of the person in which the person named therein is confined, that officer shall cause him to be taken to the Court in which his attendance is required, so as to be present in the Court at the time in such order mentioned, and shall cause him to be detained in custody in or near the Court until he has been examined or until the Judge or presiding officer of the Court authorises him to be taken back to the prison in which he was confined.

42. Power to Government to exempt certain prisoners from operation of this Part. The Provincial Government may, by notification in the Official Gazette, direct that any person or any class of persons shall not be removed from the prison in which he or they may be confined; and thereupon, and so long as such notification remains in force, the provisions of this Part, other than those contained in Sections 44 to 46, shall not apply to such person or class of persons.

43. Officer incharge of prison when to abstain from carrying out order.— In any of the following cases, that is to say,—

(a) where the person named in any order made under Section 35, Section 37 or Section 39 appears to be, from sickness or other infirmity, unfit to be removed, the officer incharge of the prison in which he is confined, shall apply to the Sessions Judge or Magistrate within the local limits of whose jurisdiction the prison is situate, and if such Court, by writing under his hand, declares himself to be of opinion that the person named in the order is, from sickness or other infirmity, unfit to be removed; or

(b) where the person named in any such order is under committal for trial; or

(c) where the person named in any such order is under a remand pending trial or pending a preliminary investigation; or

(d) where the person named in any such order is in custody for a period which would expire before the expiration of the time required for removing him under this Part and for taking him back to the prison in which he is confined; the officer incharge of the prison shall abstain from carrying out the order, and shall send to the Court from which the order has been issued a statement of the reason for so abstaining;

PROVIDED that such officer as aforesaid shall not so abstain where—

(i) the order has been made under Section 37; and

(ii) the person named in the order is confined under committal for trial, or under a remand pending trial or pending a preliminary investigation, and does not appear to be, from sickness or other infirmity unfit to be removed; and

(iii) the place, where the evidence of the person named in the order is required, is not more than five miles distant from the prison in which he is confined.

COMMISSIONS FOR EXAMINATION OF PRISONERS

44. Commissions for examination of prisoners. In any of the following cases, that is to say, —

(a) where it appears to any Civil Court that the evidence of a person confined in any prison within the local limits of the appellate jurisdiction of such Court, if it is a High Court, or if it is not a High Court, then within the local limits of the appellate jurisdiction of the High Court to which it is subordinate, who, for any of the causes mentioned in Section 42 or Section 43, cannot be removed, is material in any matter pending before it; or

(b) where it appears to any such Court as aforesaid that the evidence of a person confined in any prison so situate and more than ten miles distant from the place at which such Court is held, is material in any such matter; or

(c) where the District Judge declines, under Section 36, to countersign an order for removal; the Court may, if it thinks fit, issue a commission, under the provisions of the Code of Civil Procedure, for the examination of the person in the prison in which he is confined.

45. Commissions for examination of prisoners beyond limits of appellate jurisdiction of High Court. Where it appears to a High Court that the evidence of a person confined in a prison beyond the local limits of its appellate jurisdiction is material in any civil matter pending before it or before any Court subordinate to it, the High Court may, if it thinks fit, issue a commission under the provisions of the Code of Civil Procedure, for the examination of the person in the prison in which he is confined.

46. Commission how to be directed. Every commission for the examination of a person issued under Section 44 or Section 45 shall be directed to the District Judge within the local limits of whose jurisdiction the prison in which the person is confined is situated, and the District Judge shall commit the execution of the commission to the officer incharge of the prison, or to such other person as he may think fit.

SERVICE OF PROCESS ON PRISONERS

47. Process how served on prisoners. When any process directed to any person confined in any prison is issued from any Criminal or Revenue Court, it may be served by exhibiting to the officer-in-charge of the prison the original of the process and depositing with him a copy thereof.

48. Process served to be transmitted at prisoner's request.

(1) Every officer incharge of a prison upon whom service is made under Section 47 shall, as soon as may be, cause the copy of the process deposited with him to be shown and explained to the person to whom it is directed, and shall thereupon endorse upon the process and sign a certificate to the effect that such person as aforesaid is confined in the prison under his charge and has been shown and had explained to him a copy of the process.

(2) Such certificate as aforesaid shall be *prima facie* evidence of the service of the process, and, if the person to whom the process is directed requests that the copy shown and explained to him be sent to any other person and provides the cost of sending it by post, the officer-in-charge of the prison shall cause it to be so sent.

PART - X : MISCELLANEOUS

49. Application of Part in certain cases. Omitted by the Adaptation of Central Acts and Ordinances Order, 1949 (G.G.O. 4 of 1949), Schedule.

50. Deposit of costs. No order in any civil matter shall be made by a Court under any of the provisions of this Part until the amount of the costs and charges of the execution of such order (to be determined by the Court) is deposited in such Court:

PROVIDED that, if upon any application for such order it appears to the Court to which the application is made, that the applicant has not sufficient means to meet the said costs and charges, the Court may pay the same out of any fund applicable to the contingent expenses of such Court, and every sum so expended may be recovered by the Provincial Government from any person ordered by the Court to pay the same, as if it were costs in a suit recoverable under the Code of Civil Procedure 1882.

51. Power to make rules under this Part.

(1) The Provincial Government may make rules—

(a) for regulating the escort of prisoners to and from Courts in which their attendance is required and for their custody during the period of such attendance;

(b) for regulating the amount to be allowed for the costs and charges of such escort; and

(c) for the guidance of officers in all other matters connected with the enforcement of this Part.

(2) All rules made under sub-section (1) shall be published in the Official Gazette and shall, from the date of such publication, have the same force as if enacted by this Act.

52. Power to declare who shall be deemed officer incharge of prison. The Provincial Government may declare what officer shall, for the purposes of this Part, be deemed to be the officer incharge of a prison.

53. Repeals Repealed by the Repealing and Amending Act, 1914 (X of 1914), Section 3 and Schedule II.

THE FIRST SCHEDULE
[See Section 35 and 37]

Court of ______________________________

To the officer-in-charge of the______________________________

(*state name of prison*).

You are hereby required to produce ________, now a prisoner in ________, under safe and sure conduct before the Court of ________ at ______ on the ________ day of ________ next by ________ of the clock in the forenoon of the same day, there to give evidence in a matter now pending before the said Court, and after the said ______ has then and there given his evidence before the said Court or the said Court has dispensed with his further attendance, cause him to be conveyed under safe and sure conduct back to the prison.

The ____________________ day of ____________________

A.B.

(Countersigned) C.D.

THE SECOND SCHEDULE
[See Section 37]

Court of ______________________________

To the officer incharge of the______________________________

(*state name of prison*).

You are hereby required to produce ________, now a prisoner in ________, under safe and sure conduct before the Court of ________ at ______ on the ________ day of ________ next by ________ of the clock in the forenoon of the same day, there to answer a charge now pending before the said Court, and after such charge has been disposed of or the said Court has dispensed with his further attendance, cause him to be conveyed under safe and sure conduct back to the said prison.

The ____________________ day of ____________________

A.B.

(Countersigned) C.D.

THE THIRD SCHEDULE

Repealed by the Repealing and Amending Act, 1914 (X of 1914), Section 3 and Schedule II.

For statement of objects and reasons, *see* Gazette of India, 1899, Pt. V, p. 101; for report of the Select Committee, *see ibid.*, 1900, p. 23; for proceedings in Council, *see ibid., 1899,* Pt. VI, pp. 102 and 242; *ibid.*, 1900, p. 21.

Substituted by the Central Laws (Statute Reform) Ordinance, 1960 (XXI of 1960), Section 3 and 2nd Schedule, (with effect from the 14th October, 1955), for the original sub-section (2) as amended by the Repealing and Amending Act, 1914 (X of 1914), the Adaptation of Central Acts and Ordinances Order, 1949 (G.G.O. 4 of 1949), and the Federal Laws (Revision and Declaration) Act, 1951 (XXVI of 1951).

Sub-section (3) repealed by the Repealing and Amending Act, 1914 (X of 1914), Section 3 and Schedule II.

Substituted by the Government of India (Adaptation of Indian Laws) Order, 1937 as amended by the Government of India (Adaptation of Indian Laws) Supplementary Order, 1937, for "Local Government".

Substituted by the Adaptation of Central Acts and Ordinances Order, 1949 (G.G.O. 4 of 1949), Schedule, for the original heading "PRISONERS OUTSIDE THE PRESIDENCY-TOWN".

The words "outside the Presidency-towns", omitted, *ibid.*

Substituted the Adaptation of Central Acts and Ordinances Order, 1949 (G.G.O. 4 of 1949), Articles 3(2) and 4, for "British India".

The words "and the Federal Territory of Karachi," omitted by the Central Adaptation of Laws Order, 1964 (P.O. 1 of 1964), Article 2 and Schedule the words in crotchets were substituted by the Repealing and Amending Ordinance, 1961 (I of 1961), Section 3 and 2nd Schedule, for "Capital of the Federation".

The original words, "Her Majesty, or of the Governor-General in Council, of any Local Government", have successively been amended by the Government of India (Adaptation of Indian Laws) Order, 1937 as amended by the Government of India (Adaptation of Indian Laws) Supplementary Order, 1937 and by the Central Laws (Adaptation) Order, 1961 (P.O. 1 of 1961), Article 2 and Schedule (with effect from the 23rd March, 1956), to read as above.

Substituted by the Punjab Laws (Adaptation) Order, 1974 (Pb. A. O. 1 of 1974), for "Central Government".

Inserted by the Central Laws (Adaptation) Order, 1961 (P.O. 1 of 1961), Article 2 and Schedule (with effect from the 23rd March, 1956).

The original words, "the territories of any Native Prince or State in India", have been amended by the Government of India (Adaptation of Indian Laws) Order, 1937 as amended by the Government of India (Adaptation of Indian Laws) Supplementary Order, 1937 and the Federal Laws (Revision and Declaration) Act, 1951 (XXVI of 1951), Section 4 and III Schedule, to read as above.

Substituted by the Central Laws (Adaptation) Order, 1961, Article 2 (with effect from the 23rd March, 1956), for "Crown", which had been substituted by the Government of India (Adaptation of Indian Laws) Order, 1937 as amended by the Government of India (Adaptation of Indian Laws) Supplementary Order, 1937, for "British Government".

Substituted by the Government of India (Adaptation of Indian Laws) Order, 1937 as amended by the Government of India (Adaptation of Indian Laws) Supplementary Order, 1937, for "by the Native Prince or State".

Substituted by the Government of India (Adaptation of Indian Laws) Order, 1937 as amended by the Government of India (Adaptation of Indian Laws) Supplementary Order, 1937 for "the Governor-General in Council".

Substituted by the Punjab Laws (Adaptation) Order, 1974 (Pb. A. O. 1 of 1974) for "Central Government".

The words, "in British India or" repealed, *ibid.*

The words, "of British India", omitted by the Adaptation of Central Acts and Ordinances Order, 1949 (G.G.O. 4 of 1949), Schedule.

The words, "the Governor-General in Council or", repealed by the Government of India (Adaptation of Indian Laws) Order, 1937 as amended by the Government of India (Adaptation of Indian Laws) Supplementary Order, 1937.

Substituted *ibid.,* for "Local Government".

The words, "as the case may be", repealed, *ibid.*

The original words, "the territories of any Native Prince or State in India", have been amended by the Government of India (Adaptation of Indian Laws) Order, 1937 as amended by the Government of India (Adaptation of Indian Laws) Supplementary Order, 1937 and the Federal Laws (Revision and Declaration) Act, 1951 (XXVI of 1951), Section 4 and III Schedule, to read as above.

The words, "the Governor-General in Council or", repealed by the Government of India (Adaptation of Indian Laws) Order, 1937 as amended by the Government of India (Adaptation of Indian Laws) Supplementary Order, 1937.

Substituted *ibid.*, for "Local Government".

Inserted *ibid.*

Substituted *ibid.*, for "Native Prince".

Substituted by the Central Laws (Adaptation) Order, 1961 (P.O. 1 of 1961), Article 2 (with effect from the 23rd March, 1956), for "Crown", which had been substituted by the Government of India (Adaptation of Indian Laws) Order, 1937 as amended by the Government of India (Adaptation of Indian Laws) Supplementary Order, 1937, for "British Government".

Substituted by the Government of India (Adaptation of Indian Laws) Order, 1937 as amended by the Government of India (Adaptation of Indian Laws) Supplementary Order, 1937, for "the G.G. in C".

Substituted by the Punjab Laws (Adaptation) Order, 1974 (Pb. A. O. 1 of 1974), for "Central Government".

Substituted by the Government of India (Adaptation of Indian Laws) Order, 1937 as amended by the Government of India (Adaptation of Indian Laws) Supplementary Order, 1937, for "Local Government".

Substituted by the Adaptation of Central Acts and Ordinances Order, 1949 (G.G.O. 4 of 1949), Schedule, for "British Court".

Substituted by the Punjab Laws (Adaptation) Order, 1974 (Pb. A. O. 1 of 1974), for "Central Government".

Substituted the Adaptation of Central Acts and Ordinances Order, 1949 (G.G.O. 4 of 1949), Articles 3 (2) and 4, for "British India".

The words, "and the Federal Territory of Karachi", omitted by the Central Adaptation of Laws Order, 1964 (P.O. 1 of 1964), Article 2 and Schedule. The words in crotchets were substituted by the Repealing and Amending Ordinance, 1961 (I of 1961), Section 3 and 2nd Schedule, for "Capital of the Federation".

Substituted by the Government of India (Adaptation of Indian Laws) Order, 1937 as amended by the Government of India (Adaptation of Indian Laws) Supplementary Order, 1937, for "the G.G. in C".

Substituted by the Central Laws (Adaptation) Order, 1961 (P.O. 1 of 1961), Article 2, for "Crown" (with effect from the 23rd March, 1956).

Substituted by the Adaptation of Central Acts and Ordinances Order, 1949 (G.G.O. 4 of 1949), Articles 3(2) and 4, for "British India".

The words, "and the Federal Territory of Karachi", omitted by the Central Adaptation of Laws Order, 1964 (P.O. 1 of 1964), Article 2 and Schedule. The words in crotchets were substituted by the Repealing and Amending Ordinance, 1961 (I of 1961), Section 3 and 2nd Schedule, for "Capital of the Federation".

Substituted by the Adaptation of Central Acts and Ordinances Order, 1949 (G.G.O. 4 of 1949), Articles 3(2) and 4, for "British India".

The words, "and the Federal Territory of Karachi", omitted by the Central Adaptation of Laws Order, 1964 (P.O. 1 of 1964), Article 2 and Schedule. The words in crotchets were substituted by the Repealing and Amending Ordinance, 1961 (I of 1961), Section 3 and 2nd Schedule, for "Capital of the Federation".

Substituted by the Government of India (Adaptation of Indian Laws) Order, 1937 as amended by the Government of India (Adaptation of Indian Laws) Supplementary Order, 1937, for "shall be such as the G.G. in C. or a L.G. authorised by the G.G. in C. in this behalf".

Substituted by the Adaptation of Central Acts and Ordinances Order, 1949 (G.G.O. 4 of 1949), Schedule, for "deemed to be a British Court for the purposes of this Section".

Substituted by the Punjab Laws (Adaptation) Order, 1974 (Pb. A. O. 1 of 1974), for "Central Government".

Substituted by the Central Laws (Adaptation) Order, 1961 (P.O. 1 of 1961), Article 2 (with effect from the 23rd March, 1956), for "Crown", which had been substituted by the Government of India (Adaptation of Indian Laws) Order, 1937 as amended by the Government of India (Adaptation of Indian Laws) Supplementary Order, 1937, for "British Government".

The original words, "by any Native Prince or State in India or by the G.G. in C.", have been successively amended by the Government of India (Adaptation of Indian Laws) Order, 1937 as amended by the Government of India (Adaptation of Indian Laws) Supplementary Order, 1937, the Adaptation of Central Acts and Ordinances Order, 1949 (G.G.O. 4 of 1949), Schedule and the Federal Laws (Revision and Declaration) Act, 1951 (XXVI of 1951), Section 4 and 3rd Schedule to read as above.

Substituted by the Punjab Laws (Adaptation) Order, 1974 (Pb. A. O. 1 of 1974), for "Central Government".

Substituted by the Central Laws (Adaptation) Order, 1961 (P.O. 1 of 1961), Article 2 (with effect from the 23rd March, 1956), for "Crown", which had been substituted by the Government of India (Adaptation of Indian Laws) Order, 1937 as amended by the Government of India (Adaptation of Indian Laws) Supplementary Order, 1937, for "British Government".

Substituted by the Amending Act, 1903 (I of 1903), Section 3 and Schedule II.

Substituted by the Government of India (Adaptation of Indian Laws) Order, 1937 as amended by the Government of India (Adaptation of Indian Laws) Supplementary Order, 1937, for "G.G. in C".

The word "or", deleted by Notification No: Prs. I (M) 1572, dated 6th July, 1977.

Added *ibid.*

Substituted by the Government of India (Adaptation of Indian Laws) Order, 1937 as amended by the Government of India (Adaptation of Indian Laws) Supplementary Order, 1937, for "British India or to any prison in Berar". The words, "or to any prison in Berar" had been added by the Prisoners (Amendment) Act, 1923 (XVII of 1923), Section 2.

Substituted by the Central Adaptation of Laws Order, 1964 (P.O. 1 of 1964), Article 2 and Schedule, for "any other Province".

Added by the Prisoners (Amendment) Ordinance, 1942 (XV of 1942).

Now 'Federal Government', see P.O. 4 of 1975.

Substituted by the Adaptation of Central Acts and Ordinances Order, 1949 (G.G.O. 4 of 1949), for "by him or under his authority".

Substituted by the Federal Laws (Revision and Declaration) Act, 1951 (XXVI of 1951), Section 4 and III Schedule, for "India".

Substituted by the West Pakistan (Adaptation of Laws) Ordinance, 1962 (XXV of 1962).

Added by Act XVII of 1953.

Now "Federal Government" *see* P.O. 4 of 1975.

Ibid.

The words "where such other prison is situated in a Province not being a Chief Commissioner's Province", omitted by the Central Adaptation of Laws Order, 1964 (P.O. 1 of 1964), Article 2 and Schedule.

Substituted by the Government of India (Adaptation of Indian Laws) Order, 1937 as amended by the Government of India (Adaptation of Indian Laws) Supplementary Order, 1937, for "Local Government".

Ibid.

Substituted by the Government of India (Adaptation of Indian Laws) Order, 1937 as amended by the Government of India (Adaptation of Indian Laws) Supplementary Order, 1937, for "Local Government".

Ibid.

Ibid.

XXXVI of 1858.

Substituted by the Devolution Act, 1920 (XXXVIII of 1920), Section 2 and Schedule I.

Substituted by the Government of India (Adaptation of Indian Laws) Order, 1937 as amended by the Government of India (Adaptation of Indian Laws) Supplementary Order, 1937, for "Local Government".

Ibid.

Substituted by the Central Adaptation of Laws Order, 1964 (P.O. 1 of 1964), for "any other Province".

The original words "the territories of any Native Prince or State in India", were first substituted by the Government of India (Adaptation of Indian Laws) Order, 1937 as amended by the Government of India (Adaptation of Indian Laws) Supplementary Order, 1937 and then amended by the Federal Laws (Revision and Declaration) Act, 1951 (XXVI of 1951), Section 4 and III Schedule, to read as above.

Substituted by the Government of India (Adaptation of Indian Laws) Order, 1937 as amended by the Government of India (Adaptation of Indian Laws) Supplementary Order, 1937, for "Local Government".

Substituted, *ibid.,* for "such Native Prince or State",

Section 32 was re-numbered as sub-section (1) of that Section by the Devolution Act, 1920 (XXXVIII of 1920), Section 2 and Schedule I.

Substituted by the Government of India (Adaptation of Indian Laws) Order, 1937 as amended by the Government of India (Adaptation of Indian Laws) Supplementary Order, 1937, for "Local Government".

Substituted by the Devolution Act, 1920 (XXXVIII of 1920), Section 2 and Schedule I, for "British India".

Substituted by the Government of India (Adaptation of Indian Laws) Order, 1937 as amended by the Government of India (Adaptation of Indian Laws) Supplementary Order, 1937, for "Local Government".

Substituted by the Government of India (Adaptation of Indian Laws) Order, 1937 as amended by the Government of India (Adaptation of Indian Laws) Supplementary Order, 1937, for "Local Government".

Inserted by the Devolution Act, 1920 (XXXVIII of 1920) Section 2 and Schedule I.

Substituted by the Government of India (Adaptation of Indian Laws) Order, 1937 as amended by the Government of India (Adaptation of Indian Laws) Supplementary Order, 1937, for "Local Government".

Ibid.

Substituted by the Central Adaptation of Laws Order, 1964 (P.O. 1 of 1964), for "any other Province".

Substituted by the Government of India (Adaptation of Indian Laws) Order, 1937 as amended by the Government of India (Adaptation of Indian Laws) Supplementary Order, 1937, for "Local Government".

Substituted by the Central Laws (Statute Reform) Ordinance, 1960 (XXI of 1960), Section 3 and 2nd Schedule (with effect from the 14th October, 1955), for "Any Court which is a High Court for the purposes of the Government of India Act, 1935", which had been substituted by the Government of India (Adaptation of Indian Laws) Order, 1937 as amended by the Government of India (Adaptation of Indian Laws) Supplementary Order, 1937, for "Any court established under the Indian High Courts Act, 1861".

Substituted by the Central Laws (Adaptation) Order, 1961 (P.O. 1 of 1961), Article 2 and Schedule, for "Her Majesty" (with effect from the 23rd March, 1956).

The words, "outside a Presidency Town", omitted by the Adaptation of Central Acts and Ordinances Order, 1949 (G.G.O. 4 of 1949).

Substituted for the words "District Magistrate" by the Prisoners (Punjab Amendment) Ordinance, 2001 (XXXIX of 2001), which will remain in force under the Provisional Constitution (Amendment) Order 1999 (9 of 1999), Article 4, notwithstanding the maximum limit of three months prescribed under Article 128 of the Constitution of the Islamic Republic of Pakistan.

Ibid., for the words "District or Sub-divisional".

Ibid., for the word "Magistrate".

The words, "in a prison within a Presidency-town, or", omitted by the Adaptation of Central Acts and Ordinances Order, 1949 (G.G.O. 4 of 1949).

Substituted for the words "District or Sub-divisional" by the Prisoners (Punjab Amendment) Ordinance, 2001 (XXXIX of 2001), which will remain in force under the Provisional Constitution (Amendment) Order 1999 (9 of 1999), Article 4, notwithstanding the maximum limit of three months prescribed under Article 128 of the Constitution of the Islamic Republic of Pakistan.

The words, "or in the case of a person confined in a prison within a Presidency-town to the Commissioner of Police", omitted by the Adaptation of Central Acts and Ordinances Order, 1949 (G.G.O. 4 of 1949), Schedule.

Substituted for the word "Magistrate" by the Prisoners (Punjab Amendment) Ordinance, 2001 (XXXIX of 2001), which will remain in force under the Provisional Constitution (Amendment) Order 1999 (9 of 1999), Article 4, notwithstanding the maximum limit of three months prescribed under Article 128 of the Constitution of the Islamic Republic of Pakistan.

The words, "or Commissioner", omitted, by the Adaptation of Central Acts and Ordinances Order, 1949 (G.G.O. 4 of 1949), Schedule.

Substituted by the Government of India (Adaptation of Indian Laws) Order, 1937 as amended by the Government of India (Adaptation of Indian Laws) Supplementary Order, 1937, for "Local Government".

Ibid.

The words, "if it thinks fit" deleted by the Prisoners (Punjab Amendment) Ordinance, 1984 (XXVIII of 1984).

Substituted by the Government of India (Adaptation of Indian Laws) Order, 1937 as amended by the Government of India (Adaptation of Indian Laws) Supplementary Order, 1937, for "G.G. in C".

The words "the G.G. in C. or" repealed by the Devolution Act, 1920 (XXXVIII of 1920), Section 2 and Schedule I.

Substituted by the Government of India (Adaptation of Indian Laws) Order, 1937 as amended by the Government of India (Adaptation of Indian Laws) Supplementary Order, 1937, for "Local Government".

The words "the Gazette of India or" repealed by the Devolution Act, 1920 (XXXVIII of 1920), Section 2 and Schedule I.

Substituted by the Government of India (Adaptation of Indian Laws) Order, 1937 as amended by the Government of India (Adaptation of Indian Laws) Supplementary Order, 1937, for "local Official Gazette".

The words "as the case may be", repealed by the Devolution Act, 1920 (XXXVIII of 1920), Section 2 and Schedule I.

Substituted for the words "District or Sub-divisional" by the Prisoners (Punjab Amendment) Ordinance, 2001 (XXXIX of 2001), which will remain in force under the Provisional Constitution (Amendment) Order 1999 (9 of 1999), Article 4, notwithstanding the maximum limit of three months prescribed under Article 128 of the Constitution of the Islamic Republic of Pakistan.

Ibid., for the word "Magistrate".

XIV of 1882, subsequently replaced by the Code of Civil Procedure 1908 (V of 1908).

Ibid.

Substituted by the Government of India (Adaptation of Indian Laws) Order, 1937 as amended by the Government of India (Adaptation of Indian Laws) Supplementary Order, 1937, for "Govt".

Now the Code of Civil Procedure, 1908 (V of 1908).

Substituted by the Government of India (Adaptation of Indian Laws) Order, 1937 as amended by the Government of India (Adaptation of Indian Laws) Supplementary Order, 1937, for "Local Government".

The words, "and in cases arising under Section 40, the G.G. in C"., repealed *ibid.*

Substituted *ibid.,* for "local official Gazette".

The words, "or the Gazette of India, as the case may be", repealed, *ibid.*

Substituted by the Government of India (Adaptation of Indian Laws) Order, 1937 as amended by the Government of India (Adaptation of Indian Laws) Supplementary Order, 1937, for "Local Government".

❐❐❐

29

The Prisons Act, 1894

Act No. 9 of 1894 [22nd March, 1894]

AN ACT to amend the law relating to Prisons.

WHEREAS it is expedient to amend the law relating to prisons in 2 India except the territories which, immediately before the 1st November, 1956, were comprised in Part B States, and to provide rules for the regulation of such prison; It is hereby enacted as follows:-

CHAPTER - I : PRELIMINARY

1. Title, extent and commencement.

(1) This Act may be called the Prisons Act, 1894.

(2) It extends to the whole of India except the territories which, immediately before the 1st November, 1956, were comprised in Part B States, and

(3) It shall come into force on the first day of July, 1894.

(4) Nothing in this Act shall apply to civil jails in the State of Bombay as it existed immediately before the 1st November, 1956 outside the city of Bombay, and those jails shall continue to be administered under the provisions of Sections 9 and 16 (both inclusive) of Bombay Act 2 of 1874, as amended by subsequent enactments.

2. Repeal. Rep. by the Repealing Act, 1938 (1 of 1938), s. 2 and Sch.

3. Definitions. In this Act-

(1) "prison" means any jail or place used permanently or temporarily under the general or special orders of a State Government for the detention of prisoners, and includes all lands and buildings appurtenant thereto, but does not include-

(a) any place for the confinement of prisoners who are exclusively in the custody of the police;

(b) any place specially appointed by the State Government under Section 541 of the Code of Criminal Procedure, 1882 or (10 of 1882);

(c) any place which has been declared by the State Government, by general or special order, to be a subsidiary jail;

(2) "criminal prisoner" means any prisoner duly committed to custody under the writ, warrant or order of any Court or authority exercising criminal jurisdiction, or by order of a Court-martial.

(3) "convicted criminal prisoner" means any criminal prisoner under sentence of a Court or Court-martial, and includes a person detained in prison under the provisions of Chapter VIII of the Code of Criminal Procedure, 1882, or under the' Prisoners Act, 1871 : (10 of 1882, 5 of 1871).

(4) "civil prisoner" means any prisoner who is not a criminal prisoner.

(5) "remission system" means the rules for the time being in force regulating the award of marks to, and the consequent shortening of sentences of, prisoners in jail.

(6) "history-ticket" means the ticket exhibiting such information as is required in respect of each prisoner by this Act or the rules thereunder.

(7) "Inspector General" means the Inspector General of Prisons.

(8) "Medical Subordinate" means an Assistant Surgeon, Apothecary or qualified Hospital Assistant, and

(9) "prohibited article" means an article the introduction or removal of which into or out of a prison is prohibited by any rule under this Act.

CHAPTER -II : MAINTENANCE AND OFFICERS OF PRISONS

4. Accommodation for prisoners. The State Government shall provide, for the prisoners in the territories under such Government, accommodation in prisons constructed and regulated in such manner as to comply with the requisitions of this Act in respect of the separation of prisoners.

5. Inspector General. An Inspector General shall be appointed for the territories subject to each State Government, and shall exercise, subject to the orders of the State Government, the general control and superintendence of all prisons situated in the territories under such Government.

6. Officers of prisons. For every prison there shall be a Superintendent, a Medical Officer (who may also be the Superintendent), a Medical Subordinate, a Jailer and such other officers as the State Government thinks necessary:

> *PROVIDED that the State Government of Bombay may declare by order in writing that in any prison specified in the order the office of Jailer shall be held by the person appointed to be Superintendent.*

7. Temporary accommodation for prisoners. Whenever it appears to the Inspector General that the number of prisoners in any prison is greater than can conveniently or safely be kept therein, and it is not convenient to transfer the excess number to some other prison, or whenever from the outbreak of epidemic disease within any prison, or for any other reason, it is desirable to provide for the temporary shelter and safe custody of any prisoners, provision shall be made, by such officer and in such manner as the State Government may direct, for the shelter and safe custody in temporary prisons of so many of the prisoners as cannot be con-veniently or safely kept in the prison.

CHAPTER -III : DUTIES OF OFFICERS GENERALLY

8. Control and duties of officers of prisons. All officers of a prison shall obey the directions of the Superintendent; all officers subordinate to the Jailer shall perform such duties as may be imposed on them by the Jailer with the sanction of the Superintendent or be prescribed by rules under Section 59.

9. Officers not to have business dealings with prisoners. No officer of a prison shall sell or let, nor shall any person in trust for or employed by him sell or let, or derive any benefit from selling or letting, any article to any prisoner or have any money or other business dealings, directly or indirectly, with any prisoner.

10. Officers not to be interested in prison-contracts. No officer of a prison shall, nor shall any person in trust for or employed by him, have any interest, direct or indirect, in any contract for the supply of the prison: nor shall he derive any benefit, directly or indirectly, from the sale or purchase of any article on behalf of the prison or belonging to a prisoner.

11. Superintendent.

(1) Subject to the orders of the Inspector General, the Superintendent shall manage the prison in all matters relating to discipline, labour, expenditure, punishment and control.

(2) Subject to such general or special directions as may be given by the State Government, the Superintendent of a prison other than a central prison or a prison situated in a presidency-town shall obey all orders not inconsistent with this Act or any rule thereunder which may be given respecting the prison by the District Magistrate, and shall report to the Inspector General all such orders and the action taken thereon.

12. Records to be kept by Superintendent. The Superintendent shall keep, or cause to be kept, the following records:-

(1) a register of prisoners admitted;

(2) a book showing when each prisoner is to be released;

(3) a punishment-book for the entry of the punishments inflicted on prisoners for prison-offences;

(4) a visitors' book for the entry of any observations made by the visitors touching any matters connected with the administration of the prison;

(5) a record of the money and other articles taken from prisoners; and all such other records as may be prescribed by rules under Section 59.

Medical Officer

13. Duties of Medical Officer. Subject to the control of the Superintendent, the Medical Officer shall have charge of the sanitary administration of the prison, and shall perform such duties as may be prescribed by rules made by the State Government under Section 59.

14. Medical Officer to report in certain cases. Whenever the Medical Officer has reason to believe that the mind of a prisoner is, or is likely to be, injuriously affected by the discipline or treatment to which he is subjected, the Medical Officer shall report the case in writing to the Superintendent, together with such observations as he may think proper. This report, with the orders of the Superintendent thereon, shall forthwith be sent to the Inspector General for information.

15. Report on death of prisoner. On the death of any prisoner, the Medical Officer shall forthwith record in a register the following particulars, so far as they can be ascertained, namely:-

(1) the day on which the deceased first complained of illness or was observed to be ill,

(2) the labour, if any, on which he was engaged on that day,

(3) the scale of his diet on that day,

(4) the day on which he was admitted to hospital,

(5) the day on which the Medical Officer was first informed of the illness,

(6) the nature of the disease,

(7) when the deceased was last seen before his death by the Medical Officer or Medical Subordinate,

(8) when the prisoner died, and

(9) (in cases where a postmortem examination is made) an account of the appearances after death, together with any special remarks that appear to the Medical Officer to be required.

16. Jailer.

(1) The Jailer shall reside in the prison, unless the Superintendent permits him in writing to reside elsewhere.

(2) The Jailer shall not, without the Inspector General' s sanction in writing, be concerned in any other employment.

17. Jailer to give notice of death of prisoner. Upon the death of a prisoner, the Jailer shall give immediate notice thereof to the Superintendent and the Medical Subordinate.

18. Responsibility of Jailer. The Jailer shall be responsible for the safe custody of the records to be kept under Section 12, for the commitment warrants and all other documents confided to his care, and for the money and other articles taken from prisoners.

19. Jailer to be present at night. The Jailer shall not be absent from the prison for a night without permission in writing from the Superintendent; but, if absent without leave for a night from unavoidable necessity, he shall immediately report the fact and the cause of it to the Superintendent.

20. Powers of Deputy and Assistant Jailers. Where a Deputy Jailer or Assistant Jailer is appointed to a prison, he shall, subject to the orders of the Superintendent, be competent to perform any of the duties, and be subject to all the responsibilities, of a Jailer under this Act or any rule thereunder.

SUBORDINATE OFFICERS

21. Duties of gate-keeper. The officer acting as gate-keeper, or any other officer of the prison, may examine anything carried in or out of the prison, and may stop and search or cause to be searched any person suspected of bringing any prohibited article into or out of the prison, or of carrying out any property belonging to the prison, and, if any such article or property be found, shall give immediate notice thereof to the Jailer.

22. Subordinate officers not to be absent without leave. Officers subordinate to the Jailer shall not be absent from the prison without leave from the Superintendent or from the Jailer.

23. Convict officers. Prisoners who have been appointed as officers of prisons shall be deemed to be public servants within the meaning of the Indian Penal Code (45 of 1860).

CHAPTER -IV : ADMISSION, REMOVAL AND DISCHARGE OF PRISONERS

24. Prisoners to be examined on admission.

(1) Whenever a prisoner is admitted into prison, he shall be searched, and all weapons and prohibited articles shall be taken from him.

(2) Every criminal prisoner shall also, as soon as possible after admission, be examined under the general or special orders of the Medical Officer, who shall enter or cause to be entered in a book, to be kept by the Jailer, a record of the state of the prisoner' s health, and of any wounds or marks on his person, the class of labour he is fit for if sentenced to rigorous imprisonment, and any observations which the Medical Officer thinks fit to add.

(3) In the case of female prisoners the search and examination shall be carried out by the matron under the general or special orders of the Medical Officer.

25. Effects of prisoners. All money or other articles in respect whereof no order of a competent Court has been made, and which may with proper authority be brought into the prison by any criminal prisoner or sent to the prison for his use, shall be placed in the custody of the Jailer.

26. Removal and discharge of prisoners.

(1) All prisoners, previously to being removed to any other prison, shall be examined by the Medical Officer.

(2) No prisoner shall be removed from one prison to another unless the Medical Officer certifies that the prisoner is free from any illness rendering him unfit for removal.

(3) No prisoner shall be discharged against his will from prison, if labouring under

any acute or dangerous distemper, nor until, in the opinion of the Medical Officer, such discharge is safe.

CHAPTER -V : DISCIPLINE OF PRISONERS

27. Separation of prisoners. The requisitions of this Act with respect to the separation of prisoners are as follows:-

(1) in a prison containing female as well as male prisoners, the females shall be imprisoned in separate buildings, or separate parts of the same building, in such manner as to prevent their seeing, or conversing or holding any intercourse with, the male prisoners;

(2) in a prison where male prisoners under the age of twentyone are confined, means shall be provided for separating them altogether from the other prisoners and for separating those of them who have arrived at the age of puberty from those who have not;

(3) unconvicted criminal prisoners shall be kept apart from convicted criminal prisoners; and

(4) civil prisoners shall be kept apart from criminal prisoners.

28. Association and segregation of prisoners. Subject to the requirements of the last foregoing Section, convicted criminal prisoners may be confined either in association or individually in cells or partly in one way and partly in the other.

29. Solitary confinement. No cell shall be used for solitary confinement unless it is furnished with the means of enabling the prisoner to communicate at any time with an officer of the prison, and every prisoner so confirmed in a cell for more than twenty-four hours, whether as a punishment or otherwise, shall be visited at least once a day by the Medical Officer or Medical Subordinate.

30. Prisoners under sentence of death.

(1) Every prisoner under sentence of death shall, immediately on his arrival in the prison after sentence, be searched by, or by order of, the Jailer and all articles shall be taken from him which the Jailer deems it dangerous or inexpedient to leave in his possession.

(2) Every such prisoner shall be confined in a cell apart from all other prisoners, and shall be placed by day and by night under the charge of a guard.

CHAPTER -VI : FOOD, CLOTHING AND BEDDING OF CIVIL AND UNCONVICTED CRIMINAL PRISONERS

31. Maintenance of certain prisoners from private sources. A civil prisoner or an unconvicted criminal prisoner shall be permitted to maintain himself, and to purchase, or receive from private sources at proper hours, food, clothing, bedding or other necessaries, but subject to examination and to such rules as may be approved by the Inspector General.

32. Restriction on transfer of food and clothing between certain prisoners. No part of any food, clothing, bedding or other necessaries belonging to any civil or unconvicted criminal prisoner shall be given, hired or sold to any other prisoner; and any prisoner transgressing the provisions of this Section shall lose the privilege of purchasing food or receiving it from private sources, for such time as the Superintendent thinks proper.

33. Supply of clothing and bedding to civil and unconvicted criminal prisoners.

(1) Every civil prisoner and unconvicted criminal prisoner unable to provide himself with sufficient clothing and bedding shall be supplied by the Superintendent with such clothing and bedding as may be necessary.

(2) When any civil prisoner has been committed to prison in execution of a decree in favour of a private person, such person, or his representative, shall, within forty-eight hours after the receipt by him of a demand in writing, pay to the Superintendent the cost of the clothing and bedding so supplied to the prisoner; and in default of such payment the prisoner may be released.

CHAPTER -VII : EMPLOYMENT OF PRISONERS

34. Employment of civil prisoners.

(1) Civil prisoners may, with the Superintendents permission, work and follow any trade or profession.

(2) Civil prisoners finding their own implements and not maintained at the expense of the prison, shall be allowed to receive the whole of their earnings; but the earnings of such as are furnished with implements or are maintained at the expense of the prison shall be subject to a deduction, to be determined by the Superintendent, for the use of implements and the cost of maintenance.

35. Employment of criminal prisoners.

(1) No criminal prisoner sentenced to labour or employed on labour at his own desire shall, except on an emergency with the sanction in writing of the Superintendent, be kept to labour for more than nine hours in any one day.

(2) The Medical Officer shall from time to time examine the labouring prisoners while they are employed and shall at least once in every fortnight cause to be recorded upon the history-ticket of each prisoner employed on labour the weight of such prisoner at the time.

(3) When the Medical Officer is of opinion that the health of any prisoner suffers from employment on any kind or class of labour, such prisoner shall not be employed on that labour but shall be placed on such other kind or class of labour as the Medical Officer may consider suited for him.

36. Employment of criminal prisoners sentenced to simple imprisonment. Provision shall be made by the Superintendent for the employment (as long as they so desire) of all criminal prisoners sentenced to simple imprisonment; but no prisoner not sentenced to rigorous imprisonment shall be punished for neglect of work excepting by such alteration in the scale of diet as may be established by the rules of the prison in the case of neglect of work by such a prisoner.

CHAPTER -VIII : HEALTH OF PRISONERS

37. Sick prisoners.

(1) The names of prisoners desiring to see the Medical Subordinate or appearing

out of health in mind or body shall, without delay, be reported by the officer in immediate charge of such prisoners to the Jailer.

(2) The Jailer shall, without delay, call the attention of the Medical Subordinate to any prisoners desiring to see him, or who is ill, or whose state of mind or body appears to require attention, and shall carry into effect all written directions given by the Medical Officer or Medical Subordinate respecting alterations of the discipline or treatment of any such prisoner.

38. Record of directions of Medical Officers. All directions given by the Medical Officer or Medical Sub ordinate in relation to any prisoner, with the exception of orders for the supply of medicines or directions relating to such matters as are carried into effect by the Medical Officer himself or under his superintendence, shall be entered day by day in the prisoner' s history-ticket or in such other record as the State Government may by rule direct, and the Jailer shall make an entry in its proper place stating in respect of each direction the fact of its having been or not having been complied with, accompanied by such observations, if any, as the Jailer thinks fit to make, and the date of the entry.

39. Hospital. In every prison an hospital or proper place for the reception of sick prisoners shall be provided.

CHAPTER -IX : VISITS TO PRISONERS

40. Visits to civil and unconvicted criminal prisoners. Due provision shall be made for the admission, at proper times and under proper restrictions, into every prison of persons with whom civil or unconvicted criminal prisoners may desire to communicate, care being taken that so far as may be consistent with the interests of justicc, prisoners under trial may see their duly qualified legal advisers without the presence of any other person.

41. Search of visitors.

(1) The Jailer may demand the name and address of any visitor to a prisoner, and, when the Jailer has any ground for suspicion, may search any visitor, or cause him to be searched, but the search shall not be made in the presence of any prisoner or of another visitor.

(2) In case of any such visitor refusing to pcrmit himself to be searched, the Jailer may deny him admission; and the grounds of such proceeding, with the particulars thereof, shall be entered in such record as the State Government may direct.

CHAPTER -X : OFFENCES IN RELATION TO PRISONS

42. Penalty for introduction or removal of prohibited articles into or from prison and communication with prisoners. Whoever, contrary to any rule under Section 59 introduces or removes or attempts by any means whatever to introduce or remove, into or from any prison, or supplies or attempts to supply to any prisoner outside the limits of a prison, any prohibited article, and every officer of a prison who, contrary to any such rule, knowingly suffers any such article to be introduced into or removed from any prison, to be possessed by any prisoner, or to be supplied to any prisoner outside the limits of a prison, and whoever, contrary to any such rule, communicates or attempts to communicate with any prisoner, and whoever abets any offence made punishable by this Section, shall, on conviction before a Magistrate, be liable to imprisonment for a term not exceeding six months, or to fine not exceeding two hundred rupees, or to both.

43. Power to arrest for offence under Section 42. When any person, in the presence of any officer of a prison, commits any offence specified in the last foregoing Section, and refuses on demand of such officer to state his name and residence, or gives a name or residence which such officer knows, or has reason to believe, to be false, such officer may arrest him, and shall without unnecessary delay make him over to a Police-Officer, and thereupon such Police-Officer shall proceed as if the offence had been committed in his presence.

44. Publication of penalties. The Superintendent shall cause to be affixed, in a conspicuous place outside the prison, a notice in English and the Vernacular setting forth the acts prohibited under Section 42 and the penalties incurred by their commission.

CHAPTER -XI : PRISON-OFFENCES

45. Prison-offences. The following acts are declared to be prison-offences when committed by a prisoner:-

(1) such wilful disobedience to any regulation of the prison as shall have been declared by rules made under Section 59 to be a prison-offence;

(2) any assault or use of criminal force;

(3) the use of insulting or threatening language;

(4) immoral or indecent or disorderly behaviour;

(5) wilfully disabling himself from labour;

(6) contumaciously refusing to work;

(7) filing, cutting, altering or removing handcuffs, fetters or bars without due authority;

(8) wilful idleness or negligence at work by any prisoner sentenced to rigorous imprisonment;

(9) wilful mismanagement of work by any prisoner sentenced to rigorous imprisonment;

(10) wilful damage to prison-property;

(11) tampering with or defacing history-tickets, records or documents;

(12) receiving, possessing or transferring any prohibited article;

(13) feigning illness;

(14) wilfully bringing a false accusation against any officer or prisoner;

(15) omitting or refusing to report, as soon as it comes to his knowledge, the occurrence of any fire, any plot or conspiracy, any escape, attempt or preparation to escape, and any attack or preparation for attack upon any prisoner or prison-official; and

(16) conspiring to escape, or to assist in escaping, or to commit any other of the offences aforesaid.

46. Punishment of such offences. The Superintendent may examine any person touching any such offence, and determine thereupon, and punish such offence by—

(1) a formal warning: *EXPLANATION.* A formal warning shall mean a warning per sonally addressed to a prisoner by the Superintendent and recorded in the punishment-book and on the prisoner' s history-ticket;

(2) change of labour to some more irksome or severe form for such period as may be prescribed by rules made by the State Government;

(3) hard labour for a period not exceeding seven days in the case of convicted criminal prisoners not sentenced to rigorous imprisonment;

(4) such loss of privileges admissible under the remission system for the time being in force as may be prescribed by rules made by the State Government;

(5) the substitution of gunny or other coarse fabric for clothing of other material, not being woollen, for a period which shall not exceed three months;

(6) imposition of handcuffs of such pattern and weight, in such manner and for such period, as may be prescribed by rules made by the State Government;

(7) imposition of fetters of such pattern and weight, in such manner and for such period, as may be prescribed by rules made by the State Government;

(8) separate confinement for any period not exceeding three months;

EXPLANATION: Separate confinement means such confinement with or without labour as secludes a prisoner from communication with, but not from sight of, other prisoners, and allows him not less than one hour' s exercise per diem and to have his meals in association with one or more other prisoners;

(9) penal diet, that is, restriction of diet in such manner and subject to such conditions regarding labour as may be prescribed by the State Government:

PROVIDED that such restriction of diet shall in no case be applied to a prisoner for more than ninety-six consecutive hours, and shall not be repeated except for a fresh offence nor until after an interval of one week;

(10) cellular confinement for any period not exceeding fourteen days:

PROVIDED that after each period of cellular confinement an interval of not less duration than such period must elapse before the prisoner is again sentenced to cellular or solitary confinement;

(11) penal diet as defined in clause (9) combined with cellular confinement;

(12) whipping, provided that the number of stripes shall not exceed thirty:

PROVIDED that nothing in this Section shall render any female or civil prisoner liable to the imposition of any form of handcuffs or fetters, or to whipping.

47. Plurality of punishment, under Section 46.

(1) Any two of awarded for any such offence in combination, subject to the following exceptions, namely:-

(1) formal warning shall not be combined with any other punishment except loss of privileges under clause (4) of that Section;

(2) penal diet shall not be combined with change of labour under clause (2) of that Section, nor shall any additional period of penal diet awarded singly be combined with any period of penal diet awarded in combination with cellular confinement;

(3) cellular confinement shall not be combined with separate confinement, so as to, prolong the total period of seclusion to which the prisoner shall be liable;

(4) whipping shall not be combined with any other form of punishment except cellular and separate confinement and loss of privileges admissible under the remission system;

(5) no punishment will be combined with any other punishment in contravention of rules made by the State Government.

(2) No punishment shall be awarded for any such offence so as to combine, with the punishment awarded for any other such offence, two of the punishments which may not be awarded in combination for any such offence.

48. Award of punishments under Section 46 and 47 to be in accordance with foregoing Sections.

(1) The Superintendent shall have power to award any of the punishments enumerated in the two last foregoing Sections, subject, in the case of separate confinement for a period exceeding one month, to the previous confirmation of the Inspector General.

(2) No officer subordinate to the Superintendent shall have power to award any punishment whatever.

49. Punishments to be in accordance with foregoing Sections. Except by order of a Court of Justice, no punishment other than the punishments specified in the foregoing Sections shall be inflicted on any prisoner, and no punishment shall be inflicted on any prisoner otherwise than in accordance with the provisions of those Sections.

50. Medical Officer to certify to fitness of prisoner for punishment.

(1) No punishment of penal diet, either singly or in com-bination, or of whipping, or of change of labour under Section 46, clause (2), shall be executed until the prisoner to whom such punishment has been awarded has been examined by the Medical Officer, who, if he considers the prisoner fit to undergo the punishment, shall certify accordingly in the appropriate column of the punishment book prescribed in Section 12.

(2) If he considers the prisoner unfit to undergo the punishment, he shall in like manner record his opinion in writing and shall state whether the prisoner is absolutely unfit for punishment of the kind awarded, or whether he considers any modification necessary.

(3) In the latter case he shall state what extent of punishment he thinks the prisoner can undergo without injury to his health.

51. Entries in punishment books.

(1) In the punishment-book prescribed in Section 12 there shall be recorded, in respect of every punishment inflicted, the prisoners name, register number and the class (whether habitual or not) to which he belongs, the prison-offence of which he was guilty, the date on which such prison-offence was committed, the number of previous prison-offences recorded against the prisoner, and the date of his last prison-offence, the punishment awarded, and the date of infliction.

(2) In the case of every serious prison-offence, the names. of the witnesses proving the offence shall be recorded, and, in the case of offences for which whipping is awarded, the Superintendent shall record the substance of the evidence of the witnesses, the defence of the prisoner, and the finding with the reasons therefor.

(3) Against the entries relating to each punishment the Jailor and Superintendent shall affix their initials as evidence of the correctness of the entries.

52. Procedure on committal of heinous offence. If any prisoner is guilty of any offence against prison-discipline which, by reason of his having frequently committed such offences or otherwise, in the opinion of the Superintendent, is not adequately punishable by the infliction of any punishment which he has power under this Act to award, the Superintendent may forward such prisoner to the Court of the District Magistrate or of any Magistrate of the first class or Presidency Magistrate having jurisdiction, together with a statement of the circumstances, and such Magistrate shall thereupon inquire into and try the charge so brought against the prisoner, and, upon conviction, may sentence him to imprisonment which may extend to one year, such term to be in addition to any term for which such prisoner was undergoing imprisonment when he committed such offence, or may sentence him to any of the punishments enumerated in Section 46: Provided that any such case may be transferred for inquiry and trial by the District Magistrate to any Magistrate of the first class and by a Chief Presidency Magistrate to any other Presidency Magistrate, and Provided also that no person shall be punished twice for the same offence.

53. Whipping.

(1) No punishment of whipping shall be inflicted in instalments, or except in the presence of the Superintendent and Medical Officer or Medical Subordinate.

(2) Whipping shall be inflicted with a light ratan not less than half an inch in diameter on the buttocks, and in case of prisoners under the age of sixteen it shall be inflicted, in the way of school discipline, with a lighter ratan.

54. Offences by prison-subordinates.

(1) Every Jailor or officer of a prison subordinate to him who shall be guilty of any violation of duty or wilful breach or neglect of any rule or regulation or lawful order made by competent authority, or who shall withdraw from the duties of his office without permission, or without having given previous notice in writing of his intention for the period of two months, or who shall wilfully overstay any leave granted to him, or who shall engage without authority in any employment other than his prison-duty, or who shall be guilty of cowardice, shall be liable,

on conviction before a Magistrate, to fine not exceeding two hundred rupees, or to imprisonment for a period not exceeding three months, or to both.

(2) No person shall under this Section be punished twice for the same offence.

CHAPTER -XII : MISCELLANEOUS

55. Extramural custody, control and employment of prisoners. A prisoner, when being taken to or from any prison in which he may be lawfully confined, or whenever he is working outside or is otherwise beyond the limits of any such prison in or under the lawful custody or control of a prison-officer belonging to such prison, shall be deemed to be in prison and shall be subject to all the same incidents as if he were actually in prison.

56. Confinement in irons. Whenever the Superintendent considers it necessary (with reference either to the state of the prison or the character of the prisoners) for the safe custody of any prisoners that they should be confined in irons, he may, subject to such rules and instructions as may be laid down by the Inspector General with the sanction of the State Government, so confine them.

57. Confinement of prisoners under sentence of transportation in irons.

(1) Prisoners under sentence of transportation may, subject to any rules made under Section 59, be confined in fetters for the first three months after admission to prison.

(2) Should the Superintendent consider it necessary, either for the safe custody of the prisoner himself or for any other reason, that fetters should be retained on any such prisoner for more than three months, he shall apply to the Inspector General for sanction to their retention for the period for which he considers their retention necessary, and the Inspector General may sanction such retention accordingly.

58. Prisoners not to be ironed by jailer except under necessity. No prisoner shall be put in irons or under mechanical restraint by the Jailer of his own authority, except in case of urgent necessity, in which case notice thereof shall be forthwith given to the Superintendent.

59. Power to make rules. The State Government may by notification in the official gazette make rules consistent with this Act-

(1) defining the acts which shall constitute prison-offences;

(2) determining the classification of prison-offences into serious and minor offences;

(3) fixing the punishments admissible under this Act which shall be awardable for commission of prison-offences or classes thereof;

(4) declaring the circumstances in which acts constituting both a prison-offence and an offence under the Indian Penal Code may or may not be dealt with as a prison offence (45 of 1860);

(5) for the award of marks and the shortening of sentences;

(6) regulating the use of arms against any prisoner or body of prisoners in the case of an outbreak or attempt to escape;

(7) defining the circumstances and regulating the conditions under which prisoners in danger of death may be released;

(8) for the classification of prisons, and description and construction of wards, cells and other places of detention;

(9) for the regulation by numbers, length or character of sentences, or otherwise, of the prisoners to be confined in each class of prisons;

(10) for the government of prisons and for the appointment of all officers appointed under this Act;

(11) as to the food, bedding and clothing of criminal prisoners and of civil prisoners maintained otherwise than at their own cost;

(12) for the employment, instruction and control of convicts within or without prisons;

(13) for defining articles the introduction or removal of which into or out of prisons without due authority is prohibited;

(14) for classifying and prescribing the forms of labour and regulating the periods of rest from labour;

(15) for regulating the disposal of the proceeds of the employment of prisoners;

(16) for regulating the confinement in fetters of prisoners sentenced to transportation;

(17) for the classification and the separation of prisoners

(18) for regulating the confinement of convicted criminal prisoners under Section 28;

(19) for the preparation and maintenance of history-tickets.

(20) for the selection and appointment of prisoners as officers of prisons;

(21) for rewards for good conduct.

(22) for regulating the transfer of prisoners whose term of transportation or imprisonment is about to expire subject, however, to the consent of the State Government of any other State to which a prisoner is to be transferred;

(23) for the treatment, transfer and disposal of criminal lunatics or recovered criminal lunatics confined in prisons;

(24) for regulating the transmission of appeals and petitions from prisoners and their communications with their friends;

(25) for the appointment and guidance of visitors of prisons;

(26) for extending any or all of the provisions of this Act and of the rules thereunder to subsidiary jails or special places of confinement appointed under Section 541 of the Code of Criminal Procedure, 1882 (10 of 1882), and to the officers employed, and the prisoners confined, therein;

(27) in regard to the admission, custody, employment, dieting, treatment and release of prisoners; and

(28) generally for carrying into effect the purposes of this Act.

(29) Every rule made under this Section shall be laid, as soon as may be after it is made, before the State Legislature.

60. Power of Local Government to make rules. *Rep. by the A.O. 1937.*

61. Exhibition of copies of rules. Copies of rules, under Section 59 so far as they affect the government of prisons, shall be exhibited, both in English and in the Vernacular, in some place to which all persons employed within a prison have access.

62. Exercise of powers of Superintendent and Medical Officer. All or any of the powers and duties conferred and imposed by this Act on a Superintendent or Medical Officer may in his absence be exercised and performed by such other officer as the State Government may appoint in this behalf either by name or by his official designation.

❑❑❑

30

The Probation of Offenders Act, 1958

Act No. 20 of 1958 [16th May, 1958]

AN ACT to provide for the Release of Offenders on Probation or Afterdue Admonit

1. Short title extent and commencement.

(1) This Act may be called the Probation of Offenders Act, 1958.

(2) It extends to the whole of India except the State of Jammu and Kashmir.

(3) It shall come into force in a State on such date as the State Government may, by notification in the Official Gazette, appoint, and different dates may be appointed for different parts of the State.

2. Definitions. In this Act, unless the context otherwise requires,-

(a) "Code" means the Code of Criminal Procedure, 1898 (5 of 1898);

(b) "probation officer" means an officer appointed to be a probation officer or recognised as such under Section 13;

(c) "prescribed" means prescribed by rules made under this Act;

(d) words and expressions used but not defined in this Act and defined in the Code of Criminal Procedure, 1898 (5 of 1898), shall have the meanings respectively assigned to them in that Code.

3. Power of court to release certain offenders after admonition. When any person is found guilty of having committed an offence punishable under Section 379 or Section 380 or Section 381 or Section 404 or Section 420 of the Indian Penal Code (45 of 1860) or any offence punishable with imprisonment for not more than two years, or with fine, or with both, under the Indian Penal Code or any other law, and no previous conviction is proved against him and the court by which the person is found guilty is of opinion that, having regard to the circumstances of the case including the nature of the offence and the character of the offender, it is expedient so to do, then notwithstanding anything contained in any other law for the time being in force, the court may, instead of sentencing him to any punishment or releasing him on probation of good conduct under Section 4, release him after due admonition.

EXPLANATION. For the purposes of this Section, previous conviction against a person shall include any previous order made against him under this Section or Section 4.

4. Power of court to release certain officers on probation of good conduct.

(1) When any person is found guilty of having committed an offence not punishable with death or imprisonment for life and the court by which the person is found guilty is of opinion that, having regard to the circumstances of the case including the nature of the offence and the character of the offender, it is expedient to release him on probation of good conduct, then, notwithstanding anything contained in any other law for the time being in force, the court may, instead of sentencing him at once to any punishment direct that he be released on his entering into a bond, with or without sureties, to appear and receive sentence when called upon during such period, not exceeding three years, as the court may direct and in the meantime to keep the peace and be of good behaviour:

PROVIDED that the court shall not direct such release of an offender unless it is satisfied that the offender or his surety, if any, has a fixed place of abode or regular occupation in the place over which the court exercises jurisdiction or in which the offender is likely to live during the period for which he enters into the bond.

(2) Before making any order under sub-section (1), the court shall take into consideration the report, if any, of the probation officer concerned in relation to the case.

(3) When an order under sub-section (1) is made, the court may, if it is of opinion that in the interests of the offender and of the public it is expedient so to do, in addition pass a supervision order directing that the offender shall remain under the supervision of a probation officer named in the order during such period, not being less than one year, as may be specified therein, and may in such supervision order impose such conditions as it deems necessary for the due supervision of the offender.

(4) The court making a supervision order under sub-section (3) shall require the offender, before he is released, to enter into a bond, with or without sureties, to observe the conditions specified in such order and such additional conditions with respect to residence, abstention from intoxicants or any other matter as the court may, having regard to the particular circumstances, consider fit to impose for preventing a repetition of the same offence or a commission of other offences by the offender.

(5) The court making a supervision order under sub-section (3) shall explain to the offender the terms and conditions of the order and shall forthwith furnish one copy of the supervision order to each of the offenders, the sureties, if any, and the probation officer concerned.

5. Power of court to require released offenders to pay compensation and costs.

(1) The Court directing the release of an offender under Section 3 or Section 4, may, if it thinks fit, make at the same time a further order directing him to pay-

(a) such compensation as the court thinks reasonable for loss or injury caused to any person by the commission of the offence; and

(b) such costs of the proceedings as the court thinks reasonable.

(2) The amount ordered to be paid under sub-section (1) may be recovered as a fine in accordance with the provisions of Sections 386 and 387 of the Code.

(3) A civil court trying any suit, arising out of the same matter for which the offender is prosecuted, shall take into account any amount paid or recovered as compensation under sub-section (1) in awarding damages.

6. Restrictions on imprisonment of offenders under twenty-one years of age.

(1) When any person under twenty-one years of age is found guilty of having committed an offence punishable with imprison-ment (but not with imprisonment for life), the court by which the person is found guilty shall not sentence him to imprisonment unless it is satisfied that, having regard to the circumstances of the case including the nature of the offence and the character of the offender, it would not be desirable to deal with him under Section 3 or Section 4, and if the court passes any sentence of imprisonment on the offender, it shall record its reasons for doing so.

(2) For the purpose of satisfying itself whether it would not be desirable to deal under Section 3 or Section 4 with an offender referred to in sub-section (1), the court shall call for a report from the probation officer and consider the report, if any, and any other information available to it relating to the character and physical and mental condition of the offender.

7. Report of probation officer to be confidential. The report of a probation officer referred to in sub-section (2) of Section 4 or sub-section (2) of Section 6 shall be treated as confidential:

PROVIDED that the court may, if it so thinks fit, communicate the substance thereof to the offender and may give him an opportunity of producing such evidence as may be relevant to the matter stated in the report.

8. Variation of conditions of probation.

(1) If, on the application of a probation officer, any court which passes an order under Section 4 in respect of an offender is of opinion that in the interests of the offender and the public it is expedient or necessary to vary the conditions of any bond entered into by the offender, it may, at any time during the period when the bond is effective, vary the bond by extending or diminishing the duration thereof so, however, that it shall not exceed three years from the date of the original order or by altering the conditions thereof or by inserting additional conditions therein:

PROVIDED that no such variation shall be made without giving the offender and the surety or sureties mentioned in the bond an opportunity of being heard.

(2) If any surety refuses to consent to any variation proposed to be made under sub-section (1), the court may require the offender to enter into a fresh bond and if the offender refuses or fails to do so, the court may sentence him for the offence of which he was found guilty.

(3) Notwithstanding anything hereinbefore contained, the court which passes an order under Section 4 in respect of an offender may, if it is satisfied on an application made by the probation officer, that the conduct of the offender has been such as to make it unnecessary that he should be kept any longer under supervision, discharge the bond or bonds entered into by him.

9. Procedure in case of offender failing to observe conditions of bond.

(1) If the court which passes an order under Section 4 in respect of an offender or any court which could have dealt with the offender in respect of his original offence has reason to believe, on the report of a probation officer or otherwise, that the offender has failed to observe any of the conditions of the bond or bonds entered into by him, it may issue a warrant for his arrest or may, if it thinks fit, issue a summons to him and his sureties, if any, requiring him or them to attend before it at such time as may be specified in the summons.

(2) The court before which an offender is so brought or appears may either remand him to custody until the case is concluded or it may grant him bail, with or without surety, to appear on the date which it may fix for hearing.

(3) If the court, after hearing the case, is satisfied that the offender has failed to observe any of the conditions of the bond or bonds entered into by him, it may forthwith-

(a) sentence him for the original offence; or

(b) where the failure is for the first time, then, without prejudice to the continuance in force of the bond, impose upon him a penalty not exceeding fifty rupees.

(4) If a penalty imposed under clause (b) of sub-section (3) is not paid within such period as the court may fix, the court may sentence the offender for the original offence.

10. Provision as to sureties. The provisions of Sections 122, 126, 126A, 406A, 514, 514A, 514B and 515 of the Code shall, so far as may be, apply in the case of bonds and sureties given under this Act.

11. Courts competent to make order under the Act, appeal and revision and powers of courts in appeal and revision.

(1) Notwithstanding anything contained in the Code or any other law, an order under this Act may be made by any court empowered to try and sentence the offender to imprisonment and also by the High Court or any other court when the case comes before it on appeal or in revision.

(2) Notwithstanding anything contained in the Code, where an order under Section 3 or Section 4 is made by any court trying the offender (other than a High Court), an appeal shall lie to the court to which appeals ordinarily lie from the sentences of the former court.

(3) In any case where any person under twenty-one years of age is found guilty of having committed an offence and the court by which he is found guilty declines to deal with him under Section 3 or Section 4, and passes against him any sentence of imprisonment with or without fine from which no appeal lies or is preferred, then, notwithstanding anything contained in the Code or any other law, the court to which appeals ordinarily lie from the sentences of the former court may, either of its own motion or on an application made to it by the convicted person or the probation officer, call for and examine the record of the case and pass such order thereon as it thinks fit.

(4) When an order has been made under Section 3 or Section 4 in respect of an offender, the Appellate Court or the High Court in the exercise of its power of revision may set aside such order and in lieu thereof pass sentence on such offender according to law: Provided that the Appellate Court or the High Court in revision shall not inflict a greater punishment than might have been inflicted by the court by which the offender was found guilty.

12. Removal of disqualification attaching to conviction. Notwithstanding anything contained in any other law, a person found guilty of an offence and dealt with under the provisions of Section 3 or Section 4 shall not suffer disqualification, if any, attaching to a conviction of an offence under such law:

PROVIDED that nothing in this Section shall apply to a person who, after his release under Section 4, is subsequently sentenced for the original offence.

13. Probation officers.

(1) A probation officer under this Act shall be-

(a) a person appointed to be a probation officer by the State Government or recognised as such by the State Government; or

(b) a person provided for this purpose by a society recognised in this behalf by the State Government; or

(c) in any exceptional case, any other person who, in the opinion of the court, is fit to act as a probation officer in the special circumstances of the case.

(2) A court which passes an order under Section 4 or the district magistrate of the district in which the offender for the time being resides may, at any time, appoint any probation officer in the place of the person named in the supervision order. Explanation.-For the purposes of this Section, a presidency town shall be deemed to be a district and chief presidency magistrate shall be deemed to be the district magistrate of that district.

(3) A probation officer, in the exercise of his duties under this Act, shall be subject to the control of the district magistrate of the district in which the offender for the time being resides.

14. Duties of probation officers. A probation officer shall, subject to such conditions and restrictions, as may be prescribed,-

(a) inquire, in accordance with any directions of a court, into the circumstances or home surroundings of any person accused of an offence with a view to assist the court in determining the most suitable method of dealing with him and submit reports to the court;

(b) supervise probationers and other persons placed under his supervision and, where necessary, endeavour to find them suitable employment;

(c) advise and assist offenders in the payment of compensation or costs ordered by the court;

(d) advise and assist, in such cases and in such manner as may be prescribed, persons who have been released under Section 4; and

(e) perform such other duties as may be prescribed.

15. Probation officers to be public servants. Every probation officer and every other officer appointed in pursuance of this Act shall, be deemed to be public servants within the meaning of Section 21 of the Indian Penal Code (45 of 1860).

16. Protection of action taken in good faith. No suit or other legal proceeding shall lie against the State Government or any probation officer or any other officer appointed under this Act in respect of anything which is in good faith done or intended to be done in pursuance of this Act or of any rules or orders made thereunder.

17. Power to make rules.

(1) The State Government may, with the approval of the Central Government, by notification in the Official Gazette, make rules to carry out the purposes of this Act.

(2) In particular, and without prejudice to the generality of the foregoing power, such rules may provide for all or any of the following matters, namely:-

   (a) appointment of probation officers, the terms and conditions of their service and the area within which they are to exercise jurisdiction;

   (b) duties of probation officers under this Act and the submission of reports by them;

   (c) the conditions on which societies may be recognised for the purposes of clause (b) of sub-section (1) of Section 13;

   (d) the payment of remuneration and expenses to probation officers or of a subsidy to any society which provides probation officers; and

   (e) any other matter which is to be, or may be, prescribed.

(3) All rules made under this Section shall be subject to the condition of previous publication and shall, as soon as may be after they are made, be laid before the State Legislature.

18. Saving of operation of certain enactments. Nothing in this Act shall affect the provisions of Section 31 of the Reformatory Schools Act, 1897 (8 of 1897), or sub-section (2) of Section 5 of the Prevention of Corruption Act, 1947 (2 of 1947), or of any law in force in any State relating to juvenile offenders or borstal schools.

19. Section 562 of the Code not to apply in certain areas. Subject to the provisions of Section 18, Section 562 of the Code shall cease to apply to the States or parts thereof in which this Act is brought into force.

❑❑❑

31

The Smugglers and Foreign Exchange Manipulators (Forfeiture of Property Act 1976)

ACT NO. 13 OF 1976 [25TH JANUARY, 1976]

AN ACT to provide for the forfeiture of illegally acquired properties of smugglers and foreign exchange manipulators and for matters connected therewith or incidental thereto.

WHEREAS for the effective prevention of smuggling activities and foreign exchange manipulations which are having a deleterious effect on the national economy it is necessary to deprive persons engaged in such activities and manipulations of their ill-gotten gains;

AND WHEREAS such persons have been augmenting such gains by violations of wealth-tax, income-tax or other laws or by other means and have thereby been increasing their resources for operating in a clandestine manner;

AND WHEREAS such persons have in many cases been holding the properties acquired by them through such gains in the names of their relatives, associates and confidants;

Be it enacted by Parliament in the Twenty-sixth Year of the Republic of India as follows:-

1. Short title, extent and commencement.

(1) This Act may be called the Smugglers and Foreign Exchange Manipulators (Forfeiture of Property) Act, 1976.

(2) It extends to the whole of India except the State of Jammu and Kashmir.

(3) It shall be deemed to have come into force on the 5th day of November, 1975.

2. Application.

(1) The provisions of this Act shall apply only to the persons specified in sub-section (2).

(2) The persons referred to in sub-section (1) are the following, namely:-

(a) every person-

(i) who has been convicted under the Sea Customs Act, 1878 (8 of 1878), or the Customs Act, 1962 (52 of 1962), of an offence in relation to goods of a value exceeding one lakh of rupees; or

(ii) who has been convicted under the Foreign Exchange Regulation Act, 1947 (7 of 1947), or the Foreign Exchange Regulation Act, 1973 (46 of 1973), of an offence, the amount or value involved in which exceeds one lakh of rupees; or

(iii) who having been convicted under the Sea Customs Act, 1878 (8 of 1878), or the Customs Act, 1962 (52 of 1962), has been convicted subsequently under either of those Acts; or

(iv) who having been convicted under the Foreign Exchange Regulation Act, 1947 (7 of 1947), or the Foreign Exchange Regulation Act, 1973 (46 of 1973), has been convicted subsequently under either of those Acts;

(b) every person in respect of whom an order of detention has been made under the Conservation of Foreign Exchange and Prevention of Smuggling Activities Act, 1974 (52 of 1974); Provided that-

(i) such order of detention, being an order to which the provisions of Section 9 or Section 12A of the said Act do not apply, has not been revoked on the report of the Advisory Board under Section 8 of the said Act or before the receipt of the report of the Advisory Board or before making a reference to the Advisory Board; or

(ii) such order of detention, being an order to which the provisions of Section 9 of the said Act apply, has not been revoked before the expiry of the time for, or on the basis of, the review under sub-section (3) of Section 9, or on the report of the Advisory Board under Section 8, read with sub-section (2) of Section 9, of the said Act; or

(iii) such order of detention, being an order to which, the provisions of Section 12A of the said Act apply, has not been revoked before the expiry of the time for, or on the basis of, the first review under sub-section (3) of that Section, or on the basis of the report of the Advisory Board under Section 8, read with sub-section (6) of Section 12A, of that Act; or

(iv) such order of detention has not been set aside by a court of competent jurisdiction;

(c) every person who is a relative of a person referred to in clause (a) or clause (b);

(d) every associate of a person referred to in clause (a) or clause (b);

(e) any holder (hereafter in this clause referred to as the present holder) of any property which was at any time previously held by a person referred to in clause (a) or clause (b) unless the present holder or, as the case may be, any one who held such property after such person and before the present holder, is or was a transferee in good faith for adequate consideration.

EXPLANATION 1: For the purposes of sub-clause (i) of clause (a), the value of any goods in relation to which a person has been convicted of an offence shall be the wholesale price of the goods in the ordinary course of trade in India as on the date of the commission of the offence.

EXPLANATION 2: For the purposes of clause (c), "relative", in relation to a person, means-

(i) spouse of the person;

(ii) brother or sister of the person;

(iii) brother or sister of the spouse of the person;

(iv) any lineal ascendant or descendant of the person;

(v) any lineal ascendant or descendant of the spouse of the person;

(vi) spouse of a person referred to in clause (ii), clause (iii), clause (iv) or clause (v);

(vii) any lineal descendant of a person referred to in clause (ii) or clause (iii).

EXPLANATION 3: For the purposes of clause (d), "associate", in relation to a person, means-

(i) any individual who had been or is residing in the residential premises (including outhouses) of such person;

(ii) any individual who had been or is managing the affairs or keeping the accounts of such person;

(iii) any association of persons, body of individuals, partnership firm, or private company within the meaning of the Companies Act, 1956 (1 of 1956), of which such person had been or is a member, partner or director;

(iv) any individual who had been or is a member, partner or director of an association of persons, body of individuals, partnership firm or private company referred to in clause (iii) at any time when such person had been or is a member, partner or director of such association, body, partnership firm or private company;

(v) any person who had been or is managing the affairs, or keeping the accounts, of any association of persons, body of individuals, partnership firm or private company referred to in clause (iii);

(vi) the trustee of any trust, where-

  (a) the trust has been created by such person; or

  (b) the value of the assets contributed by such person (including the value of the assets, if any, contributed by him earlier) to

the trust amounts, on the date on which the contribution is made, to not less than twenty per cent. of the value of the assets of the trust on that date;

(vii) where the competent authority, for reasons to be recorded in writing, considers that any properties of such person are held on his behalf by any other person, such other person.

EXPLANATION 4. For the avoidance of doubt, it is hereby provided that the question whether any person is a person to whom the provisions of this Act apply may be determined with reference to any facts, circumstances or events (including any conviction or detention) which occurred or took place before the commencement of this Act.

Act not to apply to certain persons. Act not to apply to certain persons.

2A. On and from the commencement of the provisions of Chapter VA of the Narcotic Drugs andPsychotropic Substance

3. Definitions.

(1) In this Act, unless the context otherwise requires-

(a) "Appellate Tribunal" means the Appellate Tribunal for Forfeited Property constituted under Section 12;

(b) "competent authority" means an officer of the Central Government authorised by it under sub-section (1) of Section 5 to perform the functions of a competent authority under this Act;

(c) "illegally acquired property", in relation to any person to whom this Act applies, means-

(i) any property acquired by such person, whether before or after the commencement of this Act, wholly or partly out of or by means of any income, earnings or assets derived or obtained from or attributable to any activity prohibited by or under any law for the time being in force relating to any matter in respect of which Parliament has power to make laws; or

(ii) any property acquired by such person, whether before or after the commencement of this Act, wholly or partly out of or by means of any income, earnings or assets in respect of which any such law has been contravened; or

(iii) any property acquired by such person, whether before or after the commencement of this Act, wholly or partly out of or by means of any income, earnings or assets the source of which cannot be proved and which cannot be shown to be attributable to any act or thing done in respect of any matter in relation to which Parliament has no power to make laws; or

(iv) any property acquired by such person, whether before or after the commencement of this Act, for a consideration, or by any means, wholly or partly traceable to any property referred to in sub-clauses (i) to (iii) or the income or earnings from such property; and includes-

(A) any property held by such person which would have been, in relation to any previous holder thereof, illegally acquired property under this clause if such previous holder had not ceased to hold it, unless such person or any other person who held the property at any time after such previous holder or, where there are two or more such previous holders, the last of such previous holders is or was a transferee in good faith for adequate consideration;

(B) any property acquired by such person, whether before or after the commencement of this Act, for a consideration, or by any means, wholly or partly traceable to any property falling under item (A), or the income or earnings therefrom;

(d) "prescribed" means prescribed by rules made under this Act;

(e) "property" includes any interest in property, movable or immovable;

(f) " trust" includes any other legal obligation.

(2) Any reference in this Act to any law which is not in force in any area shall, in relation to that area, be construed as a reference to the corresponding law, if any, in force in that area.

(3) Any reference in this Act to any officer or authority shall, in relation to any area in which there is no officer or authority with the same designation, be construed as a reference to such officer or authority as may be specified by the Central Government by notification in the Official Gazette.

4. Prohibition of holding illegally acquired property.

(1) As from the commencement of this Act, it shall not be lawful for any person to whom this Act applies to hold any illegally acquired property either by himself or through any other person on his behalf.

(2) Where any person holds any illegally acquired property in contravention of the provisions of sub-section (1), such property shall be liable to be forfeited to the Central Government in accordance with the provisions of this Act.

5. Competent authority.

(1) The Central Government may, by order published in the Official Gazette, authorise as many officers of the Central Government (not below the rank of a Joint Secretary to the Government), as it thinks fit, to Perform the functions of the competent authority under this Act.

(2) The competent authorities shall perform their functions in respect of such persons or classes of persons as the Central Government may, by order, direct.

6. Notice of forfeiture.

(1) If, having regard to the value of the properties held by any person to whom this Act applies, either by himself or through any other person on his behalf, his

known sources of income, earnings or assets, and any other information or material available to it as a result of action taken under Section 18 or otherwise, the competent authority has reason to believe (the reasons for such belief to be recorded in writing) that all or any of such properties are illegally acquired properties. it may serve a notice upon such person (hereinafter referred to as the person affected) calling upon him within such time as may be specified in the notice, which shall not be ordinarily less than thirty days, to indicate the sources of his income, earnings or assets, out of which or by means of which he has acquired such property, the evidence on which he relies and other relevant information and particulars, and to show cause why all or any of such properties, as the case may be, should not be declared to be illegally acquired properties and forfeited to the Central Government under this Act.

(2) Where a notice under sub-section (1) to any specifies any property as being held on behalf of such person by any other person, a copy of the notice shall also be served upon such other person.

7. Forfeiture of property in certain cases.

(1) The competent authority may, after considering the explanation, if any, to the show-cause notice issued under Section 6, and the materials available before it and after giving to the person affected (and in a case where the person affected holds any property specified in the notice through any other person, to such other person also) a reasonable opportunity of being heard, by order, record a finding whether all or any of the properties in question are illegally acquired properties.

(2) Where the competent authority is satisfied that some of the properties referred to in the show-cause notice are illegally acquired properties but is not able to identify specifically such properties then, it shall be lawful for the competent authority to specify the properties which, to the best of its judgment, are illegally acquired properties and record a finding accordingly under sub-section (1).

(3) Where the competent authority records a finding under this Section to the effect that any property is illegally acquired property, it shall declare that such property shall, subject to the provisions of this Act, stand forfeited to the Central Government free from all encumbrances.

(4) where any shares in a company stand forfeited to the Central Government under this Act, then, the company shall, notwithstanding anything contained in the Companies Act, 1956 (1 of 1956), or the articles of association of the company, forthwith register the Central Government as the transferee of such shares.

8. Burden of proof. In any proceedings under this Act, the burden of proving that any property specified in the notice served under Section 6 is not illegally acquired property shall be on the person affected.

9. Fine in lieu of forfeiture.

(1) Where the competent authority makes a declaration that any property stands forfeited to the Central Government under Section 7 and it is a case where

the source of only a part, being less than one-half of the income, earnings or assets with which such property was acquired has not been proved to the satisfaction of the competent authority, it shall make an order giving an option to the person affected to pay, in lieu of forfeiture, a fine equal to one and one-fifth times the value of such part.

EXPLANATION. For the purposes of this sub-section, the value of any part of income, earnings or assets, with which any property has been acquired, shall be,-

(a) in the case of any part of income or earnings, the amount of such part of income or earnings;

(b) in the case of any part of assets, the proportionate part of the full value of the consideration for the acquistion of such assets.

(2) Before making an order imposing a fine under sub-section (1), the per-son affected shall be given a reasonable opportunity of being heard,

(3) Where the person affected pays the fine due under sub-section (1), within such time as may be allowed in that behalf, the competent authority may, by order, revoke the declaration of forfeiture under Section 7 and thereupon such property shall stand released.

10. Procedure in relation to certain trust properties. In the case of any person referred to in clause (vi) of Explanation 3 to sub-section (2) of Section 2, if the competent authority, on the the basis of the information and materials available to it, has reason to believe (the reason for such belief to be recorded in writing) that any property held in trust in illegally acquired property, it may serve a notice upon the author of the trust or, as the case may be, the contributor of thc asscts out of or by mcans of which such propcrty was acquired by the trust and the trustees, calling upon them within such time as may be specified in the notice which shall not ordinarily be less than thirty days, to explain the source of the money or other assets out of or by means of which property was acquired or, as the case may be, the source of the money or other assets which were contributed to the trust for acquiring such property and thereupon such notice shall be deemed to be a notice served under Section 6 and all the other provisions of this Act shall apply accordingly.

Explanation: For the purposes of this Section "illegally acquired property", in relation to any property held in trust, includes-

(i) any property which if it had continued to be held by the author of the trust or the contributor of such property to the trust would have been illegally acquired property in relation to such author or contributor;

(ii) any property acquired by the trust out of any contributions made by any person which would have been illegally acquired property in relation to such person had such person acquired such property out of such contributions.

11. Certain transfers to be null and void. Where after the issue of a notice under Section 6 or under Section 10, any property referred to in the said notice is transferred by any mode whatsoever such transfer shall, for the purposes of the proceedings under this Act, be ignored and if such property is subsequently forfeited to the Central Government under Section 7, then, the transfer of such property shall be deemed to be null and void.

12. Constitution of Appellate Tribunal.

(1) The Central Government may, by notification in the Official Gazette, constitute an Appellate Tribunal to be called the Appellate Tribunal for Forfeited Property consisting of a Chairman and such number of other members (being officers of the Central Government not below the rank of a Joint Secretary to the Government) as the Central Government thinks fit, to be appointed by that Government for hearing appeals against the orders made under Section 7, sub-section (1) of Section 9 or Section 10.

(2) The Chairman of the Appellate Tribunal shall be a person who is or has been or is qualified to be a Judge of the Supreme Court or of a High Court.

(3) The terms and conditions of service of the Chairman and other members shall be such as may be prescribed.

(4) Any person aggrieved by an order of the competent authority made under Section 7, sub-section (1) of Section 9 or Section 10, may, within forty-five days from the date on which the order is served on him, prefer an appeal to the Appellate Tribunal:

PROVIDED that the Appellate Tribunal may entertain any appeal after the said period of forty-five days, but not after sixty days, from the date aforesaid if it is satisfied that the appellant was prevented by sufficient cause from filing the appeal in time.

(5) On receipt of an appeal under sub-section (4), the Appellate Tribunal may, after giving an opportunity to the appellant to be heard if he so desires, and after making such further enquiry as it deems fit, confirm, modify or set aside the order appealed against.

(6) The powers and functions of the Appellate Tribunal may be exercised and discharged by Benches consisting of three members and constituted by the Chairman of the Appellate Tribunal.

(6A) Notwithstanding anything contained in sub-section (6), where the Chairman considers it necessary so to do for the expeditious disposal of appeals under this Section, he may constitute a Bench of two members and a Bench so constituted may exercise and discharge the powers and functions of the Appellate Tribunal:

PROVIDED that if the members of a Bench so constituted differ on any point or points, they shall state the point or points on which they differ and refer the same to a third member (to be specified by the Chairman) for hearing on such point or points and such point or points shall be decided according to the opinion of that member.

(7) the Appellate Tribunal may regulate its own procedure.

(8) On application to the Appellate Tribunal and on payment of the prescribed fee, the Tribunal may allow a party to any appeal or any person authorised in this behalf by such party to inspect at any time during office hours, any relevant records and registers of the Tribunal and obtain a certified copy of any art thereof.

13. Notice or order not to be invalid for error in description. No notice issued or served, no declaration made, and no order passed, under this Act shall be deemed to be invaild by reason of any error in the description of the property or person mentioned therein if such property or person is identifiable from the description so mentioned.

14. Bar of jurisdiction. No order passed or declaration made under this Act shall be appealable except as provided therein and no civil court shall have jurisdiction in respect of any matter which the Appellate Tribunal or any competent authority is empowered by or under this Act to determine and no injunction shall be granted by any court or other authority in respect of any action taken or to be taken in pursuance of any power conferred by or under this Act.

15. Competent authority and Appellate Tribunal to have powers of civil court. The competent authority and the Appellate Tribunal shall have all the powers of a civil court while trying a suit under the Code of Civil Procedure, 1908 (5 of 1908), in respect of the following matters, namely:-

(a) summoning and enforcing the attendance of any person an examining him on oath;

(b) requiring the discovery and production of documents;

(c) receiving evidence on affidavits;

(d) requisitioning any public record or copy thereof from any court or office;

(e) issuing commissions for examination of witnesses or documents;

(f) any other matter which may be prescribed.

16. Information to competent authority.

(1) Notwithstanding anything contained in any other law, the competent authority shall have power to require any officer or authority of the Central Government or a State Government or a local authority to furnishing information in relation to such persons, points or matters as in the opinion of the competent authority will be useful for, or relevant to, the purposes of this Act.

(2) Any officer of the Income-tax Department, the Customs Department or the Central Excise Department or any officer of enforcement appointed under the Foreign Exchange Regulation Act, 1973 (46 of 1973), may furnish *suo motu* any information available with him to the competent authority if in the opinion of the officer such information will be useful to the competent authority for the purposes of this Act.

17. Certain officers to assist competent authority and Appellate Tribunal. For the purposes of any proceedings under this Act, the following officers are hereby empowered and required to assist the competent authority and the Appellate Tribunal, namely:-

(a) officers of the Customs Department;

(b) officers of the Central Excise Department;

(c) officers of the Income-tax Department;

(d) officers of enforcement appointed under the Foreign Exchange Regulation Act, 1973 (46 of 1973);

(e) officers of police;

(f) such other officers of the Central or State Government as are specified by the Central Government in this behalf by notification in the Official Gazette.

18. Power of competent authority to require certain officers to exercise certain powers.

(1) For the purposes of any proceedings under this Act or the initiation of any such proceedings, the competent authority shall have power to cause to be conducted any inquiry, investigation or survey in respect of any person, place, property, assets, documents, books of account or any other relevant matters.

(2) For the purposes referred to in sub-section (1), the competent authority may, having regard to the nature of the inquiry, investigation or survey, require an officer of the Income-tax Department to conduct or cause to be conducted such inquiry, investigation or survey.

(3) Any officer of the Income-tax Department who is conducting or is causing to be conducted any inquiry, investigation or survey required to be conducted under sub-section (2), may, for the purpose of such inquiry, investigation or survey, exercise any power (including the power to authorise the exercise of any power) which may be exercised by him for any purpose under the Income-tax Act, 1961 (43 of 1961), and the provisions of the said Act shall, so far as may be, apply accordingly.

19. Power to take possession.

(1) Where any property has been declared to be forfeited to the Central Government under this Act, or where the person affected has failed to pay the fine due under sub-section (1) of Section 9 within the time allowed therefor under sub-section (3) of that Section, the competent authority may order the person affected as well as any other person who may be in possession of the property to surrender or deliver possession thereof to the competent authority or to any person duly authorised by it in this behalf within thirty days of the service of the order.

(2) If any person refuses or fails to comply with an order made under sub-section (1), the competent authority may take possession of the property and may for that purpose use such force as may be necessary.

(3) Notwithstanding anything contained in sub-section (2), the competent authority may, for the purpose of taking possession of any property referred to in sub-section (1), requisition the service of any police officer to assist the competent authority and it shall be the duty of such officer to comply with such requisition.

20. Rectification of mistakes. With a view to rectifying any mistakes apparent from record, the competent authority or the Appellate Tribunal, as the case may be, may amend any order made by it within a period of one year from the date of the order:

PROVIDED that if any such amendment is likely to affect any person prejudicially, it shall not be made without giving to such person a reasonable opportunity of being heard.

21. Findings under other laws not conclusive for proceedings under this Act. No finding of any officer or authority under any other law shall be conclusive for the purpose of any proceedings under this Act.

22. Service of notices and orders. Any notice or order issued or made under this Act shall be served-

(a) by tendering the notice or order or sending it by registered post to the person for whom it is intended or to his agent;

(b) if the notice or order cannot be served in the manner provided in clause (a), by affixing it on a conspicuous place in the property in relation to which the notice or order is issued or made, or on some conspicuous part of the premises in which the person for whom it is intended is known to have last resided or carried on business or personally worked for gain.

23. Protection of action taken in good faith. No suit, prosecution or other proceeding shall lie against the Central Government or any officers of the Central or State Government for anything which is done or intended to be done, in good faith in pursuance of this Act or the rules made thereunder.

24. Act to have overiding effect. The provisions of this Act shall have effect notwithstanding any thing inconsistent therewith contained in any other law for the time being in force.

25. Provisions of the Act not to apply to certain properties held in trust. Nothing contained in this Act shall apply in relation to any property held by a trust or an institution created or established wholly for public religious or charitable purposes if-

(i) such property has been so held by such trust or institution from a date prior to the commencement of this Act; or

(ii) such property is wholly traceable to any property held by such trust or institution prior to the commencement of this Act.

26. Power to make rules.

(1) The Central Government may, by notification in the Official Gazette, make rules to carry out the provisions of this Act.

(2) In particular and without prejudice to the generality of the foregoing power, such rules may provide for all or any of the following matters, namely:-

(a) the terms and conditions of service of the Chairman and other members of the Appellate Tribunal under sub-section (3) of Section 12;

(aa) the fees which shall be paid for the inspection of the records and registers of the Appellate Tribunal or for obtaining a certified copy of any part thereof under sub-section (8) of Section 12;

(b) the powers of a civil court that may be exercised by the competent authority and the Appellate Tribunal under clause of Section 15;

(c) any other matter which has to be, or may be, prescribed.

(3) Every rule made under this Act shall be laid, as soon as may be after it is made, before each House of Parliament, while it is in session, for a total period of thirty days which may be comprised in one session or in two or more successive sessions, and if, before the expiry of the session immediately following the session or the successive sessions aforesaid, both Houses agree

in making any modification in the rule, or both Houses agree that the rule should not be made, the rule shall thereafter have effect only in such modified form or be of no effect, as the case may be; so, however, that any such modification or annulment shall be without prejudice to the validity of anything previously done under that rule.

27. Repeal and saving.

(1) The Smuggler and Foreign Exchange Manipulators (Forfeiture of Property) Ordinance, 1975 (20 of 1975), is hereby repealed.

(2) Notwithstanding such repeal, anything done or any action taken under the Ordinance so repealed shall be deemed to have been done or taken under the corresponding provisions of this Act.

❑❑❑

32

The Supreme Court (Enlargement of Criminal Appellate Jurisdiction) Act, 1970

Act No. 28 of 1970 [9th August, 1970]

AN ACT to Enlarge the Appellate Jurisdiction of The Supreme Court in Regard to [9th August, 1970].

Be it enacted by Parliament in the Twenty- first Year of the Republic of India as follows:-

1. Short title and extent.

(1) This Act may be called the Supreme Court (Enlargement of Criminal Appellate Jurisdiction) Act, 1970.

(2) It extends to the whole of India.

2. Enlarged appellate jurisdiction of Supreme Court in regard to criminal matters. Without prejudice to the powers conferred on the Supreme Court by clause (1) of article 134 of the Constitution, an appeal shall lie to the Supreme Court from any judgment, final order of sentence in a criminal proceeding of a High Court in the territory of India if the High Court-

(a) has on appeal reversed an order of acquittal of an accused person and sentenced him to imprisonment for life or to imprisonment for a period of not less than ten years;

(b) has withdrawn for trial before itself any case from any court subordinate to its authority and has in such trial convicted the accused person and sentenced him to imprisonment for life or to imprisonment for a period of not less than ten years.

❑❑❑

33

The Terrorist and Disruptive Activities (Prevention) Act, 1987

AN ACT to make special provisions for the prevention of, and for coping with, terrorist and disruptive activities and for matters connected therewith or incidental thereto.

Be it enacted by Parliament in the Thirty-eighth year of the Republic of India as follows:-

CHAPTER - I : PRELIMINARY

1. Short title, extent, application, commencement, duration and savings.

(1) This Act may be called the Terrorist and Disruptive Activities (Prevention) Act, 1987.

(2) It extends to the whole of India, and it applies also, -

a. to citizens of India outside India;

b. to persons in the service of the Government, wherever they may be; and

c. to persons on ships and aircraft registered in India, wherever they may be.

(3) Sections 5, 15, 21 and 22 shall come into force at once and the remaining provisions of this Act shall be deemed to have come into force on the 24th day of May, 1987.

(4) It shall remain in force for a period of eight years from the 24th day of May, 1987, but its expiry under the operation of this sub-section shall not affect, -

(a) the previous operation of, or anything duly done or suffered under this Act or any rule made thereunder or any order made under any such rule, or

(b) any right, privilege, obligation or liability acquired accrued or incurred under this Act or any rule made thereunder or any order made under any such rule, or

(c) any penalty, forfeiture or punishment incurred in respect of any offence under this Act or any contravention of any rule made under this Act or of any order made under any such rule, or

(d) any investigation, legal proceeding or remedy in respect of any such right, privilege, obligation, liability, penalty, forfeiture or punishment as aforesaid.

and any such investigation, legal proceeding or remedy may be instituted, continued or enforced and any such penalty, forfeiture or punishment may be imposed as if this Act had not expired.

2. Definitions.

(1) In this Act, unless the context otherwise requires, -

(a) "*abet*", with its grammatical variations and cognate expressions, includes,-

i. the communication or association with any person or class of persons who is engaged in assisting in any manner terrorists or disruptionists;

ii. the passing on, or publication of, without any lawful authority, and information likely to assist the terrorists or disruptionists, and the passing on, or publication of, or distribution of, any document or matter obtained from terrorists or disruptionists;

iii. the rendering of any assistance, whether financial or otherwise, the terrorists or disruptionists;

(b) "*Code*" means the Code of Criminal Procedure 1973 (2 of 1974);

(c) "*Designated Court*" means a Designated Court constituted under Section 9;

(d) "*Disruptive activity*" has the meaning assigned to it in Section 4, and the expression "disruptionist" shall be construed accordingly;

(e) "*High Court*" means the High Court of the State in which a judge or an additional judge of a Designated Court was working immediately before his appointment as such judge or additional judge;

(f) "*notified area*" means such area as the State Government may, by notification in the Official Gazette, specify;

(g) "*public prosecutor*" means a Public Prosecutor or an Additional Public Prosecutor or a Special Public Prosecutor appointed under Section 13, and includes any person acting under the directions of the Public Prosecutor;

(gg) "*property*" means property and assets of any description, whether corporeal or incorporeal, movable or immovable, tangible or intangible and deeds and instruments evidencing title to, or interest in, such property or assets, derived or obtained from the terrorist Act and includes proceeds of terrorism;

(h) "*terrorist act*" has the meaning assigned to it in sub-section (1) of Section 3, and the expression "terrorist" shall be construed accordingly;

(i) words and expressions used but not defined in this Act and defined in the Code shall have the meaning respectively assigned to them in the Code.

(2) Any reference in this Act to any enactment or any provision thereof shall, in relation to an area in which such enactment or such provision is not in force, be construed as a reference to the corresponding law or the relevant provision of the corresponding law, if any, in force in that area.

CHAPTER - II : PUNISHMENTS FOR, AND MEASURES FOR COPING WITH, TERRORIST AND DISRUPTIVE ACTIVITIES

3. Punishment for terrorist acts.

(1) Whoever with intent to overawe the Government as by law established or to strike terror in the people or any section of the people or to alienate any section of the people or to adversely affect the harmony amongst different sections of the people does any act or thing by using bombs, dynamite or other explosive substances or inflammable substances or lethal weapons or poisons or noxious gases or other chemicals or by any other substances (whether biological or otherwise) of a hazardous nature in such a manner as to cause, or as is likely to cause, death of, or injuries to, any person or persons or loss of, or damage to, or destruction of, property or disruption of any supplies or services essential to the life of the community, or detains any person and threatens to kill or injure such person in order to compel the Government or any other person to do or abstain from doing any act, commits a terrorist act.

(2) Whoever commits a terrorist act, shall, -

(i) if such act has resulted in the death of any person, be punishable with death or imprisonment for life and shall also be liable to fine;

(ii) in any other case, be punishable with imprisonment for a term which shall not be less than five years but which may extend to imprisonment for life and shall also be liable to fine.

(3) Whoever conspires or attempts to commit, or advocates, abets, advises or incites or knowingly facilitates the commission of, a terrorist act or any act preparatory to a terrorist act, shall be punishable with imprisonment for a term which shall not be less than five years but which may extend to imprisonment for life and shall also be liable to fine.

(4) Whoever harbours or conceals, or attempts to harbour or conceal, any terrorist shall be punishable with imprisonment for a term which shall not be less than five years but which may extend to imprisonment for life and shall also be liable to fine.

(5) Any person who is a member of a terrorists gang or a terrorist organisation, which is involved in terrorist acts, shall be punishable with imprisonment for a term which shall not be less than five years but which may extend to imprisonment for life and shall also be liable to fine.

(6) Whoever holds any property derived or obtained from commission of any terrorist act or has been acquired through the terrorist funds shall be punishable with imprisonment for a term which shall not be less than five years but which may extend to imprisonment for life and shall also be liable to fine.

4. Punishment for disruptive activities.

(1) Whoever commits or conspires or attempts to commit or abets, advocates, advises, or knowingly facilitates the commission of, any disruptive activity or any act preparatory to a disruptive activity shall be punishable with imprisonment for a term which shall not be less than five years but which may extend to imprisonment for life and shall also be liable to fine.

(2) For the purposes of sub-section (1), "disruptive activity" means any action taken, whether by act or by speech or through any other media or in any other manner whatsoever, -

(i) which questions, disrupts or is intended to disrupt, whether directly or indirectly, the sovereignty and territorial integrity of India; or

(ii) which is intended to bring about or supports any claim, whether directly or indirectly, for the cession of any part of India or the secession of any part of India from the Union.

EXPLANATION: For the purposes of this sub-section, -

(a) "cession" includes the admission of any claim of any foreign country to any part of India, and

(b) "secession" includes the assertion of any claim to determine whether a part of India will remain within the Union.

(3) Without prejudice to the generality of the provisions of sub-section (2), it is hereby declared that any action taken, whether by act or by speech or through any other media or in any other manner whatsoever, which -

(a) advocates, advises, suggests or incites; or

(b) predicts, prophesies or pronounces or otherwise expresses, in such manner as to incite, advice, suggest or prompt, the killing or the destruction of any person bound by oath under the constitution to uphold the sovereignty and integrity of India or any public servant shall be deemed to be a disruptive activity within the meaning of this section.

(4) Whoever harbours or conceals, or attempts to harbour or conceal, any disruptionist shall be punishable with imprisonment for a term which shall not be less than five years but which may be extend to imprisonment for life and shall also be liable to fine.

2. Habeas Corpus – In habeas corpus proceedings if the detention is legal at the time of the disposal of the petition the Court cannot order release of the person detained by issuing a writ of habeas corpus. Therefore, the legality or otherwise of the detention shall also be considered on the date of final disposal of the petition. *Bacha Bora v. State of Assam*, 1991 Cr LJ 2782 (Gau).

5. Possession of certain unauthorised arms, etc. in specified areas. Where any person is in possession of any arms and ammunition specified in Columns 2 and 3 of Category I or Category III (a) of Schedule I to the Arms Rules, 1962, or bombs, dynamite or other explosive substances unauthorisedly in a notified area, he shall, notwithstanding anything contained in any other law for the time being in force, be punishable with imprisonment for a term which shall not be less than five years but which may extend to imprisonment for life and shall also be liable to fine.

6. Enhanced penalties.

(1) If any person with intend to aid any terrorist or disruptionist, contravenes any provision of, or any rule made under the Arms Act, 1959, the Explosives Act, 1884, the Explosives Substances Act, 1908 or the Inflammable Substances Act, 1952, he shall, notwithstanding anything contained in any of the aforesaid Acts or the rules made thereunder, be punishable with imprisonment for a term which shall not be less than five years but which may extend to imprisonment for life and shall also be liable to fine.

(2) For the purposes of this section, any person who attempts to contravene or abets, or attempts to abet, or does any act preparatory to the contravention of any provision of any law, rule or order, shall be deemed to have contravened that provision, and the provision of sub-section (1) shall, in relation to such person, have effect subject to the modification that the reference to "imprisonment for life" shall be construed as a reference to "imprisonment for ten years".

7. Conferment of powers.

(1) Notwithstanding anything contained the Code or in any other provision of this Act, the Central Government may, if it considers it necessary or expedient so to do, –

(a) for the prevention of, and for coping with, any offence under Section 3 or Seciton 4; or

(b) for any case or class or group of cases under Section 3 or Section 4;

in any State or part thereof, confer, by notification in the official Gazette, on any officer of the Central Government, powers exercisable by a police officer under the Code in such State or part thereof or, as the case may be, for such case or class or group of cases and in particular, the powers of arrest, investigation and prosecution of persons before any Court.

(2) All officers of police and all officers of Government are hereby required and empowered to assist the officer of the Central Government referred to in sub-section (1), in the execution of the provisions of this Act or any rule or order made thereunder.

(3) The provisions of the Code shall, so far as may be and subject to such modifications made in this Act, apply to the exercise of the powers by an officer under sub-section (1).

7-A. Powers of investigating officers. If an officer investigating an offence committed under this Act has reason to believe that any property in relation to which an investigation is being conducted is a property derived or obtained from the commission of any terrorist act and includes proceeds of terrorism he shall, with the approval of the Superintendent of Police, make an order seizing such property and where it is not practicable to seize such property, he may make an order of attachment directing that such property shall not be transferred or otherwise dealt with except with the prior permission of the officer making such order, or of the Designated Court and a copy of such order shall be served on the persons concerned:

PROVIDED that the investigating officer shall duly inform the Designated Court within forty-eight hours of the attachment of such property and the said Court shall either confirm or revoke the order of attachment so issued.

8. Forfeiture of property of certain persons.

(1) Where a person has been convicted to any offence punishable under this Act or any rule made thereunder, the Designated Court may, in addition to awarding any punishment, by order in writing, declare that any property, movable or immovable or both, belonging to the accused and specified in the order, shall stand forfeited to the Government free from all encumbrances.

(2) Where any person is accused of any offence under this Act or any rule made thereunder, it shall be open to the Designated Court trying him to pass an order that all or any properties, movable or immovable or both belonging to him, shall, during the period of such trial, be attached, and where such trial ends in conviction, the properties so attached shall stand forfeited to Government free from all encumbrances.

(3) (a) If upon a report in writing made by a police officer or an officer referred to in sub-section (1) of Section 7, any Designated Court has reason to believe that any person, who has committed an offence punishable under this Act or any rule made thereunder, has absconded or is concealing himself so that he may not be apprehended, such court may, notwithstanding anything contained in Section 82 of the Code, publish a written proclamation requiring him to appear at a specified place and at a specified time not less than fifteen days but not more than thirty days from the date of publication of such proclamation.

(b) The Designated Court issuing a proclamation under Clause (a) may, at any time, order the attachment of any property, movable or immovable or both, belonging to the proclaimed person, and thereupon the provisions of Sections 83 to 85 of the Code shall apply to such attachment as if such attachment were made under that Code.

(c) If, within six months from the date of the attachment, any person, whose property is, or has been, at the disposal of the Government under sub-section (2) of Section 85 of the code, appears voluntarily or is apprehended and brought before the Designated Court by whose order the property was attached, or the Court to which such Court is subordinate, and proves to the satisfaction of such Court that he did not abscond or conceal himself for the purpose of avoiding apprehension and that he had not received such notice of the proclamation as to enable him to attend within the time specified therein, such property or, if the same has been sold, the net proceeds of the sale and the residue of the property, shall, after satisfying therefrom all costs incurred in consequence of the attachment, be delivered to him.

(4) Where any shares in a company stand forfeited to the Government under this sub-section, then, the company shall, notwithstanding anything contained in the Companies Act, 1956, or the articles of association the company, forthwith register the Government as the transferee of such shares.

CHAPTER - III : DESIGNATED COURTS

9. Designated Courts.

(1) The Central Government or a State Government may, by notification in the official Gazette, constitute one or more Designated Courts for such area or areas, or for such case or class or group of cases as may be specified in the notification.

(2) Where a notification constituting a Designated Court for any area or areas or for any case or class or group of cases is issued by the Central Government under sub-section (1), and a notification constituting a Designated Court for the same area or areas or for the same case or class or group of cases has also been issued by a State Government under that sub-section, the Designated Court constituted by the Central Government, whether the notification constituting such Court is issued before or after the issue of the notification constituting the Designated Court by the State Government, shall have, and the Designated Court constituted by the State Government shall not have, jurisdiction to try any offence committed in that area or areas or, as the case may be, the case or class or group of cases, and all cases pending before any Designated Court constituted by the State Government shall stand transferred to the Designated Court constituted by the Central Government.

(3) Where any question arises as to the jurisdiction of any Designated Court, it shall be referred to the Central Government whose decision thereon shall be final.

(4) A Designated Court shall be presided over by a Judge to be appointed by the Central Government or, as the case may be, the State Government, with the concurrence of the Chief Justice of the High Court.

(5) The Central Government or, as the case may be, the State Government may also appoint, with the concurrence of the Chief Justice of the High Court additional Judges to exercise jurisdiction in a Designated Court.

(6) A person shall not be qualified for appointment as a Judge or an additional Judge of a Designated Court unless he is, immediately before such appointment a Sessions Judge or an additional Sessions Judge in any State.

(7) For the removal of doubts, it is hereby provided that the attainment by a person appointed a judge or an Additional Judge of a Designated Court of the age of superannuation under the rules applicable to him in the service to which he belongs, shall not affect his continuance as such Judge or Additional Judge.

(8) Where any Additional Judge or Additional Judges is or are appointed in a Designated Court, the Judge of the Designated Court may, from time to time, by general or special order, in writing, provide for the distribution of business of the Designated Court among himself and the additional Judge or Additional Judges and also for the disposal of urgent business in the event of his absence or the absence of any Additional Judge.

10. Place of sitting. A Designated Court may, on its own motion or on an application made by the Public Prosecutor, and if it considers it expedient or desirable so to do, sit for any of its proceedings at any place, other than its ordinary place of sitting :

PROVIDED that nothing in this section shall be construed to change the place of sitting of a Designated Court constituted by a State Government to any place outside that State.

11. Jurisdiction of Designated Courts.

(1) Notwithstanding anything contained in the Code, every offence punishable under any provision of this Act or any rule made thereunder shall be triable only by the Designated Court within whose local jurisdiction it was committed or, as the case may be, by the Designated Court constituted for trying such offcncc under sub-section (1) of Section 9.

(2) If, having regard to the exigencies of the situation prevailing in a State, the Central Government is of the opinion that, -

(a) the situation prevailing in such State is not conducive to a fair, impartial or speedy trial, or

(b) it is not likely to be feasible without occasioning the breach of peace or grave risk to the safety of the accused, the witnesses, the Public Prosecutor and the Judge of the Designated Court or any of them, or

(c) it is not otherwise in the interests of justice,

It may, with the concurrence of the Chief Justice of India (such occurrence to be obtained on a motion moved in that behalf by the Attorney-General), transfer any case pending before a Designated Court in that State to any other Designated Court within that State or in any other State.

(3) Where the whole or any part of the area within the local limits of the jurisdiction of a Designated Court has been declared to be, or forms part of, any area which has been declared to be a disturbed area under any enactment for the time being in force making provision for the suppression of disorder and restoration and maintenance of public order, and the Central Government is of opinion that the situation prevailing in the State is not conducive to fair, impartial or

speedy trial within the State, of offences under this Act or the rules made thereunder which such Designated Court is competent to try, the Central Government may, with the concurrence of the Chief Justice of India, specify, by notification in the official Gazette, in relation to such Court (hereafter in this sub-section referred to as the local Court) a Designated Court outside the State (hereinafter in this section referred to as the specified court), and thereupon -

(a) it shall not be competent at any time during the period of operation of such notification, for such local court to exercise any jurisdiction in respect of, or try, any offence under this Act or the rules made thereunder;

(b) the jurisdiction which would have been, but for the issue of such notification, exercisable by such local court in respect of such offences committed during the period of operation of such notification shall be exercisable by the specified court;

(c) all cases relating to such offences pending immediately before the date of issue of such notification before such local court shall stand transferred on that date to the specified court;

(d) all cases taken cognizance of by, or transferred to, the specified court under Clause *(b)* or Clause *(c)* shall be dealt with and tried in accordance with this Act (whether during the period of operation of such notification or thereafter) as if such offences had been committed within the local limits of the jurisdiction of the specified court or, as the case may be, transferred for trial to it under sub-section (2).

EXPLANATION 1: A notification under this sub-section in relation to any local court shall cease to operate on the date on which the whole or, as the case may be, the aforementioned part of the area within the local limits of its jurisdiction, ceases to be a disturbed area.

EXPLANATION 2: For the purposes of this section, "Attorney-General" means the Attorney-General of India or, in his absence, the Solicitor-General of India or, in the absence of both, one of the Additional Solicitors-General of India.

12. Power of Designated Courts with respect to other offences.

(1) When trying any offence, a Designated Court may also try any other offence with which the accused may, under the Code, be charged at the same trial if the offence is connected with such other offence.

(2) If, in the course of any trial under this Act of any offence, it is found that the accused person has committed any other offence under this Act or any rule made thereunder or under any other law, a the Designated Court may convict such person of such other offence and pass any sentence authorised by this Act or such rule or, as the case may be, such other law, for the punishment thereof.

13. Public Prosecutors.

(1) For every Designated Court, the Central Government or, as the case may be, the State Government, shall appoint a person to be the Public Prosecutor and

may appoint one or more persons to be the Additional Public Prosecutor or Additional Public Prosecutors; provided that the Central Government or, as the case may be, the State Government, may also appoint for any case or class or group of cases a Special Public Prosecutor.

(2) A person shall not be qualified to be appointed as a Public Prosecutor or an Additional Public Prosecutor or a Special Public Prosecutor under this section unless he has been in practice as an Advocate for not less than seven years or has held any post, for a period of not less than seven years, under the Union or a State, requiring special knowledge of law.

(3) Every person appointed as a Public Prosecutor or an Additional Public Prosecutor or a Special Public Prosecutor under this section shall be deemed to be a Public Prosecutor within the meaning of clause *(u)* of Section 2 of the Code and the provisions of the Code shall have effect accordingly.

14. Procedure and powers of Designated Courts.

(1) A Designated Court may take cognizance of any offence, without the accused being committed to it for trial, upon receiving a complaint of facts which constitute such offence or upon a police report of such facts.

(2) Where an offence triable by a Designated Court is punishable with imprisonment for a term not exceeding three years or with fine or with both, the Designated Court may, notwithstanding anything contained in sub-section (1) of Section 260 or Section 262 of the Code, try the offence in a summary way in accordance with the procedure prescribed in the Code and the provisions of Section 263 to 265 of the Code, shall, so far as may be, apply to such trial:

PROVIDED that when, in the course of a summary trial under this sub-section, it appears to the Designated Court that the nature of the case is such that it is undesirable to try it in a summary way, the Designated Court shall recall any witnesses who may have been examined and proceed to re-hear the case in the manner provided by the provisions of the Code for the trial of such offence and the said provisions shall apply to and in relation to a Designated Court as they apply to and in relation to a Magistrate:

PROVIDED FURTHER that in the case of any conviction in a summary trial under this section, it shall be lawful for a Designated Court to pass a sentence of imprisonment for a term not exceeding two years.

(3) Subject to the other provisions of this Act, a Designated Court shall, for the purpose of trial of any offence, have all the powers of a Court of Session and shall try such offence as if it were a Court of Session so far as may be in accordance with the procedure prescribed in the Code for the trial before a Court of Session.

(4) Subject to the other provisions of this Act, every case transferred to a Designated Court under sub-section (2) of Section 11 shall be dealt with as if such case had been transferred under Section 406 of the Code to such Designated Court.

(5) Nothwithstanding anything contained in the Code, a Designated Court may, if it thinks fit and for reasons to be recorded by it, proceed with the trial in the

absence of the accused or his pleader and record the evidence of any witness, subject to the right of the accused to recall the witness for cross-examination.

15. Certain confessions made to police officers to be taken into consideration.

(1) Nothwithstanding anything in the Code or in the Indian Evidence Act, 1872, but subject to the provisions of this section, a confession made by a person before a police officer not lower in rank than a Superintendent of Police and recorded by such police officer either in writing or on any mechanical device like cassettes, tapes or sound tracks from out of which sounds or images can be reproduced, shall be admissible in the trial of such person or co-accused, abettor or conspirator] for an offence under this Act or rules made thereunder:

PROVIDED that co-accused, abettor or conspirator is charged and tried in the same case together with the accused.

(2) The police officer shall, before recording any confession under sub-section (1), explain to the person making it that he is not bound to make a confession and that, if he does so, it may be used as evidence against him and such police officer shall not record any such confession unless upon questioning the person making it, he has reason to believe that it is being made voluntarily.

16. Protection of witnesses.

(1) Nothwithstanding anything contained in the Code, the proceedings under this Act may be held in *camera* if the Designated Court so desires.

(2) A Designated Court may, on an application made by a witness in any proceedings before it or by the Public Prosecutor in relation to such witness or on its own motion, take such measures as it deems fit for keeping the identity and address of any witness secret.

(3) In particular, and without prejudice to the generality of the provisions of sub-section (2), the measures which a Designated Court may take under that sub-section may include,-

(a) the holding of the proceedings at a place to be decided by the Designated Court;

(b) the avoiding of the mention of the names and addresses of the witnesses in it orders or judgments or in any records of the case accessible to public;

(c) the issuing of any directions for securing that the identity and addresses of the witnesses are not disclosed.

(d) that it is in the public interest to order that all or any of the proceedings pending before such a court shall not be published in any manner.

(4) Any person who contravenes any direction issued under sub-section (3) shall be punishable with imprisonment for a term which may extend to one year and with fine which may extend to one thousand rupees.

17. Trial by Designated Courts to have precedence. The trial under this Act of any offence by a Designated Court shall have precedence over the trial of any other case against the accused in any other court (not being a Designated Court) and shall be concluded in preference to the trial of such other case and accordingly the trial of such other case shall remain in abeyance.

18. Power to transfer cases to regular courts. Where, after taking cognizance of any offence, a Designated Court is of opinion that the offence is not triable by it, it shall, notwithstanding that it has no jurisdiction to try such offence, transfer the case for the trial of such offence to any court having jurisdiction under the Code and the court to which the case is transferred may proceed with the trial of the offence as if it had taken cognizance of the offence.

19. Appeal.

(1) Nothwithstanding anything contained in the Code, an appeal shall lie as a matter of right from any judgment, sentence or order, not being an interlocutory order, of a Designated Court to the Supreme Court both on facts and on law.

(2) Except as aforesaid, no appeal or revision shall lie to any court from any judgment, sentence or order including an interlocutory order of a Designated Court.

(3) Every appeal under this section shall be preferred within a period of thirty days from the date of the judgment; sentence or order appealed from:

PROVIDED that the Supreme Court may entertain an appeal after the expiry of the said period of thirty days if it is satisfied that the appellant had sufficient cause for not preferring the appeal within the period of thirty days.

CHAPTER - IV : MISCELLANEOUS

20. Modified application of certain provisions of the Code.

(1) Nothwithstanding anything contained in the Code or any other law, every offence punishable under this Act or any rule made thereunder shall be deemed to be a cognizable offence within the meaning of clause (c) of Section 2 of the Code, and "cognizable case" as defined in that clause shall be construed accordingly.

(2) Section 21 of the Code shall apply in relation to a case involving an offence punishable under this Act or any rule made thereunder subject to the modification that the reference to "the State Government" therein shall be construed as a reference to "the Central Government or the State Government".

(3) Section 164 of the Code shall apply in relation to a case involving an offence punishable under this Act or any rule made thereunder, subject to the modification that the reference in subsection (1) thereof to "Metropolitan Magistrate or Judicial Magistrate" shall be construed as a reference to "Metropolitan Magistrate, Judicial Magistrate, Executive Magistrate or Special Executive Magistrate.

(4) Section 167 of the Code shall apply in relation to a case involving an offence punishable under this Act or any rule made thereunder subject to the modifications that,-

(a) the reference in sub-section (1) thereof to "Judicial Magistrate" shall be construed as a reference to Judicial Magistrate or Executive Magistrate or Special Executive Magistrate;

(b) the reference in sub-section (2) thereof to "fifteen days," "ninety days" and "sixty days," wherever they occur, shall be construed as references to "sixty days."one hundred and eighty days] and [8][one hundred and eighty days], respectively; and

(bb) sub-section (2-A) thereof shall be deemed to have been omitted.

(bbb) in sub-section (2), after the proviso, the following proviso shall be inserted, namely:-

"PROVIDED FURTHER that, if it is not possible to complete the investigation within the said period of one hundred and eighty days, the Designated Court shall extend the said period up to one year, on the report of the Public Prosecutor indicating the progress of the investigation and the specific reasons for the detention of the accused beyond the said period of one hundred and eighty days.

(5) Section 268 of the Code shall apply in relation to a case involving an offence punishable under this Act or any rule made thereunder subject to the modifications that -

(a) the reference in sub-section(1) thereof –

(i) to "the State Government" shall be construed as a reference to "the Central Government or the State Government";

(ii) to "order of the State Government" shall be construed as a reference to "order of the Central Government or the State Government, as the case may be"; or

(b) the reference in sub-section (2) thereof, to "State Government" shall be construed as a reference to "Central Government or the State Government, as the case may be".

(6) Sections 366 to 371 and Section 392 of the Code shall apply in relation to a case involving an offence triable by a Designated Court subject to the modifications that the references to "Court of Session" and "High Court", wherever occurring therein, shall be construed as references to "Designated Court" and "Supreme Court", respectively.

(7) Nothing in Section 438 of the Code shall apply in relation to any case involving the arrest of any person on an accusation of having committed an offence punishable under this act or any rule made thereunder.

(8) Notwithstanding anything contained in the Code, no person accused of an offence punishable under this Act or any rule made thereunder shall, if in custody, be released on bail or on his own bond unless, –

(a) the Public Prosecutor has been given an opportunity to oppose the application for such release, and

(b) where the Public Prosecutor opposes the application, the Court is satisfied that there are reasonable grounds for believing that he is not guilty of such offence and that he is not likely to commit any offence while on bail.

(9) The limitations on granting of bail specified in sub-section (8) are in addition to the limitations under the Code or any other law for the time being in force on granting of bail.

20-A. Cognizance of offence.

(1) Notwithstanding, anything contained in the Code, no information about the commission of an offence under this Act shall be recorded by the police without the prior approval of the District Superintendent of Police.

(2) No court shall take cognizance of any offence under this Act without the previous sanction of the Inspector-General of Police, or as the case may be, the Commissioner of Police.

21. Presumption as to offences under Section 3.

(1) In a prosecution for an offence under sub-section (1) of Section 3, if it is proved–

(a) that the arms or explosives or any other substances specified in Section 3 were recovered from the possession of the accused and there is reason to believe that such arms or explosives or other substances of similar nature, were used in the commission of such offence; or

(b) that by the evidence of an expert the fingerprints of the accused were found at the site of the offence or on anything including arms and vehicles used in connection with the commission of such offence.

(c) * * *

() * * *

(2) In a prosecution for an offence under sub-section 3 of Section 3, if it is proved that the accused rendered any financial assistance to a person accused of, or reasonably suspected of, an offence under that section, the Designated Court shall presume, unless the contrary is proved, that such person has committed the offence under that sub-section.

22. Identification of accused. Where a person has been declared a proclaimed offender in terrorist case, the evidence regarding his identification by witnesses on the basis of his photograph shall have the same value as the evidence of a test identification parade.

23. Saving.

(1) Nothing in this Act shall affect the jurisdiction exercisable by, or the procedure applicable to, any Court or other authority under any law relating to the naval, military or air forces or other armed forces of the Union.

(2) For the removal of doubts, it is hereby declared that for the purposes of any such law as is referred to in sub-section (1), a Designated Court shall be deemed to be a Court of ordinary criminal justice.

24. Saving as to orders. Where an order purports to have been made and signed by any authority in exercise of any power conferred by or under this Act, a Court shall, within the meaning of the Indian Evidence Act, 1872, presume that such order was so made by that authority.

25. Overriding effect. The provisions of this Act or any rule made thereunder or any order made under any such rule shall have effect notwithstanding anything inconsistent therewith contained in any enactment other than this Act or in any instrument having effect by virtue of any enactment other than this Act.

26. Protection of action taken under this Act. No suit, prosecution or other legal proceeding shall lie against the Central Government or State Government or any other authority on whom powers have been conferred under this Act or any rules made thereunder, for anything which is in good faith done or purported to be done in pursuance of this Act or any rules made thereunder or any order issued under any such rule.

27. Power of the Supreme Court to make rules. The Supreme Court may, by notification in the Official Gazette, make such rules, if any, as it may deem necessary for carrying out the provisions of this Act relating to Designated Court.

28. Power to make rules.

(1) Without prejudice to the powers of the Supreme Court to make rules under Section 27, the Central Government may, by notification in the Official Gazette, make rules for carrying out the provisions of this Act.

(2) In particular, and without prejudice to the generality of the foregoing power, such rules may provide for all or any of the following matters namely:

(a) regulating the conduct of persons in respect of areas the control of which is considered necessary or expedient and the removal of such persons from areas.

(b) The entry into, and search of, -

(i) any vehicle, vessel or aircraft; or

(ii) any place, whatsoever,

reasonably suspected of being used for committing the offence referred to in Section 3 or Section 4 or for manufacturing or storing anything for the commission of any such offence.

(c) Conferring powers upon, –

(i) the Central Government;

(ii) a State Government;

(iii) an Administrator of a Union Territory under Article 239 of the Constitution;

(iv) an officer of the Central Government not lower in rank than of a Joint Secretary; or

(v) an officer of a State Government not lower in rank than that of a District Magistrate, to make general or special orders to prevent or cope with terrorist acts or disruptive activities;

(d) the arrest and trial of persons contravening any of the rules or any order made thereunder;

(e) the punishment of any person who contravenes or attempts to contravene or abets or attempts to abet the contravention of any rule or order made thereunder with imprisonment for a term which may extend to seven years or for a term which may not be less than six months but which may extend to seven years or with fine or with imprisonment as aforesaid and fine;

(f) Providing for the seizure and detention of any property in respect of which such contravention, attempt or abetment as is referred to in Clause (e) has been committed and for the adjudication of such seizure and detention, whether by any court or by any other authority.

29. Rules to be laid before Houses of Parliament. Every rule made by the Central Government under this Act shall be laid, as soon as may be after it is made, before each House of Parliament, while it is in session, for a total period of thirty days which may be comprised in one session or in two or more successive sessions, and if, before the expiry of the session immediately following the session or the successive sessions aforesaid, both Houses agree in making any modification in the rule or both Houses agree that the rule should not be made, the rule shall thereafter have affect only in such modified form or be of no effect, as the case may be; so, however, that any such modification or annulment shall be without prejudice to the validity of anything previously done under that rule.

30. Repeal and Saving.

(1) The Terrorist and Disruptive Activities (Prevention) Ordinance, 1987 (2 of 1987) is hereby repealed.

(2) Notwithstanding such repeal, anything done or any action taken under the said Ordinance shall be deemed to have been done or taken under the corresponding provisions of this Act.

❑❑❑

34

The Transfer of Prisoners Act, 1950

ACT NO. 29 OF 1950 [12TH APRIL, 1950]

AN ACT to provide for the removal from one State to another of persons confined in a prison.

Be it enacted by Parliament as follows:-

1. Short title and extent.

(1) This Act may be called the Transfer of Prisoners Act, 1950 .

(2) It extends to the whole of India

2. Definitions. In this Act,-

(a) "court" includes any officer lawfully exercising civil, criminal or revenue jurisdiction;

(b) "Government" or "State Government", in relation to a Union territory, means the administrator thereof;

(c) "prison" includes any place which has been declared by a State Government, by general or special order, to be a subsidiary jail.

3. Removal of prisoners from one State to another.

(1) Where any person is confined in a prison in a State,-

(a) under sentence of death. or

(b) under, or in lieu of, a sentence of imprisonment or transportation, or

(c) in default of payment of a fine, or

(d) in default of giving security for keeping the peace or for maintaining good behaviour: the Government of that State may, with the consent of the Government of any other State, by order, provide for the removal of the prisoner from that prison to any prison in the other State.

(2) The officer in charge of the prison to which any person is removed under sub-section (1) shall receive and detain him, so far as may be, according to the exigency of any writ, warrent or order of the court by which such person has been committed, or until such person is discharged or removed in due course of law.

4. Amendment of section 29, Act III of 1900. *Rep. by the Repealing and Amending Act, 1957 (36 of 1957), s. 2 and Sch. I.*

❑❑❑

35

The Union Territories (Stamp and Court- Fees Laws) Act, 1961

ACT NO. 33 OF 1961 [29TH AUGUST, 1961]

AN ACT to provide for the amendment and repeal of certain laws relating to stamp duties and court-fees as in force in certain Union territories.

Be it enacted by Parliament in the Twelfth Year of the Republic of India as follows:-

1. Short title. This Act may be called the Union Territories (Stamp and Court-fees Laws) Act, 1961.

2. Amendment of Indian Stamp Act, 1899, as in force in Himachal Pradesh. On such date as the Central Government may, by notification in the Official Gazette, appoint, for Schedule I-A of the Indian Stamp Act, 1899, (2of 1899) as in force in the Union territory of Himachal Pradesh immediately before that date, there shall be substituted, with such modifications as may be specified in the notification, Schedule I-A to the Indian Stamp Act, 1899, as in force in the State of Punjab on the 28th day of November, 1960.

3. Repeal of Court-fees Act, 1870 (7 of 1870) as in force in Himachal Pradesh. On the date on which the Court-fees Act, 1870, as in force in the State of Punjab, is extended to the Union territory of Himachal Pradesh by notification under Section 2 of the Union Territories (Laws) Act, 1950, (30 of 1950) the Court-fees Act, 1870, as in force in that Union territory immediately before the date of such notification, shall stand repealed.

4. Repeal of Court-fees Act, 1870 (7 of 1870) as in force in Manipur and Tripura.

(a) On the date on which the Court-fees Act, 1870, as in force in the State of Assam, is extended to the Union territory of Manipur by notification under Section 2 of the Union Territories (Laws) Act, 1950, (30 of 1950) the Court-fees

Act, 1870, as in force in that Union territory immediately before the date of such notification, shall stand repealed.

(b) On the date on which the Court-fees Act, 1870, as in force in the State of Assam, is extended to the Union territory of Tripura by notification under Section 2 of the Union Territories (Laws) Act, 1950, the Court-fees Act, 1870, as in force in that Union territory immediately before the date of such notification, shall stand repealed.

5. Repeal of Indian Stamp Act, 1899, as in force in Manipur and Tripura.

(a) On the date on which the Indian Stamp Act, 1899, (2 of 1899) as in force in the State of Assam, is extended to the Union territory of Manipur by notification under Section 2 of the Union Territories (Laws) Act, 1950, (30 of 1950), the Indian Stamp Act, 1899, as in force in that Union territory immediately before the date of such notification, shall stand repealed.

(b) On the date on which the Indian Stamp Act, 1899, as in force in the State of Assam, is extended to the Union territory of Tripura by notification under Section 2 of the Union Territories (Laws) Act, 1950, the Indian Stamp Act, 1899, as in force in that Union territory immediately before the date of such notification, shall stand repealed.

6. Validation of levy of stamp duties in Scertain cases. Any stamp duties levied and collected in the Union territory of Manipur during the period commencing on the 16th day of April, 1950, and ending on the date on which the Indian Stamp Act, 1899 (2 of 1899), as in force in the State of Assam is extended to that Union territory under Section 5, in the belief that the Indian Stamp Act, 1899, as in force in the State of Assam immediatcly bcfore the 16th day of April, 1950, was applicable to that Union territory, shall be deemed always to have been levied and collected in accordance with law.

❑❑❑

36

The Unlawful Activities (Prevention) Act, 1967

ACT NO. 37 OF 1967 [30TH DECEMBER, 1967]

AN ACT to provide for the more effective prevention of certain unlawful activities of individuals and associations and for matters connected therewith.

Be it enacted by Parliament in the Eighteenth Year of the Republic of India as follows:-

CHAPTER - I : PRELIMINARY

1. Short title and extent.

(1) This Act may be called the Unlawful Activities (Prevention) Act, 1967.

(2) It extends to the whole of India: Provided that it shall come into force in the State of Jammu and Kashmir on such date as the Central Government may, by notification in the Official Gazette, appoint.

2. Definitions. In this Act, unless the context otherwise requires,-

(a) "association" means any combination or body of individuals;

(b) "cession of a part of the territory of India" includes admission of the claim of any foreign country to any such part;

(c) "prescribed" means prescribed by rules made under this Act;

(d) "secession of a part of the territory of India from the Union" includes the assertion of any claim to determine whether such part will remain a part of the territory of India;

(e) "Tribunal" means the Tribunal constituted under Section 5;

(f) "unlawful activity", in relation to an individual or association, means any action taken by such individual or association (whether by committing an act or by words, either spoken or written, or by signs or by visible representation or otherwise),-

(i) which is intended, or supports any claim, to bring about, on any ground whatsoever, the cession of a part of the territory of India or the secession of a part of the territory of India from the Union, or which incites any individual or group of individuals to bring about such cession or secession;

(ii) which disclaims, questions, disrupts or is intended to disrupt the sovereignty and territorial integrity of India;

(g) "unlawful association" means any association-

(i) which has for its object any unlawful activity, or which encourages or aids persons to undertake any unlawful activity, or of which the members undertake such activity; or

(ii) which has for its object any activity which is punishable under Section 153A or Section 153B of the Indian Penal Code (45 of 1860), or which encourages or aids persons to undertake any such activity, or of which the members undertake any such activity:

PROVIDED that nothing contained in sub-clause (ii) shall apply to the State of Jammu and Kashmir.

2A. Construction of reference to laws not in force in Jammu and Kashmir. Any reference in this Act to a law which is not in force in the State of Jammu and Kashmir shall, in relation to that State, be construed as a reference to the corresponding law, if any, in force in that State.

CHAPTER - II : UNLAWFUL ASSOCIATIONS

3. Declaration of an association as unlawful.

(1) If the Central Government is of opinion that any association is, or has become, an unlawful association, it may, by notification in the Official Gazette, declare such association to be unlawful.

(2) Every such notification shall specify the grounds on which it is issued and such other particulars as the Central Government may consider necessary: Provided that nothing in this sub-section shall require the Central Government to disclose any fact which it considers to be against the public interest to disclose.

(3) No such notification shall have effect until the Tribunal has, by an order made under Section 4, confirmed the declaration made therein and the order is published in the Official Gazette:

PROVIDED that if the Central Government is of opinion that circumstances exist which render it necessary for that Government to declare an association to be unlawful with immediate effect, it may, for reasons to be stated in writing, direct that the notification shall, subject to any order that may be made under Section 4, have effect from the date of its publication in the Official Gazette.

(4) Every such notification shall, in addition to its publication in the Official Gazette, be published in not less than one daily newspaper having circulation in the

State in which the principal office, if any, of the association affected is situated, and shall also be served on such association in such manner as the Central Government may think fit and all or any of the following modes may be followed in effecting such service, namely:-

(a) by affixing a copy of the notification to some conspicuous part of the office, if any, of the association; or

(b) by serving a copy of the notification, where possible, on the principal office-bearers, if any, of the association; or

(c) by proclaiming by beat of drum or by means of loudspeakers, the contents of the notification in the area in which the activities of the association are ordinarily carried on; or

(d) in such other manner as may be prescribed.

4. Reference to Tribunal.

(1) Where any association has been declared unlawful by a notification issued under sub-section (1) of Section 3, the Central Government shall, within thirty days from the date of the publication of the notification under the said sub-section, refer the notification to the Tribunal for the purpose of adjudicating whether or not there is sufficient cause for declaring the association unlawful.

(2) On receipt of a reference under sub-section (1), the Tribunal shall call upon the association affected by notice in writing to show cause, within thirty days from the date of the service of such notice, why the association should not be declared unlawful.

(3) After considering the cause, if any, shown by the association or the office-bearers or members thereof, the Tribunal shall hold an inquiry in the manner specified in Section 9 and after calling for such further information as it may consider necessary from the Central Government or from any office-bearer or member of the association, it shall decide whether or not there is sufficient cause for declaring the association to be unlawful and make, as expeditiously as possible and in any case within a period of six months from the date of the issue of the notification under sub-section (1) of Section 3, such order as it may deem fit either confirming the declaration made in notification or cancelling the same.

(4) The order of the Tribunal made under sub-section (3) shall be published in the Official Gazette.

5. Tribunal.

(1) The Central Government may, by notification in the Official Gazette, constitute, as and when necessary, a tribunal to be known as the" Unlawful Activities (Prevention) Tribunal" consisting of one person, to be appointed by the Central Government:

PROVIDED that no person shall be so appointed unless he is a Judge of a High Court.

(2) If, for any reason, a vacancy (other than a temporary absence) occurs in the office of the presiding officer of the Tribunal, then, the Central Government

shall appoint another person in accordance with the provisions of this section to fill the vacancy and the proceedings may be continued before the Tribunal from the stage at which the vacancy is filled.

(3) The Central Government shall make available to the Tribunal such staff as may be necessary for the discharge of its functions under this Act.

(4) All expenses incurred in connection with the Tribunal shall be defrayed out of the Consolidated Fund of India.

(5) Subject to the provisions of Section 9, the Tribunal shall have power to regulate its own procedure in all matters arising out of the discharge of its functions including the place or places at which it will hold its sittings.

(6) The Tribunal shall, for the purpose of making an inquiry under this Act, have the same powers as are vested in a civil court under the Code of Civil Procedure, 1908 (5 of 1908), while trying a suit, in respect of the following matters, namely:-

   (a) the summoning and enforcing the attendance of any witness and examining him on oath;

   (b) the discovery and production of any document or other material object producible as evidence;

   (c) the reception of evidence on affidavits;

   (d) the requisitioning of any public record from any court or office;

   (e) the issuing of any commission for the examination of witnesses.

(7) Any proceeding before the Tribunal shall be deemed to be a judicial proceeding within the meaning of Sections 193 and 228 of the Indian Penal Code (45 of 1860) and the Tribunal shall be deemed to be a civil court for the purposes of Section 195 and Chapter XXXV of the Code of Criminal Procedure, 1898 (5 of 1898).

6. Period of operation and cancellation of notification.

(1) Subject to the provisions of sub-section (2), a notification issued under Section 3 shall, if the declaration made therein is confirmed by the Tribunal by an order made under Section 4, remain in force for a period of two years from the date on which the notification becomes effective.

(2) Notwithstanding anything contained in sub-section (1), the Central Government may, either on its own motion or on the application of any person aggrieved, at any time, cancel the notification issued under Section 3, whether or not the declaration made therein has been confirmed by the Tribunal.

7. Power to prohibit the use of founds of an unlawful association.

(1) Where an association has been declared unlawful by a notification issued under Section 3 which has become effective under sub-section (3) of that Section and the Central Government is satisfied, after such inquiry as it may think fit, that any person has custody of any moneys, securities or credits which are being used or are intended to be used for the purpose of the unlawful association, the Central Government may, by order in writing, prohibit such person from paying, delivering, transferring or otherwise dealing in any manner

whatsoever with such moneys, securities or credits or with any other moneys, securities or credits which may come into his custody after the making of the order, save in accordance with the written orders of the Central Government and a copy of such order shall be served upon the person so prohibited in the manner specified in sub-section (3).

(2) The Central Government may endorse a copy of the prohibitory order made under sub-section (1) for investigation to any gazetted officer of the Government it may select, and such copy shall be a warrant whereunder such officer may enter in or upon any premises of the person to whom the order is directed, examine the books of such person, search for moneys, securities or credits, and make inquiries from such person or any officer, agent or servant of such person, touching the origin of any dealings in any moneys, securities or credits which the investigating officer may suspect are being used or are intended to be used for the purpose of the unlawful association.

(3) A copy of an order made under this section shall be served in the manner provided in the Code of Criminal Procedure, 1898 (5 of 1898), for the service of a summons, or, where the person to be served is a corporation, company, bank or other association, it shall be served on any secretary, director or other officer or person concerned with the management thereof, or by leaving it or sending it by post addressed to the corporation, company, bank or other association at its registered office, or where there is no registered office, at the place where it carries on business.

(4) Any person aggrieved by a prohibitory order made under sub-section (1) may, within fifteen days from the date of the service of such order, make an application to the Court of the District Judge within the local limits of whose jurisdiction such person voluntarily resides or carries on business or personally works for gain, to establish that the moneys, securities or credits in respect of which the prohibitory order has been made are not being used or are not intended to be used for the purpose of the unlawful association and the Court of the District Judge shall decide the question.

(5) Except so far as is necessary for the purposes of any pro-ceedings under this section, no information obtained in the course of any investigation made under sub-section (2) shall be divulged by any gazetted officer of the Government, without the consent of the Central Government.

(6) In this section, "security" includes a document whereby any person acknowledges that he is under a legal liability to pay money, or whereunder any person obtains a legal right to the payment of money.

8. Power to notify places for the purpose of an unlawful association.

(1) Where an association has been declared unlawful by a notification issued under Section 3 which has become effective under sub-section (3) of that section, the Central Government may, by notification in the Official Gazette, notify any place which in its opinion is used for the purpose of such unlawful association.

EXPLANATION: For the purposes of this sub-section, "place" includes a house or building, or part thereof, or a tent or vessel.

(2) On the issue of a notification under sub-section (1), the District Magistrate within the local limits of whose jurisdiction such notified place is situate or any officer authorised by him in' writing in this behalf shall make a list of all movable properties (other than wearing-apparel, cooking vessels, beds and beddings, tools of artisans, implements of husbandry, cattle, grain and foodstuffs and such other articles as he considers to be of a trivial nature) found in the notified place in the presence of two respectable witnesses.

(3) If, in the opinion of the District Magistrate, any articles specified in the list are or may be used for the purpose of the unlawful association he may make an order prohibiting any person from using the articles save in accordance with the written orders of the District Magistrate.

(4) The District Magistrate may thereupon make an order that no person who at the date of the notification was not a resident in the notified place shall, without the permission of the District Magistrate, enter, or be on or in, the notified place: Provided that nothing in this sub-section shall apply to any near relative of any person who was a resident in the notified place at the date of the notification.

(5) Where in pursuance of sub-section (4), any person is granted permission to enter, or to be on or in, the notified place, that person shall, while acting under such permission, comply with such orders for regulating his conduct as may be given by the District Magistrate.

(6) Any police officer, not below the rank of a sub-inspector, or any other person authorised in this behalf by the Central Government may search any person entering, or seeking to enter, or being on or in, the notified place and may detain any such person for the purpose of searching him:

PROVIDED that no female shall be searched in pursuance of this sub-section except by a female.

(7) If any person is in the notified place in contravention of an order made under sub-section (4), then, without prejudice to any other proceedings which may be taken against him, he may be removed therefrom by any officer or by any other person authorised in this behalf by the Central Government.

(8) Any person aggrieved by a notification issued in respect of a place under sub-section (1) or by an order made under sub-section (3) or sub-section (4) may, within thirty days from the date of the notification or order, as the case may be,, make an application to the Court of the District Judge within the local limits of whose jurisdic-tion such notified place is situate-

   (a) for declaration that the place has not been used for the purpose of the unlawful association; or

   (b) for setting aside the order made under sub-section (3) or sub-section (4), and on receipt of the application the Court of the District Judge shall, after giving the parties an opportunity of being heard, decide the question.

9. Procedure to be followed in the disposal of applications under this Act. Subject to any rules that may be made under this Act, the procedure to be followed by the Tribunal in holding any inquiry under sub-section (3) of Section 4 or by a Court of the District Judge in disposing of any application under sub-section (4) of Section 7 or sub-section (8) of Section 8 shall, so far as may be, be the procedure laid down in the Code of Civil Procedure, 1908 (5 of 1908), for the investigation of claims and the decision of the Tribunal or the Court of the District Judge, as the case may be, shall be final.

CHAPTER -III : OFFENCES AND PENALTIES

10. Penalty for being members of an unlawful association. Whoever is and continues to be a member of an association declared unlawful by a notification issued under Section 3 which has become effective under sub-section (3) of that section, or takes part in meetings of any such unlawful association, or contributes to, or receives or solicits any contribution for the purpose of, any such un-lawful association, or in any way assists the operations of any such unlawful association, shall be punishable with imprisonment for a term which may extend to two years, and shall also be liable to fine.

11. Penalty for dealing with funds of an unlawful association. If any person on whom a prohibitory order has been served under sub-section (1) of Section 7 in respect of any moneys, securities or credits pays, delivers, transfers or otherwise deals in any manner whatsoever with the same in contravention of the prohibitory order, he shall be punishable with imprisonment for a term which may extend to three years, or with fine, or with both, and notwithstanding anything contained in the Code of Criminal Procedure, 1898 (5 of 1898), the court trying such contravention may also impose on the person convicted an additional fine to recover from him the amount of the moneys or credits or the market value of the securities in respect of which the prohibitory order has been contravened or such part thereof as the court may deem fit.

12. Penalty for contravention of an order made in respect of notified place.

(1) Whoever uses any article in contravention of a prohibi-tory order in respect thereof made under sub-section (3) of Section 8 shall be punishable with imprisonment for a term which may extend to one year, and shall also be liable to fine.

(2) Whoever knowingly and wilfully is in, or effects or attempts to effect entry into, a notified place in contravention of an order made under sub-section (4) of Section 8 shall be punishable with imprisonment for a term which may extend to one year, and shall also be liable to fine.

13. Punishment for unlawful activities.

(1) Whoever-

  (a) takes part in or commits, or

  (b) advocates abets, advises or incites the commission of, any unlawful activity, shall be punishable with imprisonment for a term which may extend to seven years, and shall also be liable to fine.

(2) Whoever, in any way, assists any unlawful activity of any association, declared unlawful under Section 3, after the notification by which it has been so declared

has become effective under sub-section (3) of that section, shall be punishable with imprisonment for a term which may extend to five years, or with fine, or with both.

(3) Nothing in this section shall apply to any treaty, agreement or convention entered into between the Government of India and the Government of any other country or to any negotiations therefor carried on by any person authorised in this behalf by the Government of India.

14. Offences to be cognizable. Notwithstanding anything contained in the Code of Criminal Procedure, 1898 (5 of 1898), an offence punishable under this Act shall be cognizable.

CHAPTER -IV : MISCELLANEOUS

15. Continuance of association. An association shall not be deemed to have ceased to exist by reason only of any formal act of its dissolution or change of name but shall be deemed to continue so long as any actual combination for the purposes of such association continues between any members thereof.

16. Bar of jurisdiction. Save as otherwise expressly provided in this Act, no proceeding taken under this Act by the Central Government or the District Magistrate or any officer authorised in this behalf by the Central Government or the District Magistrate shall be called in question in any court in any suit or application or by way of appeal or revision, and no injunction shall be granted by any court or other authority in respect of any action taken or to be taken in pursuance of any power conferred by or under this Act.

17. Prosecution for offences under this Act. No court shall take cognizance of any offence punishable under this Act except with the previous sanction of the Central Government or any officer authorised by the Central Government in this behalf.

18. Protection of action taken in good faith.

(1) No suit or other legal proceeding shall lie against the Government in respect of any loss or damage caused or likely to be caused by anything which is in good faith done or intended to be done in pursuance of this Act or any rules or orders made thereunder.

(2) No suit, prosecution or other legal proceeding shall lie against the District Magistrate or any officer authorised in this behalf by the Government or the District Magistrate in respect of anything which is in good faith done or intended to be done in pursuance of this Act or any rules or orders made thereunder.

19. Power to delegate. The Central Government may, by notification in the Official Gazette, direct that all or any of the powers which may be exercised by it under Section 7, or Section 8, or both, shall, in such circumstances and under such conditions, if any, as may be specified in the notification, be exercised also by any State Government and the State Government may, with the previous approval of the Central Government, by order in writing direct that any power which has been directed to be exercised by it shall, in such circumstances and under such conditions, if any, as may be specified in the direction, be exercised by any person subordinate to the State Government as may be specified therein.

20. Effect of Act and rules, etc., inconsistent with other enactments. The provisions of this Act or any rule or order made thereunder shall have effect notwithstanding anything inconsistent there-with contained in any enactment other than this Act or any instrument having effect by virtue of any enactment other than this Act.

21. Power to make rules.

(1) The Central Government may, by notification in the Official Gazette, make rules to carry out the purposes of this Act.

(2) In particular, and without prejudice to the generality of the foregoing power, such rules may provide for all or any of the following matters, namely:-

(a) the service of notices or orders issued or made under this Act and the manner in which such notices or orders may be served, where the person to be served is a corporation, company, bank or other association;

(b) the procedure to be followed by the Tribunal or a District Judge in holding any inquiry or disposing of any application under this Act;

(c) any other matter which has to be, or may be, prescribed.

(3) Every rule made by the Central Government under this section shall be laid, as soon as may be after it is made, before each House of Parliament while it is in session for a 1[total period of thirty days which may be comprised in one session or[in two or more successive sessions, and if, before the expiry of the session immediately following the session or the successive sessions aforesaid], both Houses agree in making any modification the rule or both Houses agree that the rule should not be made, the rule shall thereafter have effect only in such modified form or be of no effect as the case may be; so, however, that any such modification or annulment shall be without prejudice to the validity of anything previously done under that rule.

❑❑❑

37

The Unlawful Activities (Prevention) Amendment Act, 2004

ACT NO. 29 OF 2004 [29TH DECEMBER, 2004]

AN ACT further to amend the Unlawful Activities (Prevention) Act, 1967.

Be it enacted by Parliament in the Fifty-fifth Year of the Republic of India as follows:-

1. Short title and commencement.

(1) This Act may be called the Unlawful Activities (Prevention) Amendment Act, 2004.

(2) It shall be deemed to have come into force on the 21st day of September, 2004.

2. Amendment of long title. In the Unlawful Activities (Prevention) Act, 1967 (37 of 1967) (hereinafter referred to as the principal Act), in the long title, after the word "associations", the words, "and for dealing with terrorist activities," shall be inserted.

3. Substitution of word "Code" for "Code of Criminal Procedure, 1898". In the principal Act, for the words and figures "Code of Criminal Procedure, 1898 (5 of 1898)", wherever they occur, the word "Code" shall be substituted.

4. Amendment of Chapter I. In Chapter I of the principal Act, for Sections 1, 2 and 2A, the following Sections shall be substituted, namely:-

1. Short title, extent and application.

(1) This Act may be called the Unlawful Activities (Prevention) Act, 1967 (37 of 1967).

(2) It extends to the whole of India.

(3) Every person shall be liable to punishment under this Act for every act or omission contrary to the provisions thereof, of which he is held guilty in India.

(4) Any person, who commits an offence beyond India, which is punishable under this Act, shall be dealt with according to the provisions of this Act in the same manner as if such act had been committed in India.

(5) The provisions of this Act apply also to-
  (a) citizens of India outside India;
  (b) persons in the service of the Government, wherever they may be; and
  (c) persons on ships and aircrafts, registered in India, wherever they may be.

2. Definitions.

(1) In this Act, unless the context otherwise requires,-
  (a) "association" means any combination or body of individuals;
  (b) "cession of a part of the territory of India" includes admission of the claim of any foreign country to any such part;
  (c) "Code" means the Code of Criminal Procedure, 1973 (2 of 1974);
  (d) "court" means a criminal court having jurisdiction, under the Code, to try offences under this Act;
  (e) "Designated Authority" means such officer of the Central Government not below the rank of Joint Secretary to that Government, or such officer of the State Government not below the rank of Secretary to that Government, as the case may be, as may be specified by the Central Government or the State Government, by notification published in the Official Gazette;
  (f) "prescribed" means prescribed by rules made under this Act;
  (g) "proceeds of terrorism" means all kinds of properties which have been derived or obtained from commission of any terrorist act or have been acquired through funds traceable to a terrorist act, irrespective of person in whose name such proceeds are standing or in whose possession they are found, and includes any property which is being used, or is intended to be used, for the purpose of a terrorist organisation;
  (h) "property" means property and assets of every description, whether corporeal or incorporeal, movable or immovable, tangible or intangible and deeds and instruments evidencing title to, or interest in, such property or assets, and includes cash and bank account;
  (i) "secession of a part of the territory of India from the Union" includes the assertion of any claim to determine whether such part will remain a part of the territory of India;
  (j) "State Government", in relation to a Union territory, means the Administrator thereof;
  (k) "terrorist act" has the meaning assigned to it in Section 15, and the expressions" terrorism" and" terrorist" shall be construed accordingly;

(l) "terrorist gang" means any association, other than terrorist organisation, whether systematic or otherwise, which is concerned with, or involved in, terrorist act;

(m) "terrorist organisation" means an organisation listed in the Schedule or an organisation operating under the same name as an organisation so listed;

(n) "Tribunal" means the Tribunal constituted under Section 5;

(o) "unlawful activity", in relation to an individual or association, means any action taken by such individual or association (whether by committing an act or by words, either spoken or written, or by signs or by visible representation or otherwise),-

(i) which is intended, or supports any claim, to bring about, on any ground whatsoever, the cession of a part of the territory of India or the secession of a part of the territory of India from the Union, or which incites any individual or group of individuals to bring about such cession or secession; or

(ii) which disclaims, questions, disrupts or is intended to disrupt the sovereignty and territorial integrity of India; or

(iii) which causes or is intended to cause disaffection against India;

(p) "unlawful association" means any association,-

(i) which has for its object any unlawful activity, or which encourages or aids persons to undertake any unlawful activity, or of which the members undertake such activity; or

(ii) which has for its object any activity which is punishable under Section 153A or Section 153B of the Indian Penal Code (45 of 1860), or which encourages or aids persons to undertake any such activity, or of which the members undertake any such activity:

PROVIDED that nothing contained in sub-clause (ii) shall apply to the State of Jammu and Kashmir;

(q) words and expressions used but not defined in this Act and defined in the Code shall have the meanings respectively assigned to them in the Code.

(2) Any reference in this Act to any enactment or any provision thereof shall, in relation to an area in which such enactment or such provision is not in force, be construed as a reference to the corresponding law or the relevant provision of the corresponding law, if any, in force in that area.

5. Amendment of Section 5. In Section 5 of the principal Act, in sub-section (7), for the word and figures "Chapter XXXV", the word and figures "Chapter XXVI" shall be substituted.

6. Substitution of new Section for Section 10. For Section 10 of the principal Act, the following Section shall be substituted, namely:-

"10. Penalty for being member of an unlawful association, etc. Where an association is declared unlawful by a notification issued under Section 3 which has become effective under sub-section (3) of that Section,-

(a) a person, who-

  (i) is and continues to be a member of such association; or

  (ii) takes part in meetings of such association; or

  (iii) contributes to, or receives or solicits any contribution for the purpose of, such association; or

  (iv) in any way assists the operations of such association, shall be punishable with imprisonment for a term which may extend to two years, and shall also be liable to fine; and

(b) a person, who is or continues to be a member of such association, or voluntarily does an act aiding or promoting in any manner the objects of such association and in either case is in possession of any unlicensed firearms, ammunition, explosive or other instrument or substance capable of causing mass destruction and commits any act resulting in loss of human life or grievous injury to any person or causes significant damage to any property,-

  (i) and if such act has resulted in the death of any person, shall be punishable with death or imprisonment for life, and shall also be liable to fine;

  (ii) in any other case, shall be punishable with imprisonment for a term which shall not be less than five years but which may extend to imprisonment for life, and shall also be liable to fine."

7. Substitution of new Chapters and Schedule for Chapter IV. For Chapter IV of the principal Act, the following Chapters and the Schedule shall be substituted, namely:-'

8. Repeal and saving.

(1) The Unlawful Activities (Prevention) Amendment Ordinance, 2004 (Ord. 2 of 2004) is hereby repealed.

(2) Notwithstanding such repeal, anything done or any action taken under the principal Act, as amended by the said Ordinance, shall be deemed to have been done or taken under the principal Act, as amended by this Act.

CHAPTER -IV : PUNISHMENT FOR TERRORIST ACTIVITIES

15. Terrorist Act. Whoever, with intent to threaten the unity, integrity, security or sovereignty of India or to strike terror in the people or any Section of the people in India or in any foreign country, does any act by using bombs, dynamite or other explosive substances or inflammable substances or firearms or other lethal weapons or poisons or noxious gases or other chemicals or by any other substances (whether biological or otherwise) of a hazardous nature, in such a manner as to cause, or likely to cause, death of, or injuries to any person or persons or loss of, or damage to, or destruction of, property or disruption of any supplies or services essential to the life of the community in India or in any foreign country or causes damage or destruction of any property or equipment used or intended to be used for the defence of India or in connection with any other purposes of the Government of India, any State Government or any of their agencies, or detains any person and threatens to kill or injure such person in order to compel the Government in India or the Government of a foreign country or any other person to do or abstain from doing any act, commits a terrorist act.

16. Punishment for terrorist act.

(1) Whoever commits a terrorist act shall,-

(a) if such act has resulted in the death of any person, be punishable with death or imprisonment for life, and shall also be liable to fine;

(b) in any other case, be punishable with imprisonment for a term which shall not be less than five years but which may extend to imprisonment for life, and shall also be liable to fine.

17. Punishment for raising fund for terrorist act. Whoever raises fund for the purpose of committing a terrorist act shall be punishable with imprisonment for a term which shall not be less than five years but which may extend to imprisonment for life, and shall also be liable to fine.

18. Punishment for conspiracy, etc. Whoever conspires or attempts to commit, or advocates, abets, advises or incites or knowingly facilitates the commission of, a terrorist act or any act preparatory to the commission of a terrorist act, shall be punishable with imprisonment for a term which shall not be less than five years but which may extend to imprisonment for life, and shall also be liable to fine.

19. Punishment for harbouring, etc. Whoever voluntarily harbours or conceals, or attempts to harbour or conceal any person knowing that such person is a terrorist shall be punishable with imprisonment for a term which shall not be less than three years but which may extend to imprisonment for life, and shall also be liable to fine: Provided that this Section shall not apply to any case in which the harbour or concealment is by the spouse of the offender.

20. Punishment for being member of terrorist gang or organization. Any person who is a member of a terrorist gang or a terrorist organisation, which is involved in terrorist act, shall be punishable with imprisonment for a term which may extend to imprisonment for life, and shall also be liable to fine.

21. Punishment for holding proceeds of terrorism. Whoever knowingly holds any property derived or obtained from commission of any terrorist act or acquired through the terrorist fund shall be punishable with imprisonment for a term which may extend to imprisonment for life, and shall also be liable to fine.

22. Punishment for threatening witness. Whoever threatens any person who is a witness or any other person in whom such witness may be interested, with violence, or wrongfully restrains or confines the witness, or any other person in whom the witness may be interested, or does any other unlawful act with intent to cause any of the said acts, shall be punishable with imprisonment which may extend to three years, and shall also be liable to fine.

23. Enhanced penalties.

(1) If any person with intent to aid any terrorist contravenes any provision of, or any rule made under the Explosives Act, 1884 (4 of 1884) or the Explosive

Substances Act, 1908 (6 of 1908) or the Inflammable Substances Act, 1952 (20 of 1952) or the Arms Act, 1959 (54 of 1959), or is in unauthorised possession of any bomb, dynamite or hazardous explosive substance or other lethal weapon or substance capable of mass destruction or biological or chemical substance of warfare, he shall, notwithstanding anything contained in any of the aforesaid Acts or the rules made thereunder, be punishable with imprisonment for a term which shall not be less than five years but which may extend to imprisonment for life, and shall also be liable to fine.

(2) Any person who, with intent to aid any terrorist, attempts to contravene or abets, or does any act preparatory to contravention of any provision of any law or rule specified in sub-section (1), shall be deemed to have contravened that provision under sub-section (1) and the provisions of that sub-section in relation to such person, have effect subject to the modification that the reference to "imprisonment for life" therein shall be construed as a reference to "imprisonment for ten years".

CHAPTER -V : FORFEITURE OF PROCEEDS OF TERRORISM

24. Forfeiture of proceeds of terrorism.

(1) No person shall hold or be in possession of any proceeds of terrorism.

(2) Proceeds of terrorism, whether held by a terrorist or by any other person and whether or not such terrorist or other person is prosecuted or convicted for any offence under Chapter IV or Chapter VI, shall be liable to be forfeited to the Central Government or the State Government, as the case may be, in the manner provided under this Chapter.

25. Powers of investigating officer and Designated Authority and appeal against order of Designated Authority.

(1) If an officer investigating an offence committed under Chapter IV or Chapter VI, has reason to believe that any property in relation to which an investigation is being conducted, represents proceeds of terrorism, he shall, with the prior approval in writing of the Director General of the Police of the State in which such property is situated, make an order seizing such property and where it is not practicable to seize such property, make an order of attachment directing that such property shall not be transferred or otherwise dealt with except with the prior permission of the officer making such order, or of the Designated Authority before whom the property seized or attached is produced and a copy of such order shall be served on the person concerned.

(2) The investigating officer shall duly inform the Designated Authority within forty-eight hours of the seizure or attachment of such property.

(3) The Designated Authority before whom the seized or attached property is produced shall either confirm or revoke the order of seizure or attachment so issued within a period of sixty days from the date of such production:

PROVIDED that an opportunity of making a representation by the person whose property is being seized or attached shall be given.

(4) In the case of immovable property attached by the investigating officer, it shall be deemed to have been produced before the Designated Authority, when the investigating officer notifies his report and places it at the disposal of the Designated Authority.

(5) The investigating officer may seize and detain any cash to which this Chapter applies if he has reasonable grounds for suspecting that-

(a) it is intended to be used for the purposes of terrorism; or

(b) it forms the whole or part of the resources of a terrorist organisation: Provided that the cash seized under this sub-section by the investigating officer shall be released within a period of forty-eight hours beginning with the time when it is seized unless the matter involving the cash is before the Designated Authority and such Authority passes an order allowing its retention beyond forty-eight hours. Explanation.-For the purposes of this sub-section, "cash" means-

(a) coins or notes in any currency;

(b) postal orders;

(c) traveller' s cheques;

(d) banker' s drafts; and

(e) such other monetary instruments as the Central Government or, as the case may be, the State Government may specify by an order made in writing.

(6) Any person aggrieved by an order made by the Designated Authority may prefer an appeal to the court within a period of thirty days from the date of receipt of the order, and the court may either confirm the order of attachment of property or seizure so made or revoke such order and release the property.

26. Court to order forfeiture of proceeds of terrorism. Where any property is seized or attached on the ground that it constitutes proceeds of terrorism and the court confirms the order in this regard under sub-section (6) of Section 25, it may order forfeiture of such property, whether or not the person from whose possession it is seized or attached, is prosecuted in a court for an offence under Chapter IV or Chapter VI.

27. Issue of show-cause notice before forfeiture of proceeds of terrorism.

(1) No order forfeiting any proceeds of terrorism shall be made under Section 26 unless the person holding or in possession of such proceeds is given a notice in writing informing him of the grounds on which it is proposed to forfeit the proceeds of terrorism and such person is given an opportunity of making a representation in writing within such reasonable time as may be specified in the notice against the grounds of forfeiture and is also given a reasonable opportunity of being heard in the matter.

(2) No order of forfeiture shall be made under sub-section (1), if such person establishes that he is a bona fide transferee of such proceeds for value without knowing that they represent proceeds of terrorism.

(3) It shall be competent for the court to make an order in respect of property seized or attached,-

(a) directing it to be sold if it is a perishable property and the provisions of Section 459 of the Code shall, as nearly as may be practicable, apply to the net proceeds of such sale;

(b) nominating any officer of the Central Government or the State Government, in the case of any other property, to perform the function of the Administrator of such property subject to such conditions as may be specified by the court.

28. Appeal.

(1) Any person aggrieved by an order of forfeiture under Section 26 may, within one month from the date of the receipt of such order, appeal to the High Court within whose jurisdiction, the court, which passed the order appealed against, is situated.

(2) Where an order under Section 26 is modified or annulled by the High Court or where in a prosecution instituted for any offence under Chapter IV or Chapter VI, the person against whom an order of forfeiture has been made under Section 26 is acquitted, such property shall be returned to him and in either case if it is not possible for any reason to return the forfeited property, such person shall be paid the price therefor as if the property had been sold to the Central Government with reasonable interest calculated from the day of seizure of the property and such price shall be determined in the manner prescribed.

29. Order for forfeiture not to interfere with other punishments. The order of forfeiture made under this Chapter by the court, shall not prevent the infliction of any other punishment to which the person affected thereby is liable under Chapter IV or Chapter VI.

30. Claims by third party.

(1) Where any claim is preferred or any objection is made to the seizure or attachment of any property under Section 25 on the ground that such property is not liable to seizure or attachment, the Designated Authority before whom such property is produced, shall proceed to investigate the claim or objection:

PROVIDED that no such investigation shall be made where the Designated Authority considers that the claim or objection is designed to cause unnecessary delay.

(2) Where an appeal has been preferred under sub-section (6) of Section 25 and any claimant or objector establishes that the property specified in the notice issued under Section 27 is not liable to be forfeited under this Chapter, the said notice shall be withdrawn or modified accordingly.

31. Powers of Designated Authority. The Designated Authority, acting under the provisions of this Chapter, shall have all the powers of a civil court required for making a full and fair inquiry into the matter before it.

32. Certain transfers to eb null and void. Where, after the issue of an order under Section 25 or issue of a notice under Section 27, any property referred to in the said order or notice is transferred by any mode whatsoever, such transfer shall, for the purpose of the proceedings under this Chapter, be ignored and if such property is subsequently forfeited, the transfer of such property shall be deemed to be null and void.

33. Forfeiture of property of certain persons.

(1) Where any person is accused of an offence under Chapter IV or Chapter VI, it shall be open to the court to pass an order that all or any of the properties, movable or immovable or both, belonging to him, shall, during the period of such trial, be attached, if not already attached under this Chapter.

(2) Where a person has been convicted of any offence punishable under Chapter IV or Chapter VI, the court may, in addition to awarding any punishment, by order in writing, declare that any property, movable or immovable or both, belonging to the accused and specified in the order, shall stand forfeited to the Central Government or the State Government, as the case may be, free from all encumbrances.

34. Company to transfer shares to Government. Where any share in a company stand forfeited to the Central Government or the State Government, as the case may be, under this Chapter, then, the companyshall, on receipt of the order of the court, notwithstanding anything contained in the Companies Act, 1956 (1 of 1956), or the articles of association of the company, forthwith register the Central Government or the State Government, as the case may be, as the transferee of such share.

CHAPTFR -VI : TERRORIST ORGANISATIONS

35. Amendment of Schedule, etc.

(1) The Central Government may, by order, in the Official Gazette,-

(a) add an organisation to the Schedule;

- (b) add also an organisation to the Schedule, which is identified as a terrorist organisation in a resolution adopted by the Security Council under Chapter VII of the Charter of the United Nations, to combat international terrorism;
- (c) remove an organisation from the Schedule;
- (d) amend the Schedule in some other way.

(2) The Central Government shall exercise its power under clause (a) of sub-section (1) in respect of an organisation only if it believes that it is involved in terrorism.

(3) For the purposes of sub-section (2), an organisation shall be deemed to be involved in terrorism if it-

- (a) commits or participates in acts of terrorism, or
- (b) prepares for terrorism, or
- (c) promotes or encourages terrorism, or
- (d) is otherwise involved in terrorism.

36. Denotification of a terrorist organization.

(1) An application may be made to the Central Government for the exercise of its power under clause (c) of sub-section (1) of Section 35 to remove an organisation from the Schedule.

(2) An application under sub-section (1) may be made by-

(a) the organisation, or

(b) any person affected by inclusion of the organisation in the Schedule as a terrorist organisation.

(3) The Central Government may prescribe the procedure for admission and disposal of an application made under this Section.

(4) Where an application under sub-section (1) has been rejected the applicant may apply for a review to the Review Committee constituted by the Central Government under sub-section (1) of Section 37 within one month from the date of receipt of the order of such refusal by the applicant.

(5) The Review Committee may allow an application for review against rejection to remove an organisation from the Schedule, if it considers that the decision to reject was flawed when considered in the light of the principles applicable on an application for judicial review.

(6) Where the Review Committee allows review under sub-section (5) by or in respect of an organisation, it may make an order to such effect.

(7) Where an order is made under sub-section (6), the Central Government shall, as soon as the certified copy of the order is received by it, make an order removing the organisation from the Schedule.

37. Review Committees.

(1) The Central Government shall constitute one or more ReviewCommittees for the purposes of Section 36.

(2) Every such Committee shall consist of a Chairperson and such other members not exceeding three and possessing such qualifications as may be prescribed.

(3) A Chairperson of the Committee shall be a person who is, or has been, a Judge of a High Court, who shall be appointed by the Central Government and in the case of appointment of a sitting Judge, the concurrence of the Chief Justice of the concerned High Court shall be obtained.

38. Offence relating to membership of a terrorist organization.

(1) A person, who associates himself, or professes to be associated, with a terrorist organisation with intention to further its activities, commits an offence relating to membership of a terrorist organisation:

PROVIDED that this sub-section shall not apply where the person charged is able to prove-

(a) that the organisation was not declared as a terrorist organisation at the time when he became a member or began to profess to be a member; and

(b) that he has not taken part in the activities of the organisation at any time during its inclusion in the Schedule as a terrorist organisation.

(2) A person, who commits the offence relating to membership of a terrorist organisation under sub-section (1), shall be punishable with imprisonment for a term not exceeding ten years, or with fine, or with both.

39. Offence relating to support given to a terrorist organization.

(1) A person commits the offence relating to support given to a terrorist organisation,-

(a) who, with intention to further the activity of a terrorist organisation,-

(i) invites support for the terrorist organisation, and

(ii) the support is not or is not restricted to provide money or other property within the meaning of Section 40; or

(b) who, with intention to further the activity of a terrorist organisation, arranges, manages or assists in arranging or managing a meeting which he knows is-

(i) to support the terrorist organisation, or

(ii) to further the activity of the terrorist organisation, or

(iii) to be addressed by a person who associates or professes to be associated with the terrorist organisation; or

(c) who, with intention to further the activity of a terrorist organisation, addresses a meeting for the purpose of encouraging support for the terrorist organisation or to further its activity.

(2) A person, who commits the offence relating to support given to a terrorist organisation under sub-section (1) shall be punishable with imprisonment for a term not exceeding ten years, or with fine, or with both.

40. Offence of raising fund for a terrorist organization.

(1) A person commits the offence of raising fund for a terrorist organisation, who, with intention to further the activity of a terrorist organisation,-

(a) invites another person to provide money or other property, and intends that it should be used, or has reasonable cause to suspect that it might be used, for the purposes of terrorism; or

(b) receives money or other property, and intends that it should be used, or has reasonable cause to suspect that it might be used, for the purposes of terrorism; or

(c) provides money or other property, and knows, or has reasonable cause to suspect, that it would or might be used for the purposes of terrorism.

EXPLANATION: For the purposes of this sub-section, a reference to provide money or other property includes of its being given, lent or otherwise made available, whether or not for consideration.

(2) A person, who commits the offence of raising fund for a terrorist organisation under sub-section (1), shall be punishable with imprisonment for a term not exceeding fourteen years, or with fine, or with both.

CHAPTER -VII : MISCELLANEOUS

41. Continuance of association. An association shall not be deemed to have ceased to exist by reason only of any formal act of its dissolution or change of name but shall be deemed to continue so long as any actual combination for the purposes of such association continues between any members thereof.

42. Power to delegate. The Central Government may, by notification in the Official Gazette, direct that all or any of the powers which may be exercised by it under Section 7, or Section 8, or both, shall, in such circumstances and under such conditions, if any, as may be specified in the notification, be exercised also by any State Government and the State Government may, with the previous approval of the Central Government, by order in writing, direct that any power which has been directed to be exercised by it shall, in such circumstances and under such conditions, if any, as may be specified in the direction, be exercised by any person subordinate to the State Government as may be specified therein.

43. Officers competent to investigate offences under Chapter IV and VI. Notwithstanding anything contained in the Code, no police officer,-

(a) in the case of the Delhi Special Police Establishment, constituted under sub-section (1) of Section 2 of the Delhi Special Police Establishment Act, 1946 (25 of 1946), below the rank of a Deputy Superintendent of Police or a police officer of equivalent rank;

(b) in the metropolitan areas of Mumbai, Kolkata, Chennai and Ahmedabad and any other metropolitan area notified as such under sub-section (1) of Section 8 of the Code, below the rank of an Assistant Commissioner of Police;

(c) in any case not relatable to clause (a) or clause (b), below the rank of a Deputy Superintendent of Police or a police officer of an equivalent rank, shall investigate any offence punishable under Chapter IV or VI.

44. Protection of witnesses.

(1) Notwithstanding anything contained in the Code, the proceedings under this Act may, for reasons to be recorded in writing, be held in camera if the court so desires.

(2) A court, if on an application made by a witness in any proceeding before it or by the Public Prosecutor in relation to such witness or on its own motion, is satisfied that the life of such witness is in danger, it may, for reasons to be recorded in writing, take such measures as it deems fit for keeping the identity and address of such witness secret.

(3) In particular, and without prejudice to the generality of the provisions of sub-section (2), the measures which a court may take under that sub-section may include-

   (a) the holding of the proceedings at a place to be decided by the court;

   (b) the avoiding of the mention of the name and address of the witness in its orders or judgments or in any records of the case accessible to public;

   (c) the issuing of any directions for securing that the identity and address of the witness are not disclosed;

(d) a decision that it is in the public interest to order that all or any of the proceedings pending before such a court shall not be published in any manner.

(4) Any person who contravenes any decision or direction issued under sub-section (3) shall be punishable with imprisonment for a term which may extend to three years, and shall also be liable to fine.

45. Cognizance of offences. No court shall take cognizance of any offence-

(i) under Chapter III without the previous sanction of the Central Government or any officer authorised by the Central Government in this behalf;

(ii) under Chapters IV and VI without the previous sanction of the Central Government or, as the case may be, the State Government, and where such offence is committed against the Government of a foreign country without the previous sanction of the Central Government.

46. Admissibility of evidence collected through the interception of communications. Notwithstanding anything contained in the Indian Evidence Act, 1872 (1 of 1872) or any other law for the time being in force, the evidence collected through the inter-ception of wire, electronic or oral communication under the provisions of the Indian Telegraph Act, 1885 (13 of 1885) or the Information Technology Act, 2000 (21 of 2000) or any other law for the time being in force, shall be admissible as evidence against the accused in the court during the trial of a case:

PROVIDED that the contents of any wire, electronic or oral communication intercepted or evidence derived therefrom shall not be received in evidence or otherwise disclosed in any trial, hearing or other proceeding in any court unless each accused has been furnished with a copy of the order of the competent authority under the aforesaid law, under which the interception was directed, not less than ten days before trial, hearing or proceeding:

PROVIDED FURTHER that the period of ten days may be waived by the judge trying the matter, if he comes to the conclusion that it was not possible to furnish the accused with such order ten days before the trial, hearing or proceeding and that the accused shall not be prejudiced by the delay in receiving such order.

47. Bar of jurisdiction.

(1) Save as otherwise expressly provided in this Act, no proceeding taken under this Act by the Central Government or the District Magistrate or any officer authorised in this behalf by the Central Government or the District Magistrate, shall be called in question in any civil court in any suit or application or by way of appeal or revision, and no injunction shall be granted by any civil court or other authority in respect of any action taken or to be taken in pursuance of any power conferred by or under this Act.

(2) Notwithstanding anything contained in sub-section (1), no civil court or other authority shall have, or be entitled to exercise, any jurisdiction, powers or authority in relation to the matters referred to in Section 36.

48. Effect of Act and rules, etc., inconsistent with other enactments. The provisions of this Act or any rule or order made thereunder shall have effect notwithstanding anything inconsistent therewith contained in any enactment other than this Act or any instrument having effect by virtue of any enactment other than this Act.

49. Protection of action taken in good faith. No suit, prosecution or other legal proceeding shall lie against-

(a) the Central Government or a State Government or any officer or authority of the Central Government or State Government or District Magistrate or any officer authorised in this behalf by the Government or the District Magistrate or any other authority on whom powers have been conferred under this Act, for anything which is in good faith done or purported to be done in pursuance of this Act or any rule or order made thereunder; and

(b) any serving or retired member of the armed forces or para-military forces in respect of any action taken or purported to be taken by him in good faith, in the course of any operation directed towards combating terrorism.

50. Saving. Nothing in this Act shall affect the jurisdiction exercisable by, or the procedure applicable to, any court or other authority under any law relating to the navy, army or air force or other armed forces of the Union.

51. Impounding of passport and arms licence of person chargesheeted under the Act. Notwithstanding anything contained in any other law for the time being in force, the passport and the arms licence of a person, who is charge-sheeted for having committed any offence under this Act, shall be deemed to have been impounded for such period as the court may deem fit.

52. Power to make rules.

(1) The Central Government may, by notification in the Official Gazette, make rules for carrying out the provisions of this Act.

(2) In particular, and without prejudice to the generality of the foregoing powers, such rules may provide for all or any of the following matters, namely:-

  (a) the service of notices or orders issued or made under this Act and the manner in which such notices or orders may be served, where the person to be served is a corporation, company, bank or other association;

  (b) the procedure to be followed by the Tribunal or a District Judge in holding any inquiry or disposing of any application under this Act;

  (c) determination of the price of the forfeited property under sub-section (2) of Section 28;

  (d) the procedure for admission and disposal of an application under sub-section (3) of Section 36;

  (e) the qualifications of the members of the Review Committee under sub-section (2) of Section 37; and

  (f) any other matter which is required to be, or may be, prescribed.

53. Orders and rules to be laid before hoth Houses of Parliament. Every order and every rule made by the Central Government under this Act shall be laid, as soon as may be after it is made, before each House of Parliament, while it is in session, for a total period of thirty days which may be comprised in one session or in two or more successive sessions, and if, before the expiry of the session immediately following the session or the successive sessions aforesaid, both Houses agree in making any modification in the order or rule or both Houses agree that the order or rule should not be made, the order or rule shall thereafter have effect only in such modified form or be of no effect, as the case may be; so, however, that any such modification or annulment shall be without prejudice to the validity of anything previously done under that order or rule.

THE SCHEDULE

[See Sections 2 (1) (m) and 35]

TERRORIST ORGANISATIONS

1. BABBAR KHALSA INTERNATIONAL.
2. KHALISTAN COMMANDO FORCE.
3. KHALISTAN ZINDABAD FORCE.
4. INTERNATIONAL SIKH YOUTH FEDERATION.
5. LASHKAR-E-TAIBA PASBAN-E-AHLE HADIS.
6. JAISH-E-MOHAMMED TAHRIK-E-FURQAN.
7. HARKAT-UL-MUJAHIDEEN HARKAT-UL-ANSAR HARKAT-UL-JEHAD-E-ISLAMI.
8. HIZB-UL-MUJAHIDEEN HIZB-UL-MUJAHIDEEN PIR PANJAL REGIMENT.
9. AL-UMAR-MUJAHIDEEN.
10. JAMMU AND KASHMIR ISLAMIC FRONT.
11. UNITED LIBERATION FRONT OF ASSAM (ULFA).
12. NATIONAL DEMOCRATIC FRONT OF BODOLAND (NDFB).
13. PEOPLE' S LIBERATION ARMY (PLA).
14. UNITED NATIONAL LIBERATION FRONT (UNLF).
15. PEOPLE' S REVOLUTIONARY PARTY OF KANGLEIPAK (PREPAK).
16. KANGLEIPAK COMMUNIST PARTY (KCP).
17. KANGLEI YAOL KANBA LUP (KYKL).
18. MANIPUR PEOPLE' S LIBERATION FRONT (MPLF).
19. ALL TRIPURA TIGER FORCE.
20. NATIONAL LIBERATION FRONT OF TRIPURA.
21. LIBERATION TIGERS OF TAMIL EELAM (LTTE).
22. STUDENTS ISLAMIC MOVEMENT OF INDIA.
23. DEENDAR ANJUMAN.
24. COMMUNIST PARTY OF INDIA (MARXIST-LENINIST) PEOPLE'S WAR, ALL ITS FORMATIONS AND FRONT ORGANISATIONS.
25. MAOIST COMMUNIST CENTRE (MCC), ALL ITS FORMATIONS AND FRONT ORGANISATIONS.
26. AL BADR.

27. JAMIAT-UL-MUJAHIDDEN.
28. AL-QAIDA.
29. DUKHTARAN-E-MILLAT (DEM).
30. TAMIL NADU LIBERATION ARMY (TNLA).
31. TAMIL NATIONAL RETRIEVAL TROOPS (TNRT).
32. AKHIL BHARAT NEPALI EKTA SAMAJ (ABNES).

❑❑❑

Bibliography

AGARWAL, Rajendra Saran, "India: National Report", (1983) 54(1-2) *Revue internationale de droit pénal / International Review of Penal Law* 397-399 (Actes du Colloque International, "Conception et principes du droit pénal économique et des affaires y compris la protection du consommateur", tenu à Freiburg-en-Brisgau, République Fédérale d'Allemagne, 20-23 septembre 1982, en préparation pour le 13e Congrès international de droit pénal de l'Association internationale de droit pénal (AIDP) au Caire en 1984 / Report of the Proceedings of the International Colloquium, "Concept and Principles of Economic and Business Criminal Law", held in Freiburg i. Br., Federal Republic of Germany, September 20-23, 1983, in preparation for the 13th International Congress of Penal Law of the International Association of Penal Law (IAPL) in Crairo, 1984);

AMNESTY INTERNATIONAL, *India, persecuted for challenging injustice: human rights defenders in India*, New York: Amnesty International, USA, 2000, 96, [28] p.;

ANNOUSSAMY, David, "La torture dans l'Inde", dans, sous la direction de Bernard Durand, avec la collaboration de Leah Otis-Cour, *La torture judiciaire. Approches historiues et jurdiques*, vol. 1, Lille: Centre d'histoire judiciaire Éditeur, Faculté des Sciences Juridiques, Politiques et Sociales, 2002, aux pp. 41-62, ISBN: 2910114066; copie à l'Université d'Ottawa, MRT, HV 8593 .T678 2002 v. 1;

ARTHANARESWARAN, P., "Criminal law during the Chola period", in C.E.Ramachandran and K.V. Raman, eds. *Aspects of Indian history and culture*, New Delhi: Books & Books, 1984. 352 p., at pp. 49-52;

BALASUBRAHMANYAM, V., "Group Liability", in S. Govindarajulu, ed., *Essays on the Indian Penal Code: published on the occasion of the centenary of the Indian Penal Code*, Bombay: N.M. Tripathi, 1962, pp. 94-106; title noted in my research but article not consulted (27 April 2007);

BALASUBRAHMANYAM, V., "Jurisdiction", in S. Govindarajulu, ed., *Essays on the Indian Penal Code: published on the occasion of the centenary of the Indian Penal Code*, Bombay: N.M. Tripathi, 1962, pp. 47-55;

BANERJEE, Tapas Kumar, *Background to Indian criminal law*, Calcutta : R. Cambray, 1990, xviii, 402 p.; notes: Reprint, with new pref. Originally published: Bombay : Orient Longmans, 1963;

BANERJI, Eric H., "Strict Liability", in S. Govindarajulu, ed., *Essays on the Indian Penal Code: published on the occasion of the centenary of the Indian Penal Code*, Bombay: N.M. Tripathi, 1962, pp. 63-71; title noted in my research but article not consulted (27 April 2007);

BARNEJEE, Tapas Kamur, *Background to Indian Criminal Law*, Bombay: Orient Longmans, 1963, 389 p.; there is a second edition : Calcutta: R. Cambray, 1990, copy at the library of the Supreme Court of Canada, KF9220 ZM2 B36 1990;

BENERJI, Eric H., "Reform",, in S. Govindarajulu, ed., *Essays on the Indian Penal Code: published on the occasion of the centenary of the Indian Penal Code*, Bombay: N.M. Tripathi, 1962, pp. 166-177; title noted in my research but article not consulted (27 April 2007);

BETAI, Ramesh S., 1926-, *Evolution of law of crimes in ancient India*, Delhi : Bharatiya Kala Prakashan, 2003, x, 225 p., ISBN: 8180900207;

BHATIA, K.L., "Fair Trial in Criminal Proceedings in India" in David Weissbrodt and Rüdiger Wolfrum, eds., *The right to a fair trial*, Berlin; New York: Springer, 1997, ix, 779 p. at pp. 373 to approx.402 (Series; Beiträge zum ausländischen öffentlichen Recht und Völkerrecht ; Bd. 129), ISBN: 3540625933;

BHATTACHARYA, Chanchal A., 1942-, *The concept of theft in classical Hindu law : an analysis and the idea of punishment*, Delhi : Munshiram Manoharlal publisgers, c1990, viii, 207 p., ISBN: 8121504753;

BONNAN, J.-C., "Le roi, souverain du châtiment : l'exemple de l'Inde ancienne", (1986) 11 *Revue Droit et Cultures - Anthropologie et histoire* 123-127;

BOSE, Sukumar and Paripurnanand Varma, "Philosophical significance of Ancient Indian Penology", (1982) 10(1) *Journal of Indian Philosophy* 61-100;

BOSE, V., "The Migration of the Common Law: India", (1960) 76 *Law Quarterly Review* 59;

CAMERON, C.H. and D. Elliott, *The Indian Penal Code as Originally Framed in 1837 and the First and Second Reports Thereon*, Madras: Higginbotham, 1888

CHAKRABORTY, Tapan and Kiara Okita, "The Adult Corrections in India", in John A Winterdyk, ed., *Adult Corrections, International Systems and Perspectives*, Monsey (N.Y.): Criminal Justice Press, 2004, xi, 369 p., ISBN: 188179850X; copie à l'Université de Montréal;

CHANDRACHUD, Y.V. in collaboration with Shri V.R. Manohar, *Ratanlal & Dhirajlal Indian Penal Code*, 30th ed., Nagpur (India): Wadhwa and Company, 2004, 1250 p. (approx.);

Criminal Justice Reform in India: ICJ Position Paper Review of the Recommendations made by the Justice Malimath Committee from an international human rights perspective, Position Paper of the ICJ submitted on the occasion of the National Conference Jointly Organized by Human Rights Law Network (HRLN), New Delhi and International Commission of Jurists (ICJ), Geneva on 9th & 10th August 2003, New Delhi, 40 p.;

available athttp://www.icj.org/IMG/pdf/India_crim_justice_reform.pdf (accessed on 12 February 2006);

CROSS, Rupert, "The Making of English Criminal Law (5) Macaulay", [1978] *Criminal Law Review* 519;

CURRIE, Fendall, *The Indian Criminal Codes*, 4th ed., London: John Flack and Calcutta: Wyman, 1872;

DARESTE de la CHAVANNE, 1824-1911, *Études d'histoire du droit*, Paris : L. Larose et Forcel, 1889, xii, 419 p., voir le chapitre 4, "Les anciens codes brahmaniques", aux pp. 69-100; réimpression de ce livre: Amsterdam: Éditions Rodopi, 1971;

DAS, Ram Mohan, *Crime and punishment in ancient India : with a particular reference to the Manusmmrti*, 1st ed., Bodh-Gaya : Kanchan Publications, Can be had from R. Agrawal, 1982, xii, 171 p., ; Based on the author's thesis (D. Litt. — Magadh University, 1978); copy at the National Library, Ottawa;

DHAGAMWAR, Vasudha, 1940-, *Law, power and justice : the protection of personal rights in the Indian penal code*, 2nd ed., New Delhi ; Newbury Park : Sage Publications, 1992, 392 p., ISBN : 0803994419 (U.S. : cloth), 0803994427 (U.S. : paper), 8170362970 (India : cloth), 8170362989;

DONGALI, Damayanti, *Crime and punishment in ancient Hindu society*, Delhi : Ajanta Publications : Distributors, Ajanta Books International, 1986, xvi, 294 p., ISBN: 812020168;

DRAPKIN, Israel, 1905-, *Crime and Punishment in the Ancient World*, Lexington (Mass.): Lexington Books, c1989, xviii, 423 p., see "Ancient India and the Laws of Manu" at pp. 99-133, ISBN: 0669012793;

FISCH, von Jorg, 1947-, *Cheap lives and dear limbs : the British transformation of the Bengal criminal law 1769-1817*, Wiesbaden : Steiner, 1983, vii, 154 p., (Series; Beitrage zur Sudasienforschung ; Bd. 79), ISBN: I3515040129;

GIONA, V., "Parallèle entre la responsabilité pénale dans le droit mésopotamien, hébreu, perse, indien et chinois", (1992) 14 *Cuadernos informativos de derecho histórico público, procesal y de la navegación*; cité par Stamatios Tzitsis, *La philosophie pénale*, Paris: Presses Universitaires de France, 1996, 127 p., à la p. 57, note 2 (Collection "Que sais-je?"; no 3043), ISBN: 2130473490;

GLAZEBROOK, P.R., "Criminal Law Reform - England" in Sanford H. Kadish, ed., volume 2, New York: The Free Press, at pp. 490-501 and more particularly, "The Indian Penal Code, 1835-1860" at p. 496, ISBN: 0029181100 (for the set of 4 volumes);

GLUCKLICH, A., "Karma and social justice in the criminal code of Manu", (1982) 16(1) *Contributions to Indian sociology* 59-78;

GOUR, Hari Singh, Sir, 1869-1949, *The penal law of India : being an analytical, critical & expository commentary on the Indian penal code (Act No. XLV of 1860), as amended up to date, Diamond Jubilee - 10th ed. / revised by M.C. Desai, Gyanendra Kumar, R.B. Sethi*, Allahabad : Law Publishers, 1982-1984, 4 volumes; copy at the Government of India, Information Services, Reference Library, Ottawa;

GRANDLE, B.B., "Choosing to help or to Advance their agenda: A comparative look at how the Supreme Courts of India and the United States Approach Violence Against Women", (2003) 24(2) *Women's Rights Law Reporter* 445-477;

GUILLET-DESGROIS, *Étude sur le droit hindou: du droit de punir*, Paris: Berger-Levrault, 1878, 179 p.;

GUILLOT, P., "Administration de la justice dans l'Inde", (1845) 11 *Revue de législation et de jurisprudence* 161-187; copie à la bibliothèque de la Cour suprême du Canada, Ottawa; the article is a summary of a book written by another author; not much on criminal law;

HARTJEN, Clayton A. and Sesha Kethineni, "India" in Donald J. Shoemaker, ed., *International Handbook on Juvenile Justice*, Westport (Connecticut): Greenwood Press, 1996, xv, 327 p., at pp.175-190, ISBN: 031328895X; copy at Ottawa University, MRT General, HV 9069 .I665 1996;

HUDA, Syed Shamsul, 1862-1922, *The principles of the law of crimes in British India*, Calcutta ; Winnipeg : Butterworth, 1919, xv, 455 p. (Tagore Law Lectures - 1902);

ILBERT, C., "Indian Codification", (1889) 5 *The Law Quarterly Review* 347-369; does not deal more than one page on the codification of the criminal law;

INDIAN LAW INSTITUTE, *Essays on the Indian penal code : Published on the occasion of the centenary of the Indian penal code / Prepared under the auspices of the Indian Law Institute*, New Delhi, Bombay : N. M. Tripathi, [c1962], 188 p.;

JAIN, K.B., "Vice of bigamy and Indian penal code: ramifications of an archaic law", (1990) 32 *Journal of the Indian Law Institute* 386-399;

JAYASWAL, Kashi Prasad, *Manu and Yajnavalkya - a comparison and a contrast; a treatise on the basic Hindu law*, Calcutta: Butterworth, 1930, xxiv, 331 p. (series; Tagore law lectures, 1917); copy at the Supreme Court of Canada Library;

KOLSKY, Elizabeth, "Codification and the rule of Colonial Difference: Criminal Procedure in British India", (Fall 2005) 23(3) *Law and History Review* 631-683

KULSHRESHTHA, V. D. (Visheshwar Dayal), 1922-, *Landmarks in Indian legal history and constitutional history*, Lucknow, Eastern book co., 1989, xxiv, 518 p., ISBN: 8170123879; excellent book for background information; copy at the library of the Supreme Court of Canada, KF349 I54 K85 1989;

KUMARI, Ved, "Gender analysis of the Indian penal code", in Amita Dhanda and Archana Parashar, eds., *Engendering law: essays in honour of Lotika Sarkar*,Lucknow(India): Eastern Book Co., 1999, at pp. 139-160;

LAHIRI, Tarapada, *Crime and punishment in ancient India*, New Delhi : Radiant Publishers, 1986, xiii, 207 p., ISBN: 8170270936; copy at University of Ottawa, KPN .L327 1986 MRT;

LAUDE, Francois Nicolas, 1822-1874, *Manuel de droit indou et de législation civile et criminelle applicable dans les établissements francais de l'Inde*, Pondichery, E.-V. Geruzet, imprimeur, 1856, 3 p. l., v, 388 p.;

LAW COMMISSION OF INDIA, Indian Penal Code, June 1971, Delhi : Manager of Publications, 1971, ii, 579 p. (series; Report ; 42); available athttp://lawcommissionofindia.nic.in/1-50/Report42.pdf (accessed on 31 July 2006);

MACAULAY, Lord T.B. [Thomas Babington], 1800-1859, J.M. MacLeod, G.W. Anderson and F. Millett., "Notes [on the Indian Penal Code by the Indian Law Commissioners]", in *Miscellaneous Works of Lord Macaulay edited by his sister Lady Trevelyan, in Five Volumes*, vol. IV, New York: Harper, 1880, 669 p., pp. 177-327; these notes are part of the "Introductory Report upon the Indian Penal Code - To The Right Honorable George Lord Auckland, C.G.C.B. Governor-General of India in Council" at pp. 161-177;

MACAULAY, Lord T.B. [Thomas Babington], 1800-1859, *Speeches and Poems, with the Report and Notes on the Indian penal code*, vol. 2, New York Hurd and Houghton, 1867

MACRAE, C.C.-"Criminal Jurisdiction over Englishmen in India", (July-December 1883) 34 *The Fortnightly Review* 203-214;

MAKKAR, S. P. Singh, 1952-, *Law of culpable homicide, murder and punishment in India*, New Delhi : Deep & Deep, c1988, viii, 464 p., ISBN: 8171000827;

MALHOTRA, Monika, *Criminal jurisprudence and law of insanity*, New Delhi : Deep & Deep Publications, c1988, 171 p., ISBN: 8171000916;

MALIK, Shahdeen, *The transformation of colonial perceptions into legal norms : legislating for crime and punishment in Bengal, 1790's to 1820's*, Ph.D. thesis, University of London, 1994, 300 leaves;

MAYNE, John D., *Commentaries on the Indian Penal Code (Act of 1860)*, Madras: Higginbotham, 1869;

MAYNE, John D., *The Criminal Law of India*, Madras: Higginbotham, 1896, xl, 1028 p., copy at the University of Ottawa and at the Supreme Court of Canada library, Ottawa, KF9219 M39 1896;

MENON, N.R. Madheva, "A Note on the Law and Practice Relating to Habitual Criminals in India", (1967)13 *McGill Law Journal* 675-678;

MENSKI, Werner F., "Crime and Punishment in Hindu Law and under Modern Indian Law" dans *La peine, Quatrième partie = Punishment - Fourth Part*, Bruxelles: De Boeck, 1991, 514 p. aux pp. 295-334, (Collection; Recueils de la Société Jean Bodin; vol. 58), (series; Transactions of the Jean Bodin Society for Comparative Institutional History; vol. 58), ISBN: 2804115240;

MUKHERJEE,Mithi, "Codification and the Rule of Colonial Difference: Criminal Procedure in British India", (Fall 2005) 23(3) *Law & Historty Review* 589 to approx.630;

MUSTAFA, Faizan, *Strict liability in criminal law*, New Delhi : Deep & Deep Publications, c1992, xii, 124 p., ISBN: 8171004008;

MUSTAFA, Faizan, *Strict liability in criminal law*, New Delhi : Deep & Deep Publications, c1992, 124 p., ISBN: 8171004008;

NYPELS, Jean Servais Guillaume, 1803-1886, "Bibliographie: Essai sur l'histoire du droit des peuples anciens (Inde brahmanique, Egypte, Judée), par J.-J,Thonissen, *professeur à l'Université catholique de Louvain, memnbre de l'Académie royale de Belgique.* Bruxelles, Bruylant-Christophe et comp. — *Paris, A.*Durand et Pedone-Lauriel, 1869. In-8, 2 vol. exv-247 et 316 p."

PALKAR, Vineeta V., "National Monographs: India" in Cyrille Fijnault, ed. *International Encyclopaedia of Laws, Criminal Law*, The Hague, London, Boston: Kluwer Law International, 2001, + 200 p., ISBN: 9065449374,

PATRA, A.C., "An Historical Introduction to the Indian Penal Code", (1961) 3 *Journal of the Indian Law Institute* 351; the library of the Supreme Court of Canada, Ottawa, is missing this particular number in volume 3; with the same title in S. Govindarajulu, ed., *Essays on the Indian Penal Code: published on the occasion of the centenary of the Indian Penal Code*, Bombay: N.M. Tripathi, 1962, pp. 33-46;

PILLAI, P.S.A. (P.S. Atchuthen), *Criminal Law*, 9th ed., Butterworths, 2001;

PRINSEP, H.T., with notes by, *The code of criminal procedure (Acts X of 1872 and XI of 1874) and other laws and rules of practice relating to procedure in the criminal courts of British India, with notes, by H.T. Prinsep ...*, 5th ed., Calcutta, Thacker, Spink, 1875, xl, 23, 810 p. tables. 24 cm.;

RAGHAVEN, R.K., "World Factbook of Criminal Justice Systems - India" at http://www.ojp.usdoj.gov/bjs/pub/ascii/wfbcjind.txt (U.S. Department of Justice, Bureau of Justice Statistics - The World Factbook of Criminal Justice Systems at http://www.ojp.usdoj.gov/bjs/abstract/wfcj.htm);

RANGNATHARAO, N.S., "Freedom of expression and the law of sedition in India", in Trimbak Krishna Tope, ed., *Essays in law (published on the occasion of the centenary of the affiliation of Government Law College to the University of Bombay)*, Bombay: T. K. Tope on behalf of Government Law College, 1960, at pp. 43-72;

RANKIN, G.G., "The Indian Penal Code", (1944) 60 *Law Quarterly Review* 37-50;

RAO, K. Sreedhar, "Criminal Justice System — Required Reforms", (2001) 43(2) *Journal of the Indian Law Institute* 155-173; copy at Ottawa University;

SEN, Satadru, *Punishment and Society in Colonial India: The penal Settlement in the Andaman Islands, 1858-1898*, Ph.D. thesis, University of Washgington, 1998, 446 p.;

SHARMA, V.S., *A comparative study of the historical development and present structure of the Juvenile Courts in England, India and Japan*, Ph.D. thesis, London University, 1970;

SINGH, Mool, 1947-, *Justice Iyer's jurisconscience*, Jaipur, India : RBSA Publishers, 1993, 311 p., ISBN: 8185813078; note: Critical analysis of Justice Krishna Iyer's thoughts and contribution to Indian criminal jurisprudence; Krishna Iyer, V. R., 1915-;

SINGHA, Radhika, "Civil Authority and Due Process: Colonial Criminal Justice in the Banaras Zamindari, 1781-1795", in Michael R. Anderson and Sumit Guha, eds., *Changing concepts of rights and justice in South Asia*, Calcutta; New York: Oxford University Press, 1998, x, 288 p., chapter 3 (series; SOAS studies on South Asia);

SINGHA, Radhika, *A despotism of law : crime and justice in early colonial India*, Calcutta ; Oxford : Oxford University Press, 1998, xxix, 342 p., ISBN: 0195640497;

STARLING, M. H. (Matthew Henry) 1837-1903, *Indian Criminal Law*, 4th ed., Bombay: Education Society's Press, 1886;

STEPHEN, James Fitzjames, 1829-1894, "Codification in India and England", (July - December 1872) 18 *The Fortnightly Review* 644-672;

STOKES, Whitley, ed., 1830-1909, *The Anglo-Indian codes*, Oxford, Clarendon Press, 1887-88, 2 volumes, vol. 1, Substantive law; volume 2, Adjective law;

TEWARI, R.B., "Attempt", in S. Govindarajulu, ed., *Essays on the Indian Penal Code: published on the occasion of the centenary of the Indian Penal Code*, Bombay: N.M. Tripathi, 1962, pp. 107-116; title noted in my research but article not consulted (27 April 2007);

THONISSEN, J. J. (Jean Joseph), 1817-1891, "Le droit criminel dans les livres sacrés de l'Inde", tome 18, 1864, *Bulletins de l'Académie royale de Belgique* (2e série);

VAIDYA, Nidhi and Raghuvanshi, Raghvendra Singh, Criminality of Intention - How to Adjudge Mens REA? (February 25, 2010). Available at SSRN: http://ssrn.com/abstract=1558968; available at http://papers.ssrn.com/sol3/papers.cfm?abstract_id=1558968 (accessed on 28 February 2010);

VIBHUTE, K.I., "Adultery and the Indian Penal Code: Need for a Gender Equality Perspective", (2001) (6) *Supreme Court Cases* 16 (J);

WRIGHT, Barry, "Macaulay's Indian Penal Code: Historical Context and Originating Principles", in Wing-Cheong Chan, Barry Wright, and Stanley Yeo, eds.,*Codification, Macaulay and the Indian Penal Code : the legacies and modern challenges of criminal law reform*, Farnham, Surrey, England ; Burlington, VT, USA : Ashgate, c2011, xiii, 379 p., at pp. 19 to approx. 58; ISBN: 9781409424420 (hardback); title noted in my research but article not consulted yet (7 November 2011);

YANG, Anand A., ed., *Crime and Criminality in British India*, Tucson, , Ariz. : Published for the Association for Asian Studies by the University of Arizona Press, c1985, xi, 192 p., ISBN: ISBN: 0816509514; copy at Ottawa University, HV 7092 .C75 1985 MRT;

YEO, Stanley M.H., "Revitalising the Penal Code with a General Part", (July 2004) *Singapore Journal of Legal Studies*;

YEO, Stanley, *Fault in Homicide: Towards a Schematic Approeach to the Fault Elements for Murder and Involontary Manslaughter in England, Australia and India*, Annandale (NSW, Australia): The Federation Press and Sydney (NSW, Austrralia): The Institute of Criminology, University of Sydney, 1997, xv, 312 p., (series; The Institute of Criminology Monograph Series; No. 7), ISBN: 1862872759;

ZALKIND, Paola, 1981- and Rita James Simon, *Global perspectives on social issues : juvenile justice systems*, Lanham, Md. : Lexington Books, c2004, vii, 197 p., see "India" at pp. 145-150 and 163-164, ISBN: 0739107305; copy at Ottawa University, MRT General: HV 9069 .Z35 2004;

Index

A

B

C

D

O

P

R

S

T

U

V

W